The Twilight of Ramesside Egypt

IN MEMORY OF
KRZYSZTOF ŁUKASZEWICZ

Mirosław Barwik

The Twilight of Ramesside Egypt

Studies on the History of Egypt at the End of the Ramesside Period

Warszawa 2011

The book was published with the financial support of the Department of the Archaeology of Egypt and Nubia, Institute of Archaeology, University of Warsaw

Cover: design by Sylwia Caban, photographs by Mirosław Barwik

Agade Bis
Krasińskiego 18/252
01-581 Warsaw, Poland
Mobile +48 604 94 11 36
Tel. +48 22 701 83 95

www.ksiegarniaorientalna.pl
e-mail: agade@ksiegarniaorientalna.pl

ISBN 978-83-87111-51-9

Contents

PREFACE

In spite of the abundant documentation dating to the end of the 20th Dynasty the political history of the period remains practically unknown. All the available ostraca and papyri refer mostly to the matters of the Theban necropolis and its staff. Consequently any details concerning the political history of the period must be read between the lines, and simply inferred on the basis of a detailed analysis of these documents. In the very centre of those events were the members of the well known family of the scribes of the royal necropolis, descendants of the scribe Amennakht, who had been promoted to the post during the reign of Ramesses III. Horisheri son of Amennakht was still active when the Theban necropolis had been ravaged at the end of the reign of Ramesses IX. His son Khaemhedje succeeded his father in those hard times, when the apparent weakness of the state strongly influenced the political situation in the country. The latter's descendants, the scribe Tuthmosis and his son Butehamun, were the eyewitnesses of the final collapse of the Ramesside dynasty and emergence of the new order under the auspices of the new dynasty in the North, and the high priests of Amun in Upper Egypt. The activity of Tuthmosis as the scribe of the necropolis fell within the long reign of Ramesses XI. He had started his career as an ordinary workman already in the reign of Ramesses IX. Probably nothing foretold then the beginning of the crisis when he was promoted to the post of the necropolis scribe at the very beginning of the reign of Ramesses XI. But his subsequent involvement in the matters of the necropolis testifies to an increasing degree of instability. During the later years of his career he was assisted by Butehamun – the one "who opens the gates of the netherworld". As a matter of fact the latter belonged to the generation contemporary with a final abandonment of the royal necropolis in the Valley of the Kings, after earlier depredations of the mummies of the pharaohs and their tombs. There is a family archive of Tuthmosis and his son, which forms one of the most important sources of information on the epoch. It is a pity, however, that none of these men, devoted exclusively to their job and the matters of everyday life, were tempted to become the chroniclers of their times. In consequence the last of the Ramesside rulers disappeared from the stage of history as a shadowy person, and the history of his reign still remains the domain of literary fiction on the one hand and scientific discussion on the other.

The aim of the present book is a critical evaluation of the sources relating to the end of the Ramesside period in Egypt. The events which led to the fall of the Ramessides can be compared only with the twilight of the Tuthmosides under the last rulers of the 18th Dynasty, and to some extent also with the end of the succeeding 19th Dynasty, when usurpers and other powers behind the throne played a dominant role. If the crisis of the monarchy at the end of the 18th and 19th Dynasties was finally overcome, with the result that new ruling families started a fresh policy of revival, the very end of the 20th Dynasty marked the end of the glorious epoch of the New Kingdom and the devastating collapse of the political and social order in Egypt. In the present state of our knowledge, any attempt to formulate a coherent picture of the history of these troubled times seems to be premature. The inconsistent and complicated character of the available sources makes the task difficult. On the other hand, the discovery of new sources and their publication has given now a fresh impetus to the studies on the subject. The enormous effort of three generations of Egyptologists enables us now to verify some of the older views and put forward new hypotheses. No doubt the latter must still be submitted to verification and critical evaluation, and continuously necessitates a formulation of new hypotheses.

Nevertheless, the story of the end of the Ramesside dynasty is still hidden behind scattered remains of its previous glory. A total lack of written sources from the northern part of the country threatens to render any attempt to write a history of the epoch fragmentary and incomplete. Certainly we have to wait for further results of the excavations currently being conducted by the German mission on the site of ancient Per-Ramesse, which possibly will provide a new epigraphic evidence relating to the main protagonists of the events which led to the extinction of the royal house of the Ramessides. For the moment, we have to rely now on the sources connected mostly with the Upper Egypt, i.e. Thebes in particular, with ample documentation concerning the activity of the institutions of the royal necropolis, the acts of the robbery trials and thousands of graffiti left in the Theban mountains by those engaged in the matters of the necropolis. Unfortunately the overall number of documents significantly diminishes after the reign of Ramesses X. As a result the story of the reign of the last ruler of the dynasty as well as his personality still remain a mystery.

The most intriguing problems of the history of these times relate to the chronology of the reign of Ramesses XI, but also the chronological position and the role played by the High Priest Herihor – both subjects currently the topic of stimulating discussion and research. The aim of the author is to shed some new light on the dark period at the end of the 20th Dynasty even if final solutions are still unattainable. The polemical character of the present study should not detract from the fact that most of the sources were critically edited and thoroughly commented in the pioneering research of such respected scholars as Jürgen von Beckerath, Jaroslav Černý, Wolfgang Helck, Jacob J. Janssen and Kenneth A. Kitchen. It was their works that introduced me into a fascinating world of the Ramessides.

My thanks go to all those who helped me in the arduous task of completing the documentation and in editing this book – first of all to the editor Magdalena Kapełuś ("Agade" Publishing House), to Iwona Zych for translating the Introduction, and to Paul Barford for revising the English text of the rest of the book. I am especially grateful to Jaromír Málek of the Griffith Institute (Oxford), Robert J. Demarée of the Leiden University, and John A. Larson of the Oriental Institute of the University of Chicago, for providing me with some unpublished material, but also to the members of the Polish Archaeological Mission in the Hatshepsut Temple at Deir el-Bahari, and its director Zbigniew E. Szafrański in particular, for their assistance in my work on the "late" inscriptional evidence newly found at Deir el-Bahari and in the surrounding area. Last but not least I would like to express my sincere gratitude to my son Janusz for his invaluable help, and to my wife Monika for her unfailing patience and encouragement in all those years devoted to the study of Ramesside history.

Warsaw, December 2010

Abbreviations and Bibliography

(Abbreviations not listed here are those of the Lexikon der Ägyptologie – LÄ).

Abitz F., Der Bauablauf und die Dekoration des Grabes Ramses' IX, SAK 17, 1990, 1-40

Abitz F., The Structure of the Decoration in the Tomb of Ramesses IX, in: After Tutankhamun, 165-185

After Tutankhamun:
Reeves C.N. (ed.), After Tutᶜankhamūn. Research and excavation in the Royal Necropolis at Thebes, [Studies in Egyptology], London 1992

Aldred, Tomb Robberies:
Aldred C., More Light on the Ramesside Tomb Robberies, in: J. Ruffle et al. (ed.), Glimpses of Ancient Egypt. Studies in Honour of H.W. Fairman, Warminster 1979, 92-99

Ali, Hieratische Ritzinschriften:
Ali M.S., Hieratische Ritzinschriften aus Theben, [GOF IV, 34], Wiesbaden 2002

Allam S., Sind die nichtliterarischen Schriftostraka Brouillons?, JEA 54, 1968, 121-128

Allam S., Zur Stellung der Frau im alten Ägypten in der Zeit des Neuen Reiches, 16.-10. Jh.v.u.Z., BiOr 26, 1969, 155-159

Allam HOP:
Allam S., Hieratische Ostraka und Papyri aus der Ramessidenzeit, [Urkunden zum Rechtsleben im Alten Ägypten, Bd.1], I-II, Tübingen 1973

Allam S., Das Verfahrensrecht in der altägyptischen Arbeitsiedlung von Deir el-Medineh, [Untersuchungen zum Rechtsleben im alten Ägypten 1], Tübingen 1973

Allam S., Papyrus Moscow 127, JEA 61, 1975, 147-153

Allam S., Einige hieratische Ostraka der Papyrussammlung der Staatlichen Museen zu Berlin, FuB 22, 1982, 51-61, pls. 1-8

Allam S., A new look at the Adoption Papyrus (reconsidered), JEA 76, 1990, 189-191

Allam S., La vie municipale à Deir el-Médineh: les supérieurs (*ḥwtjw/ḥntjw*) du village, BIFAO 97, 1997, 1-17

Allam S., Vermittler im Handel zur Zeit des Neuen Reiches, SAK 26, 1998, 3-18

Allam S., Der eponyme richterliche Schreiber, ZÄS 133, 2006, 1-9

Ancient Egyptian Chronology:
Hornung E., Krauss R., Warburton D.A. (eds.), Ancient Egyptian Chronology, [Handbook of Oriental Studies, Section One, vol. 83], Leiden – Boston 2006

Antoine J.-Chr., Fluctuations of fish deliveries at Deir el-Medina in the Twentieth Dynasty. A statystical analysis, SAK 35, 2006, 25-41

Bács T.A., Amun-Re-Harakhti in the late Ramesside Royal Tombs, in: Luft U. (ed.), The Intellectual Heritage of Egypt. Studies presented to László Kákosy, [Studia Aegyptiaca 14], Budapest 1992, 43-53

Baines J., On Wenamun as a Literary Text, in: Assmann J., Blumenthal E. (eds.), Literatur und

Politik im pharaonischen und ptolemäischen Ägypten, [BdE 127], Cairo 1999, 209-233

Baines J., Eyre C.J., Four notes on literacy, GM 61, 1983, 65-96

Bakir, Epistolography:
Bakir Abd El-Mohsen, Egyptian Epistolography from the Eighteenth to the Twenty-first Dynasty, [BdÉ 48], Cairo 1970

Barguet P., Le temple d'Amon-Rê à Karnak. Essai d'exégèse, [RAPH 21], Cairo 1962

Barns J., The Nevill Papyrus: A Late Ramesside Letter to an Oracle, JEA 35, 1949, 69-71

Barta W., Bemerkungen zur Chronologie der 21. Dynastie, MDAIK 37, 1981, 35-39

Barwik M., The owner of cliff tomb MMA 1021 at Thebes, GM 165, 1998, 13-21

Barwik M., Theban Graffito no. 1572 rediscovered and some new texts from the "Valley of the Quarries", (in preparation)

von Beckerath, Tanis und Theben:
Beckerath J. von, Tanis und Theben. Historische Grundlagen der Ramessidenzeit in Ägypten, [ÄF 16], Glückstadt – Hamburg – New York 1951

Beckerath J. von, Die «Stele der Verbannten» im Museum des Louvre, RdE 20, 1968, 7-36

Beckerath J. von, Drei Thronbesteigungsdaten der XX. Dynastie, GM 79, 1984, 7-9

von Beckerath, Chronologie:
Beckerath J. von, Chronologie des ägyptischen Neuen Reiches, [HÄB 39], Hildesheim 1994

Beckerath J. von, Papyrus Turin 1898+, Verso, SAK 21, 1994, 29-33

Beckerath J. von, Zur Datierung des Papyrus Brooklyn 16.205, GM 140, 1994, 15-17

von Beckerath, Chronologie der XXI. Dynastie:
Beckerath J. von, Zur Chronologie der XXI. Dynastie, in: D. Kessler, R. Schulz (eds.), Gedenkschrift für Winfried Barta: *ḥtp dj n ḥzj*, [MÄU 4], Frankfurt a/M 1995, 49-55

Beckerath J. von, Zur Datierung des Grabräuberpapyrus Brit.Mus.10054, GM 159, 1997, 5-9

Beckerath J. von, Chronologie des pharaonischen Ägypten. Die Zeitbestimmung der ägyptischen Geschichte von der Vorzeit bis 332 v.Chr., [MÄS 46], Mainz 1997

von Beckerath, Königsnamen:
Beckerath J. von, Handbuch der ägyptischen Königsnamen, [MÄS 49], Mainz 1999 (2nd ed.)

Beckerath J. von, Bemerkungen zur Chronologie der Grabräuberpapyri, ZÄS 127, 2000, 111-116

Beckerath J. von, Überlegungen zum Zeitabstand zwischen Ramses II. und dem Ende der XXI. Dynastie, GM 181, 2001, 15-17

Bell L., Only One High Priest Ramessenakht and the Second Prophet Nesamun his Younger Son, Serapis 6, 1980, 7-27

Bellion, Catalogue:
Bellion M., Catalogue des manuscrits hiéroglyphiques et hiératiques et des dessins, sur papyrus, cuir ou tissu, publiés ou signalés, Paris 1987

Belova G.A., TT 320 and the History of the Royal Cache during the Twenty-first Dynasty, in: Hawass Z., Pinch Brock L. (eds.), Egyptology at the Dawn of the Twenty-first Century. Proceedings of the Eighth International Congress of Egyptologists, Cairo, 2000, vol. I, Cairo-New York 2003, 73-80

Berlev O., The Date of pPrakhov, GM 160, 1997, 5-15

Bierbrier M.L., A Second High Priest Ramessesnakht?, JEA 58, 1972, 195-199

Bierbrier M.L., Hrere, Wife of the High Priest Paiankh, JNES 32, 1973, 311

Bierbrier M.L., The Length of the Reign of Ramesses X, JEA 61, 1975, 251

Bierbrier LNK:

Bierbrier M.L., The Late New Kingdom in Egypt (c. 1300-664 B.C.). A Genealogical and Chronological Investigation, Warminster 1975

Bierbrier, Tomb-Builders:
Bierbrier M.L., The Tomb-Builders of the Pharaohs, London 1982

Blackman A.M., Oracles in Ancient Egypt II, JEA 12, 1926, 176-185

Bogoslovsky E.S., Hundred Egyptian Draughtsmen, ZÄS 107, 1980, 89-116

Bogoslovsky E.S., *Drevne-Egipetskie Mastera* (in Russian), Moscow 1983

Bohleke B., An Ex Voto of the Previously Unrecognized Viceroy Setmose, GM 85, 1985, 13-24

Bonhême M.-A., Hérihor fut-il effectivement roi?, BIFAO 79, 1979, 267-283

Bonhême, Noms royaux:
Bonhême M.-A., Les noms royaux dans l'Égypte de la troisième période intermédiaire, [BdE 98], Cairo 1987

Bonhême, Livre des rois I:
Bonhême M.-A., Le livre des rois de la troisième période intermédiaire, I: XXIe dynastie, [BdE 99], Cairo 1987

Boochs W., Das altägyptische Strafverfahren bei Straftaten von besonderem staatlichem Interesse, GM 109, 1989, 21-26

Borghouts J.F., A New Approach to the Late Egyptian Conjunctive, ZÄS 106, 1979, 14-24

Botti G., Frammenti di Registri di Stato Civile della XX[a] Dinastia, in: Rendiconti della Reale Accademia Nazionale dei Lincei 31, 1922-23, 391-394

Botti G., Who succeded Ramesses IX-Neferkere?, JEA 14, 1928, 48-51

Botti G., Frammenti di Papiri Ieratici della XX Dinastia nel Museo Egizio di Firenze, OrAnt 3, 1964, 221-226, pls. 102-113

Botti-Peet, Giornale:
Botti G., Peet T.E., Il Giornale della Necropoli di Tebe, Turin 1928

Bouvier-Bouvier, L'activité des gens:
Bouvier G. and K., L'activité des gens de la Nécropole à la fin de la XXe et à la XXIe dynastie, d'après les graffiti de la Montagne thébaine: le transfert des momies royales, in: Living and Writing, 21-29

Broekman G.P.F., The founders of the twenty-first dynasty and their family relationships, GM 191, 2002, 11-18

Bruyère, Rapport:
Bruyère B., Rapport sur les fouilles de Deir el Médineh, [FIFAO 1.1, 2.2, 3.3, 4.3, 5.2, 6.2, 7.2, 8.3, 10.1, 14-16, 20, 21, 26], Cairo 1924-1953

Burkard G., Ostraka aus Deir el-Medine in spätzeitliche Grabanlagen vor dem Deutschen Haus in Theben, in: Guksch H., Polz D. (eds.), Stationen. Beiträge zur Kulturgeschichte Ägyptens R. Stadelmann gewidmet, Mainz 1998, 433-442

Burkard G., «...Die im Dunkeln sieht man nicht». Waren die Arbeiter im Tal der Könige privilegierte Gefangene? in: H. Guksch et al. (eds.), Grab und Totenkult im alten Ägypten, München 2003, 128-146

Burkard G., „Oh, diese Mauern Pharaos!" Zur Bewegungsfreiheit der Einwohner von Deir el Medine, MDAIK 59, 2003, 11-39

Burkard G., Das *ḫtm n pꜣ ḫr* von Deir el-Medine. Seine Funktion und die Frage seiner Lokalisierung, in: Living and Writing, 31-42

Caminos R.A., s.v. Grabräuberprozeß, in: LÄ II (1977), 862-866

Caminos R.A., A Tale of Woe from a hieratic papyrus in the A.S. Pushkin Museum of Fine Arts in Moscow, Oxford 1977

Cannuyer, Brelan de "pharaons":
Cannuyer C., Brelan de "pharaons" Ramsès XI, Thoutmosis III, et Hatshepsout, in: S. Israelit-Groll (ed.), Studies in Egyptology presented to Miriam Lichtheim, I, Jerusalem 1990, 98-115

Cannuyer C., Encore la date de l'accession au trône de Ramsès XI, GM 132, 1993, 19-20

Capart J., Gardiner A.H., van de Walle B., New Light on the Ramesside Tomb-Robberies, JEA 22, 1936, 169-193, pls. 10-16

Capart J., Gardiner A.H., Le papyrus Léopold II aux Musées Royaux d'Art et d'Histoire de Bruxelles et le Papyrus Amherst à la Pierpont Morgan Library de New York, Bruxelles 1939

Chevereau, Prosopographie:
Chevereau P.-M., Prosopographie des cadres militaires égyptiens de la Basse Époque. Carrières Militaires et Carrières Sacerdotales en Egypte du XIe au IIe siècle avant J.C., Paris 1985

Christophe L.-A., Sur le graffito 1247 de la nécropole thébaine, BIFAO 56, 1957, 173-188

Ciccarello, Graffito of Pinutem I:
Ciccarello M., The Graffito of Pinutem I in the Tomb of Ramesses XI, Brooklyn 1979

Ciccarello M., Romer J., A Preliminary Report of the Recent Work in the Tombs of Ramesses X and XI in the Valley of the Kings, Brooklyn 1979

Cody A., The Phoenician Ecstatic in Wenamūn. A Professional Oracular Medium, JEA 65, 1979, 99-106

Cruz-Uribe E., Late Egyptian Varia, ZÄS 113, 1986, 18-20

Cruz-Uribe E., A new look at the Adoption Papyrus, JEA 74, 1988, 220-223

Černý J., Le culte d'Aménophis Ier chez les ouvriers de la Nécropole Thébaine, BIFAO 27, 1927, 159-203

Černý J., Quelques ostraca hiératiques inédits de Thèbes au Musée du Caire, ASAE 27, 1927, 183-210

Černý J., A Note on the "Repeating of Births", JEA 15, 1929, 194-198

Černý J., Zu den Ausführungen von Sethe über die *wḥm msw.t* Datierungen in den thebanischen Grabberaubungsakten der 20. Dynastie, ZÄS 65, 1930, 129-130

Černý J., Ostrakon Nr.2973 der Staatl. Ermitage zu Leningrad, ArOr 3, 1931, 395-399

Černý J., Une expression designant la réponse négative d'un oracle, BIFAO 30, 1931, 491-496

Černý J., Fluctuations in Grain Prices During the Twentieth Egyptian Dynasty, ArOr 6, 1933, 173-178

Černý, Ostraca CG:
Černý J., Ostraca hiératiques (Nos 25501-25832), [CG], fasc. 1-4, Cairo 1930-35

Černý J., La constitution d'un avoir conjugal au Nouvel Empire, CdE 11, 1936, 39-41

Černý J., Une famille de scribes de la nécropole royale de Thèbes, CdE 11, 1936, 247-250

Černý J., Restitution of, and Penalty attaching to, stolen Property in Ramesside Times, JEA 23, 1937, 186-189

Černý J., La constitution d'un avoir conjugal en Égypte, BIFAO 37, 1937-1938, 41-48

Černý LRL:

Černý J., Late Ramesside Letters, [BAe IX], Brussels 1939

Černý J., 'The Temple', as an Abbreviated Name for the Temple of Medinet Habu, JEA 26, 1940, 127-130

Černý J., Inn in Late Egyptian, JEA 27, 1941, 106-112

Černý J., Le tirage au sort, BIFAO 40, 1941, 135-141
Černý J., Studies in the Chronology of the Twenty-First Dynasty, JEA 32, 1946, 24-30
Černý, Ostraca DeM:
Černý J., Catalogue des ostraca hiératiques non littéraires de Deir el-Médineh, I-V, [DFIFAO 3-7], Cairo 1935-1951
Černý J., Prices and Wages in Egypt in the Ramesside Period, Cahiers d'Histoire Mondiale 1, no. 4, 1954, 903-921
Černý, Graffiti:
Černý J., Graffiti hiéroglyphiques et hiératiques de la nécropole thébaine, [DFIFAO 9], Cairo 1956
Černý J., review of Helck, Verwaltung, in: BiOr 19, 1962, 140-144
Černý, Ostraca DeM nos. 624-705:
Černý J., Catalogue des ostraca hiératiques non littéraires de Deir el-Médinéh, Nos. 624-705, [DFIFAO 14], Cairo 1970
Černý, Community:
Černý J., A Community of Workmen at Thebes in the Ramesside Period, [BdÉ 50], Cairo 1973 (1st ed.), 2004 (3rd ed.)
Černý, Valley of the Kings:
Černý J., The Valley of the Kings. Fragments d'un manuscrit inachevé, [BdÉ 61], Cairo 1973
Černý J., Egypt: From the Death of Ramesses III to the End of the Twenty-First Dynasty, in: CAH3 II.2, Cambridge 1975, 606-657
Černý-Gardiner HO:
Černý J., Gardiner A.H., Hieratic Ostraca, I, Oxford 1957
Černý-Groll, Late Egyptian Grammar:
Černý J., Groll S.I., A Late Egyptian Grammar, [Studia Pohl: Series Maior 4], Rome 1975
Černý J., Koenig Y., Papyrus hiératiques de Deir el-Médineh, II: Nos XVIII-XXXIV, [DFIFAO 22], Cairo 1986
Černý-Peet, Marriage Settlement:
Černý J., Peet T.E., A Marriage Settlement of the Twentieth Dynasty. An Unpublished Document from Turin, JEA 13, 1927, 30-39, pls. 13-15
Černý J., Posener G., Papyrus hiératiques de Deir el-Médineh, I: Nos I-XVII, [DFIFAO 8], Cairo 1978
Černý, Sadek et al., Graffiti:
Černý J., Sadek A.A. et al., Graffiti de la montagne thébaine, vol. III-IV, Cairo 1970-83
Daressy, Ostraca:
Daressy G., Ostraca (N°s 25001-25385), [CG], Cairo 1901
Daressy, Cercueils:
Daressy G., Cercueils des cachettes royales, [CG], Cairo 1909
Daressy G., Les titres du Grand Prêtre Piankh, ASAE 17, 1917, 29-30
Daressy G., Rapport sur le déblaiement des tombes 6 et 9 de Biban el Molouk, ASAE 18, 1919, 270-274
Daressy G., Un ostracon de Biban el Molouk, ASAE 22, 1922, 75-76
Daressy G., Quelques ostraca de Biban el Molouk, ASAE 27, 1927, 161-182
Dautzenberg N., Die Stellung Pinutems I. und die Nachfolge des Smendes, GM 142, 1994, 61-66
Davies B.G., Two many Butehamuns? Additional observations on their identity, SAK 24, 1997, 49-68

Davies, Who's Who at DeM:
Davies B.G., Who's Who at Deir el-Medina. A Prosopographic Study of the Royal Workmen's Community, [Egyptologische Uitgaven 13], Leiden 1999

Dégardin J.-C., Le Temple de Khonsou. Problèmes de destination et de propriété, in: Sesto Congresso Internazionale di Egittologia. Atti, II, Turin 1993, 93-99

DeM et la Vallée des Rois:
Andreu G. (ed.), Deir el-Médineh et la Vallée des Rois. La vie en Égypte au temps des pharaons du Nouvel Empire. Actes du colloque organisé par le musée du Louvre les 3 et 4 mai 2002, Paris 2003

DeM in the Third Millennium:
Demarée R.J., Egberts A.(eds.), Deir el-Medina in the Third Millennium AD. A Tribute to Jac. J. Janssen, [Egyptologische Uitgaven 14], Leiden 2000

Demarée R.J., Recent work on the administrative papyri in the Museo Egizio, Turin, in: Sesto Congresso Internazionale di Egittologia. Atti, II, Turin 1993, 101-105

Demarée R.J., The King is Dead – Long Live the King, GM 137, 1993, 49-52

Demarée R.J., Deir el-Medina after all?, GM 183, 2001, 5-6

Demarée, Ramesside Ostraca:
Demarée R.J., Ramesside Ostraca, London 2002

Demarée R.J., Quelques textes de la fin de la XXe et du début de la XXe dynastie, in: Deir el-Médineh et la Vallée des Rois, 235-251

Demarée, Bankes Papyri:
Demarée R.J., The Bankes Late Ramesside Papyri, [The British Museum Research Publication no. 155], London 2006

Demichelis S., Le phylactère du scribe Boutehamon, BIFAO 100, 2000, 267-273

Demidoff G., Pour une revision de la chronologie de la fin de l'epoque Ramesside, GM 177, 2000, 91-101

Demidoff, Retour sur une controverse:
Demidoff G., Hérihor-Piankhy, Piankhy-Hérihor. Retour sur une controverse, in: Gallois C. et al. (eds.), Mélanges offerts à François Neveu, [BdE 145], Cairo 2008, 99-111

Dewachter M., Contribution à l'histoire de la cachette royale de Deir el-Bahari, BSFE 74, 1975, 19-32

Dodson A., A Twenty-first Dynasty private reburial at Thebes, JEA 77, 1991, 180-182

Dodson A., Janssen J.J., A Theban Tomb and its Tenants, JEA 75, 1989, 125-138

Donnat S., Hommage d'un lettré à son épouse défunte, Égypte, Afrique & Orient No. 25, 2002, 31-42

Dorn A., Men at Work. Zwei Ostraka aus dem Tal der Könige mit nicht-kanonischen Darstellungen von Arbeitern, MDAIK 61, 2005, 1-11, pls. 1-4

Eaton-Krauss M., review of: Reeves, Valley of the Kings, in: BiOr 49, 1992, 706-717

Edwards I.E.S., The Bankes Papyri I and II, JEA 68, 1982, 126-133, pls. 12-13

Egberts A., The Chronology of *The Report of Wenamun*, JEA 77, 1991, 57-67

Egberts A., Piankh, Herihor, Dhutmose and Butehamun: a fresh look at O. Cairo CG 25744 and 25745, GM 160, 1997, 23-25

Egberts A., Hard Times: The Chronology of "The Report of Wenamun" Revised, ZÄS 125, 1998, 93-108

Egberts A., Double Dutch in the Report of Wenamun?, GM 172, 1999, 17-22

Eichler S., Untersuchungen zu den Wasserträgern von Deir-el-Medineh I, SAK 17, 1990, 135-175

Eichler S., Untersuchungen zu den Wasserträgern von Deir-el-Medineh II, SAK 18, 1991, 173-205

El-Sayed R., Piankhi, fils de Hérihor. Documents sur sa vie et sur son rôle, BIFAO 78, 1978, 197-218

Erman A., Gebete eines ungerecht Verfolgten und andere Ostraka aus den Königsgräbern, ZÄS 38, 1900, 19-41

Erman A., Ein Fall abgekürzter Justiz in Ägypten, ADAW 1, 1913, 3-18, pls. 1-5 (reedition in: Erman A., Akademieschriften (1880-1928), II, [Opuscula 13.2], Leipzig 1986, 117-132)

Erman, Neuägyptische Grammatik:
Erman A., Neuägyptische Grammatik, Leipzig 1933 (2nd ed.)

Eyre C.J., A "Strike" Text from the Theban Necropolis, in: Glimpses of Ancient Egypt. Studies in Honour of H.W. Fairman, Warminster 1979, 80-91

Eyre C.J., The Use of Data from Deir el-Medîna, BiOr 44, 1987, 21-32

Eyre C.J., The Adoption Papyrus in Social Context, JEA 78, 1992, 207-221

Eyre C.J., Irony in the Story of Wenamun: the Politics of Religion in the 21st Dynasty, in: Assmann J., Blumenthal E. (eds.), Literatur und Politik im pharaonischen und ptolemäischen Ägypten, [BdE 127], Cairo 1999, 235-252

Fecht G., Der Moskauer „literarische Brief" als historisches Dokument, ZÄS 87, 1962, 12-31

Félix-Aubriot-Kurz, Plans de position:
Félix J., Aubriot L., Kurz M., Graffiti de la montagne thébaine. Plans de position, vol. II.1-6, Cairo 1970-1977

Fischer-Elfert H.-W., Zwei Akten aus der Getreideverwaltung der XXI. Dynastie (P. Berlin 14.384 und P. Berlin 23098), in: Altenmüller H., Germer R. (eds.), Miscellanea Aegyptologica Wolfgang Helck zum 75. Geburtstag, Hamburg 1989, 39-65, pls. 1-3

Fischer-Elfert H.-W., Legenda Hieratika – I, GM 165, 1998, 105-112

Fischer-Elfert H.-W., review of Schipper, Wenamun, in: WdO 36, 2006, 219-226

Frandsen, Verbal System:
Frandsen P.J., An Outline of the Late Egyptian Verbal System, Kopenhagen 1974

Frandsen P.J., A Word for "Causeway" and the Location of "the Five Walls", JEA 75, 1989, 113-123

Frandsen P.J., The Letter to Ikhtay's Coffin: O. Louvre Inv. No. 698, in: Village Voices, 31-49

Frood, Biographical Texts:
Frood E., Biographical Texts from Ramessid Egypt, [Writings from the Ancient World 26], Atlanta 2007

Galán J.M., Four Journeys in Ancient Egyptian Literature, [LingAeg Studia monographica 5], Göttingen 2005

Gardiner A.H., A Political Crime in Ancient Egypt, JMEOS 2, 1912-1913, 57-64

Gardiner LES:
Gardiner A.H., Late-Egyptian Stories, [BAe 1], Bruxelles 1932

Gardiner A.H., Adoption Extraordinary, JEA 26, 1940, 23-29, pls. 5-7

Gardiner A.H., Ramesside Texts Relating to the Taxation and Transport of Corn, JEA 27, 1941, 19-73

Gardiner AEO:

Gardiner A.H., Ancient Egyptian Onomastica, I-III, London 1947
Gardiner RAD:
Gardiner A.H., Ramesside Administrative Documents, Oxford 1948
Gardiner, Wilbour Papyrus Comm.:
Gardiner A.H., The Wilbour Papyrus, II: Commentary, Oxford 1948
Gardiner A., A Protest Against Unjustified Tax-Demands, RdE 6, 1951, 115-127
Gasse, Domaine d'Amon:
Gasse A., Données nouvelles administratives et sacerdotales sur l'organisation du Domaine d'Amon XXe-XXIe Dynasties à la lumière des papyrus Prachov, Reinhardt et Grundbuch (avec édition princeps des papyrus Louvre AF 6345 et 6346-7), I-II, [BdÉ 104], Cairo 1988
Gasse A., Panakhtemipet et ses complices (à propos du papyrus BM EA 10054, r° 2, 1-5), JEA 87, 2001, 81-92
Gleanings from Deir el-Medîna:
Demarée R.J., Janssen Jac.J.(eds.), Gleanings from Deir el-Medîna, [Egyptologische Uitgaven 1], Leiden 1982
Gnirs, Militär und Gesellschaft:
Gnirs A., Militär und Gesellschaft. Ein Beitrag zur Sozialgeschichte des Neuen Reiches, [SAGA 17], Heidelberg1996
Goedicke H., Hieratische Ostraka in Wien, WZKM 59/60, 1963-1964, 1-8, pls. 1-22
Goedicke H., The Report of Wenamun, Baltimore 1975
Goedicke H., Wente E.F., Ostraka Michaelides, Wiesbaden 1962
Goelet O. Jr., A New 'Robbery' Papyrus: Rochester MAG 51.346.1, JEA 82, 1996, 107-127
Gohary S., A Lintel of Penherishef, Chief Agent of Amun's Leading Priests, BIFAO 86, 1986, 183-185
Goldberg J., Was Piankh the Son of Herihor after all?, GM 174, 2000, 49-58
Goldwasser O., On the Conception of the Poetic Form – A Love Letter to a Departed Wife: Ostracon Louvre 698, Israel Oriental Studies 15, 1995, 191-205
Graefe E., Über die Goldmenge des Alten Ägypten und die Beraubung der thebanischen Königsgräber, ZÄS 126, 1999, 19-40
Graefe E., Die königliche Cachette TT 320 von Deir el-Bahri. Nachgrabungen im berühmtesten Königsmumienversteck Ägyptens, Antike Welt 30.4, 1999, 369-374
Graefe E., Vorbericht über die erste Kampagne einer Nachuntersuchung der königlichen *Cachette* TT 320 von Deir el-Bahari, MDAIK 56, 2000, 215-221
Graefe E., The Royal Cache and the tomb robberies, in: Strudwick N., Taylor J.H. (eds.), The Theban Necropolis. Past, Present and Future, London 2003, 74-82
Graefe E., „Der Hügel (*qꜣy*) der Inhapi, der der Heilige Ort ist, in dem Amenhotep ruht", MDAIK 61, 2005, 207-209
Graefe E., Nochmals zur Lage des Grabes Amenhoteps I, GM 214, 2007, 9-10
Graefe E., Belova G., The Royal Cache TT 320: New investigations 1998, 2003, and 2004, ASAE 80, 2006, 207-220
Graefe E., Belova G. (eds.), The Royal Cache TT 320 – a re-examination, Cairo 2010
Grandet, Ostraca DeM:
Grandet P., Catalogue des ostraca hiératiques non littéraires de Deîr el-Médînéh, VIII-X, [DFIFAO 39, 41, 46], Cairo 2000-2006

Green M., Wenamun's Demand for Compensation, ZÄS 106, 1979, 116-120
Groll, Non-Verbal Sentence Patterns:
Groll S.I, Non-Verbal Sentence Patterns in Late Egyptian, London 1967
Groll, Negative Verbal System:
Groll S.I., The Negative Verbal System of Late Egyptian, London 1970
Groll S., review of Wente LRL, in: RdE 26, 1974, 168-172.
Guérin S., Les cercueils du scribe royal de la Tombe Boutehamon. L'art de renaître, Égypte, Afrique & Orient No. 48, 2007-2008, 17-28
Gundlach R., s.v. Wiederholung der Geburt, in: LÄ VI (1986), 1261-1264
Gundlach R., Das Königtum des Herihor. Zum Umbruch in der ägyptischen Königsideologie am Beginn der 3. Zwischenzeit, in: Minas M., Zeidler J. (eds.), Aspekte spätägyptischer Kultur. Festschrift für Erich Winter, [Aegyptiaca Treverensia 7], Mainz a/R 1994, 133-138
Gutgesell, Datierung:
Gutgesell M., Die Datierung der Ostraka und Papyri aus Deir el-Medineh und ihre ökonomische Interpretation. Teil I: Die 20. Dynastie, I-II, [HÄB 18-19], Hildesheim 1983
Hagen F., A Ramesside Administrative Document (P. Cambridge University Library MS. Add. 4167), ZÄS 135, 2008, 30-39, pls. 2-5
Hagens G., A Critical Review of Dead-Reckoning from the 21st Dynasty, JARCE 33, 1996, 153-163
Hari R., Un monument du grand-prêtre Paiankh, BSEG 7, 1982, 39-46
Häggman, Directing DeM:
Häggman S., Directing Deir el-Medina. The External Administration of the Necropolis, [Uppsala Studies in Egyptology 4], Uppsala 2002
Haring B., Libyans in the Late Twentieth Dynasty, in: Village Voices, 71-80
Haring B., Libyans in the Theban region, 20th dynasty, in: Sesto Congresso Internazionale di Egittologia. Atti, II, Turin 1993, 159-165
Haring, Divine Households:
Haring B.J.J., Divine Households. Administrative and Economic Aspects of the New Kingdom Royal Memorial Temples in Western Thebes, [Egyptologische Uitgaven 12], Leiden 1997
Haring B., The Scribe of the Mat: From Agrarian Administration to Local Justice, in: DeM in the Third Millennium, 129-158
Harris-Wente, Atlas of the Royal Mummies:
Harris J.E., Wente E.F. (eds.), An X-ray Atlas of the Royal Mummies, Chicago – London 1980
van Heel-Haring, Writing in a Workmen's Village:
van Heel K.D., Haring B.J.J., Writing in a Workmen's Village. Scribal Practice in Ramesside Deir el-Medina, Leiden 2003
Helck H.W., Die Inschrift über die Belohnung des Hohenpriesters *Imn-ḥtp*, MIO 4, 1956, 161-178
Helck, Verwaltung:
Helck W., Zur Verwaltung des Mittleres und Neuen Reiches, [PÄ 3], Leiden – Köln 1958
Helck, Thronbesteigungsdaten:
Helck W., Bemerkungen zu den Thronbesteigungsdaten im Neuen Reich, Studia Biblica et Orientalia 3 (= Analecta Biblica 12), 1959, 113-129
Helck, Materialien:
Helck W., Materialien zur Wirtschaftsgeschichte des Neuen Reiches, I-VI, Wiesbaden 1961-69

Helck W., Feiertage und Arbeitstage in der Ramessidenzeit, JESHO 7, 1964, 136-166
Helck W., Eine Briefsammlung aus der Verwaltung des Amuntempels, JARCE 6, 1967, 135-151
Helck, Wirtschaftsgeschichte:
Helck W., Wirtschaftsgeschichte des Alten Ägypten im 3. und 2. Jahrtausend vor Chr., [HdO 1. Abt., 1.Bd, 5.Abschnitt], Leiden/Köln 1975
Helck W., Chronologische Schwachstellen (III), GM 70, 1984, 31-32
Helck W., Drei Thronbesteigungsdaten der XX. Dynastie, GM 79, 1984, 7-9
Helck W., Der Anfang des Papyrus Turin 1900 und «Recycling» im Alten Ägypten, CdE 59, 1984, 242-247
Helck W., Zur Datierung der Hohenpriesterinschrift PM II^2, 174 (516), Or 53, 1984, 52-56
Helck W., s.v. Wenamun, in: LÄ VI (1986), 1215-1217
Helck W., Drei ramessidische Daten, SAK 17, 1990, 205-214
Helck OPG:
Helck W., Die datierten und datierbaren Ostraka, Papyri und Graffiti von Deir el-Medineh, [ÄA 63], Wiesbaden 2002
Hieratische Papyrus aus den Königlichen Museen zu Berlin, III, Leipzig 1911
Hofmann I., Indices zu W. Helck, Materialien zur Wirtschaftsgeschichte des Neuen Reiches, [AAWLM 1969 -13], Wiesbaden 1970
Hornung, Untersuchungen:
Hornung E., Untersuchungen zur Chronologie und Geschichte des Neuen Reiches, [ÄA 11], Wiesbaden 1964
Hornung E., Zur „Dritten Zwischenzeit" Ägyptens (review of Kees, Hohenpriester), OLZ 61, 1966, 437-442
Hornung E., New Kingdom, in: Ancient Egyptian Chronology, 197-217
Jackson H.M., "The shadow of Pharaoh, your lord, falls upon you": once again *Wenamun* 2.46, JNES 54, 1995, 273-286
Jansen-Winkeln K., Zum militärischen Befehlsbereich der Hohenpriester des Amun, GM 99, 1987, 19-22
Jansen-Winkeln K., Das Ende des Neuen Reiches, ZÄS 119, 1992, 22-37
Jansen-Winkeln K., Der Beginn der libyschen Herrschaft in Ägypten, Biblische Notizen 71, 1994, 78-97
Jansen-Winkeln K., Der Schreiber Butehamun, GM 139, 1994, 35-40
Jansen-Winkeln K., Die Plünderung der Königsgräber des Neuen Reiches, ZÄS 122, 1995, 62-78
Jansen-Winkeln K., Die thebanischen Gründer der 21. Dynastie, GM 157, 1997, 49-74
Jansen-Winkeln K., Zur Geschichte der „Cachette" von Deir el-Bahri, in: DeM in the Third Millennium, 163-170
Jansen-Winkeln K., Der thebanische 'Gottesstaat', Or 70, 2001, 153-182
Jansen-Winkeln K., Relative Chronology of Dyn. 21, in: Ancient Egyptian Chronology, 218-233
Jansen-Winkeln, InschrSp I:
Jansen-Winkeln K., Inschriften der Spätzeit. Teil I: Die 21. Dynastie, Wiesbaden 2007
Janssen J.J., Vizier Mentehetef, JEA 53, 1967, 163-164
Janssen J.J., review of: Wente LRL, BiOr 25, 1968, 37-39
Janssen, Commodity Prices:
Janssen J.J., Commodity Prices from the Ramessid Period. An Economic Study of the

Village of Necropolis Workmen at Thebes, Leiden 1975
Janssen J.J., Prolegomena to the Study of Egypt's Economic History during the New Kingdom, SAK 3, 1975, 127-185
Janssen J.J., Agrarian Administration in Egypt During the Twentieth Dynasty, BiOr 43, 1986, 351-366
Janssen J.J., On Style in Egyptian Handwriting, JEA 73, 1987, 161-167
Janssen J.J., Marriage Problems and Public Reactions (P. BM 10416), in: Baines J. et al. (eds.), Pyramid Studies and other Essays presented to I.E.S. Edwards, [Occasional Publications 7], London 1988, 134-137, pls. 25-28
Janssen LRLC:
Janssen J.J., Late Ramesside Letters and Communications, [Hieratic Papyri in the British Museum VI], London 1991
Janssen J.J., Requisitions from Upper Egyptian Temples (P. BM 10401), JEA 77, 1991, 79-94, pl. 4.2
Janssen J.J., A New Kingdom Settlement. The Verso of Pap. BM. 10068, AoF 19, 1992, 8-23
Janssen J.J., Literacy and Letters at Deir el-Medîna, in: Village Voices, 81-94
Janssen J.J., Debts and Credit in the New Kingdom, JEA 80, 1994, 129-136
Janssen, Village Varia:
Janssen J.J., Village Varia. Ten Studies on the History and Administration of Deir el-Medina, [Egyptologische Uitgaven 11], Leiden 1997
Janssen J.J., Idiosyncrasies in Late Ramesside Hieratic Writing, JEA 86, 2000, 51-56
Janssen J.J., Once Again the Accession Date of Ramesses IX, GM 191, 2002, 59-65
Janssen J.J., Donkeys at Deir el-Medîna, [Egyptologische Uitgaven 19], Leiden 2005
Janssen J.J., Pestman P.W., Burial and Inheritance in the Community of the Necropolis Workmen at Thebes (Pap. Bulaq X and O. Petrie 16), JESHO 11, 1968, 137-170
Jenni H. (ed.), Das Grab Ramses' X. (KV 18), [AH 16], Basel 2000
Junge, Neuägyptisch:
Junge Fr., Einführung in die Grammatik des Neuägyptischen, Wiesbaden 1996
Kees, Herihor:
Kees H., Herihor und die Aufrichtung des thebanischen Gottesstaates, [NGWG 2.1], Göttingen 1936, 1-20
Kees, Priestertum:
Kees H., Das Priestertum im ägyptischen Staat vom Neuen Reich bis zur Spätzeit, [PdÄ 1], Leiden – Köln 1953
Kees, Hohenpriester:
Kees H., Die Hohenpriester des Amun von Karnak von Herihor bis zum Ende der Äthiopenzeit, [PdÄ 4], Leiden 1964
Keller C.A., How Many Draughtsmen Named Amenhotep? A Study of Some Deir el-Medina Painters, JARCE 21, 1984, 119-129
Keller C.A., Un artiste égyptien à l'œuvre: le dessinateur en chef Amenhotep, in: DeM et la Vallée des Rois, 83-114
Kemp, Ancient Egypt:
Kemp B.J., Ancient Egypt. Anatomy of Civilization, London – New York 1998
Kikuchi T., Das Graffito Nr. 3981a und eine aus den Late Ramesside Letters bekannte Familie der Nekropolenschreiber, GM 160, 1997, 51-58

Kikuchi T., Graffiti Nr. 3974-3982 aus dem Gebiet des Grabes Amenophis' III im Westtal der Könige, Memnonia 7, 1996, 163-184

Kitchen K.A., Family Relationships of Ramesses IX and the late Twentieth Dynasty, SAK 11, 1984, 127-134

Kitchen TIP:
Kitchen K.A., The Third Intermediate Period in Egypt (1100-650 BC), Warminster 1986^{2}

Kitchen K.A., The Titularies of the Ramesside Kings as Expression of their Ideal Kingship, ASAE 71, 1987, 131-141

Kitchen, RamInscr:
Kitchen K.A., Ramesside Inscriptions. Historical and Biographical, I-VIII, Oxford 1969-90

Kitchen K.A., The Third Intermediate Period in Egypt: An Overview of Fact & Fiction, in: Libyan Period in Egypt, 161-202

Koenig Y., Les ostraca hiératiques inédits de la Bibliothèque nationale et universitaire de Strasbourg, [DFIFAO 33], Cairo 1997

Koenig Y., Nouveaux textes Rifaud I, CRIPEL 10, 1988, 57-60, pls. 4-7

Korostovtsev M.A., *Ieratichesky Papirus 127 iz sobranija GMII im. A.S. Pushkina*, Moscow 1961

Korostovtsev M., Grammaire du néo-égyptien, Moscow 1973

Krauss, Sothis- und Monddaten:
Krauss R., Sothis- und Monddaten. Studien zur astronomischen und technischen Chronologie Altägyptens, [HÄB 20], Hildesheim 1985

Krauss R., Ein Modell für die chronologische Einordnung der Maunier-Stele (Stele der Verbannten), GM 219, 2008, 41-48

Kruchten, Études de syntaxe:
Kruchten J.-M., Études de syntaxe néo-égyptienne. Les verbes *ꜥḥꜥ*, *ḥmsi* et *sḏr* en néo-égyptien. Emploi et signification, Bruxelles 1982

Lacovara P., Quirke S., Podzorski P.V., A Third Intermediate Period Fortress at El-Ahaiwah, CRIPEL 11, 1989, 59-68

Leblanc C., *Ta Set Neferou*. Une nécropole de Thèbes-Ouest et son histoire, I, Cairo 1989

Lefebvre G., Herihor, vizir (statue du Caire, n° 42190), ASAE 26, 1926, 63-68

Lefebvre, Grands Prêtres:

Lefebvre G., Histoire des Grands Prêtres d'Amon de Karnak jusqu'a la XXIe Dynastie, Paris 1929

Lefebvre G., Inscriptions concernant les Grands Prêtres d'Amon Romê-Roÿ et Amenhotep, Paris 1929

Lefèvre D., La fortresse d'el-Hibeh: papyrus inédits de la XXIe dynastie, BSFE 165, 2006, 32-47

Lesko, Dict. I-II:
Lesko L.H., A Dictionary of Late Egyptian, vol. I-II (2nd ed.), Providence 2002-2004

Libyan Period in Egypt:
Broekman G.P.F., Demarée R.J., Kaper O.E. (eds.), The Libyan Period in Egypt. Historical and Cultural Studies into the 21st-24th Dynasties: Proceedings of a Conference at Leiden University, 25-27 October 2007, [Egyptologische Uitgaven 23], Leiden 2009

Living and Writing:
Dorn A., Hofmann T. (eds.), Living and Writing in Deir el-Medine. Socio-historical Embodiment of Deir el-Medine Texts, [AH 19], Basel 2006

Lopez, Ostraca:
Lopez J., Ostraca Ieratici, [Catalogo del Museo Egizio di Torino, vol. III], fasc. 1-4, Milan

1978-84

Lopez J., review of Ventura, City of the Dead, in: BiOr 45, 1988, 545-551

Lorton D., The Treatment of Criminals in Ancient Egypt through the New Kingdom, JESHO 20, 1977, 2-64

Lull, Los sumos sacerdotes:
Lull J., Los sumos sacerdotes de Amón tebanos de la *wḥm-mswt* y dinastía XXI (ca. 1083-945 a.C.), [BAR IS 1469], Oxford 2006

Lull, Menkheperre:
Lull J., Beginning and End of the High Priest of Amun Menkheperre, in: Libyan Period in Egypt, 241-249

Lull G.J., Algunas cuestiones cronológicas de la *wḥm-mswt* y la Dinastía XXI. Sobre Amenhetep, Paiankh y Herihor, Trabajos de Egiptología (Papers on Ancient Egypt) 5/2, 2009, 49-61

Maspero, Momies royales:
Maspero G., Les momies royales de Déir el-Baharî, [MMAF 1], Paris 1889

McDowell, Jurisdiction:
McDowell A., Jurisdiction in the Workmen's Community of Deir el-Medîna, [Egyptologische Uitgaven 5], Leiden 1990

McDowell A., Agricultural Activity by the Workmen of Deir el-Medina, JEA 78, 1992, 195-206

McDowell, Hieratic Ostraca:
McDowell A., Hieratic Ostraca in the Hunterian Museum Glasgow (The Colin Campbell Ostraca), Oxford 1993

McDowell A.G., Contacts with the Outside World, in: Pharaoh's Workers, 41-59

McDowell, Village Life:
McDowell A.G., Village Life in Ancient Egypt. Laundry Lists and Love Songs, Oxford 2001

Meltzer E.S., Wenamun 2.46, JSSEA 17, 1987, 86-88

Meyer E., Gottesstaat, Militärherrschaft und Ständewesen in Ägypten, [SPAW 28], Berlin 1928, 495-532

Montet P., La nécropole royale de Tanis II: Les constructions et le tombeau de Psousennès à Tanis, Paris 1951

Montet, Géographie II:
Montet P., Géographie de l'Égypte ancienne. II: La Haute Égypte, Paris 1961

Morales A.J., The Suppression of the High Priest Amenhotep: A Suggestion to the Role of Panhesi, GM 181, 2001, 59-75

Morschauser S.N., "Crying to the Lebanon": A Note on Wenamun 2, 13-14, SAK 18, 1991, 317-330

Möller, Paläographie:

Möller G., Hieratische Paläographie I-III, Leipzig 1909-12

Müller H.W., Goldschmuck und ein Fayencekelch aus dem Grabe des Herihor (?), Pantheon. Internationale Zeitschrift für Kunst, 1979 – no. III, 237-246

Müller M., The "El-Hibeh"-Archive: Introduction & Preliminary Information, in: Libyan Period in Egypt, 251-264

Naguib, Le clergé féminin:
Naguib S.-A., Le clergé féminin d'Amon thébain à la 21e Dynastie, [OLA 38], Leuven 1990

Navailles R., Neveu F., Une ténébreuse affaire: P. Bankes I, GM 103, 1988, 51-60

Neveu, Grammaire:

Neveu Fr., La langue des Ramsès. Grammaire du néo-égyptien, Paris 1998 (2nd ed.)

Nims Ch.F., An Oracle Dated in "The Repeating of Births", JNES 7, 1948, 157-162

Nims Ch.F., Second Tenses in Wenamun, JEA 54, 1968, 161-164

Niwiński A., Problems in the Chronology and Genealogy of the XXIst Dynasty: New Proposals for their Interpretation, JARCE 16, 1979, 49-68

Niwiński A., The Bab el-Gasus Tomb and the Royal Cache in Deir el-Bahari, JEA 70, 1984, 73-81

Niwiński A., Butehamon – Schreiber der Nekropolis, SAK 11, 1984, 135-156

Niwiński A., Three More Remarks in the Discussion of the History of the Twenty-First Dynasty, BES 6, 1985, 81-88

Niwiński, 21st Dynasty Coffins:
Niwiński A., 21st Dynasty Coffins from Thebes. Chronological and Typological Studies, [Theben 5], Mainz 1988

Niwiński, Funerary Papyri:
Niwiński A., Studies on the Illustrated Theban Funerary Papyri of the 11th and 10th Centuries B.C., [OBO 86], Freiburg – Göttingen 1989

Niwiński A., Some Remarks on Rank and Titles of Women in the Twenty-First Dynasty Theban "State of Amun", DE 14, 1989, 79-89

Niwiński, Bügerkrieg:
Niwiński A., Bügerkrieg, militärischer Staatsstreich und Ausnahmezustand in Ägypten unter Ramses XI. Ein Versuch neuer Interpretation der alten Quellen, in: Gamer-Wallert I., Helck W. (eds.), Gegengabe. Festschrift für Emma Brunner-Traut, Tübingen 1992, 235-262

Niwiński A., Le passage de la XXe à la XXIIe dynastie. Chronologie et histoire politique, BIFAO 95, 1995, 329-360

Niwiński A., Les périodes *wḥm-mswt* dans l'histoire de l'Égypte: un essai comparatif, BSFE 136, 1996, 5-26

Niwiński A., The Twenty-first Dynasty on the Eve of the Twenty first Century, in: Hawass Z. (ed.), Egyptology at the Dawn of the Twenty-first Century. Proceedings of the Eight International Congress of Egyptologists, Cairo 2000, II, Cairo 2002, 416-422

Niwiński A., The Necropolis Scribes Butehamun in Light of Some New Material, in: Kloth N. et al. (eds.), Es werde niedergelegt als Schriftstück. Festschrift für Hartwig Altenmüller, [BSAK 9], Hamburg 2003, 295-303

Niwiński A., The Story of Thebes in the Third Intermediate Period, in: Mynářová J., Onderka P. (eds.), Thebes. City of Gods and Pharaohs, Prague 2007, 161-171

Niwiński A., review of: Jansen-Winkeln, InschrSp I, in: JEA 94, 2008, 317-319

Ohlhafer K., Zum Thronbesteigungsdatum Ramses' XI und zur Abfolge der Grabräuberpapyri aus Jahr 1 und 2 *wḥm-mswt*, GM 135, 1993, 59-72

Otto E., Topographie des thebanischen Gaues, [UGAÄ 16], Berlin – Leipzig 1952

Parker R.A., The Length of Reign of Ramses X, RdE 11, 1957, 163-164

Peden, Historical Inscriptions:

Peden A.J., Egyptian Historical Inscriptions of the Twentieth Dynasty, Jonsered 1994

Peden, Decline of Textual Graffiti:
Peden A.J., The Workmen of Deir el-Medina and the Decline of Textual Graffiti at West Thebes in Late Dynasty XX and Early Dynasty XXI, in: DeM in the Third Millennium, 287-290

Peden, Graffiti:
Peden A.J., The Graffiti of Pharaonic Egypt. Scope and Roles of Informal Writings (c. 3100-332 BC), [PÄ 17], Leiden – Boston – Köln 2001
Peet T.E., The Great Tomb Robberies of the Ramesside Age. Papyri Mayer A and B, I-II, JEA 2, 1915, 173-177, 204-206
Peet, Mayer Papyri:
Peet T.E., The Mayer Papyri A & B. Nos. M. 11162 and M. 11186 of the Free Public Museums, Liverpool, London 1920
Peet T.E., Fresh Light on the Tomb Robberies of the Twentieth Dynasty at Thebes, JEA 11, 1925, 37-55, 162-164
Peet T.E., The Supposed Revolution of the High-Priest Amenhotpe under Ramesses IX, JEA 12, 1926, 254-259
Peet T.E., The Chronological Problems of the Twentieth Dynasty, JEA 14, 1928, 52-73
Peet, Tomb Robberies:
Peet T.E., The Great Tomb-Robberies of the Twentieth Egyptian Dynasty, I-II, Oxford 1930
Peet T.E., The Egyptian Words for "Money", "Buy", and "Sell", in: Studies presented to F.Ll. Griffith, London 1932, 122-127
Peust, Indirekte Rede:
Peust C., Indirekte Rede im Neuägyptischen, [GOF IV, 33], Wiesbaden 1996
Pharaoh's Workers:
Lesko L.H. (ed.), Pharaoh's Workers. The Villagers of Deir el-Medina, Ithaca – New York 1994
Pleyte-Rossi, Papyrus de Turin:
Pleyte W., Rossi F., Papyrus de Turin, Leiden 1869-1876
Polz D., The Ramesesnakht Dynasty and the Fall of the New Kingdom: A New Monument in Thebes, SAK 25, 1998, 257-293
Posener G., Un papyrus d'El-Hîbeh, JEA 68, 1982, 134-138
Quack J.F., Eine Revision im Tempel von Karnak (Neuanalyse von Papyrus Rochester MAG 51.346.1), SAK 28, 2000, 219-232
Quack J.F., Ein neuer Versuch zum Moskauer literarischen Brief, ZÄS 128, 2001, 167-181
Quack J.F., Henuttawis machtlose Unschuld. Zum Verständnis von LRL Nr. 37, in: Gallois Chr. et al. (eds.), Mélanges offerts à François Neveu, [BdE 145], Cairo 2008, 259-263
Quirke S.G.J., Tait W.J., Egyptian Manuscripts in the Wellcome Collection, JEA 80, 1994, 145ff., pls. 13-14
Redmount C.A., El Hibeh: A Brief Overview, in: Hawass Z.A., Richards J. (eds.), The Archaeology and Art of Ancient Egypt. Essays in Honor of David B. O'Connor, [CASAE 36], Cairo 2007, II, 303-311.
Reeves C.N., Excavations in the Valley of the Kings, 1905/6: a Photographic Record, MDAIK 40, 1984, 227-235, pls. 24-36
Reeves, Valley of the Kings:
Reeves C.N., Valley of the Kings. The decline of a royal necropolis, London – New York 1990
Reeves-Wilkinson, The Complete Valley of the Kings:
Reeves N., Wilkinson R.H., The Complete Valley of the Kings. Tombs and Treasures of Egypt's Greatest Pharaohs, Cairo 2002 (2nd ed.)
Romer J., Valley of the Kings, London 1981
Roth A.M., Some New Texts of Herihor and Ramesses IV in the Great Hypostyle Hall at

Karnak, JNES 42, 1983, 43-53

Römer M., Der Handel und die Kaufleute im alten Ägypten, SAK 19, 1992, 257-284

Römer, Gottes- und Priesterherrschaft:
Römer M., Gottes- und Priesterherrschaft in Ägypten am Ende des Neuen Reiches. Ein religionsgeschichtliches Phänomen und seine sozialen Grundlagen, [ÄAT 21], Wiesbaden 1994

Rößler-Köhler U., Pianch – Nedjmet – Anchefenmut – eine Kleinigkeit, GM 167, 1998, 7-8

Ryholt K., A Pair of Oracle Petitions Addressed to Horus-of-the-Camp, JEA 79, 1993, 189-198

Ryholt K., Two New Kingdom Oracle Petitions, O. BMFA 72.659, 72.666, RdE 48, 1997, 279-282

Sabek Y., Der hieratische Papyrus Berlin P 10497, ZÄS 129, 2002, 75-84, pls. 15-16

Sadek A.A., Varia Graffitica, VA 6, 1990, 109-120

Sass B., Wenamun and his Levant – 1075 BC or 925 BC?, Ägypten und Levante 12, 2002, 247-255

Satzinger, Neuägyptische Studien:
Satzinger H., Neuägyptische Studien. Die Partikel ir. Das Tempussystem, [Beihefte zur WZKM 6], Wien 1976

Satzinger H., Übersetzungsvorschläge und Anmerkungen zu einigen neuägyptischen Texten, in: Bryan B.M., Lorton D. (eds.), Essays in Egyptology in honor of Hans Goedicke, San Antonio 1994, 233-242

Satzinger H., How good was Tjeker-Baʿl's Egyptian? Mockery at foreign diction in the Report of Wenamūn, LingAeg 5, 1997, 171-176

Sauneron, Ostraca DeM:
Sauneron S., Catalogue des ostraca hiératiques non littéraires de Deir el-Médineh (nos. 550-623), [DFIFAO 13], Cairo 1959

Scheepers A., Le voyage d'Ounamon: un texte «littéraire» ou «non-littéraire»?, in: C. Obsomer, A.L. Osthoek (eds.), Amosiadès. Mélanges offerts au Prof. C. Vandersleyen, Leuven 1992, 355-365

Schipper, Wenamun:
Schipper B.U., Die Erzählung des Wenamun. Ein Literaturwerk im Spannungsfeld von Politik, Geschichte und Religion, [OBO 209], Freiburg – Göttingen 2005

Schneider T., Ramses X.: Person und Geschichte, in: Jenni H. (ed.), Das Grab Ramses' X. (KV 18), [AH 16], Basel 2000, 81-108

Sethe K., Die angebliche Rebellion des Hohenpriesters Amenhotp unter Ramses IX, ZÄS 59, 1924, 60-61

Sethe K., Sethos I. und die Erneuerung der Hundessternperiode (mit einem Exkurs über das *wḥm msw.t* der thebanischen Grabberaubungsakten), ZÄS 66, 1931, 1-7

Smith, Royal Mummies:
Smith G.E., The Royal Mummies, [CGC], Cairo 1912 (1st ed.), London 2000 (2nd ed.)

Spens R. de, Droit international et commerce au début de la XXIe dynastie. Analyse juridique du rapport d'Ounamon, in: N. Grimal, B. Menu (eds.), Le commerce en Égypte ancienne, [BdÉ 121], Cairo 1998, 105-126

Spiegelberg, Correspondances:
Spiegelberg W., Correspondances du temps des rois-prêtres publiées avec autres fragments épistolaires de la Bibliothèque Nationale, in: Notices et extraits des manuscrits de la Bibliothèque Nationale et autres bibliothèques publiés par Institut de France, vol. 34, Paris 1895, 199-317, pls. I-VIII

Spiegelberg W., Briefe der 21. Dynastie aus El-Hibe, ZÄS 53, 1917, 1-30
Spiegelberg W., Eine zurückgezogene Pachtkündigung, ZÄS 53, 1917, 107-111
Spiegelberg, Graffiti:
Spiegelberg W., Ägyptische und andere Graffiti (Inschriften und Zeichnungen) aus der thebanischen Nekropolis, Heidelberg 1921
Spiegelberg W., Die Empörung des Hohenpriesters Amenhotpe unter Ramses IX, ZÄS 58, 1923, 47-48
Stučevsky I.A., "The «First Priest» of Amun and Ramses IX" (in Russian), Vestnik Drevney Istorii 3 (157), 1981, 3-20
Stučevsky I.A., "The «Persecution» of Amenhotep, «First Priest» of Amun, and the Incursion of the Troops of Panehsi, «King's-son of Kush»" (in Russian), Vestnik Drevney Istorii 1 (163), 1983, 3-20
Stučevsky, Ramses II and Herihor:
Stučevsky I.A., *Ramses II i Herihor. Iz istorii drevniego Egipta epochi Ramessidov* (in Russian), Moscow 1984
Sturtewagen C., Studies in Ramesside Administrative Documents, in: S. Israelit-Groll, (ed.), Studies in Egyptology presented to Miriam Lichtheim, II, Jerusalem 1990, 933-942
Sweeney D., Involvement Category in Late Egyptian, in: S. Israelit-Groll, (ed.), Studies in Egyptology presented to Miriam Lichtheim, II, Jerusalem 1990, 943-979
Sweeney D., Women's correspondence from Deir el-Medineh, in: Sesto Congresso Internazionale di Egittologia. Atti, II, Turin 1993, 523-529
Sweeney, Idiolects:
Sweeney D., Idiolects in the Late Ramesside Letters, LingAeg 4, 1994, 275-324
Sweeney D., Henuttawy's guilty conscience (gods and grain in Late Ramesside Letter no. 37), JEA 80, 1994, 208-212
Sweeney D., review of: Village Voices, in: DE 30, 1994, 205-210
Sweeney D., Offence and Reconciliation in Ancient Egypt. A Study in Late Ramesside Letter No. 46, GM 158, 1997, 63-79
Sweeney, Letters of Reconciliation:
Sweeney D., Letters of Reconciliation from Ancient Egypt, in: I. Shirun-Grumach (ed.), Jerusalem Studies in Egyptology, [ÄAT 40], Wiesbaden 1998, 353-369
Sweeney, Women and Language:
Sweeney D., Women and Language in the Ramesside Period or, Why Women Don't Say Please, in: Eyre C.J. (ed.), Proceedings of the Seventh International Congress of Egyptologists, Cambridge, 3-9 September 1995, [OLA 82], Leuven 1998, 1109-1117
Sweeney, Correspondence and Dialogue:
Sweeney D., Correspondence and Dialogue. Pragmatic Factors in Late Ramesside Letter Writing, [ÄAT 49], Wiesbaden 2001
Taylor, Valley of the Kings in the TIP:
Taylor J.H., Aspects of the History of the Valley of the Kings in the Third Intermediate Period, in: After Tutankhamun, 186-206
Taylor, Horemkenesi:
Taylor J.H., Unwrapping a Mummy. The Life, Death and Embalming of Horemkenesi, London 1995
Taylor, The End of the New Kingdom:

Taylor J.H., Nodjmet, Payankh and Herihor. The End of the New Kingdom reconsidered, in: Eyre C.J. (ed.), Proceedings of the Seventh International Congress of Egyptologists, Cambridge, 3-9 September 1995, [OLA 82], Leuven 1998, 1143-1155

The Temple of Khonsu 1:
The Temple of Khonsu 1: Scenes of King Herihor in the Court, with Translations of Texts, [OIP 100], Chicago 1979

The Temple of Khonsu 2:
The Temple of Khonsu 2: Scenes and Inscriptions in the Court and the First Hypostyle Hall, with Translations of Texts and Glossary, [OIP 103], Chicago 1981

Theodorides A., Le testament d' Imenkhâou, JEA 54, 1968, 149-154

Thiers Ch., Civils et militaires dans lest temples. Occupation illicite et expulsion, BIFAO 95, 1995, 493-516

Thijs A., Two Books for one Lady. The mother of Herihor reconsidered, GM 163,1998, 101-110

Thijs A., Piankh's second Nubian campaign, GM 165, 1998, 99-103

Thijs A., Reconsidering the End of the Twentieth Dynasty, Part I: The fisherman Pnekhtemope and the date of BM 10054, GM 167, 1998, 95-108

Thijs A., Reconsidering the End of the Twentieth Dynasty, Part II, GM 170, 1999, 83-99

Thijs A., Reconsidering the End of the Twentieth Dynasty, Part III: Some hitherto unrecognised documents from the *wḥm mswt*, GM 173, 1999, 175-191

Thijs A., Reconsidering the End of the Twentieth Dynasty, Part IV: The Harshire-family as a test for the shorter chronology, GM 175, 2000, 99-103

Thijs A., "Please tell Amon to bring me back from Yar", Dhutmose's visits to Nubia, GM 177, 2000, 63-70

Thijs A., Reconsidering the End of the Twentieth Dynasty, Part V: P.Ambras as an advocate of a shorter chronology, GM 179, 2000, 69-83

Thijs A., Reconsidering the End of the Twentieth Dynasty, Part VI: Some minor adjustments and observations concerning the chronology of the last Ramessides and the *wḥm mswt*, GM 181, 2001, 95-103

Thijs A., Reconsidering the End of the Twentieth Dynasty, Part VII: The history of the viziers and the politics of Menmare, GM 184, 2001, 65-73

Thijs A., The Troubled Careers of Amenhotep and Panehesy: The High Priest of Amun and the Viceroy of Kush under the Last Ramessides, SAK 31, 2003, 289-306

Thijs A., Pap. Turin 2018, the journeys of the scribe Dhutmose and the career of the Chief Workman Bekenmut, GM 199, 2004, 79-88

Thijs A., In Search of King Herihor and the Penultimate Ruler of the 20th Dynasty, ZÄS 132, 2005, 73-91

Thijs A., „I was thrown out from my city" – Fecht's views on pap. Pushkin 127 in a new light, SAK 35, 2006, 307-326

Thijs A., King or High Priest? The problematic career of Pinuzem, GM 211, 2006, 81-88

Thijs A., The scenes of the High Priest Pinuzem in the Temple of Khonsu, ZÄS 134, 2007, 50-63

Thijs A.A.J., The Second Prophet Nesamun and his claim to the High-Priesthood, SAK 38, 2009, 343-353

Thomas E., *P3 Ḫr Ḫnỉ H̱nw/ n H̱nw Ḫnỉ*, A Designation of the Valley of the Kings, JEA 49, 1963, 57-63

Thomas, Royal Necropoleis:

Thomas E., The Royal Necropoleis of Thebes, Princeton 1966

Thomas E., The *k3y* of Queen Inhapy, JARCE 16, 1979, 85-92

Toivari J., Man versus Woman. Interpersonal Disputes in the Workmen's Community of Deir el-Medina, JESHO 40, 2, 1997, 153-173

Trigger et al., A Social History:
Trigger B.G. et al., Ancient Egypt: A Social History, Cambridge 1983

Turayev B.A., Papyrus Prachov *sobranija B.A. Turayeva*, Leningrad 1927

Valbelle D., Remarques sur les textes néo-égyptiens non littéraires (§1-5), BIFAO 76, 1976, 101-109

Valbelle D., Remarques sur les textes néo-égyptiens non littéraires (§6-10), BIFAO 77, 1977, 129-136

Valbelle D., Catalogue des poids à inscriptions hiératiques de Deir el-Médineh, N°s 5001-5423, [DFIFAO 16], Cairo 1977

Valbelle, Ouvriers:
Valbelle D., «Les Ouvriers de la Tombe». Deir el-Médineh à l'Époque Ramesside, [BdÉ 96], Cairo 1985

Valbelle D., Les archives de la Tombe, aujourd'hui, in: DeM et la Vallée des Rois, 157-171

Valley of the Sun Kings:
Wilkinson R.H. (ed.), Valley of the Sun Kings. New Explorations in the Tombs of the Pharaohs. Papers from the University of Arizona International Conference on the Valley of the Kings, Tucson 1995

Vandersleyen, L'Égypte II:
Vandersleyen Cl., L'Égypte et la Vallée du Nil, vol. II: De la fin de l'Ancien Empire à la fin du Nouvel Empire, Paris 1995

Ventura, City of the Dead:
Ventura R., Living in a City of the Dead. A Selection of Topographical and Administrative Terms in the Documents of the Theban Necropolis, [OBO 69], Freiburg – Göttingen 1986

Ventura R., On the Location of the Administrative Outpost of the Community of Workmen in Western Thebes, JEA 73, 1987, 149-160

Vernus, Affaires et scandales:
Vernus P., Affaires et scandales sous les Ramsès. La crise des valeurs dans l'Égypte du Nouvel Empire, [Bibliothèque de l' Égypte Ancienne], Paris 1993

Village Voices:
Demarée R.J., Egberts A.(eds.), Village Voices. Proceedings of the Symposium "Texts from Deir el-Medîna and their Interpretation", Leiden, May 31-June 1, 1991, Leiden 1992

Vittmann G., Die Hymne des Ostrakons Wien 6155 + Kairo CG 25214, WZKM 72, 1980, 1-6

Waddell W.G., Manetho with an English Translation, [The Loeb Classical Library], Cambridge Mass. – London 1964

Warburton D.A., State and Economy in Ancient Egypt. Fiscal Vocabulary of the New Kingdom, [OBO 151], Fribourg – Göttingen 1997

Weeks, Atlas:
Weeks K.R. (ed.), Atlas of the Valley of the Kings. Study Edition, [Publications of the Theban Mapping Project: III], Cairo – New York 2003

Wenig S., Einige Bemerkungen zur Chronologie der frühen 21. Dynastie, ZÄS 94, 1967, 134-139

Wente E.F., The Late Egyptian Conjunctive as a Past Continuative, JNES 21, 1962, 304-311

Wente E.F., The Suppression of the High Priest Amenhotep, JNES 25, 1966, 73-87

Wente LRL:

Wente E.F., Late Ramesside Letters, [SAOC 33], Chicago 1967

Wente E.F., On the Chronology of the Twenty-First Dynasty, JNES 26, 1967, 155-176

Wente E.F., Was Paiankh Herihor's son?, in: Drevny Vostok 1, Moscow 1975, 36-38

Wente, Letters:

Wente E.F., Letters from Ancient Egypt, [Writings from the Ancient World 1], Atlanta 1990

Wente-van Siclen, Chronology:

Wente E.F., Van Siclen III Ch.C., A Chronology of the New Kingdom, in: J.H. Johnson, E.F. Wente (eds.), Studies in Honor of George R. Hughes, [SAOC 39], Chicago 1976

Williams R.J., review of: Wente LRL, in: JNES 28, 1969, 137-139

Wimmer, Hieratische Paläographie:

Wimmer S., Hieratische Paläographie der Nicht-Literarischen Ostraka der 19. und 20. Dynastie I-II, [ÄAT 28], Wiesbaden 1995

Winand J., Le voyage d'Ounamon. Index verborum, concordance, relevés grammaticaux, [Aegyptiaca Leodiensia 1], Liège 1987

Winand, Études:

Winand J., Études de néo-égyptien, 1. La morphologie verbale, [Aegyptiaca Leodiensia 2], Liège 1992

Winand J., Derechef *Ounamon* 2, 13-14, GM 139, 1994, 95-108

Winand J., La grammaire au secours de la datation des textes, RdE 46, 1995, 187-202

Winand J., Les constructions analogiques du futur III en néo-égyptien, RdE 47, 1996, 117-145

Winand J., La négation *bn ... iwn3* en néo-égyptien, LingAeg 5, 1997, 223-236

Winand J., La progression au sein de la narration en égyptien. Éléments d'une grammaire du texte, BIFAO 100, 2000, 403-435

Winand J., À la croisée du temps, de l'aspect et du mode. Le conjonctif en néo-égyptien, LingAeg 9, 2001, 293-329

Winand J., L'ironie dans Ounamon: les emplois de *mk* et de *ptr*, GM 200, 2004,105-110

Winlock H.E., The Tomb of Queen Inhapi. An Open Letter to the Editor, JEA 17, 1931, 107-110

Young E., Some Notes on the Chronology and Genealogy of the Twenty-First Dynasty, JARCE 2, 1963, 99-112

Yoyotte J., Pharaons, guerriers libyens et grands prêtres. «La Troisième Période Intermédiaire», in: Tanis. L'or des pharaons. Catalogue de l'exposition au Grand Palais, Paris 1987, 51-76

The abbreviations LRL and LRLC (with successive numbers) are used here both to denote particular letters in the editions of J. Černý and J.J. Janssen respectively, but the former also as a convenient designation of the corpus of late Ramesside letters in general.

Introduction

Egypt and Thebes before the Accession of Ramesses XI

Ramesses VIII Setiherkhepeshef is believed to be the last son of Ramesses III to ascend the pharaoh's throne. He ruled for such a short time[1] that very few sources can actually be linked with his reign.[2] Even the location of his tomb is unknown,[3] although there is a hypothesis according to which KV 19 in the Valley of the Kings started to be built for him.[4] The ephemeral character of his reign stands at the root of the difficulties in determining his position within the Dynasty. In the list of princes from Medinet Habu he is ranked fourth, right after Ramesses VI,[5] but the view that he was this pharaoh's immediate successor is hardly acceptable anymore.[6]

Upon his death, power passed into the hands of Neferkare Setepenre Ramesses IX. Based on records in the Journal of the Necropolis, the date of his accession to the throne can be set between I *akhet* 18 and 23.[7] It is possible that the event took place on I *akhet* 21.[8] Ramesses IX was presumably a nephew of his predecessor and son of the prince Montuherkhepeshef (the Elder).[9] His mother is assumed to be Queen Takhat, who was buried in the Valley of the Kings, in the re-opened tomb of the usurper Amenmesse (KV 10).[10]

---

1 Most probably little more than a year, cf. von Beckerath, Chronologie, 86f.

2 Kitchen, RamInscr VI, 438-47; VII, 370; see also A.M. Amer, A Unique Theban Tomb Inscription under Ramesses VIII, GM 49, 1981, 9-12; Kitchen, in: LÄ V (1984), 124f.

3 Reeves, Valley of the Kings, 119, 271. It cannot be excluded that he was buried in the north, at Per-Ramesse, cf. Schneider in: H. Jenni (ed.), Das Grab Ramses' X. (KV 18), [AH 16], Basel 2000, 104-108.

4 Cf. ibid., 125 n. 54; Thomas, Royal Necropoleis, 131, 152. According to what E. Brock observed, the construction started while he was still only a prince; cf. Reeves-Wilkinson, The Complete Valley of the Kings, 167, 170. But the tomb was most certainly not taken into consideration as a burial place for the pharaoh Ramesses VIII.

5 The Epigraphic Survey. Medinet Habu V, Chicago 1957, pls. 299, 301. Cf. also comments provided by K. Seele, JNES 19, 1960, 184f., 186f., 203: Ramesses Setiherkhepeshef identified with the son of Ramesses VI; J. Monnet, BIFAO 63, 1965, 233.

6 See now von Beckerath, Chronologie, 83.

7 Cf. Helck, Analecta Biblica 12, 1959, 128.

8 Cf. J. von Beckerath, Drei Thronbesteigungsdaten der XX. Dynastie, GM 79, 1984, 7-8; id., Chronologie, 87, 117; Janssen, GM 191, 2002, 59ff.

9 K.A. Kitchen, Family Relationships of Ramesses IX, SAK 11, 1984, 127-134.

10 Reeves, Valley of the Kings, 104f.; A. Dodson, The Tomb of King Amenmesse: Some Observations,

During the reign of this particular king, the Valley of the Kings appears to have been turned into a burial ground for the royal family, which could mean that no new tomb construction was taking place in the Valley of the Queens.[11] It is a fact that the wife of Ramesses IX, Queen Baketwernel was laid to rest in KV 10, next to this ruler's mother.[12] The oldest son of the pharaoh, prince Montuherkhepeshef (the Younger), was interred in a tomb that was never finished (KV 19) and which could have started to have been built possibly for prince Setiherkhepeshef (the later Ramesses VIII).[13] In this context one is tempted to ask whether the objects found in connection with the burial of prince Montuherkhepeshef, in the tomb of the chancellor Bay (KV 13),[14] should not be linked to the father of Ramesses IX, that is, prince Montuherkhepeshef (the Elder), son of Ramesses III, ranked sixth in the list of princes from Medinet Habu.[15] The fragmentary cartouche of Queen Nubkhesebed,[16] wife of Ramesses VI, discovered in this tomb, indicates the time of burial of one of the two princes buried in KV 13 (prince Amonherkhepeshef beside Montuherkhepeshef);[17] the uncertainty of attribution is due to the fact that the cartouche cannot be linked conclusively with either one. Since the sarcophagus of Amonherkhepeshef (usurped from Queen Tauseret) was found in the sarcophagus chamber of the

DE 2, 1985, 7ff. (esp. p. 10); id., The Takhats and some other royal ladies of the Ramesside period, JEA 73, 1987, 224ff. As regards the scene in chamber "E", cf. O. Schaden, Some Observations on the Tomb of Amenmesse (KV-10), in: B.M. Bryan, D. Lorton (eds.), Essays in Egyptology in honor of Hans Goedicke, San Antonio 1994, 248 (in chamber "E"; this is chamber "D" in PM I/2², 518 (4), and plan on p. 510).

11 Cf. A. Dodson, JEA 73, 1987, 226. The tomb of Queen Tyti (QV 52) could be of later date, if K.A. Kitchen is right to see in her the wife of Ramesses X and mother of his heir, cf. Kitchen, SAK 11, 1984; 131f.; Dodson, JEA 73, 1987, 227ff. (opting against a hypothesis regarding Tyti as a daughter-wife of Ramesses III, cf. J. Grist, The identity of the Ramesside Queen Tyti, JEA 71, 1985, 71-81). Similarly, the question of the location of the tomb of Queen Baketwernel ("Royal Wife of Menmaatre") of papMayer A, 4, 3-4, cannot be resolved, although it is commonly suggested that it was one of the tombs in the Valley of the Queens, cf. Dodson, DE 2, 1985, 10; id., JEA 73, 1987, 225; Vernus, Affaires et scandales, 42.

12 In chamber "F", cf. Schaden, op.cit., 248f. (chamber "E" in PM I/2², 518 (8), and plan on p. 510).

13 Cf. above, n. 4.

14 H. Altenmüller, SAK 19, 1992, 33-6; id., SAK 21, 1994, 8-13, 17-18.

15 And not the son of Ramesses VI, as H. Altenmüller would have it, cf. id., Prinz Mentu-her-chopeschef aus der 20. Dynastie, MDAIK 50, 1994, 1-12. In his discussion of the genealogical position of this prince H. Altenmüller refers to an idea already propounded by K. Sethe, according to which the princes from the Medinet Habu list (nos 4-10) are the sons of Ramesses VI and not Ramesses III. The cartouche of Queen Nubkhesebed (see below) cannot be taken as a decisive argument for this. Moreover, the fact that Montuherkhepeshef was buried in KV 13 after Amonherkhepeshef does not mean necessarily that he belonged to a younger generation than the latter.

16 On the north wall of the second corridor, cf. ibid., 5f., figs. 5-6.

17 H. Altenmüller, SAK 21, 1994, 4ff., 15ff. (with discussion regarding the tomb of prince Amonherkhepeshef in the Valley of the Queens, QV 55); A.J. Peden, GM 181, 2001, 86.

tomb and that of Montuherkhepeshef in the corridor preceding this chamber,[18] it is equally possible to assume that the tomb was also the burial place of Queen Nubkhesebed (perhaps in the second corridor of KV 13). This recalls to some extent the situation existing in the tomb of Amenmesse reused in the reign of Ramesses IX, when successive rooms of the tomb were occupied. Chronological assumptions do not exclude the possibility that at least the queen could have been buried during the reign of Ramesses IX (the two princes being buried probably earlier). Neither can it be excluded that the decision to bury members of the royal family in the Valley of the Kings was made in direct consequence of the robberies that plagued the Valley of the Queens at the time (on this, see below).

The Journal of the Necropolis, extensive sections of which have survived, reflects the intensive activities undertaken by the crew of the royal necropolis during this period. Papyri fragments containing the records for the years 8-10 and 13-17 of the reign of Ramesses IX[19] show that the work in the necropolis matched in intensity that of earlier periods although not without impediments. Interestingly, there is continuous mention of Libyan marauders or "desert people" (*ḫ3s.tyw*) seen in the Thebaid. Texts refer to the Meshwesh and Rebu tribal groups which are also known from earlier sources. Despite the absence of detailed information, there can be no doubt that the appearance of the Libyans must have filled the local population with terror, causing periodic stoppages at the royal necropolis.[20] The incessant pressure by the desert nomads during the rule of the last three pharaohs of the dynasty is surely a mark of the ineffectiveness of the central administration and military weakness of the state, unable to mount any action on a broader scale against the menace from the west. The alleged trade with the newcomers, assuming that such relations were actually

[18] See Altenmüller, SAK 21, 1994, fig. 1.

[19] For the sequence of preserved fragments of the journal, see now Valbelle, Ouvriers, 39-43, 53; Helck OPG, 465ff. Most of the fragments are still unpublished, cf. Valbelle, Ouvriers, 39ff.; id., in: DeM et la Vallée des Rois, 167f.; Bellion, Catalogue, 84ff.; R.J. Demarée, Les archives de la Tombe, in: B. Gratien, R. Hanoune (eds.), Lire l'écrit. Textes, archives, bibliothèques dans l'Antiquité, "Ateliers" 12, 1997, 68. New additions have been made recently, as announced by R.J. Demarée, Recent work on the administrative papyri in the Museo Egizio, Turin, in: Atti di Sesto Congresso Internazionale di Egittologia, II, Turin 1993, 104f. (pap Turin 2074); id., News from the Turin archives of Ramesside papyri, in: L'Impero Ramesside, Rome 1997, 67-69; see also F. Tiradritti, in: L'Egitto a Milano. Nuove Acquisizioni e Restauri, Milan 1991, 15-17, 44, figs. 2-3.

[20] See especially Černý, CAH[3] II.2, 616-619; K. Kitchen, Les suites des guerres libyennes de Ramsès III, RdE 36, 1985, 177-179; B. Haring, Libyans in the Late Twentieth Dynasty, in: Village Voices, 71-80 (= id., Libyans in the Theban Region, 20th Dynasty, in: Atti di Sesto Congresso Internazionale di Egittologia, II, Turin 1993, 159-165); id., Divine Households, 271; Jansen Winkeln, BN 71, 1994, 88ff.; Ch. Booth, The Role of Foreigners in Ancient Egypt. A study of non-stereotypical artistic representations, [BAR Int. Series 1426], Oxford 2005, 40.

initiated at a later date (in the reign of Ramesses XI and the Renaissance Era),[21] are presumably testimony to the changed conditions of life in the Thebaid on the threshold of a new age characterized by the growing role of peoples of Libyan origin. Unpublished parts of the Journal of the Necropolis of year 8 of the reign of Ramesses IX seem to bear this out, mentioning a woodcutter Khonsumose, who received something from the Rebu.[22]

There is nothing to indicate any changes in the structure of the necropolis crew despite periodic perturbations in its work. On the contrary. Surviving fragments of the Journal of the Necropolis confirm the same number of crew members and, more importantly, mention all the key officers. Records of grain distribution in the Journal of the Necropolis for year 17 of the pharaoh's reign, dated to I *peret* (day 12?), reflect the full number of the crew in this period:[23] 62 men and three captains and one overseer of draughtsmen, that is, 66 in all. At this time the chiefs of the crew were Harmose son of Anherkhau (on the left side) and Userkhepesh, acting perhaps on behalf of his elderly father Nekhemmut (on the right side),[24] while Horisheri, son of the famous scribe Amennakht, was the necropolis scribe. The latter's brother Amenhotep son of Amennakht was head of the draftsmen.[25] The document also mentions two door-keepers, meaning guards of some kind, responsible for the crew's contacts with the outside world.[26] The presumed door-keepers during this time were Khonsumose (son of Panehesy) and probably Tuthmosis son of Ramose.[27]

For the moment little can be said of the "Stato Civile", a document which, once it is published, will surely enlighten our knowledge of the royal necropolis

21 Cf. Haring, in: Atti di Sesto Congresso, 162.

22 Cf. Haring, in: Village Voices, 73f.; id., in: Atti di Sesto Congresso, 162 (this is a fragment recently attached to pap Turin 2074 by R.J. Demarée). Haring suggested that the Rebu mentioned in the text could have been immigrants who settled in the region and not necessarily hostile invaders.

23 Botti-Peet, Giornale, pl. 11: year 17, ro. A 4, 11-12=Kitchen, RamInscr VI, 568, 15-16. See also Helck OPG, 522; Valbelle, Ouvriers, 105 (tab. III).

24 Cf. Černý, Community, 308-310; Bierbrier LNK, 33f., 38; Davies, Who's Who at DeM, 57, 279.

25 Cf. Davies, Who's Who at DeM, 112f.; see also below.

26 On the role of door-keepers within the institution of the royal necropolis, see Černý, Community, 161ff. Ventura, City of the Dead, 107ff., 161; McDowell, Jurisdiction, 41-46; id., in: Pharaoh's Workers, 45; G. Burkard, «...Die im Dunkeln sieht man nicht». Waren die Arbeiter im Tal der Könige privilegierte Gefangene? in: H. Guksch et al. (eds.), Grab und Totenkult im alten Ägypten, München 2003, 133; id., MDAIK 59, 2003, 12.

27 Cf. Černý, Community, 167f., 170. As regards the latter, cited in the journal of year 16, cf. Kitchen, RamInscr VI, 652, 1; Helck OPG, 515; and probably in the journal of year 17, cf. Kitchen, RamInscr VI, 589, 5; Helck OPG, 518: Tuth[mosis]; the other possible candidate would be the door-keeeper Tuthmosis son of Kadjore.

crew structure at the end of the 20th Dynasty.[28] Recent research has demonstrated that the surviving fragments are parts of at least a few separate documents. The dating of these records remains an open issue,[29] but at least some of them should be referred to the reign of Ramesses IX.

There is again nothing to indicate the transfer of the crew from the village in Deir el-Medina to Medinet Habu at such an early date.[30] The list of residents of the temple complex in Medinet Habu in pap.BM 10068vo., dating undoubtedly from the beginnings of the reign of Ramesses XI, does not include any members of the crew. On the other hand, the smaller number of ostraca from the Deir el-Medina settlement starting with the rise to the throne of Ramesses IX is surely not the criterion by which to judge whether the crew left the village or not. It can be perceived as no more than proof of possibly less intensive operations by the crew and its supervising institution. Difficulties in dating such "late" documents undoubtedly play a role here as well.[31] Neither is it probably a mere coincidence that the decline in the number of ostraca from this area is paralleled by a simultaneous appearance of extensive versions of the Journal of the Necropolis on papyrus. It may be merely accidental, but the fact is that from this point onwards the necropolis crew and its scribes were less prone to using either limestone or ceramic ostraca to make notes (in spite of the facility in obtaining these kinds of writing materials).

The relatively small group of ostraca from this period originating from Deir el-Medina (and the nearest vicinity) presumably include oDeM 570[32] and oDeM 571, both documenting the functioning of the necropolis staff at the very end of the 20th Dynasty. The latter refers to a strike or else a demonstration of some kind on the part of the necropolis staff. It is noteworthy that on this particular occasion the workmen appealed directly to the high priest of Amun himself, following in this precedents from earlier times:[33]

---

[28] Cf. G. Botti, Frammenti di Registri di Stato Civile della XXª Dinastia, in: Rendiconti della Reale Accademia Nazionale dei Lincei 31, 1922-1923, 391-394; Valbelle, Ouvriers, 56ff.; id., in: DeM et la Vallée des Rois, 162. The document(s) will be published soon by R.J. Demarée and D. Valbelle.

[29] Cf. Demarée, in: Atti di Sesto Congresso Internazionale di Egittologia, II, Turin 1993, 105.

[30] As suggested by Eyre, BiOr 44, 1987, 25; see also Peden, Graffiti, 189 n. 357; McDowell, Jurisdiction, 84.

[31] Cf. Janssen, in: Village Voices, 86 n. 25.

[32] Sauneron, Ostraca DeM, pl. 11-11a; Kitchen, RamInscr VI, 664; cf. also Ventura, City of the Dead, 87, 105; McDowell, Jurisdiction, 98. As regards its dating to the reign of Ramesses IX, cf. Kitchen, loc.cit.; it must be noted, however, that Gutgesell (Datierung, 406) has suggested a much earlier date (Ramesses III/IV).

[33] As regards the role of the high priest of Amun in the matters of the necropolis during the 20th Dynasty, cf. Valbelle, Ouvriers, 142f.; McDowell, Jurisdiction, 10; Janssen, Village Varia, 1f.; Demarée, GM 183, 2001, 5f.; Häggman, Directing DeM, 185ff.

"[...] (2) [of] Amun-Ra king of the gods [Montu-tawy? ...] (3) They passed guard-posts (*inb.w*)[34] and they spent the day (4) (at) the fortress of the necropolis (*p3 ḫtm n p3 ḫr*),[35] but it was not noticed [...]. (5) They repeated (it) once again, and they descended to the riverbank (*mry.t*)[36] in regnal year 9, fourth month of *shemu*, day 26[37]. [...] (6) the fortress of the necropolis. They summoned the high priest [of Amun ...], (7) and he came to them (to) the fortress of the necropolis. [...] (8) and he has spoken to [them ...]" (oDeM 571).[38]

This important document is undoubtedly of late 20th Dynasty date, but a more precise attribution of it to the reign of Ramesses IX[39] or that of Ramesses XI remains an open question.[40] The reading of the year date given in the middle of the text as a change of date (i.e., before IV *shemu*, 26) is dubious, but were it indeed the case, then a dating to the reign of Ramesses XI cannot be excluded, bearing in mind that the pharaoh ascended the throne on III *shemu* 20 (see Chapter 1). It is much more probable, however, that there was another date originally at the beginning of the text, thus referring simply to an earlier phase of the workmen's strike (namely, the first crossing of the walls) described earlier in the text. In consequence, the date given in line 5 refers to a subsequent demonstration, when the workmen of the necropolis descended to the port located somewhere on the riverbank. As a matter of fact, there is nothing in the text itself to date it to the reign of Ramesses XI. A highly doubtful reading of the name of an official of the

[34] The number of "four walls", suggested in the transcription of S. Sauneron, must be emended now, see Lopez, BiOr 45, 1988, 551; Janssen, BSEG 16, 1992, 49 n. 59.

[35] For the sake of convenience I have retained here the traditional meaning of the term in spite of serious objections against it presented by Ventura (City of the Dead, 83ff.), and others. Alternatively, it can be translated as "enclosure of the necropolis", cf. McDowell, Village Life, 6, 267. For the meaning of the term, see below.

[36] As regards the meaning of *mry.t* as the marketplace or the port, see now McDowell, in: Pharaoh's Workers, 46; G. Burkard, «...Die im Dunkeln sieht man nicht». Waren die Arbeiter im Tal der Könige privilegierte Gefangene? in: H. Guksch et al. (eds.), Grab und Totenkult im alten Ägypten, München 2003, 141ff. For its possible location, cf. B. Kemp, D. O'Connor, An ancient Nile harbour. University Museum excavations at the 'Birket Habu', The International Journal of Nautical Archaeology and Underwater Exploration, 1974, no. 3.1, 133f.

[37] Numeral 26 given by the editor may be possibly emended to 27, cf. Helck, Materialien IV, (585); compare however, id., OPG, 22, 497.

[38] Sauneron, Ostraca DeM, pl. 11-11a; with emendations proposed by Lopez, in: BiOr 45, 1988, 550f. The text has been translated several times: cf. Frandsen, JEA 75, 1989, 122; Helck, Materialien IV, (585); and quite recently, id., OPG, 497; Burkard, in: Grab und Totenkult, 134; compare also some comments and partial translations in: Ventura, City of the Dead, 93, 104, 123 (Ex. 12), 137f.

[39] Cf. Valbelle, Ouvriers, 142 n. 9; Janssen, Village Varia, 172; id., BSEG 16, 1992, 49 n. 59; Helck OPG, 22, 497.

[40] Cf. Frandsen, JEA 75, 1989, 122 n. 51; Ventura, City of the Dead, 135 n. 83; Helck, Materialien IV, (585); similarly Burkard, MDAIK 59, 2003, 26; see also Vernus, Affaires et Scandales, 215 n. 53.

domain of Amun adds nothing to the discussion on its dating.[41] More probably the name of the high priest of Amun should be restored here (thus possibly Ramessesnakhte?).

Notwithstanding its precise dating, the ostracon is an important source documenting the existence of an administrative centre of the necropolis (*pꜣ ḫtm n pꜣ ḫr*) at the very end of the 20th Dynasty. According to recent studies on the topography of the Theban necropolis, it should be located somewhere between the settlement at Deir el-Medina and the Ramesseum.[42] The functioning of this centre at such a late date seems to suggest that the institution of the royal necropolis still existed in its previous form. The issuing of provisions and distribution of wages took place right there,[43] but it was also a convenient place for contacts between the crew and the necropolis authorities.[44]

As for the location of the "fortress of the necropolis", as described in the text of oDeM 571, we should take into consideration suggestions made recently by A. McDowell that the lacuna at the end of line 5 of the text could be restored with words referring to the gang returning back to the fortress.[45] As a consequence, the fortress of the necropolis need not be situated on the riverbank and the region in the close proximity of the necropolis should be taken into consideration (see above).

Similarly, the very existence of fortified posts or guard houses, mentioned in the above-cited text as "walls" (*inb.w*),[46] leaves no doubt that the necropolis

---

41 Assuming Sauneron's proposed reading, no plausible explanation can be offered here in regard of his identity; certainly he cannot be identified with the well known overseer of the treasury Montuemtawy, who was active in the first half of the 20th Dyn., cf. Černý, in: CAH³ II.2, 627; Helck, Verwaltung, 413f., 518f. (no. 30); Janssen, Village Varia, 163 n. 103; A.J. Peden, The Reign of Ramesses IV, Warminster 1994, 57f.; Polz, SAK 25, 1998, 278; M. Römer, ZÄS 131, 2004, 77 n. 23. For the latter's involvement in provisioning the crew of the necropolis, see especially papDeM XXIV: J. Černý, Y. Koenig, Papyrus hiératiques de Deir el-Médineh, II, [DFIFAO 22], Cairo 1986, pl. 9-9a; Allam HOP, pl. 87=Kitchen, RamInscr VI, 134f. (A.47).

42 Cf. R. Ventura, On the Location of the Administrative Outpost of the Community of Workmen in Western Thebes, JEA 73, 1987, 149-160; id., City of the Dead, 83ff.; Sturtewagen, in: S. Israelit-Groll (ed.), Studies in Egyptology presented to Miriam Lichtheim, II, Jerusalem 1990, 938 (4); McDowell, Jurisdiction, 93-105; see now G. Burkard, in: H. Guksch, D. Polz (eds.), Stationen. Beiträge zur Kulturgeschichte Ägyptens R. Stadelmann gewidmet, Mainz 1998, 438 n. 17; id., in: Grab und Totenkult, 133-36, fig. 2; id., Das *ḫtm n pꜣ ḫr* von Deir el-Medine. Seine Funktion und die Frage seiner Lokalisierung, in: Living and Writing, 31-42.

43 This is why it was sometimes interpreted as an open space where distribution of wages took place, cf. McDowell, Jurisdiction, 101f.; id., in: Pharaoh's Workmen, 58 ("enclosure of the tomb"); similarly Eyre, BiOr 44, 1987, 278; Lopez, BiOr 45, 1988, 550. Nonetheless, its suggested role as an outpost controlling the crew's contacts with the outside world cannot be doubted either, cf. Burkard, MDAIK 59, 2003, 37ff.

44 Cf. Ventura, City of the Dead, 98ff.

45 McDowell, Jurisdiction, 105; otherwise Helck, OPG, 497: "Sie wiederholten das und stiegen zum Hafen herunter und [erreichten] die Festung...".

46 For the meaning of the term as guard-posts or watchposts, see Ventura, City of the Dead, 120

(including the royal tombs in the Valley of the Kings) was still effectively protected, although the purpose and character of the posts cannot be explained precisely and there is no certainty about their exact location.[47] Elsewhere the system of watch posts has been described more precisely as "the five walls" (*tꜣ 5 inb.t*)[48] or "walls of the Pharaoh" (*inb.wt n pr-ꜥꜣ*).[49] Texts sometimes mention only "the walls" (*nꜣ inb.wt*) or just "a wall" (*wꜥ inb.t*),[50] raising serious doubts as to whether these designations referred to a planned system of fortifications or rather to some guard posts located in strategic points of the necropolis. It is safe to imagine that these were not successive protective walls or watch posts forming a planned defence system,[51] but rather a number of guard posts dispersed in the whole area of the necropolis.

The available texts provide, for example, information about the guard-post (*tꜣ inb(.t)*)[52] located possibly somewhere in the region to the north of the village of Deir el-Medina, in the vicinity of the causeway (*pꜣ sṯꜣ*) of one of the temples,[53] but also the walls (*inb.w*) to the north (or else the northern wall?)[54] of the royal tomb (*tꜣ s.t pr-ꜥꜣ*),[55] located perhaps in the Valley of the Kings, if not in a more extensive area of the necropolis (possibly the eastern part?),[56] assuming the rest of the text has any connection with it whatsoever:[57] "from the great place of

(referring however to the fem. form *inb.t*).

47 Cf. Vernus, Affaires et scandales, 84f.; Valbelle, in: DeM et la Vallée des Rois, 165; McDowell, in: Pharaoh's Workers, 58; Burkard, in: Grab und Totenkult, 136-139.

48 Ventura, City of the Dead, 120ff. (with further references); Frandsen, JEA 75, 1989; 113ff.; see also Burkard, in: Grab und Totenkult, 136-139; id., in: DeM in the Third Millennium, 59 n. 20.

49 As for the latter, see oQurna 691vo., 5: Burkard, in: DeM in the Third Millennium, 55ff.

50 For the latter, see e.g. Gardiner RAD, 56, 13; cf. a comment by Ventura, City of the Dead, 122f. (Ex. 7) – "one *inbt*"; Frandsen, JEA 75, 1989, 121.

51 As suggested by Ventura, City of the Dead, 120ff., fig. 1; cf. Lopez, BiOr 45, 1988, 550.

52 For the meaning of the term as guard post, cf. W.F. Edgerton, JNES 10, 1951, 139 n. 10; Thomas, JEA 49, 1963, 61; K. Baer, Or 34, 1965, 431 n. 3; Lesko, Dict. I, 33; Valbelle, in: DeM et la Vallée des Rois, 165.

53 O. Varille 39+IFAO 1255: Kitchen, RamInscr VII, 301, 4-5; cf. Frandsen, JEA 75, 1989, 117 (translation); it has been suggested that the causeway of the temple of king Mentuhotep III Sankhkare was meant here, cf. ibid., 120f.; id., in: S. Israelit-Groll (ed.), Studies in Egyptology presented to Miriam Lichtheim, I, Jerusalem 1990, 174f. (n. 21).

54 So Ventura, City of the Dead, 22, 124; Helck OPG, 523. On the other hand, it must be noted that Ventura (op.cit., 142 n. 104) does not interpret the "walls" mentioned here in relation to the royal tomb in his Exx. 14-16 (ibid., 124) as elements of the royal tomb.

55 Necropolis Journal of Year 17, ro. B 1, 3: Botti-Peet, Giornale, pl. 14=Kitchen, RamInscr VI, 570, 13-14.

56 As a matter of fact one wonders whether the region described here is that of the royal necropolis of the 17th Dynasty at Dra Abu el-Naga, bearing in mind that investigations undertaken in years 16 and 17 of Ramesses IX took place mostly in this region of the Theban necropolis.

57 Which is highly doubtful indeed, because the following text may be taken as simply a description of the inspecting tour, comparable to that described in papAbbott, cf. McDowell, Jurisdiction, 196.

Pharaoh (*t3 s.t ꜥ3.t n pr-ꜥ3*),[58] l.p.h, down to the garden of king [Amenhot]ep, l.p.h., the great god, (and) down to the southern valley (*t3 int rsy*),[59] as far as the edge (*wꜥr.t*)[60] of a flood(plain)".[61]

The ruins of some buildings in the region of the "Vallée du Dolmen", including the structure still standing near the so-called "menhir" on the ridge dividing the "Vallée du Dolmen" from the valley of the village at Deir el-Medina,[62] may be interpreted as an archaeological remnant of such a defence system for the royal necropolis.[63] As a matter of fact, the structure in question may be interpreted as a guard house of the Madjoy-policemen, placed in a strategic location above the Valley of the Queens and near the start of the road leading from the village of Deir el-Medina to the Valley of the Kings.

One way or another, it cannot be denied that fortified posts of some kind were meant to assure the security of the royal necropolis. The system was apparently effective still in the late years of Ramesses IX, as exemplified by the testimony of one of the thieves: "I was going far beyond the fortress (*itḥ*) of the west of the City according to my custom regularly, in year 13 of the Pharaoh" (papBM 10054vo. 1, 5-6).[64] Although the true meaning of the term used here cannot be explained precisely,[65] the text demonstrates explicitly that fortified posts of some sort were still in place at the end of the Ramesside period, marking distinctly the limits of an area forbidden to trespassers.

---

58 For the meaning of the term *s.t ꜥ3.t* referring directly to the royal tomb (less possibly the royal necropolis in general, cf. especially Černý, Community, 69ff.; Wente, JNES 32, 1973, 225ff.; Thomas, JARCE 16, 1979, 90, 92 n. 40; Ventura, City of the Dead, 142; Reeves, Valley of the Kings, 231.

59 Doubtful in meaning, cf. Ventura, City of the Dead, 152; it can be identified possibly as the Valley of the Queens, cf. Ch. Leblanc, Ta Set Neferou. Une nécropole de Thèbes-Ouest et son histoire, I, Cairo 1989, 4.

60 For the meaning of this obscure term as "desert" or else "desert plateau", see Černý, JEA 15, 248 n. 30; Lesko, Dict. I, 95.

61 Necropolis Journal of Year 17, ro. B 1, 4-5: Botti-Peet, Giornale, pl. 14=Kitchen, RamInscr VI, 570, 15-571, 1; the passage has been translated in Ventura, City of the Dead, 124 (Ex. 17); Helck OPG, 523.

62 Cf. Leblanc, op.cit., 5f., fig. 4, pls. 30-31; see also Bruyère, Rapport (1945-1946 et 1946-1947), 74f., fig. 58; it is worth noting here that Bruyère suggested a Ramesside date for the structure near the "menhir" and proposed a religious function for the establishment at the same time, cf. ibid., 75.

63 For other structures of this kind located in the vicinity of the Valley of the Kings, see also Thomas, JEA 49, 1963, 61. A building located to the south of the village at Deir el-Medina, supposed to be a guardhouse of the Madjoy police (cf. Bruyère, Rapport (1934-1935), 34f., fig. 5) is doubtful in character and function. As regards the brick structures near Gurna tomb 1152, to the north of Deir el-Medina, mentioned by Frandsen, JEA 75, 1989, 121 n. 49, these are in fact the ruins of the Coptic monastery, currently being excavated by T. Górecki of the Polish Center of Mediterranean Archaeology, cf. PAM 15, 2003, 173.

64 Peet Tomb Robberies, pl. 7=Kitchen, RamInscr VI, 490, 8-10.

65 As for the meaning of *itḥ*, cf. Lesko, Dict.I, 52.

It is not without significance that the high priest of Amun played such a prominent role in matters concerning the necropolis and this is well in accord with the new situation, being the result of a gradual diminishing of the significance and effectiveness of the central administration.[66] Actually, the events of the end of the reign of Ramesses IX led to a substantial weakening of the role played by the vizier at Thebes, especially as there is nothing in the sources about the institution of the southern viziers.[67] His frequent absence from the region must have been at the root of this situation, with other high ranking officials taking over his responsibilities, mostly those connected with the supervision of the royal necropolis and sustaining the necropolis staff. In the words of the Mayor of the West, Paweraa: "It was a (serious) offence on the part of these two scribes of the necropolis that they have approached this Mayor of Thebes to report to him, although their predecessors (lit. fathers) had never reported to him. But they used to report to the vizier when he was staying in the southern district. And if he happened to be in the northern district the Madjoy of the necropolis – (these) servants of His Majesty, l.p.h, used to go downstream to the place where the vizier was, carrying their memoranda" (papAbbott 6, 20-23).[68]

As in earlier times, these were probably heavy irregularities in delivery of provisions, which prompted the protest of the necropolis staff described in the text of oDeM 571. With so few sources at hand we can only guess that the economic crisis of the period caused a number of similar incidents and we cannot fill out with details the general picture of the situation in the region. It is noteworthy that oSydney R97, doubtful in dating, also refers to a workmen's strike,[69] as do also some slightly later fragments of the necropolis journal of year 3 of Ramesses X.[70]

While the number of ostraca from the village is very limited for this period, the same cannot be said of the ostraca found in the Valley of the Kings. A substantial number was discovered during the cleaning of the tomb of Ramesses

[66] See above, note 33.

[67] On the role of viziers in this period, cf. Häggman, Directing DeM, 231ff.

[68] Peet, Tomb Robberies, pl. 4=Kitchen, RamInscr VI, 479, 6-11.

[69] Cf. C.J. Eyre, A "Strike" Text from the Theban Necropolis, in: Glimpses of Ancient Egypt. Studies in Honour of H.W. Fairman, Warminster 1979, 80-91; J. Ray, in: K.N. Sowada, B.G. Ockinga (eds.), Egyptian Art in the Nicholson Museum, Sydney, Sydney 2006, 214-216, pl. 39. As regards its dating to the reign of Ramesses IX, see Gutgesell, Datierung, 357f.; Janssen, BSEG 16, 1992, 49; Helck OPG, 514; more probably, however, the text must be dated to the middle of the 20th Dynasty, see now Kitchen, RamInscr VI, 151 (A.96); P. Tallet, BIFAO 99, 1999, 419; Haring, in: DeM in the Third Millennium, 147; id., Divine Households, 271; Häggman, Directing DeM, 172.

[70] Cf. Häggman, Directing DeM, 173f.

IX (KV 6) in the spring of 1888.[71] No detailed records exist and unfortunately the ostraca were mixed up during the transport of the finds to Cairo with a set found in the tomb of Ramesses VI (KV 9).[72] The latter circumstance could explain why ostraca from the reign of Ramesses IX turned up in the tomb of Ramesses VI – for example, oCG 25184, which is believed to be a plan of the tomb of Ramesses IX[73] – but according to G. Daressy this particular ostracon was discovered during the cleaning of KV 9.[74] J. Černý has suggested that G. Daressy was simply mistaken, but there is another tempting possibility for explaining the presence of this as well as other ostraca in this location. In this respect oCG 25017 is particularly significant; according to G. Daressy it was found in KV 9, but a matching fragment from New York (oMMA 14.6.215), from the excavations of Th. Davis, bears a cartouche of Ramesses IX.[75] In this case as well K. Keller suggested a mistake on Daressy's part that could be derived from the mix up which occurred during the transport to Cairo.[76] Yet the very presence of the ostraca inside any of these tombs is difficult to explain assuming that they would have been left there once the preparation of the tomb had been completed.

After all, all such artefacts would need to have been removed from the tomb prepared for receiving a burial. The fact that they were found inside a royal tomb must be attributed to secondary movement of rock rubble which penetrated into the tomb on some later occasion, most probably after the tomb had been plundered.

These ostraca could have come originally from the central part of the Valley of the Kings where it is only natural to expect ostraca connected with the building of surrounding tombs, that is, among others, KV 6 and 9.[77] Ostraca were also found in this area during excavations carried out by E. Ayrton for Th. Davis in

[71] G. Daressy, Rapport sur le déblaiement des tombes 6 et 9 de Biban el Molouk, ASAE 18, 1919, 270-274. Only some of the ostraca found at the time are included in: Daressy, Ostraca. The provenance of three ostraca found by Daressy and published by Černý, Ostraca CG, 126 (oCG 25626, 25628, 25629) is not known.

[72] Cf. Daressy, Ostraca, 112 (index IV).

[73] Ibid., 35, pl. 32; id., Un plan égyptien d'une tombe royale, RAr 32, 1898, 235-240; Černý, Valley of the Kings, 23 (no. 1); Kitchen, RamInscr VII, 378f.; C. Rossi, The Plan of a Royal Tomb on O.Cairo 25184, GM 184, 2001, 45-53; id., JEA 87, 2001, 74.

[74] Daressy, Ostraca, 35; but in another place he said that the ostracon had been found (in four pieces) in the tomb of Ramesses IX (KV 6), cf. id., RAr 32, 1898, 239.

[75] Keller, in: Deir el-Médineh et la Vallée des Rois, 93f., 107 (fig. 8).

[76] Ibid., 101 n. 21.

[77] Of special importance is the case of the two ostraca with cartouches of Ramesses IX found recently during the clearance of the tomb of Ramesses VII (KV 1), cf. E.C. Brock, in: Valley of the Sun Kings, 61.

1907/08,[78] and then by H. Carter in the 1920, 1920/21 and 1922/23 seasons.[79] At least part of the material found here could have been brought from even a considerable distance, for example, ostraca discarded near the tomb of Merenptah (KV 8), in the vicinity of which there were some workmen's huts. Some of the ostraca could have been brought down by flash floods following heavy rainfall.[80] If at any moment the entrances to KV 6 and 9 were below the level in the centre of the valley, limestone chips (including ostraca) would have easily penetrated the interior of these lower-lying tombs. But this could not have happened before the tombs had been plundered and abandoned.

This explanation, however, does not fit the case of ostraca connected, as G. Daressy believed, with the tomb of Ramesses X (KV 18),[81] which is found after all in the eastern part of the valley at some distance. It is possible that ostraca with cartouches of Ramesses X[82] were somehow brought to the spot at the time of the burial of his predecessor. But the concentration of ostraca found in KV 6 and 9 (about one hundred in the former case and two hundred in the latter) could suggest that there were other, more persuasive reasons for this state of affairs. Namely, it cannot be excluded that the "workmen's huts", situated at the entrance to KV 9,[83] in the area of KV 55[84] and also at the entrance to KV 10 as indicated by recent research, had a part in it. There are no grounds for dating these structures,[85] but they were surely in use during the building of the Ramesside

78 Cf. Reeves, Valley of the Kings, 307f. (oCG 25615, 25617, 25627a).

79 Ibid., 327 (site 6: nos. "244, 246-247"), 328f. (sites 9, 12, 14), 330 (site 16), 331 (site 18: no. "434").

80 This was presumably what happened to oCG 25581 (from year 2 of Merenptah), found by Carter in the area of the shelters at the entrance to KV 9. Similarly in the case of oCG 25671 (mentioning the scribe Ramose of the time of Ramesses II); Carter mistakenly believed that it "probably dates the level of the huts of this part of the valley", cf. Reeves, Valley of the Kings, 325.

81 Daressy, ASAE 18, 1919, 272f. It is naturally impossible for the chips left from cutting the tomb of Ramesses X to have been used as fill in the entrance to the tomb of Ramesses IX. G. Daressy noted already that such an assumption is contrary to what is imagined today about access to the royal tombs during this period.

82 These are: oCG 25190-93, 25210.

83 H. Carter, A.C. Mace, The Tomb of Tut.Ankh.Amen I, London 1923, 82, 87, pl. 10; Reeves, Valley of the Kings, 61, pl. 14 (Carter's plan = Carter MSS, I.G.52).

84 Cf. Carter, Mace, op.cit., 87; J. Romer, Valley of the Kings, London 1981, 247.

85 H. Carter thought that the structures around the entrance to the tomb of Ramesses VI (KV 9) were of rather early date, cf. supra, note 80; see however Carter, Mace, op.cit., 87 ("workmen's huts, used probably by the labourers in the tomb of Rameses"). Contradictory opinions were also expressed by Romer, op, cit., 247 (19th Dynasty), 253 (Ramesses VI). Reeves (Valley of the Kings, 61) dates them to the time of the building of KV 9. It should be noted by the way that Carter's "huts" were located considerably below the entrance to the tomb of Ramesses VI, presumably because the entrance to the tomb was located at a high level in order to prevent flooding of the complex during heavy rain, cf. Romer, op.cit., 247.

tombs located in this part of the Valley of the Kings, foremost KV 9 and then also perhaps KV 6. It is not to be excluded then that the huts were still in use in the terminal years of the 20th Dynasty, and also at the time when the construction of the tomb of Ramesses X (KV 18) commenced which would explain the presence of ostraca dated to the reign of this king in the area (especially as the huts situated near KV 18 appear to be dated to a slightly earlier period).[86] It should be noted, however, that the available documentation does not settle the question whether the clusters of huts in the central part of the Valley of the Kings, in the neighbourhood of KV 6, 9 and 55 were contemporary, thus leaving open the possibility that they were built successively in different periods.[87]

Even if sporadically these huts in different parts of the Valley of the Kings were used as provisional shelters for the gang working in the valley or for its supervisors, which is not very likely in any case,[88] it is possible to assume for them an administrative function connected with the construction of the royal tombs. The traditional view that the gang spent the week near their work location and returned to the village in Deir el-Medina only for the days free of work,[89] is no longer tenable, especially since the two locations were separated by no more than half an hour march on foot.

The considerable concentration of ostraca in this part of the Valley of the Kings is proof of intensive administrative activities carried out on the spot of the actual work. Surely there must have also existed some kind of stores (*p3 wḏ3*),[90] which could have held tools, but also wicks and oil for the lamps, as well as pigments and other materials necessary in tomb decoration. Many of the documents from the area can be dated to the reign of Ramesses IV and the time when his tomb (KV 2) was under construction. Determining provenance

86 Cf. E. Paulin-Grothe, T. Schneider, New workmen's huts in the Valley of the Kings, Egyptian Archaeology 19, 2001, 5: Ramesses IV-VI; similarly A. Dorn, MDAIK 61, 2005, 1: Ramesses IV-VII.

87 According to Romer's information (op.cit., 247), the structures by KV 9 and 55 were on the same level, that is, "about 3 feet above the bedrock, and 12 feet below the entrance to KV 9". According to Reeves (Valley of the Kings, 61): "The entrance to KV 62 was situated 13 feet below the 20th Dynasty ground level, beneath a series of huts..."; this opinion seems to be in apparent contradiction to the previous one.

88 Workmen and their superiors working in the valley could rest in shelters situated in the shade at the foot of the rock wall. This is proved by the numerous graffiti found in different parts of the Valley of the Kings, cf. e.g. graffiti nos. 423, 431, 438, 442, 1400; see also no. 2188.

89 Cf. Bruyère, Rapport (1934-1935), 345f.; see also Valbelle, Ouvriers, 239; McDowell, Village Life, 17.

90 On their existence in the Valley of the Kings: Černý, CAH[3] II.2, 621; id., Community, 227; Janssen, Commodity Prices, 457f.; Ventura, City of the Dead, 88f. (esp. notes 35-36). It is debatable whether the name is identical with *p3 wḏ3 n Pr-ꜥ3*, or else it refers to a separate institution. As regards the meaning of the term, see also Janssen, Pestman, JESHO 11, 1968, 153f. (d).

for particular ostraca is also very difficult in this case.[91] The much later oCG 25577,[92] which is dated to the beginning of the 21st Dynasty,[93] mentions [*wḏ*]*ꜣ n Ḥḳꜣ-mꜣꜥt-Rꜥ*, "[storehous]e of Hekamaatre (i.e., Ramesses IV)." If we accept J. Černý's reconstruction as correct, then it would be a clue as to the name of the storehouse situated in this part of the Valley of the Kings. The storehouse could have been erected in the reign of Ramesses IV in connection with the project for building this king's tomb. What is surprising is that the name, but also a specific building lasted through the onset of the 21st Dynasty. Not improbably, oCG 25577 could be connected with works carried out in KV 4 in connection with its usurpation for the projected burial of Paynudjem I or other activities of a similar nature prevalent in the Valley of the Kings at the beginning of the 21st Dynasty.

It should be noted that the large numbers of limestone ostraca left at the "building site" in the Valley of the Kings means by necessity that the official reports on papyrus must have been written largely on the spot. Otherwise it is difficult to imagine that large amounts of these ostraca would have been transported out of the valley to wherever such reports were written in their final form.[94] True, at least some of the ostraca should be treated not as drafts or provisional notes, but as original documents.[95] But even so, their presence in a given location indicates where they were filed.[96] This is enough to prompt a search for places inside the valley which could have served as local administrative centres. The extensive complex (?) in the centre of the Valley of the Kings is an ideal location for such activity, although it cannot be excluded that other structures of the type found in the valley served the same role but perhaps in different periods.[97] Quite

[91] Cf. Janssen, Village Varia, 164-167.

[92] Černý, Ostraca CG, 51*, pl. 40. The ostracon was found during Th. Davis' excavations in 1902, cf. Reeves, Valley of the Kings, 293.

[93] Cf. Černý, op.cit., 28; Valbelle, Ouvriers, 346; Häggman, Directing DeM, 356ff. (year 14, most probably from the time of Paynudjem I).

[94] Cf. Sauneron, Ostraca DeM, X n. 4; XVIIf. But this must have taken place as well, considering that among the ostraca found in the village at Deir el-Medina there are examples that are connected directly with the works carried out in the Valley of the Kings.

[95] Cf. S. Allam, Sind die nichtliterarischen Schriftostraka Brouillons?, JEA 54, 1968, 121-128.

[96] Ibid., 127f.

[97] Apart from the mentioned one should also note smaller concentrations of huts that could have served as watch posts for the guards (?). This groups could possibly include the huts situated to the east of the entrance to the tomb of Siptah (KV 47), cf. Félix-Aubriot-Kurz, Plans de position, pl. 47; Weeks, Atlas, 16, 22. Of equally enigmatic nature are the huts in the Western Valley; for the latter, see Thomas, Royal Necropoleis, 61; Félix-Aubriot-Kurz, op.cit., pls. 88, 89, 90, 93, 95, 99, 100; R. Wilkinson, The Other Valley of the Kings. Exploring the Western Branch of the Theban Royal Necropolis, KMT 2 (3), 1991, 52, and fig. on p. 51; Weeks, Atlas, 12, 14.

possibly these buildings were generally termed as *t3 wḥy.t n p3 ḫr*.[98] It is open to discussion then whether there were actually any structures inside the valley that belonged to the workmen. Information about *t3 ʿ.t nty m sḫ.t(-ʿ3.t?)*,[99] that is, houses (or else shelters or huts),[100] need not refer to buildings inside the Valley of the Kings, for they could equally well designate any kind of architecture of this type localized outside the Deir el-Medina village, whether in the near vicinity of the settlement[101] or even in the countryside or near the port (*mry.t*).[102] They are mentioned, among others, in oGardiner 23,[103] dated to the reign of Ramesses IX: the "house/hut (*ʿ.t*) in the field (*sḫ.t*)" (l. 6), and the "house/hut (*ʿ.t*) in the field (*sḫ.t*) of the workman Mose" (l. 7-8). Sometimes the location of these huts was given more precisely in relation to the well known buildings of the Theban west side: "the house/hut (*ʿ.t*) beside (*r-gs*) the temple of Ah[mes] Nefer[t]ary, l.p.h., of Menset" (papTurin 2070/154vo. 2, 4).[104] In the case of huts inside the Valley of the Kings[105] or in its immediate vicinity, it is difficult to assume that they were the private property of individual labourers working on the royal tombs. Quite the contrary, it seems that these buildings were part of an administrative and logistics centre for the works carried out in the Valley.[106]

It has been pointed out recently that the "village du col"[107] was not a group of huts inhabited by workmen while away from the village in Deir el-Medina,

---

[98] See Černý, Community, 92; cf. also Valbelle, Ouvriers, 89; id., in: P. Posener-Kriéger (ed.), Mélanges Gamal Eddin Mokhtar, II, [BdÉ 97/2], Cairo 1985, 316.

[99] Cf. Janssen, Village Varia, 97f., n. 75 (sources).

[100] For the meaning of *ʿ.t* as a house in general, cf. Gardiner AEO II, 206*f.; id., Wilbour Papyrus Comm., 34; Janssen, Commodity Prices, 397. A distinction has been suggested between the "official" houses (*pr*) in the village of Deir el-Medina (being a state property), and huts/shelters (*ʿ.t*) located outside the village (apparently private possessions of the workmen), cf. Helck, Materialien III, (340); Janssen, Pestman, JESHO 11, 1968, 160; M. Muszynski, OrAnt 16, 1977, 189 (r); H.-W. Fischer-Elfert, in: Miscellanea Aegyptologica Wolfgang Helck zum 75. Geburtstag, Hamburg 1989, 57 (d); see, however, some reservations expressed by E.S. Bogoslovsky, *Drevne-Egipetskie Mastera*, Moscow 1983, 256; G. Bouvier et al., JEA 87, 2001, 99f. (q). As a matter of fact, it is hardly probable that all the huts (*ʿ.t*) were the private property of workmen, especially those located in the Valley of the Kings.

[101] Cf. Valbelle, Ouvriers, 120f.; L. Meskell, in: DeM in the Third Millennium, 267f.

[102] Valbelle, op.cit., 253; see also Černý, Community, 91 on two possible meanings of *sḫ.t*.

[103] Černý-Gardiner HO, pl. 43.4 (=Kitchen, RamInscr VI, 663); Allam HOP 153f. (no. 149); see also Janssen, Pestman, JESHO 11, 1968, 160; Helck, Materialien III, (337)f.; as for its dating cf. Gutgesell, Datierung, 308f., and Helck OPG, 502.

[104] Cf. Allam HOP, 327f. (no. 281), pl. 121; M. Muszynski, P. Turin Cat. 2070/154, OrAnt 16, 1977, 183ff., esp. p. 186, fig. 2, pl. 10.

[105] Cf. Bogoslovsky, op.cit., 255 n. 30; Janssen, Village Varia, 97f.; Y. Koenig, BIFAO 81, 1981, 42 n. 3.

[106] Cf. Bogoslovsky, op.cit., 256.

[107] PM I/2^2, 588f.; Bruyère, Rapport (1934-1935), 345-64, pls. 35-40; id., CdE 11, 1936, 338-340; Weeks, Atlas, 13, 16.

as believed so far, but could have been a place where specific administrative duties were discharged, presumably as a checkpoint on the road to the Valley of the Kings[108] (it remains to be determined in which period).[109] Interestingly, B. Bruyère who worked there in 1935, found a surprisingly small number of ostraca.[110] A similar function in the Valley of the Queens could have been played by the village (*tȝ wḥyt*) situated in its western part.[111] Although its existence is documented in an earlier time, it could have still been in existence in the end of the 20th Dynasty, as indicated perhaps by Paykharu's testimony recorded in year 16 of Ramesses IX, following an inspection in the Valley of the Queens: "I do not know any place here among these tombs, except this tomb, which is open, and this house/hut (*tȝy* ˁ*.t*), which (I) pointed out to you" (papAbbott 5, 7-8).[112] Too little is known unfortunately about these "workmen huts", whether in the Valley of the Kings or in other parts of the Theban necropolis, as most of the structures of this kind were dismantled and removed during earlier excavations. Their chronology and function must remain therefore the object of hypothetical considerations. Some hope draws from recent work in the vicinity of KV 10 and KV 18. This research may help to understand better the mechanism governing the operations of the crew and the administrative staff of the royal necropolis.

It seems that many of the ostraca found in the central part of the Valley of the Kings can be linked directly with the gang and the building of the tomb of Ramesses IX. There are lists of workmen, records concerning supplies for them as well as receipts for deliveries of materials (such as oil for the lamps and papyrus), not to mention other records that can be classified generally as fragments of the Journal of the Necropolis.[113] Beside the ostraca mentioned above (oCG 25184

[108] Cf. L. Meskell, in: DeM in the Third Millennium, 266f.; G. Burkard, «...Die im Dunkeln sieht man nicht». Waren die Arbeiter im Tal der Könige privilegierte Gefangene? in: H. Guksch et al. (eds.), Grab und Totenkult im alten Ägypten, München 2003, 139-41. The absence of evidence related to the occupation of these shelters was noted already by Bruyère, Rapport (1934-1935), 349; id., CdE 11, 1936, 340; see also McDowell, Village Life, 17. Neither can the cultic function of the place be excluded entirely, see now N. Toye, Amon-de-la-bonne-rencontre, GM 211, 2006, 89ff.

[109] Dating to the 19th-20th Dynasty: Bruyère, Rapport (1934-1935), 346.

[110] Cf. Bruyère, op.cit., 362f., fig. 212. One naturally cannot exclude that other museum ostraca of undetermined provenance actually came from here.

[111] Cf. Černý, Community, 92; C. Leblanc, *Ta Set Neferou*. Une nécropole de Thèbes-Ouest et son histoire I, Cairo 1989, 5, 63 n. 15, fig. 3, pls. 16-17; Janssen, Village Varia, 156f. See also "the hut (ˁ*.t*) in the Valley of the Queens (*tȝ s.t nfr.w*)", as written in oDeM 112vo. 5: Černý, Ostraca DeM I, pl. 62; Helck, Materialien III, (338).

[112] Peet, Tomb Robberies, pl. 3=Kitchen, RamInscr VI, 475, 7-8; cf. Peden, Historical Inscriptions, 234f. It was "the house (*tȝ* ˁ*.t*) of the workman of the necropolis Amenemone son of Huy" (papAbbott 5, 4); for the comment, see Černý, Community, 89.

[113] See, for example, documents compiled by Helck OPG, 465-67; as regards the activity of the crew

and oCG 25017+oMMA 14.6.215), one can also include oCG 25252 with a letter addressed to the mayor Paser[114] and oGardiner 164 with a draft of a letter to the pharaoh himself.[115] One should also note an ostracon with the text of a hymn to the night sun (oWien 6155+oCG 25214),[116] and an ostracon with the text of an eulogy (?) of Ramesses IX (oCG 25199).[117]

Other ostraca of unknown provenience can also be connected presumably with the building of the tomb of Ramesses IX. The text of oErmitage 2973 (two separate pieces purchased in Luxor)[118] records deliveries of pigments used in the decoration of the tomb in year 14 (III *akhet*, 14). The ostracon oBM 5672+oCG 25649, which was written only a month later, mentions deliveries of pigments and notes that some of them were leftovers from the decoration of the tomb of Ramesses VII (Itamun).[119]

A hieratic graffito on the right wall of the third corridor, covered with a coat of whitewash, must have been written undoubtedly when work commenced on the decoration of the tomb.[120] It is a brief note without a year date: "Fourth month of *akhet*, day 22: laying plaster in the corridor (*p3 st3-nṯr*)". It is by chance that the same work, carried out in the four month of *achet*, days 1-3, was recorded on oCG 25299, also found in KV 6.[121] Much later mentions of gypsum being

in this period, see Valbelle, Ouvriers, 207-215.

114 Daressy, Ostraca, 66, pl. 53; also found in KV 6.

115 Kitchen, RamInscr VII, 380f. (A.54); for its dating, see Gutgesell, Datierung, 454.

116 Cf. Kitchen, RamInscr VII, 379f.; Erman, ZÄS 38, 1900, 29f. (IV); G. Vittmann, Die Hymne des Ostrakons Wien 6155+Kairo 25214, WZKM 72, 1980, 1-6. According to Vittmann, a whole group of ostraca published by A. Erman (ZÄS 38, 1900, 19-41) was found in KV 6 and can be dated to the rule of this pharaoh (he also includes oCG 25120 in this group).

117 Daressy, Ostraca, 38 (no photo; mention of year 10 rather doubtful); Erman, op.cit., 40 (XII). Found in KV 6 according to Daressy.

118 J. Černý, Ostrakon Nr. 2973 der Staatl. Ermitage zu Leningrad, ArOr 3, 1931, 395-99; Kitchen, RamInscr VI, 659f.; Helck OPG 506.

119 Černý-Gardiner HO, pl. 69.1 (=Demarée, Ramesside Ostraca, 20, pls. 43-44); see also Kitchen, RamInscr VI, 660f.; Helck, Materialien VI, 49.

120 Cf. E. Lefébure, Les hypogées royaux de Thèbes, II: Notices des hypogées, [Annales du Musée de Guimet 16], Paris 1889, pls. 8 (location of the graffito), 9 [A]; PM I/2^2, 503 (18); transcription: Černý, Valley of the Kings, 41 (with a comment); Kitchen, RamInscr VI, 676, 7-8 (based on Černý's transcription). See also Helck OPG, 473; McDowell, Village Life, 211 (no. 161). The entirely different character of the other hieratic graffiti on the walls of this corridor (Lefébure, op.cit., 9 [B], 23) should be noted; like similar graffiti in KV 19, these are religious texts.

121 Daressy, Ostraca, 76, pl. 55; Kitchen, RamInscr VI, 666 (A42); Helck OPG, 507 (transl.). Dating of the ostracon is difficult in view of unsatisfactory publication; but see Černý, Valley of the Kings, 40 n. 6, where the ostracon is dated to year 14 of Ramesses IX and linked to the construction of KV 19. For a similar dating: Helck, loc.cit.

prepared for the finishing works in this, or more likely another tomb, are included in the necropolis journal dated to year 17.[122]

During this period the community on the western bank of Thebes was shocked by robberies that occurred in the necropolis, especially as members of the gang took part in them. The crime investigation that was conducted in years 16 and 17 of the reign of Ramesses IX uncovered gross negligence in the functioning of the local administration.[123] We hear that the robberies had been taking place for a long time. One group of robbers was active already in year 13 of the king's reign, that is three or four years before the affair came to light (cf. papBM 10054vo. 1, 6; papLeopold-Amherst 1, 17-18). The robbers had been plundering tombs in West Thebes for some time by then. For the most part the tombs were privately owned, but the investigation in year 16 revealed that they had robbed the tomb of king Sebekemsaf. A list of the eight robbers from this gang is given in both papLeopold-Amherst and papBM 10054vo.[124]

Interestingly, the tomb of the royal wife Isis[125] was robbed two years earlier, in year 14 (Ramesses IX) and the coppersmith employed in the funerary temple of Ramesses III, Paykharu son of Khary,[126] who was caught red-handed with two of his associates, was now interrogated again and taken to the Valley of the Kings for an inspection of the scene of the crime (papAbbott ro. 4, 11ff.). Unexpectedly, the inspection, carried out under the supervision of the vizier Khaemwese himself, showed that the tomb had not been disturbed. The suspects were cleared of all suspicion, which was undoubtedly the effect of clever politics by the mayor of the West Paweraa and his followers.[127]

More facts concerning the robberies in the necropolis came to light just a year later. A group of workmen employed in the royal necropolis were charged with robberies in the Valley of the Queens (papBM 10068ro. 1, 3-4; papBM

[122] Necropolis Journal of Year 17, vo. B 3, 1-8: Botti-Peet, Giornale, 31f., pl. 31=Kitchen, RamInscr VI, 583, 11-14; translated in McDowell, Village Life, 211 (no. 160); and Helck OPG, 531.

[123] Generally on these events: Vernus, Affaires et Scandales, 17-36; as regards the sequence of events, see Valbelle, Ouvriers, 210ff.

[124] Cf. Peet, Tomb Robberies, 47f.

[125] This is presumably the tomb of the wife of Ramesses III in the Valley of the Queens (QV 51); cf. I. Mahmoud Soliman, M. Tosi, La tombe de la reine Isis [VdR 51], Grande Épouse de Ramsès III, Memnonia 7, 1996, 213ff.; see below Chapter 2.

[126] His mother was Mytsheri (papAbbott ro. 4, 13); cf. Haring, Divine Households, 451; Helck, Materialien I, (112). It is naturally impossible to identify him with the coppersmith Paykharu, son of Tjara, whose house in a later period was located close to the temple of Ramesses III, as indicated by the list in papBM 10068 (vo. 3, 23).

[127] Cf. G.A. Wainwright, JEA 24, 1938, 59-62; Vernus, op.cit., 23ff.

10053ro. 1, 4).[128] It is difficult to show any connection between the two groups of robbers, and it is more likely that the two gangs acted independently. A surviving fragment of the necropolis journal for year 17 tells of assembling all the staff working in the necropolis and reading out from a papyrus roll the names of all eight robbers.[129] One of the documents concerning supplies for the crew gives their names with the annotation "imprisoned" (*s3w*) on the margin.[130] They seem to have been members of two families living in the village of Deir el-Medina: on one hand there is the draughtsman Amenwa son of Hori and his three sons – the deputy Paanken, Hori and Peison (alternatively Nekhemmut), and on the other Pentawer son of Amennakht, assisted by his three sons – "deputy" Amenhotep, Mose and Nakhtmin.[131] One can wonder indeed whether some of them were not mentioned in the unique group of scraps of papyrus for drawing lots, found in the vicinity of the village in Deir el-Medina.[132]

The surviving documents demonstrate that the authorities were interested not only in finding those guilty of the crime, but also in recovering the stolen items. The records of the investigation contain detailed lists of objects and the names of those who had them in their possession. These lists were included in the necropolis journal,[133] as well as in the acts of the investigation (papBM 10068ro.; and papBM 10053ro.). Nothing is known of the fate of the indirect and direct perpetrators of the robbery. They were taken to the prison near the temple of Maat in Karnak.[134] A week later an unusual event took place with the recovered objects being returned in the presence of the vizier Khaemwese and the High Priest Amenhotep himself in the great courtyard (*p3 wb3*) of the temple of Amun in Karnak.[135] The objects

[128] This also appears to refer to the tomb of Isis, judging by the record in the Necropolis Journal of Year 17, ro. B 8, 5-6; for this, see below, and Valbelle, Ouvriers, 212 n. 7.

[129] Botti-Peet, Giornale, pl. 12: ro. A 5, 1-11=Kitchen, RamInscr VI, 569, 1-10; cf. Helck OPG, 522.

[130] Botti-Peet, Giornale, pls. 8-10: ro. A 1-3=Kitchen, RamInscr VI, 567f.; cf. Peet, Tomb Robberies, 72f.; Helck OPG, 521f. A rather curious annotation was written before the name of Anherkhau son of Setehi – "fugitive" (*wʿr*), cf. Botti-Peet, Giornale, pl. 11: ro. A 4, 4; Helck OPG, 522, interpreted it as "Inspector (*wʿrtw*)".

[131] For a genealogical investigation, cf. Bierbrier LNK, 30 (chart VIII), 34; Davies, Who's Who at DeM, 111f., 172-4. The latter may in fact have originated from a different family, cf. Davies, op.cit., 112. As regards some differences in the extant lists of thieves, see Peet, Tomb Robberies, 73ff.; Bierbrier LNK, 126 n. 126; Valbelle, Ouvriers, 212 n. 6. Quite possibly Peet was right supposing that also some innocent members of the community were temporarily "under suspicion".

[132] Cf. J. Černý, Le tirage au sort, BIFAO 40, 1941, 135ff., fig. 1.

[133] Cf. Helck OPG, 525-8.

[134] Cf. Botti-Peet, Giornale, pl. 13: ro. A 6, 3-8; see also ibid., pls. 14 (ro. B 1, 10), 15 (ro. B 1, 17), and papBM 10068ro. 1, 8-10; as regards the prison in the temple of Maat, see P. Grandet, Ramsès III. Histoire d'un règne, Paris 1993, 254.

[135] Botti-Peet, Giornale, pl. 15: ro. B 1, 21-25=Kitchen, RamInscr VI, 572, 13-573, 4; Peet, Tomb

were deposited subsequently in the storerooms of the temple of Ramesses III in Medinet Habu, while the robbers were surrendered into the custody of the mayor of the West, the scribe of district and the two *ꜣṯw*-officers.[136]

In the course of the investigation the vizier Khaemwese personally supervised an inspection of the tomb of the royal wife Isis in the Valley of the Queens. The inspectors opened the tomb and "found the stone (sic!) of red granite,[137] which was broken by the eight thieves in the entrance (?) (*tꜣ mnniwt*);[138] they (i.e., the thieves) caused a ruthless destruction on everything which was therein, and smashed [the western door, and they] made [...]".[139] At this point the text is broken, so we know no further details of the robbery, because the robbers' testimony that has been preserved concerns only a list of robbed items.

It is possible, however, that an undated fragment of the necropolis journal from papTurin 2106+2107[140] contains more of the robbers' testimony: "(1) [Inter]-rogation of the thief Nakhtmin, son of Pentawere, of the necropolis, (2) [about the] thieves: The thief Amenwa and the thief Pentawere [said to us: «Go] into this tomb (*tꜣy s.t*) and remove the corner stones of the tomb» – so they said to us. [«Then you go] up and hack up (*bꜣ*) opposite the [corne]r stone of the tomb» – so they said to us. We went up to the tomb [and we] reached the blockage (*pꜣ mkt*)[141] [and we op]ened the door and we entered [it, and we took:] 4 bronze [...]-vessels, [...of] bronze, 2 *sema*-vessels of bronze, 2 *meḥbek*-vessels of bronze [...]".

These notes are identical in character with the records of the robbers' interrogations. At the same time there is no reason why this fragment should be excluded from the necropolis journal. Information on the trial and the interrogations of the robbers were included in the necropolis journal presumably because

Robberies, 74; Helck OPG, 525; cf. also papBM 10068ro. 4, 1-3: Peet, op.cit., pl. 11.

[136] Cf. McDowell, Jurisdiction, 57.

[137] Probably not fragments of the granite sarcophagus, cf. Thomas, Royal Necropoleis, 269; see however I. Mahmoud Soliman, M. Tosi, op.cit., 214.

[138] For the meaning of *mnniwt*, cf. Wb.II, 82 (8); Lesko, Dict.I, 188; J.E. Hoch, Semitic Words in Egyptian Texts of the New Kingdom and Third Intermediate Period, Princeton 1994, 129: "part of granite sarcophagus or part of tomb".

[139] Botti-Peet, Giornale, 26, pl. 24: ro. B8, 7-11=Kitchen, RamInscr VI, 579, 8-11; cf. also Peet, Tomb Robberies, 77; Thomas, Royal Necropoleis, 269; McDowell, Village Life, 198 (no. 151 A); Helck OPG, 529.

[140] Cf. Botti-Peet, Giornale, 41f., pl. 49; Kitchen, RamInscr VI, 598, 6ff.=868, 15ff. (in the second case the document wrongly included in the sources from the reign of Ramesses XI; Kitchen clearly failed to observe that the text in Černý's Notebook is identical with a fragment of the necropolis journal(?) published earlier); for the comments and translation of the passage in question, see Peet, Tomb Robberies, 78; Gutgesell, Datierung, 147; Thomas, Royal Necropoleis, 270; McDowell, Jurisdiction, 195; id., Village Life, 198f. (no. 151 B); Helck OPG, 528.

[141] Thus possibly "protection" or "defence", rather than "proper place"; the latter meaning suggested by McDowell and Helck; cf. also Wb.II, 160f.; Lesko, Dict I, 211.

the gang consisted exclusively of workmen employed in the royal necropolis. People from the crew and members of their families are mentioned also among those to whom the robbers handed the stolen goods.[142]

It is difficult to estimate the effect that these events had on the functioning of the institution of the royal necropolis. Much has been written on the ambiguous role in the whole matter of the mayor of West Thebes, Paweraa. His presence in sources from a later period appears to indicate that the investigation failed to reveal the story behind the scene and to punish the chief culprits. It is perhaps this circumstance that kept the robbers going, bringing back the robberies in full force later on during a deep political crisis.

The surviving documents clearly demonstrate that dealing in objects from tomb robbing became quite common not only among inhabitants of the west bank but also the Thebans living in the city on the east bank. Interestingly, most of the people who came into the possession of the copper or bronze objects were of low social status, but the luxury objects made of precious metals passed through the hands of the middle class, that is, scribes and lower rank officials. Merchants were the most involved, however, in this trade and obviously had no qualms about risking their reputation with ordinary fencing.[143] It may be surprising that golden and silver objects were found in the possession of indigent people, because it was surely impossible for a simple gardener or weaver to own such pieces under ordinary circumstances. It certainly demonstrates the scale of the robbing that was taking place at the time. It is noteworthy that this was not an isolated incident, but that robberies perpetrated by different groups of robbers occurred over a number of years.

Should the situation be interpreted as efforts on the part of sluggish authorities to cover up inconvenient facts of an affair that involved local notables? Quite possibly so, considering the role played in the whole matter by the scribe of the necropolis Horisheri. It was Horisheri informed the town's mayor Paser about matters obviously connected with the robberies, but he did this avoiding official channels, that is, his direct superior, the vizier, in this case. Little is known about the career of the vizier Khaemwese beside his role in the investigations and a few remarks in the necropolis journal.[144] It may be assumed that during his term

[142] Cf. papBM 10053ro. 2, 17-19; ro. 3, 3, 18; ro. 5, 6, 8, 10; ro. 6, 14-15; ro. 7, 2 – since not all of the mentioned individuals can be identified securely as members of the crew, it is possible that some of them were actually workers of the necropolis in a broader sense.

[143] On merchants in papBM 10068 (ro. 4, 1-21) and papBM 10053ro. (passim), both documents of year 17 of Ramesses IX, cf. D. Kessler, SAK 2, 1975, 128-30; Allam, SAK 26, 1998, 14ff.

[144] Cf. Helck, Verwaltung, 465 (43).

in office he stayed mostly in the north of the country and it is perhaps this circumstance that can explain why in the following period the high priest of Amun played an important, if not decisive role in matters concerning the administration of the royal necropolis.

Whether the robberies also touched the Valley of the Kings in this period remains an issue open to debate. We would be better equipped to say were we to know the results of the inspection carried out in the Valley of the Kings by the vizier Khaemwese and the high priest of Amun on III *peret* 23, in year 17 of the reign of Ramesses IX, that is, exactly two days after the inspection of the tomb of queen Isis: "On this day the vizier, the high priest (of Amun), the royal butler and overseer of the treasury Nesamun, and the scribe of Pharaoh, l.p.h., ascended to the Great Field (*sḫ.t ꜥ3.t*) to receive [the] commission (*šsp* [*p3*?] *sḥnw*) in the great and noble Necropolis of Millions of Years of Pharaoh, l.p.h. And the crew of the necropolis reported to them, saying: «We are lacking (the payments) and we are hungry, (and) the wages, guaranteed to be given to us by Pharaoh, l.p.h., has not been given to us either». And the vizier, the high priest (of Amun), the (royal) butler and overseer of the treasury of Pharaoh said: «The workmen of the crew of the necropolis are right». [And we] said: «Our brothers have committed robbery and they are imprisoned now, but oth[er brothers] of ours [...]»".[145] It looks as if the inspection was part of routine supervision of work in the royal necropolis and there is nothing to show that any irregularities were noted on this occasion. Of prime importance apparently were matters connected with provisioning of the crew. It would mean that security at the royal necropolis had not been meaningfully disturbed yet, although it is clear that some of the royal tombs in the valley had been robbed previously.[146]

It is apparently groundless to assume that the "cache" in KV 55 was disturbed during the building of the tomb of Ramesses IX.[147] The unfinished state of one of the lateral chambers in the first corridor of the tomb of Ramesses IX[148] laves no

[145] Necropolis Journal of Year 17, ro. B 9, 6-12: Botti-Peet, Giornale, pl. 25=Kitchen, RamInscr VI, 580, 3-11; cf. also Helck OPG, 529 (translation).

[146] Cf. Reeves, Valley of the Kings, 274.

[147] Cf. ibid., 44, 59 n. 166. See also A. Dodson, On the Origin, Contents and Fate of Biban el-Moluk Tomb 55, GM 132, 1993, 28; L. Pinch Brock, Theodore Davis and the Rediscovery of Tomb 55, in: Valley of the Sun Kings, 39. Even more controvesial is the question of such activity in WV 23, dated tentatively to the reign of Ramesses IX as well, cf. Reeves, op.cit., 72 n. 138; for a different point of view, see A. Dodson, Antiquity 64, 1990, 964; Jansen-Winkeln, ZÄS 122, 1995, 64. It is possible, however, that the Western Valley started being evacuated earlier than the central part of the royal necropolis. This may have been due to the impossibility of ensuring the security of this distant part of the burial ground.

[148] Cf. Reeves, op.cit., 48 (fig. 18); see now Weeks, Atlas, 42-43 (Sheet 16/70) – chamber Bd.

doubt that the builders were aware of the existence of KV 55 and decided not to complete the room in an effort to avoid a collision. The stage at which the work was broken off indicates that the stonecutters must have heard an echo coming from the chamber below. Had KV 55 indeed been penetrated on this occasion, then it stands to reason that all the remaining gold in this tomb would have been removed and yet it was not.[149] For the same reason it seems equally untenable to claim that the tomb was penetrated at a later date when mass robberies were common in the Valley of the Kings.[150] Nevertheless, the jars, which are possibly the remnants of an embalming cache left after the burial of Ramesses IX and which E. Ayrton found near KV 55,[151] certainly cannot be used to argue against a later penetration of KV 55 as their archaeological context has not been recorded.

No conclusive evidence can be put forward regarding the last penetration of KV 55. Such a late opening of the tomb is postulated only to explain the attempt to evacuate objects connected with the burial of Queen Tiye, including her mummy, which eventually found its way to the cache in KV 35. In that case, the confused history of KV 55 would have been in direct relation with the inauguration of the cache in KV 35, unless N. Reeves' theory of a transitional cache where Tiye's remains would have been taken (still "before the end of the Twentieth Dynasty")[152] before reaching KV 35 is accepted. Arguing in favour of such a connection are two fragments of glass vessels, said to have been found in KV 55, which are thought to be part of vessels discovered in KV 35. The provenance of these fragments is not certain however.[153] Consequently, there is no reason to hold that Tiye's mummy was transferred to the cache in KV 35 directly from KV 55. Moreover, it seems that W. Helck's reasonable and sober views suggesting that the last penetration of KV 55 occurred in the reign of Horemheb and that the condition of the tomb contents at the time of discovery has nothing to do with the robberies from the late 20th Dynasty have not received enough attention so far.[154]

---

[149] Cf. W. Helck, GM 60, 1982, 44; M. Gabolde, D'Akhenaton à Toutânkhamon, Paris 1998, 273-275.

[150] According to Pinch Brock (op.cit., 39) the last penetration could have occurred in the 21st Dynasty; similarly M.R. Bell, JARCE 27, 1990, 136f. Compare Gabolde, op.cit., 274.

[151] E.R. Ayrton, in: Th.M. Davis et al., The Tomb of Queen Tîyi, London 1910, 7; Reeves, Valley of the Kings, 56 n. 130, 172 (KV C), 178 n. 72, 306; Gabolde, op.cit., 273f. n. 1923. On the possible location of the "cache" or rather deposit, cf. Pinch Brock, op.cit., 36.

[152] Cf. N. Reeves, A Reappraisal of Tomb 55 in the Valley of the Kings, JEA 67, 1981, 53.

[153] Cf. K. Bosse-Griffiths, JEA 47, 1961, 68, pl. VII.5; M.R. Bell, JARCE 27, 1990, 108 (N), 109 (P), 136; see however Reeves-Wilkinson, The Complete Valley of the Kings, 120 ("Items from the 'Harold Jones collection' in Swansea have no demonstrable connection with KV 55").

[154] W. Helck, Was geschah in KV 55?, GM 60, 1982, 43-46; see also Dodson, Antiquity 64, 1990, 964;

At least one royal tomb outside of the Valley of the Kings, that of Sekhemre-Shedtawy Sebekemsaf II from the 17th Dynasty, is known to have been robbed in the reign of Ramesses IX, not to mention attempts to penetrate the tombs of Antef V Nubkheperre and Antef VI Sekhemre-Wepmaat reported in papAbbott (2, 12-18). The investigation also indicated that two tombs of singers from the domain of the Divine Votaress of Amun-Ra were robbed, as well as a number of tombs belonging to other private persons (papAbbott 3, 17-4, 4). One wonders whether the corruption in the necropolis reported in sources for years 16 and 17 of Ramesses IX had actually been much more dramatic than hitherto assumed. It does seem difficult to move all the acts of robbery in the royal tombs in the Valley of the Kings to a later period. The unique testimony of the robbing of the tomb of Ramesses VI (KV 9) recorded in papMayer B,[155] seems to be of crucial importance in this case. The surviving fragment does not contain a date and the names of the robbers are also not enlightening with regard to the dating, as these were men of low status in the social hierarchy, hence seldom mentioned in the sources. In this case, they were the foreigners (i.e., probably slaves) Pais and Nesamun, and two coppersmiths, Pentahetnakht and Hori. The latter two names are sufficiently popular to raise doubts about a possible identity with the elsewhere attested coppersmith Pentahetnakht (papBM 10068 vo. 5, 10) and coppersmith Hori, called Kadjadja (papBM 10052, 16,16).[156] Similarly no relevant information can be obtained from the mention of a certain Pabak the younger,[157] who was killed in rather obscure circumstances, together with an unnamed "child of the tomb" (*ms-ḫr*), possibly to prevent them from betraying the robbers to external authorities: *mtw.f tm dỉ.tw.n r-bnr* "and not to let him give us away" (papMayer B, 9).[158]

The dating of papMayer B cannot be examined separately from a graffito found on the ceiling of the sarcophagus chamber inside the tomb of Ramesses

Eaton-Krauss, BiOr 49, 1992, 710; Jansen-Winkeln, ZÄS 122, 1995, 64.

155 Peet, Mayer Papyri, 19-20 (with phot. and transcr.); Kitchen, RamInscr VI, 515f.; see also Peet, JEA 2, 1915, 204-6; McDowell, Village Life, 199f. (no. 152).

156 Cf. Peet, Mayer Papyri, 20; id., Tomb Robberies, 176. The coppersmith Hori son of Kadjaja was found not guilty (papBM 10052, 16, 16-17), so it is rather improbable that we are dealing with the same person who was involved in the violation of the royal tomb of Ramesses VI, regardless of the date of the two documents. Compare, however, Thijs, GM 179, 2000, 78, as regards Pentahetnakht.

157 Peet (Tomb Robberies, 176) hesitates with regard to the true meaning of the words *pꜣ bꜣk šri* (papMayer B, 9), although he interpreted them earlier as a personal name (cf. JEA 2, 1915, 206). See also the interpretation of this fragment by Ranke PN I, 104 (21): "*pꜣ- bꜣk* der Jüngere" (not attested elsewhere); similarly W. Spiegelberg, RT 17, 1895, 99.

158 Compare Neveu, Grammaire, 137 (15).

VI, in year 9 of Ramesses IX.[159] Regardless of the possibility that it is not proof of earlier robbery,[160] it does not seem tenable that anybody could have entered the sarcophagus chamber of a royal tomb before it had been plundered. The nature of the text also excludes the possibility that it was meant to commemorate an official inspection of the tomb connected with its re-sealing.[161] The graffito is obviously the effect of a visit by a draughtsman (here referred to as a "scribe") Amenhotep son of Amennakht, together with his son Amennakht (designated here as "scribe and deputy of the draughtsmen of the necropolis").[162] This was hardly an official inspection,[163] although it is possible that the visit of representatives of the necropolis authorities had been prompted by the recent (?) robbing of the tomb.[164] There can be no doubt that the writing of the graffito on the ceiling of the sarcophagus chamber[165] was possible only after a scaffolding had been built (possibly a ladder?) to reach the rock surface located 6 m above the floor; even today access to it is difficult. Knowing today that the ancient builders of the royal tombs used such scaffoldings,[166] we should discard A. Peden's peculiar notion that elements of the tomb's furnishings had been piled up for the purpose.[167] In any case, there is no plausible explanation for why Amenhotep wanted to put his graffito on the ceiling of the sarcophagus chamber, especially as he had to have special scaffolding to do it.

---

[159] Champollion, Notices Descriptives II, 635; Spiegelberg, Graffiti, 92f. (II); Kitchen, RamInscr VI, 658f. (A.24); Gutgesell, Datierung, 137 (f.); Reeves, Valley of the Kings, 125 n. 40, 233; McDowell, in: Pharaoh's Workers, 53; id., Village Life, 242 (no. 195); C.A. Keller, JARCE 21, 1984, 124; id., in: Deir el-Médineh et la Vallée des Rois, 96.

[160] Cf. Niwiński, BIFAO 95, 1995, 331.

[161] See N. Grimal, A History of Ancient Egypt, Oxford – Cambridge, Mass. 1999, 289. Similarly, it is simply not possible that the tomb had not been completed at that time, as noted by E.S. Bogoslovsky, Hundred Egyptian Draughtsmen, ZÄS 107, 1980, 95; for this see also Keller, JARCE 21, 1984, 124 n. 65.

[162] Gutgesell, Datierung, 137 (f).

[163] Cf. C.A. Keller, Un artiste égyptien à l'œuvre: le dessinateur en chef Amenhotep, in: Deir el-Médineh et la Vallée des Rois, 96.

[164] Cf. Aldred, Tomb Robberies, 92; Reeves, Valley of the Kings, 117, 119; Bierbrier, Tomb-Builders, 111; and Davies, Who's Who at Deir el-Medina, 112f.

[165] PM I/2^{2}, 517; Thomas, Royal Necropoleis, 130. The exact location of the graffito, nowhere stated explicitly, is a matter of a serious confusion, as E. Lefébure stated that it is not in the tomb of Ramesses VI, cf. Les Hypogées royaux de Thèbes, II: Notices des hypogées, [Annales du Musée Guimet 16], Paris 1889, 80, 190f. As a matter of fact, its location or even existence in modern times could not have been verified by anybody.

[166] See now Dorn, MDAIK 61, 2005, 7, pls. 1-2. On the use of scaffoldings in ancient Egypt see D. Arnold, Building in Egypt. Pharaonic Stone Masonry, Oxford 1991, 231ff.

[167] Peden, Graffiti, 205 n. 447. The idea that the tomb contains other graffiti of similar content is equally unlikely (cf. ibid., n. 450).

In his text Amenhotep clearly says that he had come with his son "to see the mansion(s) of the Two Truths (*ḥw.(w)t M3ʿ.ty*)[168] [when][169] they executed the decoration in the tomb (*mʿḥʿ.t*) [of the chief of the] temple [archives] of the estate of Amun Iymiseba. They came and walked about (?)[170] (to) look at the mountains". It is highly probable that the visitors were interested only in the ceiling paintings which Amenhotep himself may have executed in his youth.[171] It is demonstrable that Amenhotep painted, among others, scenes from the Book of the Day and Night decorating the huge ceiling of the sarcophagus chamber, along with the very characteristic figures of the sky goddess Nut embracing the entire horizon with her naked body. Amenhotep may have wished to show to his son these particular scenes, which are considered among the most beautiful in the Valley of the Kings. He may have simply wished to boast his talents or to show to his son some model scenes.[172] At the time they were both working on the decoration of the nearby tomb of Ramesses IX (KV 6) and consequently, the visit may have been purely professional in character, searching for model paintings. The professionalism of draughtsmen working on the decoration of the royal tombs cannot be put in doubt. Suffice it to mention all the sketches on ostraca that they left in the Valley of the Kings, even if some of them were painted only for entertainment and to train the hand. Some of the sketches were executed by Amenhotep himself.[173] Amenhotep, assuming it was he in this case, must have had the same objectives in mind when he visited the tomb of Tuthmosis III (KV 34), scratching a graffito in the vicinity of one of the scenes of the fourth hour of Amduat in the sarcophagus chamber: "Amenhotep. A thousand (times) beautiful is the figure on the right!".[174]

168 Cf. infra for the discussion on the meaning of the term.

169 See, however, a doubtful restoration proposed by Spiegelberg, loc.cit.; criticised by Keller, JARCE 21, 1984, 124 n. 67.

170 Compare G.T. Martin, The Memphite Tomb of Horemheb Commander-in-Chief of Tut'ankhamūn, I, London 1989, 157 (Gr.5); M. Barwik, SAK 38, 2009, 46 (b).

171 Cf. McDowell, Village Life, 242.

172 On the career of Amenhotep, cf. C.A. Keller, How Many Draughtsmen Named Amenhotep? A Study of Some Deir el-Medina Painters, JARCE 21, 1984, 119-129.

173 Cf. Keller, in: Deir el-Médineh et la Vallée des Rois, 83ff., figs. 1-10.

174 Cf. J. Osing, in: J. Romer, The Tomb of Tuthmosis III, MDAIK 31,1975, 349f. (no. 4), fig. 8 (4), pl. 106a; for a possible identification of the author with the famous draughtsman Amenhotep, cf. ibid., 351 n. 95. For the difficulties connected with the "scribe Amenhotep" and the "draughtsman Amenhotep", see Černý, Community, 197f.; Davies, Who's Who at Deir el-Medina, 112f. The "scribe Amenhotep" is mentioned also in a nearby graffito in the tomb of Tuthmosis III, cf. Osing, loc.cit., no. 3. Reeves exercises caution in the interpretation of both the graffiti in connection with the plundering of the tomb (Valley of the Kings, 23), whereas J. Romer sees it as a clue left by members of the "reburial commission" removing the royal mummy from the tomb, cf. Valley of the Kings, London 1981, 165. The tenor of this text, however, does not seem to fit plausibly any of these circumstances.

Interestingly, there are elements of iconography apparently derived from the decoration of royal tombs in the tomb of Iymiseba (TT 65), the decoration of which is mentioned by Amenhotep in the graffito on the ceiling in KV 9.[175]

Is the visit by the artist Amenhotep in the tomb of Ramesses VI sufficient proof for dating to an earlier period the robbery described in papMayer B, assuming that the testimony given by the robbers recorded in papMayer B can at all be referred to a robbery taking place at such an early date?[176] Indeed, there are no grounds for dating this document which remains a completely isolated piece of evidence. It could equally well be much later, referring to times when the tombs in the Valley of the Kings were being robbed on a grand scale (see below). True, the operations described in the papyrus do not seem to attain any bigger format. The robbers admit to taking only some less precious objects, mainly bronze vessels and linen garments, which could be disposed of with relative ease. C. Aldred's view that the traces of resin residue on the inside walls of the outer sarcophagus in the tomb of Ramesses VI are proof of robbery occurring shortly after the ruler's burial, at which time the sarcophagus was overturned, cannot be maintained today.[177] It is much more likely that the residue formed at the time of the burial and was clearly due to the uneven surface of the sarcophagus bottom.[178]

The robbing of the tomb of Ramesses VI, which is described in papMayer B, could have indeed preceded in time the mass plunder from the end of the 20th Dynasty (see below, Chapter 2). The text informs that five robbers needed four days to penetrate into the tomb (papMayer B, 9-10). The necropolis guards could not have failed to notice anything, if the royal necropolis was still functioning in a regular way. But we know of earlier actions of this kind, the two penetrations of the tomb of Tutankhamun by robbers being an excellent example. F. Abitz has demonstrated how robbers could have proceeded unnoticed by the guards,[179] but

[175] Cf. Keller, in: Deir el-Médineh et la Vallée des Rois, 96f. As regards other sources for the motifs appearing in the decoration of this tomb, see also T. Baćs, Art as material for later art: the case of Theban Tomb 65, in: W.V. Davies (ed.), Colour and Painting in Ancient Egypt, London 2001, 94-100; id., A Royal Litany in a Private Context, MDAIK 60, 2004, 1-16.

[176] Thus Aldred, Tomb Robberies, 96; Reeves, Valley of the Kings, 117-119, 274 (no. 11); Reeves-Wilkinson, The Complete Valley of the Kings, 192. As a matter of fact, it is only by reason of a "gentleman's agreement" that papMayer B is dated to the early years of Ramesses IX, cf. Kitchen, RamInscr VI, 515 ("Year 9-x"). As regards its dating to the reign of Ramesses XI, cf. Thomas, Royal Necropoleis, 265, 268.

[177] Cf. Aldred, op.cit., 96-98, pl. 1.

[178] Cf. E. Graefe, Über die Goldmenge des Alten Ägypten und die Beraubung der thebanischen Königsgräber, ZÄS 126, 1999, 36-40, figs. 1-4.

[179] F. Abitz, Baugeschichte und Dekoration des Grabes Ramses' VI, [OBO 89], Freiburg – Göttingen 1989, 53, fig. 9.

his explanation concerns only the early shaft and corridor tombs in the Valley of the Kings which were bricked up and covered with sand. In the case of the tombs of the Ramesside pharaohs (starting with Ramesses II and Merenptah), the entrance to which were not filled with sand, but closed with massive doors protected by seals [180] and guarded by the Madjoy police, robbers had to devise a completely different approach. If we assume an earlier date for the robbing of the tomb of Ramesses VI, a much simpler explanation can be proposed of how the robbers actually entered the tomb. It is very likely that they simply used a hole that had appeared at the point of the collision of the tomb of Ramesses VI (KV 9) with the anonymous tomb KV 12.[181] They could have simply knocked out a hole where the wall was just 20 cm thick[182] or else enlarged a hole that had been made during the building of the tomb. Through this opening (which is presently bricked up), which was approx. 61 by 85 cm,[183] the robbers could escape with relatively small objects only, exactly like the ones mentioned in the testimony recorded in papMayer B. Additional proof of KV 9 being robbed through KV 12 is provided by alabaster ushebti of Ramesses VI found at the entrance to KV 12.[184]

This reconstruction of events connected with the robbery of KV 9 explains also the presence of Amenhotep's graffito on the ceiling of the sarcophagus chamber. Protective texts and representations designed to protect the tomb from evil forces were painted at the end of the fifth corridor (below the ceiling) of the tomb of Ramesses VI, above the entrance to the vestibule preceding the sarcophagus chamber, exactly on the spot of the collision.[185] It has been noted rightly that there is no way to know whether the hole between the tombs was made already during the construction of KV 9 or was cut by the robbers from KV 12.[186] The

[180] Ibid., 50ff.; Thomas, Royal Necropoleis, 108, 130, 268; C.H. Roehrig, Gates to the Underworld: The Appearance of Wooden Doors in the Royal Tombs in the Valley of the Kings, in: Valley of the Sun Kings, 92ff. It remains open to debate whether in this situation the outer parts of a tomb (up to the hall with four pillars) were actually accesible for mortuary rituals possibly celebrated inside the tomb; on this, see Thomas, op.cit., 130, 275; Roehrig, op.cit., 104.

[181] Weeks, Atlas, 55 (sheet 22/70), 66 (sheet 28/70); cf. also Abitz, op.cit., 30, figs. 4-5.

[182] Abitz, op.cit., 28; Thomas, Royal Necropoleis, 135 n. 87.

[183] Abitz, op.cit., 28.

[184] Reeves, Valley of the Kings, 131, 309.

[185] Cf. A. Piankoff; N. Rambova, The Tomb of Ramesses VI, [Bollingen Series XL.1], New York 1954, 407, fig. 141, pls. 101-102, 182; E. Hornung, Zum Schutzbild im Grabe Ramses' VI, in: J.H. Kamstra et al. (eds.), Funerary Symbols and Religion. Essays dedicated to Prof. Heerma van Voss, Kampen 1988, 45-51; Abitz, op.cit., 157f., fig. 39. The decoration is in essence unique, in terms of both the iconography and the accompanying inscriptions.

[186] Cf. Thomas, Royal Necropoleis, 130, 135 n. 87.

builders of KV 9 could have been responsible[187] (similarly as in KV 11), but it is also possible that hearing the echo, they changed their plans and lowered the level of the next chambers of the tomb (possibly already in a following building phase). If the hole was the work of the robbers, who thus destroyed the decoration in this area (which could have been meant to be apotropaic right from the start), then it would have been understandably bricked up at the moment the theft was discovered (although today there is no evidence of such ancient repairs). In such a case, Amenhotep's visit inside the tomb, recorded in his graffito left on the ceiling of the sarcophagus chamber, could have been in connection with this work. It would have been enough to move the scaffolding from the end of the fifth corridor through the vestibule to the nearby sarcophagus chamber. Otherwise it is difficult to explain why such scaffolding would have been made at all, surely not just for the purpose of leaving a graffito on the ceiling of the sarcophagus chamber. It is pure speculation whether the wooden beams found in KV 9[188] are the remains of this scaffolding or should rather be connected with later robbers who could have been responsible for more disastrous actions like smashing the stone sarcophagus.[189]

Note should be taken here of a well discussed graffito no. 1860a of year 8 (of an unspecified reign), scratched above the entrance to KV 35,[190] mentioning the "closing (*ḫnỉ*) of the tomb (*p3 ḫr*)"[191] by some important officials headed by the High Priest Remessesnakht himself. The graffito can no longer be dated to the reign of either Ramesses XI or the more so Ramesses X.[192] Its connection with the cache in KV 35 has been suggested,[193] but it is difficult to understand why the tomb was closed so early on unless the inspection recorded by the graffito was

[187] See Abitz, op.cit., 27f., figs. 3-4; Reeves, Valley of the Kings, 130.

[188] Cf. Daressy, ASAE 18, 1919, 272 (JdE 29003); see also Dorn, MDAIK 61, 2005, 7 n. 29 (who does not exclude the possibility that the beams are modern).

[189] In keeping with the hypothesis proposed by Aldred, Tomb Robberies, 98.

[190] Černý, Sadek et al., Graffiti III, pl. 35; IV, 21; Félix-Aubriot-Kurz, Plans de positions, pl. 8. An emendation proposed by Bell, Serapis 6, 1980, 7, must be noted, cf. also Peden, Graffiti, 199 n. 421. For a detailed comment on its dating, see now Davies, Who's Who at DeM, 58-61; Peden, Graffiti, 199ff.

[191] On the possible meaning of the passus, cf. Bell, Serapis 6, 1980, 15.

[192] Cf. M.L. Bierbrier, A Second High Priest Ramessesnakht?, JEA 58, 1972, 195ff.; id., JEA 61, 1975, 251; similar dating in Kitchen, RamInscr VI, 681 (Ramesses XI); Peden, Graffiti, 199ff. (Ramesses X); Davies, Who's Who at DeM, 60 (Ramesses X or XI). In consequence, the High Priest Ramessesnakht II, postulated by Bierbrier, becomes definitely a "ghost" figure, not only because of the estimated duration of the reign of Ramesses X, but also to avoid problems with the chronology of the suppression of the High Priest Amenhotep, an event which certainly cannot be placed in the reign of Ramesses IX, cf. Jansen-Winkeln, ZÄS 119, 1992, 32.

[193] See Reeves, Valley of the Kings, 199, 222 n. 139; Davies, Who's Who at DeM, 58 n. 757.

prompted by its earlier robbing,[194] of which however nothing certain can be said. Similarly, there is no reason to connect this operation with the tomb of Ramesses VI (KV 9),[195] situated at a considerable distance after all, even if it is assumed that the tomb could have been finished and closed provisionally before the ruler's death. On the other hand, it is possible that the sealing referred to the nearby tomb KV 12, this because the steep cliff above KV 35 is the only convenient place in the neighbourhood of KV 12 for such a graffito to be placed. The rock around KV 12, which is cut into the talus slope,[196] is of poor quality and there are no ancient graffiti in this area. Therefore, the inspectors sealing KV 12 could have chosen to commemorate their actions on the rock face just 30 m further on to the west of the tomb.

This hypothesis has some serious consequences for the chronology of the period. First of all, it would mean that Ramessesnakht was still the high priest of Amun in year 8 of Ramesses IX,[197] and that his son Amenhotep did not succeed him until sometime between year 8 and 10 of the reign of this king (see below). In addition, there is no place whatsoever for the High Priest Nesamun in the period prior to the pontificate of his brother Amenhotep,[198] especially if he is identical with the second prophet of Amun of the same name, known from the sources dating to the reign of Ramesses IX (see below). Moreover, from the viewpoint of the community in Deir el-Medina one needs to consider the chief workman Amennakht, whose name appears among the notables listed in graffito 1860a as carrying out the inspection. A foreman of this name is recorded in the

[194] Cf. Reeves, op.cit., 199.

[195] In this case apparently one should also reject the dating of the graffito to year 8 of Ramesses VI, proposed by Bell, Serapis 6, 1980, 15f.; followed by Amer, JEA 71, 1985, 69f.; Ventura, City of the Dead, 183 n. 38; Krauss, Sothis- und Monddaten, 133 (revision of his earlier opinion on the subject: id., GM 70, 1984, 42f.); Janssen-Winkeln, ZÄS 119, 1992, 32f.; Reeves, Valley of the Kings, 233 (2); von Beckerath, Chronologie, 82.

[196] Thomas, Royal Necropoleis, 148.

[197] The present hypothesis has the advantage over that formulated by M.L. Bierbrier of retaining the possibility to identify this Rameessesnakht with the well known high priest of that name.

[198] See Kees, Priestertum, 128. For a summary of an earlier discussion on the chronological position of the High Priest Nesamun, cf. Bell, Serapis 6, 1980, 16; Polz, SAK 25, 1998, 282. Anyway, Nesamun's tenure as high priest of Amun must have been fairly short, if only one monument has been preserved, i.e., the statue CG 42162, representing his father, and inscribed with Nesamun's (secondary?) dedication inscription, which testifies distinctly to his tenure of office rather than merely his claims to it, cf. G. Legrain, Statues et statuettes des rois et des particuliers, II, [CG], Cairo 1909, 29, pl. 26; id., ASAE 6, 1905, 133f. (XXI); Kitchen, RamInscr VI, 531. The chronological position of the High Priest Nesamun still remains open to question and there is no certainty about his identity with the second prophet Nesamun of the oracle text dated to year 7 of the Renaissance Era, as suggested by Bell, Serapis 6, 1980, 17ff.

necropolis journal during the reign of Ramesses X.[199] To assume that he is the same person as the man mentioned in graffito 1860a complicates considerably the chronological framework for the institution of crew foremen. Neither an extension of his tenure until the extremely doubtful year 8 of Ramesses X (or year 8 of his successor),[200] nor does an interpolation of the second Amennakht during the reign of Ramesses VI[201] give any plausible results in reconstructing the chronology of the chief workmen. Thus the more likely solution seems to be an interpolation of another Amennakht into the line of the foremen of the left side between Anherkhau (II) and his son Harmose. The latter's tenure is firmly attested in year 17 of Ramesses IX, but he appeared as foreman much earlier, probably still at the end of the reign of Ramesses VII (during his year 8), if the dating of papTurin 1883+2095 to this reign will be accepted,[202] or even earlier – in regnal year 4 of Ramesses VII.[203] Anyway, Harmose's tenure in office can be safely attested in year 6 of Ramesses IX,[204] alongside the chief workman Nekhemmut, and subsequently in year 7,[205] and also in year 9.[206] So we should rather assume that the chief workman Amennakht took on the position of foreman, if at all, for a brief time during Harmose's period in office.[207]

[199] Cf. Černý, Community, 310 n. 4; Davies, Who's Who at DeM, 58, 279; one can postulate his identity with the deputy Amennakht son of Hay, cf. Davies, op.cit., 71 (with a proposed reconstruction of his complicated career).

[200] In the grain accounts for year 8 of Ramesses XI, Khonsu (right side) and Kenna (left side) are mentioned as the chief workmen, cf. e.g. papTurin 2018ro. A 2, 1; A 3, 16: Kitchen, RamInscr VI, 852, 10; 853, 11.

[201] See Bell, Serapis 6, 1980, 8ff.; strongly criticised by Davies, Who's Who at DeM, 59f.

[202] Pleyte-Rossi, Papyrus de Turin, pl. 29 (right): ro. 6=Kitchen, RamInscr VI, 431, 16; cf. Davies, Who's Who at DeM, 27-29, 54. On the dating of papTurin 1883+2095, see also ibid., 27 n. 346; C.J. Eyre, JEA 66, 1980, 170; Gutgesell, Datierung, 248f. It must be noted, however, that the dating of the papyrus was based mostly on the interpretation of the king's name written at the beginning of the document (but without a clear context, unless it will be understood as an extention of a date written below, cf. however T.E. Peet, BIFAO 30, 1931, 490 n. 2). Significantly enough, the prosopographical data provided by the papyrus does not exclude at all a dating in the reign of Ramesses IX, cf. Eyre, op.cit., 169; Gutgesell, op.cit., 248. It was dated indeed to the reign of Ramesses IX by Valbelle, Ouvriers, 39, 53, 345.

[203] See Eyre, JEA 66, 1980, 169.

[204] Cf. papTurin 1930/2050ro. 1, 5; 12=Kitchen, RamInscr VI, 600, 3-4, 13. For a dating of the papyrus, cf. Černý, Community, 308; Bellion, Catalogue, 290; Gutgesell, Datierung, 134f. The inventory numbers of the papyrus must be corrected now, cf. Demarée, Bankes Papyri, 25.

[205] Cf. papTurin 1881ro. 4, 3=Kitchen, RamInscr VI, 612, 15.

[206] Cf. papTurin 2072/142ro. 1, 8=Kitchen, RamInscr VI, 631, 13; cf. Allam HOP, 330, pl. 128.

[207] Although at first glance the hypothesis raises objections, it should be noted that just a few years later the foreman Nekhemmut was assisted by his son Userkhepesh (see above). Anyhow, in both cases perturbations connected with filling the post of chief of the crew could have been caused by robberies in the royal necropolis. There is no certainty naturally that Amennakht was related to Harmose. Adopting this idea also leaves open the question of the relation between this Amennakht and the foreman of the same name recorded during the reign of Ramesses X. The hypothesis is undoubtedly weakened by the

Beside the other difficulties connected with the dating of graffito 1860a one may wonder why 15 months had to pass between the possible inspection in year 8 of Ramesses IX and the date of the graffito on the ceiling of the sarcophagus chamber in the tomb of Ramesses VI. Naturally, the first thing after discovering the robbery would be to seal the tomb through which the robbers penetrated the royal tomb. But why should so many months have to pass before protective action was taken in the plundered tomb of Ramesses VI? Hypothetically it can be assumed that robbery in KV 12 was easily detected because it was a small corridor tomb and the robber's shaft attracted attention soon after it had been made. The fact that the tomb was used to rob a neighbouring royal tomb may not have been observed at once, hence the difference in time between the two graffiti (assuming that both can be dated to the reign of Ramesses IX).

The text of the graffito from the tomb of Ramesses VI indicates clearly that Amenhotep and his son came here "to see the mansion(s) of the Two Truths (*ḥw.(w)t M3ᶜ.ty*)" (l. 4),[208] meaning presumably the room preceding the sarcophagus chamber which was called the "Hall of Maat" (*wsḫ.t M3ᶜ.t*)[209] or the "Hall of the Two Truths" (*wsḫ.t M3ᶜ.ty*).[210] The name probably derives from the specific decoration of these chambers in which the predominant motifs are borrowed from the Book of the Dead (Chapters 124-127), including scenes of judgment of the dead.[211] In the tomb of Ramesses VI the decoration contains (on the right wall) a representation of the king worshipping Maat and the text of a hymn to Maat.[212] The hole which was caused by the collision with KV 12 is above the entrance to this particular chamber.

Iymiseba, who usurped an 18th Dynasty tomb (TT 65) in Sheikh Abd el-Qurna, was the descendant of an influential family connected with the temple

absence of any other form of confirmation of the existence of a foreman of this name in the said period.

208 The emendation proposed by Keller, JARCE 21, 1984, 124 n. 66 ("the Places of Truth") is not really necessary and rather not justified; compare Kitchen, RamInscr VI, 658, 15. Similarly, "the temples of truth (perhaps royal tombs)", as suggested by McDowell, Village Life, 242, seems to be unfounded. Even less plausible is the translation proposed by Davies, Who's Who at DeM, 112f.: "the Mansions of the Just Ones".

209 Thus in papTurin CGT 55002, cf. S. Demichelis, Le projet initial de la tombe de Ramsès IV?, ZÄS 131, 2004, 114ff., esp. 118f.(H), 120 (N); papTurin 1923 (+fragments), vo. 9: Kitchen, RamInscr VI, 367, 8; cf. R. Ventura, The Largest Project for a Royal Tomb in the Valley of the Kings, JEA 74, 1988, 137ff. (esp. p. 139, 142); Černý, Valley of the Kings, 32. See also Demarée, in: Village Voices, 16-17 (=fig. 1).

210 Cf. Demichelis, op.cit., 129 n. 133. It is worth noting that one of the side niches in the tomb of Ramesses III (KV 11) is also termed as "(hall? of) the Two Truths", cf. Černý, Valley of the Kings, 33; M. Marciniak, ET 12, 1983, 304f.

211 E. Naville, Tb (Einleitung), 112; H. Grapow, ZÄS 72, 1936, 16.

212 PM I/2², 515 (29-30); Piankoff, Rambova, op.cit., 319-325, pls. 104-107, 109-110; Abitz, op.cit., 110-116.

of Amun at Thebes, members of which served over three generations as "chief of the temple archives of the estate of Amun".[213] For this reason presumably the decoration in his tomb included depictions of the most influential persons in Thebes of his times: the High Priest of Amun Amenhotep, second prophet Tjanefer (II), third prophet Penparei, and fourth prophet Kha[emope].[214] The fact that Nesamun is also mentioned in the decoration of Iymiseba's tomb with the title of second prophet[215] is important for the dating of the tomb decoration as he was Tjanefer's successor as second prophet (the change is presumed to have taken place while Iymiseba's tomb was being decorated). Nesamun is known to have been the younger son of the High Priest Ramessesnakht and brother of the High Priest Amenhotep. The earliest testimony of his office of second prophet of Amun, contained in papLeopold-Amherst, can be referred to year 13 of Ramesses IX;[216] here he simultaneously bears the title of *sem*-priest in the temple of Medinet Habu (taken over presumably from his brother Amenhotep).[217] It is also known that Amenhotep could not have been promoted to the office of the high priest of Amun earlier than in the second year of Ramesses IX when the pontifical office was filled still by his father Ramessesnakht[218] and later than year 10 when he appears together with Ramesses IX in the famous scene from the Karnak temple (see below).[219] Therefore, the tomb of Iymiseba had to have been usurped and decorated between years 2 and 13 of the reign of Ramesses IX, most probably in the same year 9 as the graffito in the tomb of Ramesses VI. Therefore, the mention of and representation of the High Priest Amenhotep in

213 Bierbrier LNK, 14f.

214 Cf. Champollion, Notices Descr. I, 862; Kitchen, RamInscr VI, 550 (14-16), 551 (15)-552 (1); H. Murray, J. Málek, GM 37, 1980, 32.

215 Kitchen, RamInscr VI, 551, 15.

216 See Bierbrier LNK, 12; cf. also Bell, Serapis 6, 1980, 17 n. 124.

217 Cf. Capart et al., JEA 22, 1936, pl. 12 (2,1)=Kitchen, RamInscr VI, 483, 5-6; see also papLeopold-Amherst 3, 9; 4, 12.

218 For the papyrus in The Egyptian Society of Papyrology, being the latest testimony regarding the High Priest Ramessesnakht, see Helck, JARCE 6, 1967, 137 (Text B), 139, 147 (l. 22)=Kitchen, RamInscr VI, 518, 11. In consequence, a graffito from Karnak representing Amenhotep as the *sem*-priest (of the temple in Medinet Habu, as it seems) can be dated possibly to the very beginning of the reign of Ramesses IX, whose cartouches were written on the offering table represented in the scene, cf. Kitchen, RamInscr VI, 534 (3); for the photograph, see R.A. Schwaller de Lubicz, Le Temple de l'Homme. Apet du Sud à Louqsor, II, Paris 1957, pl. 96B; see also a comment by Haring, Divine Households, 449. Even earlier in date (i.e., beginning of the reign of Ramesses VII) is an occurence of the *sem*-priest Amenhotep in papIFAO (no number), docs.A+B, cf. Y. Koenig, in: Hommages à la mémoire de Serge Sauneron, I, [BdE 81], Cairo 1979, 185ff., esp. p. 208; with a missing part of the papyrus published by Koenig, BIFAO 83, 1983, 249ff.; Kitchen, RamInscr VI, 397ff. (no. 14); Haring, Divine Households, 217, 220 n. 3, 449 n. 5.

219 Cf. Helck, CdE 59, 1984, 244f.; Bierbrier LNK, 13.

the tomb of Iymiseba appears to be the earliest known.[220] In the scene from the Amun temple in Karnak from year 10 of Ramesses IX he can be seen in front of the statue of the ruler,[221] who had presented him with valuables in return for his services.[222] The accompanying text speaks, among others, of land donations.[223] The text constitutes valuable evidence for the importance and activity of the high priest in administering the domain of Amun; neither should his efforts to beautify the temple in Karnak be forgotten.[224]

Despite the unstable situation in the Theban necropolis, caused by sporadic tomb robberies and threat of attack by desert nomads, security at the royal necropolis was still not significantly disturbed. When Ramesses IX died, his tomb (KV 6) was completed sufficiently[225] for his body to be deposited in it.[226] There is no reason to doubt that Ramesses IX was indeed buried in this tomb,[227] especially as several elements of undoubtedly the original equipment were found in it.[228] The missing stone cover of the sarcophagus, comparable to that used earlier in KV 1 to cover up the hollow in the centre of the burial chamber, is disturbing. It must have been taken from the tomb for reuse elsewhere. It is not without importance for the fact that this was the last royal tomb in the Valley of the Kings which was built and decorated sufficiently for the ruler to be buried in it. At the time of the pharaoh's death only a small part of the planned complex

[220] Cf. T.A. Bács, GM 148, 1995, 9f., who suggests year 4 for his introduction to the office, thus following Wente, JNES 25, 1966, 83 n. 27; cf. also Bell, Serapis 6, 1980, 18. Obviously, a mere mention of the name of Ramessesnakht in the tomb of Setau in El-Kab (no. 4), dated to year 4 of Ramesses IX in the "artist's signature", is not necessarily a contradiction for such a hypothesis, compare Kitchen, RamInscr VI, 557, 3; 558, 4; cf. also LD III, 236b; Spiegelberg, RT 24, 1902, 185f. (a). Setau was the father-in-law of Meribaste (II), one of the sons of Ramessesnakht, and the latter's name appears in the filiation of Meribaste.

[221] See W. Federn, CdE 34, 1959, 214; cf. Niwiński, BIFAO 95, 1995, 332; for the photograph, see e.g. A. Hermann, ZÄS 90, 1963, pl. 10; Lull, Los sumos sacerdotes, fig. 2.

[222] G. Lefebvre, Inscriptions concernant les Grands Prêtres d'Amon Romê-Roÿ et Amenhotep, Paris 1929, 47ff.; Helck, MIO 4, 1956, 161ff.; Kitchen, RamInscr VI, 455ff.; Frood, Biographical Texts, 68ff.

[223] Cf. Frood, op.cit., 71, 237 n. 51.

[224] The texts from the temple in Karnak stand in evidence of this, cf. Kitchen, RamInscr VI, 532ff., as does also a text from the base of a statue of the high priest found in front of pylon VII, cf. G. Legrain, ASAE 5, 1904, 21; Kitchen, RamInscr VI, 542, 11-543, 3 (no. 10); Frood, Biographical Texts, 60f.

[225] Cf. Thomas, Royal Necropoleis, 131f.

[226] The mummified remains of Ramesses IX were found in the coffin of Nesikhonsu included in the cache at Deir el-Bahari, cf. Maspero, Momies royales, 567f.; Reeves, Valley of the Kings, 250; E. Graefe, G. Belova (eds.), The Royal Cache TT 320 – a re-examination, Cairo 2010, 59, 70.

[227] See ramrks on the subject: A. Dodson, C.N. Reeves, A casket fragment of Ramesses IX in the Museum of Archaeology and Anthropology, Cambridge, JEA 74, 1988, 223-226; Reeves, Valley of the Kings, 119f., 250.

[228] These are objects from the previous Salt collection, cf. Reeves, Valley of the Kings, 125 n. 56.

had been achieved, reaching the hall of the four pillars which was provisionally adapted for the sarcophagus chamber.[229] The decoration had reached the second corridor. Even before his death, when it became obvious that the undertaking could not be completed according to the original plan, decisions were made to alter the decoration program. Interestingly, the remaining parts of the tomb were decorated, albeit with less attention to quality, in the short time between the pharaoh's death and his burial. The size of the tomb and the volume of stone removed (1076.35 cubic meters)[230] indicate a slower pace of the work than in the case of the unfinished tomb of Ramesses X (KV 18), the preparation of which started in the beginning of the reign of his son and successor.

The last year of the reign of Ramesses IX is attested in exceptionally few documents from the Theban necropolis.[231] This is surely pure chance, but the robbing affair must have bitterly affected the necropolis staff. Changes took place among the management of the crew. Contrary to a once held opinion,[232] it is not very likely that the scribe Horisheri kept his office through this stormy period. His actions going over the heads of his direct superiors apparently had their consequences. Yet it is not very probable that the accusations against him of accepting a bribe for promoting a boy to the necropolis staff (oCG 25800)[233] and of seizing some furnishings (oTurin 57356)[234] had anything to do with it. The former ostracon may be dated to a much earlier period, as it gives the names of the crew's foremen Nekhemmut and Anherkhau.[235] The latter one is not dated certainly,[236] hence one can have doubts as to whether the "affair" actually helped to end his career – it does not seem likely somehow. Of decisive importance

[229] On the building and decoration of the tomb, cf. F. Abitz, The Structure of the Decoration in the Tomb of Ramesses IX, in: After Tutankhamun, 165-185; id., Der Bauablauf und die Dekoration des Grabes Ramses' IX., SAK 17, 1990, 1-40; id., Die Veränderung von Schreibformen im Königsgrab Ramses' IX., in: H. Altenmüller, R. Germer (eds.), Miscellanea Aegyptologica, W. Helck zum 75. Geburtstag, Hamburg 1989, 1-5.

[230] After the Theban Mapping Project, Atlas of the Valley of the Kings: http://www.thebanmappingproject.com. As regards the dimensions, cf. also E. Hornung, ZÄS 105, 1978, 61; C. Rossi, GM 184, 2001, fig. 3; compare however Abitz, SAK 17, 1990, 7.

[231] Cf. Helck OPG, 532f.

[232] Cf. Capart et al., JEA 22, 1936, 191; Černý, CdE 11, 1936, 249; Thomas, JEA 49, 1963, 60.

[233] Černý, Ostraca CG, 114*, pl. 109 (=Kitchen, RamInscr VI, 257); cf. Černý, Community, 255, 354; McDowell, Village Life, 230 (no. 181).

[234] Lopez, Ostraca, fasc. 3, 19 (suppl. no. 9572), pl. 105-105a; cf. Černý, Community, 354; McDowell, Jurisdiction, 233.

[235] Kitchen (RamInscr VI, 257) places it among the documents from the reign of Ramesses V. See also Gutgesell, Datierung, 436 (R IV-R VI/VII); Janssen, Commodity Prices, 36 (after the reign of R IV); Černý, Ostraca CG, 92 (a note on the palaeography).

[236] Gutgesell (Datierung, 371) dates oTurin 57356 also to an early period of the 20th Dynasty.

in this respect was a case described in papAbbott and Horisheri's role in these events. Anyway, the name of the scribe Horisheri appears in the documents for the last time in year 17. His son Khaemhedje succeeded him undoubtedly, having already appeared at his side earlier as a necropolis scribe, just as Horisheri himself appeared in this role by the side of his father, the scribe Amennakht. It is noteworthy that it is Khaemhedje and not his father who accompanies the necropolis inspectors during the inspection of the royal burial ground in year 17.[237]

Another name that disappears from documents for the period that followed the investigation into the robberies is that of the scribe Paybes, a colleague of Horisheri.[238] More importantly, the two foremen of the crew were also changed at this time.[239] Shortly after the events we find Nebnefer and Amennakht as foremen (both attested in sources from the reign of Ramesses X).[240] It remains an open issue whether the personal changes in the necropolis staff were the result of members of the crew being involved in the robberies or whether the changes should be referred to the change in power and the ascension to the throne of Ramesses X.

J. von Beckerath has shown that the records of fish supplied to the crew, contained in the necropolis journal from the end of the reign of Ramesses IX and the beginning of the rule of his successor, establish the date of ascension to the throne of Ramesses X to the period between day 25 and 27 of the first month of *peret*, most probably day 27 of this month.[241] The short, merely three years long, rule of this pharaoh[242] is documented by a continuous sequence of records in the Theban necropolis journal, the continuity being something not encountered in the other periods.[243] The crew numbered about 32(+x) workmen,[244] which is

[237] Botti-Peet, Giornale, pl. 14: ro. B 1, 2=Kitchen, RamInscr VI, 570, 12.

[238] For the career and responsibilities of the scribe Paybes, cf. Černý, Community, 203 (25); Davies, Who's Who at DeM, 120, 135, 146f.

[239] As suggested by Černý, Community, 310; Bierbrier LNK, 34; id., CdE 59, 1984, 208; Bell, Serapis 6, 1980, 14f.; otherwise Davies, op.cit., 57.

[240] Cf. Černý, Community, 310; Davies, Who's Who at DeM, 279.

[241] PapTurin 2075+2056/55-56+2096/268 vo. 1, 8-9=Kitchen, RamInscr VI, 655, 4; 683, 8. Cf. von Beckerath, GM 79, 1984, 8f.; see also id., Chronologie, 87f. (with a comment on a suggested emendation of numeral 27 into 28).

[242] Contra Parker's suggestion (RdE 11, 1957, 163f.) proposing an extension of the reign of Ramesses X to nine years, cf. Helck, GM 70, 1984, 31f.; Krauss, Sothis- und Monddaten, 135; von Beckerath, SAK 21, 1994, 29ff.; id., Chronologie, 88.

[243] A detailed analysis of this part of the journal: Valbelle, Ouvriers, 43f., 216-219; Helck OPG, 538-554; Schneider in: H. Jenni (ed.), Das Grab Ramses' X. (KV 18), [AH 16], Basel 2000, 87-104. On the new fragments complementing the parts known earlier, cf. Demarée, GM 137, 1993, 49f.; Peden, in: DeM in the Third Millennium, 289.

[244] Valbelle, Ouvriers, 105 (tab. III), 219.

about the same number as in the last years of Ramesses IX. Overall, there exist records of 37 working days and 184 days during which the work in the Valley of the Kings was not carried out for a variety of reasons.[245] The number of working days in these records is surprisingly low (merely 17%).

In year 3 of Ramesses X (III *peret* 18) the vizier Khaemwese personally visited the royal necropolis, more specifically *tꜣ ỉnt*.[246] Graffito 1756 on the rocks of the Western Valley, in a region called "Vallon de la chambre de Hay", close to the steps ending the path leading from the eastern branch of the Valley of the Kings and the huts[247] of the necropolis guards(?) perhaps, is direct evidence of this visit. The localization of the graffito is not necessarily an indicator of any work being done in the region. It is noteworthy that on the day of the inspection the necropolis journal recorded a break in the work due to the presence of Bedouin (*ẖꜣstyw*),[248] most likely Libyan nomads. It cannot be excluded that the vizier's presence in this part of the necropolis was the result of several reports relating to nomads from the beginning of the month,[249] and the menace that this constituted.

The pharaoh's death came at a moment when the work on his tomb was not much advanced. The first corridor in the entrance had been made when the work was suddenly interrupted.[250] The total volume of removed rock (319.73 cubic meters)[251], compared to the time that it took to get to this point in the project, shows a rather ordinary pace of work. Therefore, the most likely reason for the tomb not to have been finished was the ruler's premature death. There was, however, a year before the pharaoh's demise, a surprisingly long stoppage in the work at the necropolis (72 days), apparently caused by problems with supplies for the crew and possibly some jurisdiction disputes of more or less unidentified nature regarding administration of work at the necropolis.[252] There

[245] Schneider, op.cit., 104.

[246] The term is used to refer to the Valley of the Kings, but also the Western Valley, cf. Černý, Community, 92f. For other meanings of the term, cf. Ventura, City of the Dead, 145ff.; see however C.J. Eyre, CdE 67, 1992, 279.

[247] Černý, Sadek et al., Graffiti III, pl. 20; IV, 15; Félix-Aubriot-Kurz, Plans de positions, pls. 93, 94. Structures of undetermined date.

[248] Cf. Botti-Peet, Giornale, pl. 50: ro. 1, 11=Kitchen, RamInscr VI, 688, 7; Schneider, op.cit., 90. As regards the arrival of Libyans in year 3 of Ramesses X, see Černý, CAH^3 II.2, 618; Haring, Divine Households, 271.

[249] See Peden, Graffiti, 199 n. 418; see also Haring, in: Village Voices, 76.

[250] Cf. H. Jenni (ed.), Das Grab Ramses' X (KV 18), [AH 16], Basel 2000, 26ff., figs. 10, 13, 15.

[251] After the Theban Mapping Project, Atlas of the Valley of the Kings: http://www.thebanmappingproject.com.

[252] See Schneider, op.cit., 100-104.

can be no doubt that the stage in which the work in the tomb was interrupted did not permit the pharaoh to be buried in it. Neither his mummy nor any furnishings that could be connected with his burial have ever been found,[253] hence it seems probable that he was not buried in Thebes.[254]

[253] Cf. Reeves, Valley of the Kings, 120.
[254] Cf. Schneider, op.cit., 104ff.

1. Chronology of the reign of Ramesses XI – before the Renaissance Era

The date of accession, or more precisely the proclamation of the reign of Ramesses XI, the last of the Ramesside rulers, is apparently explicitly stated in the preamble of the so-called Adoption Papyrus, papAshmoleanMus 1945.96, (ro. 1-3):[1] "Year 1, third month of *shemu*, day 20 under the Majesty of the King of Upper and Lower Egypt Ramesses-Khaemwese, l.p.h., Meriamun, the god, ruler of Heliopolis, l.p.h., given life eternally. On this day: proclamation to Amun of the appearance of this noble god, when he (i.e. the king) arose[2] and made offerings to Amun".[3]

The hypothesis put forward by W. Helck, on the basis of the sequence of dates of papMayer A and papTurin 1888+2085, that the day of accession of this sovereign fell between IV *shemu* 18 and IV *shemu* 23,[4] was finally discarded by the author himself. His later assumption, however, based on data provided by the unpublished papTurin 2097/161+2105vo., that it fell upon IV *shemu* 27 or 28,[5] must be dismissed as well. In both cases W. Helck proposed some arbitrary emendations of the dates given in these sources, which cannot be upheld any more and this brings into doubt his assertions regarding the date of the accession, as clearly demonstrated by C. Cannuyer,[6] and recently also by K. Ohlhafer.[7]

---

1 See Gardiner, JEA 26, 1940, 23 n. 3, 25; Allam HOP, 260 n. 2; Wente-van Siclen, Chronology, 245; Eyre, JEA 78, 1992, 207, 209; Cannuyer, GM 132, 1993, 19f.; Vandersleyen, L'Égypte II, 643; von Beckerath, Chronologie, 89, 91; cf. J.J. Janssen, Grain Transport in the Ramesside Period. Papyrus Baldwin (BM EA 10061) and Papyrus Amiens, [HPBM 8], London 2004, 5 n. 27.

2 The inchoative character of the phrase cannot be overlooked, cf. Kruchten, Études de syntaxe; id., GM 84, 1985, 33-40; Junge, Neuägyptisch, 87f.; Cannuyer, Brelan de "pharaons", 101f.; id., GM 132, 1993, 19. For the passage in question see also Satzinger, Neuägyptische Studien, 246; Allam HOP, 258.

3 Gardiner, JEA 26, 1940, pl. 5, 1-3=Kitchen, RamInscr VI, 735, 10-12. For the meaning and translation of the entire passage, cf. Cannuyer, Brelan de "pharaons", 100-102, 104f.; id., GM 132, 1993, 19f.; von Beckerath, Chronologie, 89.

4 Helck, Thronbesteigungsdaten, 128f.; accepted by others, cf. e.g. Hornung, Untersuchungen, 100; Kitchen, in: LÄ V (1984), 125.

5 Helck, SAK 17, 1990, 211f.; id., OPG, 555.

6 Cf. Cannuyer, Brelan de "pharaons", 98ff.; id., GM 132, 1993, 19f.

7 Cf. Ohlhafer, GM 135, 1993, 59ff. PapTurin 2097/161+2105 has been excluded from the dossier relating

Nothing is known about the origin of the new ruler and family relationship with his immediate predecessors, except the mere fact that he directly succeeded Ramesses X, as documented by the verso of papTurin 1898+ (papChabas-Lieblein).[8] Also the circumstances accompanying the change of the reign are completely unknown, as we have practically no knowledge about the interests of court coteries in distant Per-Ramesse in those times. By mere chance of survival of the records, the personalities of the last Ramesside rulers and their political aspirations are reflected mostly in their engagement in Theban affairs and such a character of the sources must be viewed as a serious obstacle in the studies on the political history of the period. Even if the very beginning of the reign of Ramesses XI is scarcely documented, there can be no doubt that his sovereignty was recognised in Thebes in the early years of his reign. As a matter of fact some dated documents testify to his sovereignty over Upper Egypt and the Thebaid in his early years, and these are the following:

– The Adoption Papyrus originating probably from Spermeru in the XIXth nome of Upper Egypt[9] certainly has a quite exceptional character, especially because Spermeru is located near the historical border dividing both parts of the country in the subsequent period. In its present form, the document was compiled in year 18 of Ramesses XI, but an older document dated to the very beginning of the reign was incorporated in it (see above).

– A significant number of the documents originating from the Theban necropolis can be dated to years 1, 3, 8-10, 12, and 14-15 of this sovereign.[10] An attempt to redate all of them to the Renaissance Era, as suggested recently by A. Thijs,[11] is thoroughly unfounded (see below, Chapter 4).

On the other hand, however, it must be noted that there are no dated official or monumental inscriptions in Thebes for the early years of his reign. The scarcity of such sources may be due to the relative weakness of the royal administration in Upper Egypt, a direct consequence of the trouble-

to the reign of Ramesses XI and Renaissance Era, since it was dated by him to the reign of Ramesses IX (ibid., 61f.); see however, Demarée, GM 137, 1993, 49f. (dating to year 2 of the reign of Ramesses X).

8 Cf. Helck, GM 70, 1984, 32; von Beckerath, SAK, 21, 1994, 29-33; id., Chronologie, 88.

9 Allam HOP, 262; cf. Gardiner, AEO II, 110*f. (no. 388).

10 Not to mention the documents later in date. As regards their dating and chronological sequence, cf. Helck, GM 70, 1984, 31; id., OPG, 557.

11 See for example his: Reconsidering the End of the Twentieth Dynasty, Part III: Some hitherto unrecognised documents from the *wḥm mswt*, GM 173, 1999, 175ff. (see esp. a list of dates on pp. 190f.); cf. also id., GM 184, 2001, 72.

some events of the reign of Ramesses IX. It is strange that no dedication inscriptions of Ramesses XI whatsoever are known from the Theban temples (except of course the magnificent reliefs of the Khonsu temple in Karnak, partly decorated during this reign, although no dates are available there). Outside Thebes too, the evidence relating to the reign of this sovereign is extremely rare and devoid of any dates.[12] Significantly enough there are no data concerning his activity in Lower Egypt, except three shabtis connected with the Apis burials.[13] Quite possibly a fortress in El-Ahaiwah (on the east bank of the Nile north of Girga) was already functioning as a "royal outpost" by the reign of Ramesses XI.[14] Of course this is not support for a thesis about the military background of king's rule in the south.

A. Thijs has recently suggested that Ramesses IX and X on the one hand, and Ramesses XI on the other represented two concurring lines of the royal family and consequently that they were ruling simultaneously for some time.[15] This cannot be accepted in the light of the available documentation,[16] and the "short chronology" which results from this assumption does not withstand criticism.[17] First of all the fragment of the necropolis journal of year 3 of Ramesses X (papChabas-Lieblein) gives also information pertaining to year 1 of Ramesses XI (with the name of the king partly preserved),[18] following the entries dated to year 3 of Ramesses X. Certainly the sequence of dates provided by this document does not confirm the chronological scheme proposed by A. Thijs, according to which year 17 of Ramesses XI started during year 3 of Ramesses X.[19] On the other hand, the restoration of the date relating to

[12] This is the cartouche in a usurped tomb in Hierakonpolis, cf. Kitchen, RamInscr VI, 731 (13); Gauthier LR III, 222 n. 2; and also the gold earrings and funerary statuette from Abydos, cf. Kitchen, RamInscr VI, 702 (2B); Gauthier LR III, 222 (XI) n. 3. The stela of Hori from Abydos has been omitted here, as it is dated to the end of this reign. For objects from Assuan and Buhen, see below, Chapter 7.

[13] Cf. PM III, 207 (E"); Kitchen, RamInscr VI, 701 (1); id., in: LÄ V (1984), 125.

[14] See P.V. Podzorski, in: P. Lacovara et al., CRIPEL 11, 1989, 66; an opinion based solely on a fragment of faience sherd with the cartouche of Ramesses XI, cf. ibid., 65f., fig. 4.

[15] See the series of his papers enumerated in the bibliography; cf. also Gasse, JEA 87, 2001, 81.

[16] If his rule was restricted to Upper Egypt, it would be difficult to explain for example the objects bearing cartouches of Ramesses IX found in Memphis and Heliopolis (attesting possibly his building activity and religious foundations); cf. Kitchen, in: LÄ V (1984), 125; id., RamInscr VI, 449-451 (nos. 2-4). A stela from Memphis dated to year 13 of this sovereign is especially significant in this regard, cf. A.M. Amer, GM 57, 1982, 11f., 16 (fig.). As regards the objects from Heliopolis, cf. ibid., 15 n. 8; Vandersleyen, L'Égypte II, 641.

[17] For the critics, see now von Beckerath, ZÄS 127, 2000, 111-116; id., GM 181, 2001, 17; Demidoff, GM 177, 2000, 91ff. See also a general note on the question by Hornung, in: Ancient Egyptian Chronology, 217.

[18] PapTurin 1898+1937+2094/244vo.: Botti-Peet, Giornale, pl. 63: texts a-c=Kitchen, RamInscr VI, 850f.; Helck OPG, 561.

[19] Cf. e.g., his revised chronological scheme, in GM 173, 1999, 181ff.; id., SAK 38, 2009, 345 (fig. 1).

Ramesses XI in this papyrus, as made by J. von Beckerath, leaves no place for any mention of *wḥm msw.t*.[20] Such a dating formula, as presented here, does not fit any of the constructions used by the scribes in reference to the Renaissance Era.[21] Thus we evidently have a reference to the regnal years of Ramesses XI – more precisely year 1 of Ramesses XI. Certainly a scribal error must be excluded, if even the provincial scribe of the Adoption Papyrus properly recognised the regnal years of Ramesses XI, and at the same time he was fully aware of the date of king's accession. Similarly the very beginning of grain accounts of papTurin 2018 was dated explicitly to "year 8, [4] month of *akhet*, day [5] under the Majesty of the King of Upper [and Lower Egypt, lord of Two Lands] Menmaat[re]-Setepenptah, l.p.h., son of Ra, lord of diadems Ra[mes] ses-Khaemwese Meriamun, beloved of all the gods of Waset" (ro. A1, 1-2).[22] Thus it is well in accord with the datation system according to regnal years of the pharaoh, and a lack of any reference to the Renaissance Era makes a redating of these documents to a later period highly dubious.[23] Moreover, the supposition of A. Thijs that "year 1" following year 3 of Ramesses X, refers to the Renaissance Era,[24] cannot be upheld because of the names of the scribes Efnamun and Khaem[hedje],[25] neither of whom has been attested at such a late date.[26]

The main reason to postulate the "short chronology" was, as it seems, a need to reconcile some apparent contradictions observed in the documentation concerning the robberies in the Theban necropolis at the end of the 20th Dynasty. As a matter of fact this documentation referring to the robberies is an abundant source of information on the history of the period. Just a general review of the contents of the papyri forming this exceptional dossier points out to the conclusion that the extant documentation in fact covers a much longer span of time than postulated by A. Thijs, and there is no evidence whatsoever for his "short chronology".

---

20 Cf. von Beckerath, SAK 21, 1994, 31, 33 (fig. 1); id., ZÄS 127, 2000, 113; cf. Thijs, GM 170, 1999, 95.

21 Contra Thijs, GM 170, 1999, 95f. His proposal to take as such the date in the Turin Taxation Papyrus (GM 173, 1999, 187) must be viewed as a simple misunderstanding, since we have here a regular dating according the regnal years of the pharaoh, and nothing at all permits us to see in it a reference to the Renaissance Era (see also below, note 23).

22 Kitchen, RamInscr VI, 851, 11-12; cf. Helck OPG, 562.

23 This is also the case with other pre Renaissance Era documents dated according the same patterns – Turin Taxation Papyrus (papTurin 1895+2006) of years 12-14: Pleyte-Rossi, Papyrus de Turin, pl. 65c; Gardiner RAD, 36, 1-2; cf. also Gauthier LR III, 220 (IV); and similarly papBerlin 10460 of year 14: Kitchen, RamInscr VI, 863, 9-10; Allam HOP, pls. 78-79.

24 Thijs, GM 170, 1999, 95.

25 Botti-Peet, Giornale, pl. 63 a, 7 and 10; the latter name wrongly restored as Khaemwese by Helck OPG, 561.

26 Cf. e.g. Davies, Who's Who at DeM, 284.

Certainly too much significance has been attached hitherto to the case of the fisherman Panakhtemope, a person well documented during the later phase of the tomb-robbery trials. His depositions given in the year 1 of the Renaissance Era were written in papBM 10052, 14, 10-18 and in papMayer A ro. 5, 9-12. Panakhtemope's "reappearance" in the text of papBM 10054 ro. 2, {1}-6 (cf. also the text of ro. 3, 1-6, and the list of the thieves – vo. 5, 6), written among the texts dated unequivocally to the year 16 of Ramesses IX (papBM 10054 ro. 1, {1}-12, and ro. 2, 7-16) does not necessarily mean that the former text is also so "early" in date.[27]

As a matter of fact, the chaotic arrangement of the texts written on papBM 10054 and their distinctly heterogeneous character give the strongest evidence against taking it as a "real" document relating to the trial of the thieves and court proceedings. The texts copied on the papyrus look rather like a collection of excerpts from the original documents and not their complete versions. Certainly this is not an official report, nor even a draft of such a document. In every respect it differs clearly from other legal documents dealing with the robbery trials, even if some of them may have undergone also an editing of sorts.[28] More probably the texts collected in papBM 10054 were simply a kind of a rough notes,[29] made by someone who was connected in some way with the trials, probably one of the court assistants or lesser necropolis officials.[30] It has been pointed out that different parts of the text were written in fact by one and the same hand,[31] and this may suggest indeed that someone compiled a selection of loosely connected legal texts relating to the robberies, but dealing also with other administrative duties (such as grain and bread supplies recorded on vo. 2-4).[32] In fact, it cannot be excluded that the document in its entirety was rather a kind of a miscellany or even a source book useful for a

[27] See J. von Beckerath, Zur Datierung des Grabräuberpapyrus Brit.Mus.10054, GM 159, 1997, 4ff.; compare however his later assertion in ZÄS 127, 2000, 114, where he dated all the robbery texts from papBM 10054 to the reign of Ramesses IX.

[28] Cf. Sweeney, Correspondence and Dialogue, 8.

[29] Cf. Capart et al., JEA 22, 1936, 191 ("The composition is as scrappy as that of Mayer A"); Gasse, JEA 87, 2001, 82 ("un document provisoire, une sorte d'aide-mémoire"); von Beckerath, GM 159, 1997, 8.

[30] The best candidate could have been possibly one of the scribes of the necropolis. Concerning the role of Nesamenope and Tuthmosis in the investigations and trials at the beginning of the Renaissance Era, see below Chapter 5.

[31] Cf. Capart et al., loc.cit.; Gasse, loc.cit. (an opinion based on an unpublished study of H. Musnik, regarding the palaeography of the hieratic texts written on the papyrus); see however, von Beckerath, GM 159, 1997, 8.

[32] It cannot be excluded, however, that the latter texts were in fact the real notes made by the owner of the scroll. Anyway, it is hardly imaginable that someone had ever copied such lists of persons supplied with grain as a model text.

scribe engaged in the matters of the necropolis and the legal proceedings in particular. In consequence, the absolute dating of the texts need not necessarily agree with the order in which they were copied onto the papyrus (see below).

Consequently, one cannot accept the very controversial hypothesis presented by A. Thijs, that papBM 10054 provides an intermediary link between some rough notes made by the scribe during the trial and the official document in its final form achieved by the reworking and restyling of the actual notes made directly during examinations of the thieves.[33] The chaotic character of the compilation represented by the papyrus certainly does not favour such an interpretation. We should rather expect a series of interrelated consecutive depositions, reflecting the most important stages of the trial, and investigation of facts, whereas here we are dealing only with a scattered episodes and such a degree of inconsistency in regard of the composition that it would be hardly possible to accept this as any kind of official document. In its form, due to some inconsistencies discernible in the text, papBM 10052 for example would perhaps fit much better the term of an "intermediary document"[34] as defined by A. Thijs. In this document some of the depositions are evidently not complete (cf. the deposition of Montusankh – 12, 22-23; Pakeneny – 13, 10-14; Suaamun – 15, 19-20), or else nothing was ever written about them, as for example the missing deposition of the sailor Nesamun (9, 7-8 followed by a blank space with traces of a line of text);[35] there are also subsequent notes or extrapolations inserted into the main corpus of the text (cf. e.g.1a, 1-5; a note after 3, 15;[36] 5, 1).[37]

In addition, there is an obvious contradiction created by the interpretation of A. Thijs concerning the chronology of the tomb robberies. First of all there is the well known case of the sons of Paykharu, whose houses were listed in papBM 10068vo. 2, 17-19, as located in the vicinity of the mortuary temple of Ramesses II.[38] The list of houses dated to year 12 of an unnamed sovereign must now be related decisively to the reign of Ramesses XI.[39] In consequence,

[33] Cf. Thijs, GM 167, 1998, 105f.

[34] Certainly the question still needs a further study, since we are not acquainted with the real procedures adopted by Egyptian clerks.

[35] Cf. Peet, Tomb Robberies, 151. It can be argued that the text was simply washed out but this would also be an argument in favour of the provisional character of the document. As for another erasure in the text, see also 4, 19 (ibid., 147, pl. 28).

[36] Written in red ink, cf. Peet, Tomb Robberies, 145, pl. 27. Certainly this was a simple correction of the text.

[37] For an explanation of the latter insertion, cf. ibid., 162 n. 36.

[38] Cf. ibid., 116.

[39] As demonstrated convincingly by J.J. Janssen, A New Kingdom Settlement. The Verso of Pap. BM.

this testimony cannot be reconciled with their involvement in the robberies committed in the temples of the west bank of Thebes, documented in every detail in papBM 10053vo. (dated to "year 9" of an unnamed sovereign), if the latter belonged also to the reign of Ramesses XI, year 9 (for this see below). Redating of both texts to the Renaissance Era, as proposed by A. Thijs,[40] does not remove an apparent contradiction. The persons accused of such a serious crime could never have escaped punishment, which is exactly what would have been the case if they had still been on duty three years later according to the reasoning of A. Thijs. A solution may be sought perhaps in a reversal of both dates: thus one can suggest that only "year 9" should be related to the Renaissance Era. This however does not remove the contradiction either, this time because of the mention of the scribe of the royal records Setekhmose (papBM 10053vo. 3, 13-15; 5, 5-6), about whom we know that he was accused already in year 18 (of Ramesses XI, cf. papBM 10054ro. 3, 15) – it is impossible of course that his trial could have lasted for a decade or so, especially because one can assume that the trials of year 1 and 2 of the Renaissance Era would certainly brought this to a conclusion.[41]

Moreover, the preserved sources certainly support the widely accepted thesis about two successive phases of tomb robberies separated from each other by a considerable time. The testimony of a certain Tjawenany of papBM 10052vo. 8, 19-20, if interpreted correctly,[42] leaves no doubts about it: "(I) have seen the punishment which was done to the thieves in the time of the vizier Khaemwese. Indeed, what would be the point in my going to seek out death, (now) when I know it?".[43] The testimony was given in year 1 of the Renaissance Era,[44] and the punishment of the thieves he witnessed must have

10068, AoF 19, 1992, 8ff. (esp. p. 9); cf. also Černý, Community, 263; Davies, Who's Who at DeM, 201.

[40] Cf. e.g. Thijs, GM 173, 1999, 184-186, 191; id., GM 179, 2000, 75-77, 83; id., GM 181, 2001, 97f.; id., GM 199, 2004, 84; cf. also Peet, Tomb Robberies, 180.

[41] It will not help us in solving the inconsistencies to ignore this problem, as did Thijs (GM 173, 1999, 185 n. 48). As regards the case of Setekhmose, see also Peet, Tomb Robberies, 115. It is noteworthy that Thijs (ibid., 185f.) wrongly interprets data concerning the chief warehouseman Djehutyemhab, whose house was recorded in papBM 10068vo. 3, 18 (his name appears also in the Turin Taxation Papyrus ro. 4, 7, and possibly also in papBM 10068vo. 1, 12) – a supposition that he is the same person as the warehousman from the Montu temple in Armant (papBM 10052, 12, 12-13) is unfounded, because the former was presumably a member of the staff in the temple complex of Medinet Habu.

[42] Cf. Aldred, Tomb Robberies, 92; Jansen-Winkeln, ZÄS 122, 1995, 63.

[43] Peet, Tomb Robberies, pl. 30=Kitchen, RamInscr VI, 787, 6-8; see also Černý-Groll, Late Egyptian Grammar, 23 (Ex. 49); 116 (Ex. 400); Peden, Historical Inscriptions, 274f.

[44] The person in question is documented also in papAbbott dockets, vo. A, 6; B, 7; and in papMayer A vo. 9, 22; 12, 23.

taken place much earlier, probably still during the reign of Ramesses IX (i.e. ca. 25 years earlier, according to the traditional chronology). Even though the estimation of the length of the interval between both occurrences is the subject of controversy, certainly there is no way to interpret the deposition of Tjawenany in favour of the shorter span of time.[45]

The case of "the gardener (*k3my*)[46] Pay[kha]ru the younger, son of Amenem-[hab of the temple of] Khonsu of Amenope",[47] apparently provides a more direct link between these two phases of robberies. Interrogated twice in year 1 of the Renaissance Era, he was found innocent of the thefts and finally set free. In his earlier testimony Paykharu reported in full detail the circumstances of the robberies committed once by his father: "My father crossed to the island of Amenope, and he found a coffin in the possession of the *wab*-priest Hapy(?),[48] of the chapel (*ḳniw*) of king Menkheper(u)re,[49] l.p.h., and the *wab*-priest Kaemwese of this temple (*pr pn*).[50] They said to him: «Ours is this coffin which belonged to our rich people.[51] We were hungry and we went and brought it. (Now) you be quiet! And we will give you a *d3iw*-cloth» – so they said to him. And they gave him a *d3iw*-cloth. But my mother said to him: «You are a silly[52] old man – stealing is that what you (really) did!»".[53]

There are good reasons to identify Amenemhab, Paykharu's father, with one of the thieves of the times of Ramesses IX[54] involved in the robberies in the tomb of king Sekhemre-Shedtawy Sebekemsaf (II) and in other tombs in

[45] As suggested by Thijs, GM 170, 1999, 85; id., GM 184, 2001, 66.

[46] Lesko, Dict. II, 168, 170; Gardiner AEO I, 96*f.

[47] PapBM 10052vo. 10, 1: Peet, Tomb Robberies, 151, pl. 31, and similarly in papMayer A ro. 3, 12: Peet, Mayer Papyri, 12, pl. 3 [for the sake of convenience Peet's "pages" are rendered here simply as plates].

[48] Less probably Mery(?). For the reading of the name, cf. also Peet, Tomb Robberies, 152, 165 n. 70; Helck, Materialien I, (120) – no. 1. As for the reading adopted here, see Ranke PN I, 234 (7); compare also the names of the type Hapy-wer or Hapy-aa, cf. ibid., 234 (8 and 9).

[49] Cf. Helck, Materialien I, (120); contra Peet, Tomb Robberies, 152, pl. 31 (10, 5) – sign Z3 should be possibly read instead of G7 in the royal cartouche; compare hieratic forms of the signs: Möller, Paläographie II, nos. 188 and 563. It cannot be excluded, however, that the name of Menkheperre was given here as a result of an error made by Paykharu (see below). Anyway, the correction proposed here is supported by papLeopold-Amherst 2, 3; 3, 14, where the water-pourer (*w3ḥ mw*) Kaemwese of the chapel of Menkheperure was referred to (see also papBM 10054vo. 1, 7-8). As regards the chapel or portable shrine (*ḳniw*) of Tuthmosis IV, cf. Otto, Topographie, 67. For *ḳniw* as the ceremonial throne of the king or a palanquin, see Helck, op.cit., (119)ff.; Janssen, JEA 52, 1966, 91 (f); Haring, in: DeM in the Third Millennium, 148; id., Divine Households, 26f.

[50] On this locution cf. Haring, Divine Households, 246 n. 1.

[51] Cf. Černý, JEA 27, 1941, 107 (6).

[52] Or: "doddering", cf. Lesko, Dict. II, 137.

[53] PapBM 10052vo. 10, 4-8: Peet, Tomb Robberies, pl. 31=Kitchen, RamInscr VI, 789, 3-10.

[54] Cf. Capart et.al., JEA 22, 1936, 181f.; Peet, Tomb Robberies, 47.

the Theban necropolis as well: "the field worker (*iḥwty*) Amenemhab of the temple of Amenope, who is employed (*nty sḥn.Ø*) in the island of Amenope in the charge of the high priest of Amun".[55] In another part of the same document he was described as "inspector (*rwḏ*) of the temple of Amenope, who was employed (*wn* (*ḥr*) *sḥn*) in the island of Amenope in the charge of the high priest of Amun-Ra, king of the gods".[56] Again in papBM 10054vo. 5, 11 he was mentioned as brought to the trial or to the prison, together with other thieves: "Brought. The field worker Amenmehab (of) the temple of Khonsu of Amenope".[57] Significantly, the independent testimony given by the quarryman Amenpnufer, son of Anhernakht, also concerns the activity of the gang in which this Amenemhab and his comrades participated: "I was going far beyond fortress (*itḥ*) of the west of Ne according to my custom regularly (*m dwn sp-sn*),[58] in year 13 of Pharaoh – (for) four years until this (year).[59] I was with the quarryman Hapywer, the field worker Amen[emhab], the craftsman (*ḥmww*) Setekhnakht, the craftsman Irenamun of the overseer of hunters of Amun,[60] the stonecutter (*nšdy*)[61] Hapyaa, the water pourer Kaemwese of the chapel of king [Menkheperu]re. Total: men 7. We [destroyed?][62] the tombs of the west of the City (Ne) and brought away their inner coffins which were in them, stripping off their gold and their silver which was on them, [and we] stole it and I divided it between myself and my companions" (papBM 10054vo. 1, 5-9).[63]

An anonymous testimony relating to the violation of the tomb of the third prophet of Amun Tjanefer at Dra Abu el-Naga (TT 158), being a continuation of the preceding text,[64] gives some additional details resembling to a surprising degree those recalled later by Paykharu: "We [...] went to the tomb of Tjanefer, who was the third prophet of Amun. We opened it and we brought out his

55 PapLeopold-Amherst 3, 13: Capart et al., JEA 22, 1936, pl. 15=Kitchen, RamInscr VI, 487, 1-2; similarly in papLeopold-Amherst 2, 2.

56 PapLeopold-Amherst 4, 6: Capart et al., JEA 22, 1936, pl. 16=Kitchen, RamInscr VI, 488, 11-12.

57 Peet, Tomb Robberies, 63, pl. 8=Kitchen, RamInscr VI, 495, 2.

58 As regards the reading, see Kitchen, RamInscr VI, 490, 9; for the adverb in question, cf. Černý-Groll, Late Egyptian Grammar, 138f.; Gardiner, JEA 42, 1956, 14; Lesko, Dict. II, 243.

59 Compare Peet, Tomb Robberies, 60; Neveu, Grammaire, 8. For a similar expression in papLeopold-Amherst 1, 17-18, see Capart et al., JEA 22, 1936, 176f.

60 This was the "overseer of the hunters of the temple of Amun-Ra, king of the gods, Nesamun", according to papLeopold-Amherst 3, 12; cf. Helck, Materialien I, (41).

61 Lesko, Dict. I, 250; cf. Capart et al., JEA 22, 1936, 177.

62 Cf. Peet, Tomb Robberies, 60, 66 n. 4; Kitchen, RamInscr VI, 490 n. 13d; Wb. I, 578 (9); Lesko, Dict. I, 358 (*ḫfy*).

63 Peet, Tomb Robberies, pl. 7=Kitchen, RamInscr VI, 490, 8-16.

64 For the sequence of texts written on papBM 10054, see below.

inner coffins, and we took his mummy, and we threw it there in a corner of his tomb. We took his inner coffins to this boat (*ꜥḳꜣ*) together with other things, to the island of Amenope. We set fire to them by night, and we gathered the gold which we had found on them" (papBM 10054ro. 1, 3-7).[65]

The case of Paykharu and his father Amenemhab seems to provide the most important evidence concerning the chronology of the robberies in the Theban necropolis. There are no grounds of course to suppose that the action described by Paykharu and violation of the tomb of Tjanefer were the same events. In both cases, however, the stolen coffins were brought from the tombs in the west of Thebes to the island of Amenope, a place of unknown location, possibly part of the domain of the Khonsu temple in Karnak.[66] The place was accessible by boat so it should be located either on a Nile island or else somewhere on the east bank (perhaps in the vicinity of Luxor or maybe Karnak).[67] The coffins were burned there, as it was an easy method of separating the gold foil from the wooden surface of the coffin.[68] A mention of the island of Amenope forms a direct link between the affair described by Paykharu and that related by the anonymous thief of papBM 10054ro. 1. It can be surmised that it was a distant and desolate place, well suited for the shady business of the gang of the quarryman Amenpnufer. The fact that it was the place of work of the field labourer Amenemhab would have had an effect on the choice of this particular place by the gang.

There can be no doubt about the identity of Amenemhab, Paykharu's father, with the man of the same name accused in year 16 of Ramesses IX. In contrast to the conclusions achieved by A. Thijs,[69] the case of Paykharu and Amenemhab in no way contradicts the assumption that two different phases of robberies were documented in the sources, and these were separated in time, to the effect

[65] Peet, Tomb Robberies, pl. 6=Kitchen, RamInscr VI, 491, 2-9.

[66] Cf. Capart et al., JEA 22, 1936, 182. As regards other possibilities of identification of the "temple of Amenope" and the "temple of Khonsu of Amenope", see P. Barguet, Le temple d'Amon-Rê à Karnak, Cairo 1962, 10 n. 1; Otto, Topographie, 40; Helck, Materialien I, (79).

[67] Compare the meaning of the Arabic *gezirah*. For the location of the place, cf. Capart et al., JEA 22, 1936, 181 ("a name of cultivable lands round Karnak or between Karnak and Luxor"); Otto, Topographie, 43 ("in der Nähe des Chonstempels"); Montet, Géographie II, 73 ("vraisemblablement l'île en face de Louxor"; Helck, loc.cit. ("im Strom liegende Nilinsel, die, jetzt mit dem Westufer verwachsen, auf älteren Karten noch zu erkennen ist".

[68] Cf. A.J. Spencer, Death in Ancient Egypt, London 1982, 97.

[69] Thijs, GM 170, 1999, 87. The argument that "Peikharu's whole story seems completely irrelevant since the officials specifically asked him to tell about his own actions", certainly loses its intrinsic value if one realize that the sole aim of Paykharu was to clear his own name. This is why he felt necessary to dissociate from the deeds of his father who was notorious for his activity, no matter how distant in time.

that the experiences of two successive generations were recalled in them.[70] This seems to be rather an additional argument against the "short chronology".

Presumably Paykharu was recollecting events distant in time and his memory obviously failed in some details. Significantly he mentioned the *wab*-priest Kaemwese of the chapel of Menkheper(u)re,[71] whereas in the sources dating to the reign of Ramesses IX the latter was titled as water-pourer (*wꜣḥ mw*), i.e. a *chaochyte*,[72] of the chapel of Menkheperure in the City (Ne), being under the direction of a certain unnamed person (possibly the high priest of Amun himself).[73] The mistake cannot be explained satisfactorily, because there are no special relation between the two priestly functions.[74] Quite possibly, Paykharu's memory had faded over the years dividing him from the events described. The same concerns also the name of the king, which he gave as Menkheperre instead of Menkheperure. If the robberies committed by the gang of Amenpnufer started in year 13 of Ramesses IX then, according to the "traditional" chronology, the interval of years would amount to ca. 27 years. This is indeed well in accord with the fact that representatives of two generations were involved in the events described. Amenemhab was already an old man when he participated in the robberies, and there are good reasons to suppose that his son was then a mere boy (as was Ahautynefer, whose testimony relating to the deposition of the high priest Amenhotep was written down at the beginning of the Renaissance Era – see Chapter 2).

In addition there are two similar cases which were brought to light in depositions written in papMayer A at the beginning of the Renaissance Era. This time, however, an interpretation of the entire context is not so obvious, and one can only guess about the exact date of events recalled in the following way:

"The *Wab*-priest Nesamun, son of Paybaki, was brought on account of his father.[75] He was examined by beating with the stick. He was told: «Tell the manner of your father's going with the men who were with him!» He said: «Indeed my father was there, when I was a little child (*ꜥḏd-šri*), (but) I have

[70] See von Beckerath, ZÄS 127, 2000, 115.

[71] If the locution *m pr pn* (papBM 10052vo. 10, 6) can be taken rightly as referring to the preceding *pꜣ ḳniw n nsw Mn-ḫpr(.w)-Rꜥ*; cf.supra, n. 50.

[72] For the ritual meaning of the title, cf. K. Donker van Heel, Use and meaning of the Egyptian term *wꜣḥ mw*, in: Village Voices, 19-30 (with the references to Kaemwese on pp. 25, 30-Tab. II).

[73] Cf. papLeopold-Amherst 2, 3; 3, 14; and papBM 10054vo. 1, 7-8.

[74] It cannot be excluded, however, that "pouring the water" was one of the acts fulfilled by the *wab*-priests; as regards their other activities, cf. Kemp, Ancient Egypt, 307; Janssen, AoF 19, 1992, 18f.

[75] This probably means that Paybaki was already dead at the time of the trial, cf. Peet, JEA 12, 1926, 256 n. 6; id., JEA 14, 1928, 67.

no knowledge of what he did»" (papMayer A ro. 2, 10-12).[76] At first glance it is difficult to say whether Nesamun spoke here about events which were remote in time or whether his testimony concerned more recent occurrences. If he was brought to the court as a young man at the beginning of his career (ca. 20 years old) then his father's deeds recalled here could have taken place 10 or even 15 years earlier.[77] On the other hand, if he was older, his testimony could possibly have concerned robberies from the reign of Ramesses IX, though the latter seems less probable as there are no data relating to the robberies of this period included in papMayer A (nor in other documents of this period either). As a consequence we may infer that this is a testimony of later phase of robberies, which not were prosecuted until the Renaissance Era. Strangely enough the further examination of this man clearly refreshed his memory to the effect that he disclosed the names of three of the thieves, whom he saw "in this place where this portable shrine was" (papMayer A ro. 2, 13).[78] What is more, he expressed an opinion that they are the persons who would know the ultimate fate of gold which could have been robbed: "If gold was collected, they are the ones who know (it)" (papMayer A ro. 2, 15).[79] Just two days later he withdrew his accusations, saying: "They were seen while hastening to this well-equipped (*ḏbȝ.tw*)[80] place. What does it mean (when you say) that they were seen while they opened this seal? I did not see them opening this seal! It was out of fear that I (ever) said it" (papMayer A vo. 6, 15-17).[81] Now Nesamun unexpectedly occurs in the role of an eyewitness contemporary with the events described, so one cannot escape the conclusion that the subject of the present document is an investigation regarding quite recent robberies. It looks rather as if these robberies lasted for a substantial span of time, starting still during Nesamun's childhood and continued in the following period, when he already reached adulthood.

Among the names of the three thieves accused by Nesamun (these are the workman Ahautynefer; Meniunefer,[82] son of Hapywer; and the craftsman

[76] Peet, Mayer Papyri, 11, pl. 2=Kitchen, RamInscr VI, 807, 3-8; cf. Peet., JEA 2, 1915, 176; see also Černý-Groll, Late Egyptian Grammar, 312 (Ex. 854).

[77] A much shorter span of time has been postulated by Peet, JEA 12, 1926, 256f.; id., JEA 14, 1928, 67; Jansen-Winkeln, ZÄS 119, 1992, 28f.; Niwiński, Bürgerkrieg, 246f.

[78] Peet, Mayer Papyri, pl. 2=Kitchen, RamInscr VI, 807, 9.

[79] Peet, Mayer Papyri, pl. 2=Kitchen, RamInscr VI, 807, 11-12; cf. Černý-Groll, Late Egyptian Grammar, 224 (Ex. 600); Junge, Neuägyptisch, 192.

[80] Cf. Wb.V, 558 (1).

[81] Peet, Mayer Papyri, 13, pl. 6=Kitchen, RamInscr VI, 816, 4-7; cf. also Černý-Groll, Late Egyptian Grammar, 239f. (Ex. 642), 245 (Ex. 666), 380 (Ex. 1064); Groll, Negative Verbal System, 8f. (Ex. 11).

[82] I prefer such a reading instead of "the herdsman Nefer", because in papMayer A vo. 6, 2, the thieves accused

Wenmedihuy, son of Ahauty)[83] only that of workman (*k3wty*)[84] Ahautynefer seems to be known elsewhere.[85] He may be the same person as the owner of a house in the complex of Medinet Habu: "the chief of the workmen (*ḥry k3wty.w*) Ahautynefer", included in the list of houses of papBM 10068 (vo. 8, 3), dated to year 12, undoubtedly of Ramesses XI. If so, we should draw the conclusion that by that year he was already the chief of the workmen. For unknown reasons in later documents dating to the years 1 and 2 of the Renaissance Era he was termed simply as the "workman".[86] It is hardly possible that he was demoted in this way because of his participation in the robberies.

More probably, the later texts refer to his activities in the period when he was still just a workman, and this would date the events connected with the robberies to the period before year 12 of Ramesses XI. In the LRL no. 36, written by the scribe of the necropolis Nesamenope, we can find an isolated mention of the "workman Ahautynefer", the only one in the whole corpus of LRL.[87] The early dating of the letter will be demonstrated below (Chapter 6), here it will suffice to note that it must predate significantly the Renaissance Era and the trials documented in papMayer A and papBM 10403, if the identification of the "workman Ahautynefer" is justifiable.

The early stage of Ahautynefer's career is documented also by the marriage settlement of his father, preserved in papTurin 2021(+Genève D 409), presumably also predating the Renaissance Era.[88] He appears here together with his brother: "the *wab*-priest and chief of the workmen (*wʿb ḥry k3wty.w*) Ahautynefer, and the *wab*-priest Nebnefer – the children of the god's father

by Nesamun, including Meniunefer, were enumerated without mentioning their functions or professions.

83 PapMayer A ro. 2, 13-14; similarly vo. 6, 2; for the correction of the older reading of the name of Hapywer, cf. Peet, Tomb Robberies, pl. 24 (papMayer A ro. 2, 14).

84 For the meaning of the term, cf. Lesko, Dict. II, 167f.; Spiegelberg, ZÄS 63, 1928, 151; Gardiner, AEO I, 59*f. (132); Steinmann, ZÄS 107, 1980, 142 (1.1.3.1); Haring, Divine Households, 238f.

85 For the person in question and sources concerning him, see Černý-Peet, Marriage Settlement, 31; Helck, Materialien I, (113); Haring, Divine Households, 223, 450 n. 2.

86 Cf. papMayer A ro. 2, 13; vo. 6, 2 (no title), 3 (with father's name), 17 (no title): Peet, Mayer Papyri, pls. 2, 6=Kitchen, RamInscr VI, 807, 8-9; 815, 2-4; 816, 7. See also his more elaborate title in papBM 10403ro. 1, 3: Peet, Tomb Robberies, pl. 36=Kitchen, RamInscr VI, 828, 13-14.

87 Černý LRL, 56, 9; cf. Haring, Divine Households, 450 n. 2.

88 An attempt to date this papyrus more precisely has been made by Wente LRL, 9: "no later than Year 19 of Ramesses XI"; cf. also Valbelle, Ouvriers, 77, 125 n. 3. Wente's reasoning must be corrected now on the basis of our knowledge regarding the chronology of the scribes of the necropolis: the position of the scribe Efen[khonsu] of papTurin 2021ro. 4, 10 (instead of Efn[amun], as wrongly restored by Wente LRL, 9 n. 31) cannot be established convincingly; cf. however Davies, Who's Who at DeM, 138f., 284: post year 20 of Ramesses XI. Quite hypothetically a period between years 10 and 12 of Ramesses XI may be taken into consideration as well.

Amenkhau, who stood in front of him (i.e. the vizier), the eldest brothers (among) his children" (ro. 3, 5-6).[89] The identity of this Ahautynefer cannot be doubted because the name of his father was given also in papMayer A vo. 6, 3.[90] It is important to say that the legal deposition of papTurin 2021 was written still during the lifetime of Ahautynefer's father on the occasion of the latter's second marriage. Although there is no certainty about identity of the god's father Amenkhau, he may be the same person as one of the two god's fathers of that name in the list of houses of papBM 10068vo. (3,27; 5, 28).[91]

The value of papTurin 2021 for the present discussion lays mostly in the fact that it provides detailed information regarding the "chief of the workmen" Ahautynefer and his family – all of them were the members of the temple staff in Medinet Habu. At the same time the "early" dating of the papyrus does not necessarily disturb the chronological framework of his career. Some confusion may be caused perhaps by the fact that he attained the function of the "chief of the workmen" by year 12 of Ramesses XI, whereas later documents dating to the Renaissance Era present him as an ordinary workman.[92] His functions were in fact more varied at the time preceding the interrogations, since we are informed that he was also a porter: "There was brought workman Ahautynefer of the temple of king Usermaatre-Meriamun, l.p.h., in the estate of Amun. They said to him: «You are the porter (*p3 mnty*) of this place. Tell (us), please,[93] about every man whom you saw entering into this place and doing damage to the fittings (*n3 ip.(w)t*)[94] of this portable shrine (*p3y pr-n-st3*)»" (papBM

[89] Černý-Peet, Marriage Settlement, pl. 14, 5-6=Allam HOP, pls. 116-117=Kitchen, RamInscr VI, 740, 14-16; cf. also Černý, BIFAO 37, 1937-1938, 42; Allam, op.cit., 321 (translation).

[90] Peet, Mayer Papyri, pl. 6=Kitchen, RamInscr VI, 815, 4.

[91] Cf. Černý-Peet, Marriage Settlement, 31; these are sons of Tjenery and Bakenptah respectively. The god's father of that name is also known from papAmbras 1, 5 (no parentage given), and from an unpublished papPhiladelphia (Pennsylvania University Museum), being the missing lower part of papBM 10383: Černý Notebook 157.3, and 5 (by courtesy of the Griffith Institute, Oxford), cf. Haring, Divine Households, 231, 450. A *wab*-priest Amenkhau son of Bakptah was accused of robberies too, as demonstrated by papBM 10053vo. 1, 11-12, but the information cannot be properly evaluated in the context of the above discussion (Peet, Tomb Robberies, 113, 115, suggested his identity with the god's father Amenkhau of papTurin 2021).

[92] At first sight such a strange situation could be taken as an argument in favour of the hypothesis presented by A. Thijs, and his "reverse" dating of the documents cited, cf. GM 181, 2001, 96-99 (tab. II). Even then a contradiction remains, namely why the workman Ahautynefer, accused at the beginning of the Renaissance Era (years 1-2), survived the prosecution and finally attained the post of the chief of the workers (in hypothetical "year 12"). Another aspect of the question is that the guilt or innocence of Ahautynefer cannot be ascertained beyond any doubt. If we take into consideration the information provided by LRL no. 36, which must predate the Renaisance Era and the trials, he was indeed a simple workman then. It cannot be excluded, however, that the chief of the workmen and the workman of that name were in fact different persons.

[93] As regards an ironical meaning of the particle, see Sweeney, Women and Language, 1116.

[94] Rendered as "fittings" or "(metal) covering" by Peet, Tomb Robberies, 162 n. 39, 173 n. 2; cf. also

10403ro. 1, 3-6).[95] In the light of this text, his function can be compared perhaps to that of the door-keeper or guardian, and this finds another exemplification in LRL no. 36, according to which Ahautynefer was obliged to deliver (presumably not as his personal debt) a certain amount of tin for manufacturing of weapons (*ḫꜥw*).[96] First of all this variety of functions can be satisfactorily explained not only by the very character of the job of the worker or porter (i.e. *kꜣwty*) but also by the fact that as a *wab*-priest he was obliged to take on more humble duties as well.[97]

All of the persons accused by Nesamun had been examined in connection with the violation of the portable shrine (*pꜣ pr-n-sṯꜣ*) and the portable chest (*pꜣ gs-pr*) from the temple in Medinet Habu,[98] but only the testimony of Ahautynefer was included in papMayer A (vo. 6, 3ff). Strangely enough their names do not appear at all in the dockets of papAbbott where, however, we find a mention of: "The scribe Paybaki of the temple of Usermaatre-Meriamun, son of Nesamun, his mother being Isis" (papAbbott-dockets, vo. A, 14).[99] In the light of the depositions written in papMayer A "the scribe Paybaki, son of Nesamun, of this temple"[100] evidently played a prominent role as he was one of the six robbers who had violated portable shrines (*nꜣ pr.w-(n)-sṯꜣ*), deposited in the treasury in Medinet Habu temple.[101] No doubt this Paybaki was the father of the *wab*-priest Nesamun son of Paybaki, mentioned above, which means that Nesamun was named after his grandfather. The latter may be identified more precisely with a deputy of the temple in Medinet Habu because of the information provided by papBM 10403, concerning also violations of the portable shrine: "the scribe Paybaki, son of [de]puty Nesamun of the temple".[102] In all probability the "house of deputy Nesamun" in the complex of Medinet

Lesko, Dict. I, 25.

95 Peet, Tomb Robberies, pl. 36=Kitchen, RamInscr VI, 828, 13-829, 1; cf. Haring, Divine Households, 450 n. 2.

96 Černý LRL, 56, 9ff.; cf. Helck, Materialien VI, (987).

97 See detailed comments by Haring, Divine Households, 238f.; Janssen, AoF 19, 1992, 12f., 18f.

98 Cf. papMayer A ro. 1, 1-3 and vo. 6, 1.

99 Peet, Tomb Robberies, 132, pl. 23=Kitchen, RamInscr VI, 765, 1. For this Paybaki, cf. Haring, Divine Households, 451; Helck, Materialien I, (112) – father's name read erroneously.

100 PapMayer A ro. 1, 11; he was mentioned also in papMayer A ro. 2, 6 (bare name only) and vo. 6, 22 (the "scribe Paybaki").

101 PapMayer A ro. 1, 10; counted among main culprits by Haring, Divine Households, 276f.

102 PapBM 10403ro. 1, 17-18: Peet, Tomb Robberies, pl. 36=Kitchen, RamInscr VI, 829, 15-16; cf. also Haring, Divine Households, 451 n. 3, 453. Obviously the temple of Ramesses III in Medinet Habu is meant here, cf. Černý, JEA 26, 1940, 127ff. The identification of Nesamun seems to be quite certain, although the name was written here in its full form (*Nsy-sw-Imn*), cf. Ranke PN I, 173 (19).

Habu, mentioned in papBM 10068vo. 6, 22,[103] can be connected with the same person. Thus we can say for certain that the affair of the portable shrines came to light during the lifetime of the next generation after that of deputy Nesamun, documented in year 12 (of Ramesses XI). It was the Nesamun's son Paybaki, who actively participated in the robberies, when the latter's son Nesamun was only a child. Then Nesamun son of Paybaki had witnessed some subsequent, probably slightly later robberies. This does not necessarily mean that there was a long interval between year 12 (when Nesamun, father of Paybaki, was living in Medinet Habu) and the time of the robberies committed by Paybaki (and those witnessed by Nesamun as well). As a matter of fact it can be restricted just to several years, and the robberies committed during the lifetime of Nesamun son of Paybaki must be connected with the second phase of robberies in the Theban necropolis. Significantly none of the persons accused in relation to the robberies carried out in the temple of Medinet Habu were involved explicitly in other robberies reported by the extant sources – those of the reign of Ramesses IX in particular.

Further on in papMayer A we read the following: "There was brought the weaver Wennekhu, son of Tatay, of the temple. He was examined by beating with the stick. The screw was put very tight on his feet and his hand. There was given to him an oath by the Lord, l.p.h., not to speak falsehood. (Then) he was told: «Now tell the manner of your father's going when he made a damage to[104] this(?) portable shrine, together with his companions!» He said: «I was only a child (*šri*) when my father was killed. And my mother said to me: The chief of Madjoy Nesamun gave some (pieces?)[105] of copper to your father. Then when the troop-commanders (*n3 ḥr.(y)w-pḏ.t*) of the foreigners[106] killed your father, they took me for interrogation (*r smtr*). Nesamun took the (pieces of) copper he gave me (earlier). It was deposited [...]»" (papMayer A ro. 2, 17-21).[107] Here too some doubts arise as regards the precise dating of the events referred to in the text. At first sight it would seem that the father of the witness was killed much earlier than the trial which took place in year 1 of the Renaissance Era. As in the

[103] Peet, Tomb Robberies, pl. 16=Kitchen, RamInscr VI, 753, 6. There is no mention of Paybaki in the list.

[104] Or else: "appropriated", cf. Lesko, Dict. I, 285; Wb.II, 478 (17).

[105] Reading *m33* rather doubtful.

[106] An alternative interpretation of this passage as proposed by A.R. Schulman, Military Rank, Title and Organization in the Egyptian New Kingdom, [MÄS 6], Berlin 1964, 124 (239), is incorrect.

[107] Peet, Mayer Papyri, 11, pl. 2; with corrections in: id., Tomb Robberies, pl. 24; Kitchen, RamInscr VI, 807, 14-808, 7; cf. also Černý-Groll, Late Egyptian Grammar, 367 (Ex. 1038), 379 (Ex. 1063), 485 (Ex. 1373); Junge, Neuägyptisch, 103; Neveu, Grammaire, 167 (Ex. 12).

preceding case the reference to the childhood of Wennekhu does not necessarily mean, however, that the robberies took place during the reign of Ramesses IX, when the first wave of the robberies in the necropolis occurred. We find neither the name of father nor son in the list of houses of year 12 (papBM 10068vo. 2ff.) and unfortunately they are unknown elsewhere.[108] However, the very circumstances described in this deposition shed some light on the date of the violation of the portable chests. The role played by the "troop-commanders of the foreigners", who did violence to the member of the temple staff in Medinet Habu points clearly to the period of disturbances connected with the civil war and deposition of the High Priest Amenhotep.

As a consequence of the analysis of the sources presented above, at least two different waves of robberies in the Theban necropolis can be discerned in this period. The first of them had taken place in the last years of the reign of Ramesses IX (the earliest information dates however to year 13 of Ramesses IX),[109] and found its finale in the series of investigations undertaken by the authorities just three or four years later, i.e. in years 16 and 17 of Ramesses IX. It was the vizier Khaemwese himself who presided over the court proceedings and administered justice. Significantly none of these "early" robberies concerned the royal necropolis in the Valley of the Kings itself,[110] nor any of the Theban temples. As a result of the investigations a great amount of the stolen property was recovered from the hands of the thieves and other persons involved. In addition, the thieves were certainly punished as evidenced by the testimony of Tjawenany mentioned above. This clearly means that legal procedures had been definitely closed and there is no reason to look for a continuation of the legal proceedings in the later period.

The dating of the second phase of robberies has an essential bearing on our understanding of the events which finally led to the proclamation of the Renaissance Era, when the robbers were brought to the court and prosecuted by the tribunal appointed by the pharaoh. Again, it was the vizier Nebmarenakht (II),[111] who supervised the investigations, accompanied by a

---

[108] For Wennekhu, see Haring, Divine Households, 450. Certainly the *wab*-priest and coppersmith Wenennekhu of papBM 10068vo. 3, 29 cannot be the same person.

[109] PapLeopold-Amherst 1, 17-18; papBM 10054vo. 1, 6.

[110] Excluding the isolated case of the tomb of Ramesses VI (KV 9).

[111] Cf. Černý, BiOr 19, 1962, 143, as regards the two viziers of that name; the second one identified by the nickname Sahnefer, cf. Kitchen, RamInscr VI, 841. For the role of Nebmarenakht, see Helck, Verwaltung, 342ff.; Gnirs, Militär und Gesellschaft, 202. It is worth noting here that the hypothetical career of Nebmarenakht, the same person as his namesake from the reign of Ramesses IX, looks rather unconvincing in the light of the "short chronology", cf. Thijs, GM 184, 2001, 70f.; compare however Häggman, Directing DeM, 40f.

group of high-ranking royal officials (cf. papBM 10383, 1, 1-3). The lists of the thieves prepared by the mayor of the west of the city Paweraa had been presented directly to the king and the vizier (papAbbott-dockets, vo. A, 1-2, 19-20). Apparently the temple officials and the mayor of the city[112] were simply excluded from the investigations. The absence of the high priest of Amun in these proceedings[113] can be possibly explained by the fact that the bulk of the robberies had taken place in the Theban temples. The available sources leave no doubt that now all the Theban area, including the tombs and also the temples (including Karnak temple), had been severely ravaged.

The wholly different character of both phases of robberies is a major obstacle to accepting the "short chronology". The thieves of the second wave were more numerous and much better organized (see Chapter 2). Hardly any of the stolen goods were recovered this time – this is probably due to the span of time dividing the robberies and the trials, but also as a result of the vicissitudes of the civil war, when the authorities were losing control of circulation of goods, and their supervision of the matters of the necropolis appeared to be ineffective. Those participating in the events could have been scattered throughout the country, and some of them probably disappeared completely from the stage.

As has already been noticed, an inevitable consequence of the hypothesis formulated by A. Thijs would be an urgent need to redate all the sources dating to the years 1-16 of Ramesses XI (according to the "traditional" chronological scheme). The results of applying this idea to the interpretation of the late Ramesside sources, as presented by A. Thijs in a series of papers, are highly doubtful in fact.[114] It will suffice to recall here the case of papBM 10068vo. 2ff., dated to year 12 – undoubtedly of the reign of Ramesses XI and not of the Renaissance Era. To the arguments presented above, the following observation can be added: the scribe of the treasury Setekhmose, whose house was enumerated there (vo. 3, 1), was accused of participating in the robberies committed in the temple in Medinet Habu and interrogated in year 2 of the Renaissance Era (papBM 10383, 1, 6-7); it is hardly possible that he was still active ten years later (i.e. in a hypothetical year 12 of the Renaissance Era).

[112] The office is hardly attested in the sources dating to the reign of Ramesses XI, cf. Helck, Verwaltung, 429, 531 (21-22); Wente LRL, 9; Häggman, Directing DeM, 257f.

[113] The sole exception seems to be an investigation described in papBM 10053vo. – for this, however, see below.

[114] For a detailed discussion on the subject, see below, Chapter 4.

Last but not least, A. Thijs' supposition that two parts of the country were ruled independently by two royal lines of the dynasty (i.e., Ramesses IX-X and XI), can be undermined by the following argument. What would be the reason for the sarcastic comment expressed by the mayor of the west Paweraa about the difficulties in contacts with higher authority (namely the vizier himself) in year 16 of the reign of Ramesses IX (papAbbott 6, 20ff.), if at least some representatives of pharaoh were present at Thebes, not to speak about Pharaoh himself? Anyway, it is hardly imaginable that the actual ruler of Upper Egypt as a distinct political entity could have really established his residence outside Thebes at such an early period (as would be done by some of the high priests of Amun during the following 21st Dynasty, who at least temporarily resided in el-Hibeh). In other words, what would be the reason for sending a report to the vizier staying in the north (so probably in Lower Egypt or even in Per-Ramesse) if that part of the country was under the rule of Ramesses XI – the king belonging to a rival royal line? Last but not least, it was the vizier Khaemwese who in the same year 16 of Ramesses IX said in relation to his inspection of the necropolis: "I had been there myself as vizier of the country (*ṯ3ty n p3 t3*)" (papAbbott 7, 10).[115]

There are some additional details which may be helpful in elucidating some problems concerning the chronology of the documents of the reign of Ramesses XI. Thus one can notice that in the time of the distribution of grain text of papBM10054vo. 2, dated to "year 6" of unnamed pharaoh, the Madjoy Nesamun was apparently just a simple policeman: "the Madjoy Nesamun son of(?) the chieftain of Madjoy".[116] An enigmatic expression "the chieftain of the Madjoy (*p3 wr n n3 Mḏ3y*)" cannot be explained satisfactorily in this context, and it cannot be taken literally as a designation of a native prince of the Madjoy tribe.[117] An alternative interpretation based on reading a determinative A1 (according the Gardiner's sign list) instead of the sign *s3*,[118] is even less probable: "the Madjoy Nesamun, the chieftain of the Madjoy". It must be noticed that in a similar list connected with a distribution of bread loaves of papBM 10054vo. 4, 1-14 he was already "the chief (*ḥry*) of the Madjoy".[119]

---

[115] Peet, Tomb Robberies, pl. 4=Kitchen, RamInscr VI, 480, 15; for a comment, see Demidoff, GM 177, 2000, 94f. n. 32. Compare a similar locution in papLouvre 3169: Kitchen, op.cit., 523, 3 (vizier's name unpreserved).

[116] Peet, Tomb Robberies, pl. 7 (vo. 2, 18)=Kitchen, RamInscr VI, 744, 6.

[117] As suggested by Černý, Community, 261 n. 2. Compare Wb.II, 186 (13) and sources cited in Wb, Belegst. II, 272.

[118] Cf. Peet, loc.cit., note 18; similarly Kitchen, loc.cit. An interpretetation of the passage is obscured by the fact that group *šd* (?) was written above *p3*.

[119] Peet, Tomb Robberies, pl. 8 (vo. 4, 2) – the name only partly preserved.

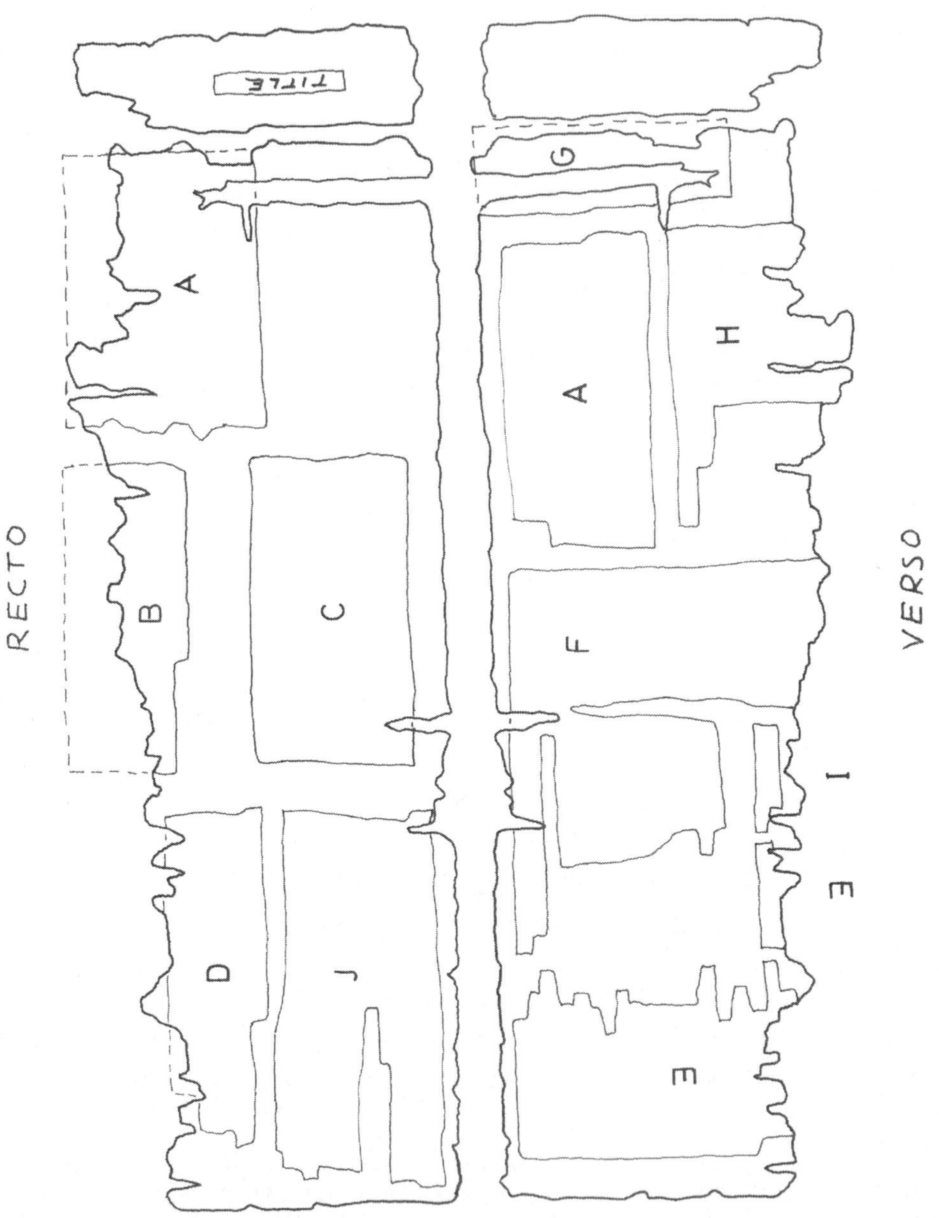

Fig. 1. Papyrus BM 10054 – diagram showing the layout of the texts.

The difference in the status attained by Nesamun seems to be reflected in the amount of grain given to him on both occasions. As an ordinary Madjoy he received ½ *khar*, just as the women enumerated in the list, and only half of the amount of grain given to the men from the top of the list (1 *khar*). In the latter case, he was grouped among upper ranks, as receiving ⅞ *khar*, making 50 loaves of bread.[120] Indeed, if he is referred to as a simple Madjoy in the previous text, then the latter text must be later in date. Although a precise dating of this list in relation to the distribution of grain text of year 6 cannot be established convincingly (this concerns also the partly preserved list of vo. 3, 1-18), both must be close in time. Not only does the committee supervising the distribution of the grain in both cases include the prince Paweraa, the scribe of the quarter Wennefer and district officer Anynakht (only the district officer Amenkhau was omitted in the second list),[121] but also some of the names in the lists are the same (besides Nesamun, these are: Ashathebsed, Seramun, and Ahay). The short note of vo. 2, 37-38 dated to the "year 10" must be slightly later than vo. 2, 1-36, and probably of the same reign, and such an idea can be supported by the name of the washerman Amenmose, son of Bak[...],[122] whose house in the complex of Medinet Habu was listed in papBM 10068 (vo. 4, 8).[123] Significantly he is also present among the members of the *semdet*-staff of the right side of the crew, in years 8-10 of Ramesses XI in papTurin 2018 (ro. A1a, 8; A4, 20; vo. A1, 4; ro. B2, 7; ro. D17).[124]

The chronology of the texts of papBM 10054 has a crucial significance for our understanding of the history of the period. Thus the establishment of the correct sequence of the texts must be attempted. The spatial relation of the texts (Fig. 1),[125] taken in accord with the preserved dates, can lead to

[120] This is much more than rations given to the simple Madjoy in the second list, who received only ½ *khar*, making 30 loaves (vo. 4, 5 and 6). The case of the chief of the stable Ashathebsed is confusing: the numbers in both lists also differ, and these are respectively 1 *khar* (vo. 2, 4), and ½ *khar*, making 30 loaves (vo. 4, 7); some doubts arise, however, in regard of the identity of the latter beneficiary. Similarly in the case of Seramun (respectively 1 *khar* and ¾ *khar*).

[121] As for Nesmut, the steward (*wr pr*) of the songstress of Amun, and the scribe of the army Kashuty, these two officials were responsible for provisioning, whereas Paweraa and others were simply intermediaries (*m-ḏr.t*) who performed the duty of distribution of the grain. On the meaning of *m-ḏr.t*, see Valbelle, BIFAO 76, 1976, 101ff.; P. Tallet, BIFAO 99, 1999, 411; J.J. Janssen, Grain Transport in the Ramesside Period. Papyrus Baldwin (BM EA 10061) and Papyrus Amiens, [HPBM 8], London, 2004, 13 n. 8.

[122] The name should be restored as Bak[(en)amun], cf. Peet, Tomb Robberies, pl. 7: vo. 2, 38 (note 29); Kitchen, RamInscr VI, 745, 8; Helck OPG, 564.

[123] Peet, Tomb Robberies, pl. 15=Kitchen, RamInscr VI, 751, 9; no parentage given.

[124] Kitchen, RamInscr VI, 852, 7; 854, 11; 854, 13; 856, 14; 863, 1; cf. Helck OPG, 562; no parentage given.

[125] Cf. Peet, Tomb Robberies, pl. 39; von Beckerath, GM 159, 1997, 5ff. For the photograph of the *recto*, see now N. Strudwick, The British Museum. Masterpieces of Ancient Egypt, London 2006, 234.

the following reconstruction of a sequence in which particular texts had been written on the papyrus (the absolute dates they mention have evidently nothing to do with their sequence on the papyrus; those based on internal evidence are given here in brackets):

Text A – Year 16 (of Ramesses IX): vo. 1, 1-9 (probably written merely by mistake on the *verso*,[126] so the scribe decided to return to the *recto* of the sheet, turning the papyrus upside down) – ro. 1, {1}-12;[127] the text comprises depositions concerning the activities of the gang of the quarryman Amenpnufer, son of Anhernakht, whose mother was Mery from Kush;[128] the appearance of Amenpnufer (and other accomplices known from this text) in papLeopold-Amherst leaves no doubt about the absolute dating of this entry.

Text B – (pre Renaissance Era?): ro. 2, {1}-6;[129] the deposition of the fisherman Panakhtemope, whose interrogations are documented also in papBM 10052, 14, 10-18 and papMayer A ro. 5, 9-12, both dated explicitly to the year 1 of the Renaissance Era.

Text C – (Year 16 of Ramesses IX): ro. 2, 7-16; a second deposition of Amenpnufer, son of Anhernakht; thus the text must be related directly to text A and has nothing in common with the text B, from which it is indeed separated by an empty space.

Text D – (pre Renaissance Era?): ro. 3, 1-6; the deposition of the coppersmith of the necropolis Pakhyhat, son of Kedakhtef, a member of the gang, for which the fisherman Panakhtemope also worked;[130] thus the text can be safely related to text B in regard to its absolute dating.

Text E – (pre Renaissance Era?): vo. 5, x+1-x+20 – vo. 6, x+1-x+3 – a list or lists of names; the docket on the right margin of the *recto* was probably written at the same time, when the papyrus was rolled up, after the list(s) were com-

[126] Cf. Peet, Tomb Robberies, 53; it has been suggested, however, that the *recto* was already occupied by another text, which was subsequently washed away when a scribe turned his attention to the *recto* to continue his work, cf. Capart et al., JEA 22, 1936, 191; Thijs, GM167, 1998, 104f.; the latter author, however, rejects the notion that the text of vo. 1, 1-9 was the earliest entry recorded. Unfortunately no traces of an earlier text on the *recto* has ever been reported until now; compare photographs published by N. Strudwick and A. Gasse.

[127] Originally 13 lines of the text (one line added to those documented once by Peet), cf. Gasse, JEA 87, 2001, 82.

[128] For the members of this gang, cf. Peet, Tomb Robberies, 47f., 57. As a matter of fact there is no certainty about the precise relation of both texts, because that of the *recto* did not preserve any name of the thief. Quite possibly, however, the text of the *recto* forms a direct continuation of that written first on the *verso*: thus A.J. Spencer, Death in Ancient Egypt, London 1982, 96f.; see also my comments above.

[129] Originally eight lines of the text (two lines must be added to those documented by Peet), cf. Gasse, JEA 87, 2001, 85 n. 11, fig. 1, pl. 11.

[130] As for the members of the gang, cf. Gasse, JEA 87, 2001, 89-91.

piled: "The examination of the thieves";[131] vo. 5-6 comprises the names of the thieves contemporary with Amenpnufer (vo. 5: 4, 11, 12, 20), mixed up with those of the accomplices of Panakhtemope and Pakhyhat (vo. 5: 6-9, 14, 15).[132]

Text F – Year 6 (of Ramesses XI): vo. 2,1-36; baking accounts.

Text G and H – (Year 6(?) of Ramesses XI or slightly later): vo. 3, 1-18 – vo. 4,1-13; continuation of baking accounts, thus possibly of the same date as text F or slightly later.

Text I – Year 10 (of Ramesses XI): vo. 2, 37-38; just a short note regarding the washerman Amenmose and his boat.

Text J – Year 18 (of Ramesses XI): ro. 3, 7-17. Possibly this is the last of the texts written on the papyrus, regardless of the date recorded within the passage. Significantly none of the names recorded in this text were included in the list of the thieves of vo. 5-6 (Text E). Thus, it is reasonable to assume that the latter had been compiled before the text J was written on the papyrus. Text J concerns robberies apparently committed in the temple of Ramesses II,[133] and the culprits were mostly temple priests. Some of them can be identified indeed with persons mentioned in the list of houses of pap.BM 10068vo. – this is certainly the case of the *sem*-priest Khaemope from the Ramesseum, and the god's father Hapywer of the temple in Medinet Habu.[134] We are informed that both of them received gold stripped from the statue of Nefertum, and the latter actively participated in the robberies.[135] As a consequence, text J cannot be earlier than the list of houses of papBM 10068vo. If the latter can be dated to year 12 of Ramesses XI then the dating of the present text to year

[131] Peet, Tomb Robberies, pl. 7 (below ro. 3)=Kitchen, RamInscr VI, 490, 1. The docket was in accord with the contents of the papyrus at this moment, even if the new text on the *verso* (5-6) does not contain any depositions of the thieves. Anyway the docket is parallel to the title of vo. 1, 1-2 (text A). On the other hand, if the title was written after text of ro. 3, 7-17 was completed, then we would rightly expect the title placed rather on the *verso*; cf. a comment by Peet, JEA 11, 1925, 164 n. 2.

[132] The rest of the names cannot be found in the extant tomb robbery papyri. On the other hand, however, some of the names mentioned in texts A-D do not appear in the list(s).

[133] Cf. Haring, Divine Households, 276 (1).

[134] Cf. papBM 10068vo. 2, 15 and 7, 21 respectively: Peet, Tomb Robberies, pls. 14, 16=Kitchen, RamInscr VI, 749, 3; 754, 6. The identity of the god's father Paysen, son of Hapywer (papBM 10054ro. 3, 8; possibly the same person as *wab*-priest Pa(y)sen, son of Hapywer of papBM 10054ro. 3, 16), with the "*wab*-priest Paysen of the temple of Usermaatre-Setepenre" (papBM 10068vo. 3, 19) is rather doubtful. Similarly, the identity of the scribe of the royal records Setekhmose (papBM10054ro. 3, 15), with the scribe of the treasury (of the Ramesseum?) of the same name (papBM 10068vo. 3, 1), must be excluded beyond any doubt, because the latter was titled in the same way much later – in papBM 10383, 1, 6, which is dated to year 2 of the Renaissance Era, although obviously relates to the earlier events.

[135] Cf. papBM 10054ro. 3, 8-9, 15: Peet, Tomb Robberies, 62, pls. 6-7.

18 of the same ruler seems to be well justified.[136] As a consequence of such a reasoning, we should inevitably reach the conclusion that the absolute date of the texts B, D, and E must be earlier than text J (apparently the last written on the papyrus). They were approximately of the same period, and thus predating the trials of the Renaissance Era. It is completely unknown what would be the bearing of such an assumption on the meaning of the words regarding one of the thieves, namely the *wab*-priest Panekhtresi son of Iyemnofre: "he is (in) the northern province (*ꜥ-mḥ.ty*)" (papBM 10054vo. 5, 17).[137] Certainly the statement simply explains why he has not been brought to the court, but the actual reason of his stay in the north remains obscure. The toponym in question is known also from papMayer A vo. 13, B2, in relation to the fifteen thieves, who were killed there.[138] Quite possibly both references should be taken together as a testimony of the internal policy of Panehesy during his stay in Upper Egypt, and the mechanism of recruitement of the soldiers into his army.

In his edition of the papyrus, T.E. Peet arranged the sequence of columns of vo. 2-4 (Texts F-H), with a consequence that he dated all of them to year 6 (of Ramesses XI or Renaissance Era).[139] Some observations regarding such an arrangement of the texts can be made: 1) The text of vo. 3 does not reach the bottom margin of the papyrus and thus vo.4 cannot be taken as its direct continuation. 2) A number of women were enumerated in the list of vo. 3 just like in vo. 2, and three of the preserved names are probably identical in both lists (cf. vo. 2, 13, 25; and vo. 3, 3, 8); so it cannot be excluded that vo. 3 is not a simple continuation of vo. 2, 1-36, but rather a separate list, although a lacuna at the beginning of vo. 3 does not enable us to draw the conclusion that it was preceded by any heading.[140] 3) On the other side, vo. 4 has a specific heading if *p3 wp* "specification" can be taken as such.[141] The list of vo. 4 seems to be of a different character than that of

[136] And the dating to the reign of Ramesses IX must be definitely discounted, cf. e.g. Gutgesell, Datierung, 145 (f); Kitchen, RamInscr VI, 495, 13; Haring, loc.cit.; Helck OPG, 532.

[137] Peet, Tomb Robberies, pl. 8=Kitchen, RamInscr VI, 495, 7.

[138] See below, Chapter 2.

[139] Cf. Peet, Tomb Robberies, 59; similarly Helck, Materialien IV, (609) (*wḥm-msw.t*), and id., OPG, 557, 561 (Ramesses XI); Haring, Divine Households, 231 n. 4, 279 (here preference is given to a dating within the Renaissance Era); Kitchen, RamInscr VI, 743 (Ramesses XI or *wḥm-msw.t*); von Beckerath, GM 159, 1997, 5f., 7 (year 6 and 10 of the Renaissance Era); see however Valbelle, Ouvriers, 60, 89 n. 8 (Ramesses XI). Peet did not comment explicitly the position of vo. 2, 37-38 (Text I) in relation to other texts of this group, except the mere fact that its numbering places it directly after Text F. It is possible in fact that Text I was inserted here after the texts G-H were written.

[140] Cf. Peet, Tomb Robberies, pl. 8: vo. 3, 1=Kitchen, RamInscr VI, 745, 9.

[141] Peet, Tomb Robberies, 65, 71 n. 40, pl. 8 (vo. 4, 1); cf. Wb. I, 303; Wente LRL 51 (j); Lesko, Dict. I, 97; van Heel-Haring, Writing in a Workmen's Village, 116f.

vo. 2, because it enumerates a distribution of the bread loaves, not a grain as in the case of vo. 2 (and possibly also vo. 3). Thus there are no serious objections against the arrangements of Texts F-H and their relative sequence as adopted by T.E. Peet. However, the short note of vo. 2, 37-38, dated to the year 10, cannot be related explicitly to any of the three lists (Texts F-H). Text H (and possibly also G) must be dated around year 6 or maybe later, because some of the officials enumerated in it appear also in Text F and in the list of houses of papBM 10068vo. 3, 5-9, arranged exactly in the same sequence as here (papBM 10054 vo. 2, 1-2; compare also vo. 4, 1).[142] The sequence apparently reflects the order in which the houses of these persons, belonging to the local elite, were arranged within the complex of Medinet Habu.[143] The name of Nesamun the chief of the Madjoy appears in both documents (papBM 10068vo. 7, 7; and papBM 10054vo. 4, 2), thus providing a solid argument for dating the lists of papBM 10054 to the early decade of the reign of Ramesses XI.[144]

At the same time the dating of the lists of papBM 10054vo. 2-4 (Texts F-H) to the Renaissance Era must be definitely excluded, as there are no members of the crew in these lists, whereas we know that the crew was already living in Medinet Habu by that period.[145] The heading of the first enumeration (Text F) informs that the inhabitants of the complex of Medinet Habu were taken into consideration beside others living on the west bank:[146] "The name-list of the people of the land (*rmṯ n pꜣ tꜣ*)[147] to whom wheat was [giv]en for making into bread, by the steward of the singer of Amun Nesmut (and) the scribe of the army Kashuty, being all the people from every house which is within enclosure of the temple of Usermaatre-Meriamun, by the hand (*m-ḏr.t*) of the mayor Paweraa, scribe of the quarter Wennefer, the district officer (*ꜣṯw*) Anynakht and the district officer Amenkhau, from the temple of Seti (I) to the temple of Usermaatre-[Meriamun]" (papBM 10054vo. 2, 1-3).[148]

---

[142] Cf. Peet, Tomb Robberies, 59.

[143] Cf. Janssen, AoF 19, 1992, 15f.

[144] The chief of Madjoy Nesamun was noted also in the Turin Taxation Papyrus (ro. 5, 3), in its part dated to year 12, cf. Gardiner RAD, 41, 13; cf. id., JEA 27, 1941, 33.

[145] For the contrary view cf. Thiers, BIFAO 95, 1995, 494 (a).

[146] Cf. Häggman, Directing DeM, 284 n. 1902.

[147] For the meaning of this phrase, see Peet, Tomb Robberies, 70 n. 34; cf. also J.J. Janssen, in: E. Teeter, J.A. Larson (eds.), Gold of Praise. Studies on Ancient Egypt in Honor of Edward F. Wente, [SAOC 58], Chicago 1999, 189.

[148] Peet, Tomb Robberies, 64, pl. 7=Kitchen, RamInscr VI, 743, 3-8; cf. also Helck OPG, 561; id., Materialien IV, (609); J.F. Borghouts, SAK 8, 1980, 76 n. 52; Thiers, BIFAO 95, 1995, 493f.; Haring, Divine Households, 279.

Thus the dating of the lists to the reign of Ramesses XI, and more precisely to the period still before the move of the crew to Medinet Habu, seems highly probable. All these four documents seem to be *ad hoc* written notes,[149] made on the *verso* of the papyrus with the texts connected with the trials of the thieves from the reign of Ramesses IX and the slightly later investigations dating to the reign of Ramesses XI. It does not seem however that the lists are complete, for the number of names included is not even comparable to that of the houses enumerated in papBM 10068vo. 2-8. The completely irregular arrangement of these texts was caused of course by the very presence of the slightly earlier text on the *verso* of the papyrus (Text A: vo. 1, 1-9). It could be possibly argued that Text E (vo. 5, x+1-x+20 – vo. 6, x+1-x+3) does not necessarily predate Texts F-I, because one can imagine indeed that Text F was written by someone who found an older papyrus, and unrolled it (from right to left?) while looking through its contents and searching for an empty space. In consequence Text F would have been written in the wide empty space directly to the left of an existing beginning of Text A on the *verso*. In such a case the remaining three texts (G-I) were written successively while rolling up of the papyrus, thus leaving blank space only on the left margin of the papyrus, which was filled later. In such a case, however, we should rather expect that the following lists (G-H) would have been written directly to the left of Text F (if there was a blank space), as this was a natural sequence of writing. Certainly the unusual character of the arrangement of the texts prevents us from finding a satisfactory solution. The matter is even more complicated if we take into consideration the position of Text I, which is four years later than Text F. Meanwhile, it can be assumed that Text E already existed here at the moment when an attempt to write Texts F-I had been made, thus restricting the blank space available for the scribe who wrote on the *verso* of the papyrus.[150] This may explain in fact the rather strange arrangement of Text F, which has been inserted between Texts A and E, and the relative position of Texts G-H, which were written in the remaining empty space on the *verso*.

It has been observed that the list of the thieves (Text E), must have had some practical purpose at the time when it was compiled.[151] All the entries

[149] Certainly there was no reasonable purpose, other than purely practical, to write down the texts of this kind, being a simple lists of provision.

[150] A consequence of the contrary assumption would be far reaching indeed. It would simply mean that there is no direct connection (in regard of the relative sequence of their copying) between Text E (the list of thieves) and the compilation of Texts A-D, which seems hardly probable, although not impossible.

[151] Peet, Tomb Robberies, 54, 58; Thijs, GM 167, 1998, 103f.; cf. also Capart et al., JEA 22, 1936, 191.

were preceded by a black dot, and the word "brought" was written against some of the names, which can be interpreted as an annotation indicating those who were brought into the court or simply imprisoned. One may wonder why the scribe who wrote this text did not use the empty space directly below the last column of *recto* (i.e. ro. 3, 1-6), if it was filled later, as proposed above. Unfortunately there is no convincing explanation for this, unless we admit that Text J was written here much earlier than suggested above (which seems hardly probable). On the other hand, there can be offered an easy explanation for the atypical orientation of Text E, being turned upside down in relation to other texts of the *verso*. After writing the last lines of Text D on the *recto*, the scribe decided perhaps to compile an additional list of the thieves, including those whose depositions form the contents of texts A-D. For this purpose he simply folded the papyrus on the left side in a way that he had easy access to the contents of the texts written on the *recto*, while writing Text E on the *verso* without the necessity of rotating the entire sheet (116 cm in length).[152] The only exception would be the beginning of text A, written on *verso*, being now upside down – and here possibly only three or four names have been copied (three of the omitted names are not preserved in the list).

The sequence of the names included in the list is highly instructive, as it gives a mixture of the robbers' names connected with two different gangs – that of papLeopold-Amherst (of year 16 of Ramesses IX) on the one hand, and the gang whose activity was described also in papBM 10052 from the very beginning of the Renaissance Era.[153] In addition, not all of the names contained in list E appear in texts A-D, so it is possible that the latter were not the sole source for the compilation of the list. Quite probably there were also other documents used by a scribe for the present compilation. On the other hand, some of the names contained in the texts of the depositions (texts A-D) were not included in the list E either.

Two explanations are possible in regard to this: 1) The names in question could have been written in the missing parts of the *recto*, which seems hardly probable, because as revealed by recent studies of the document, only a few lines are missing there;[154] 2) Or, more probably, it was simply a result of a

[152] For dimensions of the papyrus (116x41cm), cf. Strudwick, loc.cit. Rotation was necessary, however, to read the text of vo. 1, 1-9 (text A).

[153] For a convenient juxtaposition of data, cf. Thijs, GM 167, 1998, 102.

[154] Doubt may be expressed in fact about the hypothesis formulated by Thijs (ibid., 101 n. 29) that these names were written in the missing parts of columns vo. 5-6. See now Gasse, JEA 87, 2001, 89: four lines can be added at the top of vo. 5, and six lines at the top of vo. 6, but there are no traces of the missing names.

mistake on the part of the scribe who had compiled the list. As a consequence doubt should be cast on the notion of an official character of the list in its present form. It may be interpreted rather as an artificial compilation, comparable to the unusual collection of unconnected and fragmentary texts A-D. If so, the list need not be contemporary with the trials of the reign of Ramesses IX, as supposed by A. Thijs.[155] Moreover, the date of this compilation may be significantly earlier than suggested hitherto – its compilation probably took place around year 6 of Ramesses XI (i.e. the date of Text F).[156]

The role played by Nesamun the chief of the Madjoy in the robberies committed in the region of Imyotru[157] has an essential meaning for an absolute dating of texts F and H of papBM 10054vo., where his name appears. During the examinations of the thieves in year 1 of the Renaissance Era, one of the suspects (i.e. the slave Sekhahatyamun) gave the following testimony: "I was on the west of Imyotru together with Nesamun who was the chief of the Madjoy (*wn m ḥry Mḏ3y*),[158] and I was on the west of of the City (Ne) with him also" (papBM 10052, 8, 14-15).[159] This testimony taken together with the information provided by papMayer A in regard to his supposed participation in the violation of the portable shrines,[160] leave no doubt that severe accusations made against him definitely exclude a dating of any of the documents mentioning Nesamun to the period later than the trials of the beginning of the Renaissance Era. Let us note that in papBM 10052 Nesamun does not appear as the chief of the Madjoy, but as a man who was a chief of the Madjoy.[161] If he started his office before year 12 of Ramesses XI, when he was certainly a chief of the Madjoy, as exemplified by the entries in papBM 10068vo. 7, 7 and

[155] Thijs, GM 167, 1998, 107f.: as a matter of fact all of his conclusions (enumerated there as nos. 1-5) may be disproven in the light of the analysis presented here. The dots and marks "brought" reveal only an interest on the part of a scribe in the details contained in the texts partly copied by him, and probably in other texts unrelated otherwise to the present compilation.

[156] See below.

[157] Near Gebelein, cf. K. Sethe, ZÄS 47, 1910, 45, 47 (6); Gardiner AEO II, 21* (no. 331); Otto, Topographie, 94, 100; Montet, Géographie II, 52. As for the Madjoy Nesamun, see also above.

[158] For the preterite participle *wn* in relative constructions, cf. Junge, Neuägyptisch, 171; Černý-Groll, Late Egyptian Grammar, 465; Frandsen, Verbal System, § 97A.

[159] Peet, Tomb Robberies, pl. 30 (8, 14-15)=Kitchen, RamInscr VI, 786, 14-16.

[160] This is the deposition of a certain Wennekhu, son of Tatay, of papMayer A ro. 2, 17-21: Peet, Mayer Papyri, pl. 2=Kitchen, RamInscr VI, 807, 14-808, 7; see above for the translation. In the same document Nesamun was mentioned twice as a witness for the prosecution (papMayer A ro. 1, 3, and ro. 1, 13). This does not necessarily mean, however, that he was truly innocent.

[161] A good parallel can be found in the Turin Judicial Papyrus, where one of the criminals was mentioned as: *ḫrw ꜥ3 P3y-bs wn m wdpw* "great criminal Paybes who was a butler" (papTurin 1875, 6, 2=Kitchen, RamInscr V, 360, 3).

Turin Taxation Papyrus (ro. 4, 9), then his participation in the affairs described in papBM 10052 must be placed also in the time of his tenure, i.e. between years 12 of Ramesses XI and the very beginning of the Renaissance Era.[162] It is impossible of course that he was still the chief of Madjoy just five years after the trials, if Text F really could be dated to the Renaissance Era.

Similarly, the *sem*-priest Khaemope of the temple of Ramesses II, mentioned in Text J of papBM 10054ro. 3, 7-17, provides a convenient starting point for a discussion on the dating of this document. Certainly the text cannot be dated to the reign of Ramesses IX,[163] and at the same time it must be the latest of the texts written on papBM 10054 (as a matter of fact at least 24 years later than text A, written as the first). The text dated to year 18 concerns the ransacking of the statue of Nefertum, founded by Ramesses II in one of the Theban temples (quite possibly the Rameseum).[164] The gold foil stolen by the thieves was received by some priests, one of them was the *sem*-priest Khaemope, to whom 1 *deben* of gold was given.[165] His position of the *sem*-priest of the Ramesseum is firmly attested already in the list of houses of papBM 10068 (vo. 2, 15): "The house of the temple of Usermaatre-Setepenre in the domain of Amun, under the authority (*r-ḫt*) of the *sem*-priest Khaemope".[166] This means that he occupied the distinguished position of the chief administrator of the temple property and the head of its personnel.[167] He was also mentioned in an unpublished papPhiladelphia (Pennsylvania University Museum), being the missing lower part of papBM 10383,[168] concerning the robberies committed in the temple of Ramesses III.[169]

The role he played in the complicated story of the copper statue from the Ramesseum is dubious in fact, and there are no compelling reason to admit his guilt. Anyway, it was a certain Paseny,[170] who was accused of damaging the

[162] Cf. Černý, Community, 267f. (no. 15); Gutgesell, Datierung, 268.

[163] See Peet, Tomb Robberies, 58; Kitchen, RamInscr VI, 495; Helck OPG, 532. In fact we hear nothing about ransacking the Theban temples at such an early date.

[164] See the comment by Haring, Divine Households, 276 (1).

[165] PapBM 10054ro. 3, 15: Peet, Tomb Robberies, pl. 7=Kitchen, RamInscr VI, 496, 13.

[166] Peet, Tomb Robberies, pl. 14=Kitchen, RamInscr VI, 749.

[167] Haring, Divine Households, 215, 447; cf. also Helck, Materialien I, (105).

[168] Transcription in Černý Notebook 157.5 (by courtesy of the Griffith Institute, Oxford). Fragment following papBM 10383ro. 2, 5, according to Haring, Divine Households, 231 n. 7.

[169] Cf. ibid., 277 (4).

[170] Here without any title. It is doubtful indeed, whether he was the same person as the *wab*-priest and guard mentioned in papBM 10383ro. 2, 4; or else one of the *wab*-priests from Ramesseum, whose houses are listed on papBM 10068vo. 2, 17; 3, 3; 3,19; not to mention two *wab*-priests from Medinet Habu (papBM 10068vo. 3, 26; 5, 26).

statue. According to the testimony given by the god's father Amenkhau the statue had been brought to the temple in Medinet Habu, and subsequently it was handed over to Panehesy, possibly at the instigation of the *sem*-priest Khaemope, while Paseny was simply an intermediary. It seems that it was Panehesy who in turn did damage to the statue or else appropriated it (*ỉw.f (ḥr) ỉr.t h3w.f*).[171] Though papBM 10383 is dated to the year 2 of the Renaissance Era,[172] the events recalled in the depositions had certainly occured earlier, and there is no obstacle to dating some of them to the period of the viceroy Panehesy's stay in Thebes.[173]

The scribe of the royal records (*sš mḏ3.t-nsw*) Setekhmose[174] appears side by side with Khaemope and others, as a person who received 6 *kite* of gold stripped from the statue of Nefertum from the Ramesseum (papBM 10054ro. 3, 15). This time, however, his participation in the robberies was documented much better thanks to the parallel testimonies written down on papBM 10053vo. The "*wab*-priest and gardener (*k3my*) Kari of the temple",[175] who described in detail repeated robberies apparently committed in the temple of Ramesses II,[176] also gave the following testimony: "The scribe of the royal records Setekhmose heard his speech and he quarrelled with us saying: «I am going to report to the high priest of Amun». (So) we brought 3 *kite* of gold and we gave it to the scribe of the royal records Setekhmose. Again we went once more and gave him 1½ *kite* of gold. The total sum of gold given to the scribe of the royal records Setekhmose: 4½ *kite* of gold"(papBM 10053vo. 3, 13-15).[177] Later on in the same papyrus we are informed about "a charge concerning [the shri]ne of cedar, the *šśm*,[178] and the wood which the scribe of the royal records Setekhmose has stolen. He sold it (*ỉw.f (ḥr) dỉ.t.f r-bnr*) in Ne and received its price" (papBM 10053vo. 5, 5-6).[179]

---

171 For a different interpretation of the events, see Haring, Divine Households, 220, 231f., 277.

172 Cf. e.g. Peet, Tomb Robberies, 123; Thijs, SAK 38, 2009, 352.

173 It must be noted, however, that Panehesy's name was determined here in a regular way (i.e. without a determinative naming him an enemy).

174 See above.

175 PapBM 10053vo. 3, 6: Peet, Tomb Robberies, pl. 20=Kitchen, RamInscr VI, 759, 2. It is hardly likely that this is the same man as the "*wab*-priest Kar, son of Khaemope" from the staff of the temple of Ramesses II (papBM 10068vo. 2, 23), see however Peet, op.cit., 116. The attribute "of the temple" would rather suggest the temple of Ramesses III, cf. Haring, Divine Households, 244f., 454; Helck, Materialien I, (111). So it cannot be excluded, that a member of the temple staff in Medinet Habu was living in the vicinity of the Ramesseum, and vice versa (compare the case of the *wab*-priest Paysen of papBM 10068vo. 3, 19).

176 Cf. Valbelle, Ouvriers, 74, 219; Haring, Divine Households, 276 (2).

177 Peet, Tomb Robberies, pl. 20=Kitchen, RamInscr VI, 760, 5-9.

178 *Hapax legomenon*, meaning unknown, cf. Lesko, Dict. II, 137.

179 Peet, Tomb Robberies, pl. 21=Kitchen, RamInscr VI, 763, 14-16; see also a comment by Peet, in:

Much has been said about the dating of a document written on the *verso* of papBM 10053. A date written on the top of page 2 ("year 9, II *akhet*, day 23[+x]") can be related to the reign of Ramesses XI.[180] The date has been connected with the period of viceroy Panehesy's stay at Thebes, because the latter's name, it would seem, has been preserved at the beginning of the document, although in a badly damaged context (vo. 1, 2).[181] Here too again the person of Sedi, the temple scribe from the temple of Ramesses II, mentioned several times in the text, seems to provide a solid basis for a relative dating of this important document. His serious involvement in the robberies cannot be denied in the light of the present text, being in fact a grave indictment levelled against this temple official: "It was found that the scribe of the temple Sedi and the *wab*-priests of the temple had committed damage. He made a record about all the thefts he had committed in every inspection of his".[182] He appears here alongside the scribe of the royal records Setekhmose and other priests of the Medinet Habu temple involved in the robberies. Some of the thieves are known from the list of houses of papBM 10068vo. – this is the case of the *wab*-priest Amenkhau son of Bakptah (in the list of houses, vo. 5, 28: the god's father Amenkhau, son of Bakenptah),[183] and first of all a group of the *wab*-priests of the temple of Ramesses II, i.e. three sons of Paykharu (Paysen, Hori and Nesamun, in the list of houses, vo. 2, 17-19), but possibly also Kar son of Khaemope (in the list of houses, vo. 2, 23).[184] It is hardly imaginable that any of the persons accused could have survived the trial in question,[185] so it must rather be assumed that the list of houses must be earlier than depositions documented in papBM 10053vo. In such a case, however, year 9 of Ramesses XI must be necessarily dismissed, unless we date the list of houses to the year 12 of Ramesses IX, which seems to be impossible. Quite obviously there are only two possibilities as regards the

Studies presented to F.Ll. Grifftith, London 1932, 124.

[180] PapBM 10053vo. 2, 1: Peet, Tomb Robberies, pl. 20=Kitchen, RamInscr VI, 756, 5; as regards dating to the reign of Ramesses XI, cf. ibid., 755 (no. 23); Valbelle, Ouvriers, 219; Helck OPG, 557, 564.

[181] Cf. e.g. Peden, Historical Inscriptions, 265; Niwiński, Bürgerkrieg, 245; see also below, Chapter 2.

[182] PapBM 10053vo. 1, 8-10: Peet, Tomb Robberies, pl. 19; for a grammatical comment cf. also Černý-Groll, Late Egyptian Grammar, 571 (Ex. 1633). For the temple scribe Sedi, see Peet, Tomb Robberies, 115; Helck, Materialien I, (107); Haring, Divine Households, 231, 447.

[183] Certainly the identity of both persons is not so obvious, but the father's name cannot be disregarded. If so, this may be possibly the same person as the god's father Amenkhau (no parentage) from papTurin 2021+Geneva D 409 (see above, note 91); and more clearly the god's father Amenkhau (without parentage too) of papAmbras 1, 5.

[184] As regards the latter, see above, note 175.

[185] As suggested by Niwiński, Bürgerkrieg, 246.

dating of papBM 10053vo. – either its “year 9” relates to the Renaissance Era or else the date should be emended to “year <1>9”, and thus related to the reign of Ramesses XI.[186] In such a case an omission of the numeral 10 could be explained as a mere mistake made by a scribe.[187]

The latter solution has an important advantage over the former one as it would explain satisfactorily the case of the scribe of the royal records Setekhmose (see above). We are informed that he participated in the robberies in the Theban temples, investigated (less possibly committed)[188] in “year 9” (papBM 10053vo.), but he appears also in a testimony given in the controversial “year 18” (papBM 10054ro. 3, 15), as a man who had received gold stripped from the statue of Nefertum (possibly as a bribe or simply as his share in the loot?). No matter how we arrange these texts in regard of their relative chronology, in any case a span of ca. 9-10 years would separate these investigations, if we take “year 9” literally. It is possible of course that such a procedure as the looting the temples could have continued for years, or else that the criminals were judged a long time after their deeds had been committed, especially in the period of turmoil. It cannot be denied, however, that both dates relate to the investigations if not the very trials of the thieves, and then a 10-years duration of such proceedings cannot be explained satisfactorily, unless we take as granted that the prolonged investigation was caused by the civil war (see below). On the other hand, as a result of proposed redating of papBM 10053vo. to year 19 of Ramesses XI, the two documents are separated by scarcely a year. It has been already demonstrated that “year 9” of papBM 10053vo. cannot be related satisfactorily to the Renaissance Era, as proposed by A. Thijs.[189] First of all, there is no available information regarding robberies or legal proceedings at such a late date; certainly papAmbras dated to year 6 of the Renaissance Era cannot be taken as evidence to contradict

[186] Therefore one day earlier than list 2 of papAbbott-dockets (II *akhet* 24), or else one or two days later if the numeral in papBM 10053vo. 2, 1 is emended. In such a case, however, the omission of any reference to the Renaissance Era must raise some doubts.

[187] Similarly in papTurin 2034, cf. Kitchen, RamInscr VI, 865, 4; here the date is correlated with year 1 of the Renaissance Era (thus the entry dated to IV *akhet* 5 would be over one month later than that of papBM 10053vo. 2, 1).

[188] Such a possibility cannot be denied automatically. One can imagine that after an introduction (papBM 10053vo. 1) and a blank space below (half a page), the second column of the text started with the depositions of the thieves. Nevertheless, the date placed at the beginning of this column cannot be taken as a part of such a speech – quite obviously it has an official character and must be taken as the date of interrogation.

[189] For example Thijs' dating of papyri BM 10053vo. and BM 10068vo. 2-8 respectively to years 9 and 12 of the Renaissance Era does not remove the problem with the sons of Paykharu commented upon earlier; for references see above n. 40.

this.[190] More important, however, are inevitable contradictions caused by such a redating of the entire group of documents of years 1-16 of Ramesses XI to the Renaissance Era.

The role of the scribe of the army Kashuty in the affair described in papBM 10053 (vo. 4, 10) cannot be evaluated properly, so it does not affect directly the question of the dating of this document. There are no grounds, however, to suppose his direct involvement in the robberies, and in fact we learn from the sources that he was still on duty at the beginning of the Renaissance Era. Significantly enough, he was interrogated in year 2 of the Renaissance Era in relation to the affair of the silver vase-stand from the temple in Medinet Habu: "There was brought the scribe of the army Kashuty of the temple, and the matter of this vase-stand[191] of 86 *deben* of silver, which had been stolen, and which the god's father Payseni of the temple reported to Pharaoh, was examined. He said: «I did not see what happened to it; so what if I (ever) heard of it?»" (papBM 10383, 1, 4-5).[192] The contents of the text do not enable us to decide whether he was really involved, but quite possibly, the accusation was serious enough to cause his disappearance from the scene after this date.[193]

In the text on the distribution of grain of papBM 10054vo. 2, 1-36, dated to "year 6", the temple scribe Sedi was still responsible for provision of the staff of the temple of Ramesses II.[194] Evidently this document must be earlier in time than the trial documented in papBM 10053vo., when Sedi had been accused of participation in the robberies. Another person which appears in both texts is "the craftsman Ahauty of the temple (*ḥw.t* or *ḥw.t-kꜣ*) of Huy",[195] who provides an additional argument in regard of the relative dating of both documents.

---

[190] Let us note that papAmbras relates to "Making a list inventory (*šnw*) of the records of examinations (*nꜣ sš n nꜣ ḥy*) which were in the jars, which the chief taxing master (*ꜥꜣ n št*) brought, (as) bought from the people of the country" (papAmbras 1, 1-2). I reject here Peet's reading *ḥsyw* "the men of old" or simply "blessed ones", adopted also by Lesko, Dict. I, 330 (here erroneously: papBM 10403); Peden, Historical Inscriptions, 278f. For *šnw* "list", "inventory" or else "inspection", "survey", see Lesko, Dict. II, 127; Gardiner, JEA 45, 1959, 14-15 (with a translation of the passage in question).

[191] Or: vase for unguents, cf. J. Winand, in: C. Gallois et al. (eds.), Mélanges offerts à François Neveu, [BdE 145], Cairo 2008, 301 (Ex. 50).

[192] Peet, Tomb Robberies, pl. 22=Kitchen, RamInscr VI, 833, 16-834, 3; cf. Černý-Groll, Late Egyptian Grammar, 242 (Ex. 645); Frandsen, Verbal System, 10 (Ex. 5); Sweeney, Correspondence and Dialogue, 139 (Ex. 65).

[193] Cf. Peet, JEA 14, 1928, 70; id., Tomb Robberies, 59. The data provided by the unpublished papPhiladelphia (Pennsylvania University Museum) are not helpful in regard of this.

[194] According to Haring, he was supposedly an administrator of the temple at that time, cf. Divine Households, 231.

[195] Cf. papBM 10054vo. 2, 6 and papBM 10053vo. 4, 16.

In consequence of the arguments presented above the absolute dating of papBM 10054vo. 2, 1-36 to year 6 of the Renaissance Era[196] must be definitely rejected, thus weakening significantly the idea of the "short chronology" proposed by A. Thijs. A more precise review of the documents dating to the early years of the reign of Ramesses XI will be necessary to corroborate the results achieved in the reasoning presented here, and this will be the subject of the Excursus in Chapter 4.

The history of the compilation of the texts written on papBM 10054 may now therefore be reconstructed in the following way:

1) The earliest group of the texts copied on the papyrus deals with the matters of the tomb robberies during the reign of Ramesses IX (Texts A and C), but these hardly were the texts of the actual depositions of those times, as we are clearly dealing with scrappy fragments of them, undoubtedly copied in later times.

2) Obviously the baking accounts of vo. 2-4 (Texts F-H) cannot be copies of earlier texts, for these were documents connected with the everyday life of the community of the west bank of Thebes, and as such were not susceptible to be copied for any other purpose than the record keeping. This means that Text F was written exactly in year 6 (of Ramesses XI), III *akhet* 10.

3) Text A (vo. 1, 1-9) must have been written before the texts F-H, because their irregular arrangement can be explained only by the earlier existence of vo. 1, 1-9 (anyway it is unimaginable that F-H were written first, thus leaving an empty space in the middle).[197] Texts A-D on the *recto* form a natural continuation of vo. 1, 1-9, and there is no way to separate Texts A and C (relating to the reign of Ramesses IX) and Texts B and D (relating to later events, probably of the reign of Ramesses XI). This dates the events described in Texts B and D before year 6 (of Ramesses XI). One should assume that Texts A-D were copied earlier or at least approximately at the time, when the lists F-H were drawn up. It is possible that a scribe who wrote the latter was an author of the compilation of the robbery texts.

4) It may be only surmised that the list E is contemporary with Texts A-D, on which it clearly depends. On the other hand, it must predate the latest of the texts copied on the papyrus (Text J), dated to year 18 (of Ramesses XI), and relating to the ransacking of the temple of Ramesses II. The dating of the

[196] See Helck, Materialien I, (107); compare however, id. OPG, 557, 561; von Beckerath, GM 159, 1997, 7; id., ZÄS 127, 2000, 114; Thijs, GM 179, 2000, 79 (based however on his redating of the sources).

[197] A hypothesis can be put forward that these are remnants of the texts (partly erased?), which were already written on the papyrus when it was appropriated by someone who used it to write a compilation relating to the robberies. It cannot be substantiated anyway, without more detailed research.

latter provides an indication as regards a dating of the entire compilation– it cannot be related to the reign of Ramesses IX, and accordingly it must predate the Renaissance Era.

The thoroughly heterogeneous character of the texts written down on papBM 10054 can be explained only as a result of an artificial compilation of texts found by someone who was connected in some way with administration of the Theban necropolis, and being a person interested enough in the legal proceedings to copy some fragments of them. In fact, these are probably just excerpts from the original documents (or their drafts) related to the investigations conducted in three different periods. The earliest of them had taken place at the end of the reign of Ramesses IX; the next in the early years of Ramesses XI, probably during the civil war; and the others on the eve of the Renaissance Era. The depositions of Panakhtemope and his accomplice belong to the second group of investigations, thus providing precious information relating to the dark period of the civil war. If the case of Panakhtemope had its finale 13-14 years later, when he was brought to the tribunal once again, it can be explained only by the vicissitudes of the civil war. The text of year 18 of Ramesses XI (papBM 10054ro. 3, 7-17) can be related now to the latest stage of the civil war (or rather its aftermath), slightly preceding the inauguration of the Renaissance Era. Similarly, the story of the robberies committed in the Theban temples, described in papBM 10053vo., can be related approximately to the same stage of the robberies, if the proposed redating to year 19 of Ramesses XI is accepted.[198] Significantly one of the culprits, the scribe of the royal records Setekhmose, appears in both documents, thus providing a firm link in regard to their respective dating.

The title of the compilation clearly indicates such an ambiguous character of the scroll – there are no additional details relating to neither the date nor place of the robberies (as in other legal documents), and in fact it would be extremely difficult to summarize aptly its contents. An interesting parallel can be provided to some extent by papAmbras, the dating of which also has nothing to do with its contents. As it is highly improbable that any legal proceedings has taken place at such a late date (i.e., in year 6 of the Renaissance Era), it would seem that the finding of the two jars with old scrolls, related in papAmbras, was accidental. In consequence the sole reason for drawing up the contents of the documents found in the jars was the interest, or just the

[198] A conclusion which make us aware of the relatively short span of time between an expulsion of Panehesy and the beginning of the Renaissance Era (see below, Chapter 2).

meticulousness, of the person who was entrusted with the papyri. It was not the official character of the archive, which had evidently been abandoned by those responsible for it.

One of the most important factors relating to the proper understanding of the unusual compilation of texts preserved on papBM 10054 is the complete lack of any references to the thefts committed by the gangs of Bukhaaf and Efnamun, duly investigated at the beginning of the Renaissance Era. At the same time, it documents the deeds of the group of the robbers which was active still during the reign of Ramesses XI – namely the gang to which belonged the fisherman Panakhtemope.[199] The reappearance of Panakhtemope in the dossier dating to the beginning of the Renaissance Era necessarily means that the charges were brought against him and his accomplices while Panehesy was still present himself in the Thebaid, but he was finally judged in year 1 of the Renaissance Era. This seems to be the sole case of such an extraordinary prolongation of the judicial procedure, possibly due to the turbulent events following the suppression of the High Priest Amenhotep. All of the companions of Panakhtemope were simple craftsmen, and they certainly had no support on the part of the personnel of the Theban temples nor the officers of the military garrison of Thebes, as was the case of the gangs of Bukhaaf and Efnamun. It is not surprising that Panakhtemope and his accomplices fell the prey of prosecutors still during the occupation of Thebes by Panehesy. Others (i.e. the members of the gangs of Bukhaaf and Efnamun), were more fortunate, or else simply covered up by some influential representatives of the local administration or temple hierarchy, and were not accused of robberies until appearance of the new regime after the civil war.

Contrary to the members of the gangs of Bukhaaf and Efnamun, whose depositions were at least partly preserved, those relating to deeds committed by the colleagues of Panakhtemope are practically non existent. The sole source of our knowledge on their business remains the rather strange compilation of heterogeneous documents written down in papBM 10054, comprising depositions of Panakhtemope and his accomplice Pakhyhat son of Kedakhtef,[200] and short passages in papBM 10052, 14, 10-18,[201] and papMayer A 5, 9-12.[202]

[199] Concerning the members of the gang, cf. Gasse, JEA 87, 2001, 89-91.

[200] PapBM 10054ro. 2, {1}-6 and ro. 3, 1-6 respectively. An unpreserved document mentioned in papAmbras 2, 8, may be possibly connected with this gang as well, if the coppersmith Uaresi is the same person as the coppersmith Pauaresi. As a matter of fact, the name of the latter was cited also as Uaresi, cf. papBM 10052, 14, 15.

[201] Peet, Tomb Robberies, pl. 34=Kitchen, RamInscr VI, 798, 7ff.

[202] Peet, Mayer Papyri, 13, pl. 5=Kitchen, RamInscr VI, 813, 14ff.

The latter two testimonies, being depositions of Panakhtemope, were simply inserted into a lengthy reports relating to the examinations of the thieves of the gangs of Bukhaaf and Efnamun, and actually have nothing to do with the latter two.[203] One cannot exclude that Panakhtemope was in fact the sole member of the gang who had survived earlier (i.e. pre Renaissance Era) prosecutions, and finally was brought to the trial in year 1 of the Renaissance Era. Anyway it would be a reasonable explanation of his repeated interrogations in year 1 of the Renaissance Era (in the evening of IV *shemu* 8, and on IV *shemu* 17)[204], after that documented by papBM 10054 (ro. 2, {1}-6), apparently earlier in time. It is worth noting that in the list of the thieves of papBM 10054vo. 5, comprising also the colleagues of Panakhtemope, the name of the latter has not been preceded by the adnotation "brought",[205] which only accompanies the names of two of his accomplices (i.e. the coppersmith Ytnefer and Panakhtres son of Pawenesh).[206] It is hard to say whether this really means that Panakhtemope had not been arrested then, or else that he was examined simply as a witness, not a culprit. On the other hand, however, he is apparently incriminated by the actual contents of his deposition as recorded in papBM 10054. He admitted explicitly that 3 *kite* of gold were given to him for his services (papBM 10054ro. 2, 6), although its connection with the thefts has not been proven, except the deposition of Pakhyhat, who accused him in the following words: "It was the fisherman Panakhtemope of the mayor of the City, who ferried us to the west of the City. And his share was exactly the same as ours" (papBM 10054ro. 3, 5f.).[207] It is true that still in year 1 of the Renaissance Era Panakhtemope sturdily declared his own innocence, maintaining that he did not know what the men whom he ferried had really done (papBM 10052, 14, 18), whereas a few days later he was forced by beating with the stick to testify that he ferried the thieves, and that they rewarded him (papMayer A 5, 11f.).

Quite possibly his interrogations can be related to two different affairs,[208] and this may be viewed as another reason why he was standing trial for the second time at the beginning of the Renaissance Era. The circumstances of the examinations of the fisherman Panakhtemope do not, however, necessarily

[203] See Peet, Tomb Robberies, 141, 167 (n. 94).

[204] Respectively papBM 10052, 14, 10, and papMayer A 3, 6.

[205] PapBM 10054vo. 5, 6: Peet, Tomb Robberies, pl. 8=Kitchen, RamInscr VI, 494f.; cf. however Thijs, GM 179, 2000, 78 n. 53; where he mentions (after J.J. Janssen) a lacuna preceding his name.

[206] PapBM 10054vo. 5, 14-15. As regards identity of the latter, cf. Gasse, JEA 87, 2001, 90f.

[207] Peet, Tomb Robberies, pl. 6=Kitchen, RamInscr VI, 494, 5-7.

[208] See Thijs, GM 167, 1998, 99; Gasse, JEA 87, 2001, 88, contra Peet, Tomb Robberies, 167 n. 94.

indicate that the two affairs came to light at the same time. On the contrary, some time had elapsed between the two occasions, and this is a period marked by the events of the crucial meaning for the situation in the region on the eve of the Renaissance Era. Significantly, in his testimony of year 1 of the Renaissance Era Panakhtemope gave the titles of two of his accomplices wrongly: "*wab*-priest Panakhtres son of Pawenesh, of the temple of (Aa)-kheper-(ka)-re,[209] and craftsman (*ḥmww*) Ytnefer",[210] so he clearly forget that the former was in fact the member of the *semdet*-staff of the temple of king Aa-kheper-(ka)-re, and the latter was a coppersmith of the temple of Montu of Tod.[211] The apparent mistake can only be explained by the lapse of time.[212]

Finally, the case of the craftsman (*ḥmww*) Setekhnakht (no parentage), recalled by Pakhyhat (papBM 10054ro. 3, 2)[213] in relation to Panakhtemope and his accomplices cannot be evaluated properly unless we assume that there were two different persons of that name.[214] The second one was the son of Penanket and Iset, a craftsman from the complex in Medinet Habu, involved in the affair of the reign of Ramesses IX, as documented in papLeopold-Amherst (1, 18-2, 1 and 4, 12),[215] and also in papBM 10054vo. 1, 7 (no parentage given), a person much earlier in time than the thief accused by his colleagues Pakhyhat and Panakhtemope. There is no apparent reason to postulate that the names of both would have been inserted into the lists of the thieves of papBM 10054vo. 5-6,[216] as there are others omitted as well. On the contrary, the special character of the document in question makes its reliability highly suspicious.

---

[209] The name of the king written defectively, cf. Gasse, JEA 87, 2001, 90 n. 31; Haring, Divine Households, 425 n. 2, 456 n. 7; Kitchen, RamInscr VI, 798, 15. Wrongly read by Peet (Tomb Robberies, 168 n. 97) as Khepermaatre (Ramesses X).

[210] PapBM 10052, 14, 15f. For the discussion of the titles, cf. Gasse, JEA 87, 2001, 90f.

[211] As indicated in papBM 10054ro. 3, 3; see also papBM 10054vo. 5, 14.

[212] Cf. von Beckerath, ZÄS 127, 2000, 114f.

[213] Peet, Tomb Robberies, pl. 6=Kitchen, RamInscr VI, 493, 16; the name and title now destroyed, cf. Strudwick, loc.cit. (photograph). He appears also in the deposition of Panakhtemope: ro. 2, {1}, cf. Gasse, op.cit., 83, pl. 11.

[214] See von Beckerath, GM 159, 1997, 7; otherwise Thijs, GM 167, 1998, 101; cf. also Gasse, JEA 87, 2001, 90 n. 29.

[215] Capart et al., JEA 22, 1936, pls. 12, 16=Kitchen, RamInscr VI, 483, 4-5; 489, 8-9. Cf. Helck, Materialien I, (112)f. (dated to the reign of Ramesses XI by mistake); evidence regarding both persons mingled in Haring, Divine Households, 454. The craftsman Setekhnakht son of Anket and Iset (papBM 10054vo. 5, 20) is evidently the same person.

[216] See the discussion by von Beckerath, GM 159, 1997, 7; Thijs, GM 167, 1998, 101.

2. The so-called war of the High Priest Amenhotep

A series of documents connected with the trials of the thieves who ravaged the tombs and memorial temples on the west bank of Thebes provides the sole evidence of the events which brought an end to a period of relative peace in the region. Therefore a brief review of this material seems to be necessary here to reconstruct an overall picture of those troubled times. The most important information for this purpose can be found in the lengthy testimony of the workman Ahautynefer, son of Amenkhau, accused of stealing a portable shrine from the temple in Medinet Habu: "The foreigners (*ꜣꜥꜥ.w*) came and they seized the temple, while I was in charge of some donkeys belonging to my father. Pehety, a foreigner, seized me and he took me to Epep (*Ỉpip*). [1] (This was) when Amenhotep, who was the High Priest of Amun, had been attacked for six months. It so happened that it was after nine whole months of the suppression (*thꜣ*) of Amenhotep,[2] who was the High Priest of Amun, that I returned; (this was) when this portable shrine (*pꜣy pr-n-sṯꜣ*) was damaged and set on fire. Now when order was restored, the mayor of the West of Thebes and the scribe of the treasury Pasemennakht and the scribe of the army Kashuty said: «Let us collect the wood, and then those who are in charge of the workshop will not set fire to it». (So) they gathered the remains and put a seal on it, and it is intact today" (papMayer A vo. 6, 4-12).[3]

The violent character of the events described here cannot escape our attention. The foreigners seized the fortified complex of the temple in Medinet

1 No exact location possible; there are no grounds to accept its location in the region of the Theban necropolis, as suggested by Gauthier, DG I, 66; cf. von Beckerath, Tanis und Theben, 91 n. 499; Fecht, ZÄS 87, 1962, 22 n. 3.

2 Or else: "an offence made (against)", cf. Sethe, ZÄS 59, 1924, 60f.; Peet, JEA 12, 1926, 255f.; Kees, Herihor, 4; id., Hohenpriester, 4. Anyway it may be taken for certain that Amenhotep was a victim, and not an instigator of the civil war.

3 Peet, Mayer Papyri, pl. 6=Kitchen, RamInscr VI, 815, 5-15; see also Peet, JEA 12, 1926, 254ff.; Černý-Groll, Late Egyptian Grammar, 245f. (Ex. 667), 367 (Ex. 1039), 386 (Ex. 1079), 447 (Ex. 1215); Groll, Negative Verbal System, 188 (Ex. 422); Frandsen, Verbal System, 141 (Ex. 11); Wente, JNES 21, 1962, 304 n. 5; Winand, Études, 336 (Ex. 823).

Habu after its persistent defence.[4] Unfortunately the date of the events cannot be deduced, except the mere fact that the occurrence took place much earlier than the trials of the beginning of the Renaissance Era, when the testimony was given (see Chapter 1). Certainly the suppression of the high priest was only a relatively short time before the devastation of the portable shrine, which must have been only one of the symptoms of chaos prevailing in the region in the time of turmoil and disorder. Obviously K. Jansen-Winkeln was right when he observed that the wooden remnants of the shrine could hardly have been kept under lock and key for decades.[5] Nevertheless, it is possible that the precious wood was kept in the times of confusion in the hope that better times will come to restore the shrine.

Much has been said about the career of Ahautynefer. Here we have to focus our attention on the mere fact that the events described apparently predate all the later documents, in which he appears in the role of the "workman" (*k3wty*) or the "chief of the workmen" (*ḥry k3wty.w*) in the complex of Medinet Habu, while during the attack on the temple (of Medinet Habu) he was simply "in charge of some donkeys" (*m-s3 nh3 n ˁ3.w*) belonging to his father, thus possibly a mere boy or a youth.[6] An official function is evidently out of question here, and we can imagine that he had taken care of the donkeys belonging to his father, of whom nothing certain can be said except the fact that he was probably identical with one of the god's fathers of that name documented in papBM 10068 (vo. 3, 27; 5, 28).[7]

One can possibly doubt the honesty of Ahautynefer's testimony, but it finds a confirmation in the words of Nesamun son of Paybaki, extensively commented above in Chapter 1. Here Nesamun had tried to clear his own name saying that he was only a child when his father had committed a crime. One can perhaps doubt the honesty of Nesamun as well, having in mind that he was trying perhaps to belittle his own role in the affair.[8] Nonetheless, it would be unwise to suppose that both culprits adopted such a crude strategy to defend

4 As regards the possible archaeological testimony of the destruction, cf. U. Hölscher, Medinet Habu. Ausgrabungen des Oriental Institutes der Universität Chicago, Leipzig 1933, 32, 50; id., in: Work in Western Thebes 1931-1933, [OIC 18], Chicago 1934, 100f.; id., The Excavation of Medinet Habu V: Post-Ramessid Remains, [OIP 66], Chicago 1954, 6; Černý, JEA 26, 1940, 129.

5 Jansen-Winkeln, ZÄS 119, 1992, 32f.

6 Cf. Kees, Herihor, 5.

7 See Chapters 1 and 6 for more details regarding the persons in question.

8 Cf. Peet, JEA 14, 1928, 67; Jansen-Winkeln, ZÄS 119, 1992, 28f.

themselves against the accusations. Anyway such an argument would have completely failed if the span of time dividing the robberies and the trial was reasonably short. It would seem that at least several years must have passed if the culprits tried to persuade the judges in this way. As a matter of fact, it has been demonstrated in the previous chapter that the robberies following the deposition of the High Priest Amenhotep had been committed by the fathers of those who were taken to the trial at the beginning of the Renaissance Era – this is the case of the *wab*-priest Nesamun, and his father Paybaki, but also the weaver Wennekhu and his father Tatay. Both Nesamun and Wennekhu declared that they had been just children or youngsters at the time of the events described (*ʿḏd-šri* and *šri* respectively).[9] We are also informed that the workman Ahautynefer son of Amenkhau participated in the robberies. However, this does not mean that his testimony relating to the beginning of the civil war and his relative age at that time was false. On the contrary, the robberies evidently also continued after the deposition of the high priest. No doubt the period of destabilization lasted longer than has hitherto been assumed, and we should consider that those events during the first two decades of the reign of Ramesses XI were a bit more complicated than it has been thought.

Let us return to the ancient sources relating to this. One of the guardians of the royal palace (perhaps in Medinet Habu?) gave the following testimony before the tribunal: "I left the house of Pharaoh after Panehesy came and attacked my superior (*pꜣy.i ḥry*), though there was no fault in him" (papBM 10383, 2, 5).[10] In the words of a woman also implicated in the robbery affairs, the rather vague term "the war of the high priest" is used to describe these events: "After the war of the high priest (*pꜣ ḫrwy n pꜣ ḥm-nṯr tpy*) broke out,[11] this man had stolen property belonging to my father" (papBM 10052vo. 13, 24-5).[12]

Although not explicitly stated in the available documentation, the opponent of the high priest must have been Panehesy, the viceroy of Kush.[13] Later on, at the beginning of the Renaissance Era, his name was written with a

[9] K. Jansen-Winkeln' s (ibid., 29 n. 64) doubts about the meaning of the latter are only partly justified, as the term can be simply taken as a common designation of a child; cf. Cody, JEA 65, 1979, 100; Lesko, Dict. I, 85.

[10] Peet, Tomb Robberies, pl. 22=Kitchen, RamInscr VI, 835, 7-9; see also Černý-Groll, Late Egyptian Grammar, 371 (Ex. 1050); Frandsen, Verbal System, 23 (Ex. 31), 160 (Ex. 29), 212 (Ex. 25).

[11] Lit. "one made the war" (*iry.tw pꜣ ḫrwy*), so Frandsen, Verbal System, 23 (Ex. 34), 98 (Ex. 12) and Junge, Neuägyptisch, 278; see however Černý-Groll, Late Egyptian Grammar, 411 (Ex. 1135): "the war ... had finished"; similarly Groll, Negative Verbal System, 145 (Ex. 321).

[12] Peet, Tomb Robberies, pl. 33=Kitchen, RamInscr VI, 797, 4-6.

[13] See, however, Bierbrier, in: LÄ IV (1982), 661f.

determinative pointing out to his status of public enemy number one.[14] None of the preserved sources explain the reason why the hostilities broke out, and this is due to the very character of the Egyptian historical texts, which seldom inform us about the political background of the events. Actually there are no official sources which would shed light on the events of this dark period of late Ramesside history. Thus we are ignorant of the most important factor concerning the civil war: which one of the protagonists caused it to break out. Two possibilities must be taken into consideration. The culprit may have been the High Priest Amenhotep, a descendant of a powerful family exercising control over the most important sectors of administration and economy in the Theban area and in other parts of the country as well.[15] In such a case, his deposition by Panehesy[16] could be viewed possibly as a reaction on the part of the king against the exaggerated ambitions of the high priest.[17] If this was the situation, however, Panehesy's retreat and his subsequent history would remain wholly incomprehensible. For this reason, the opposite view must be considered instead. A course of events with Panehesy in the role of the real instigator of the disturbances much better fits the scattered mosaic of pieces of the historical record.[18] Thus it seems that, no matter who really stood behind these military operations, pharaoh and his northern forces finally defeated Panehesy and subsequently forced him to retreat to his Nubian stronghold. One way or another, Panehesy's relations with the Residence were not necessarily the same all the time during his stay in Upper Egypt.

Panehesy's presence in Thebes is well documented in year 12 of Ramesses XI at the earliest,[19] but the exact date of the fall of the High Priest Amenhotep cannot be established beyond any doubt. It is possible that it occurred shortly before year 12 of Ramesses XI,[20] or earlier (i.e., before year 9).[21] An even earlier

[14] Cf. e.g. papBM 10052vo. 10, 18; papMayer A vo. 13, B3; the sign in question is: Gardiner, Sign-list Z6. See also Helck, Verwaltung, 396.

[15] Cf. e.g. Černý, CAH[3] II.2, 626ff.; O'Connor, in: Trigger et al., A Social History, 229ff.

[16] Less possibly that it was caused by "a local faction" (whatever that could really mean), as proposed by D. O'Connor, op.cit., 231; cf. also Morales, GM 181, 2001, 62 (about the possible involvement of "internal enemies of the high priest at Thebes"). As regards the hypothethis about a rising or revolt, see Kees, Herihor, 7; id., Hohenpriester, 5f.; and a critical comment by Niwiński, Bürgerkrieg, 250f.; id., BIFAO 95, 1995, 336.

[17] See Helck, Wirtschaftsgeschichte, 242; O'Connor, loc.cit.

[18] Compare Sethe, ZÄS 59, 1924, 60f.

[19] This is Turin Taxation Papyrus, ro. 1, 4-5: Gardiner RAD, 36, 4-5.

[20] So Černý, CAH[3] II.2, 636; Helck, MIO 4, 1956, 176; id., Materialien I, (109); id., Verwaltung, 395; Fecht, ZÄS 87, 1962, 25f.; Janssen, BiOr 25, 1968, 38; similarly Junge, Neuägyptisch, 278 (about year 11); cf. also Morales, GM 181, 2001, 64f., 70, 73.

[21] Cf. Wente, JNES 25, 1966, 85f.; Aldred, Tomb Robberies, 94; Janssen, AoF 19, 1992, 14f.

dating (i.e., before year 6) may be suggested on the basis of the reconstructed chronology of the texts of papBM 10054 (cf. Chapter 1). As presented above, the activity of the gang of the fisherman Panakhtemope may be placed at such an early period, thus suggesting that the robberies committed by the gang were a direct consequence of the destabilization caused by the attack of Panehesy. Significantly the latest evidence relating to High Priest Amenhotep (the name only partly preserved) can be dated to the reign of Ramesses X (year 2).[22] In spite of the severe reservations concerning the "short chronology" of A. Thijs, expressed in the preceding chapter, the latter's hypothesis on the date of the civil war at the very end of the reign of Ramesses X deserves special attention.[23] Anyway, the hypothesis explains perfectly the tensions between the high priest and the vizier in connection with the administration of the royal necropolis, as documented in the sources dating to year 3 of Ramesses X.[24] Quite possibly the source of the conflict with Panehesy should be sought for at such an early date.[25] If so, this would be the most important factor lying behind the abandonment of the royal tomb in the Valley of the Kings. Consequently there is further, albeit circumstantial, evidence for an extremely early dating of the suppression of Amenhotep.

On the other hand, an attempt to date these events to the period between years 17 and 19 of Ramesses XI[26] does not withstand criticism. Such a late dating of the revolt of Panehesy does not explain satisfactorily the very character of Panehesy's presence in Thebes in the period preceding the royal

Bierbrier's assertions in regard of this were influenced by his hypothesis on existence of the High Priest Ramessesnakht II, cf. JEA 58, 1972, 199; id., in: LÄ IV (1982), 662.

[22] PapTurin 1932+1939vo. 1, 3: Kitchen, RamInscr VI, 686, 4; Helck OPG, 539 (year [1]); cf. Černý, CAH³ II.2, 629 n. 4; Gutgesell, Datierung, 149; Valbelle, Ouvriers, 43, 216; Peden, Decline of Textual Graffiti, 289 n. 19; see however Schneider, in: H. Jenni (ed.), Das Grab Ramses' X. (KV 18), [AH 16], Basel 2000, 88. There are other references to the high priest in the Necropolis Journal of this period but without giving his name, cf. Lull, Los sumos sacerdotes, 29 n. 120; Valbelle, Ouvriers, 216ff.

[23] Cf. Thijs, GM 184, 2001, 66; id., SAK 31, 2003, 291ff.; id., SAK 35, 2006, 308; id., SAK 38, 2009, 350. The sequence of events resulting from the "short chronology" will not be discussed here in full detail. See also Jansen-Winkeln, BN 71, 1994, 90.

[24] Cf. Schneider, op.cit., 101f.; Thijs, SAK 31, 2003, 293; Morales, GM 181, 2001, 61f.; Lull, Los sumos sacerdotes, 24.

[25] See also Niwiński, Bürgerkrieg, 250.

[26] Cf. e.g. Jansen-Winkeln, ZÄS 119, 1992, 28; Polz, SAK 25, 1998, 285 n. 109 ("Probably before Herihor's first attested year as High Priest of Amun (year 19 Ramses XI)"); Niwiński, Bürgerkrieg, 241, 250; id., BIFAO 95, 1995, 338; Vandersleyen, L'Égypte II, 644; Vernus, Affaires et scandales, 39; Häggman, Directing DeM, 274; Lull, Los sumos sacerdotes, 35, 58; Thijs, SAK 31, 2003, 289ff.; id., SAK 38, 2009, 345. Compare also von Beckerath, Tanis und Theben, 93 n. 512 (a few years before the Renaissance Era, and after year 12); and Kees, Herihor, 10 (between years 12 and 15).

decree of year 17, unless one accept that he acted formally on behalf of Pharaoh before the outburst of an armed conflict. Unfortunately a possible shift of political alliances cannot be evaluated properly in the light of the available sources.

Certainly a great deal of time elapsed before the final forcing of the troops of Panehesy out of his Theban stronghold. A letter of Pharaoh to Panehesy (papTurin 1896),[27] dated to year 17 seems to show that the latter's presence in the Thebaid lasted at least several years (minimum 5 years).[28] Panehesy's titles attested by this unique document present him as "the King's Son of Kush, royal scribe of the army, overseer of the granaries, and commander of the troops of Pharaoh, l.p.h.".[29] No doubt the control of the army and provincial administration remained his prerogatives. In fact, he imposed a military administration in the Thebaid, and the prolonged occupation of Thebes by the Nubian army of Panehesy had a serious impact on the internal situation in the region.[30] This aspect of the period of the civil war will be thoroughly investigated in this chapter. Obviously the 'suppression' of Amenhotep and subsequent defeat of Panehesy were different events separated significantly in time.[31] This hypothesis has an advantage over other reconstructions of the events, as it explains perfectly the scarcity of sources dating to the first decade of the reign of Ramesses XI, being a period of strife and chaos caused by the military action undertaken by Panehesy, no matter what kind of relations between Pharaoh and Panehesy prevailed in the subsequent period. The Pharaoh's letter of year 17 seems to suggest, however, that soon before the second stage of the civil war, their relations were peaceful if not amicable. Nothing at all indicates that Pharaoh's sovereignty had been openly denied in those times. On the other hand, however, there are no official royal monuments in the Theban area which could be dated to this period. Significantly, no part of the decoration of the temple of Khonsu can be dated plausibly to such an early period, and in the decoration of the hypostyle hall, Ramesses

[27] Bakir, Epistolography, pls. 24-25, 31; Kitchen, RamInscr VI, 734f. As for the recent translations of the text, cf. Wente, Letters, 39f. (no. 39); Peden, Historical Inscriptions, 111-114.

[28] About seven years according to O'Connor, op.cit., 231; similarly Zibelius-Chen, SAK 16, 1989, 331; Morales, GM 181, 2001, 65 ("as long as ten years").

[29] He held also a honorific title of the "fanbearer on the right of the king" (Turin Taxation Papyrus, ro. 1, 4), cf. I. Pomorska, Les flabellifères à la droite du roi en Égypte ancienne, Warsaw 1987, 211f. (no. 126).

[30] Quite properly A.Niwiński describes the action undertaken by him as a military *coup d'état*, cf. Bürgerkrieg, 251, 255.

[31] Cf. e.g. A. Gardiner, Egypt of the Pharaohs, Oxford 1961, 301f.; see also Helck, in: LÄ I (1975), 221.

XI appears in company with Herihor. Strangely enough, these two decades of the reign left no visible traces in Thebes, and this must be viewed as the effect of a general diminution of royal power and collapse of economic stability in the country. Above all, it seems one cannot overlook that it was the period of occupation of Thebes by the army of Panehesy, subsequent to the suppression of the high priest of Amun.

An obscure passage from an unpublished papyrus in the Turin collection, cited by J. Černý, may be recalled here, as it gives possibly unique testimony of the arrival of the Nubian soldiers of Panehesy's army at Thebes: "the Ethiopians (Kush) [came] to Ne".[32] An apparent scarcity of the contemporary sources relating directly to Panehesy cannot be explained by a *damnatio memoriae*, imposed not until the very beginning of the Renaissance Era. An exception seems to be oStrasbourg H 175,[33] mentioning the "general Panehesy" alongside some other persons whose identity cannot be established beyond any doubt.[34] A record of the arrival (?) of an unnamed Royal Son of Kush in oCG 25289 in year 6, III *peret* 13 is rather ambiguous.[35] A revised version of the text suggests it was rather the revenues from Kush (*inw n Kš*) that were arriving at Thebes,[36] and in addition the document is dated unequivocally to the middle of the 20th Dynasty (the reign of Ramesses IV).[37] In the opinion of the present author, its later dating (to the reign of Ramesses XI?) cannot be excluded, mostly because of the partly preserved word, which can be possibly read as *wʿ[w]* "soldier" (l. 2), thus placing the text in the warlike context of the civil war of the reign of Ramesses XI.

It may be also argued that a group of foreigners (*ꜣʿʿ.w*) mentioned in the grain accounts of year 9 of Ramesses XI[38] has no precedents in the earlier documentation referring to the sustenance of the necropolis crew, and their presence in Thebes at such an early date can be explained only

32 Černý, CAH³ II.2, 618: according to Černý the text was written on the *verso* of a small papyrus fragment belonging among other fragments of the necropolis journal (of the reign of Ramesses IX, as suggested by him); cf. Gutgesell, Datierung, 340; Helck OPG, 502f. (year 10 of Ramesses IX).

33 Y. Koenig, Les ostraca hiératiques inédits de la Bibliothèque nationale et universitaire de Strasbourg, [DFIFAO 33], Cairo 1997, pls. 88-89, 132; cf. Allam, WdO 30, 1999, 142.

34 Those of lines 2-4 being probably soldiers – *wʿw* (only the determinative is preserved); the title of the royal scribe of the army is at the end.

35 Cf. Daressy, Ostraca, 73=Kitchen, RamInscr VI, 147, 8-10 (A.81). The ostracon was found in the Valley of the Kings.

36 Kitchen, RamInscr VII, 454, 4-6 (A.81).

37 See Kitchen, loc.cit.; Janssen, Village Varia, 167; Häggman, Directing DeM, 201.

38 PapTurin 2018vo. A, 5, 2-3, 5-6; and vo. E, 2-3: Kitchen, RamInscr VI, 856, 5-6, 863, 4-5.

as a result of the sack of Thebes by Panehesy's Nubian army.[39] From this period onwards, the number of these foreigners significantly increases in the available documentation from the Theban necropolis.[40] A number of them appear also in the documents of the robbery trials from the beginning of the Renaissance Era (but referring to the earlier period), figuring among those against whom the charges of involvement in the robberies were brought.[41] There were among them two soldiers of the Kushite battalion or garrison – Ahautynefer, living in Opet (papBM 10052ro. 4, 27-28), and "the foreigner (sic!) Pentawere" (papBM 10052vo. 8, 25).[42] Besides these, several foreigners mostly of undifferentiated function were mentioned by the name,[43] as well as a group of foreigners from Hefau (papBM 10052vo. 8, 15).

Having gained a firm hold over his Theban stronghold, Panehesy was able to establish his supremacy over other parts of Upper Egypt as well. An obscure passage in papBM 10052vo. 12, 3-4,[44] relating no doubt to the period subsequent to Panehesy's attack and the 'suppression' of the high priest of Amun, gives interesting information about the possible extent of the territory controlled by his forces – two toponyms were referred to in this context: the Wall-of-the-Valiant-(Arm) (*ỉnb p3 ḥ̜pš*),[45] and the settlement of *Pa-wedj-mehty-en-Nemtywy* (*P3 wḏ mḥ.ty n Nmty.wy*).[46]

After the occupation of Thebes, the Nubian army of Panehesy moved northward, although the exact date of this action remains unknown. It does not seem, however, that it was a revolt in the XVIIth nome of Upper Egypt, which

[39] For an earlier occurence, dating to the reign of Ramesses IX, cf. papBM 10068ro. 6, 15. More explicit reference to the "soldier (*wʿw*) of the Kushite batallion/garrison (*t3 ỉwʿy.t*) Bakwerel, cf. papBM 10053ro. 5, 11; 7, 5.

[40] Cf. e.g. in the Turin Taxation Papyrus: Gardiner RAD, 90 (index).

[41] One wonders why they did not accompany Panehesy while he retreated to the south.

[42] The soldier (*wʿw*) Pentawere appears in papMayer A vo., 11, 19; 13, B7.

[43] These were Userhatnakht (papBM 10052, 1, 11; 3, 2, and 25; 6, 2), possibly identical (?) with the person of the same name in 2, 9; Panehesy the younger (ibid., 7, 13); Paykamen (ibid., 9, 1); Pentasekhenu (ibid., 10, 18-19); Panehesy son of Tjat (ibid., 11, 4); and Ahautynefer son of Nakhy (ibid., 15, 21). For those in papMayer A, see Peet, Mayer Papyri, index (30, 57, 63, 70, 71, 85, 93, 135, 156, 162, and others without a title). See also papAbbott-dockets, vo. A, 16-17, 25; B, 6-10, 16.

[44] Peet, Tomb Robberies, pl. 32.

[45] Location unknown; it could be the designation of a stronghold or fortifications somewhere in Upper Egypt (possibly to the south of the Xth nome?).

[46] In the Xth nome of Upper Egypt (or to the north of it?), cf. Montet, Géographie II, 121; Gardiner AEO II, 64*-66* (nos. 365-366); III, pls. 11-11a (5, 3-4); Gasse, Domaine d'Amon I, 35 (64). As for the reading of the god's name within the toponym, see also O. Berlev, GM 160, 1997, 6ff., contra K. Sethe, ZÄS 47, 1910, 48ff.

caused the attack, as suggested recently by Ch. Thiers.[47] More likely Panehesy was endeavouring to subjugate the territories belonging to the domain of the temple of Amun (papWilbour provides detailed information about Theban dependencies in Middle Egypt). We can only surmise that the offensive of the Nubian army was directed against the forces loyal to Pharaoh residing in the north.[48] According to the unique testimony given several years later by a slave Paynekh, bought by one of the robbers: "When Panehesy had destroyed Hardai (*Ḥr-dy*; Cynopolis),[49] the young Nubian Butehamun bought me, and (then) foreigner Pentsekhen bought me from him; he gave two *deben* of silver for me. And when someone killed him, the gardener Karo bought me for my price" (papBM 10052vo. 10, 18-20).[50] Certainly there is no urgent need either to suppose that the slave was ever taken northward (compare however the case of Ahautynefer, who was enslaved and then taken to Epep) or else that he was one of the inhabitants of Hardai, taken captive after the city was seized, and subsequently sold.[51] It seems that the sole aim of his testimony was to provide information about the silver and the amount that had been the price paid for him. Quite possibly he was in Thebes when hostilities broke out in the north, and soon afterwards he was bought by the gardener Karo in exchange for silver of doubtful provenance (originating perhaps from the robberies committed in the Theban necropolis). Obviously the success of Panehesy's army in the north was widely known among the citizens of Thebes, as documented by the text under discussion. Such important occurrences were always a convenient point of reference for those referring to the course of events occurring in the past.[52]

The information concerning a certain Pentsekhen, who was killed after the destruction of Hardai (Cynopolis), is a little bit ambiguous as we are not informed whether he was killed in a war or else in other circumstances. Quite possibly, however, he was a soldier of the army of the viceroy, and then we

---

47 Cf. BIFAO 95, 1995, 510 n. 100; cf. also P. Montet, Le drame d'Avaris, Paris 1941, 179; see also below.

48 Or else against the remnants of the army supporting the high priest, cf. Helck, MIO 4, 1956, 175.

49 In the XVIIth nome of U.E., cf. Montet, Géographie II, 169f.; Gardiner AEO II, 98*-103*; id., Wilbour Papyrus Comm., 39f., 50ff.; id., JEA 27, 1941, 51; F. Gomaà, Hardai, in: LÄ II (1977), 962. There was a "mooring-place of Pharaoh" in the city in the Ramesside period, cf. Gardiner, Wilbour Papyrus Comm., 18; Kemp, Ancient Egypt, 218.

50 Peet, Tomb Robberies, pl. 31=Kitchen, RamInscr VI, 790, 7-10; cf. also Černý-Groll, Late Egyptian Grammar, 279 (Ex. 759), 423 (Ex. 1152); Groll, Negative Verbal System, 145f. (Ex. 323); Frandsen, Verbal System, 60 (Ex. 41); Sweeney, Correspondence and Dialogue, 140 (Ex. 70)

51 Cf. Černý, in: CAH[3] II.2, 631.

52 Well in accord with an ancient method of dating, amply documented not only in the annals of the Palermo Stone, but also in later periods, cf. W. Spiegelberg, ZÄS 53, 1917, 106f.

can draw the conclusion that the hostilities continued still after destruction of Hardai. It is not without significance that the border between the Theban state of Amun and northern state of Smendes was later drawn a little further to the north, namely in the region of Teudjoy (modern El-Hibeh). A mention of the robbers killed in the north could be taken as evidence of the hostilities which broke somewhere in the northern part of Egypt (but hardly in Lower Egypt): "Thieves who were killed in the fight (*m pꜣ ḫrwy*)[53] in the northern province (*ʿ-mḥ.ty*)[54]: 15 men. Thieves whom Panehesy slew: 3 men; those who were (...):[55] 2 men; total: 5 men" (papMayer A vo. 13, B2-3).[56] Unfortunately no further details can be drawn from this terse and isolated testimony. We can only guess that those killed by Panehesy were probably the victims of the punishment carried out by him after his final retreat from the north, thus probably during his second stay in Thebes.[57]

Consequently there is no plausible explanation of an obscure passage mentioning a slave belonging to one of the robbers: "My father bought a servant (*bꜣk*) and called him H[...]enamun by name, but Panehesy took him" (papBM 10052, 15, 12).[58] We can only guess whether the slave was taken to be punished for his crimes, or else he was conscripted into Panehesy's army. The latter possibility seems to be less probable, as the sentence is a direct answer to the vizier, questioning whether the father of the witness was doing his job with his own hand. Thus we can only surmise that he used that servant of his while robbing the tombs and temples in Thebes. It cannot be excluded, however, that the slave could have indeed been conscripted but not necessarily as a consequence of his earlier engagement in the shady business of his patron.

---

[53] Not necessarily a "rebellion" or "revolt", cf. Kees, Herihor, 8-10; von Beckerath, Tanis und Theben, 94. The supposed role of Herakleopolis (and Libyans) in these events cannot be substantiated, cf. Helck, MIO 4, 1956, 175.

[54] The term appears also in LRL no. 37: Černý LRL, 59, 11; for its meaning and location cf. Sethe, ZÄS 44, 1907-8, 7 ("die Nordgegend"); Kees, Herihor, 8 ("'nördliche Hälfte' ... d.h. Unterägypten bedeuten, aber auch in engerem Sinne die 'nördliche Hälfte' von Oberägypten"); and more precisely von Beckerath, op.cit., 93f.: "nördlich Siût beginnenden Amtsbereich des unterägyptischen Wezîrs". According to Jansen-Winkeln (ZÄS 119, 1992, 27, 30f.) this is just a designation of Lower Egypt. The latter's suposition that Panehesy attacked (and destroyed) the Ramesside capital in Per-Ramesse cannot be substantiated at all; compare now the critical comments by Lull, Los sumos sacerdotes, 32f.

[55] The doubtful *nty ḥr n ḥr.w* cannot be explained satisfactorily.

[56] Peet, Mayer Papyri, pl. 13=Kitchen, RamInscr VI, 827, 6-7.

[57] Once again the available information is too scanty to infer from this testimony that Panehesy suppressed a rising in Thebes, cf. H. Kees, Ancient Egypt. A Cultural Topography, London 1961, 281.

[58] Peet, Tomb Robberies, pl. 35=Kitchen, RamInscr VI, 801, 3-5.

None of the preserved sources mentions any battle which had forced Panehesy to retreat southwards. One of the documents concerning the robbery trials preserved the vague words of one of the thieves (i.e. Bukhaaf), which could possibly shed some light on these obscure events: "I went away before/because of *n3 mdw-ʿn*, after Panehesy had made *n3 mdw-ʿn*" (papMayer A ro. 4, 4-5).[59] Unfortunately, the actual character of the action undertaken by Panehesy cannot be evaluated properly, and no satisfactory translation of the term *mdw-ʿn* can be offered in the present state of our knowledge. Having in mind the actual meaning of the adverb *ʿn*,[60] one can suggest a general meaning "retreat" for the entire compound (not attested elsewhere). As for *mdw* or *md.t* the meaning "to quarrel" or "affair" may be taken into consideration.[61] Interestingly, the words cited above are an answer directed to the vizier himself, who asked Bukhaaf about the place where he had concealed the silver stolen from the tombs in the Valley of the Queens. The continuation of this utterance suggests that Bukhaaf was forced to leave his house subsequent to the action undertaken by Panehesy:[62] "and the servant (*sḏmy*) Nesyaashefyt, this (man) who was a steward (*imy-r pr*), seized my house (*mḥ m p3y.i pr*). (Thus) he took three *deben* of silver, 150 *deben* of copper (in the form) of vessels ..." (papMayer A ro. 4, 5-6).[63] What follows this is a detailed register of the goods appropriated by Nesyaashefyt, being undoubtedly a part of the robber's loot.[64] We can only speculate about the circumstances of the action undertaken by Nesyaashefyt, but one thing seems to be clear enough: he acted

[59] Peet, Mayer Papyri, pl. 4=Kitchen, RamInscr VI, 811, 5-6; cf. Groll, Negative Verbal System, 82 (Ex. 178); 146 (Ex. 328); Frandsen, Verbal System, 67 (Ex. 1).

[60] Černý-Groll, Late Egyptian Grammar, 134f.; cf. also J. Winand, «Déjà», «aussi», «toujours» et «encore» ... *ʿn* en néo-égyptien, in: Chr. Gallois et al. (eds.), Mélanges offerts à François Neveu, [BdE 145], Cairo 2008, 289ff.

[61] Lesko, Dict. I, 216f. Compare Černý-Groll, Late Egyptian Grammar, 411 (Ex. 1136): "after A had intrigued again". See also oGardiner 5, 6 (Černý-Gardiner HO, pl. 18.1): *wnn.k (ḥr) mdw ʿn* "if you start wrangling again", cf. S. Israelit-Groll, in: Studies in Egyptology presented to Miriam Lichtheim, I, Jerusalem 1990, 365ff. (esp. pp. 367f., 373 (Ex. 5)). For *mdw ʿn* as enforced recruitment to Panehesy's army, cf. Niwiński, Bürgerkrieg, 243; id., BIFAO 95, 1995, 337. Lull (Los sumos sacerdotes, 32) suggests the meaning "conquest", thus implying that Bukhaaf fled before the conquest of Thebes by Panehesy. Compare also Fecht, ZÄS 87, 1962, 22f. n. 4.

[62] It is open to question whether it had happened after the sack of Thebes by Panehesy (thus Lull, Los sumos sacerdotes, 31f.), or else during his final retreat.

[63] Peet, Mayer Papyri, 12, pl. 4=Kitchen, RamInscr VI, 811, 6ff.

[64] It is rather difficult to reconcile this record with another list which records Bukhaaf's share being in the hands of several persons enumerated in papBM 10052, 2, 17ff. Supposedly the latter concerns the metals handed over to certain persons as a gifts or more probably as a payment given in exchange for other commodities and goods. Strangely enough the name of Nesyaashefyt does not appear among those documented by other papyri relating to the robberies.

in the period of disorder caused by the operations of the army of Panehesy. Evidently the accompanying events had happened suddenly, as if Bukhaaf had left his house in a hurry, abandoning the precious things which were concealed in it. First of all we do not know whether or not Nesyaashefyt's deeds were legal. It cannot be excluded, however, that he acted as a representative of a new regime introduced by Panehesy, several years earlier when Thebes fell prey to his Nubian army.

A detailed analysis of the sources concerning the later phase of robberies committed in the Theban necropolis enables us to say that most of them had taken place indeed in the time of troubles caused by the action undertaken by the viceroy of Kush. One of the culprits was none other than "the brander of cattle (*ṯ3y-3bw*)[65] Ahautynefer, being in the charge of (*r-ḫt*) the Royal Son of Kush" (papMayer A ro. 4, 15).[66] No doubt robberies committed on such a scale were caused to some degree by the disturbances of the civil war and a complete breakdown of the administrative system. One of the texts informs explicitly that it had happened "in the year of the hyenas, when there was a famine" (papBM 10052vo. 11, 8).[67] Disorder in the functioning of the local administration, and the famine as the final result of the political and economic crisis in the country – these were the vital factors prompting and at the same time facilitating the activities of the gangs of robbers ravaging the Theban region.

Surprisingly enough, some of the workmen of the royal necropolis were also implicated in the robberies at this stage of the decay of the institution of the royal necropolis, when clearly no works had been conducted in the Valley of the Kings and the crew itself was unemployed and finally dispersed. Some of those who escaped recruitment into the army were particularly apt candidates to join the robbers and in this way to survive the period of stagnation. One of them was a certain Pawerakhtef, son of Hormin,[68] who is barely documented in the contemporary sources.[69] An incense-roaster (*ps-*

[65] For the meaning of the term, cf. Gardiner, JEA 27, 1941, 32 n. 3; Lesko Dict. II, 224.

[66] Peet, Mayer Papyri, pl. 4=Kitchen, RamInscr VI, 812, 7f.

[67] Peet, Tomb Robberies, pl. 32=Kitchen, RamInscr VI, 791, 7; cf. Spiegelberg, ZÄS 53, 1917, 107 (III). The meaning of the term "hyenas" in this context cannot be properly evaluated; cf. however, Kees, Herihor, 6, who explained the phrase as relating to eating of hyenas by hungry people. More likely the increasing number of hyenas in the Nile valley had been caused by the increased availability of carrion in the period of famine, cf. Niwiński, Bürgerkrieg, 243f.

[68] PapBM 10052, 2, 2; 6, 17: Peet, Tomb Robberies, pls. 25, 29.

[69] Cf. Davies, Who's Who at DeM, 171, 175, chart 12; Gutgesell, Datierung, 207, 219. The earliest source concerning him (apparently as a member of the crew) is an unpublished papTurin 2072/142vo. 1, 11: Allam HOP, pl. 129, line 11 (Černý's transcription)=Kitchen, RamInscr VI, 633, 1; an occurrence

sntr) Nesamun incriminated him with the following testimony: "Pawerakhtef, this workman of the necropolis came, and he went to the place where was Amenkhau, son of the singer of the offering-table Hori. Then he said to him: «Come out, that I can give you this bread[70] and you shall give (me) my share of it! But do not give me too much lest my fellow necropolis workers (*msw-ḫr*) denounce me»" (papBM 10052ro. 6, 17-20).[71] Of course, the exact date of these events is unknown, we cannot assess either its impact on the functioning of the institution of the royal necropolis. Significantly the text mentions only a subsidiary group of necropolis workers, being in fact no more than members of the community not registered on the official lists of the necropolis crew but still functioning in some relation to it.[72] It is impossible that Pawerakhtef was one of them at the time of the robberies, as he was counted among the members of the crew already in year 9/10 of Ramesses IX, and subsequently at the end of the reign of Ramesses IX (or during the reign of his successor).[73]

We know that Pawerakhtef represented the third generation after that of his grandfather Hori,[74] the latter being a contemporary of the famous scribe of the necropolis Amennakhte. This makes Pawerakhtef a contemporary or maybe a peer of Khaemhedje son of Horisheri, and in fact we know that both had started their careers already in the reign of Ramesses IX (Khaemhedje a bit later, it seems). At the time of the robberies described in the text, Khaemhedje had already been succeded by his son Tuthmosis, and Pawerakhtef was certainly an adult possibly aged in his thirties or forties at least. If we accept the hypothesis put forward by B.G. Davies that he was depicted on the stela from the Ôhara collection,[75] he must have been still a

dated to year 9 of Ramesses IX, cf. however Helck OPG, 500 (year 10; father's name given wrongly; in fact the name is given here without filiation). There is also a stela representing him as a boy in company with other members of his family, as suggested by Davies, Who's Who at DeM, 171; cf. M. Suzuki, Les Antiquités égyptiennes dans la collection Ôhara, Orient 16, 1980, 126f. (no. 12), pl. 12.

[70] No doubt a jargon designation of the robbers' loot.

[71] Peet, Tomb Robberies, pl. 29=Kitchen, RamInscr VI, 783, 6-11; see also Wente, JNES 21, 1962, 304 n. 5; Černý-Groll, Late Egyptian Grammar, 448 (Ex. 1217); Frandsen, Verbal System, 141f. (Ex. 12).

[72] For the meaning of the term, see Černý, Community, 28, 117-120; Ventura, City of the Dead, 35-37. To the classical comments on the subject add also J.F. Borghouts, in: Gleanings from Deir el-Medîna, 81 (n. 29); A. Mahmoud, *Msw-ḫr* = the sons of the Tomb, in: Mamdouh Eldamaty, Mai Trad (eds.), Egyptian Museum Collections around the World. Studies for the Centennial of the Egyptian Museum, Cairo, Cairo 2002, 763-776; Häggman, Directing DeM, 66f.

[73] PapTurin 2053/49-50+2028+1914 (unpublished; Černý Notebook 15, 34-35); cf. Gutgesell, Datierung, 342f.; Helck OPG, 531; Bellion, Catalogue, 301; the *verso* of the papyrus can be dated on the basis of a cartouche of Ramesses X: Pleyte-Rossi, Papyrus de Turin, pl. 65a, 2; cf. Valbelle, Ouvriers, 68.

[74] Cf. Davies, Who's Who at DeM, 171, chart 12.

[75] Under the name Werakhetamun, cf. Davies, loc. cit. He was represented here with a side lock of youth

boy when his older brother Hori (son of Hormin) had already attained the status of the chief draftsman of the crew. As we know very little about the career of the draftsman Hori, son of Hormin, we can only surmise that it was not earlier than the beginning of the reign of Ramesses XI that he held the function of the chief draftsman (if ever).[76] Thus the stela cannot provide a very precise point of reference for the chronology of the life and activity of Pawerakhtef, his younger brother. Certainly, the latter could have achieved maturity before the time of the robberies at the end of the reign of Ramesses IX, and he was an adult man at the time of the second stage of the robberies in the Theban necropolis.[77] If he had not been conscripted into the Panehesy's army, this would have been because of his relatively advanced age or else due to other unknown circumstances.

No firm conclusion can be drawn either from the mere fact that the text cited above does not mention other men of the gang proper (*rmṯ-ỉs.t*). As a matter of fact, the workmen of the crew are almost absent from the extant documentation concerning the second phase of the robberies committed in the Theban necropolis. Of course, this does not necessarily mean that the crew in its entirety remained loyal to the government and its representatives. We know that some of them did indeed join the thieves. The documents shed some light on the behaviour of the necropolis workmen in those much troubled times. One of them, the workman of the necropolis Pawer (Paser) was pointed out by the thieves as the person "who showed us the tomb of Queen Hebaldje(ne)t" (papBM 10052, 1, 15-16).[78] Another member of the workmen's community also played a prominent role in the robberies. This was Panefer, who according to papBM 10052, 7, 10-13 joined the gang of the robbers under the leadership of the commander of troops (*ḥry-pḏ.t*) Efnamun. One of the accomplices gave the following testimony referring to him: "I gave some barley to a workman (*rmṯ-ỉs.t*) Panefer, and he gave me 2 *kite* of silver. (But) I found them (i.e., silver) to be an evil (thing), and I went to return them to him" (papBM 10052, 8,

and holding a scribal palette of an apprentice, thus cannot be older than 10 years.

76 Cf. Bogoslovsky, ZÄS 107, 1980, 104; id., *Drevne-Egipetskie Mastera*, Moscow 1983, 12f.; Davies, Who's Who at DeM, 144 n. 732; 170f. Anyway, in the years 9 (and 10?) of Ramesses IX and 1 (or 2) of Ramesses X it seems he was enumerated among the simple workmen, cf. papTurin 2072/142 ro. 1, 8; vo. 1, 4 and papTurin 1932+1939 vo. 3, 1: Kitchen, RamInscr VI, 631, 11f.; 632, 7; 686, 14; Helck OPG, 497, 499, 539.

77 This can be an additional argument against the hypothesis put forward by A. Thijs, relating to the chronology of the robberies.

78 Peet, Tomb Robberies, pl. 25=Kitchen, RamInscr VI, 768, 11-12. We can only guess the identity of this Pawer – for a possible candidate cf. Davies, Who's Who at DeM, 174f. (draftsman); Valbelle, Ouvriers, tab. X.

6-7).[79] It is worth noting that the incident was reported also in papMayer A vo. 9, 16-18,[80] although here Panefer was just termed a "craftsman" (*ḥmww*).[81] Of the two possible candidates which can be taken into consideration as regards identity of this Panefer,[82] more likely is Panefer son of Meryre.[83] There are no solid grounds to identify the unnamed son of Panefer, apparently involved in the same affair (cf. papBM 10052, 8, 10-11).[84]

One can imagine that the necropolis crew could not continue to carry out their work during this unstable period, and in fact there is no information available regarding any building operations in the royal necropolis in this period. We can only surmise that some of the workmen were possibly conscripted into the army, while others were simply left to their own fate, and such would be the case of the workman Pawerakhtef, who joined the gang of Bukhaaf, as stated explicitly in papBM 10052, 2, 1-2. A much debated question regarding the true meaning of the phrase *n3 iṯ3.w n p3 ḫr* (found in the robbery papyri)[85] must be taken here into consideration. A current analysis of the extant sources leads to the conclusion that it denotes simply the thieves operating in the necropolis, and not those recruited among the men of the crew. Evidently men connected with institutions other than the royal necropolis appear under such a headings.[86]

A closer examination of the documents pertaining to the robberies investigated in the early years of the Renaissance Era (i.e., relating to the second phase of robberies) enables us to create a vivid picture of the events at Thebes in the period of the civil war and prolonged occupation of the Upper Egypt by the Nubian army of the viceroy Panehesy. The very character of the sources pertaining to the two phases of robberies in the Theban necropolis enables us to say that those responsible for the second one were prosecuted long after

[79] Peet, Tomb Robberies, pl. 30=Kitchen, RamInscr VI, 786, 1-3.

[80] Peet, Mayer Papyri, pl. 9=Kitchen, RamInscr VI, 821, 10-12; as for the text, cf. Groll, Negative Verbal System, 175 (Ex. 391); Frandsen, Verbal System, 86 (Ex. 3).

[81] Cf. Steinmann, ZÄS 107, 1980, 139.

[82] These are respectively the sons of Meryre and Pahemnetjer, cf. Gutgesell, Datierung, 220; Davies, Who's Who at DeM, 95ff.; 232, chart 20 and 43. As regards Panefer son of Pahemnetjer he should be rather excluded, because he was already accused in year 17 of Ramesses IX, cf. papBM 10053ro. 6, 14.

[83] Cf. Gutgesell, 207, 442 (without filiation); Valbelle, Ouvriers, tab. IX-X; Davies, Who's Who at DeM, 232, chart 20.

[84] It was possibly [Pa]ankhau, cf. Davies, loc.cit.

[85] PapAbbott-dockets, vo. A, 1; 19-20: Kitchen, RamInscr VI, 764, 3-4; 765, 6-7; papMayer A ro. 3, 6; vo. 12, 1: ibid., 808, 15-16; 824, 14. Similarly in papBM 10068ro. 4, 1 and 18; 5, 18; 6, 20 – entries dated to the reign of Ramesses IX.

[86] Cf. Černý, Community, 19; Ventura, City of the Dead, 34f.

their deeds had taken place, when the peace was finally restored. This contrasts with the situation concerning the first phase when, even if some of the robberies started some years earlier, the prosecution and trials were a direct response to the events in question. The second phase of the robberies, as displayed in the depositions given by the thieves themselves, evidently involved a much larger scale of plundering than those of the reign of Ramesses IX. Not only were the temples plundered now by the soldiers from the Nubian army of Panehesy and the members of the temple staff, but gangs of robbers looted the necropolis on the west side of Thebes as well as in other cemeteries in the region.

It is to this phase in particular that the first attempts to plunder the royal necropolis in the Valley of the Kings, as well as that of the Valley of the Queens, may be possibly attributed. It has been already noted that only one of the tombs in the Valley of the Queens was disturbed during the reign of Ramesses IX, and if we exclude the tombs of the ancient necropolis of Dra' Abu el-Naga, none of the royal tombs had been attacked by the thieves at those times. The documents dating to the beginning of the Renaissance Era provide detailed information about the disturbance of the tomb of "Queen Hebaldje(ne)t" (papBM 10052ro. 1, 15ff.),[87] probably the same person as the wife of Ramesses III, the Queen Isis Ta-Hemdjeret.[88] There can be little doubt that this tomb can be identified with the tomb of Queen Isis (QV 51),[89] which was reported as disturbed already in year 16 of Ramesses IX, although the robbery itself had taken place much earlier, i.e. in year 14 of Ramesses IX, as it seems.[90] The suggestion made by K.A. Kitchen that the tomb "was only rumoured to be robbed under Ramesses IX, but was later entered and found "open"[91] by robbers under Ramesses XI" seems quite improbable.[92] More likely

[87] Peet, Tomb Robberies, pl. 25=Kitchen, RamInscr VI, 768, 10ff.

[88] Cf. J. Černý, Queen Ēse of the Twentieth Dynasty and Her Mother, JEA 44, 1958, 31-37; cf. also K. Seele, JNES 19, 1960, 191ff.; J. Monnet, BIFAO 63, 1965, 217f.; K.A. Kitchen; JEA 58, 1972, 189-192; id., JEA 68, 1982, 123-125; J. Grist, JEA 71, 1985, 77 n. 25; P. Grandet, Ramsès III. Histoire d'un règne, Paris 1993, 60.

[89] Contra Peet, Tomb Robberies, 34, 77; Černý, JEA 44, 1958, 32 ("now either completely destroyed or one of the numerous anonymous tombs in the Valley"); W. J. Murnane, JARCE 9, 1971-1972, 128 n. 35 ("the tomb itself has apparently not survived"); see however I.M. Soliman, M. Tosi, Memnonia 7, 1996, 213.

[90] PapAbbott, ro. 4, 11ff.; Peet's supposition that other documents of his Group III also deal with the same affair is highly probable (cf. Tomb Robberies, 72ff.). Certainly this is the case of the necropolis journal of year 17 of Ramesses IX, where the tomb of Queen Isis was mentioned explicitly, cf. Botti-Peet, Giornale, 26, pl. 24: ro. B8, 5-6=Kitchen, RamInscr VI, 579, 6-7.

[91] As stated in papBM 10052, 1, 16-17: *i.ir.i gm.t.s wn.tw ꜥn* "It was already open when I found it". For a discussion on the passage, cf. Peet, Tomb Robberies, 158 (5); Černý-Groll, Late Egyptian Grammar, 193f. (Ex. 533), 368f. (Ex. 1042); Frandsen, Verbal System, 157 (Ex. 14), 162 (Ex. 5).

[92] Kitchen, JEA 58, 1972, 191f. Even less probable are the conclusions reached by Thijs, GM 170, 1999, 87-89; cf. von Beckerath, ZÄS 127, 2000, 115.

the robbers entered it twice, although investigators of the time of Ramesses XI were evidently not persuaded by statements of one of the robbers, that the tomb was already open when they entered it.[93] As a result of the first robbery, an investigating party found "the stone (sic!) of red granite" smashed into the pieces at the tomb entrance.[94] A number of objects made of precious metals were taken from the tomb on this occasion, as well as linen and other valuable items.[95] Significantly, many of the objects were recovered by the authorities supervising the first investigation undertaken still in the reign of Ramesses IX. Quite possibly the mummy of the queen had at this time escaped profanation.[96] But several years later the robbers were able to lay their hands on the coffins made of silver and gold,[97] and this means that a mummy must have been looted at that moment. Other tombs located in the Valley of the Queens could have been robbed as well, as exemplified by the reasoning of the scribe Tuthmosis and scribe Nesamenope documented in papBM 10052, 5, 14-15, 21-22.[98] As a matter of fact, at least one more tomb in the Valley of the Queens was entered at this time by the same gang of the robbers – this was the tomb of Queen Nesymut, and similarly the burial of Queen Baketwernel was robbed as well: "I opened this tomb (*p3y ḫr*) of the Royal Wife Nesymut. He said (also): It was I who opened this tomb (*p3y ḫr*) (of) the Royal Wife Bak(et)wernel of the King Menmaatre, l.p.h.; total three" (papMayer A ro. 4, 2-4).[99] If the latter cannot be the same person as the Royal Wife Baketwernel

93 As clearly demonstrated by the words of the scribe Nesamenope, participating in the interrogation: "If I went and stole a goat-skin from a stable, and then someone else went after me, would not I accuse him in order to make the punish[ment] fall on him as well as on me?" (papBM 10052, 1, 19-21=Kitchen, RamInscr VI, 769, 2-5); cf. Černý-Groll, Late Egyptian Grammar, 435 (Ex. 1187), 552 (Ex. 1570); Sweeney, Correspondence and Dialogue, 111.

94 Botti-Peet, Giornale, 26, pl. 24: ro. B8, 7-9=Kitchen, Ram Inscr VI, 579, 8-9; fragments of the granite sarcophagus were not necessarily meant, cf. Thomas, Royal Necropoleis, 269; see also above, Introduction.

95 See the comment by Peet, Tomb Robberies, 78; Thomas, Royal Necropoleis, 269-271; Reeves, Valley of the Kings, 280 n. 70.

96 Some elements of the coffin(s), made of ivory and ebony, mentioned in papBM 10068ro. 6, 5-7, must be viewed rather as canopic containers (?) or maybe small coffins/containers for ushebti figures (?). As regards the meaning of *k3pw*, see Janssen, Commodity Prices, 392 n. 22.

97 PapBM 10052, 1, 18. As for the meaning of *wt* and *swḥ.t* in this context, cf. e.g. Janssen, Commodity Prices, 213 n. 36.

98 Peet, Tomb Robberies, 148; cf. Thomas, Royal Necropoleis, 270f.; Vernus, Affaires et scandales, 42.

99 Peet, Mayer Papyri, 12, pl. 4, 2-4=Kitchen, RamInscr VI, 811; cf. a comment by Thomas, Royal Necropoleis, 271. J. Černý (Community, 19) suggested that the third of the tombs was the tomb of the reigning king (i.e., Ramesses XI) – a conclusion based on a misunderstanding of the passage in question. Some doubts arise, however – why the royal wife had been buried in Thebes in such an unstable period, when the work on the royal tomb had not been completed?

of KV 10, as suggested by A. Dodson,[100] then we should assume that the tomb was located elsewhere in the Valley of the Queens. Anyway, it cannot be excluded that the tomb in question was located in the Valley of the Kings (KV 10).[101]

In such a case, however, the old hypothesis that the royal tombs in the Valley of the Kings had been ravaged already by the soldiers of Panehesy's army,[102] should be evaluated in every detail. Certainly the sole term *pꜣ ḫr*, commonly used in relation to the robberies in the Theban necropolis (of the two phases discussed), cannot solve indisputably the question, as we know that this is a common designation not only of the royal tomb, but also of the royal necropolis in general, including the tombs in the Valley of the Queens.[103] One of the testimonies seems to suggest, however, that the royal tombs in the Valley of the Kings were indeed attacked by the thieves. One Ahautynefer, being in the charge of the Royal Son of Kush was asked about it: "What have you to say about the tombs of Pharaoh(s) (*nꜣ ḫr.w n pr-ꜥꜣ*) which you robbed?" (papMayer A ro. 4, 16-17).[104] The tomb of the reigning king is out of question here, as we know that the tomb was never completed, and the plural form clearly refers to the royal tombs in general.[105]

At least two distinct groups of thieves can be discerned in the sources pertaining to these events during the reign of Ramesses XI. They formed, as it seems, two well organised gangs of robbers, each of them headed by its own leader. The herdsman (*mniw*) Bukhaaf of the domain of Amun was the son of certain Jutji, and he came from Epep,[106] not far from Thebes, as

[100] A. Dodson, DE 2, 1985, 10; id., JEA 73, 1987, 225; cf. also Vandersleyen, L'Égypte II, 642.

[101] See Thomas, loc.cit.; Vernus, Affaires et scandales, 42. The hypothesis must be taken seriously, because arguments in favour of different queens of that name are in fact meagre. The consequences of such hypothesis would be far reaching in regard of the history of the pillaging the royal tombs in the Valley of the Kings.

[102] Cf. Aldred, Tomb Robberies, 96, 98. Certainly, the case of the portable shrines cannot be related to the supposed violation of the tombs in the Valley of the Kings, as suggested earlier by Thomas, Royal Necropoleis, 271. A quite different view of the events has been presented recently by Jansen-Winkeln, ZÄS 122, 1995, 62-78.

[103] For a discussion on the subject, cf. e.g. Černý, Community, 7ff.; Ventura, City of the Dead, 1ff.; Lopez, BiOr 45, 1988, 546ff.

[104] Peet, Mayer Papyri, 12, pl. 4=Kitchen, RamInscr VI, 812, 10-11. As regards the use of the term *pr-ꜥꜣ* in relation to a deceased king, cf. Wente, JNES 25, 1966, 83f. n. 34.

[105] Contra Černý, Community, 15.

[106] PapAbbott-dockets, vo. A, 11: Peet, Tomb Robberies, pl. 23=Kitchen, RamInscr VI, 764, 14. The extant sources also preserved the names of other members of his family, namely his brother and sister: these were the herdsman Paysy (papBM 10052, 4, 19, 28, 29), and Nesymut (papMayer A, 4, 11).

it seems.[107] No doubt he was a self-made man, who took great advantage of the confusion caused by the civil war. His ruthless and clever conduct led to him achieving the position of an influential personality in the criminal underworld in this time of turmoil. A complete list of his companions can be drawn up on the basis of his own testimony: "The list of the men given by the herdsman Bukhaaf, (those) who were in his gang of the thieves: the workman (of the necropolis) Pawerakhtef, son of Hormin; the scribe of the divine records Nesamun; the incense-roaster Shedsukhonsu; the incense-roaster Nesamun called Tjaybay; Amenkhau, son of the singer of the offering-table Hori; the incense-roaster Ankhefenkhonsu; the young slave (*ms-ḥm*) Amenkhau son of Mutemheb; the foreigner Userhatnakht, being in the charge of (*r-ḫt*) the overseer of the hunters of Amun – he (i.e., the latter?)[108] is in the service (*m-di͗*) of the mayor of Thebes (Ne); the sailor (*nfw*) Paweraa of the domain of Amun; the measurer (*ḫ3y*)[109] Paweraa son of Kaka (of) the domain of Amun; the measurer Paaemtaumet; the trumpeter (*ḏd m šnb*)[110] Perpatjau.[111] Total: 13 men.[112] (And) he said: «They were with me in the tomb (*t3 s.t*)». He implicated them (in it), and he said (also): «As Amun lives, and as the Ruler, l.p.h., lives, if there be found a man who was with me and whom I have concealed, let his punishment be imposed on me (lit. him)»" (papBM 10052ro. 2, 1-16).[113] Being only a humble "field-worker" (*i͗ḥwty*), as Bukhaaf introduced himself during the interrogations,[114] he gained the support of some representants of the middle class personnel from the domain of Amun,[115] but also a significant group of the so-called "foreigners" (*3ᶜᶜ.w*), whoever they might have been.[116] It must remain an open question whether

[107] As regards the location of Epep, see above, n. 1.

[108] Cf. however Peet, Tomb Robberies, 144; A. Gasse, JEA 87, 2001, 87.

[109] For the meaning of the title and function, cf. Gasse, Domaine d'Amon, I, 208; S.S. Eichler, Die Verwaltung des "Hauses des Amun" in der 18. Dynastie, [SAK Beihefte 7], Hamburg 2000, 42ff.

[110] For the title cf. J.E. Hoch, Semitic Words in Egyptian Texts of the New Kingdom and Third Intermediate Period, Princeton 1994, 281f.; Lesko, Dict. II, 276.

[111] As regards Perpatjau, he must be the same person as Perpatjauemope, son of Paweraa, from the temple of Amun, cf. papAbbott-dockets, vo. A, 4; for other references cf. Peet, Tomb Robberies, 132.

[112] Including Bukhaaf himself.

[113] Peet, Tomb Robberies, pl. 25=Kitchen, RamInscr VI, 769, 11-770, 10; cf. also Peust, Indirekte Rede, 110 (Ex. 115); Winand, RdE 47, 1996, 136 (Ex. 79).

[114] PapBM 10052ro. 1, 8.

[115] Not necessarily of the temple of Amun in Karnak, but rather the members of the temple staff of the memorial temples on the west bank of Thebes.

[116] As regards to their status and role in relation to the memorial temples in Thebes, cf. Haring, Divine Households, 246, 366. For the meaning of the term, see Peet, JEA 14, 1928, 68; Gardiner, JEA 27, 1941, 25 n. 4; id., Wilbour Papyrus Comm., 80; H. Goedicke, ZÄS 52, 1966, 172-174; Warburton, State and

some of them were soldiers of the army of Panehesy, settled in the Theban nome,[117] or else a group of land owners recruited from the prisoners of war, well attested in the system of land holding during the New Kingdom.[118] Anyway, a group of foreigners settled south of Thebes is attested as early as year 14 of Ramesses XI, as documented by the Turin Taxation Papyrus.[119] And this may be an additional point of reference for the dating of the events described as "the war of the high priest (of Amun)".

A list of those who participated in the distribution of the goods stolen by the gang of Bukhaaf was of course much more lengthy, and we can imagine that this process was an economically significant activity for a substantial group of the inhabitants of Thebes,[120] but also for outsiders, such as a merchant or trader (*šwy.ty*) coming from such a distant place as *Mer-wer* in Middle Egypt (at the entrance to the Fayum oasis).[121]

Slightly more is known about the leader of the second group of robbers – this was the troop commander (*ḥry-pḏ.t*) Efnamun (nowhere is his parentage given). We can only imagine that his position as an officer of the army had indeed facilitated his activities, especially since we learn that he surrounded himself with other military men – Efnamun, son of Ptahemheb, and his brother Ankhefenamun, both scribes of the army (in the domain of Amun).[122] Hori, son of Efnamun, who was the scribe of the army in the "Place (Beloved) of Thoth in the domain of Amun" (*tꜣ s.t (Mry)-Ḏḥwty m*

Economy, 174 n. 508; L. Bell, Once more the *ꜥw*: 'interpreters' or 'foreigners'?, NARCE 87, 1973, 33 (cited after Trigger et al., A Social History, 400).

[117] See Valbelle, Ouvriers, 221; Peden, Historical Inscriptions, 114; Niwiński,BIFAO 95, 1995, 333; Morales, GM 181, 2001, 66.

[118] Cf. e.g. foreigners settled in Middle Egypt, as documented by papWilbour, see Gardiner, Wilbour Papyrus Comm., 77-79. Settlements inhabited by Syrians in the vicinity of Thebes (or in Thebes?) were mentioned during the reign of Amenhotep III, no doubt as a part of his mortuary foundation, cf. Urk. IV, 1649, 12; for a comment cf. Haring, Divine Households, 40f.; J.K. Winnicki, Late Egypt and Her Neighbours. Foreign Population in Egypt in the First Millennium BC, [JJP Suppl. 12], Warsaw 2009, 62.

[119] Cf. e.g. Gardiner RAD, XIV, 43f.; id., JEA 27, 1941, 25 n. 4. Significantly none of the owners of the houses listed in papBM 10068vo. can be identified as belonging to this group.

[120] We are informed that even a servant of the high priest of Amun was among them, cf. papBM 10052ro. 2a, 3.

[121] Cf. papBM 10052ro. 5, 11-12. For their role in connection with the robberies, see Kemp, Ancient Egypt, 244, 257; Vernus, Affaires et scandales, 72f.; Römer, SAK 19, 1992, 279f.; Allam, SAK 26, 1998, 14ff.

[122] As for Efnamun, cf. papBM 10052vo. 11, 10-11; papAbbott-dockets, vo. B, 19. For Ankhefenamun cf. papBM 10052, 11, 9; papMayer A vo. 8, 16; 12, 14; papAbbott-dockets, vo. B, 18. As regards the title of the "army scribe" within the domain of Amun, see S.S. Eichler, Die Verwaltung des "Hauses des Amun" in der 18. Dynastie, [SAK Beihefte 7], Hamburg 2000, 174, 324 (no. 543); Haring, Divine Households, 246f.; Gnirs, Militär und Gesellschaft, 171 n. 1100, 198.

pr-Ỉmn),[123] examined together with other culprits on account of his father, was not implicated directly in the robberies, as stated explicitly in papMayer A vo. 10, 22-23 (see below). Although the identity of Hori's father cannot be determined satisfactorily, possibly he was not the same man as the chief of the robbers.[124] It is worth noting here that the case of Hori and his father Efnamun provides another point of reference in regard to the chronology of the events: "They (i.e. the magistrates)[125] said: «He (i.e., Hori's father) was in the Tomb (*p3 ḫr*) and in (*m*) the portable shrine (*p3 pr-n-sṯ3*), but this one (i.e., Hori) did not go (there), (because) he was then a child (*ỉw.f m šrỉ*)» (papMayer A vo. 10, 21-23).[126] Thus we can see again that the robberies must have occurred significantly earlier than the time of the trials of the beginning of the Renaissance Era.[127]

There are good reasons to assume that the "Place (Beloved) of Thoth" was in fact a military post or a fortress located somewhere in Thebes or in its immediate vicinity. As a matter of fact, this is one of the earliest mentions of the fortress or military establishment, well known from the sources dating mostly to the III Intermediate Period.[128] It must be noted, however, that its mention in papBM 10052 does not necessarily mean that it also existed at the time of the robberies documented by this papyrus (i.e. several years before the trials of the year 1 of the Renaissance Era). Quite possibly, however, it was the same military foundation as that created by Merenptah, the location of which cannot be established beyond any doubt, but possibly it was a place located somewhere on the west side of Thebes (within the domain of Amun).[129] It cannot be excluded that the foundation, with its distinctly military character, had indeed something to do with the military operations conducted by Panehesy, and the occupation of Thebes by his forces. The strategic role of such a military outpost could hardly have been overlooked when he decided

---

[123] Cf. papBM 10052, 15, 10: Peet, Tomb Robberies, pl. 34=Kitchen, RamInscr VI, 800, 16-801, 1. As regards Hori son of Efnamun, see Haring, Divine Households, 246 n. 8.

[124] Peet, Tomb Robberies, 133 (B 19), suggested that this was Efnamun son of Ptahemheb.

[125] *n3 sr.w* (papMayer A vo. 10, 23); for the meaning cf. Lesko, Dict. II, 57.

[126] Peet, Mayer Papyri, 16, pl. 10=Kitchen, RamInscr VI, 823, 11-13; cf. Černý-Groll, Late Egyptian Grammar, 104 (Ex. 358), 570 (Ex. 1632); Groll, Negative Verbal System, 83 (Ex. 180), 84 (Ex. 183); Neveu, Grammaire, 8 (Ex. 2).

[127] Cf. Helck, MIO 4, 1956, 177f.

[128] Cf. G. Legrain, ASAE, 1907, 254-256; Chevereau, Prosopographie, 25ff.; Gnirs, Militär und Gesellschaft, 170f.

[129] Cf. J. Yoyotte, RdE 7, 1950, 63-66; Montet, Géographie II, 64; Gnirs, Militär und Gesellschaft, 9, 170 n. 1094; Häggman, Directing DeM, 274f.

to move northward. Quite possibly the garrison of the "Place Beloved of Thoth" enabled him to exercise control over the Thebaid during his northern campaign.

The behaviour of the soldiers left in the south is quite a different question. Certainly some of the soldiers of the garrison had taken a full advantage of their semi independent position. Thus the robberies committed in the necropolis were partly the result of a striking abuse of the power on the part of those who were left behind far from the front line. It is worth noting that the sources mention one more person connected with this military post – this was the foreigner Efnamun, whose daughter had an amount of silver which was part of the treasures stolen from the tombs by the gang of Bukhaaf.[130]

A thorough knowledge of the area of the Theban nome would have been advantageous with regard the effectiveness of the gang. Indeed, we may suspect that prior to his enlistment into the army (and promotion to the rank of troop commander) Efnamun had been a simple priest of Montu, well acquainted with the situation in the Thebaid and in the surrounding area. He started to plunder the tombs at the time when he was still a priest of Montu, and it seems that some of his accomplices were also connected with the Montu temple of Hermonthis (Armant). His connection with Armant, nowhere stated explicitly, can be inferred from the statement of Montusankh, god's father in the Montu temple: "I was in Hermonthis (in the temple of) Montu. I have heard that Efnamun (...)"[131] (papBM 10052, 12, 22-23).[132] In the words of Efenmontu, the storekeeper (*šnʿ*) of the temple of Montu, Lord of Hermonthis: "Efnamun was (then) a priest (*ḥm-nṯr*) of Montu; Pasemdet[133] of the temple of Montu was with him, when I was in the house of Efnamun together with other men: Panakhtemniut and Adjar of the temple of Montu, workman Panefer of the necropolis, and foreigner Panehesy-the younger" (papBM 10052, 7, 12-13).[134] Certainly this is not a complete list of those working for Efnamun, but a significant number of them originated from nearby Armant (Hermonthis), which must have facilitated their activity

[130] PapMayer A ro. 4, 9: Peet, Mayer Papyri, 12, pl. 4=Kitchen, RamInscr VI, 811, 13. Peet's transcription of the relevant passage should be emended, as noted by Černý, JEA 32, 1946, 28 n. 5; the text should be read as follows: *t3 n 3ʿʿ iw.f-n-Ỉmn n t3 s.t (Mry)-Ḏḥwty ḥḏ ḳd.t 5*. The term *3ʿʿ* could simply mean a foreign soldier (of the Theban garrison).

[131] The text ends here abruptly.

[132] Peet, Tomb Robberies, pl. 33=Kitchen, RamInscr VI, 794, 14.

[133] Peet (Tomb Robberies, 164 n. 54) was probably right supposing that this is a personal name and not a vague reference to one of the *semdet*-staff.

[134] Peet, Tomb Robberies, pl. 30=Kitchen, RamInscr VI, 784, 15-785, 2.

in the region to the south of Thebes. One of them testified that in the following words: "I was on the west of Imyotru (*Im-itrw*)[135] together with Nesamun who was a chief of the Madjoy, and I was on the west of Thebes (Ne) with him also; I was (also) on the west of Hefau (*Ḥfꜣw*)[136] with all the foreigners (*nꜣ ꜣʿʿ.w*) of Hefau" (papBM 10052, 8, 14-16).[137] Clearly all the region south of Thebes had been ransacked by the gang of Efnamun. The picture of events would be more comprehensible if we could learn who those "foreigners of Hefau" were. It must not be overlooked, however, that it was "foreigners" who had attacked and seized the temple in Medinet Habu.[138] The substantial number of mentions of foreigners in the documents of this period must be viewed not only as the result of assault of Thebes by the army of Panehesy but also as evidence of the prolonged stay of his garrison in this region.

It was not then a mere coincidence that Efnamun and his comrades had felt at their ease at the very moment when Panehesy's army marched out of the town on their way to the north: "When Efnamun had killed the brothers of my superiors, I went down into the boat with him and I went to [the] Wall-of-the-Valiant-(Arm) (*inb pꜣ ḫpš*). Now when he reached the settlement of *Pa-wedj-mehty-en-Nemtywy* (*Pꜣ wḏ mḥ.ty n Nmty.wy*)[139] they said to him: «Your men have been robbing the West.» And he replied: «Be quiet! Do not talk about it!» And when (he) returned and reached the City (Ne) they came in order to say to me: «Kerbaal! Go with your accomplices and bring this ox from Ihumeh, his brother» (papBM 10052, 12, 2-7).[140] It was Ihumeh, Efnamun's brother, who was his deputy and leader of the group operating in Thebes at the time when Efnamun himself, conscripted into the army, was in the north with Panehesy's army: "What have you to say about the affair of the tombs, which you attacked together with the men whom Efnamun who was a troop captain sent, with Ihumeh his brother at their head?" (papBM 10052, 7, 10-11).[141] And elsewhere: "A messenger/retainer

[135] For its location, cf. supra Chapter 1 note 157.

[136] Probably the same place as Hefat (now el-Moalla), near Gebelein, cf. Sethe, ZÄS 47, 1910, 47; Montet, Géographie II, 49f.

[137] Peet, Tomb Robberies, pl. 30=Kitchen, RamInscr VI, 786, 14-787, 1; cf. Peden, Historical Inscriptions, 272f.

[138] Cf. papMayer A vo. 6, 4; cf. supra for the passage in question.

[139] On the location of the toponyms enumerated here, see above, n. 45, 46.

[140] Peet, Tomb Robberies, pl. 32=Kitchen, RamInscr VI, 793, 4-11; cf. also Černý-Groll, Late Egyptian Grammar, 109 (Ex. 373), 348 (Ex. 972); Groll, Negative Verbal System, 10 (Ex. 14), 145 (Ex. 322); Frandsen, Verbal System, 67 (Ex. 15), 97 (Ex. 8); Neveu, Grammaire, 106 (Ex. 14), 182 (Ex. 18).

[141] Peet, Tomb Robberies, pl. 30=Kitchen, RamInscr VI, 784, 12-14; cf. Černý-Groll, Late Egyptian Grammar, 405 (Ex. 1124).

(*wꜥ šmsw*) of Efnamun came ... . «Which messenger of Efnamun was he, who came to you?» He said: «It was Ihumeh, his brother, who had come to me»" (papBM 10052, 13, 3-8).[142]

Understandably enough, soon after his return to Thebes, Efnamun decided to take over the loot stolen earlier by his comrades. The enigmatic mention of an ox (or a bull)[143] in one of the texts cited above can perhaps be interpreted as a jargon designation of the robbers' spoils,[144] otherwise the obstinate refusal on the part of the slave Kerbaal would be wholly incomprehensible. Significantly, neither the deposition of Efnamun nor his brother has been preserved in the extant sources, which possibly means that they had been killed earlier, still before the trials, or had simply fled.[145]

Undoubtedly, Thebes must have been disturbed once again, at the moment when the retreating army of Panehesy moved southward. It seems inevitable that the retreating (and possibly also defeated) army must have stopped at Thebes on its way through the region. It is quite possible that the city and its necropolis were plundered once again by the undisciplined soldiers of Panehesy. It cannot be excluded, however, that Panehesy had taken measures to put a stop to the thefts made by the demoralized soldiers of his army. One way or another, it is hardly imaginable that he had had enough time to investigate and finally to prosecute all those who had participated in this shady business. Finally, as we know, they were brought to court in the first two years of the Renaissance Era, and it must be credited to the new administration established in the region that the unstable situation was finally settled down successfully. It is, nonetheless, still open to question whether any of the preserved documents relating to the robbery investigations can be dated back to the period of Panehesy's rule over the Thebaid. It has been suggested that this is the case of papBM 10053vo., with the name of Panehesy mentioned explicitly, unfortunately only in the fragmentarily preserved beginning of the text.[146] Certainly the dating of the document, based on the mention of the "year 9", at the beginning of vo. 2, must be submitted to critical review. As

[142] Peet, Tomb Robberies, pl. 33=Kitchen, RamInscr VI, 795, 9ff.

[143] Cf. Peust, Indirekte Rede, 113 (Ex. 128).

[144] Just like the word "bread" used elsewhere, cf. e.g. Jansen-Winkeln, ZÄS 122, 1995, 69.

[145] A mention of the robbers killed by Panehesy (cf. papMayer A vo. 13, B1-3) can perhaps be taken as an explanation of the absence of Efnamun and his brother during the trial. We are also informed that six of the thieves escaped (papMayer A vo. 13, B5).

[146] Peet, Tomb Robberies, pl. 19 (vo. 1, 2)=Kitchen, RamInscr VI, 755, 12. The final determinative(s) unpreserved so one cannot decide whether at the time of writing he was treated as an enemy or not.

demonstrated above (see Chapter 1) the year date can be possibly emended into <1>9 instead of 9, thence it seems that the text may possibly be referred to the very beginning of the Renaissance Era. At the same time, the text of vo. 1 can be slightly earlier – in such a case, however, the identity of an unnamed high priest of Amun mentioned in it (vo. 1, 13) as the person who had undertaken an investigation of the thefts, must necessarily provoke an acute controversy. Certainly, the extraordinary role played by the high priest in the administration of the necropolis is not a new factor in the history of the late Ramesside period.[147] This time, however, quite new circumstances must be taken into consideration. First of all this is the weakened role of the central administration in the Thebaid, the most visible result of this seems to be a complete lack of references to the office of the vizier during seventeen years of the reign of Ramesses XI. Unfortunately, our understanding of these perturbations is too fragmentary due to the insufficient data on the subject. The sequence of the viziers of that time has not yet been ascertained satisfactorily.[148] Nonetheless it is known for certain that vizier Nebmarenakht (II) held his office already in year 19 (=1 of the Renaissance Era), IV *akhet*, day 5.[149] Other tomb robbery documents show explicitly that Nebmarenakht (II) presided, together with other officials, over the court sessions held on IV *shemu* 5-8 and 10 (papBM 10052), IV *shemu* 15 and 17 (papMayer A), and subsequently in year 2, IV *shemu* 25 (papBM 10383).[150] Thus the only possible explanation of the role played by the high priest of Amun in the investigations would be the mere fact that the case of Amankhau directly concerned the temple(s) of the Theban west bank and not the matters of the necropolis proper,[151] the latter being inevitably under direct supervision of the vizier.

On the other hand, there is no certainty as regards the actual character of the two texts written in papBM 10053vo. and their respective dating. The arrangement of the texts casts doubt upon its apparent homogeneity: there is half a page blank below vo. 1, 1-13, and the fact that the name of the main culprit referred to in the text (the *wab*-priest Amenkhau, son of Bakptah) does

[147] Cf. Häggman, Directing DeM, 261ff.; Valbelle, Ouvriers, 216; Allam, BIFAO 97, 1997, 10.

[148] Cf. Helck, Verwaltung, 335ff. As regards the chronological position of the ephemeral tenure of the office by Montuerhatef, see Černý, BiOr 19, 1962, 142; Janssen, JEA 53, 1967, 163f. Thijs' reconstruction of the sequence of viziers (GM 184, 2001, 65ff.) is determined by his "short chronology", and cannot be accepted in its entirety.

[149] Cf. papTurin 2034: Kitchen, RamInscr VI, 865, 4.

[150] As regards the chronological sequence of dates, see Ohlhafer, GM 135, 1993, 59ff.

[151] See, however, my comments above, in Chapter 1.

not even occur in the remaining texts of the *verso*. Additionally, the robberies committed by the temple scribe Sedi, and other priests, are referred to in both parts of the text written on the *verso*. The latter circumstance may indeed suggest that there is some connection between the texts of vo. 1 and vo. 2-4, although their respective date is not necessarily the same (it is possible that vo. 1 may be slightly earlier). Thus the date placed at the top of vo. 2 cannot be related confidently to the investigation referred to in vo. 1. Moreover, the text of vo. 1 seems to be only a fragment of a more lengthy document, less possibly that mentioned in papAmbras 1, 5, which refers perhaps to the routine procedures connected with the temple administration rather than the plundering: "The record of the examination (*p3 sš n n3 sip.t*) of the garlands of Amun-United-with-Eternity, which the god's father Amenkhau made".[152] If Amenkhau son of Bakenptah, the god's father in the temple of Medinet Habu, was still on duty in year 12 of Ramesses XI (as attested by papBM 10068vo. 5, 28), then we can deduce that his involvement in the matters mentioned in papBM 10053vo. 1 occurred after year 12 of Ramesses XI,[153] and must be probably earlier than the beginning of the Renaissance Era, when the main investigations took place.

The second document which can attest an earlier (i.e., pre Renaissance Era) prosecution of the thieves who had been active in the region of the Theban necropolis, is possibly papBM 10054, or rather the unpreserved documents used in its compilation (see Chapter 1). Here too again the absolute dating of the proceedings cannot be estimated precisely, although the text dated to year 18 (of Ramesses XI) seems to be the latest among them, and it contains a deposition relating to the robberies committed in the Ramesseum (ro. 3, 7-17). Unfortunately no details were given as regards the investigating authorities,[154] thus one cannot decide whether the interrogations had taken place still during Panehesy's stay in Thebes or after his expulsion. The latter possibility seems to be more likely.

An exact estimation of the duration of Panehesy's rule over Thebaid is hardly possible. General problems with the chronology of the period make it extremely difficult to date particular documents properly. The most astonishing is an apparent absence of contemporary sources relating to the daily life

[152] Peet, Tomb Robberies, pl. 38; with corrections in: Kitchen, RamInscr VI, 836, 12f.; see also Peden, Historical Inscriptions, 278f.

[153] Provided that the *wab*-priest Amenkhau is the same person as the god's father of that name; cf. supra.

[154] Cf. Haring, Divine Households, 276 (1).

on the west bank of Thebes at that time. One can argue that the institution of the royal necropolis practically ceased to function in its normal way when the disturbances broke out. Later on, in the middle period of Panehesy's supremacy in Thebes, the situation was at least partly stabilised, as exemplified by the preserved fragments of the necropolis journal of years 8-10 (papTurin 2018).[155] As a matter of fact, the above cited text of papMayer A clearly informs that order was restored within several months after a military action undertaken by Panehesy against the high priest of Amun: "Now when order was restored..." (vo. 6, 9).[156] There is some evidence, however, to suggest that quite unusual means of supply of the necropolis crew had been adopted in those times, as documented by the Turin Taxation Papyrus dated to years 12 and 14. This seems to cast some doubt upon the effectiveness of the new regime introduced in the aftermath of the suppresssion.

At the same time there are good reasons to assume that relations between Panehesy and the king were at least partly normalized in the subsequent period. The royal decree of year 17 (IV *akhet* 25) seems to leave an impression that the relations were friendly, but one cannot exclude that it was only an element of the political game between two opponents. Although the political status of Panehesy cannot be properly determined on the basis of this unique text, the unusual combination of titles makes him a prominent person and a virtual "governor" of the Thebaid.[157] Nevertheless, his subordinate position cannot escape our attention: "Do not be neglectful concerning this commission which I have sent to you. Look, I am writing to instruct you" (papTurin 1896ro., 13-14).[158] Not only the royal butler Yenes had been send to the south (*ꜥ-rsy*), but also cooperation with him had been demanded by the Pharaoh. Soon afterwards, but still in year 17, the vizier Wennefer arrived in Thebes on "his first journey (*wḏy(.t)*)" (papTurin 1888+2085ro. 1, 5).[159] He was already in Thebes by IV *peret* 11 (papTurin 1888+2085ro. 1, 9), and the most significant results of the actions undertaken by the vizier, accompanied by the overseer of the treasury Menmarenakht, was commissioning the

155 Kitchen, RamInscr VI, 851ff. (41); cf. Helck OPG, 562f.; Gutgesell, Datierung, 150f.; Valbelle, Ouvriers, 68f.

156 Peet, Mayer Papyri, pl. 6=Kitchen, RamInscr VI, 815, 12; cf. Wente, JNES 25, 1966, 73.

157 Cf. Peden, Historical Inscriptions, 114.

158 Bakir, Epistolography, pls. 24-25; Kitchen, RamInscr VI, 735, 5-6; cf. Peden, op.cit., 112f.; Wente, Letters, 40 (no. 39).

159 Gardiner RAD, 64, 8-9.

crew followed by distribution of bread, beer and ox, in the great court of the Medinet Habu temple.[160]

It is open to question whether the occurence took place before the expulsion of Panehesy from Egypt. More likely, however, the vizier's visit postdated the military operations, and aimed at the reorganization of the social and political situation in the Thebaid.[161] The available data do not allow us to establish the exact date of the war against the viceroy Panehesy. As a matter of fact, the documents of the second decade of the reign of Ramesses XI leave no place for the final clash of forces which finally led to Panehesy's retreat from Thebes. Four possibilities, however, must be taken into consideration as regards the date of these events:

(1) The period before the date of the Pharaoh's letter to Panehesy, which due to the general tenor of the royal decree seems hardly probable. Nothing in fact implies that Panehesy was defeated in the preceding period.

(2) The period between the date of the Pharaoh's letter and Wennefer's arrival at Thebes – i.e. about three months or even less, which seems to be too short a period for any military operation. In any case an unexpected attack of the royal forces immediately after the letter was sent to Thebes seems unlikely.

(3) The very short period of just two months between the latest date of the necropolis journal of papTurin 1888+2085 (year 18, IV *shemu* 24) and the date of the earliest robbery investigations documented in papBM 10054ro. 3, 7-11 (year 18, II *akhet* 24). It may be only surmised that the investigations of the temple robberies undertaken in year 18 postdate the expulsion of Panehesy's troops from Thebes. Quite possibly, this was the first stage of the investigations undertaken when the order was restored after the civil war. A conjecture proposed above (Chapter 1) as regards the date of papBM 10053vo. (year 19 instead of 9) would inevitably mean that Panehesy's name placed in the fragmentary beginning of the text has nothing to do with his supposed participation in the early investigations of the thieves.[162] On the contrary, one can even suppose the deep involvement of his wife in the robberies or, more precisely, that she presumably profited from the robberies in question.

---

[160] Cf. Helck OPG, 565; Häggman, Directing DeM, 242f.; Haring, Divine Households, 257.

[161] According to Niwiński (Bürgerkrieg, 256) it was an attempt to impose royal control on administration in Thebes already during Panehesy's presence in Upper Egypt.

[162] As suggested by Wente, JNES 25, 1966, 86; Aldred, Tomb Robberies, 94; Niwiński, Bürgerkrieg, 245; id., BIFAO 95, 1995, 334; Gnirs, Militär und Gesellschaft, 194, 198 n. 55. For a hypothetical restoration of this part of the text, where the name of Panehesy appears, see now Thijs, SAK 31, 2003, 297.

In one of the robbery papyri, the wife of the viceroy Panehesy is mentioned among those who received gold from the thief Bukhaaf: "Nesmut the wife of Panehesy: 5 *deben* of gold" (papBM 10052, 2, 29).[163] The identity of Panehesy cannot be doubted because his name has been determined here by the sign Z6 (in the Gardiner EG, Sign-list).[164]

(4) The period between the interrogations of year 18, II *akhet* 24, and the beginning of the Renaissance Era in year 19 of Ramesses XI.[165] For the reasons presented above it is hardly possible that Panehesy was still in Thebes at such a late period.

In spite of the reservations presented above, the period before the date of the Pharaoh's letter seems to be the most suitable to place the war against Panehesy. In such a case one can interpret the letter as an attempt on the part of Pharaoh to impose his sovereignty over Upper Egypt as a result of a battle of which virtually nothing else is known. As a matter of fact this could explain the harsh superiority openly demonstrated by Pharaoh in the letter.[166] It may be also suggested that the letter was written soon after forcing Panehesy to retreat, while he temporarily stayed at Thebes on his way southwards.[167]

It is in the relatively short period of ca. 2 years, between Panehesy's retreat and the proclamation of the new era, that we should possibly place a visit of Pharaoh himself at Thebes,[168] although no date of the event has been preserved in the extant sources. The relevant information relates to the promotion of certain Hori to the office of the *sem*-priest of the temple in Medinet Habu. Significantly the promotion was made by Pharaoh himself, who had arrived in Thebes: "Now when (*ḫr ỉr*) Pharaoh our Lord, l.p.h., had

[163] Peet, Tomb Robberies, pl. 26=Kitchen, RamInscr VI, 771, 7.

[164] Cf. also Niwiński, Bürgerkrieg, 244; id., BIFAO 95, 1995, 335; Thijs, SAK 31, 2003, 299 n. 67. Tentnub attested in the tomb at Aniba must have beeen his second wife (?); for the latter's name, cf. Kitchen, RamInscr VI, 843, 1; Helck, Verwaltung, 505.

[165] The document in question (papBM 10054ro. 3, 7-17) partially conflicts with the period suggested by Niwiński (Bürgerkrieg, 257) as regards the date of the suppression of Amenhotep.

[166] Cf. A. Gardiner, Egypt of the Pharaohs, Oxford 1961, 302. At the same time there is nothing in the letter which would support the thesis that Panehesy has been ordered to leave Thebes on a mission entrusted by Pharaoh, as suggested by Niwiński, Bürgerkrieg, 255f.; id., BIFAO 95, 1995, 335.

[167] Although nowhere stated explicitly, the letter was probably received by him in Thebes, cf. e.g. Peden, Historical Inscriptions, 111. The provenance of the letter is unknown.

[168] See however Helck, Verwaltung, 396 (the beginning of the Renaissance Era); Niwiński, Bürgerkrieg, 262; id., BIFAO 95, 1995, 341 (the king in question being Herihor); Lull, Los sumos sacerdotes, 33f. (the very beginning of the Renaissance Era); similarly Morales, GM 181, 2001, 63 (year 2 of the Renaissance Era). Thijs' supposition (SAK 31, 2003, 303 n. 92) that Pharaoh's visit took place at the moment when he assumed control over Upper Egypt, retains its value only in the frame of the "short chronology".

come to the City (Ne), he (lit. One) appointed the *sem*-priest Hori as the *sem*-priest of the temple (i.e., Medinet Habu temple). He (i.e., Hori) came to the temple and he [caused] this vase-[stand] to be brought [...] 26, and he appropriated (or: damaged?) it" (papBM 10383, 1, 10-11).[169] The dating of this event remains rather dubious, but it presumably had happened during, or just after the robberies committed in the temple of Medinet Habu – the case of the silver vase-stand was the main subject of the investigation, and Hori also played a part in this, as it seems.[170] One can assume that he is the same person as the *sem*-priest Hori of the chapel (*ḳniw*) or the temple (*ḥw.t*) of king Nebmaatre, mentioned thrice in papBM 10053ro. 2, 10; 3, 5 and 19,[171] dated to year 17 of Ramesses IX. PapBM 10383 informs us explicitly that Hori was already the *sem*-priest (thus possibly in the temple/chapel of Nebmaatre), at the moment of his promotion. This is probably the same Hori who appears in the Necropolis Journal of year 17 of Ramesses IX: "*sem*-priest Hori [of the temple of ...]" (ro. B 9, 15-16).[172] Nothing certain can be said about the predecessor of Hori in the function of the *sem*-priest in the Medinet Habu temple. It is possible, however, that it was Nesamun, the younger brother of the High Priest Amenhotep, from whom he took over the office, presumably after the latter's promotion to the post of the high priest of Amun.[173] Nesamun's activity as the *sem*-priest in Medinet Habu, alongside that of the second prophet of Amun, is well attested during the reign of Ramesses IX.[174] There are no grounds to suppose that Hori directly followed Nesamun. As a matter of fact, some documents dating apparently to the early years of Ramesses XI seem to

---

[169] Peet, Tomb Robberies, pl. 22=Kitchen, RamInscr VI, 834, 11-14; cf. Černý-Groll, Late Egyptian Grammar, 97 (Ex. 317); Frandsen, Verbal System, 66 (Ex. 13).

[170] Cf. Haring, Divine Households, 220.

[171] Cf. Peet, Tomb Robberies, 123; Gardiner, Wilbour Papyrus Comm., 143 (§127); Haring, Divine Households, 218, 440.

[172] Botti-Peet, Giornale, pl. 26=Kitchen, RamInscr VI, 580, 12; cf. Helck OPG, 529 (the restoration of the lacuna with the name of Ramesses IX seems to be unfounded).

[173] Amenhotep was promoted as the *sem*-priest in Medinet Habu during or prior the reign of Ramesses VII, cf. Haring, Divine Households, 449 n. 5; 455 n. 1; id., in: DeM in the Third Millennium, 147 n. 100. Quite possibly he was still in office at the beginning of the reign of Ramesses IX, see above, Introduction (note 218).

[174] PapLeopold II-Amherst 2, 1; 3, 9; 4, 12 – titled as the second prophet of Amun-Ra and *sem*-priest in the temple in Medinet Habu; (and possibly also 1,17 – only the *sem*-priest; name unpreserved). In papAbbott, 7, 3-4, he appears in company with his brother, the High Priest Amenhotep, although the temple of Ramesses IX was mentioned (instead of that of Ramesses III?), cf. Peet, Tomb Robberies, 42, 45 n. 24, pl. 4; Haring, Divine Households, 452, 456 (with references). His name can be found also in a newly published fragment of the necropolis journal, cf. F. Tiradritti, in: L'Egitto a Milano. Nuove Acquisizioni e Restauri, Milan 1991, 16, figs. 2-3 (x+8).

suggest that the office of the *sem*-priest was at least temporarily vacant. There is no other explanation for such an unusual situation than a destabilization caused by the civil war.

Significantly no person responsible for the temple in Medinet Habu was indicated in the list of houses in papBM 10068vo. 2-8, dated to year 12 (of Ramesses XI).[175] It seems that the highest officials of the complex in Medinet Habu were enumerated at the top of the list pertaining to this temple. These were: the army scribe Kashuty, the mayor of the west of the City Paweraa, the scribe of the quarter Wenennefer, and two *ꜣṯw*-officers, Anynakht and Amenkhau. A distribution of grain text of papBM10054vo. 2 (of year 6 of Ramesses XI), gives the names of these officials exactly in the same order, as the persons responsible for providing for those living in "every house which is within enclosure of the temple of Usermaatre-Meriamun". Here we can find one more name – that of the steward (*wr pr*) of the chantress of Amun Nesmut, acting no doubt in company with the scribe Kashuty. The role of Kashuty cannot be overestimated, as it points out to the distinctly military background of the temple administration at those troubled times. More intriguing, however, is the name of the steward of the singer of Amun, placed at the top of the list of the officials responsible for grain distribution. Certainly, it is somewhat astonishing that there was no mention of the *sem*-priest of the temple among those responsible for the provision of the temple and its staff, and the only explanation seems to be an assumption that there was no *sem*-priest in Medinet Habu at that time. Evidently the documents cited indicate that at that time the administration of Medinet Habu was in the hands of other persons. It is noteworthy that at this time it was the temple scribe Sedi who then was at the head of the temple of Ramesses II: "The temple of Usermaatre-Setepenre in charge (*m-ḏr.t*) of the temple scribe (*sš ḥw.t-nṯr*) Sedy" (papBM 10054vo. 2, 35),[176] to be followed by the *sem*-priest Khaemope, who is attested six years later (papBM 10068vo. 2, 15).

There are virtually no reasons to admit that any family ties existed between the new ruling family of the High Priest of Amun, Herihor (and his direct successors) on the one hand, and the members of the house of Meribastet

[175] Contrary to the case of the temples of Seti I and Ramesses II, being respectively in the charge (*m-ḏr.t*) of the prophet (*ḥm-nṯr*) Hapywer (papBM 10068vo. 2, 4), and under supervision (*r-ḫ.t*) of the *sem*-priest Khaemope (vo. 2, 15), cf. Peet, Tomb Robberies, pl. 14=Kitchen, RamInscr VI, 749.

[176] Peet, Tomb Robberies, pl. 7=Kitchen, RamInscr VI, 745, 5. It is noteworthy that no superior or agent was named in the following entry (vo. 2, 36) relating to the temple of Seti I.

on the other.[177] In such circumstances Amenhotep, dead or alive, must have been removed by the representatives of a new regime. Anyway, this seems to be the only possible answer to the question about the fate of the High Priest Amenhotep after his deposition. He left the stage in such obscure circumstances that nothing can be said about his demise nor a burial place.[178] It is in this particular context that the much debated question of a supposed reinstatement of Amenhotep[179] must be discussed. First of all there is a highly fragmentary inscription written on the rear wall of the Tuthmoside chapel near the VIIth pylon in Karnak,[180] which must be dated to the period after the deposition of the high priest, because the text apparently commemorates these events.[181] Anyway, a different timespan of the suppression, as expressed in papMayer A vo. 6, 7 (nine months), and in the inscription from the Tuthmoside chapel (eight whole months), cannot be taken as an argument against the identity of the two events.[182] It cannot be excluded that Amenhotep had been reinstated for some time at least, although virtually nothing can be said about this, except perhaps the obscure ending of the text mentioning an appeal to Pharaoh (col. 21).[183] Moreover, it is not obvious that it was Amenhotep himself who founded the commemoration inscription, being an example of the kind of autobiography (written in the 1st person singular) which was more usually inscribed in a tomb. More likely it was created at the instigation of his unnamed direct successor of whom we learn more from

[177] For a contrary view, see A.H. Gardiner, Egypt of the Pharaohs, Oxford 1961, 303; Černý, in: CAH[3] II.2, 636; Hornung, OLZ 61, 1966, 438f.; Helck, in LÄ I (1975), 221f.

[178] There are no grounds whatsoever to ascribe to him the coffins from Paris and Cannes, cf. Lefebvre, Grands Prêtres, 202-204; Niwiński, 21st Dynasty Coffins, 164 (no. 329) (dating to the late 21st Dynasty); id., Bürgerkrieg, 254; for a different view, see Fecht, ZÄS 87, 1962, 23f. n. 2.

[179] Cf. eg. von Beckerath, Tanis und Theben, 93; Wente, JNES 25, 1966, 85; Kitchen TIP, 247 (it was Panehesy "who may have reinstated Amenhotep on behalf of the king"); Bierbrier, in: LÄ IV (1982), 661f.; Gundlach, in: LÄ VI (1986), 1263; Vernus, Affaires et scandales, 39; Niwiński, Bürgerkrieg, 254f.

[180] Cf. Wente, JNES 25, 1966, 73-87; Kitchen, RamInscr VI, 536-538; Frood, Biographical Texts, 77ff. (translation).

[181] An earlier dating of the inscription (to the reign of Ramesses VI), proposed by Helck (JARCE 6, 1967, 138; Or 53, 1984, 52ff.) seems to be unfounded; for the critics, see Jansen-Winkeln, ZÄS 119, 1992, 33f. Quite unconvincingly Stučevsky (*Vestnik Drevney Istorii* 3 (157), 1981, 3ff.) placed the text in the reign of Ramesses IX (between years 2 and 10), thus implying two separate 'suppressions' of Amenhotep.

[182] For a plausible explanation of the difference, cf. Wente, JNES 25, 1966, 82; Morales, GM 181, 2001, 70.

[183] We are informed that after the 'suppression', Amenhotep had appealed to Pharaoh himself. It must be observed, however, that in conclusion (cols.23ff.) a kind of an appeal to the living (i.e., successors of Amenhotep) has been formulated.

several texts from the beginning of the Renaissance Era.[184] The identity of the direct successor of Amenhotep is, however, open to question. Some authors suggested that it could have been Herihor.[185] Two other possibilities must be taken into consideration here. First of all this the highly enigmatic figure of the brother of Amenhotep – the High Priest Nesamun (not necessarily the same person as the second prophet of that name documented during the Renaissance Era).[186] From the texts mentioned earlier, relating to his role as the second prophet of Amun and the *sem*-priest in Medinet Habu, we can well imagine that after deposition of his brother he was temporarily at least appointed to the office of the high priest of Amun. The other possibility is provided by the name of the high priest of Amun, mentioned in the unpublished papPhiladelphia (Pennsylvania University Museum),[187] which has not hitherto been commented upon more extensively. Quite possibly these were the two successors of Amenhotep, who were active still during the period of Panehesy's supremacy in Upper Egypt.[188]

A literary composition contained in papMoscow 127 (the so called Tale of Woe)[189] cannot be satisfactorily related to the historical events discussed above.[190] The toponyms which occur in the text relate it very strongly with

[184] Cf. e.g. papBM 10052ro. 2a, 3; 4, 28f.; papBM 10053vo. 3, 14; papMayer A ro. 4, 12; the high priest of Amun appears here in relation to the persons involved in the robberies, no doubt earlier than the beginning of the Renaissance Era.

[185] Cf. e.g. Černý, CAH^3 II.2, 636, suggesting an early appearance of Herihor in Thebes, in the period "shortly before the year 12 of Ramesses XI, and the nineteenth year of this same Pharaoh". There are no grounds for a hypothesis formulated by H. Kees (Herihor, 10f.) that Herihor became the high priest with the support of Panehesy, cf. Helck, MIO 4, 176f. For a discussion on the subject, see also Niwiński, Bürgerkrieg, 241f., 255.

[186] Cf. Bierbrier LNK, 12f.; Kitchen TIP, 253 n. 52; for a different point of view, see Bell, Serapis 6, 1980, 16ff.; Thijs, SAK 38, 2009, 343ff.

[187] To be published by D.P. Silverman (personal communication). Transcription in Černý Notebook 157.3, line 8 (by courtesy of the Griffith Institute, Oxford): *Ny(-sw)-Mwt wn m ḥm-nṯr tpy (n) Ỉmn* "Nesymut who was the high priest of Amun". In Černý's transcription the name of the high priest is Nesymut (!), and not Nesamun, as suggested recently by Häggman, Directing DeM, 276 n. 1845; followed by Thijs, SAK 38, 2009, 352. Only the feminine form of the name was recorded by Ranke PN I, 176 (10).

[188] It was already G. Fecht (ZÄS 87, 1962, 25) who postulated an existence of an "ephemeral" high priest of Amun between Amenhotep and Herihor. The purely hypothetical Ramessesnakht II must be definitely discarded (see above).

[189] R.A. Caminos, A Tale of Woe from a hieratic papyrus in A.S. Puskin Museum of Fine Arts in Moscow, Oxford 1977; compare also M.A. Korostovtsev, *Ieratichesky Papirus 127 iz sobranija GMII im. A.S. Pushkina*, Moscow 1961; Allam, JEA 61, 1975, 147ff. (translation); Quack, ZÄS 128, 2001, 167ff. (translation and detailed philological commentary); B. Schad, Die Entdeckung des " Briefes" als literarisches Ausdruckmittel in der Ramessidenzeit, Hamburg 2006, 63ff.

[190] Cf. Wente, JNES 25, 1966, 73 n. 3; Caminos, op.cit., 13 n. 3; Quack, ZÄS 128, 2001, 181 n. 130

Lower and Middle Egypt, and the region of the Great Oasis.[191] Strangely enough Thebes itself is not even mentioned in the text, and it seems hardly probable that the story has anything to do with the history of the High Priest Amenhotep after his deposition by Panehesy.

Schad, op. cit., 146. For a different view, see G. Fecht, Der Moskauer "literarische Brief" als historisches Dokument, ZÄS 87, 1962, 12ff.; Niwiński, Bürgerkrieg, 252ff.; id., BIFAO 95, 1995, 337; Thijs, SAK 31, 2003, 294 n. 48; id., SAK 35, 2006, 307ff. An interesting hypothesis has been proposed by Stučevsky (*Vestnik Drevney Istorii* 1 (163), 1983, 14ff.), according to whom the text has nothing to do with the High Priest Amenhotep, being at the same time a reflection of the incursion of Panehesy's forces in Egypt.

[191] Cf. Caminos, op.cit., map on p. 100.

3. Herihor and his Theban "kingship"

Panehesy's retreat from Egypt did not necessarily mean a complete restoration of the pharaoh's rule over the Thebaid. No doubt the unknown people who achieved the military success ensured for themselves an influential position in the region. Unfortunately the history of this period is obscured by the fragmentary state of the preserved sources and their mostly ambiguous character. This concerns not only the chronology of the period but also the identity of the main personages involved in the political events at this time. As so often is the case in Egyptian history, we search in vain for the motives of their deeds or even to outline the political background of the events. All that can be done is to submit the preserved sources to a critical review. A tentative picture of events emerges, and that is all that can be offered in the present state of research on the subject. At the same time, we cannot avoid creating new theories and ideas which would explain the most intricated problems of the history of the period, even if these sometimes appear to be somewhat controversial. Some new working ideas will be presented here, and their verification must be postponed to the moment when new documents throw some light on the questions discussed.

The picture of the events of these troubled times would be much more comprehensible if at least the name of the person who inflicted defeat on Panehesy had been transmitted by the available sources. Unfortunately this is not the case and this has led to the recent formulation of a number of precarious hypotheses. The unexpected appearance of the High Priest Herihor on the political scene makes him the best candidate for this role. No doubt his position at this early period of his career was distinguished by his military titles, naming him as commander in chief of the pharaoh's army. One of the most important among them, that of "great general of the army of the Upper and Lower Egypt", was held by him presumably in a relatively early stage of his career, although documented only on a statue from Karnak,[1] and in

[1] On his statue from the Karnak cachette (CG 42190), cf. G. Legrain, Statues et statuettes de rois et de particuliers,[CG], Cairo 1909, 59 (CG 42190), pl. 52; Lefebvre, ASAE 26, 1926, 65; Bonhême, Livre des rois I, 127 (Doc. 21 H.253); Kitchen, RamInscr VI, 843. See below on its presumed dating.

the inscriptions from the hypostyle hall of the Khonsu temple.[2] Similarly another of his titles suggesting his official functions comprising two parts of Egypt – that of the "controller (*ḫrp*) of the Upper and Lower Egypt" – is attested only once, on one of the columns in the hypostyle hall of the temple of Khonsu.[3] It is possible of course that both titles constitute only an element of the political propaganda dating to the period when the political ambitions of Herihor had established him in the position of the real "governor" of the Thebaid. Significantly, however, the latter is attested extremely rarely, so it refers presumably rather to Herihor's earlier career when he was only the pharaoh's representative in both parts of Egypt, no matter whether we relate this to a period immediately preceding the war against Panehesy or else to the period after the latter's expulsion from Egypt. Other titles mentioning the king (for example that of the fan-bearer on the King's right)[4] can be related to the same period when the pharaoh's sovereignty was still recognised in the South, and the role played by Herihor can be compared possibly to that of a regent or even a crown-prince.[5]

Such a rough reconstruction of Herihor's early career is in apparent contradiction to the hypothesis formulated recently by K. Jansen-Winkeln.[6] According to him, the sequence of pontificate of Herihor and Payankh, as commonly accepted until now, should be reversed to the effect that it was Payankh who excercised his pontifical office earlier, starting his career with the expulsion of Panehesy, and attaining the high priest's office in year 7 of the Renaissance Era (or slightly earlier), while Herihor succeeded him as

[2] Usually in connection with that of *ḥ3wty* "army-leader". Only once it was used without the latter, cf. Bonhême, Livre des rois I, 110f. (Doc. 21 H.192).

[3] Bonhême, Livre des rois I, 104f. (Doc. 21 H.183); Römer, Gottes- und Priesterherrschaft, 38, 41.

[4] Not to mention other purely honorific titles mentioning the lord of Two Lands. K. Jansen-Winkeln is certainly right (ZÄS 119, 1992, 23) while pointing out that Herihor's military titles never include a component *pr-ʿ3*, contrary to the usage observed in relation to Payankh. The sole possible explanation is the assumption that the titles of Payankh simply reflect his lower military rank, in comparison with the titles borne by Herihor.

[5] Cf. Römer, Gottes- und Priesterherrschaft, 40ff., 74. I cannot fully agree, however, with the thesis that the notion of the king in the Herihor's titulary was significantly reduced, as several of his titles actually refer to the king. It would be tempting of course to argue that those of the titles referring to the king are earlier in date than their equivalents lacking such a direct reference (thus suggesting perhaps his independent position?), but there are no grounds for such a sharp differentiation.

[6] Cf. Jansen-Winkeln, ZÄS 119,1992, 22-26; id., GM 157, 1997, 49ff.; id., in: Ancient Egyptian Chronology, 225f.; this hypothesis widely accepted by others (A. Thijs, G. Demidoff, A. Egberts, S. Häggman, J. Taylor; see bibliography for further references), was submitted to critical review by J. von Beckerath, A. Gnirs, K.A. Kitchen, and A. Niwiński.

the high priest of Amun (still during the lifetime of Ramesses XI) and subsequently as the king (after Ramesses' XI demise). Consequently, Herihor's tenure of office would be put forward to the late years of the Renaissance Era and the very beginning of the 21st Dynasty.[7] Admittedly Herihor as a hypothetical successor of Payankh on the pontifical throne of Thebes could also have borne all the military titles while starting his career at Thebes, as these merely point out to his military background. In such a case, however, it would be rather strange to find a direct reference to both parts of Egypt in his titles, at the time when a political split between the two parts of Egypt had been de facto committed.[8] Moreover, it would be difficult to explain in particular why he was titled the "great general (generalissimo) of the army of the Upper and Lower Egypt" already at a relatively early stage of his career (as documented in the hypostyle hall of the Khonsu temple), unless it was merely an element of political propaganda. But then we must notice that this could have been even higher rank than that documented in regard of Payankh himself.[9] None of the documents connected with Payankh allow us to draw the conclusion that other high ranking officials promoted by the king (i.e. Ramesses XI) were present at Thebes in his times, whereas documents connected with the robbery trials of the beginning of the Renaissance Era give the names of several of them.[10] On the contrary, we can find a number of lesser officials related directly to him in the documentation of the period.[11] Nothing explains such a degree of independence on the part of Payankh's administration without acknowledgement of the role played previously by Herihor in the Theban area.

[7] Cf. Jansen-Winkeln, ZÄS 119,1992, 25. As regards an extremely late dating of Herihor's kingship, being a direct consequence of the "short chronology", see now also Thijs, ZÄS 132, 2005, 73ff.; the conclusions arrived at by A. Thijs cannot be accepted in the light of the discussion presented below, and reservations raised against his "short chronology" scheme.

[8] It is true that titles of this kind were held also by the successors of Herihor on the pontifical throne. It cannot be overlooked, however, that at least some of the high priests of Amun of the 21st Dynasty had indeed close relations with the representatives of the Tanite dynasty in the North.

[9] Here the highest of the military titles borne by him seems to be that of the "general (of Pharaoh)" and the "army-leader of the Pharaoh's troops", cf. Černý LRL, 76 (index); Römer, Gottes- und Priesterherrschaft, 47. The highest military titles of Herihor and Payankh appear in oCG 25744 and 25745: "the leader NN, who is at the head of all the troops of Egypt" (*ḥ3wty* NN *nty* <*r-*>*ḥ3.t n3 mšꜥ(.w) n Km.t* (*r-*) *ḏr.w*); cf. Jansen-Winkeln, GM 99, 1987, 19ff.; Gnirs, Militär und Gesellschaft, 196f. It must be noted, however, that this is the sole reference for the title in question, attached to both personages, not attested elsewhere in any of the monumental inscriptions.

[10] Cf. e.g. Peet, JEA 14, 1928, 70.

[11] These were: *idnw n p3 imy-r mšꜥ*; *ḥsy n p3 imy-r mšꜥ*; *rwḏ p3 imy-r mšꜥ*; *sš n* (*p3*) *imy-r mšꜥ*; all of them attested in LRL, cf. Černý LRL, 75ff. (index).

K. Jansen-Winkeln's reasoning was based mainly on the observation that the tenure of Payankh inserted between that of Herihor and Paynudjem I interrupts the sequence of titles borne by them.[12] One cannot escape the impression that such a chronological scheme appears to be strongly determined by a sort of evolutionary point of view. It must be stressed, however, that the apparent abnormal position of Payankh, as presented in the available sources, was determined mostly by his role as a military leader (and more precisely the commander in chief of the army operating in Nubia). First of all it must be noted that his tenure of the high priest's office is attested only four times (!) in the contemporary sources,[13] and certainly it cannot be placed on the same basis as that of Herihor in regard of its duration. It must inevitably lead to the conclusion that either his priestly functions were very faintly accentuated (possibly because of his permanent stay outside Thebes, in Nubia), or else (which seems more probable in fact) that his pontifical office was only episodic and very short in time. Both assumptions explain very well all the obvious peculiarities of his position, as expressed by his titles and a traces of his activity in Thebes.

The point of departure for the present discussion on the sequence of the pontificates of Herihor and Payankh must be the fact that the career of the former (or at least part of it) can be placed in the shadow of the reigning king, i.e. Ramesses XI,[14] whereas Payankh's name is met only once in connection with the name of the reigning pharaoh (i.e. Ramesses XI). It is in the oracular decree from the Karnak temple (chapel of Amenhotep II between pylons IX and X),[15] given in favour of the storehouse scribe Nesamun, that we can find a reference to the "general" Payankh, dated explicitly to the 7th year of the Renaissance Era, which can be equated with year 25 of the reign of Ramesses XI.

It has been aptly suggested that there are no earlier references to general Payankh than LRL no. 14, dated approximately to year 6 of the Renaissance Era.[16] It is also true that all the dated references to Herihor are no earlier than

---

12 Jansen-Winkeln, ZÄS 119, 1992, 24f.; id., in: Ancient Egyptian Chronology, 226.

13 Cf. Bell, Serapis 6, 1980, 25; the sources in question are the following: LRL no. 28, votive stela from Abydos, Karnak oracular decree of year 7 of the Renaissance Era, and a statuette published by R. Hari; see below for the documents cited. The *post mortem* sources related to Paynudjem I are not taken into consideration here.

14 See also Römer, Gottes- und Priesterherrschaft, 11ff.

15 C.F. Nims, An Oracle Dated in "The Repeating of Births", JNES 7, 1948, 157ff., pl. 8; Kitchen, RamInscr VI, 702f.; Römer, op.cit., 467 (20.c)

16 Cf. Demarée, Bankes Papyri, 24; as regards the supposed dating of the letter, see also Wente LRL, 6-7, 16.

year 6 (of the Renaissance Era) either.[17] Thus the dated documents cannot enable us to solve directly the problem of the sequence of the tenure of office in this period. There are no positive arguments whatsoever in favour of the old hypothesis that Payankh was Herihor's son.[18] The sole exception seems to be a controversial inscription from his statuette, naming him as "the king's bodily son" (*s3-nsw n ẖ.t.f*).[19]

As regards the significance of the decree of year 7 for the chronology of the period, it has been suggested that the oracle text mentioning the "general" Payankh (col. 15), and the adjoining figure of the "fan-bearer on the King's right, viceroy of Kush, high priest of Amun-Ra, king of the gods, general and army-leader Payankh" (cols. 1-2) are not necessarily of the same date.[20] The apparent contradiction between the two sets of Payankh's titulature attested here raise some doubts as regards the contemporary character of both parts of the inscription.[21] Strangely enough, Payankh's figure is located in the background of the scene (in its upper right-hand corner), and not in front of the bark of Amun – the position more appropriate for the high priest of Amun himself as the chief celebrant.[22] It has been already observed that he was represented in a secular garb and not as the high priest of Amun.[23] The quite unusual role played by the second prophet of Amun Nesamun, represented in front of the bark as the main officiate, cannot escape our notice either. These apparent discrepancies led L. Bell to the conclusion that the entire inscription, though forming an unity, reflects the ambiguity of Payankh's role

[17] These are hieratic dockets on the coffins of Seti I and Ramesses II, dated respectively to "year 6, II *akhet* 7", and "year 6, III *peret* 15", cf. Reeves, Valley of the Kings, 234 (nos. 5 and 9); Kitchen TIP, 17, 417 (nos. 2 and 3); as regards an emendation of the month-name in the latter, cf. von Beckerath, Chronologie der XXI. Dynastie, 51; Demidoff, Retour sur une controverse, 103; contra Jansen-Winkeln, ZÄS 119, 1992, 26. See below for a discussion on the date preserved in the "Story of Wenamun".

[18] Cf. Wente, Was Paiankh Herihor's son?, in: *Drevny Vostok* 1, Moscow 1975, 36ff.; compare now Goldberg, GM 174, 2000, 49ff., fig. 3 (opting for Payankh as Herihor's son); Kitchen TIP, 535ff. (attributing to him the role of Herihor's son-in-law). As regards Payankh as Herihor's brother, cf. Taylor, The End of the New Kingdom, 1152f.

[19] Cf. Goldberg, loc.cit., 56. Unfortunately, the argument looses its apparent validity due to the questionable authenticity of the inscription; see below. Compare however a comment by Gnirs, Militär und Gesellschaft, 196, providing a possible explanation of the title in question.

20 Cf. Kees, Hohenpriester, 13-15; El-Sayed, BIFAO 78, 1978, 201 (Doc. 2).

[21] Cf. however, objections raised by Černý, CAH[3] II.2, 639; Kitchen (TIP, 18-20) concluded that both parts of the inscription were executed at the same time; as regards the "anachronistic" character of Payankh' s titles, suggesting that the inscription was executed later than the actual date of the oracle, cf. Nims, op.cit., 161; Young, JARCE 2, 1963, 112 n. 64; Hornung, Untersuchungen, 102 n. 5; id., OLZ 61, 1966, 439.

[22] In this role he was replaced by the second prophet of Amun Nesamun; for a comment, see Kees, Hohenpriester, 14; Bell, Serapis 6, 1980, 18ff.

[23] Cf. Kees, loc.cit.; Bell, Serapis 6, 1980, 19.

at the time of the oracle and soon afterwards.[24] In other words he admitted that Payankh "was not yet High Priest at the time of promulgation of the oracle in III *shemu* 28, but that he soon succeeded to that office, presumably upon the death of the aged Nesamun, before the execution of the memorial graffito".[25] According to L. Bell, Theban graffito no. 714 (dated to III *shemu* 23+x),[26] mentioning "the arrival of the General in (his) journeying north", can be related to these events.[27] The weak point of the hypothesis is the extremely short period of tenure of the High Priesthood by Herihor (only 6 years),[28] and consequently there is no place for his alleged "kingship". As a matter of fact, the period of his effective rule in the Thebaid gets even shorter if one acknowledge that it was representatives of the royal administration who played a dominant role at the very beginning of the Renaissance Era (during years 1-2 at least).

It may be suggested, however, that figure of the High Priest Payankh had been added slightly later to the already existing oracle text and representations accompanying it. The most vital consequence of such a conjecture would be an inevitable shift of the assumption of the pontificate by Payankh to a period slightly later than promulgation of the oracle, but not later than ca. year 10 of the Renaissance Era, when he was first titled as such (in LRL no. 28). At the same time, there are no grounds to postulate that Herihor was already deceased by the time of promulgation of the oracular decree, more precisely between year 6, III *peret* 15 (the latest attested date for Herihor), and year 7, III *shemu* 28 (the date of the oracle),[29] thus opening the way for his successor on the pontifical throne.[30] On the contrary, it may be suggested that Herihor's pontificate

[24] Bell, Serapis 6, 1980, 18ff.

[25] Ibid., 24. According to this hypothesis, Nesamun, a descendant of the high priest's family (as Amenhotep's younger brother), was appointed the high priest after the death of Herihor, and general Payankh was able then to introduce his own son Hekanefer to the office of the second prophet. The latter remained in office under the High Priest of Amun Payankh.

[26] Cf. Spiegelberg, Graffiti, 57, pl. 76; Kitchen, RamInscr VI, 849 (no. 3).

[27] As regards its dating to a later period (ca. year 10), which seems much more probable, cf. e.g. Peden, Graffiti, 191f. n. 372. PapPrakhov informs that in year 7, II *peret* 19, Payankh was in Middle Egypt; see below.

[28] Even if he had already attained the office before the Renaissance Era.

[29] These are the dates of the docket on the coffin of Ramesses II, and that of the oracle text respectively; cf. Kees, Hohenpriester, 14 (the latter date given wrongly). As regards the former date, cf. Maspero, Momies royales, 557, fig. 15.

[30] See A. Gardiner, Egypt of the Pharaohs, Oxford 1961, 305; cf. also Kitchen TIP, 18; Römer, Gottes-und Priesterherrschaft, 49f.

lasted significantly longer, probably till the very end of the Renaissance Era, then followed presumably by his assuming of the royal prerogatives.

It is worth noting that the most developed titulary of Payankh, as attested in LRL, is that written in the address of LRL no. 28: "fan-bearer on the King's right, royal scribe, general, high priest of Amun-Ra, [king of the gods, vice]-roy of Kush, overseer of the southern countries, overseer of the granaries of Pharaoh's granaries, and [leader] of Pharaoh's troops".[31] Here the omission of the title of "the mayor of the city and vizier" cannot be without significance and it can be inferred from this that he simply did not held this office at this stage. There can be no doubt that LRL no. 28 belongs to the "core group" of Nubian letters, thus dated to year 10 of the Renaissance Era.[32] It must be one of the latest sources relating to Payankh so it is rather ambiguous that the letter does not corroborate Payankh's vizierate. Taking into consideration that the title is absent also in the inscriptions on the statuette of Payankh (of unknown provenance),[33] and also on his votive stela from Abydos,[34] one cannot escape the impression that his tenure of the vizier's office is in fact quite illusory.

On the other hand, an address in a draft letter to Payankh, written on oCG 25745,[35] omits the most important among his titles – that of the high priest of Amun, while the title of the vizier is present in his titulature. It cannot be a mere coincidence that the most important of the titles attached elsewhere to Payankh has been omitted here. An attempt to explain this phenomenon by a mere fact that these documents reflects the chronology of the career of Payankh is rather unconvincing, because one could not explain satisfactorily how he would have "lost" the vizierate while attaining the status of the high priest of Amun (providing that he ever was the vizier before his assumption

---

31 Černý LRL, 44, 3-5. Quite possibly a similar set of titles was written at the beginning of papBM EA 75019+10302 ro. 1 (scanty ramains have been preserved), referring presumably to Payankh, cf. Demarée, Bankes Papyri, 14f., pl. 14.

32 Cf. Wente LRL, 12, 16. It is a pity that no titles of Payankh were given in the LRL no. 9, dated explicitly to year 10 (of the Renaissance Era), when he was campaigning in Nubia.

33 Cf. Hari, BSEG 7, 1982, 39ff.; compare however the arguments raised against the authenticity of the inscription (unfortunately no detailed photographs of the inscription are available): M. Dewachter, BSEG 11, 1987, 3-5 (the historical arguments are not persuasive after all); compare also Römer, Gottes- und Priesterherrschaft, 48; for the contrary view, see now Goldberg, GM, 174, 2000, 56; Gnirs, Militär und Gesellschaft, 196.

34 A. Mariette, Abydos. Description des fouilles exécutées sur l'emplacement de cette ville, II, Paris 1880, pl. 57 (b); El-Sayed, BIFAO 78, 1978, 197-199 (Doc. 1), pl. 66; R.J. Demarée, The *ꜣḫ iḳr n Rꜥ*–Stelae. On Ancestor Worship in Ancient Egypt, [Egyptologische Uitgaven 3], Leiden 1983, 39f. (A11).

35 Černý, Ostraca CG, 75f., 90*, pl. 92=Kitchen, RamInscr VI, 849; Daressy, ASAE 17, 1917, 29f.; as regards its provenience, cf. Reeves, Valley of the Kings, 306.

of the pontifical dignity).[36] More likely he never assumed the office of vizier, which in fact is attested only once in the sources pertaining to him (i.e. on oCG 25745).[37] In such a case oCG 25745 loses its validity for our understanding of the chronology of career of Payankh, being possibly only a draft letter comparable to the similar text written on oCG 25744 (containing the titulary of Herihor),[38] and it is open to question whether the text of oCG 25745 was ever written accurately.[39]

Much has been said about the ostraca mentioned above, and their relevance for the chronology of the period. Paleographical assessments vary from the opinion expressed by J. Černý pointing out to the similarity of the handwriting of both ostraca,[40] to that of A. Egberts, who attributed oCG 25745 (the draft letter to Payankh) to the scribe Tuthmosis, and oCG 25744 (the draft letter to Herihor) to his son Butehamun.[41] A. Egberts' conclusions do not support convincingly the thesis about the sequence of the high priests proposed by K. Jansen-Winkeln. A suggestion that the former of the two ostraca must be earlier in date cannot be substantiated anyway, having in mind that for some time Tuthmosis and his son were colleagues, working side by side in the matters of the necropolis. The titulature applied here to Payankh would rather suggest the period preceding his assumption of the pontifical dignity, whereas other titles borne by him are exactly the same as those attested in relation to Herihor in oCG 25744. At that time the throne of the high priest of Amun in Karnak could have been occupied by no other person than Herihor.[42]

It has been suggested that Payankh took over the titles previously held by Panehesy,[43] and this would certainly explain the absence of the two most

36 For a contrary view, see Häggman, Directing DeM, 214 (suggesting a reversed sequence of vizierate and high priesthood).

37 Cf. I. Pomorska, Les flabellifères à la droite du roi en Égypte ancienne, Warsaw 1987, 216f. (no. 137); El-Sayed, BIFAO 78, 1978, 213.

38 Černý, Ostraca CG, 75, 90*, pl. 92=Kitchen, RamInscr VI, 847f.; as regards its provenience, cf. Reeves, Valley of the Kings, 293.

39 Cf. Bell, Serapis 6, 1980, 25 n. 193. Compare also a comment on the ostraca in: Römer, Gottes- und Priesterherrschaft, 48f.

40 Černý, Community, 371. The name of the author of oCG 25744 was explicitly given in the text – it was the scribe Butehamun, placed as the first among the senders/authors.

41 Egberts, GM 160, 1997, 23ff.

42 The idea had been formulated already by E.F. Wente, see below; compare also Römer, Gottes- und Priesterherrschaft, 48f.; Gnirs, Militär und Gesellschaft, 211; a hypothesis unconvincingly challenged by Jansen-Winkeln, GM 157, 1997, 56.

43 See Jansen-Winkeln, ZÄS 119, 1992, 24, 31; id., GM 157, 1997, 50-54; Häggman, Directing DeM, 214.

prominent titles at the early stage of his career, which actually were never borne by Panehesy. On the other hand, on succeeding Herihor, Payankh must have adopted the latter's titles and functions, although this does not necessarily mean that all of them were given to him simultaneously. It was E.F. Wente who suggested first that Herihor as king could have relinquished to his successor Payankh all the titles except that of the high priest of Amun.[44] This seems to be supported by the fact that the priestly title of Herihor is included in his royal titulary. In such a case, however, he would have inherited the high priesthood only after Herihor's demise, although this does not explain all the problems with the chronology of the latter's career, therefore the contrary view cannot be arbitrarily dismissed either. In the light of the sources discussed above the beginning of the pontificate of Payankh may be securely shifted till the later years of the Renaissance Era, i.e. to the period between years 7 and 10, provided that the figure of the High Priest Payankh had been added later to the inscription commemorating the oracle decree of year 7 (more probably sooner than later).

As regards Paynakh's military rank documented in the contemporary sources, he was "the [leader] of Pharaoh's troops" in the text of the LRL no. 28, and "the leader who is at the head of all the troops of Egypt" on an ostracon (oCG 25745, 5-6). In addition, in both cases he was titled simply as the "general", but nowhere "general in chief/generalissimo", with the sole exception of papPrakhov (see below).[45] The military background of Payankh's power cannot escape our attention. In most of the letters of the family archive of scribe Tuthmosis, he was titled simply as the "the general" – most often in the formula of greetings found in the letters written to Tuthmosis by his colleagues and relatives, who used to wish "very many favours before the general, your lord".[46] It seems quite unusual that there is a complete omission of any titles of Payankh in LRL no. 13,[47] written by the stonemason Amenopenakht to the scribe Tuthmosis, and it is hardly possible that the

[44] Cf. Wente LRL, 3 n. 13; see also Bell, loc.cit.

[45] But not in papRifaud D, as suggested by Gnirs, op.cit., 200 n. 78; cf. Koenig, CRIPEL 10, 1988, pl. 5, 6=Kitchen, RamInscr VII, 399, 1; see also a comment by Jansen-Winkeln, GM 157, 1997, 50.

[46] Cf. e.g. Černý LRL, 14, 5-6; Demarée, Bankes Papyri, pl. 18, 3-4.

[47] Černý LRL, 26, 4: "Paynakh, your lord (*p3y.k nb*)". For the meaning of the term *nb* in the administrative context, see Häggman, op.cit., 127. The letter is dated approximately to year 10 of the Renaissance Era, and belongs to the core group of the Nubian letters, cf. Wente LRL, 17; see however reservations raised by the latter in regard to its dating and authorship (ibid., 14; and Černý, Community, 253). The stonemason Amenopenakht is attested in year 2 of the Renaissance Era (papTurin 2094ro. 3), cf. Kitchen, RamInscr VI, 866, 2-3; Gutgesell, Datierung, 153, 207.

person of the high priest of Amun himself could have been addressed in such an abrupt way.[48] More probably he had not yet attained the position of the high priest. Significantly the title of the high priest of Amun is omitted in most of the LRL, and predominance was given there to that of the general.[49] It looks as if the latter title had been preferred in the contemporary sources relating to Payankh, possibly because of his role of the commander in chief during the Nubian war against Panehesy. More interestingly even in the *post-mortem* sources ordered by his son Paynudjem I, he was titled not only as the high priest and generalissimo, but also simply as the general.[50] An apparent negligence in correct reference to the titles held by Paynakh may be explained only by his involvement in the military operations against the arch-enemy Panehesy.[51] On the other hand the omission of the title of the high priest of Amun cannot be interpreted as a mere coincidence or else a simple mistake, and the supposition that it reflects his real status at the moment a letter was written cannot be dismissed. In such a case LRL no. 28 can be definitely counted among those documents which are later in date, i.e. postdate his assumption of the pontifical office. The latter occurrence obviously had taken place not earlier than year 7 of the Renaissance Era (II *peret* 19), as documented by papPrakhov, where Payankh holds only the title of "the generalissimo" (*imy-r mšꜥ wr*),[52] and this is in apparent contradiction to the common view that he was already the high priest of Amun by that year, when the oracle for Nesamun had been given in the Karnak temple (III *shemu* 28).[53]

The relatively limited data concerning the genealogy of the high priests' family at the end of the 20th Dynasty creates another serious obstacle in our understanding of the history of the period, and the problem of succession of

---

48 Compare, however, the cases when Herihor's name was written without any titles in the Theban graffito no. 2977 (cf. Peden Graffiti, 218), and possibly also no. 3913b (ibid., 236).

49 Cf. Gardiner, JMEOS 2, 1912-13, 58f. According to Lull (Los sumos sacerdotes, 65) Payankh's subordinates quite naturally referred to him as to the general, thus omitting his priestly title.

50 Cf. Epigraphic Survey. Medinet Habu IV, [OIP 51], Chicago 1940, pl. 247f. (D-E, I-J); Römer, Gottes- und Priesterherrschaft, 553 (no. 21); see also Lull, Los sumos sacerdotes, 67f.

51 Cf. Bell, Serapis 6, 1980, 25, for the possibility that he may have exercised the office of the high priest "in absentia, through the agency of Hekanefer".

52 Cf. Berlev, GM 160, 1997, 5, 11 n. 6; unfortunately, this important document remains unpublished until now, and only extracts were used by Gasse, Domaine d'Amon I, 123-138, pls. 58-69 (transcription of vo. 8, and 11); the photographs in the work published by B.A. Turayev (Papyrus Prachov *sobranija B.A. Turayeva*, Leningrad 1927) are virtually illegible (!). As regards the title of Payankh, this is the sole reference to it in his entire dossier.

53 Of course, the sequence of dates cannot be established properly due to the unknown date of the beginning of the Renaissance Era.

the high priests in particular. One of the most discussed issues is the genealogical position of the women connected with the high priest's family. It has been recently suggested, contrary to older genealogical reconstructions,[54] that the existence of two ladies bearing the name Nodjmet (A and B) should be postulated in the light of the available material.[55]

In the representation on the Abydos stela from Leiden (V 65) Herihor is accompanied by "the lady, chief of the harem (*nb(.t) pr wr.t ḫnr.t*) of Amun-Ra, king of the gods, Nodjmet".[56] Her funerary papyrus from the royal cache in Deir el-Bahari[57] represents Nodjmet in company with her presumably already deceased husband as a king.[58] It is rather surprising that the title of the "king's wife" never appears among those attested in regards to her, except the inscriptions in the forecourt of the Khonsu temple.[59] Instead, her name is usually preceded by the title of "king's mother"[60] (var. "of the Lord of the Two Lands)", and by the title "the Lady of the Two Lands" (*nb.t tꜣ.wy*) placed directly before the cartouche with her name. In addition the titles of "the chief of the harem of Amun-Ra, king of the gods, and chief noblewoman" are attested on the funerary papyrus and on the coffins from the royal cache at Deir el-Bahari.[61] Strangely enough, a doubtful title, once read as *wbꜣ-nsw* "royal attendant" by A.W. Shorter, has been added to her titulature on papBM

[54] Cf. Kitchen TIP, 536; compare now genealogical reconstructions based on the reverse order of the high priests: Taylor, The End of the New Kingdom, 1145ff.; Broekman, GM 191, 2002, 14; both authors postulate that Nodjmet married Payankh and subsequently Herihor.

[55] Cf. e.g. Thijs, GM 163, 1998, 101ff. (Nodjmet A – mother of Herihor, and Nodjmet B – Herihor's wife, daughter of Payankh and Hrere); Goldberg, GM 174, 2000, 49ff. (with references to the earlier discussion on the subject).

[56] Cf. P. Boeser, Beschreibung der ägyptischen Sammlung des niederländischen Reichsmuseums der Altertümer in Leiden, VI, The Hague 1913, 13, pl. 28; Kitchen, RamInscr VI, 846f.

[57] Fragments now in Louvre (E 6258), British Museum (10541), and in the former "Mook" collection, now in Munich (ÄS 825), cf. Niwiński, Funerary Papyri, 337f., 362, 377 ("London 60"), pls. 8-10 (papLouvre E 6258); id., DE 20, 1991, 39; E. Naville, Das aegyptische Totenbuch der XVIII. bis XX. Dynastie. Einleitung, Berlin 1886, 108f. (Pq); I. Munro, Untersuchungen zu den Totenbuch-Papyri der 18. Dynastie. Kriterien ihrer Datierung, [Studies in Egyptology], London – New York 1988, 301 (no. 24); Jansen-Winkeln, InschrSp I, 32f.

[58] Cf. E. Naville, ZÄS 16, 1878, pl. 2; E.A. Wallis Budge, The Book of the Dead, II, London 1960 (2nd ed.), pl. 10; Lull, Los sumos sacerdotes, fig. 18. Interestingly enough in the British Museum portion he was also represented and titled as the high priest of Amun (but with an uraeus on the brow!), cf. Niwiński, Funerary Papyri, pl. 10b.

[59] Cf. Kitchen TIP, 41 n. 168.

[60] Written inside a cartouche or without it.

[61] As regards her titles in papBM 10541 cf. A.W. Shorter, Catalogue of Egyptian Religious Papyri in the British Museum. Copies of the Book *pr(t)-m-hrw* from the XVIIIth to the XXIInd Dynasty, I: Description of Papyri with Text, London 1938, 14f.; for the fragment in the Louvre: Naville, ZÄS 16, 1878, 29f. For the coffins, see Daressy, Cercueils, 40ff., pls. 25-27 (CG 61024).

10541.[62] Anyway, the special status of Nodjmet was indicated not only by her titles but also by the fact that she was buried with two funerary papyri (hieroglyphic and hieratic copies). One of them (i.e. the hieratic copy) included scenes adopted from the Books of the Underworld.[63] Thus it would seem that the custom of providing two funerary papyri during the IIIrd Intermediate Period was probably started at such an early date,[64] and there is no real reason to suppose that the two papyri belonged to two different persons, both titled the mother of the king.

The Lady of the House, Chief of the Harem of Amun (*nb.t pr wr.t* [*ḫnr.t*] *n Imn*) Nodjmet is shown in the Luxor graffito, where she was represented besides the High Priest Paynudjem I and his brothers (and the obliterated figure of Payankh).[65] This can possibly be identified with Herihor's wife as well ("Nodjmet A" according to J. Goldberg).[66] Her position, just behind the figure of Amun, represents her as the object of veneration on the part of the living members of the high priest's family (thus J. Goldberg), or else a vivid manifestation of her priestly function in the clergy of Amun, being at the same time one of the most important titles for her veneration (either *post-mortem* or still during her lifetime).[67] It is hardly likely that she was a representative of a younger generation, a contemporary of Paynudjem I (as his sister, and daughter

[62] Cf. Shorter, op.cit., 14f.; see, however, reservations expressed by Kitchen TIP, 42 n. 179 (who suggested the reading: *ḥm.t-nsw*); and severe criticism in: Jansen-Winkeln, InschrSp I, 32. Notwithstanding the paleographical problems with the reading of the title, it is worth noting that it would refer accurately to the extraordinary role played by Nodjmet in the Theban administration, as revealed by the LRL.

[63] PapBM 10490: E.A. Wallis Budge, Book of the Dead. Facsimiles of the Papyri of Hunefer, Anhai, Kerasher and Netchemet, with supplementary text from the papyrus of Nu, London 1899, pls. 1-10; cf. Niwiński, Funerary Papyri, 209ff., 337, pls. 49a-c; S.G.J. Quirke, Owners of Funerary Papyri in the British Museum, [British Museum Occasional Paper 92], London 1993, 18.

[64] A. Niwiński's suggestion that papBM 10490 could have been connected with her supposed reburial, and thus later in date than her original burial (see below), cannot be evaluated properly. The utterly exceptional character of papBM 10490 in regards of its style and contents raise the question of its workmanship as relevant for the history of Nodjmet's career, and possibly the date of her funeral. At the same time one can imagine that her "earlier" funerary papyrus had been prepared still during the pontificate/kingship of Herihor, and the latter's figures (in two iconographic conventions) appearing in the vignettes seem to confirm this.

[65] G. Daressy, RT 14, 1893, 32f. (LIII); Gauthier LR III, 245 (IX); Römer, Gottes- und Priesterherrschaft, 53 (La), 550f. (no. 18); Jansen-Winkeln, InschrSp I, 17 (no. 22b); id., DE 38, 1997, 29f.

[66] Goldberg, GM 174, 2000, 55. It is noteworthy that unlike three of the men represented in the scene only Nodjmet's name, and that of Paynudjem I, are not followed by an epithet *mꜣꜥ-ḫrw*. Anyway, a lack of any refences to her as the wife of Herihor is a little bit astonishing. It must be noticed, however, that the title of the "great chief of the harem of Amun" in the period of the 21st Dyn. belonged *ex officio* to the wife or daughter of the high priest of Amun, cf. Kitchen TIP, 430f.; Niwiński, DE 14, 1989, 80f.; Naguib, Le clergé féminin, 203; Broekman, GM 191, 2002, 13f.

[67] As regards the second possibility, cf. Peden, Graffiti, 273 n. 39.

of Payankh; i.e. "Nodjmet B" according to J. Goldberg).[68] In fact, nothing else is known about the latter, and it is hardly likely that she would be an owner of the second (later in date?) of the two funerary papyri hitherto ascribed to Nodjmet, Herihor's wife – i.e. papBM 10490.[69]

The titulature given by the above cited documents leave no doubt that Nodjmet, owner of the funerary papyri, was indeed Herihor's wife and mother of an unnamed king.[70] If her funeral had taken place at the beginning of the pontificate of Paynudjem I or rather his kingship,[71] it would simply mean that she outlived her husband for at least several years. In other words, if she was really venerated as a living member of the family (?) in the Luxor graffito, then her funeral should be possibly dated to the beginning of the "kingship" of Paynudjem I, under whom she was probably buried (see below, Chapter 8).

An unnamed female intermediary who passed a message from general Payankh to the scribe Tuthmosis, as recorded in LRL no. 28,[72] must be

---

[68] Cf. Goldberg, GM 174, 2000, 49ff., figs. 2-3. It cannot be excluded, however, that "Nodjmet B" was one and the same person as Nedjemmut, daughter of Paynudjem I, mentioned only once in another graffito from the Luxor temple, cf. Daressy, RT 14, 1893, 32 (LII); Römer, Gottes- und Priesterherrschaft, 53 (Lb), 551f. (no. 19); Jansen-Winkeln, InschrSp I, 17 (no. 22a); for an epigraphic commentary, cf. Niwiński, JARCE 16, 1979, 52. On the other hand, the existence of a younger Nodjmet (daughter of Payankh and Hrere, and sister of Paynudjem I) may be postulated on the grounds of the Luxor graffito, but her identity with Herihor's wife (cf. Niwiński, loc.cit., 52ff.), and consequently her ownership of the coffins from the royal cache or any of the two funeral papyri is definitely out of the question.

[69] The most important objection against such an attribution of papBM 10490 is the problem with identification of the royal relatives of a hypothetical "Nodjmet B", cf. Kitchen TIP, 44; Goldberg, GM 174, 2000, 50 n. 6, fig. 2. This is because in the opening vignette of the papyrus she was titled: "the Lady of the Two Lands (Nodjmet)| justified, daughter of the king's mother Hrere", and "king's mother who bore the Strong Bull, the Lady of the Two Lands (Nodjmet)| justified, born of Hrere, justified before the great Ennead". As regards her unique title *ms.t k3 nḫt*, see Rößler-Köhler, GM 167, 1998, 8; Naguib, Le clergé féminin, 137-9. It must be noted that the apparent advantage of the hypothesis proposed by J. Goldberg (i.e. identification of his "Nodjmet B" with the owner of papBM 10490) would be a convenient explanation of the supposed late dating of the papyrus in question ("probably middle 21st Dyn.", according to Niwiński, Funerary Papyri, 337). On the other hand, the high status attained by her owner (the title *nb(.t) t3.wy*, and the name written in the cartouche) seems to deny such a possibility.

[70] The king in question was probably Amenemnisu Neferkheres, cf. Niwiński, JARCE 16, 1979, 53f.; id., BES 6, 1985, 81f. As regards the position of Amenemnisu within the dynasty, cf. von Beckerath, Chronologie, 48 (12), 62f.; Jansen-Winkeln, in: Ancient Egyptian Chronology, 218f. The hypothesis according to which it was Smendes who was the son of Herihor and Nodjmet (cf. Wente, JNES 26, 1967, 174f.; Kitchen TIP, 538ff.: "Scheme B"), causes too much trouble in interpreting the pertinent sources, cf. Kitchen, loc.cit.

[71] According to Niwiński (Funerary Papyri, 209ff., 337) she was buried in the early years of Psusennes I and subsequently reburied during the pontificate of Paynudjem II, thus ca. 50 years after her death. As regards the date of Nodjmet's demise, compare also Niwiński, 21st Dynasty Coffins, 43; id., JARCE 16, 1979, 52f.; Taylor, The End of the New Kingdom, 1148; E. Loring, in: E. Graefe, G. Belova (eds.), The Royal Cache TT 320 – a re-examination, Cairo 2010, 61.

[72] Černý LRL, 46, 8ff.; cf. Wente, Letters, 195; Sweeney, Correspondence and Dialogue, 66f.

Nodjmet herself or possibly Hrere? Anyway, her identity is hidden there under a conventional sobriquet *t3y.n ḥnw.t* "our mistress".[73] Undoubtedly she was a person well acquainted with the plans of general Payankh, and it would be difficult to explain such an extraordinary confidence, he displayed in her, if she was not his closest relative.[74]

LRL nos. 38 and possibly also 39 show Hrere explicitly involved in the administrative matters of the necropolis, and this makes her another candidate for the role played by an anonymous woman in LRL no. 28.[75] According to LRL no. 30 she was in the position of intermediary who had been obliged to hand over five servants to the captains of the necropolis staff (see below, Chapter 4). We are also informed (LRL no. 2) that she had accompanied Payankh during his stay in Elephantine while he was campaigning in Nubia (see below, Chapter 7). It was argued that if she was able to accompany the general in such a distant and dangerous country, she was possibly his wife ("Hrere B") and not an elder member of his family (i.e. "Hrere A", mother of Nodjmet).[76] Unfortunately the badly preserved name (*Ḥ*[...]) of Paynudjem's I mother in the Luxor graffito,[77] cannot solve positively the question of identity of Payankh's wife,[78] although such a spelling of the name Hereret may be accepted perhaps in the light of diversity of writings of the related word *ḥrr.t* "flower".[79]

On the other hand, the close relations between Payankh and Nodjmet are best documented in a group of letters concerning the affair of two Madjoy discussed later in this book (LRL nos. 21, 34 and 35). It would be difficult to avoid the conclusion that Payankh had every confidence in her.[80] Significantly, Payankh adressed the letter to Nodjmet (LRL no. 35) titled as the "chief of the

---

73 Cf. Černý LRL, 46, 8, 9 and 11-12.

74 This is well in accord with the prominent role played by the women of the high-priests' family during the 21st Dyn., possibly an element of specific Libyan cultural background, as pointed out by Jansen-Winkeln, BN 71, 1994, 92f.

75 See a comment by Sweeney, Idiolects, 290 n. 163; compare, however, id., Correspondence and Dialogue, 67 n. 157, where she pointed rather vaguely to Nodjmet.

76 Thus Kitchen TIP, 45; cf. also Bierbrier, JNES 32, 1973, 311. As a consequence a distinction was made between Hrere A (Nodjmet's mother), and Hrere B (wife of Payankh).

77 G. Daressy, RT 32, 1910, 185f.; Gauthier LR III, 246 (X); Römer, Gottes- und Priesterherrschaft, 53 (Lc), 552 (no. 20); Jansen-Winkeln, InschrSp I, 18 (no. 23); for an epigraphic comment, see Wente, JNES 26, 1967, 160 n. 44; Taylor, The End of the New Kingdom, 1149f. (with a doubtful reading of the sign as *nḏm* – Gardiner, Sign-list M29).

78 As regards the two surmised marriages of Payankh (to Hrere and Nodjmet), cf. Rößler-Köhler, GM 167, 1998, 7f.; see also Goldberg, GM 174, 2000, 58, fig. 3 (to Hrere and an unnamed descendant of the Ramesside dynasty).

79 Cf. Wb III, 149; Ranke PN I, 254 (4).

80 Cf. Sweeney, Idiolects, 302.

harem (*wr.t ḫnr.t*) of Amun-Ra, king of the gods",[81] and not as the queen.[82] The letters of this group give an insight into the mechanisms of power in those times, but at the same time these documents provide a precious testimony of the state of affairs in Thebes during the Nubian war of general Payankh. Nodjmet appears here to be the most influential person at Thebes during the absence of the general campaigning in Nubia, and it has been suggested that she was the widow of Herihor at the moment when the letters had been written.[83]

Unfortunately, research into relative dating of these two groups of letters – those connected with Hrere on the one hand, and those mentioning Nodjmet on the other, does not provide any convenient criterion for establishing an overall chronology of the LRL, and the pontificate of Herihor and Payankh in particular. A genealogical investigation of the high priest's family must also take into consideration the second funerary papyrus belonging to Nodjmet (papBM 10490), where the name of her mother was given as the "king's mother Hrere" (no cartouche).[84] The identity of this Hrere as a different person than Payankh' s wife is highly doubtful, as there are no other sources relating to her, and her role as the "king's mother" is not otherwise attested.[85] Accordingly an "economical" genealogical scheme emerges with only one Hrere – the mother of Nodjmet and wife of Payankh, and only one Nodjmet – the wife of Herihor, and consequently the sister of Paynudjem I,[86] whose royal status would explain the title of his presumed mother Hrere. It does not affect directly the inversed chronological scheme of their respective priesthoods, even if it moves Payankh and his wife to the older generation than that represented by Herihor and Nodjmet. One can imagine indeed the subordinate role of Payankh in relation to his presumed son-in-law, during the latter's pontificate. At the same time it would explain an apparently short period of tenure of the pontifical office by Payankh, being possibly the result of late assumption of the office when he was relatively aged.

81 Černý LRL, 54, 5, and 16. Elsewhere in the corpus of the LRL without any title, cf. ibid., 78 (no. 90).

82 For the comment, see Kitchen TIP, 21 n. 92.

83 Cf. Janssen, JEA 73, 1987, 166. Another possible explanation would be the temporary absence of Herihor in Thebes, providing that he was still living at the time (?).

84 Cf. Budge, Facsimiles of the Papyri of Hunefer, Anhai, Kerasher ... (etc.), London 1899, pls. 1, 5; Niwiński, Funerary Papyri, pl. 49a; cf. Jansen-Winkeln, InschrSp I, 32 (d).

85 For the assumption that she was king's mother-in-law in relation to Herihor, or else the latter's mother, see Kitchen TIP, 44; Wente, JNES 26, 1967, 173f.

86 Thus well in accord with the hypothesis presented by Niwiński, JARCE 16, 1979, 52, 62 n. 21; similarly Thijs, GM 163, 1998, 106 (tab. 4) – with "Nodjmet A" as mother of Herihor; and despite objections raised by Kitchen TIP, 536.

As virtually nothing can be said about later stages of his career, its prolongation to the post-Renaissance Era period remains purely hypothetical,[87] and Paynudjem's I succession directly after Herihor cannot be rejected after all (this would be in accord with K. Jansen-Winkeln's hypothesis).[88]

One more question needs elucidation in regard of the role played by Payankh in the period of the LRL, still during the Renaissance Era: this is the legitimacy of his superior position in relation to the institution of the Theban necropolis, as revealed clearly by the extant LRL. First of all, it was hardly the office of the vizier, attested only once in relation to him. Accordingly it was the authority invested in him as the high priest of Amun which had placed him on the top of the administrative system in the Thebaid. Unfortunately, none of the assertions presented above can be helpful in precise dating of the period of tenure of the office of high priest by Payankh.

A sharp divergence between the information provided by the administrative documents, and the scheme of decoration of the Khonsu temple in Karnak cannot be overlooked in the discussion on the subject. The information provided by the temple reliefs leaves no doubt that Herihor's career should in fact be divided into two different periods. The decoration of the hypostyle hall and that of the court of the temple, present two different images – that of the high priest on the one hand and that of the "king" on the other. The period of Herihor's "kingship" must in fact have been preceded by a period when he played the role of high priest and general still at the side of Ramesses XI as a legitimate ruler of Egypt. If the evidence of the papyri dating to this period does not conform convincingly to such a picture, it must be explained as the result of the specific character of Herihor's kingship (and possibly also the short period of his independent rule). It is well known that Herihor was never represented as a king in the papyri and ostraca originating from Thebes, and it is only in the Karnak precinct that he appears in the role of the reigning pharaoh.[89] The same is also true, however, in regard of Ramesses XI, the reigning pharaoh whose sovereignty over the Thebaid was recognised at least

[87] There are no dated documents relating to Payankh, which postdate the Renaissance Era.

[88] For this see also Römer, Gottes- und Priesterherrschaft, 49; and quite recently Kitchen, in: Libyan Period in Egypt, 200 (§100): an alternative version of the chronology of the period. As regards the possibility of the parallel activity of Herihor and Payankh, cf. Gnirs, Militär und Gesellschaft, 211.

[89] See Kitchen TIP, 20f. His royal status was emphasised also in the funerary context, as revealed by some of the objects of the funerary equipment of his wife Nodjmet.

officially in the early years of the Renaissance Era, when he was supervising the robbery trials not only through the agency of his officials.[90]

Nothing is known about the very beginning of the career of Herihor. We can only guess that he was one of the military men in the service of the king, and the military titles mentioned above could be possibly related to this early period of his career, when presumably he was participating in the military campaign directed against Panehesy. One can only speculate that, as a descendant of a Libyan family, he had come from the north (i.e. from Lower or Middle Egypt).[91] It could be also argued that he was introduced into the office of the high priest of Amun soon after the defeat of Panehesy, although no details regarding his priestly promotion are known. The earliest dated documents referring to him may be placed not until year 6 of the Renaissance Era (these are the oldest dockets on the coffins of Seti I and Ramesses II).[92] The aforementioned statue from the Karnak cachette seems to be one of the earliest monuments of Herihor, and the inscription incised on the papyrus unrolled on his knees seems to specify his position at a relatively early stage of his career as the high priest of Amun. One of the phrases points possibly to the temporary unification of Egypt and pacification of the country: *sḥtp t3.wy n nb.f Ỉmn* "he who pacifies the two lands for his lord Amun".[93] We can only guess whether it is an allusion to the unification (and pacification) of the country after expulsion of Panehesy or whether the phrase must be viewed simply in the frame of the new ideology of the Renaissance Era – in such a

[90] Cf. McDowell, Jurisdiction, 243.

[91] There are only the names of Herihor's sons which could be taken as an argument in regard of the ethnic origin of the family; for this see a comment by von Beckerath, RdE 20, 1968, 32f.; Kitchen, TIP, 540f.; Naguib, Le clergé féminin, 140f.; Jansen-Winkeln, BN 71, 1994, 79, 84. For the controversial view, that it was Nodjmet, who was a descendant of a Libyan family, see Ch. Booth, The Role of Foreigners in Ancient Egypt. A study of non-stereotypical artistic representations, [BAR IS 1426], Oxford 2005, 40. Middle Egypt has been pointed out as a possible place of origin of Herihor and his family, cf. Kees, Hohenpriester, 9. Similarly, there are no grounds to suggest any ties of Herihor with the ruling family, cf. Peet, JEA 14, 1928, 52; even less can be said in regard of a postulated royal descent of Nodjmet, what seems to be mere speculation.

[92] Against referring them to the reign of Smendes, cf. von Beckerath, Chronologie der XXI. Dynastie, 51. For the contrary view, see now Demidoff, Retour sur une controverse, 100, 102f., 111.

[93] Cf. supra, note 1. See also Römer, Gottes- und Priesterherrschaft, 38, 41; Lull, Los sumos sacerdotes, 68 n. 441. A similar epithet (*sḥtp t3.wy*) was also held by Ramesses XI (cf. von Beckerath, Königsnamen, 175; Kitchen, ASAE 71, 1987, 139f.), and Paynudjem I (cf. Römer, op.cit., 60; Jansen-Winkeln, InschrSp I, 20, 21). Paynudjem I attributed also the title to his (then deceased) father Payankh, cf. Epigraphic Survey. Medinet Habu IV, [OIP 51], Chicago 1940, pl. 247 (E). It is worth noting here that an older version of the Horus and *nebti* name of Amenemhat I was *sḥtp ib t3.wy*, cf. von Beckerath, Königsnamen, 82f. (later on: *wḥm-msw.t*); for other parallels, see also N. Grimal, A History of Ancient Egypt, Oxford – Malden 1999, 80; Römer, op.cit., 77.

case it could be taken as a purely stereotypical phrase lacking any real political significance.

Soon after Panehesy's retreat from the Thebaid, the victorious general assumed all of the titles which he had held, including that of the Viceroy of Kush.[94] At the same time his formal dependence on the king was not refuted completely, so a number of his honorific titles still refer to pharaoh.[95] It is true that this particular group of titles could be explained only in the light of traditional formulation of the honorific titles of court or state officials. More probably, however, they reflect the real status of Herihor at the very moment of reinstating the pharaoh's sovereignty over the Thebaid. The status of Herihor, as reflected by those titles, can be compared to the role played once by Horemheb before his accession to the throne.[96] Indeed we have to note the extraordinary position attained by Herihor already before his assumption of the royal paraphernalia, no doubt due to the revolutionary changes which put an end to the old order guaranteed once by the Ramesside rulers, and the role played now by the military establishment.

Significantly nowhere in the hypostyle hall of the Khonsu temple is the title of vizier included among the titulature of Herihor.[97] This may reflect his real status at the time of the decoration of this part of the temple,[98] soon after the expulsion of Panehesy, whose titles were simply taken over by Herihor in addition to the military and priestly titles which he had previously held. Quite possibly it was a period of restitution of the royal authority over the Thebaid, in the aftermath of the civil war. No doubt the assumption of the high-priesthood by Herihor was the turning point in the course of these events. The oracular decree of Herihor, inscribed near the entrance to the

---

[94] K. Zibelius-Chen, SAK 16, 1989, 334; K. Jansen-Winkeln's argument (GM 157, 1997, 50-2), that the combination of titles borne by Payankh makes him the better candidate to be placed as a direct successor of Panehesy, does not take into consideration that the titles of Panehesy and Herihor are similar to the same extent. As a matter of fact only one of the titles of Panehesy appears only in relation to Payankh and not to Herihor – *ḥ3wty n* (*n3*) *pḏ.wt pr-ꜥ3*; that of *imy-r šnw.ty n pr-ꜥ3*, shared both by Panehesy and Payankh, appears in Herihor's titulature as well (not necessarily devoid of an extension *n pr-ꜥ3*; cf. below, note 95).

[95] Contra Jansen-Winkeln, GM 157, 1997, 53; cf. Bonhême, Livre des rois I, Docs. 21 H.182, 183, 185, 191 (with references to *nb t3.wy*, *nṯr-nfr*, and *nsw*). It is true that the sole possible exception in regard to the administrative titles, is provided as it seems by oCG 25744 (l.3): *imy-r šnw.ty n šnw.ty* [*n pr-ꜥ3*]; compare the restoration proposed by Kitchen, RamInscr VI, 847, 11f. (based on the parallel formulation of oCG 25745); for a comment, see also Gnirs, Militär und Gesellschaft, 200 (2).

[96] Cf. Kees, Herihor, 2; Römer, Gottes- und Priesterherrschaft, 40ff. (§38); id., ZÄS 131, 2004,78.

[97] Cf. Stučevsky, Ramses II and Herihor, 123, 143.

[98] Cf. Römer, Gottes- und Priesterherrschaft, 7, 9.

hypostyle hall of the Khonsu temple,[99] may be related to this very moment of his career when he first appeared as the high priest of Amun.[100] Such an early dating of the promulgation of the decree seems to be supported by the titles borne by Herihor – besides that of the high priest of Amun, these are: the King's Son of Kush, and Overseer of the Granaries. The royal cartouche of Ramesses XI (nomen) has been partly preserved at the beginning of the text, thus excluding the possibility that the text commemorates an assumption of kingship by Herihor himself. Unfortunately, a reference to "20 years" which Amun-Ra granted (ll. 11, 15) cannot be interpreted properly,[101] mostly due to the fragmentary state of preservation of the stela. It is open to question whether the decree had any direct connection with an introduction of the new era.[102]

It seems that a temporary strengthening of the central administration in Upper Egypt was achieved and this was marked by the reappearance of the high ranking officials of the civil government at Thebes. It seems as if the civil administration of the Thebaid remained mostly in the hands of royal representatives, the most influential among them was the vizier Nebmarenakht II (there can be no certainty, however, whether he was officially the vizier of the South). The robbery papyri dating to the first two years of the Renaissance Era show him as presiding (on behalf of pharaoh) over the court sessions, just like his predecessor(s) in the times of Ramesses IX. The vizier's concern with the matters of the west bank of Thebes, and the necropolis in particular, does not surprise us. His involvement in the case of the robberies committed in the temple of Amun at Karnak however is puzzling. The role of the vizier may, however, be inferred clearly from papRochester MAG 51.346.1, which is: "Copy of the document of the thefts (*mitt n sš n nꜣ ṯꜣ.wt*) which the chief doorkeeper Djehutyhotep, of the temple of Amun, committed in the great forecourt (*pꜣ wbꜣ ꜥꜣ*)[103] of Amun-Ra, king of the gods; what was delivered

[99] The Temple of Khonsu 2, 14-17, pl. 132; Kitchen, RamInscr VI, 709f.; Peden, Historical Inscriptions, 181-186.

[100] Cf. Kitchen TIP, 250 n. 33; von Beckerath, Tanis und Theben, 95f.; see however Römer, op.cit., 8. There are no grounds whatsoever to relate it to Herihor's "usurpation" (as suggested by E. Meyer, Gottesstaat, Militärherrschaft und Ständewesen in Ägypten, [SPAW], Berlin 1928, 495f.), cf. Sethe, ZÄS 66, 1931, 6 n. 2; Kees, Herihor, 12.

[101] See, however, Černý, BIFAO 30, 1931, 492; von Beckerath, Tanis und Theben, 95 n. 520. Even less can be said about the enigmatic "30 years" also mentioned in the text (l. 10), cf. Bell, Serapis, 6, 1980, 18 n. 131; Niwiński, Bürgerkrieg, 238f.; id., BIFAO 95, 1995, 350; Römer, op.cit., 8 n. 21.

[102] See Černý, CAH[3] II.2, 641; Peden, op.cit., 181; Niwiński, BIFAO 95, 1995, 340; cf. however Römer, op.cit., 6f.

[103] No doubt this refers to the open (at that time) courtyard before the second pylon in Karnak, cf. P. Spencer, The Egyptian Temple, A Lexicographical Study, London 1984, 4ff.; C. Wallet-Lebrun, GM 85,

to him after it was reported to the vizier by the mayor of the City (Ne)" (A, 2-4).[104] Such an exceptional role of the vizier in the matters concerning the temple of Amun may be explained only by a mere fact that the main culprit (i.e. Djehutyhotep) was seriously implicated also in the robberies on the west bank of Thebes (probably in the memorial temples belonging to the domain of the temple of Amun),[105] and as such he appears among other thieves in both lists of the papAbbott-dockets (vo. A, 5 and B, 17),[106] and in the list of papMayer A (list B4: 12, 26).[107] The unnamed vizier, mentioned in the text, may be identified with Nebmarenakht (II), of whom we know that he presided over the court proceedings documented in papBM 10052, papMayer A, and papBM 10383, dated to years 1 and 2 of the Renaissance Era. According to the papAbbott-dockets it was vizier Nebmarenakht (II) who received the copy of the documents, i.e the list of the thieves of the necropolis (*mỉtt sš n nꜣ ỉṯꜣ n pꜣ ḫr*),[108] from the mayor of the West of the City Paweraa.[109]

The balance of power between the high priest of Amun on the one hand, and the representatives of the civil administration on the other (besides the vizier, these were the Overseer of the Granaries of Upper and Lower Egypt, the Overseer of the Treasury, and Chief Taxing Master),[110] must have had a vital significance for the effectiveness of the new policy inaugurated by the Renaissance Era, introduced in year 19 of Ramesses XI. The lack of any references to the high priest of Amun in the acts of the robbery trials of the beginning of the Renaissance Era seems to suggest that the position of Herihor at the beginning of his pontificate was not so strong as suggested earlier. Thebes and Upper Egypt were at least nominally under royal administration, with

1985, 67ff.; as regards other possibilities, cf. Goelet, JEA 82, 1996, 120.

[104] The publication of the papyrus by Goelet, JEA 82, 1996, 107-127, pls. 9-10, must be augmented now by some corrections made by Fischer-Elfert, GM 165, 1998, 107f., and a new reading of the papyrus proposed by Quack, SAK 28, 2000, 219-232.

[105] As regards the role of Djehutyhotep in the wider context of the robberies, cf. Goelet, op.cit., 121f.

[106] Peet, Tomb Robberies, 132f., pls. 23-24=Kitchen, RamInscr VI, 764, 8; 766, 14.

[107] Peet, Mayer Papyri, pl. 12, 26=Kitchen, RamInscr VI, 826, 9.

[108] Peet, Tomb Robberies, pl. 23 (A, 19-20)=Kitchen, RamInscr VI, 765, 6-7.

[109] Cf. Peet, Tomb Robberies, 130. Consequently the unnamed mayor mentioned in papRochester MAG 51.346.1 may be safely identified with Paweraa, although he was titled here simply as the Mayor of the City; cf. Goelet, op.cit., 113 (e). Otherwise Quack, op.cit, 230 n. 15, who suggested that it was Mayor of the City Paser; it must be noted, however, that Paser does not appear in the sources after year 16 of Ramesses IX, cf. Peet, JEA 14, 1928, 70; Helck, Verwaltung, 428f., 531; apparently he was in disgrace soon after the open conflict with Paweraa had broken out, as described vividly in papAbbott, cf. Vernus, Affaires et scandales, 21ff.

[110] As regards the structure of the administrative system during the New Kingdom, cf. D. O'Connor, in: Trigger et al., A Social History, 208 (fig. 3.4).

the vizier at the head. The apparently predominant role of the vizier would grow even stronger, when the office of the vizier and that of the high priest were united in the hands of Herihor himself.[111] And it is to this particular period (not later than year 6, and after year 2)[112] that the statue of Herihor from the Karnak cachette (see above) may now be ascribed. Represented in the secular garb of the scribe and vizier, with a pectoral hanging on his breast, and a papyrus roll on his knees, Herihor is represented like those of his predecessors who united the office of the high priest of Amun and that of the vizier in their hands.[113] It is not without significance that according to the text written on the papyrus unrolled on his knees, it was Amun himself who granted the statue besides the other privileges retained by Herihor, without any mention of the reigning pharaoh![114] The early stage of the doctrine of the so-called "Gottesstaat des Amun"[115] finds perhaps its best exemplification in this interesting document, which mark out the new policy of the high priest of Amun. From that moment onwards, the political position of Herihor had been strengthened significantly enough to the effect that the way to assuming the "kingship" was wide open. His governorship wielded on behalf of Amun is expressed in a rather fanciful expression, relating it seems to his (newly acquired?) vizierate: *ỉry-pꜥ.t ḥr(y)-tp-tꜣ.wy smr ꜥꜣ m tꜣ* (*r*) *ḏr.f ṯꜣty wp-mꜣꜥ.t* "the hereditary prince, having authority over (i.e. the chief)[116] the Two Lands,

[111] Herihor seems to have acquired the title of vizier after Nebmarenakht (II), cf. Kitchen TIP, 248. The earliest reference to the office held by him is the docket on the coffin of Seti I (CG 61019), dated to year 6 (of the Renaissance Era), cf. Maspero, Momies royales, 553, pl. 10B; Daressy, Cercueils, 30, pl. 18; cf. Kitchen TIP, 417 (no. 2); Reeves, Valley of the Kings, 234 (no. 5); Helck OPG, 572. As regards an earlier (and false) interpretation of the docket, relating it to the vizier Nebmarenakht, cf. Peet, JEA 14, 1928, 65 n. 4; Kees, Herihor, 15; von Beckerath, Tanis und Theben, 92.

[112] If an unnamed vizier and high priest of Amun of papTurin 1903 ro. 7 (Kitchen, RamInscr VII, 397, 3) are one and the same person, then he could be identified perhaps as Herihor; cf. Römer, Gottes- und Priesterherrschaft, 7, 10 n. 31. The entry should be dated to year 5 of the Renaissance Era (the date given in vo. 2, 6-7); it is noteworthy that only the vizier was mentioned in vo. 2, 3, dated to year 4 of Renaissance Era. The titles are treated separately by Janssen, Commodity Prices, 456f.; Häggman, Directing DeM, 277.

[113] Cf. a comment by Stučevsky, Ramses II and Herihor, 143.

[114] Cf. ibid., 144f.

[115] As regards the term, it was used first by E. Meyer, Gottesstaat, Militärherrschaft und Ständwesen in Ägypten, [SPAW 28], Berlin 1928, 495ff.

[116] For the title in question, used as a divine epithet, but also as a title attributed to the king, king's son, or the vizier to whom the royal priviledge had been ceded (thus according to L.-A. Christophe, see below), cf. Römer, Gottes- und Priesterherrschaft, 38, 40f., 62, 74; Christophe, ASAE 51, 1951, 339f.; Jansen Winkeln, DE 38, 1997, 33f. The most interesting parallel is provided by the coronation inscription of Horemheb, where it precedes the royal cartouche: Urk IV, 2117, 9; cf. Gardiner, JEA 39, 1953, 15, 19 (ii), pl. 2 (l. 15); W.J. Murnane, Texts from the Amarna Period in Egypt, [WAW 5], Atlanta 1995, 232. It also appears in the Luxor graffito of Paynudjem I, cf. Jansen-Winkeln, InschrSp I, 17 (no. 22a);

great *semer* in the entire country, the vizier who justly judges" (inscription on the base).[117]

It is worth noting in this context that the status of Herihor as reflected in the decoration of the hypostyle hall of the Khonsu temple does not fit the role traditionally ascribed to the high priests of Amun. The scenes representing Herihor were intermingled with those representing the king in his traditional roles widely documented in the iconography of Egyptian temples. Strangely enough Herihor was always represented in the scenes reserved solely for the monarch,[118] although his accompanying titles never acknowledge that. In this part of the temple he was usually titled as the high priest and general. Herihor's name and figure are absent only in the uppermost parts of the hypostyle hall – i.e. on the ceiling, on the architraves and on abaci of the columns, where the names of Ramesses XI are unchallenged.[119] It is on the architraves of the hypostyle hall that one can also find original dedication inscriptions in the name of the reigning king – Ramesses XI.[120] In addition, a dedication inscription was ordered by the High Priest Herihor himself.[121] It was written in two versions in both halves of the hypostyle hall (starting near the door in its northern wall), directly below the lower register of scenes decorating its walls. That in the western half of the hall totally omits the name of Ramesses XI, and gives the name of the hall: "Assuming the diadems (*wṯs ḫʿw*)".[122] The inscription in the eastern half was written apparently on behalf of Ramesses XI: "The High Priest of Amun-Re, king of the gods, the generalissimo of

Gardiner, JEA 48, 1962, 68. For other parallels of the 19th Dyn., cf. also Wb II Belegst., 615f.; Helck, Verwaltung, 452f., 458, 472.

117 Kitchen, RamInscr VI, 844, 1; Bonhême, Livre des rois I, 127 (Doc. 21 H.253b); cf. also Stučevsky, op.cit., 144. Partial parallels are also available in the inscriptions from the hypostyle hall of the Khonsu temple, cf. Bonhême, op.cit., 115 (Doc. 21 H.222); Römer, op.cit., 38. As regards *wp-mȝʿ.t* it refers usually to the vizier or to the king, cf. Wb I, 299 (10-11); Römer, op.cit., 62, 77.

118 Cf. Römer, op.cit., 11ff., 22ff., for a detailed comment.

119 Cf. The Temple of Khonsu 2, pls. 202-205. It cannot be decisively stated that these parts of the hypostyle hall were already decorated before the civil war, thus in the early years of Ramesses XI. Anyway it seems highly probable that the decoration of the hypostyle hall was started well in accord with traditional iconographic patterns, but soon afterwards the new iconographic elements were introduced.

120 The Temple of Khonsu 2, 69f., pl. 202.

121 Or three, if that written in the eastern part of the hall is divided into two parallel texts – one relating to the high priest, another to the king, cf. Römer, op.cit., 28f., 34.

122 The Temple of Khonsu 2, 64, pl. 196. The priestly and military titles of Herihor definitely exclude the possiblity that the name of the hall reflects the assumption of the kingship by him. As regards the meaning of the expression, cf. P. Barguet, Le temple d'Amon-Rê à Karnak, Cairo 1962, 316ff. (esp. p. 318); Otto, Topographie, 31f.; J.-Cl. Dégardin, in: Atti di Sesto Congresso Internazionale di Egittologia, II, Turin 1993, 96; Römer, op.cit., 4f.

Upper and Lower Egypt, the army-leader Herihor, justified. He has made as his monument for Khonsu-in-Thebes Neferhotep, (...) [being that which] a son [does] who is beneficial to his [father Khonsu] who fashioned him (*ms sw*): (namely) the Lord of the Two Lands, Menmaatre-Setepenptah, the Lord of Diadems, Ramesses (XI), given life".[123] It seems that the thoroughly atypical character of the inscription reveals a delicate equilibrium in regard of the authority wielded both by the king and his formal representative at Thebes – the high priest of Amun,[124] and must be related to the period of the rule of the high priest at Thebes under tutelary, albeit purely formal, authority of the pharaoh. It looks as if the king had delegated some of the royal prerogatives to the "heir" to the throne or regent still during his lifetime, but without the latter attaining the royal paraphernalia. There is another dedication formula, unusual in its form, written in the hypostyle hall on the lintel above the gate leading from the court: "Done under (*ẖr-ʿ*) his Majesty's instructions".[125] What a difference in comparison to a dedication inscription of Herihor in the court of the Khonsu temple, where his royal prerogatives were fully displayed in the traditional phraseology of the kingship![126]

In the 19th year of the reign of Ramesses XI the "Renaissance Era" or more precisely the "Repeating of Births" (*wḥm-msw.t*) was inaugurated. According to the traditional view it was the High Priest Herihor who initiated a new era in opposition to the reigning king.[127] An alternative view, that it was made on behalf of the king,[128] must be evaluated now in more detail. It is noteworthy that the throne name (prenomen) of Ramesses XI is the same as that of Seti I, so parallels with other elements of the royal protocol of the latter may be rightly sought for.[129] As we know the initiation of the earlier "Renaissance Era" (as a political entity) can be attributed to Seti I,[130] who might be viewed indeed

[123] The Temple of Khonsu 2, 63f., pl. 195; with partial restorations proposed by the editors. Cf. also Römer, op.cit., 28ff.

[124] As regards Herihor as a mere representative of the king in the South, cf. Kitchen TIP, 541; id., in: Libyan Period in Egypt, 193.

[125] The Temple of Khonsu 2, 37, pl. 153 (A); cf. Wb III, 387 (2); Belegst., 112.

[126] Cf. The Temple of Khonsu 2, 23ff., pls. 139-140.

[127] Cf. Kees, Herihor, 18f.; Niwiński, Bürgerkrieg, 238; id., BIFAO 95, 1995, 340; compare also Römer, op.cit., 30-34, where he objects to the idea of the open political conflict between two protagonists at the moment of proclamation of the new era.

[128] Cf. von Beckerath, Tanis und Theben, 91; Lull, Los sumos sacerdotes, 55f., 59f. Compare Helck, Verwaltung, 396 ("Durch einen Besuch des Königs wurde sie gebilligt.").

[129] Cf. e.g. Römer, op.cit., 31; Demidoff, GM 177, 2000, 97f.; Lull, Los sumos sacerdotes, 55.

[130] Cf. Gundlach, in: LÄ VI (1986), 1263 (D). As regards the meaning of the so called "Era of Menophres", as referred to by Theon of Alexandria, see W. Struve, ZÄS 63, 1928, 45-50 (the name related to

as a precursor of the policy of restoration of the collapsed order in the country in the aftermath of the Amarna period. On the other hand, there are no visible references in the titulature of Ramesses XI himself which emphasize his own role in the inauguration of the new era.[131] There are, for example, no changes discernible in the royal protocol which could be related to this particular event. The same can be said in regard to the iconographic scheme adopted to represent him in the decoration of the Khonsu temple. Herihor however clearly appears as quite an exceptional personage in the decoration of the hypostyle hall of the Khonsu temple (not to mention his distinctly royal image prevalent in the court). Even more important is the presence of the notion *wḥm-msw.t* in Herihor's dedication inscription in the western half of the hall, as demonstrated recently by M. Römer.[132] No doubt the actions undertaken by Herihor to protect the desecrated royal mummies and restore the Theban temples (and possibly also cult statues) were pious acts, which were the direct consequence of the idea of "Repeating of Births" (*wḥm-msw.t*).

In addition, a new dating system was started. This was independent from the older one relating to the regnal years of Ramesses XI, and this was achieved by introducing the new era – *wḥm-msw.t*, as it was labelled in the contemporaneous sources. The dates from the papAbbott-dockets demonstrate it explicitly: "Year 1, first month of *akhet*, day 2, corresponding to (*ḫft*) regnal year 19" (vo. A, 1),[133] and similarly in the unpublished papTurin 2034.[134] All these cases present the new era as distinctly parallel to the regnal years of Ramesses XI, but not necessarily relating to the king.[135]

the epithet of Seti I's nomen – Merenptah); K. Sethe, ZÄS 66, 1931, 1-7; J. Černý, JEA 47, 1961, 150-152 (related to the prenomen of Ramesses I); von Beckerath, Tanis und Theben, 105-7 (related to Memphis and not to the king's name); id., ZDMG 126, 1976, 5-9; id., Chronologie, 13f.

[131] Cf. Gundlach, in: LÄ VI (1986), 1263.

[132] Römer, op.cit., 32ff.; thus reflecting, according to him, the restoration of the temple of Khonsu after the vicissitudes of the civil war; compare also Dégardin, loc.cit.

[133] And similarly vo. A, 19; cf. Peet, Tomb Robberies, pl. 23=Kitchen, RamInscr VI, 764, 3; 765, 6; see also Černý, JEA 15, 1929, 194; Černý-Groll, Late Egyptian Grammar, 103 (Ex. 354).

[134] Cf.Kitchen, RamInscr VI, 865, 4 (A1).

[135] The dating scheme of the oracle of year 7 (see above) cannot be interpreted unambiguously in this context: "Year 7 (of) the Repeating of Births ... under (*ḫr*) the majesty of the king of Upper and Lower Egypt Menmaatre-Setepenptah"; see however von Beckerath, Chronologie, 89 n. 543; Demidoff, GM 177, 2000, 98f. (in the framework of his extremely doubtful "alternative" chronology of the period). Anyway the meaning of the formula is not so clear as an expression used in the text dated to the reign of Seti I (oCG 25704): "Year 2 (of) the Repeating of Births (of) the king of Upper and Lower Egypt Menmaatre", cf. Černý, JEA 15, 1929, 196f.; as regards its date, see now S. Wimmer, in: C.J. Eyre (ed.), Proceedings of the Seventh International Congress of Egyptologists, [OLA 82], Leuven 1998, 1230f.

The competitive character of the new datation system cannot escape our attention, because two independent systems of counting years are simply incomprehensible. It is hardly likely that a parallel system of datation could have been accepted in the frame of the traditional ideology of the royal authority in ancient Egypt. A new dating practice can be viewed instead as a direct reference to a new regime, the one represented by the High Priest of Amun Herihor, formally acting on behalf of the reigning king whose sovereignty had not been seriously challenged in those times. One way or another, soon after its introduction the new system completely dominated the scheme of dating documents in the Thebaid.

The earliest of the documents dated to the new era are the acts concerning the trials of the robbers who had ransacked the temples and tombs on the west bank of Thebes in the period of the civil war. It might be a mere chance that this was the first step to re-establish order in the southern province. It is possible, however, that the trials were in fact only part of a more ambitious programme of reform of the internal affairs and restitution of order in the region. No doubt the new regime acted formally under the auspices of the pharaoh, and it was his representatives – namely the royal butlers (*wbꜣ-nsw/wdpw*),[136] who were incorporated into the tribunals appointed to judge the thieves.[137] Even if the royal patronage cannot be entirely denied, possibly Herihor was the real initiator of instigating the trials.

A. Niwiński is certainly right in underlying the great significance of religious motives lying behind inauguration of the new era.[138] This becomes clearly visible if one compares it with two earlier periods of transition following the periods of turmoil and disaster – one at the beginning of the 12th Dynasty, and subsequently at the beginning of the 19th Dynasty. Consequently it seems highly probable that a central figure of the new movement was Amun himself, being the virtual head of the new "theocratic" Theban state, and "the lord of the Two Lands" (*pꜣ nb n nꜣ tꜣ.wy*).[139]

[136] For the meaning of the term, cf. Gardiner AEO I, 43*f. (no. 122); Helck, Verwaltung, 269; Lesko, Dict.I, 96; as regards the reading see A.R. Schulman, JARCE 13, 1976, 127 n. 11; id., CdE 61, 1986, 192 (l); F. Colin, BIFAO 98, 1998, 94-97.

[137] Concerning their participation in the proceedings, cf. Helck, Verwaltung, 276, 343; B. Schmitz, in: LÄ VI (1986), 772.

[138] Niwiński, BSFE 136, 1996, 5-26; cf. also Römer, op.cit., 31ff.

[139] Wenamun 1, 15: Gardiner LES, 62, 7-8; cf. Green, ZÄS 106, 1979, 119; Römer, op.cit., 80ff.; Winand, GM 200, 2004, 110 (Ex. 13); compare however, H. Goedicke, The Report of Wenamun, Baltimore 1975, 31f., 84f.; Schipper, Wenamun, 175.

The exact date of the introduction of the new era has not been explicitly given in the extant sources, and the problem is much debated until now. Two possibilities have been pointed out, depending on the interpretation of the actual character of the Renaissance Era: those emphasizing the pharaoh' s initiative in its introduction postulate the date as the anniversary of his accession, while A. Niwiński assumed the beginning of the civil year (i.e. I *akhet* 1).[140] Anyway, the sequence of dates provided by papMayer A informs us that within the Renaissance Era a change of date took place within the broad span of time between IV *shemu* 17 (papMayer A ro. 3, 6) and [IV] *shemu* 15 (vo. 8, 1).[141] The same document definitely excludes, however, placing its beginning at I *akhet* 1, because after the entry dated to year 2, [IV] *shemu* 15 (vo. 8, 1), follows a date relating to year 2, I *akhet* 13 (vo. 11, 1). At the same time there are no decisive arguments against a supposition that within the Renaissance Era the yearly change of date fell upon the day of accession of Ramesses XI,[142] or else that it marks that of the assumption of power (the high priesthood) by Herihor.[143]

Even if the proclamation of the Renaissance Era aimed at restoration of the social order and political stability, the situation of the country did not change suddenly. Herihor holding his Theban governorship firmly was unable to maintain the political unity of Egypt. On the contrary, a political split became sharply outlined at the very moment of his assumption of pontifical office. As a consequence the way was wide open to create a pontifical state of Amun. From this moment onwards, the high pontiffs of Amun started to play the role of a real sovereign or governor over the Thebaid, even if sometimes they recognised an authority of Ramesses XI and subsequently that of his successors – the Tanite pharaohs of the 21st Dynasty. Thus the idea of an independent dating of their "pontifical" or even "regnal" years seems to be an

[140] Niwiński, Bürgerkrieg, 239; id., BIFAO 95, 1995, 340.

[141] Peet, Mayer Papyri, pls. 3, 8=Kitchen, RamInscr VI, 808, 15; 817, 8; the latter date written above the line. As regards the sequence of dates relating to the robbery trials, and an extension of the entire time span, cf. Ohlhafer, GM 135, 1993, 59ff. (see esp. 71); von Beckerath, Chronologie, 90f.; without the necessity of emending the latter date, as suggested by Helck, Thronbesteigungsdaten, 129. If one can take it at face value, then the period in question may be slightly restricted: between II *akhet* 24 (papAbbott-dockets, vo. A, 19) and [IV] *shemu* 15; cf. Lull, Los sumos sacerdotes, 57.

[142] Cf. Ohlhafer, GM 135, 1993, 72; von Beckerath, Tanis und Theben, 91; id., Chronologie, 89 n. 546; see also the discussion by Lull, op.cit., 57, 59.

[143] See Kees, Hohenpriester, 7f.; Hornung, Untersuchungen, 100; Helck, Verwaltung, 396; Cannuyer, GM 132, 1993, 20; Niwiński, BIFAO 95, 1995, 340f. Compare also Fecht, ZÄS 87, 1962, 26ff. concerning the position of Herihor in the context of the political action undertaken by the king with the aim to restore the undermined authority of the Ramesside dynasty; for Herihor as supervisor of the new movement and the king as its instigator, cf. Vandersleyen, L'Égypte II, 643.

unavoidable result of the political independence of the high priests of Amun. This in fact appears to be the sole explanation possible of the proclamation of the Renaissance Era, as reflecting the assumption of power by the High Priest Herihor (later represented as the king).

Smendes in the north was possibly in a much better position, having appropriated all the prerogatives of the representative of the declining royal dynasty.[144] Although no military titles were applied to him in the preserved sources, it seems possible that he was one of those military men responsible for a successful result of the offensive operations undertaken against the rebel Panehesy. Nonetheless the role of Smendes during the Renaissance Era cannot be followed in more detail. Supposedly, the subsequent relations between Herihor and his successors on the one hand, and Smendes on the other were in principle friendly. The undated stela of king Smendes from Dababieh (near Gebelein)[145] seems to be a unique attestation of such a state of relations (if not Smendes' sovereignty over Thebes at a slightly later period; see below Chapter 8), although it clearly refers to a later period. At the same time, the spheres of their respective rule were precisely defined, as the border between the two was marked somewhere in the vicinity of Teudjoy (*Tꜣy.w-ḏꜣy*; now el-Hibeh) in Middle Egypt.[146] According to one opinion the significance of the region can be traced back to the period of the Libyan wars of the New Kingdom pharaohs.[147] Quite probably Teudjoy became an important strategic point on the eve of the 21st Dynasty as a result of the split between Theban state of the high priests of Amun and the Northern state of Smendes.[148]

[144] For discussion of the supposition that he married Tentnamun, a descendant of the Ramesside dynasty (daughter of Ramesses XI), see Kitchen TIP, 537ff.; cf. however Niwiński, JARCE 16, 1979, 50f.; id., BIFAO 95, 1995, 343 (wife of Ramesses XI, daughter of certain Nebseny).

[145] Daressy, RT 10, 1888, 133-138; Jansen-Winkeln, InschrSp I, 1-3 (1.3).

[146] On the history of the place, see G.A. Wainwright, ASAE 27, 1927, 76-104; E. Graefe, s.v. El Hibe, in: LÄ II (1977), 1180f.; for the history of archaeological investigation on the site, cf. Redmount, in: Z.A. Hawass, J. Richards (eds.), The Archaeology and Art of Ancient Egypt. Essays in Honor of David B. O'Connor, [CASAE 36], Cairo 2007, II, 303-311.

[147] Cf. Wainwright, ASAE 27, 1927, 84ff.

[148] From this moment on the fortress in el-Hibeh was functioning as the headquarters of the "great army commanders" and sometimes a residence of the high priests themselves, cf. D. O'Connor, in: Trigger et al., A Social History, 235; von Beckerath, BiOr 49, 1992, 704; Jansen-Winkeln, BN 71, 1994, 82; id., Or 70, 2001, 156f., 170. For an opinion that the fortress or centre could have been established already before Paynudjem I, cf. Jansen-Winkeln, BN 71, 1994, 82 n. 17; Kitchen TIP, 248 n. 32, 541 (the hypothesis is based, however, on false presumptions regarding the dating of the papyrus with the Story of Wenamun; noteworthy Teudjoy does not appear in the story itself); Gasse, Domaine d'Amon I, 173 n. 2; Naguib, Le clergé féminin, 140f. (a reference to "Horus-of-the-Camp" in the temple of Khonsu!); Lull, Los sumos sacerdotes, 61f.; see also Lefèvre, BSFE 165, 2006, 34ff.

The only document which attests the contemporary activity of both protagonists is provided by the "Story of Wenamun" (papMoscow 120), a literary composition of the period.[149] Herihor appeared here in the role of the high priest of Amun,[150] and the direct superior (*nb*)[151] of "the elder of the portal" Wenamun, while Smendes and Tentamun were only the administrators (lit. foundations of the land) (*snṯ-t3/snntyw-t3*) of the Amun's domain in Lower Egypt.[152] A possible relationship of the literary text to a hypothetical official report made by Herihor's envoy to foreign countries is still a matter of discussion,[153] but this does not diminish at all the historical value of the source in question.[154] Strangely enough the text does not even mention Ramesses XI,[155] although it cannot be seriously doubted that he was still living at that time, i.e. in year 5 of the Renaissance Era.[156] An attempt to shift this year 5 to the period after the death of Ramesses XI, and accordingly to relate it to the

---

[149] For a general comment on the question, see Scheepers, in: Amosiadès. Mélanges offerts au Prof. C. Vandersleyen, Leuven 1992, 355ff. (with the earlier literature); Baines, in: Literatur und Politik im pharaonischen und ptolemäischen Ägypten, 209ff. The affected language of Tjeker-Baal has been aptly described by Satzinger, LingAeg 5, 1997, 171ff.; for a critical view, cf. however Egberts, GM 172, 1999, 17ff.

[150] Wenamun 1, 52; 2, 61; in both instances without giving Herihor's name.

[151] Wenamun 1, 15; 2, 26; cf. Bonhême, Livre des rois I, 134f. (Doc. 21 H.321).

[152] Wenamun 2, 35: Gardiner LES, 70, 9-11. For the meaning of the term, see J. Yoyotte, AEPHE 91, 1982-1983, 204; Naguib, Le clergé féminin, 139f. (with further references); J. Winand, Le voyage d'Ounamon, Liège 1987, 20; D.B. Redford, Egypt, Canaan, and Israel in Ancient Times, Cairo 1995 (2nd ed.), 285 n. 8; Römer, Gottes- und Priesterherrschaft, 75; Schipper, Wenamun, 199f.

[153] Cf. J. Černý, Paper and Books in Ancient Egypt, London 1952, 22 ("it is almost certainly the original report").

[154] See now de Spens, in: Le commerce en Égypte ancienne, 105ff.; Schipper, Wenamun, 111ff. As regards the relatively late date of the literary composition (beginning of the 22nd Dynasty and the reign of Sheshonq I in particular), see Helck, in: LÄ VI (1986), 1216; Sass, Ägypten und Levante 12, 2002, 247ff.; Schipper, Wenamun, 308ff.; see, however, objections raised by Fischer-Elfert, WdO 36, 2006, 224.

[155] It is hardly likely that the Khaemwese mentioned twice in the text (2, 51 and 53) may be identified with Ramesses IX or XI, as suggested e.g. by von Beckerath, Tanis und Theben, 99f.; Schipper, Wenamun, 207f. The name in question is written without a cartouche and no distinct determinative has been attached to it either, which cannot be explained by mere reduction of the role of pharaoh, as suggested by von Beckerath (loc.cit.) and Schipper (op.cit., 209, 308). In 2, 53-4 he was explicitly referred to as a normal mortal (*ḫr rmṯ ḥ˓.t.f*). More probably he was the vizier of that name, attested in the sources of the reign of Ramesses IX and X; compare also the unconvincing thesis formulated by H. Goedicke, The Report of Wenamun, Baltimore 1975, 106f. (identifying him with the famous son of Ramesses II).

[156] For the chronological problems posed by the text, cf. Egberts, JEA 77, 1991, 57ff. (places the events narrated in the story during the Renaissance Era); and his corrected view in: ZÄS 125, 1998, 93ff. (the story reflects the situation of Egypt in the early years of the 21st Dynasty, and independent reign of Herihor in particular).

independent reign of king Herihor or Smendes,[157] is contradicted by the lack of a mention of the royal status of both protagonists as presented in the story.

At the same time the text provides an argument in favour of the thesis about the purely fictitious character of the royal sovereignty in Egypt at that very moment. This is the ironic remark of prince's of Byblos steward which sheds some light on an intricate context of the political situation in the Levant and that of Egyptian envoy in particular: "The shadow of Pharaoh, l.p.h., your Lord, falls upon you".[158] Similarly in the words of Tjeker-Baal, the prince of Byblos, the pharaoh appears to be just a shadowy figure deprived of effective power and a strong political position in the region, traditionally in the Egyptian sphere of influence: "As for the ruler (*pꜣ ḥkꜣ*) of Egypt, is he the lord of what is mine, and I his servant as well? (If so) would he not have had sent silver and gold in order to say «Carry out the commission of Amun!»? ...".[159] As a matter of fact Herihor and Smendes came to power as the representatives of the king in both parts of the country, and both wielded the royal prerogatives some time before the full appropriation of the royal trappings.[160] The situation aptly depicted in the "Story of Wenamun" reveals the weakened role then played by the pharaoh. By that time, the latter's influence vanished to such an extent that political ambitions of both prominent dignitaries in Tanis and Thebes led them to take the political initiative. And it is to this very period that we can relate perhaps the process of the consolidation of Herihor's power in Thebes. The most prominent sign of the new situation was his

[157] As regards referring it to the regnal years of Smendes or Herihor, cf. von Beckerath, Tanis und Theben, 99f.; Jansen-Winkeln, ZÄS 119, 1992, 25f.; see also Schipper, Wenamun, 165 (compare however, p. 329). It must be noted, however, that an attempt to relate it to the independent reign of Herihor by Jansen-Winkeln is a direct result of an arbitrary reversal of the order of the high priests Herihor and Payankh; cf. a critical comment by Goldberg, GM 174, 2000, 52. The obscure figure of the king Khakheperre Paynudjem (different from Paynudjem son of Payankh), being a hypothetical predecessor of Herihor, whose existence has been postulated by Thijs (ZÄS 132, 2005, 73ff.; ZÄS 134, 2007, 50ff.; SAK 38, 2009, 345, fig. 2), must be classified as a pure historical fiction.

[158] Wenamun, 2, 46: Gardiner LES, 71, 12f.; for the comments on its meaning, see Černý, CAH^3 II.2, 643; Meltzer, JSSEA 17, 1987, 86ff.; Jackson, JNES 54, 1995, 273ff.

[159] Wenamun, 2, 10ff.: Gardiner LES, 68, 3ff.; I follow the solution proposed by Neveu, Grammaire, 227 (Ex. 54); similarly E.F. Wente, in: W.K. Simpson (ed.), The Literature of Ancient Egypt, Cairo 2005, 120; compare however Nims, JEA 54, 1968, 162; Barns, JEA 58, 1972, 164; Černý-Groll, Late Egyptian Grammar, 566 (Ex. 1625); Frandsen, Verbal System, 164f. (Ex. 4), 179 (Ex. 25); Satzinger, Neuägyptische Studien, 56, 68; the passage is commented upon by Eyre, in: Literatur und Politik im pharaonischen und ptolemäischen Ägypten, 235ff.; Schipper, Wenamun, 193f., 266ff. According to another interpretation, Tjeker-Baal did not deny the formal, at least, sovereignty of the pharaoh, cf. Winand, GM 139, 1994, 95ff.; see also Goedicke, op.cit., 76ff.; Morschauser, SAK 18, 1991, 319, 327 n. 20.

[160] The concept of a triumvirate describes the political situation at that very moment very well, cf. Naguib, Le clergé féminin, 99-101, 139.

seizure of the office of vizier, and this was achieved by him in the following year at the latest. An attempt to shift the dating of the pontificate of Herihor and his subsequent kingship to the post Renaissance Era period does not fit the contemporary evidence – the decoration of the hypostyle hall of the Khonsu temple in particular. All the chronological problems relating to the "Story of Wenamun" disappear, however, if the events described are referred to the Renaissance Era. Thus the mention of the hewing out of "the bark of cedar of Lebanon" in the inscriptions of the court of the Khonsu temple,[161] quite naturally must be transferred to the period of Herihor's kingship, at least several years after the events described in the story, relating to the import of lumber for its workmanship.[162] A direct consequence of such an assumption would be the redating of Herihor's demise, which should be placed at a period significantly later than that suggested hitherto. Similarly his subsequent role as the Theban "king" should be placed in the later years of the Renaissance Era at the earliest, if not after the death of Ramesses XI (thus in accordance with K. Jansen-Winkeln's hypothesis).

In such a case, however, the role played by general Payankh and the chronological position of his pontificate must be evaluated in more detail. First of all, none of his military or priestly titles decisively excludes the supposition that he could have acted as contemporary of Herihor. On the contrary, his administrative activity documented in year 7 of the Renaissance Era (papPrakhov and the Karnak oracle) can be conveniently placed at the height of Herihor's pontificate, still attested in year 6. In those times, Payankh's position was determined by his military rank and abilities which had led to his personal engagement in the Nubian war against Panehesy. There are no documents to date precisely his promotion to the office of the high priest of Amun. As mentioned above, the earliest well dated reference to his priestly titles can be found in LRL no. 28 of year 10 of the Renaissance Era. It is possible of course that he was promoted to the office soon after the Karnak oracle of year 7 was given, thus in the relatively short period between the promulgation of the oracle and an execution of the commemorating inscription. In such a case, however, we should rather assume that it was the very moment when Herihor laid his claims to the kingship, thus opening the way to Payankh's pontificate. On the other hand, the inclusion of the priestly title in Herihor's royal titulary

[161] The Temple of Khonsu 1, 8, pl. 21; 2, 30, pl. 143 (C.2).

[162] Then the period needed to execute the bark need not be restricted to the short timespan of one or two years, as suggested earlier, cf. below.

would rather suggest that he did not relinquish his priestly prerogatives to Payankh at the very moment of his assumption of the trappings of kingship.[163] If so, Payankh's pontifical investiture must be placed after Herihor's demise. Quite probably it took place at the very end of the Renaissance Era, in year 10 or earlier. According to the alternative scenario, Herihor could have outlived Ramesses XI, and then his assumption of "kingship", as a "legitimate" successor, would be possible not until the latter's death.

The duration of Herihor's kingship is undetermined and the problem cannot be solved properly in relation to such a chronological scheme, as there are no dates referring explicitly to Herihor's own rule, contrary to the opinion maintained by K. Jansen-Winkeln (who redated some documents of the Renaissance Era to the later period). That Payankh's tenure of the office of the high priest lasted for only a very short period cannot be seriously doubted, as there is so little evidence relating to it. At present it cannot be decisively determined whether it was entirely comprised within the period of Herihor's kingship, or else it was possible only after the latter's demise. For the time being, the most plausible solution of the problem of the succession of the high priests Herihor and Payankh lies in the presumptive ephemeral character of the pontificate of Payankh. In such a case, however, the apparent absence of mentions of Herihor in the sources relating directly to Payankh must be taken into consideration. An advantage of the hypothesis presented here is it provides a coherent explanation of the chronology of the decoration of the temple of Khonsu, but also of the exceptional character of the pontificate of Payankh, remaining apparently in the shadow of the "king" Herihor.

The reported surprisingly disrespectful attitude of Tjeker-Baal, the prince of Byblos, towards the Egyptian envoy to Syria can be explained only in the wider context of the international relations of the period. The threat posed by Assyria, being a reaction to the Aramaean invasions, was widely felt in the Near East. The military campaign of Tiglath-Pileser I (1115-1077 B.C.) brought the Assyrians to the Syrian coast already in the reign of Ramesses IX.[164] Later on the king of Egypt – Ramesses XI at the very end of his reign,[165] or more probably one of his immediate successors (Smendes or even

[163] K. Jansen-Winkeln (in: Ancient Egyptian Chronology, 223 n. 33) rightly observes that "a HP's and a king's office do not exclude each other in dynasty XXI."

[164] Cf. Redford, op.cit., 296f. n. 65.

[165] See Kitchen TIP, 252; Niwiński, Bürgerkrieg, 260; J.M. Galán, Four Journeys in Ancient Egyptian Literature, [LingAeg, Studia monographica 5], Göttingen 2005, 141.

Psusennes I)[166] – sent diplomatic gifts to Assurbelkala (1073-1056 B.C.), king of Assyria: "The king of Egypt sent a large female monkey, a crocodile, (and) a "river-man", beasts of the Great Sea".[167]

In one of the letters of general Payankh sent to the scribe Tuthmosis we can find a sole reference relating perhaps to the late years of the reign of Ramesses XI: "As for Pharaoh, l.p.h., how could he reach this country (*pꜣy tꜣ*)? But Pharaoh, l.p.h., whose master (is he) after all?" (LRL nr 21).[168] The letter cannot be dated precisely but it is evident from its contents that it was written during the Nubian campaign of Payankh, so at the very end of the reign of Ramesses XI.[169] It cannot be excluded of course, that the passage in question refers only to the weakened control of the Pharaoh over Nubia.[170] More probably, however, it can be interpreted in the framework of the legality of the oppressive actions undertaken against two Madjoy policeman – the affair referred to in LRL nos. 21, 34, 35.[171] In such a case, the passage in question cannot be simply taken as a firm evidence of the complete extinction of the Pharaoh's formal sovereignty over Upper Egypt and the Nubian province. Even more, the Pharaoh's rights to the throne were not questioned in any way. On the other hand, the independent position of the high priest of Amun might be traced back to the period of Herihor's pontificate, and more precisely to the later years of the Renaissance Era, when he accumulated in his hands the most important offices, including that of the vizier. It is noticeable that Ramesses' XI activity in Theban temples is limited exclusively to the Khonsu temple (even here jointly with the high priest), whereas the cartouches of Herihor appear also in his restoration inscriptions in the southern part of the Great Hypostyle Hall at Karnak (on the column bases and on the east wall).[172]

---

[166] Cf. Redford, loc.cit.

[167] The text from the so-called "Broken Obelisk", found at Niniveh, cited after A.K. Grayson, Assyrian Rulers of the Early First Millennium BC, I: 1114-859 BC, Toronto 1991, 103f. It seems that the supposed dating of the text to year 5 or 6 of Assurbelkala (or even later), cf. ibid., 99, would allow it to be placed in the reign of Smendes.

[168] Černý LRL, 36, 11-12; cf. also Gardiner, JMEOS 2, 1912-13, 61f.; Černý-Groll, Late Egyptian Grammar, 139 (Ex. 478), 557 (Ex. 1596); Groll, Non-Verbal Sentence Patterns, 14 (Ex. 43); Junge, Neuägyptisch, 179; Sweeney, Correspondence and Dialogue, 106 (Exx. 3-4); id., Idiolects, 302.

[169] It is hardly probable that these words could be referred to the "king" Herihor. No doubt the letter was written before the latter's assumption of kingship, and this is one more reason to move Herihor's kingship to the end of the Renaissance Era at the earliest.

[170] See K. Zibelius-Chen, SAK 16, 1989, 332; cf. also Häggman, Directing DeM, 213.

[171] McDowell, Jurisdiction, 242.

[172] Kitchen, RamInscr VI, 730 (no. 11); cf. Roth, JNES 42, 1983, 43-45, figs. 1, 2, 5. The renewal text on the sphinx before the tenth pylon was written in the name of Herihor as the high priest, cf. Kitchen,

The very end of the rather illusory reign of Ramesses XI, as it appears to be in the light of the Theban sources of this period, is completely veiled behind the scattered remains of the former glory of the Ramesside dynasty. Well in accord with the tradition of the New Kingdom royalty he started the building of his tomb in the Valley of the Kings in his early years, but it was never completed. There are no data whatsoever confirming his final burial in Thebes – his mummy has never been found and nothing is known about his mortuary cult in Thebes either.[173] This is certainly in agreement with what we know about the diminishing role of the Pharaoh. It cannot be overlooked that the events which can now be connected with the later years of the Renaissance Era unequivocally indicate the weakness of the Pharaoh's position in Thebes and abroad, reflected both by the ruthless comments of Tjeker-Baal in year 5, and finally by the famous passus from the letter of general Payankh (LRL no. 21). It is worth noting that the latest dated Theban document mentioning the titulature of Ramesses XI falls in year 7 of the Renaissance Era, when the oracle for Nesamun son of Ashakhet was given.

The latest date referring to his reign has been preserved on a votive stela of a certain Hori, found in Abydos.[174] If its reading is right (regnal year 27, IV *shemu*, day 8),[175] then we can draw the conclusion that Ramesses XI had been living at least 9 years after the introduction of the Renaissance Era, and perhaps at least one more year should be added to this number (i.e. year 10, I *shemu* 25, explicitly documented by LRL no. 9).[176] It is worth noting that his reign was formally recognised in Upper Egypt until its very end. Significantly, the date written on the Abydos stela does not give any reference to the Renaissance Era, and this forms the basis for an assumption that the system of datation according to the Renaissance Era was generally given up at that time.[177] Unverifiable, as it is, the hypothesis can be put forward that the Renaissance Era had actually already ended before the demise of the king.[178]

RamInscr VI, 847 (no. 5); similarly in other partly preserved inscriptions from Karnak: Jansen-Winkeln, InschrSp I, 4 (1-2).

[173] Cf. R. Stadelmann, MDAIK 27, 1971, 119; Schneider, in: Jenni H. (ed.), Das Grab Ramses' X. (KV 18), Basel 2000, 104ff.; see also Haring, Divine Households, 425.

[174] A. Mariette, Abydos. Description des fouilles exécutées sur l'emplacement de cette ville, II, Paris 1880, pl. 62; id., Catalogue, 442f. (no. 1173); Gauthier LR III, 221 (VI); Kitchen, RamInscr VI, 701 (no. 2).

[175] Cf. von Beckerath, Chronologie, 91.

[176] Černý LRL, 17, 11; cf. Kitchen TIP, 22f.

[177] See the comment by Gundlach, in: LÄ VI (1986), 1264 n. 27.

[178] As there are no explicit reasons for such a return to the dating according to the regnal years,

As a consequence of such an assumption the prolongation of the length of the Renaissance Era, as postulated sometimes (up to 14 or 15 years),[179] must be considered as highly suspicious. Anyway, the highest date attributed securely to the Renaissance Era is year 10 of LRL no. 9.[180]

As a result of this, the 29 or even 30 years,[181] assigned to Ramesses XI on the basis of the so-called "Book of Sothis" cannot be substantiated. The identification of "Ramesses, son of Uaphres" (to whom 29 years of reign were assigned there)[182] with Ramesses XI is in fact doubtful.[183] Actually nothing is known about celebration of the king's jubilee, so it seems possible that he did not enter the fourth decade of his reign.[184] Thus a minimum of 28 full years assigned to Ramesses XI seems to be plausible although not wholly confirmed hypothesis.[185]

Regardless of the place of his residence at the very end of the reign (Per-Ramesse or maybe a new capital in Tanis?) quite probably he remained under the political tutelage of Smendes, soon the founder of a new dynasty on his own. The role played by Tentamun (being a daughter or less possibly wife of the last Ramesside ruler) at Smendes' side would seem to suggest that Ramesses XI had no male offspring,[186] and indeed some of the princes of the III Intermediate Period called themselves the "king's sons of Ramesses" – i.e. apparently only the legal successors of the Ramesside dynasty with no genealogical links with their predecessors of the New Kingdom.[187]

---

exemplified by the Abydos stela, it is possible that the datation system according to the Renaissance Era was functioning only in Thebes, or else in that part of the country which was subject to the direct control of the high priest of Amun (in such a case, however, Abydos' territory cannot be exluded anyhow!).

[179] Cf. e.g. Thijs, SAK 38, 2009, figs. 1-2 (the recent application of his chronological system); Lull, Los sumos sacerdotes, 59, 308f.; id., Trabajos de Egiptología 5/2, 2009, 58; von Beckerath, Chronologie des pharaonischen Ägypten, 107f.

[180] For the possibility of prolongation of the Era until year 12, see Wente LRL, 15, 17 (with hesitation; an opinion based on his wrong dating of Theban graffito no. 1393; compare, Peden, Graffiti, 261); similarly Kitchen TIP, 23 (based on the "Book of Sothis"); von Beckerath, Chronologie, 91 n. 562; compare also Niwiński, Bürgerkrieg, 238f.

[181] See Kitchen TIP, 22f.; Hornung, Untersuchungen; 100; id., in: Ancient Egyptian Chronology, 217; von Beckerath, Chronologie, 91; id., GM 181, 2001, 16.

[182] Cf. Waddell, Manetho, 236f.

[183] Cf. Kitchen TIP, 23 n. 99; compare, however, W. Helck, Untersuchungen zu Manetho und den ägyptischen Königslisten, [UGAÄ 18], Berlin 1956, 45, 71.

[184] Cf. Wente-van Siclen, Chronology, 246.

[185] Cf. Krauss, GM 219, 2008, 44, 46.

[186] As regards Tentamun and her geneaological position, see Broekman, GM 191, 2002, 16f. (with references to earlier literature).

[187] Cf. Jansen-Winkeln, DE 38, 1997, 32f.; Broekman, GM 191, 2002, 17; see also Collombert, GM 151, 1996, 23-35, on the military significance of the title.

Presumably it was the death of Ramesses XI which finally opened a way to the realization of the political ambitions of his immediate successors – i.e. the High Priest Herihor in the south and Smendes in the north. Quite possibly their assumption of kingship can be viewed in the framework of the new situation in the aftermath of the death of the last Ramesside ruler. Obviously such a supposition would lengthen considerably the duration of Herihor's pontificate to the very end of the Renaissance Era, and as a result, there would be no place to locate the pontificate of his successor still within this era. Anyway an attempt to date Herihor's death to year 6 of the Renaissance Era (see also above) on the basis of papLouvre AF 6345+Griffith fragments, and more precisely to the period between III *peret* 15 (the docket of Ramesses' II coffin),[188] and purely hypothetical and highly doubtful "III *shemu*" (as the presumed date of assumption of the office of high priest by Payankh),[189] cannot withstand critique. The weak point of this hypothesis is the partly preserved name of the high priest of Amun (identified as that of Payankh by A. Gasse) in papLouvre AF 6345+Griffith fragments,[190] a document dated to year 6 of an unspecified reign or of the Renaissance Era.[191]

The pontifical background of Herihor's "kingship" finds its most powerful confirmation in the fact that he appears with all the trappings of his kingly status only within the precinct of the Amun temple in Karnak (i.e. in the Khonsu temple and in the Great Hypostyle Hall).[192] The inclusion of his priestly title into the royal protocol (prenomen)[193] appears to be a visible manifestation of the ideological background of the new regime, being at the

---

[188] Cf. Maspero, Momies royales, 557, fig. 15; Daressy, Cercueils, 32, pl. 22; Kitchen, RamInscr VI, 838 (30B); cf. Kitchen TIP, 417 (no. 3); Reeves, Valley of the Kings, 234 (no. 9). This is the latest preserved record relating to Herihor.

[189] Gasse, Domaine d'Amon I, 172. A suggestion being a consequence of a reading of the date of the Griffith fragments, ro. 1, 2 (ibid., I, 5, pl. 1; II, pl. 81) remains untenable in fact – only the year number seems to be partly preserved, and no traces of the month number nor season (III *peret* according to Gasse), cf. Gardiner RAD, 68a (14[a]); id., JEA 27, 1941, 65.

[190] The identification of the high priest of Amun mentioned in ro. 9, 5 as Pa[yankh] (cf. Gasse, ibid., I, 11, 34 n. 57, 172, pl. 11; II, 88) is highly questionable, although not impossible.

[191] The "Griffith fragments" are dated to the end of the 20th Dynasty by Fischer-Elfert, in: Miscellanea Aegyptologica, 40. As regards the possibility of a later dating of the "Griffith fragments", see now Katary, in: DeM in the Third Millennium, 197 n. 65 – in such a case the high priest in question could be possibly Paynudjem I or one of his successors of the 21st Dynasty: Paynudjem II or Psusennes (III). A partly preserved royal cartouche of ro. 1, 1 (cf. Gasse, ibid, I, 23 (1), pl. 1) cannot be taken as a decisive argument in regard of an earlier dating, cf. Gardiner, JEA 27, 1941, 65.

[192] The latter viewed possibly as an extension of the Khonsu temple (or the latter's entrance?), cf. Roth, JNES 42, 1983, 43, 46ff.; see also The Temple of Khonsu 1, X.

[193] Cf. Bonhême, Noms royaux, 31f.; see also id., BIFAO 79, 1979, 271ff.

same time the most sophisticated paradigm of the sovereignty of Amun-Ra in the new theocratic state. Significantly Herihor's nomen had been extended by the title "Son-of-Amun" inserted into the cartouche,[194] and this seems to be a vivid exemplification of the royal ideology developed during the New Kingdom, if not a supposed "coregency" of the god, and the king in person of the high priest of Amun.[195]

Nevertheless, there are no serious reasons to interpret the "kingship" attained by Herihor as a kind of a political fiction, as is commonly maintained in the recent research on the subject.[196] As a matter of fact, the Egyptian doctrine regarding the ideology and theological background of the kingship does not provide us with any concept of such a "transitional" or else "semi"–kingship, except of course the cases of mere usurpation or regency (although the latter never ignored requirements of legality either).[197] All the reservations regarding the exceptional character of Herihor's "kingship" must be referred rather to his earlier career as the high priest of Amun, when the decoration of the hypostyle hall of the Khonsu temple was executed. Anyway, such an idea of incomplete or simply a fictitious kingship seems to be a thoroughly alien element in the "Egyptian way of thinking", with the institution of the Pharaoh playing a dominant role in every aspect of ancient Egyptian civilization. Quite a different question, however, was the political reality of usurpation with its urgent necessity to support the rights to the throne through an elaborate dogma of the kingship and royal propaganda. One of the most reliable elements of such a propaganda was a direct reference to the theological background of the kingship. The oracle text from the Khonsu temple apparently cannot be placed in this particular context, as it nowhere does it give the royal titulary of Herihor, and the text was dated explicitly in the name of Ramesses XI.[198] In other texts, however, such a royal ideology was

[194] Cf. ibid., 32. An intermediary state in the formulation of the nomen can be found in the graffito of the high priest Herihor, written at the the south approach of the Karnak temple (between the eight and ninth pylons), where Herihor's name is preceded by such a title, cf. Barguet, Temple d'Amon-Rê, 257; Kitchen, RamInscr VI, 846 (no. 3); Roth, loc.cit., 47; Bonhême, Livre des rois I, 124f. (Doc. 21 H.252).

[195] See Niwiński, BIFAO 95, 1995, 341.

[196] See Kitchen TIP, 20f.; Gundlach, in: M. Minas, J. Zeidler (eds.), Aspekte spätägyptischer Kultur. Festschrift E. Winter, [Aegyptiaca Treverensia 7], Mainz a/R 1994, 133ff.; Bonhême, BIFAO 79, 1979, 267ff.; Kitchen, in: Libyan Period in Egypt, 194 (§80). Compare however the contrary view presented by Thijs, GM 163, 1998, 107; id., ZÄS 132, 2005, 75ff. (an opinion based on different presumptions than those presented here).

[197] Cf. e.g. H. Goedicke, Wahlkönigtum, in: LÄ, VI (1986), 1139f.; W. Helck, Usurpator, in: LÄ, VI (1986), 904f.; A. Gardiner, JEA 39, 1953, 21.

[198] Cf. The Temple of Khonsu 2, XVIII; otherwise Gundlach, op.cit., 135. More probably the oracle was

drawn up according to the traditional patterns of an Egyptian kingship: "Live Horus: Mighty-Bull Son-of-Amun, who has made monuments efficiently for the one who bore him; the king of Upper and Lower Egypt, great ruler of Egypt, the lord of the Two Lands (High-Priest-of-Amun)|. He has made as his monument for [his] father Amun-Ra, king of the gods, (...) (this) being what a son does with a willing heart for the father who placed him on his throne and gave him eternity as king of the Two Lands, the king of Upper and Lower Egypt, the Lord of the Strong Arm, the lord of the Two Lands (High-Priest-of-Amun)|, beloved of Amun-Ra, king of the gods, lord of heaven, ruler of the Ennead".[199] In the light of such declarations it is hardly possible to suppose the "fictitious" character of his kingship, not only because of the royal titulature placed at the beginning of the text (other elements of which are contained in other parts of the architrave inscriptions). Thus we can speak only about the apparent weakness of the royal position of Herihor, being an inevitable result of his presumed usurpation. There is no possibility whatsoever to interpret his sovereignty in terms of "incomplete kingship" of sorts, wholly restricted to the sphere of the rituals celebrated in Karnak, but rather as a new and quite original development of an old paradigm of Egyptian kingship.[200]

Another matter of crucial significance for the history of the period is how long king Herihor exercised his royal power. According to K.A. Kitchen the six years commonly attributed to Herihor[201] would have been an ample time to complete his works in the Khonsu temple.[202] It must be noted, however, that the overall surface of decoration made in the temple during the reign of Ramesses IV (6 full years on the throne) was significantly smaller in comparison with that made on behalf of Herihor. If we accept the idea that

---

given at an earlier stage of Herihor's career, when he consolidated his political position in Thebes (see above).

[199] The Temple of Khonsu 2, 24, pl. 140 (1), cf. also Bonhême, Livre des rois I, 3ff.

[200] Compare Römer, Gottes- und Priesterherrschaft, 454f.

[201] Compare Jansen-Winkeln, ZÄS 119, 1992, 37 (10 years); id., in: Ancient Egyptian Chronology, 228f., 230 (5-8 years); Krauss, GM 219, 2008, 44, 46 (6 years). The estimation is based on the highest recorded date for Herihor (year 6, III *peret* 15) – according to the present author it refers however to the Renaissance Era and the period of Herihor's tenure of the pontifical office. At present no dates referring to his kingship are available, and the idea of independent counting of Herihor's years, being a direct result of the reversed order of the high priests, cannot be substantiated convincingly, cf. Demidoff, Retour sur une controverse, 111.

[202] Kitchen TIP, 23; id., in: Libyan Period in Egypt, 194 (§81) – a comparison with the building activity of Seti I sounds unconvincingly due to the substantial divergence in the economic potential of Egypt in both periods.

hypostyle hall was decorated during the pontificate of Herihor (or, according to the traditional view, in its early years), and the peristyle court in later years when presumably he laid his claims to the kingship, then we can reach the conclusion that both periods were not equal at all. A tentative estimation of the proportion of the overall surface of both parts of the temple decorated on behalf of Herihor (and the number of scenes) is ca. 1:2.[203] It sheds some new light on the reconstructed chronology of the pontificate and subsequent kingship of Herihor as proposed in the present study. The most visible result is the conclusion that the period of wielding the royal prerogatives by Herihor was significant enough to enable him to commission a complete set of scenes in the peristyle court of the Khonsu temple, representing him in the traditional roles of the reigning king, including the scenes of his coronation.[204] In addition, the time needed to achieve this goal must have been significantly longer than ascribed to Herihor previously. It seems that it would have comprised also a significant span of time after the death of Ramesses XI.[205] This would make Herihor the first king of the 21st Dynasty (besides Smendes in the North), notwithstanding the fact that he has not been credited with kingship in Manetho's king list.

Nevertheless one can imagine that the period of Herihor's kingship was relatively short, and it comprised just the time needed to decorate the columns of the peristyle court of the Khonsu temple and some parts of its walls.[206] The relative brevity of the period must be viewed perhaps as a direct reason for the scarcity of sources pertaining to the personal presence of king Herihor in Thebes. It cannot be excluded, however, that he would have exercised his control over Thebes from outside, and the headquarters of the high priests of Amun of the 21st Dynasty located in Teudjoy may provide a possible location

[203] This is just a rough estimate based on the number of scenes in both parts of the temple; an exact calculation of the ratio of the decorated surfaces in both parts of the temple would be perhaps more informative in regard of this.

[204] The works in the court were continued under Paynudjem I, and there are no parts of the decoration which could be attributed to Payankh – this seems to be another confirmation of an ephemeral status of his pontificate.

[205] For the possibility that Herihor outlived Ramesses XI, cf. Hornung, Untersuchungen, 102; an assumption criticized by Kitchen, CdE 40, 1965, 320. Obviously, in the chronological schemes proposed by K. Jansen-Winkeln and A. Thijs, such an assumption does not provoke any controversy.

[206] According to C.F. Nims the Opet-feast scenes in the court (west wall, bottom register) could have been executed within a year (!), cf. Wente LRL, 4 n. 13; compare however an estimate given by Kitchen TIP, 252 n. 45 (ca. two years). As suggested above the period needed to execute the decoration of the court must have been significantly longer.

of his residence, connected or not with his place of origin (?).[207] One of the papyri found in El-Hibeh provides interesting information about "this house belonging to (?) Payankh (?)" (papStrasbourg 31, ro. 9),[208] and the partly preserved name of the viceroy Payankh is possibly mentioned in papStrasbourg 32 (ro. 1).[209] Understandably the strategic significance of the region was not without significance as regards the location of the high priest's headquarters.

The new rulers of Egypt were obliged to face a complicated situation in the internal affairs of both Northern and Southern states. The international position of Egypt declined markedly if one compares it with that of the previous epoch. The rulers of the 21st Dynasty residing in its new capital in Tanis were incapable of maintaining their political influence over the northern neighbours of Egypt. This is also true in regard to the petty kingdoms and principalities of the coastal region of Syria and Palestine, as demonstrated by the vivid narration of the "Story of Wenamun". The situation in the south was even worse, and the rebellion of the viceroy Panehesy led finally to the independence of the Nubian province with its gold-mining regions, and a free access to other raw materials sought-after in Egypt for centuries.

[207] Unfortunately no traces datable to this period have been excavated in el-Hibeh until now (see above). Another candidate would be Heracleopolis; as regards the significance of the latter in the internal policy of the Libyan period, cf. Jansen-Winkeln, BN 71, 1994, 82ff.; id., Or 60, 2000, 10; Lefevre, BSFE 165, 2006, 44. It is possible that the region of Middle Egypt was a place of origin of Herihor, and possibly also of Payankh. The supposed location of the latter's tomb in Heracleopolis (see below, Chapter 8) is not without significance, as it gives a possible hint to the location of the burial ground of his family, cf. Jansen-Winkeln, BN 71, 1994, 84f.

[208] Spiegelberg, ZÄS 53, 1917, 6f., pl. 1; Jansen-Winkeln, InscrSp I, 199; as regards identification of the person in question with general Payankh, see Jansen-Winkeln, BN 71, 1994, 82; id., Or 70, 2001, 156; compare however Wente, Letters, 207 (read as a personal name Saupaankh); similarly Sweeney, Correspondence and Dialogue, 74 (Ex. 53).

[209] Spiegelberg, ZÄS 53, 1917, 19, pl. 7; Römer, Gottes- und Priesterherrschaft, 45; compare however Jansen-Winkeln, InschrSp I, 207 (41); Lefèvre, BSFE 165, 2006, 42.

4. The administration of the Thebaid at the end of the Ramesside period

Certainly Jac. J. Janssen was right when he observed that compared with the fairly clear picture relating to the earlier periods, our view of the administration and history of Deir el-Medina after the death of Ramesses VI still needs further study.[1] The same is also true in regard to the history of Thebes and Egypt in general and we have to acknowledge that what we can determine of the mechanisms of functioning of the administrative system at the end of the 20th Dynasty does not match exactly what we know about earlier periods.

It is difficult to say whether the royal titulary of Ramesses XI ever reflected the programme of his policy, formulated at his accession: "Horus: Mighty bull, beloved of Ra; Nebty: Strong of (his) arm, punishing the multitudes; Horus of Gold: Great of strength, who makes the Two Lands live, sovereign, l.p.h., who makes content (his heart) with truth, who pacifies the Two Lands; King of Upper and Lower Egypt, lord of the Two Lands Menmaatre-Setepenptah, l.p.h., son of Re, lord of diadems Ramesses Khaemwese-Meriamun, the god-ruler of Heliopolis, l.p.h.".[2] Anyway it is worth noting that the Horus-name is the same as that of Ramesses II, while his prenomen is that of Seti I, both kings who initiated a new policy and acted as restorers and at the same time as the illustrious founders of the new dynastic line.[3]

The royal sovereignty over the Thebaid and Upper Egypt in this period is scarcely attested by official royal inscriptions, except those in the hypostyle hall of the Khonsu temple in Karnak, the most important monument of

[1] Janssen, Village Varia, 173.

[2] For the beginning of his titulary, see e.g. his inscription in the Khonsu temple: Kitchen, RamInscr VI, 705, 4; for the rest of the royal protocol: papTurin 1896: Pleyte-Rossi, Papyrus de Turin, pl. 66, 1-3; Bakir, Epistolography, pl. 24f., phot.-pl. XXXI; Kitchen, RamInscr VI, 734, 7-9. See also von Beckerath, Königsnamen, 174f.

[3] The *Nebty*-name of Ramesses XI finds an exact parallel in the same element of titulary of Ramesses VI; for a discussion of the titulary of Ramesses XI, cf. Kitchen, ASAE 71, 1987, 139f.; Vandersleyen, L'Égypte II, 643.

the reign (which must be dated, however, to a slightly later period of the pontificate of Herihor and the Renaissance Era).[4] At the same time it should be realized that the building of the royal tomb in the Valley of the Kings must be interpreted also as a manifestation of the royal authority (especially in Thebes) as well as a vivid continuation of the traditions of the Ramesside dynasty. A partly preserved figure of Ramesses XI standing in front of Amun-Ra-Harakhte and the goddess personifying the West can be found on the right wall of the first corridor in KV 4, while on the left wall he was represented in a similar, but now mostly destroyed scene.[5] The tomb and in particular its decoration were never finished, and the size of the tomb seems to point to a relatively short construction period. Nothwithstanding, foundation deposits with objects bearing the cartouches of Ramesses XI, found by J. Romer near the mouth of the shaft at the end of the tomb, suggest that the tomb in its present form was hewn out during the reign of this sovereign.[6] The shaft, being an unusual feature of the royal tomb architecture, had never been completed.[7] It is difficult to say whether the tools and implements found in the tomb were left by the workmen of the time of Ramesses XI, or whether they are later in date, and thus can be connected with subsequent activity undertaken inside the tomb in the following period (see below, Chapter 8). This is especially true in regards of the stick, which "bears an inscription of the «deputy of the crew», Neferhor".[8] As a matter of fact the identity of this Neferhor remains entirely obscure. It is possible, however, that he belonged to

[4] It is possible that its decoration was started at the very beginning of the Renaissance Era, when the royal representatives in Thebes acted on behalf of the king. Anyway the royal name is unchallenged in the decoration of the ceiling and upper registers, while going downwards the titles and representations of Herihor appear to be more substantial.

[5] For the scenes decorating both walls of the entrance corriodor, cf. PM I/2[2], 501 (2-3); LD III, pl. 239a; E. Lefébure, Les Hypogées royaux de Thèbes, II, [Annales du Musée Guimet 16], Paris 1889, 13; Kitchen, RamInscr VI, 730 (no. 12). The decoration is parallel to that from the right wall of the first corridor in the tomb of Ramesses IX (KV 6), cf. PM I/2[2], 502 (6); B. Bruyère, Mert Seger à Deir el Médineh, [MIFAO 58], Cairo 1930, 258-260, fig. 129. For the meaning of the scenes in question, cf. Abitz, SAK 17, 1990, 9f.; Lüscher, in: Jenni H. (ed.), Das Grab Ramses' X. (KV 18), Basel 2000, 54f.; T.A. Bács, Amun-Re-Harakhti in the Late Ramesside Royal Tombs, in: U. Luft (ed.), The Intellectual Heritage of Egypt. Studies presented to L. Kákosy, [Studia Aegyptiaca 14], Budapest 1992, 43-53.

[6] M. Ciccarello, J. Romer, A Preliminary Report of the Recent Work in the Tombs of Ramesses X and XI in the Valley of the Kings, Brooklyn 1979, 4-7.

[7] Ibid., 4.

[8] Ibid., 7, fig. 6; unfortunately no detailed photograph or drawing of the piece and its inscription has been provided, so that all what is known about it is just the general remark quoted here.

the family of Khonsu, the foreman of the right side,[9] and as such he should be placed perhaps among deputies of the gang some time in the early years of Ramesses XI.[10]

A comparison of the tomb's volume (ca. 1682.19 cubic metres)[11] with that of the other tombs in the Valley of the Kings leads to the conclusion that it was built for the period of time approximately comparable to that needed to excavate the tomb of Ramesses V/VI (KV 9: 1572.26 cubic metres), built under the two successive pharaohs. Certainly the period estimated on the basis of the parallel with the dimensions of the tomb of Ramesses V/VI must be carefully corrected, having in mind that the latter, although not completed in its entirety, had been lavishly decorated.[12] The approximate period of its building can be estimated at ca. 10.5 years,[13] and the work had been done by a crew numbering approximately 60 men.[14] One more factor must be considered, a significant reduction of the strength of the tomb-workforce in the early years of the reign of Ramesses XI. It is known that during the reign of Ramesses IX the overall number of the crew can be estimated at ca. 62 workmen in year 17, whereas just two years later the crew had been drastically reduced to 29 workmen, assisted by a group of 18 youths (*mnḥ.w*). At the end of the reign of Ramesses X, the crew comprised ca. 32 men,[15] when the work on the royal tomb did not go beyond the second corridor.

[9] Cf. ibid., note 7. He can be possibly identified with the workman Neferhor (VII), brother of the foreman Khonsu, and son of Ipuy, cf. Černý, Community, 127; Gutgesell, Datierung, 222; Davies, Who's Who at DeM, 52, 53, chart 7. Or else he was simply a descendant of this family, and as such can be counted perhaps among the following generation(s).

[10] Providing that the workman Neferhor son of Ipuy did not die in year 17 of Ramesses IX, as suggested by Botti-Peet, Giornale, 19 n. 5; Davies, Who's Who at DeM, 53. As a matter of fact a hieratic sign (written in red) placed in front of his name in the necropolis journal of that year (cf. Botti-Peet, Giornale, pl. 9, 4) cannot necessarily be read as sign: Gardiner EG, A 13-14 = Möller, Paläographie II, 4 (A 49). It may be noted that, according to the present text, he received the same amount of grain as other workmen, so the question is: why should he receive grain if he was really dead at the moment when the list of supplies was drawn up? Moreover, it is hardly imaginable that documents of this kind were written long after the distribution of grain, and the notes in the right margin were added presumably at the moment (or soon after) the distribution really had taken place.

[11] After the Theban Mapping Project, Atlas of the Valley of the Kings: http://thebanmappingproject.com. As regards the tomb dimensions, cf. also E. Hornung, ZÄS 105, 1978, 61, 65.

[12] As regards its building history, cf. F. Abitz, Baugeschichte und Dekoration des Grabes Ramses' VI [OBO 89], Freiburg – Göttingen 1989, 23-25, 35ff., 40ff.

[13] Cf. ibid., 45f. It must be noted that most of the time was devoted apparently to its decoration; for this compare Abitz, SAK 17, 1990, 7f.

[14] Cf. Valbelle, Ouvriers, 104.

[15] Ibid., 105, 219; Peden, Decline of Textual Graffiti, 289 n. 19 (a note relating to a temporary increase of the size of the crew at the very beginning of the reign).

By the year 8 of Ramesses XI the size of the crew had drastically fallen[16] to 16 simple workmen (total 26, including 2 foremen, 2 scribes, 2 scribes of the *semdet*-staff, 1 guardian, 2 doorkeepers, and 1 doctor),[17] the lowest ever recorded in the history of the royal necropolis in the Ramesside period. It is hardly possible, indeed, that such a workforce was able to continue effectively the work on the royal hypogeum. In the face of a complete absence of data relating to the chronology of work on the royal tomb, one can admit that the tomb was excavated within just a few years.[18] Having in mind the serious political disturbances during the three decades of the reign of Ramesses XI, its very beginning seems to be the most suitable period (probably still before the intervention of viceroy Panehesy).

The final abandonment of work on the royal tomb in the Valley of the Kings must be explained by some important political factors, such as internal strife caused by the war of the High Priest Amenhotep. Certainly the cause was not intrusions of the Libyans, although their appearance at Thebes was also noted during the reign of Ramesses XI and soon afterwards.[19] It is impossible to say whether work on the tomb was ever resumed after the civil war and disturbances of the period.[20] It seems, however, that there was no convenient time for such work in the later two decades of the reign, which inevitably led to the final abandonment of the royal necropolis at Thebes.

Apparently the period of the building of the royal tomb was so restricted that only some sketches of the decoration at its entrance were made (see above). As a matter of fact only a scanty sources can be connected directly with the building process of the royal tomb, and there are no extant fragments of the necropolis journal relating to this. One of the documents which can be possibly connected with it is the undated oCG 25243, found in the Valley of the Kings in the tomb of Ramesses IX.[21] A sequence of daily dates was

[16] As for the reduction of the workforce under Ramesses XI, cf. Černý, Cahiers d' Histoire Mondiale 1, no. 4, 1954, 920; S. Allam, Das Verfahrensrecht in der altägyptischen Arbeitsiedlung von Deir el-Medineh, Tübingen 1973, 12 n. 4; Valbelle, Ouvriers, 69 n. 1, 105, 219; Peden, Decline of Textual Graffiti, 289; Lull, Los sumos sacerdotes, 16. Černý (Community, 108) aptly observed that such an enormous reduction of the crew may be explained by the civil war and conscription into the army.

[17] The numbers can be drawn from papTurin 2018 of years 8-10: Kitchen, RamInscr VI, 851ff.; Helck OPG, 562f.; cf. Valbelle, Ouvriers, loc.cit.

[18] Compare with the estimated 8 years needed to excavate the tomb of Ramesses IX (KV 6), according to Abitz, SAK 17, 1990, 7f.

[19] Cf. Haring, in: Village Voices, 77f.; id., Libyans in the Theban region, 20th dynasty, in: Sesto Congresso Internazionale di Egittologia. Atti, II, Turin 1993, 162f.; Häggman, Directing DeM, 293ff.

[20] Cf. Häggman, Directing DeM, 215.

[21] Daressy, Ostraca, 62f., pl. 52; Kitchen, RamInscr VI, 870ff. (A11); VII, 462f. (emendations); Helck

written on both sides of it with annotations referring to some important events with which the workmen were preoccupied, and they cover a span of time of nearly two months. Marginal notes refer to the days of work and the days when the crew was idle.[22] The name of the Madjoy Anher[tore][23] (vo. 15) strongly supports its dating to the reign of Ramesses XI, because he is attested in the Turin Taxation Papyrus, in the year 12 of this sovereign.[24] If the proposed dating of the ostracon is right then it would seem we obtain important information concerning activity of the crew in the early years of Ramesses XI. First of all this concerns the existence of the *semdet* labour force at the time when it was written: "Day 8: Giving the men of *semdet*[25] to my [...]" (vo. 6). What is more, a supply of grain for the right side of the crew was recorded on *verso* 3: "Day 5: Giving grain rations (to) the right-side [...] (*di.t di.w (n) wnmy*)". This simply means that institution of the royal necropolis was still functioning according to the patterns of the previous period, although some disturbances can also be noted, as for example the coming of Meshwe(sh) on "day 21" (ro. 21).[26]

Quite probably J.J. Janssen was right while suggesting that the work on KV 4 was mentioned also in one of the earliest LRL (no. 47):[27] "Indeed, what is the use of speaking with you, if you do not listen and remain [idle] (in) this commission (*sḥnw*) of Pharaoh, l.p.h., your good lord, in which you are (engaged)?".[28] Significantly no other preserved letters relates directly to the work on the royal tomb and this can be explained by the fact that the work on it probably stopped soon after the LRL no. 47 was written. Anyway it provides in addition interesting information concerning some difficulties

OPG, 572f. For its dating to the reign of Ramesses IX, cf. Valbelle, Ouvriers, 92; Wimmer, Hieratische Paläographie I, 38f.; similarly Haring, in: Village Voices, 76. See however Helck OPG, 557, where the ostracon is dated to the reign of Ramesses XI; for a discussion see also Lull, Los sumos sacerdotes, 47, 61; Römer, Gottes- und Priesterherrschaft, 36; and Chapter 8 below.

22 For the signs used here, cf. Helck OPG, 573 (bottom); Janssen, Village Varia, 93.

23 H. Ranke notes only two names of this type, cf. PN I, 61 (29) , and 62 (1); as a matter of fact the former (*ꜥn-ḥr-iꜣw.t.f*) cannot be taken into consideration here, as it is not attested in the sources relating to the Madjoy policemen.

24 Gardiner RAD, 36, 15-16; cf. Černý, Community, 271 (no. 6). An undated document (of religious character) referring probably to the same person was commented upon by D. Meeks, Mots sans suite ou notations rituelles? (O. DeM 1696 et O. Petrie 36), in: DeM in the Third Millennium, 236; add possibly also oTurin 57372 ro., 4: Lopez, Ostraca 3, pl. 116-116a; Kitchen, RamInscr VII, 397f. (no. 63).

25 See Černý, Community, 184 n. 6; otherwise Helck OPG, 573: "der Leute und des Angestellten".

26 For the comments, see above.

27 Janssen LRLC 19; cf. also Černý, Community, 85; Peden, Graffiti, 234 n. 699; Häggman, Directing DeM, 208. For a discussion on its dating, see below Chapter 6.

28 Černý LRL, 69, 1-3; cf. Frandsen, Verbal System, 33 (Ex. 5); Borghouts, ZÄS 106, 1979, 22 (17).

in functioning of the staff of the necropolis: "As for the men who are sitting there confined (*ḏdḥ*), give [...] them as well. If they will not work there can be no work (*b3kw*)[29] for the men".[30] And in another place of the same text: "If your commissions (*n3y.k sḥnw*) are too much for you, you will not be able to take part in this commission of Pharaoh, l.p.h.".[31] The nature of these disturbances remains wholly unknown but we may suspect that it was connected in some way with irregularities in distribution of the payment: "The fishermen came to the place where the men of the necropolis were, saying: «We have been waiting till today», and saying (also): «We are confined (*ḏdḥ*) in your charge[32]». And they have said while entering (lit. breaking through), when the sky was low in elevation(?),[33] saying: «You have taken our men earlier(?)[34] and you exacted(?) (their) work. See, you have taken our men again and you exacted (their) work (again). We are going to spend a day here and we will go tomorrow to the place where the vizier is» – so they said".[35] The term *ḏdḥ* used twice in the letter apparently cannot be interpreted in its literal sense.[36] It should rather refer to the status of the fishermen and *semdet*-staff in general, in relation to their work obligation. Less probably the status of the

---

[29] According to Häggman (Directing DeM, 102) the *b3k*-payment is meant here, providing that the work of the *semdet*-staff and payment of the workmen of the crew are referred to in this passage, cf. ibid., 84f. It is possible, however, that the situation described here concerns rather the workmen of the crew, who will not work, if the *semdet*-staff cease doing their job. For the meaning of *b3kw* as "product (of the work)", see J.J. Janssen, *B3kw*: From work to product, SAK 20, 1993, 81-94; compare also Haring, Divine Households, 479 ("(obligatory) produce"); P. Grandet, Le Papyrus Harris I, Glossaire, [BdE 129], Cairo 2000, 47.

[30] Černý LRL, 69, 4-6; cf. Groll, Negative Verbal System, 94 (Ex. 187); Černý-Groll, Late Egyptian Grammar, 329 (Ex. 902); Wente, Letters, 172 (no. 288).

[31] Černý LRL, 69, 15-16; as regards the translation of the passage, compare Černý, JEA 27, 1941, 108 (17); Groll, Negative Verbal System, 59 (Ex. 118); Frandsen, Verbal System, 34 (Ex. 5); 48 (Ex. 22); Černý-Groll, Late Egyptian Grammar, 563 (Ex. 1611); Sweeney, Correspondence and Dialogue, 224f. (Ex. 76).

[32] For the meaning of *m-ḏr.t* in this context, see Valbelle, BIFAO 76, 1976, 101ff.; Gasse, Domaine d'Amon I, 220; cf. Frandsen, Verbal System, 62 (Ex. 9).

[33] An attempt to elucidate this obscure passage: Wente LRL, 73 (i), 82 (f, g); Winand, Études, 117 (Ex. 279); Häggman, Directing DeM, 103. For *wn sḏm.f* as a perfective form cf. M. Korostovtsev, BIFAO 45, 1947, 167 (9). I take *wtnw.Ø* as the stative.

[34] Cf. Wb.III, 22 (7). Wente LRL, 81: "at the beginning"; id., Letters, 172: "initially', cf. also Lesko, Dict. I, 296. Possibly this adverb relates to the previous state of affairs relating to work and payment of the *semdet*-staff. An assumption that the passage relates to the robbing of these people seems highly improbable, cf. Černý-Groll, Late Egyptian Grammar, 215 (Ex. 571).

[35] Černý LRL, 69, 8-14; cf. Frandsen, Verbal System, 118 (Ex. 1); Sweeney, LingAeg 9, 2001, 278 (Ex. 57).

[36] Lesko, Dict. II, 277; see also McDowell, Jurisdiction, 221.

workmen of the crew is related here.[37] It seems that a delay in the payments for the fishermen from the *semdet*-staff caused some disturbances referred to in the letter,[38] being at the same time the reason why the author of the letter advised its recipient to send some officials to fetch the grain, as a payment for the fishermen (and by the way to the crew as well?).[39]

LRL no. 47 was written probably by the scribe Tuthmosis himself or some other person connected with the necropolis staff. It has been suggested, however, that the sender could have been the vizier himself or some other person of high status from his immediate entourage.[40] No matter who was the author of the letter, certainly he was well acquainted with all the matters of the royal necropolis and its administrative background. This is why his primary concern was a provisioning of the necropolis staff, a task entrusted to one of his subordinates, the recipient of the letter. Similarly it is not easy to identify the recipient either. Apparently he was an official of relatively high status, having at his disposal a clerk or secretary, termed here simply as "your scribe": "Dispatch Nessobek, your scribe. And cause him to go with the doorkeeper (and) guardian Tuthmosis and the scribe Efnamun and have the grain fetched".[41] Further on in the same letter, a similar order can be found: "Dispatch your scribe together with Ef[namun], the scribe of the necropolis, and the doorkeeper Tuthmosis or the doorkeeper Khonsumose. Let them go to fetch the grain lest the men become hungry and idle in the commission of Pharaoh, l.p.h., and cast any blame on you".[42] As Nessobek, apparently a subordinate of the recipient, is scarcely known from other LRL, we can only presume he may be identified with a deputy of the temple (*idnw n tꜣ-ḥw.t*) of Medinet Habu (LRL no. 36);[43] in such a case his superior would be possibly one of the temple officials from the complex at Medinet Habu. Perhaps however some other type of the official relations can be presumed in this

37 Thus contrary to Häggman, Directing DeM, 102f.

38 Häggman (Directing DeM, 103ff.) suggested that the fishermen were in fact employed by the crew rather by any external authority.

39 As the following words seem to suggest: "lest the men become hungry and idle in the commission of the Pharaoh"; see below.

40 Häggman, Directing DeM, 101f., 207f.; see, however, Sweeney, Idiolects, 313f., attributing it tentatively to the scribe Tuthmosis on the basis of the analysis of its style.

41 Černý LRL, 69, 6-8.

42 Černý LRL, 69, 16-70, 3; cf. D.A. Warburton, State and Economy in Ancient Egypt. Fiscal Vocabulary of the New Kingdom, [OBO 151], Fribourg-Göttingen 1997, 170; Winand, BIFAO 100, 2000, 415 (Ex. 19).

43 Černý LRL, 55, 8; cf. also Helck, Materialien I, (112); Haring, Divine Households, 453.

context. No doubt the letter was written while the crew was still living in the settlement of Deir el-Medina, although one of the persons mentioned in the letter is noted also in the list of the houses from papBM 10068vo. 2-8 – this is Efnamun, titled as the "scribe of the necropolis",[44] and his presence here (vo. 7, 8) can be explained by the fact that he was responsible for the *semdet*-staff of the left side of the crew. PapTurin 2018, dating to years 8-10, gives a complete list of his subordinates besides those supervised by the scribe Wennefer son of Ankhtu,[45] responsible for the *semdet*-staff of the right side.[46] As has been already observed, there are no water-carriers in the lists of papTurin 2018, and this has led to the false conclusion that the crew had already been transferred to the complex in Medinet Habu, where access to the water was much easier than in the desert *wadi* in the old settlement of Deir el-Medina, and the water-carriers were no longer needed.[47]

Such an early dating of the abandonment of the settlement in Deir el-Medina cannot be proven. It seems that nearly two years later, in year 12 of Ramesses XI, all the members of the crew still lived in Deir el-Medina. Though the location of the settlement (*t3 wḥy.t*) of *Maiunehes* (papBM 10068vo. 2, 3) nowhere has been stated explicitly, it cannot be seriously doubted indeed that it was the settlement in the complex of the Medinet Habu temple,[48] namely in "the house of the temple of Usermaatre-Meriamun in the estate of Amun" (papBM 10068vo. 3, 4),[49] whose inhabitants were listed in the papyrus (vo. 3, 4-8, 15). There can also be little doubt that the list itself was compiled in

[44] Cf. Černý, Community; 193f. It is not clear whether scribe Efnamun performing some services for an agent Amenkhau from the temple of Amun-Ra in Karnak is the same person, cf. Demarée, Bankes Papyri, 8 (papBM EA 75015 ro. 13).

[45] Scribe Wennefer is not documented by any of the LRL, and his house was not listed in papBM 10068vo. either. He is known from some Theban graffiti, cf. Peden, Graffiti, 189, and n. 358.

[46] Cf. Černý, Community, 189f., 200f.; Davies, Who's Who at DeM, 284; Helck OPG, 562.

[47] See Černý, Community, 190 (compare also pp. 168, 281); Janssen, AoF 19, 1992, 13f. (before year 8; an occurence compelled by the war of the High Priest Amenhotep); similarly Katary, in: DeM in the Third Millennium, 206f.; for the contrary view, cf. Häggman, Directing DeM, 320ff. (with an assumption that the entire crew never moved to Medinet Habu); as regards a move of the crew in the early years of Ramesses XI, see also Ventura, City of the Dead, 116 n. 56; McDowell, in: Pharaoh's Workers, 57. According to Ch. Thiers (BIFAO 95, 1995, 510) the occurence has taken place probably at the beginning of the reign of Ramesses X. Černý's suggestion (loc.cit., 228) that the crew was living in Medinet Habu at the time of papTurin 2021 cannot be evaluated properly, mostly because of the problems with dating of the papyrus in question (see however, Chapter 1 above).

[48] Contra Otto, Topographie, 50; Černý, Community, 281. See however, Kemp, Ancient Egypt, 306. A possible relation of this toponym with a personal name attested in the reign of Ramesses IX is still open to question; for the latter cf. Botti-Peet, Giornale, pl. 40 (vo. 8, 4)=Kitchen, RamInscr VI, 591, 1.

[49] Peet, Tomb Robberies, pl. 14.

year 12 of Ramesses XI.[50] It is interesting in this connection to observe that most of the members of the *semdet*-staff of the crew, documented in papTurin 2018, were living in Medinet Habu,[51] as we can find their houses in the list of papBM 10068vo.[52]

These are the members of the *semdet*-staff of the right side, as documented in papTurin 2018, with reference to the houses in Medinet Habu of papBM 10068 (given in brackets): scribe Wennefer son of Ankhtu; potter (*ḳd*) Bakenmut son of Ahauty(nefer) (vo. 5, 13; no parentage); woodcutter (*šʿd-ḫt*) Sedy (vo. 6, 10); gypsum-worker (*ḳḏ*) Nesamun; washerman (*rḫty*) Amenmose (vo. 4, 8); washerman Ptahkhau (vo. 7, 18); coppersmith (*ḥmty*) [...].

The members of the *semdet*-staff of the left side are the following: scribe Efnamun (vo. 7, 8);[53] potter Ahauty (vo. 6, 25); gardener (*k3my*) Ahautynefer (vo. 5, 7); woodcutter Kenamun (vo. 6, 6); gypsum-worker Pakharu; washerman Ahaunefer (vo. 5, 3); fisherman (*wḥʿ*) Meri[...].[54]

As we can see the number of the serfs of both sides is the same, but their composition differs, because we know that representatives of some professions were usually attached to one side of the gang – the fishermen for example.[55] Only four of them are not mentioned in the list of houses (excluding a coppersmith whose name has not been preserved), among them the scribe responsible for the right side, namely Wennefer son of Ankhtu.[56] The latter's absence may be explained most probably by the mere fact that he was replaced in his function by another scribe responsible for the *semdet*-staff some time before the compilation of the list of houses.[57] At this particular moment (i.e.

---

50 Cf. Janssen, AoF 19, 1992, 8ff.; Davies, Who's Who at DeM, 201.

51 So definitely outside the settlement in Deir el-Medina, as postulated once by Janssen, Commodity Prices, 167 n. 10.

52 Cf. Katary, in: DeM in the Third Millennium, 206.

53 Certainly not "the scribe of the necropolis" as given here (Peet, Tomb Robberies, pl. 16), cf. Davies, Who's Who at DeM, 136f.

54 PapTurin 2018 ro. B2,16: Kitchen, RamInscr VI, 856, 14. None of the fishermen whose houses were recorded in papBM 10068vo. can be taken into consideration as a person mentioned here. This is well in accord with the hypothesis proposed once by Janssen, Commodity Prices, 536, that the fishermen and gardeners "did not even dwell in the valley". We can expect indeed that they were living somwhere in countryside, and in the vicinity of the river, although the houses of some fishermen were also located in Medinet Habu; for this question, see also Katary, in: DeM in the Third Millennium, 207; Kemp, Ancient Egypt, 307.

55 Antoine, SAK 35, 2006, 25 (with earlier literature on the subject).

56 Cf. Janssen, AoF 19, 1992, 13.

57 The latest document mentioning Wennefer son of Ankhtu is papTurin 2018: the entries dated to years 8-9 of Ramesses XI; cf. Černý, Community, 200 n. 9; Gutgesell, Datierung, 150f., 212; Helck OPG, 562f.; compare, however Davies, Who's Who at DeM, 101f. (admits possibility that the period

in year 12 of Ramesses XI) it could have been the scribe Tuthmosis,[58] whose house in Medinet Habu was located not far from that belonging to his colleague Efnamun.[59]

In addition, one fisherman and two gypsum-workers are absent from the list of houses as well. Significantly no member of the crew of the royal necropolis possessed then his house within the precinct of Medinet Habu, and this inevitably leads to the conclusion that they were still dwelling in Deir el-Medina at that particular time. Thus we can only surmise that the transfer of the crew happened soon afterwards. No doubt the crew was already installed in the complex of Medinet Habu at the time of most of the LRL, i.e. during the Renaissance Era.[60] There are good reasons to believe that the move of the crew had taken place at the end of the second decade of the reign of Ramesses XI, but not later than early years of the Renaissance Era, as documented presumably by LRL no. 12: "Now we are dwelling here in the "temple" (*ẖr tw.n dy ḥms.ti m t3 ḥw.t*) and you know the conditions in which we live both inside and outside" (see Chapter 6). It is hardly possible that it was the danger caused by an unstable situation among the desert tribes which prompted the transfer of the crew.[61] Instead, the reason should be searched for in the political situation on the eve of the Renaissance Era, in relation to the later phase of the civil war.[62] Quite possibly D. Valbelle was right, when she suggested that the crew was already living in the complex of Medinet Habu when the workmen received payment in the great court of the temple in Medinet Habu in year 17 of Ramesses XI (papTurin 1888+2085, 1, 7).[63]

It is important to acknowledge that the latest extant pages of the necropolis journal, preserved in papTurin 1888+2085, attest not only the existence of

of his activity was significantly longer; an assumption contradicted on p. 284).

[58] Not recorded, however, in the lists of the scribes connected with Deir el-Medina, cf. Černý, Community, 191ff. (esp. page opposite p. 230). Certainly he cannot be identified with the well known scribe of the necropolis, cf. Černý, Community, 361 (otherwise id., CdE 11, 1936, 249); Valbelle, Ouvriers, 124.

[59] PapBM 10068vo. 6, 21. As regards the character of this compilation, i.e. the list of houses, cf. Kemp, Ancient Egypt, 308.

[60] Cf. Černý, Community, 378 n. 4.; Valbelle, Ouvriers, 124f.

[61] See McDowell, in: Pharaoh's Workers, 57.

[62] But not the war against the High Priest Amenhotep, the occurence which should be dated to a much earlier period. I agree with J.J. Janssen (AoF 19, 1992, 14) that LRL no. 12 slightly postdates the abandonment of the village in Deir el-Medina, provided that the letter in question is much later than suggested by him (see below, Chapter 6).

[63] Gardiner RAD, 64, 12-65, 1; cf. Valbelle, Ouvriers, 125; Janssen, AoF 19, 1992, 13f.; Haring, Divine Households, 279; the passage wrongly interpreted by Ch. Thiers, BIFAO 95, 1995, 494 (b) and n. 6.

the *semdet* labour force, but also some other officials, whose function remains inseparable from the institution of the royal necropolis. Thus we can be sure that the crew was still functioning along the administrative patterns of the previous years although its goals were fundamentally different from those of the earlier times – quite obviously it was not the building of the royal tomb, since virtually no mention of it can be found in the text. The extant fragment of the journal gives the names of a group of the necropolis workmen, and also some members of the *semdet*-staff, working together to fulfil some tasks, apparently not connected either with the necropolis or the royal tomb in particular.[64] Among the men of the *semdet*-staff enumerated there we can see the gypsum-worker Pakharu (2, 3; 2, 11),[65] already met in papTurin 2018 (see above). The document in question has a special significance for our understanding of the situation in the Theban region on the eve of the Renaissance Era. Among the highest officials mentioned in the papyrus we can see the overseer of the treasury Menmarenakht, and the vizier Wennefer – both representing a newly reinstated royal administration over the Thebaid.

According to the Turin Taxation Papyrus (papTurin 1895+2006),[66] two scribes of the necropolis (at that time) actively participated in the collection of taxes in the vast agricultural area south of Thebes. If this document can be taken as proof of the existence of the institution of the royal necropolis in its previous form, it enables us to draw the conclusion that the procedures of its provisioning changed profoundly in comparison with that of the preceding periods, as the quite exceptional role of the scribes of the necropolis clearly shows.[67] Anyway, the Turin Taxation Papyrus, dated to the period of Panehesy's supremacy in the Thebaid (years 12 and 14), and other similar documents testify to a considerable effort to sustain the crew of the necropolis and other Theban institutions. The preamble of the document gives the royal protocol at the beginning and the name of viceroy Panehesy as responsible for collection of taxes.[68] The fiscal system was efficient even if it led sometimes to some disturbances or evident irregularities in the framework of the fiscal procedures, as exemplified clearly by LRL no. 37 of approximately the same date,

[64] Cf. Černý, Community, 190; Valbelle, Ouvriers, 44.

[65] Gardiner RAD, 66, 11; 67, 10-11.

[66] Pleyte-Rossi, Papyrus de Turin, pls. 65, 100, 154-157; Gardiner RAD, 35ff.; id., JEA 27, 1941, 22-37 (§2); Helck, Materialien IV, (564)ff.

[67] Cf. McDowell, JEA 78, 1992, 196; Sweeney, JEA 80, 1994, 209 n. 12.

[68] Gardiner RAD, 36, 1-5; cf. id., JEA 27, 1941, 23; Helck, Materialien IV, (571).

as it would seem (see Chapter 6).[69] Apparent irregularities were also reported by papValençay I,[70] being in fact a protest of the mayor of Elephantine to the Chief Taxing-Master (*ꜥ3-n-št*) Menmarenakht[71] apparently against some unjustified tax demands.[72] The latter document is especially interesting because of the role played by the domain of the Divine Adoratress of Amun in exacting the taxes from the fields in the region of Kom Ombo (Ombos). Anyway the role of the domain of Amun (and the high priest himself) in administering the necropolis and provisioning of its staff, at the end of the 20th Dynasty, cannot escape our attention, although it cannot be substantiated in more detail as regards the reign of Ramesses XI itself.[73]

Unfortunately, no exact date can be inferred on the basis of the text of papBM 10401,[74] except a general dating of the document to the late 20th Dynasty. As a consequence it cannot be established whether the tax collected by an anonymous Chief Taxing-Master from the temples south of Thebes, between Elephantine and Esna, had anything to do with the exceptional situation following the civil war, or maybe it illustrates a normal practice of the fiscal policy.[75] Here too it was the scribe of the necropolis Nesamenope,[76] who again participated in collecting the tax.

If the proposed dating of the LRL no. 47 approximately to year 12 of Ramesses XI is retained,[77] then we should assume that the movement of the crew from Deir el-Medina to Medinet Habu happened probably several years later. It has been suggested that a decreasing number of ostraca from the village of Deir el-Medina itself can be connected directly with the transfer of the crew to the dwellings in Medinet Habu.[78] Let us note, however, that

[69] For the meaning of the text, and possible manipulation with a grain measure, cf. Helck, Materialien IV, (580); Allam HOP I, 306; Janssen, Commodity Prices, 549; Sweeney, JEA 80, 1994, 208ff.; Toivari, JESHO 40.2, 1997, 160; Quack, in: Mélanges offerts à F. Neveu, 259ff.

[70] Gardiner RAD, 72f.; id., RdE 6, 1951, 115ff.; Helck, Materialien II, (237), (283)f.

[71] Probably the same person as the overseer of the treasury of slightly later documents, cf. Peet, JEA 14, 1928, 66, 70; Gardiner, RdE 6, 1951, 123; Helck, Verwaltung, 418, 505 (22). As regards the title of the chief taxing master, cf. Gardiner AEO I, 34* (no. 110); Helck, Verwaltung, 143f.; Janssen, JEA 77, 1991, 83f.

[72] As a result of the fact that a difference existed between *khato*-lands of Pharaoh and private landholdings obliged to pay taxes directly to the treasury, cf. Gardiner, Wilbour Papyrus Comm., 206; id., RdE 6, 1951, 123f.; Malinine, BiOr 16, 1959, 217; Kemp, Ancient Egypt, 310.

[73] For this, see Häggman, Directing DeM, 261ff.; Janssen, JEA 77, 1991, 93.

[74] Janssen, JEA 77, 1991, 79ff., pl. 4.2.; see also Warburton, op.cit., 151, 288.

[75] Or else an acquisition of some goods for a specific purpose (a festival?), cf. Warburton, op.cit., 290f.

[76] As regards his identity, see Černý, Community, 214; Janssen, loc.cit., 90.

[77] See Wente LRL, 1-2; Davies, Who's Who at DeM, 136.

[78] A jar label from Deir el-Medina, dated tentatively to the Renaissance Era, is rather doubtful

the number of preserved ostraca dating to the reign of Ramesses IX is not significantly higher in number than those of later date, although the crew was still dwelling in Deir el-Medina. Besides, such a reasoning does not explain satisfactorily why the ostraca disappear also from the working chantier in Valley of the Kings and Valley of the Queens, where the scribes could have easily made their notes on the limestone flakes according to their common habit. Apparently the reason for the transfer of the crew must be sought rather in the changed structure and organization of the staff of the royal necropolis in those troubled times when Panehesy's army occupied the Thebaid and the rest of Upper Egypt. It would be pointless to discuss it without any reference to the political situation in Egypt in those times.

It is hardly possible that the move of the crew from the village of Deir el-Medina to the nearby complex in Medinet Habu was instigated by a simple weakening of the security of the Theban necropolis and its staff. Administrative inefficiency and most of all the substantial weakening of the state during the reign of Ramesses XI, and especially in the period of the civil war of Panehesy, must be viewed as main factors laying behind the final decision of the abandonment of the royal necropolis in the Valley of the Kings. No doubt, it was the cessation of work on the royal tomb which was the direct reason for the profound changes in the structure and function of the necropolis staff.[79] This must be viewed as the main factor which put an end to the administrative practice of the detailed recording of the progress of work of the crew and its logistics.

The attitude of the members of necropolis staff themselves towards these undertakings remains completely unknown, unless we take as such an obscure affair relating to the words of two unnamed Madjoy, as referred to in LRL nos. 21, 34-35, though much later in date (i.e., of the Renaissance Era). One can only surmise whether this ever referred to some irregularities in the administrative system, or else to even more scandalous depredations occurring in the royal necropolis? Nothing is known either about internal troubles comparable to those documented still in the reign of Ramesses IX. Thus it remains only a matter of mere speculation that repeated delays in the

---

evidence, cf. Y. Koenig, Catalogue des étiquettes de jarres hiératiques de Deir el-Médineh, II, [DFIFAO 21/2], Cairo 1980, 91, pl. 62 (no. 6488); the dating proposed by P. Tallet, in: Z. Hawass (ed.), Egyptology at the dawn of the Twenty-first Century. Proceedings of the Eight International Congress of Egyptologists, I, Cairo 2002, 495f.

[79] Cf. also Häggman, Directing DeM, 323ff.

delivery of provisions (if not subsequent workmen's strikes) were possibly still a significant factor during the reign of Ramesses XI as well.[80]

Anyway, the organization of the system of the tax collecting in this period reveals some unprecedented irregularities, as summarised above. In this context the very meaning of the *šrmt*-list of papBM 10068vo. 1, cannot be evaluated properly, although it seems to record some kind of tax levied on a group of inhabitants of the West Bank.[81] This unique document gives the names of those who took part in the collection of the tax. Some of them at least were the members of the temple staff in Medinet Habu, who were active in the years following the deposition of the High Priest Amenhotep – the scribe Tuthmosis (not necessarily the same person as the well known scribe of the necropolis),[82] the army scribe Kashuty, and the scribe Pentahutnakht. The document in question was written after the list of houses of year 12 of Ramesses XI, on II *peret* 16 of an unknown year (the numeral omitted by mistake), thus it can postdate the former by seven months at least (or maybe more).[83] According to an interesting hypothesis, the tax or a kind of fine could have been levied on those who had participated in the riots of the preceding years.[84]

The small number of ostraca which can be dated confidently to the reign of Ramesses XI[85] make any attempt to reconstruct the realities of the everyday

---

80 Note for example a suggested "collapse of fish delivery under Ramesses IX and X" (Antoine, SAK 35, 2006, 35).

81 Cf. Černý, Community, 361; Janssen, JEA 77, 1991, 93; id., AoF 19, 1992, 20-23. As regards the meaning of the term, cf. Lesko, Dict. II, 133; J.E. Hoch, Semitic Words in Egyptian Texts of the New Kingdom and Third Intermediate Period, Princeton 1994, 286f. (409).

82 Cf. Černý, loc.cit.; contrary to the view expressed by Janssen, AoF 19, 1992, 20 (similarly Haring, Divine Households, 246 n. 6); he is not titled as the scribe of the necropolis, and his colleagues – the scribe Khonsumose and attendant (*šmsw*) Shedamenwa – cannot be linked to the necropolis staff either.

83 Cf. Janssen, AoF 19, 1992, 8, 20 n. 88; Davies, Who's Who at DeM, 201.

84 Janssen, AoF 19, 1992, 22. It is hardly likely that it was a recovery of the property stolen from the tombs during the war against the High Priest Amenhotep, as suggested earlier by Aldred, Tomb Robberies, 94; cf. also Jansen-Winkeln, ZÄS 122, 1995, 63 n. 17.

85 Cf. Janssen, in:Village Voices, 86 n. 25. Those of a doubtful dating are the following: (1) oTurin 57049=Lopez, Ostraca 1, 32, pls. 32-32a, mentioning Amenhotep son of the scribe Amennakht, who was active still at the beginning of the reign of Ramesses XI, but the ostracon can be dated to a much earlier period, cf. Gutgesell, Datierung, 476. (2) oTurin 57121=Lopez, Ostraca 2, 17, pls. 57-57a, dated by Gutgesell (Datierung, 478) definitely to the reign of Ramesses XI, can be also much earlier in date, cf. Davies, Who's Who at DeM, 52f. (3) oDeM 10085=Grandet, Ostraca DeM X, 89, 277, mentioning possibly the name of the daughter of the scribe Khaemhedje, thus a dating to the very beginning of the reign of Ramesses XI cannot be wholly excluded. (4) oPetrie 51=Černý-Gardiner HO, pl. 28.1; Kitchen, RamInscr VI, 869f.; Allam HOP I, 241; as regards its dating to the earlier period, cf. Gutgesell, Datierung, 415f.; Janssen, Commodity Prices, 67f.; id., JEA 80, 1994, 130. Doubtful in dating are also: oBerlin 12405, cf. Gutgesell, Datierung, 444; oGardiner 249, cf. ibid., 456.

life of the crew in this period highly controversial. As a consequence our knowledge of the functioning of administration in the area is extremely fragmentary. Let us turn our attention to those rare ostraca which can add some vivid details to the picture of the general disorder in those troubled times.

Thus for example the identity of the scribe Hori,[86] who did harm (*th3 nb*) to deputy Seny (oCG 25236),[87] remains a little bit obscure.[88] Although the ostracon was found in the tomb of Ramesses IX (KV 6),[89] the name of the vizier Ramesses Montu-er-hatef may be useful in dating of this document to the later reign as it seems, most probably the early years of Ramesses XI.[90] The scanty documentation concerning vizier Montu-er-hatef, the father of the vizier Wennefer, includes papTurin 2084+2091 (ro. 3, 10),[91] not to mention an inscription from Karnak North.[92] The same also concerns the deputy Seny, who is mentioned only in two other extant documents.[93] We also know that the door-keeper Khonsumose (ro. 8),[94] was active from year 7 of Ramesses IX (papTurin 1906+2047/132+1939, ro. 2, 10)[95] until at least year 12 of Ramesses XI, as documented by the Turin Taxation Papyrus (ro. 4, 3).[96] The chronolo-

[86] So Daressy (see below), followed by Kitchen, RamInscr VI, 839, 7; Davies, Who's Who at DeM, 72 n. 137; more plausibly Černý (Community, 354) gives here the name of the scribe Horisheri; similarly Bell, Serapis 6, 1980, 13; McDowell, Jurisdiction, 233; Kitchen, RamInscr VII, 460, 13.

[87] Daressy, Ostraca, 59f., pls. 49-50; Kitchen, Ram Inscr VI, 839f.; VII, 460f. (revised version based on Černý's transcription); for a general comment, cf. Černý, loc.cit.

[88] Nevertheles the scribe Hori may be the same person as the scribe of the *semdet*-staff (father of the well known scribe Efnamun), mentioned very often in the sources from the Theban necropolis dating as late as the reign of Ramesses IX, cf. Černý, Community, 216ff. (no. 51); Davies, Who's Who at DeM, 284. For the general problem of the identity of the scribes called Hori, see Davies, op.cit., 143ff.

[89] Daressy, Ostraca, 59.

[90] Cf. Janssen JEA 53, 1967, 163f.; Vandersleyen, L'Égypte II, 649.

[91] Kitchen, RamInscr VI, 605, 3; cf. Gutgesell, Datierung, 245ff.; Helck OPG, 492; the document dated unequivocally to the early decade of the reign of Ramesses IX.

[92] Kitchen, RamInscr VI, 840f.; PM II^2, 13 (40). As regards an unpublished ostracon from Carnarvon-Carter excavations, cf. Černý, BiOr 19, 1962, 142.

[93] These are the following: oCG 25742: Černý, Ostraca CG, 89*, pl. 90; Černý (Community, 157) dated the ostracon to the reign of Ramesses XI; as for its dating to the reign of Ramesses IX, see however Valbelle, Ouvriers, 345; Davies, Who's Who at DeM, 72, 200. Deputy Seny son of Khaemhedje appears also in papTurin 1891vo. 4: Pleyte-Rossi, Papyrus de Turin, pl. 50=Kitchen, RamInscr VI, 636, 15; as regards its dating to year 11 of Ramesses IX, see Gutgesell, Datierung, 137f., and 389 (suggested chronology of the deputies during the reign of Ramesses IX); Valbelle, Ouvriers, 81; Bellion, Catalogue, 286; Černý, Community, 127, 157; compare however ibid., 143f., where he suggested a date within the reign of Ramesses XI.

[94] Certainly not Khonsuemheb, as suggested by Daressy's transcription, cf. Černý, Community, 168 n. 1; not corrected in Kitchen, RamInscr VI, 839, 13; VII, 461, 4.

[95] Kitchen, RamInscr VI, 625, 11; cf. Gutgesell, Datierung, 255f.; Helck OPG, 481.

[96] Gardiner RAD, 40, 8; cf. Gutgesell, Datierung, 258, 299; Černý, Community, 167f., 170; Davies, Who's Who at DeM, 201.

gical position of guardian Kadjore, mentioned twice in the text of the ostracon (ro. 7, 10), may be securely determined as between year 9 of Ramesses IX and the Renaissance Era.[97] This is well enough as it seems to date oCG 25236 to the late 20th Dynasty – most probably the reign of Ramesses IX,[98] or else (less possibly perhaps?) that of Ramesses XI.[99]

The case of oCG 25236 exemplifies all the problems with interpretation of the prosopographic data relating to the reign of Ramesses XI, and as a consequence with a dating of the available documents. More conclusive perhaps in regard to its dating is the information provided by oCG 25232 from KV 9,[100] with a hymn to a goddess (?), and a protective formula on behalf of "the scribe of the necropolis Penparei" at the end (vo. 1-4). The chronological position of this Penparei among the scribes of the necropolis can be placed, with some degree of uncertainty, within the reign of Ramesses XI (in its later part).[101] In addition, some scraps of information on the crew and its activity can be obtained from some undated ostraca, which can be attributed to this period on the basis of a prosopographic study.[102]

No doubt, the situation of the local community of the West Bank changed dramatically at the moment of occupation of Thebes by the army of the viceroy Panehesy. One can only speculate about the exact date of an ostracon with a short oracle text of unknown provenance, but connected probably with the community of the West Bank, and Deir el-Medina in particular: "Have the soldiers of the army (*nꜣ rmṯ pꜣ mšꜥ*) robbed (or: taken) it?".[103] Other texts (see Chapter 2) inform us that "foreigners" (*ꜣꜥꜥ.w*) were among those who had ransacked the Theban temples and tombs during the civil war.[104] It is still open to question whether at least some of them were soldiers of the army of

---

97 Davies, op.cit., 200ff.; cf. also Černý, Community, 157ff. For the dating of LRL no. 1, see below Chapter 6.

98 Gutgesell, Datierung, 247f., 258f.; see now Kitchen, RamInscr VII, 460; Davies, op.cit., 72; similarly Thijs, GM 184, 2001, 68 n. 28.

99 Cf. Černý, Community, 143, 168 n.1.; id., BiOr 19, 1962, 142; Kitchen, RamInscr VI, 839.

100 Erman, ZÄS 38, 1900, 38 (IX); Daressy, Ostraca, 57, pl. 49; Kitchen, RamInscr VII, 403.

101 Cf. Davies, Who's Who at DeM, 104, 284, chart.46: Penparei (II) son of Paherentahatnakhte (I).

102 These are the following: oTurin 57372: Lopez, Ostraca 3, pl. 116-116a=Kitchen, RamInscr VII, 397f.; oCG 25648: Černý, Ostraca CG, 69*, pl. 65; Gutgesell, Datierung, 431f. (years 8-18 of Ramesses XI); oCG 25708: Černý, Ostraca CG, 86*, pl. 83; Gutgesell, Datierung, 433; oGardiner 63: Černý-Gardiner HO, pl. 59.3; Gutgesell, Datierung, 474.

103 Cf. J. Černý, Troisième série des questions adressées aux oracles, BIFAO 72, 1972, 52 (no. 42), pl. 16 (oBrussels E 317).

104 As regards of their status and role in relation to the memorial temples in Thebes, cf. Haring, Divine Households, 246, 366. For the term in general, see above Chapter 2.

Panehesy, settled in the Theban nome.[105] Anyway, when the hostilities broke out, it was "foreigners" who attacked the temple in Medinet Habu. One can imagine that some of them were stationed in Thebes in the garrison left by Panehesy to protect the fragile stability in the region. Eventually some of these soldiers could have been rewarded with fields in Thebes and its vicinity, as documented presumably by the Turin Taxation Papyrus (vo. 2-4), enumerating a group of foreigners as landholders in the region to the south of Thebes.[106] Significantly, one of these men – the foreigner Paykamen son of Pawaamun (vo. 2, 5)[107] – reappears several years later in the judicial documents of the beginning of the Renaissance Era as one of the culprits.[108] This is additional evidence relating to the role played by the soldiers of Panehesy's troops in ravaging the Theban nome, related to in more detail above (Chapter 2).

Apparently the new administrative system in this period had all the traits of a military regime imposed upon Thebes and its community, and some evident anomalies in its functioning may be explained perhaps in the framework of the extraordinary means adopted by the viceroy Panehesy. Administrative patterns elaborated at the moment of internal crisis survived the transition to the 21st Dynasty, when the new military organization typical for the Libyan period had been developed.[109] In this context, a temporary imposition of the royal administration after the expulsion of Panehesy, and at the beginning of the Renaissance Era, may be viewed only as an unsuccessful attempt of departure from rules prevailing in the period of occupation of Thebes by Panehesy's army. The role of the royal butlers in this period can be described as that of personal representatives of the king.[110] Even though the impact of the central administration in Thebes cannot be doubted, the power of the high priest

[105] As suggested by Valbelle, Ouvriers, 221.

[106] Cf. Pleyte-Rossi, Papyrus de Turin, pl. 96; Gardiner RAD, 43f.; see also id., JEA 27, 1941, 35-7, for an identification of the place names. According to Helck, Materialien IV, (571), these were prisoners of war; compare however Janssen, SAK 3, 1975, 172f. and n. 212.

[107] Gardiner RAD, 43, 4.

[108] PapAbbott-dockets, vo. B, 8: Peet, Tomb Robberies, pl. 23=Kitchen, RamInscr VI, 766, 5. Quite possibly he is the same person as the skipper (*nfw*) of that name (papAbbott-dockets, vo. A, 7); in both cases his brother was enumerated directly after him, cf. Peet, op.cit., 132f. If this is the case, his depositions were written in papMayer A, vo. 9, 20-21; and papBM 10052vo. 9, 1-6; in addition his name was given in the list of papMayer A, vo. 12, 22 – here as a simple crew member (*is.t- wsḫ*).

[109] As regards the Libyan background of the 21st Dynasty, see now Jansen-Winkeln, BN 71, 1994, 78ff.

[110] For the role of royal butlers, cf. Helck, Verwaltung, 275f.; Schulman, CdE 61, 1986, 198f.; O'Connor, in: Trigger et al., A Social History, 231; as regards their role in the necropolis matters in the earlier periods, see Häggman, Directing DeM, 110.

of Amun at this period cannot be evaluated properly.[111] Presumably, it was the political ambitions of Herihor which finally disturbed the state of fragile equilibrium of power.

Any conclusions regarding the organization of the institution of the royal necropolis in the early years of the Renaissance Era must be based on extremely fragmentary sources. These are limited mostly to LRL and the dossier relating to the later phase of the tomb robbery trials. Unfortunately there are no documents comparable to the journal of the necropolis of the preceding period, except some rare papyri relating to the activity of the crew and its provisioning.[112] Numerous ostraca of the earlier periods were replaced now by the graffiti dispersed in the Theban area, which constitute the primary source of our knowledge on the activities of the necropolis crew and its composition. The nearly complete lack of ostraca in this period inevitably leads to the conclusion that the administrative practice of the period had changed radically. This does not necessarily mean, however, that administration of the necropolis was ineffective or else that it ceased to function completely. On the contrary, an imposition of the "military rule" acted as a stabilizing factor, at least temporarily.[113] The new administration of the Theban west bank was responsible also for new projects connected with the security of the royal necropolis. One can only surmise that the work on new tombs destined for the high priests themselves and their close relatives was also one of the objectives of the necropolis crew at those times,[114] although the range of its activity cannot be compared with that of the previous generations. For years the proper activity of the crew appears to have ceased, with the effect that in the late 21st Dynasty little is heard of the royal necropolis and its crew.

Three distinct periods can be distinguished in regard of the functioning of the Theban administration during the Renaissance Era:[115]

---

[111] For a general comment, see Gasse, Domaine d'Amon I, 221f.; Eyre, SAK 11, 1984, 205f.

[112] These are papyri Turin 2034 (year 1), 2094 (year 2), and 1903 (years 4-5), cf. Kitchen, RamInscr VI, 865ff.; VII, 395ff.; Helck OPG, 568ff. As regards an unpublished papTurin 2097/161 (+2105)vo., dated by Helck to year 2 of the Renaissance Era (ibid., 569f.; SAK 17, 1990, 211f.), and to the reign of Ramesses IX by Ohlhafer (GM 135, 1993, 61), it has been redated now to year 2 of Ramesses X, cf. Demarée, GM 137, 1993, 49f.; for its contents, see Häggman, Directing DeM, 263.

[113] Cf. Kemp, Ancient Egypt, 244.

[114] Cf. Valbelle, Ouvriers, 226; Warburton, op.cit., 171; McDowell, in: Pharaoh's Workers, 57; Peden, Decline of Textual Graffiti, 290.

[115] More detailed discussion on these questions will be presented in the succeeding chapters.

(1) The period of the royal administration established temporarily at least in the region after depredations of the civil war. Unfortunately no data relating to the royal necropolis may be explicitly discerned from the sources of the early Renaissance Era.

(2) Attaining the vizierate by the High Priest Herihor and the beginning of his effective rule in the Thebaid. The beginning of the actions aiming at preservation of the royal mummies may be placed in this very period in the light of the coffin dockets presented in the preceding chapter.

(3) The relatively dark period of the high priesthood of Payankh, and presumably the parallel kingship of Herihor for which there are no datable references in the material originating from the Theban necropolis (see Chapter 3).

The existence of the regular *semdet*-staff, supporting the men of the crew in later years of the Renaissance Era cannot be proven beyond any doubt. A reference to "my people (*n3y.i rmṯ*) and my *semdet*-staff (*n3y.i smd.t*) as well" (LRL no. 45),[116] in an unpreserved letter written probably by the scribe Tuthmosis,[117] may indicate indeed that the system of the auxiliary labour force still existed at that time.[118] One can only surmise what kind of servants was mentioned in LRL no. 30, sent by "Pharaoh's general" Payankh to "the two chief workmen, the scribe Butehamun, guardian Kar(oy), and all the workmen of the necropolis": "Now as for the matter of these five maidservants (*t3y 5 b3k.w*) whom I gave, they are yours, all of them, from the captains down to all the workmen of the crew. But do not let anyone tyrannize his fellow among you. And do not give any of them to Heramenpenaf; indeed, I have already given to him. If you have not received them, you shall go to the place where Hrere is and you shall receive them from her".[119] It has been assumed that these were female servants (possibly women slaves?) given to the community of the necropolis workmen to fulfil the simple task of grinding the grain rations into flour.[120] Thus we are informed, that the captains of the crew were authorized by Payankh to contact with Hrere to exact

[116] Černý LRL, 66, 11.

[117] The words cited in the letter addressed supposedly to the scribe Tuthmosis, cf. Wente LRL, 5, 17.

[118] See Häggman, Directing DeM, 323.

[119] Černý LRL, 50, 13-51, 2; cf. Černý-Groll, Late Egyptian Grammar, 361 (Ex. 1023), 546 (Ex. 1546); Groll, Negative Verbal System, 75 (Ex. 160); Frandsen, Verbal System, 12 (Ex. 1), 83 (Ex. 21); Neveu, Grammaire, 193 (Ex. 3); for the recent translations of the text, cf. Wente, Letters, 198; McDowell, Village Life, 234f. (no. 186).

[120] Cf. Černý, Community, 178f.; McDowell, Village Life, 234; cf also Junge, Neuägyptisch, 320: a comment on five female servants ("Hausmädchen"; *ḥm.t*), being members of the *semdet*-staff.

this generous donation, if it was not yet carried out. Besides, an unspecified number of the serfs was given earlier to Heramenpenaf, who appears to have cooperated with the gang in the matters concerning manufacture of some bronze objects, as attested in the same letter: "Another matter for the scribe Butehamun and the guardian Kar(oy). Please, join up with Heramenpenaf and receive the copper from him and (then) send it to the coppersmith Tutuy and the coppersmith Hori, when he finishes, and to the two coppersmiths of mine. And cause them to make this kni[fe] and two *tkꜣ*-vessels. There is tin in your possession to add (it) to the copper".[121]

The role of the general Payankh as exemplified by the letter cited above can be defined indeed as that of the immediate supervisor of the necropolis staff:[122] "And you will not be neglectful in any matters of mine; and you will preserve my letter so that it may serve for you as testi[mony]".[123] It is doubtful, however, what kind of work the crew was obliged to do under his supervision. Anyway, it was hardly the regular work in the necropolis that was meant here, but rather the manufacture of some objects for general's personal use, as it seems. Thus we can only presume that the servants (or slaves) handed over by general Payankh to Heramenpenaf were in fact a reward for metal used for the production of the objects enumerated in the letter. It cannot be excluded, however, that production of the weapons for the army operating in Nubia is referred to in the letter. As we know this was a duty of the guardian Karoy,[124] and possibly also other members of the necropolis staff were delegated to fulfil this urgent task. This is not the case, however, of the coppersmith Hori, working on the production of the weapons,[125] of whom nothing is known as regards his relation to the gang except the mere fact that he was working under direction of the scribe Tuthmosis and his son.[126]

Payankh's responsibility for collecting the taxes (in year 7 of the Renaissance Era) in the region of Xth Upper Egyptian nome is amply documented by

[121] Černý LRL, 51, 4-8; cf. Frandsen, Verbal System, 109f. (Ex. 4), 115 (Ex. 1); Winand, Études, 223 (Ex. 524); Wente, Letters, 198.

[122] But not the actual ruler or the highest authority in the Thebaid, as aptly observed by Vandersleyen, L'Égypte II, 649; for a different point of view, see Demarée, Bankes Papyri, 18f.; Gnirs, Militär und Gesellschaft, 210f.

[123] Černý LRL, 51, 2-3; cf. Winand, Études, 222 (Ex. 521); Neveu, Grammaire, 135 (Ex. 11); McDowell, Village Life, 235; Sweeney, Correspondence and Dialogue, 236.

[124] Cf. Černý, Community, 159f.; Häggman, Directing DeM, 216f., 329f.; as regards the manufacture of spears see also Černý, op.cit., 379.

[125] As referred to in LRL nos. 8, 9, 10, 16, and 50; see also Chapter 7 below.

[126] Cf. Valbelle, Ouvriers, 129.

papPrakhov.[127] In addition, according to papTurin 1903 some extraordinary measures[128] were undertaken to pay the necropolis workmen in some precious commodities (copper, garments and oil) in years 4-5 of the Renaissance Era.[129] This time the collection and delivery of goods was conducted under the auspices of an unnamed vizier, and the overseer of the treasury Wennefer was in charge of it, but it was the deputy of the (royal) treasury Hori who carried it out. We are informed that a great amount of copper was taken then from the mortuary temples of the West Bank of Thebes, whereas other goods were provided by the temples of the East Bank as well.

It is hardly possible that those cooperating with general Payankh ever entered the military ranks, but we can imagine instead, that they were connected in some way or another with the military personnel of the temple of Medinet Habu, which played such a prominent role in the local administration in Western Thebes during the Renaissance Era.[130] This is not an unusual situation, if army officials were connected with Theban temples and the necropolis even in much earlier times.[131] Certainly the role of an unnamed "general from the temple of the king of Upper and Lower Egypt Usermaatre-Meriamun", being in contact with the crew during the unrest in the necropolis in the reign of Ramesses III (oVarille39+oIFAO 1255),[132] cannot be viewed as an exception in regard of the administrative patterns of the epoch. Nonetheless the military administration expanded remarkably during the unsafe period of the civil war and afterwards.[133]

---

[127] Cf. Gasse, Domaine d'Amon I, 123-138; Berlev, GM 160, 1997, 5ff. As regards the undated papLouvre AF 6345+Griffith fragments, relating to the taxation of corn in the same region, cf. Gardiner RAD, 68ff.; id., JEA 27, 1941, 64-70; Gasse, op.cit., I, 3ff., pls. 1-31; II, pls. 78-98; see also my comments above, Chapter 3.

[128] See Häggman, Directing DeM, 277.

[129] Cf. Kitchen, RamInscr VII, 395ff.; Helck OPG, 571; for the comment, see Janssen, Commodity Prices, 456f.; id., Village Varia, 2; Haring, Divine Households, 228f., 264-266, 275; Häggman, Directing DeM, 246, 248, 277f.

[130] Haring, Divine Households, 246f.; Gnirs, Militär und Gesellschaft, 170ff. As regards the role of the complex in Medinet Habu as an administrative centre of the West Bank, cf. e.g. Černý, JEA 26, 1940, 129f.; Haring, Divine Households, 278ff.; Häggman, Directing DeM, 281ff.

[131] Haring, op.cit., 247; Gnirs, op.cit., 9.

[132] Cf. Kitchen, RamInscr VII, 300, 15-301, 1; cf. also P.J. Frandsen, Editing Reality: The Turin Strike Papyrus, in: Israelit-Groll S. (ed.), Studies in Egyptology presented to M. Lichtheim, I, Jerusalem 1990, 174; Häggman, Directing DeM, 165; Gnirs, Militär und Gesellschaft, 170 (as regards the dating, see n. 1088).

[133] Gnirs, op.cit., 139f., 172.

Excursus: A comment on redating of the documents of the reign of Ramesses XI (of years 1-16) to the Renaissance Era, as proposed by A. Thijs

To uphold the hypothesis of the partial overlapping the reigns of Ramesses IX-X and XI, A. Thijs did not hesitate to redate all the documents connected hitherto with the early decades of Ramesses XI to the Renaissance Era. Unfortunately the results of such a procedure hardly withstand criticism.[134] A review of the assertions proposed by A. Thijs will be presented here in more detail, although only the most crucial points in the discussion can be covered, besides those commented above in the preceding chapters. The apparent contradictions resulting from Thijs' chronological scheme have a crucial meaning for our understanding of the history of the period and its chronology. As a matter of fact the documents enumerated below have a bearing on our understanding of the functioning of the institution of the royal necropolis during the two decades of the reign of Ramesses XI:

PapTurin 1898+, vo. – fragment of the necropolis journal of year 1 (date preserved),[135] with partly legible name of Ramesses XI. Dating of the text to year 1 of the Renaissance Era is practically impossible, because of the name of the scribe of the *semdet*-staff Efnamun, at this particular period responsible for the *semdet*-staff of the left side of the crew.[136] The latest of the securely dated documents with the name of the scribe Efnamun is papBM 10068vo. 7, 8 of year 12 (called here the scribe of the necropolis).[137] Moreover, such a late dating of the text must be excluded on the basis of the mention of the "scribe Khaem[hedje]",[138] whose name never appears in the documents of the Renaissance Era, except those cases perhaps, when it was mentioned by his son and successor to the post, the scribe Tuthmosis of the necropolis.

PapTurin 2003 – document dated to year 3 (related now to the reign of Ramesses XI rather than Ramesses X).[139] In this case the supposition

[134] Similarly in the case of the alternative chronological scheme proposed by Demidoff, GM 177, 2000, 96ff.

[135] Botti-Peet, Giornale, pl. 63=Kitchen, RamInscr VI, 850, 14-851, 5; for the new edition, cf. von Beckerath, SAK 21, 1994, 29ff., fig. 1.

[136] Cf. Botti-Peet, Giornale, pl. 63 (vo. a, 7)=Kitchen, RamInscr VI, 850, 16.

[137] Peet, Tomb Robberies, pl. 16=Kitchen, RamInscr VI, 754, 5; quite possibly a reference in papBM 9997 (1, 2) of year 15 should be added, cf. Kitchen, RamInscr VII, 389, 6, where certain Efnamun (without a title) appears alongside the scribe Efenkhonsu, and the scribe Pentahutnakhte.

[138] Botti-Peet, Giornale, pl. 63 (vo. a, 10)=Kitchen, RamInscr VI, 851, 1.

[139] Pleyte-Rossi, Papyrus de Turin, pl. 91; Kitchen, RamInscr VI, 851, replaced now by: ibid. VII, 388; cf. also Helck, Materialien V, (846)f.; id. OPG, 561; Eichler, SAK 17, 1990, 158ff.; for its dating, see Černý, ArOr 6, 1933, 175 (12); Valbelle, Ouvriers, 81 n. 6 (Ramesses X or XI); Helck OPG, 557 (year

that it should be dated to the Renaissance Era[140] cannot be discarded after all,[141] especially because of the names of the workmen (?) Paankhau and Pennestytawy, both attested in the sources from the reign of Ramesses IX,[142] but also from LRL nos. 12 and 15 (Pennestytawy), oCG 25574 (Pennestytawy), and oCG 25575 (Paankhau),[143] documents much later in time.[144] The names of the scribe Tuthmosis and the water carrier Pakharu cannot provide a decisive argument in regard of this; the document concerns a private transaction, so one cannot ascertain convincingly the role of the water carrier Pakharu in relation to the crew; in the case of a later dating of the papyrus he could hardly belong to the *semdet*-staff of the crew.[145]

PapTurin 2018 – this document gives among others the name of Bakenmut son of Khonsu as a simple workman in years 8, 9 (ro. A2, 8; ro. A3, 7; ro. A4, 9; vo. B1, 9),[146] and possibly also in year 10 (vo. A2, 10a);[147] just as much earlier (year 2? of Ramesses X) in papTurin 1932+1939 (vo. 2, 1),[148] and slightly later in the necropolis journal of papTurin 1888, in years 17 and 18 of Ramesses XI (2, 11).[149] Yet he appears as a foreman in the undated papTurin 2021(+Genève D 409), and also in LRL no. 1 (see below Chapter 6). None of the documents explicitly dated to the Renaissance Era mentions him at all, but he appears in LRLC no. III, securely placed in the period

3 of Ramesses XI).

140 See Thijs, GM 173, 1999, 190.

141 Cf. Janssen, Commodity Prices, 97; Gutgesell, Datierung, 496 (year 3 of Ramesses XI or of the Renaissance Era); Davies, SAK 24, 1997, 60.

142 Cf. Gutgesell, Datierung, 220f.; Valbelle, Ouvriers, tab. IX.

143 Černý LRL, 23,16; 30,3; id. Ostraca CG, 49*, 50*, pls. 38, 39. It is difficult to decide, however, which one of the two workmen by the name Paankhau should be identified with the man mentioned in oCG 25575, cf. Valbelle, loc.cit. (these are respectively the sons of Panefer and Hormes); the possibility exists that this is quite a different person than his namesakes from the reign of Ramesses IX.

144 As regards dating of LRL nos. 12 and 15 to the Renaissance Era, cf. Wente LRL, 8f., 13, 16f. For a dating of oCG 25574-5 to the late 20th/early 21st Dynasty, see Valbelle, Ouvriers, 49 n. 5, 54, 346; Reeves, Valley of the Kings, 107f.; Peden, Decline of Textual Graffiti, 290 n. 25; Häggman, Directing DeM, 356ff.; van Heel-Haring, Writing in a Workmen's Village, 145; a dating of oCG 25575 to year 7 of the reign of Ramesses XI (thus Janssen, Village Varia, 96) is highly doubtful indeed.

145 See however Häggman, Directing DeM, 101 (with a dating to the reign of Ramesses IX).

146 Kitchen, RamInscr VI, 852, 12; 853, 6; 854, 5; 857, 8; for other occurrences (not explicitly dated), see ibid., 858, 12 (without parentage); 860, 8; 862, 4. His namesake, the builder or potter (*ḳd*) Bakenmut son of Ahauty(nefer), appears in the document alongside, as a member of the *semdet*-staff, cf. Davies, Who's Who at DeM, 53.

147 Kitchen, RamInscr VI, 855, 13 (without parentage).

148 Kitchen, RamInscr VI, 686, 9; cf. Gutgesell, Datierung, 149; Helck OPG, 539; Schneider, in: Jenni H. (ed.), Das Grab Ramses' X. (KV 18), Basel 2000, 88; Peden, Decline of Textual Graffiti, 289 n. 19.

149 Gardiner RAD, 67, 11 (no parentage given).

of the Renaissance Era.[150] Consequently his tenure of office can be placed plausibly during the third decade of the reign of Ramesses XI, provided that he succeeded the foreman Penparei (I), son of Nebnefer, in the post of the foreman of the right side.[151] Such an assumption, however, clearly contradicts the early dating of papTurin 2021, suggested above (see Chapter 1). Such an early dating of papTurin 2021 would simply mean that the foreman Bakenmut started his career significantly earlier (i.e. after year 17 of Ramesses XI, if not earlier).[152] Thus it is open to question whether Bakenmut's foremanship must be divided into two parts, being interrupted by the period of tenure of Penparei (I) son of Nebnefer, or else it may be surmised that for an unknown reason he was transferred to the left side of the crew, thus not interferring with the tenure of the latter. The latter solution seems highly improbable indeed, as we know that in years 8-10 of Ramesses XI (papTurin 2018) the workman Bakenmut son of Khonsu worked in the right side of the crew under the foreman Khonsu (being presumably his father), alongside the workman Penparei son of Nebnefer.[153] In addition, such a transfer must be excluded on the basis of the fact, that according to LRL no. 1 Bakenmut's colleague was a foreman Amen[hotep],[154] who held the post probably on the left side, if he is the same person as the deputy Amenhotep son of Aapatjau, attested in the pre-Renaissance Era sources.[155]

Although the case of the foreman Bakenmut does not contradict explicitly the hypothesis about redating of papTurin 2018, other persons enumerated here provide more clear data in regard of this. So the name of the scribe of the *semdet*-staff of the left side Efnamun has been given in this part of the necropolis journal (papTurin 2018, vo. A1, 10-11; ro. B2, 10; vo. B2, 16),[156] alongside that of his colleague Wennefer son of Ankhtu (on the right side), in addition to the two scribes of the necropolis – Paweraa son of Thutemhab, and

---

150 Cf. Janssen, LRLC, 24; see also Chapter 6 below.

151 See now Davies, Who's Who at DeM, 55, 104, 114, 138f., 280; id., SAK 24, 1997, 62-64; Häggman, Directing DeM, 246 n. 1648, 348f. (the Renaissance Era and the beginning of the 21st Dynasty).

152 Cf. Bierbrier LNK, 35; Davies, Who's Who at DeM, 55.

153 Cf. Helck OPG, 562f.

154 Cf. Černý LRL, 1, 1-2 (with note 1[d]-2[a]); for the photograph, see Janssen LRLC, pl. 65; and M.J. Raven, in: DeM in the Third Millennium, pl. 43. As regards the proposed restoration of the name, see Černý, Community, 311 n. 4; Davies, Who's Who at DeM, 55; see also Wente, Letters, 179.

155 Černý, Community, 142, 146. The latest evidence relating to deputy Amenhotep is the Necropolis Journal of year 17 of Ramesses XI: papTurin 1888+2085, 2, 9, cf. Gardiner RAD, 67, 5; for the comment, see Davies, loc.cit.

156 Kitchen, RamInscr VI, 854, 16; 856, 8; 858, 1; cf. Černý, Community, 193.

Tuthmosis son of Khaemhedje. Both scribes of the *semdet*-staff are the latest documented in the sources from the Theban necropolis and no data of the Renaissance Era relating to them are available.[157] The latest dated reference to the scribe Efnamun is recorded in the list of houses of year 12 of Ramesses XI.[158] The hypothetical redating of papTurin 2018 to the Renaissance Era[159] causes a serious contradiction regarding the scribe Paweraa, who is attested as early as year 1 or 2 of Ramesses X, and papTurin 2018 is the latest source relating to him.[160] His dubious reappearance in the period of the Renaissance Era does not find any corroboration in the data provided by extant LRL. Finally, such a late dating of papTurin 2018 would mean that the *semdet* labour force was operating then on a scale comparable to that of the earlier reigns,[161] which seems virtually impossible having in mind the decidedly reduced status of the crew during that era.

PapBM 10068vo. 2ff. – the case of the treasury scribe Setekhmose (vo. 3, 1) may be recalled among the arguments already raised against its redating (cf. Chapter 1).

PapTurin 1895+2006 (Turin Taxation Papyrus) – the most embarrassing result of its redating to years 12 and 14 of the Renaissance Era would be the quite unexpected "reappearance onto the Theban stage of the former viceroy Panehesy",[162] whose name with his complete official titulature were given in the opening of the document just after the protocol of the reigning king Ramesses XI.[163] In spite of an apparent belittling of the very significance of this factor by A. Thijs,[164] it remains wholly incomprehensible why Panehesy would have ever returned to Thebes after being defeated on the eve of the Renaissance Era. Similarly there are no arguments in favour of the second viceroy of Kush by that name (as suggested by Thijs!).[165] Similarly the case of the foreigner Paykamen son of Pawaamun (vo. 2, 5), who was accused several

[157] As regards the careers of both, cf. Černý, Community, 193f., 200f.; Davies, Who's Who at DeM, 101f., 116, 136, 284.

[158] It is doubtful whether a reference to a certain Efnamun in papBM 9997, 1, 2 (=Kitchen, RamInscr VII, 389, 6), can be related to the scribe of the *semdet*-staff of that name; for this see Davies, Who's Who at DeM, 101. As regards an undated LRL no. 47, see Chapter 6.

[159] Cf. e.g. Thijs, GM 181, 2001, 98; id., GM 199, 2004, 81f., 88.

[160] Cf. Černý, Community, 203 (23); Gutgesell, Datierung, 212 (dubious year 19 of Ramesses IX); Davies Who's Who at DeM, 136f., 147, 175, 284.

[161] Cf. Valbelle, Ouvriers, 131.

[162] As noted by Thijs, GM, 199, 2004, 85; cf. also my comment above (Chapter 2).

[163] Cf. Gardiner RAD, 36, 1ff. (ro. 1, 1-5).

[164] Cf. Thijs, GM 199, 2004, 85; compare also Demidoff, GM 177, 2000, 100.

[165] Cf. Thijs, SAK 31, 2003, 299 (2).

years later (papAbbott-dockets, vo. B, 8),[166] does not match the chronological scheme proposed by Thijs.

PapBerlin 10460 – contrary to Thijs' supposition,[167] it is firmly dated to year 14 of Ramesses XI, whose name was explicitly given in the preamble of this judicial protocol.[168] A Theban provenience of the document (possibly Deir el-Medina)[169] cannot be denied because of the names of some of the Theban officials,[170] and most of all partly preserved name of the guardian Ka[djore] (ll. 3, 5) connected directly with the institution of the royal necropolis. A hypothetical redating of the document to the Renaissance Era would lead to a significant lengthening of its duration, and the reign of Ramesses XI would be extended beyond his year 28, which seems to be hardly probable in the light of the extant sources, although postulated by A. Thijs. However, such a late dating of papBerlin 10460 may be doubted in the light of the arrangements regarding the career of the guardian of the necropolis Ka[djore], whose latest appearance in the sources may be securely placed still at the end of the second decade of the reign of Ramesses XI and the early Renaissance Era.[171]

PapBM 9997 – dated explicitly to years 14 and 15. As observed already by J. von Beckerath, the three chiefs of Madjoy, mentioned in the text: Sermontu (5A, 2), Nesamun (5A, 4), and Amenwahsu (5A, 5),[172] were active from year 12 of Ramesses XI till the very beginning of the Renaissance Era at the latest.[173] It is worth noting that Sermontu was active as late as LRL no. 5, which can be securely dated to the early years of the Renaissance Era.[174] Some available dates relating to the career of Nesamun are especially significant for the dating of this document. He was attested as a simple Madjoy already in

[166] Peet, Tomb Robberies, pl. 23=Kitchen, RamInscr VI, 766, 5; cf. Černý, JEA 15, 1929, 196 (3).

[167] Cf. Thijs, GM 173, 1999, 191; id., GM 199, 2004, 80.

[168] Allam HOP, 275f., pls. 78-79 (ro. 1-2)=Kitchen, RamInscr VI, 863, 9-10; as regards the dating, cf. Allam, BiOr 24, 1967, 17; for the meaning of the text, cf. id., SAK 26, 1998, 12; McDowell, Jurisdiction, 47.

[169] Cf. Römer, SAK 19, 1992, 275.

[170] Allam HOP, 276 (n. 9); the god's father Amenkhau (l. 13) may be the same person as the owner of a house in the list of papBM 10068vo. 3, 27.

[171] Cf. Černý, Community, 157ff.; Davies, Who's Who at DeM, 200; see also Chapter 6 below.

[172] Kitchen, RamInscr VII, 393, 2-4.

[173] Cf. von Beckerath, Chronologie, 91; Ohlhafer, GM 135, 1993, 62; see also Černý, Community, 263 (1), 267f. (15), 270 (22); as regards the three chiefs of Madjoy police at one time, see McDowell, Jurisdiction, 64.

[174] Černý LRL, 9, 13; as regards its dating, see Chapter 6.

year 10 of Ramesses IX (papTurin 2049/141+),[175] and subsequently in year 3 of Ramesses X.[176] His tenure of the office of the chief of Madjoy is attested at the earliest in papBM 10054vo. 4, 2 slightly postdating, as it seems, the text of vo. 2 dating to year 6 (apparently of Ramesses XI), where he was still an ordinary Madjoy (cf. Chapter 1). Subsequently, in year 12 he was the chief of Madjoy (papBM 10068vo. 7, 7; and Turin Taxation Papyrus, ro. 4, 9).[177] The "reverse" dating of the documents assigning the chief of Madjoy Nesamun to the Renaissance Era makes no sense, because in papBM 10052 (8, 14-15), dating to year 1 of the Renaissance Era, he was referred to as a man, who "was a chief of Madjoy" (*wn m ḥry Mḏ3y*), though in papMayer A (ro. 1, 3, and 13; 2, 20)[178] he was titled as the chief of Madjoy. Yet the tomb robbery documents leave no doubt that he was guilty of the thefts, so it is fairly improbable that he was active fifteen years after the trials, and still as the chief of Madjoy!

The scribe Pentahutnakhte (papBM 9997, 1, 2), firmly attested since the reign of Ramesses IX,[179] subsequently became the army scribe of the Medinet Habu temple in place of the scribe Kashuty, whom he succeeded in the early years of the Renaissance Era (still during or after year 2).[180] His appearance in the document of year 14 just as the scribe (and not explicitly as the scribe of the army),[181] makes a dating of the document to the Renaissance Era utterly impossible. It is rather doubtful whether Sobeknakhte, father of Pentahutnakhte according to LRL no. 5,[182] is the same person as the scribe Sobeknakhte mentioned in a newly found graffito in the "Vallée des Carrières", where the latter appears as a contemporary of Ankhefenamun, Butehamun's son, or else merely acting at the same time.[183]

[175] Kitchen, RamInscr VI, 633ff.; cf. Helck OPG, 498ff.; Gutgesell, Datierung, 268f.

[176] Botti-Peet, Giornale, pl. 53 (ro. 2, 16)=Kitchen, RamInscr VI, 691, 4; cf. Schneider, in: Jenni H. (ed.), Das Grab Ramses' X. (KV 18), [AH 16], Basel 2000, 93; Niwiński, BIFAO 95, 1995, 332; Valbelle, Ouvriers, 217.

[177] Peet, Tomb Robberies, pl. 16; Gardiner RAD, 41, 4.

[178] Peet, Mayer Papyri, pls. 1-2=Kitchen, RamInscr VI, 803, 15-16; 805, 1; 808, 4.

[179] For the earliest reference in papTurin 1881ro. 8, 11, see Pleyte-Rossi, Papyrus de Turin, pl. 10; Allam HOP, 313ff., pl. 110; Peet, in: Studies presented to F.Ll. Griffith, pl. 10; Kitchen, RamInscr VI, 615, 5-6; as regards the career of Pentahutnakhte, cf. Černý, Community, 209f.; Davies, Who's Who at DeM, 121f.

[180] Cf. Chapter 6 below.

[181] Cf. Kitchen, RamInscr VII, 389, 6.

[182] Černý LRL, 10, 2-3. Černý (Community, 210, 219) suggested his identity with his homonym found in graffito 1267, cf. id., Graffiti, 15, pl. 41.

[183] Cf. Barwik, Theban Graffito no. 1572 rediscovered and some new texts from the "Valley of the

Last but not least such a dating of papBM 9997 within the Renaissance Era can be excluded on the basis of the presence of other officials of the West Bank of Thebes: the scribe Efenkhonsu (passim), overseer of the quarter Seramun (5A, 3),[184] and first of all the mayor of the west of the City Paweraa (5B, 3-4)[185] – all of them well known from the sources dating to the reign of Ramesses XI and the beginning of the Renaissance Era.[186]

Quarries" (in preparation). As a matter of fact, his career would be too long.

[184] Kitchen, RamInscr VII, 393, 3.

[185] Ibid., 393, 7-8.

[186] As regards Efenkhonsu, see Davies, Who' s Who at DeM, 137-139, 284; id., SAK 24, 1997, 63f.; as regards Seramun he was mentioned in papBM 10054 vo. 2, 11; 4, 4, and in papBM 10068vo. 5, 11 (see above Chapter 1 for dating of the documents); for Paweraa, see Helck, Verwaltung, 429-432, 532f. Among other persons recorded in papBM 9997 the *wab*-priest Nespamedushepes (3, 5) may be identified with the overseer of the estate of Amun (*p3 imy-r pr n Imn*) and the *wab*-priest of LRL no. 37, cf. Černý LRL, 59, 2; dated wrongly to the beginning of the 21st Dynasty by Helck, Materialien I, (30).

5. The career of Tuthmosis the scribe of the necropolis

The scribe of the necropolis Tuthmosis started his career at the beginning of the reign of Ramesses XI, when he was promoted to the post of the scribe of the royal necropolis. Although the exact date of this promotion remains unknown,[1] it is possible of course that it has happened just after the death of his father Khaemhedje or else a little bit earlier, providing that both of them exercised the office together for some time in the early years of the reign of Ramesses XI.[2] Anyway, in the preserved documentation he appeared for the first time as the scribe of the necropolis of the left side of the crew in year 8 of this sovereign.[3]

In the earlier period we find Tuthmosis mentioned as a simple workman of the "right side". He started his work in the gang already under the reign of Ramesses IX, and the earliest reference is provided by papTurin 2004+2007+2057/58+2106/396 of year 16,[4] and subsequently by the Necropolis Journal of year 17.[5] He was probably still a young man at the time of his promotion to the office of the scribe of the royal necropolis. Nothing is known about his marital status at that time. Anyway, in the Stato Civile he was mentioned as the sole occupant of a house,[6] located as it seems still in the

---

1 Cf. Peden, Graffiti, 189f. n. 355, 365; compare Bierbrier LNK, 41.

2 The latest firm evidence relating to the scribe Khaemhedje dates to year 3 of Ramesses X: Botti-Peet, Giornale, pls. 53, 57 (ro. 2, 21; 4, 13)=Kitchen, RamInscr VI, 691, 13-14; 695, 5; Helck OPG, 545, 549; Schneider, in: Jenni H. (ed.), Das Grab Ramses' X. (KV 18), Basel 2000, 93, 98. As regards a possible reference dated to year 1 of Ramesses XI: "the scribe Khaem[hedje]", see papTurin 1898+1937+2094/244vo.: Botti-Peet, Giornale, pl. 63a (10)=Kitchen, RamInscr VI, 851, 1; wrongly restored by Helck OPG, 561 (Khaem[wese]).

3 As exemplified by papTurin 2018ro. A, 3, 14; ro. C, 3, 15=Kitchen, RamInscr VI, 853, 10; 860, 15; cf. Černý, Community, 360; Helck OPG, 562.

4 Pleyte-Rossi, Papyrus de Turin, pl. 90 (II, 9); Kitchen, RamInscr VI, 651, 15 (ro. 3, 1); Helck OPG, 515; cf. Černý, Community, 360 n. 2.

5 Botti-Peet, Giornale, pl. 11 (ro. A 4, 2)=Kitchen, RamInscr VI, 568, 9; Helck OPG, 522. As regards a reference in the journal of year 19, see Kitchen, RamInscr VI, 687, 1 (papTurin 1932+1939vo. 3, 6).

6 SC 1, II, 6 (according to R. Demarée; personal communication); cf. G. Botti, Frammenti di Registri di Stato Civile della XX[a] Dinastia, in: Rendiconti della Reale Accademia Nazionale dei Lincei 31, 1922-1923, 392; Černý, Community, 357.

settlement in Deir el-Medina. In most of the LRL he was named not only by his "official" name but also by the nickname Tjaroy.[7] It remains doubtful whether he adopted the latter to make a distinction between him and another Tuthmosis (son of Userhat?),[8] living in the necropolis area, apparently in the complex of Medinet Habu, or whether this was a name he had had since his childhood. This original sobriquet cannot be taken as a simple abbreviation of his name, but seems to be meaningless, and different spellings of this seem to testify this clearly.[9] It has been postulated that the form Tjaroy/Tjary could be connected with a place name Tjaru (Sile) but the reason for this would remain completely unexplained, as we know nothing about any connection between this family or individual with the town located in the eastern Delta.[10] A foreign origin of the name must be taken into consideration as well, and a Syrian (possibly Hurrian?) origin has been recently suggested.[11] Less possibly this form of the sobriquet can be connected with a personal name of the type Tjunroy/Tjunero/Tjenery,[12] apparently of a Semitic origin.[13]

It is unknown when he got married, but we can assume that at time of his promotion he was already married. We know the name of his wife – this was Baketamun (her father's name has not been preserved in the extant sources). She was the mother of his (presumably eldest) son Butehamun,[14] who com-

---

[7] Contrary to the letters, his secondary personal name never appears in the graffiti left in the Theban area – an exception is the newly found graffito no. 3981a, cf. Kikuchi, Memnonia 7, 1996, 175f., fig. 4, pl. 49B; id., GM 160, 1997, 51ff. – here besides his "official" name, apparently as a real signature of Tuthmosis; so contrary to the opinion expressed once by Černý, Community, 363f.

[8] See below.

[9] Cf. Janssen LRLC, 20. For the variant spellings, see Erman, ADAW 1, 1913, 17; Černý LRL, 79f. (no. 143); id., Community, 366; Wente LRL, 7 n. 25; id., Letters, 171; Junge, Neuägyptisch, 260.

[10] Černý, Community, 365f.; see however Th. Schneider, Asiatische Personennamen in ägyptischen Quellen des Neuen Reiches, [OBO 114], Freiburg 1992, 255.

[11] Cf. Schneider, op.cit., 253 (N 543); compare also N 540-542, 544-548. See also J.K. Winnicki, Late Egypt and her Neighbours. Foreign Population in Egypt in the First Millennium BC, [The Journal of Juristic Papyrology Suppl. 12], Warsaw 2009, 47-49. Otherwise W.A. Ward, in: Pharaoh's Workers, 73 (no. 27).

[12] Cf. Ranke PN I, 381 (24); W.C. Hayes, JEA 46, 1960, 47, pl. 13 (21ro., 5); Helck, JARCE 6, 1967, 144, 151 (l. 85). See also a draughtsman's name apparently from the late 18th Dynasty: T. Handussa, A Funerary Statutte from a Private Collection, MDAIK 37, 1981, 203ff.; not included in Ranke PN.

[13] Cf. Schneider, op.cit., 251f. (N 537-538); Winnicki, op.cit., 51, 57, 61.

[14] It is doubtful whether the scribe Ankhefenamun of graffito no. 1012 (Spiegelberg, Graffiti, 84f., pl. 114), was really Butehamun's elder brother, who predeceased his father, as suggested by Davies, Who's Who at DeM, 58; id., SAK 24, 1997, 68 (fig. 1). Even less probable was a hypothesis that the scribe of the necropolis Nesamenope was another son of Tuthmosis, cf. Wente LRL, 4; for a comment, see Janssen, BiOr 25, 1968, 38.

memorated her name on a lintel of his house in the administrative complex in Medinet Habu.[15] There are good reasons to suppose that lady Baketamun predeceased her husband, and this could had happened relatively early. Anyway, at the height of Tuthmosis' career during the Renaissance Era, we can see another woman at his side. Her name – Hemshire – appears several times in the corpus of LRL,[16] always in connection with her small unnamed daughter, apparently the youngest offspring of the elder Tuthmosis. The sole exception seems to be LRL no. 4, where the girl is not explicitly mentioned at all, although Hemshire was mentioned again as the object of his special care.

Being a descendant of the well known scribe Amennakht, son of Ipuy, he proudly expressed his family ties with forefathers in the inscription scratched (by his own hand) on the rock in the "Vallée de l'Aigle": "King's scribe of the necropolis (*sš-nsw n ẖnw*) Tuthmosis, son of the king's scribe Khaemhedje, son of the king's scribe Horisheri, son of the king's scribe of the necropolis (*sš-nsw n ẖnw*) Amennakht" (graffito no. 1109).[17] When the text was written in the year 18 of Ramesses XI, scribe Tuthmosis had been fulfilling his duties for a number of years, as a successor of his father. The apparently short period of activity of Khaemhedje as the scribe of the necropolis does not necessarily mean that he died prematurely. More probably it was a consequence of the long lifetime of the scribe Horisheri, who remained in the office of the necropolis scribe from the beginning of the reign of Ramesses VI until year 17 of Ramesses IX.[18] Scanty information can be provided on Tuthmosis' mother. It is only from the Stato Civile that we learn her name – Tentkhenuemheb.[19]

Presumably, well in accord with ancient Egyptians customs, father and son were working together for some time. And to this period may be related now an unpublished papTurin 2097/161+2105, dating to year 2 of Ramesses

[15] Cf. Kitchen, RamInscr VII, 399, 13; Černý, Community, 358.

[16] Černý LRL, 78 (index: no. 92).

[17] Černý, Graffiti, 4, pl. 8=Kitchen, RamInscr VI, 864; Černý, Community, 339. As regards the meaning of *ẖnw*, see Ventura, City of the Dead, 64ff.

[18] For the necropolis scribe Horisheri, see Černý, Community, 352-355; J.J. Janssen, in: Gleanings from Deir el-Medîna, 149ff.; Davies, Who's Who at DeM, 114-117. As regards the estimated age of Khaemhedje at the moment of death, cf. Bierbrier LNK, 41.

[19] SC 1, II, 2 (according to R. Demarée; personal communication); cf. Černý, Community, 357. Certainly an obscure passage in LRL no. 50 has nothing to do with her: "Now you should give your attention to this(?) mother (of?) Tanettabekhen, (and?) the daughter [...]", cf. Černý LRL, 73, 7-8. As regards other offspring of Khaemhedje and Tentkhenuemheb, we are informed about a daughter by the name Tentpaope, cf. Davies, Who's Who at DeM, 118, and Chart 9; for the deputy Seny, a putative brother of the scribe Tuthmosis, see ibid., 70ff., 118, 281; Černý, Community, 143f.

X, as demonstrated recently by R. Demarée.[20] The scribe Tuthmosis was mentioned here in a period before becoming the scribe of the necropolis.[21] Similarly papTurin 2003, dated to year 3 (of Ramesses XI), mentions "the scribe Tuthmosis",[22] which could be identified perhaps with the well known son of Khaemhedje.[23] No doubt this was a most important time for his training, and preparation to his fulfilling the duties of the necropolis scribe. We can only surmise that relations between father and son were close enough, if in some of his graffiti Tuthmosis mentioned the name of his (then probably deceased) father, as for example in graffito no. 1107 in the "Vallée de l'Aigle" not far from graffito no. 1109, and another one mentioning once again "Year 18" (graffito no. 1108).[24] Besides these signs of piety and commemoration on the part of his devoted son, the name of Khaemhedje is known from just a few graffiti, which could have been written possibly by his own hand,[25] not to mention the references in the necropolis journal and a handful of ostraca relating to him.[26]

Tuthmosis was the last in the long line of the scribes of the royal necropolis who effectively participated in the building of the royal tomb in the early years of Ramesses XI. No doubt these were bad times not only for Tuthmosis, but also for other members of the local community of western Thebes. Internal

[20] See Demarée, GM 137, 1993, 50; contra Ohlhafer, GM 135, 1993, 61 (dating to the reign of Ramesses IX). See also Helck, SAK 17, 1990, 211f.; id. OPG, 569f. (questionable dating to the Renaissance Era).

[21] Cf. Demarée, loc.cit. (n. 5). The scribe "Twrj3jj (? Lesung unsicher)", cited by Ohlhafer (loc.cit.) has nothing to do with the scribe Tjaroy/Tuthmosis; compare Helck OPG, 569 ("Schreiber *Turapê* des 2. Propheten [des Amun]"). It is highly questionable whether the scribe of the necropolis Tuthmosis was mentioned in the Necropolis Journal of year 3 of Ramesses X, as suggested by Helck in his restored version of the text (OPG, 550); cf. Botti-Peet, Giornale, 53 n. 2, pl. 58 (ro. 5, 10-11)=Kitchen, RamInscr VI, 696, 11; Schneider, in: Jenni H. (ed.), Das Grab Ramses' X. (KV 18), Basel 2000, 100 and n. 319.

[22] Pleyte-Rossi, Papyrus de Turin, pl. 91 (ro. 1, 1); Kitchen, RamInscr VI, 851, 7-8; and a revised version, ibid., VII, 388, 5. As regards its dating, see Chapter 4 (Excursus).

[23] See Černý, ArOr 6, 1933, 175 (12); id., Community, 361; similarly Davies, SAK 24, 1997, 60.

[24] Černý, Graffiti,4, pl. 9. All three graffiti (nos. 1107-1109) are written in the same handwriting and this, together with their proximity to each other (cf. Félix-Aubriot-Kurz, Plans de position, pl. 58), seems to suggest the same date, most probably year 18 of Ramesses XI. As regards other graffiti of Tuthmosis mentioning his father's name, see Černý, Community, 357 and n. 1.

[25] These are for example graffiti nos. 2059, 2183, and 2185 from the Valley of the Kings (cf. Félix-Aubriot-Kurz, Plans de position, pls. 41, 43), all of them giving only his name and title, cf. Kitchen, RamInscr VI, 700 (B.III.1); Peden Graffiti, 189 and n. 356.

[26] Cf. oTurin 57387ro., 2: Lopez, Ostraca 3, pl. 123-123a; oTurin 57396ro., 6: ibid., pl. 128-128a; Kitchen, RamInscr VII, 386; oParker H8, 3 (unpublished), cf. Černý, Community, 356 n. 10; Gutgesell, Datierung, 382. As regard those predating his tenure of the necropolis scribe, see oLeipzig 1658: Kitchen, RamInscr VI, 669, 6-7.

strife had plunged the country into a deep economic and social crisis. There are good reasons to suppose that economic situation of the Thebaid interfered with the effectiveness of administrative system of the necropolis. It cannot be excluded that some irregularities in the system of supply of the necropolis staff led to a temporary food shortage, although there are no exact data on the subject. This would probably explain the involvement of some of the men of the gang in the robberies, which had proliferated in the Theban region in those dark years. It is in these years of the early decade of the reign of Ramesses XI that he was also engaged in the work on the royal tomb, the last to be built in the Valley of the Kings. The available documentation is scanty in fact, and we have to note that the role played by Tuthmosis in regard of this is practically unknown. His activity in the Theban area is hardly documented by the graffiti left in the distant desert wadis. In contrast to his well known son Butehamun he was not interested in this kind of commemoration, except one or two places, where he decided to leave his own signatures. The distribution of the graffiti left by Tuthmosis himself must lead to the conclusion that he was mostly preoccupied with the building of the royal tomb. If we take into consideration the role played by his predecessors[27] in regard to the planning and supervision of work on the royal tomb we can surmise that he was probably also seriously involved in this undertaking.

There is an apparent contradiction in the fact that a relatively substantial number of graffiti was left by him in the Valley of the Kings and in the adjacent area, but nearly no ostraca with his name are preserved not only in that area, but also on the whole of the Theban West Bank.[28] Apparently both kinds of sources could be directly connected with the building of the royal tomb, and its administrative background. The explanation of a scarcity of sources of both kinds, seems to be quite simple – this must be the result of the cessation of work on the royal tomb relatively early during the reign of the Pharaoh.[29] Unfortunately, none of the graffiti scratched by Tuthmosis on the rocks in the Valley of the Kings can be dated precisely. Most of those which can be attributed to him are located in the rocky bay with the tomb of Seti II

27 The role played by the scribe of the necropolis Amennakht son of Ipuy is an eminent example as regards his engagement in the supervision of work and possibly also its planning.

28 The sole exception seems to be oCG 25745, which is dated, however, to a much later period; see above, Chapter 3.

29 For other reasons (i.e. abandonment of the settlement at Deir el-Medina, and low size of the crew), cf. Peden, Decline of Textual Graffiti, 287-290.

(KV 15),[30] far from the building chantier in the region of KV 4. It is still open to question whether the bay of the tomb of Seti II was a convenient place of rest for the workmen during their work on the tomb of the reigning king (KV 4),[31] or whether the graffiti date to the subsequent period of salvaging the royal burials in the Valley of the Kings.[32] One way or another, the distribution of graffiti in the Valley of the Kings clearly points to the intensive activity of the crew in the bay of the tomb of Seti II during the Renaissance Era.[33] And this seems to favour the hypothesis of C.N. Reeves that a transitional royal mummy cache had been organized then in the tomb of Sethnakhte (KV 14).[34] Significantly none of the graffiti located in the distant desert wadis of the Theban area can be attributed convincingly to the scribe Tuthmosis.[35] This would mean that he did not operate on such a scale as his son and successor in the following period of the Renaissance Era and later. In other words, there was apparently no necessity to make any research or inspection in these distant desert regions of the Theban necropolis at the time of the early activity of the scribe Tuthmosis. However, an opinion has been presented recently by A.J. Peden that Tuthmosis participated in these inspections together with his son Butehamun in the period of the Renaissance Era.[36]

In the period following the war against the High Priest Amenhotep, Tuthmosis became involved in the provisioning of the crew. This seems to reflect the new circumstances of the Theban administration in those years of confusion and disorder. Thus in the 12th year of Ramesses XI, Tuthmosis was

[30] Cf. Peden, Graffiti, 190f.; Häggman, Directing DeM, 227 n. 1514. As regards other graffiti of Tuthmosis, see also Kitchen, RamInscr VI, 877f.

[31] Peden (loc.cit.) suggested that the "Vallon de la tombe de Sethi II" was a convenient resting place, offering shade for those working on the royal tomb (KV 4).

[32] Cf. Peden, loc.cit.

[33] Cf. Bouvier-Bouvier, L'activité des gens, 23 (I), 26, fig. 7.1.

[34] Reeves, Valley of the Kings, 109-111, 248, 259 (tab. 11), 277; for a critical review of relevant epigraphic evidence, see Eaton-Krauss, BiOr 49, 1992, 714f.; and Chapter 8 below.

[35] Certainly there are no grounds to attribute to him the graffito no. 1305 (=3929) in Wadi Qubbanat el-Gurud, as suggested by Peden, Decline of Textual Graffiti, 288 n. 8; id., Graffiti, 235; id., in: Ch. Lilyquist, The Tomb of Three Foreign Wives of Tuthmosis III, New York 2003, 8, 340; Kitchen, RamInscr VI, 878, 1. Much more probably it was written by his son Butehamun (or one of his grandsons?), who left his own signature 0.50 m to the left (graffito no. 1304), cf. Černý, Graffiti, 19 (without a facsimile). The name of Tuthmosis, as written here with a sign representing a sitting figure of the ibis-headed Thoth (with moon on his head), finds parallels among other graffiti written by Butehamun or one of his descendants, cf. e.g. nos. 48, 685b, 912, 1006, 1018, 1023, 1287, 1938, 1940, 2038, 2055, 2107; cf. Ali, Hieratische Ritzinschriften, pl. 37 (C.3).

[36] Cf. Peden, Graffiti, 234, 237.

travelling to the south of Thebes, to tax the fellahin of the region,[37] accompanied by the two door-keepers as his assistants.[38] The preserved copy of the report was written by Tuthmosis himself, as stated explicitly in the preamble of the document.[39] Collecting the taxes seems to be quite a unusual task compared to the usual duties of the necropolis scribe. No doubt it indicates the extraordinary means adopted by the Theban administration in the period of occupation of Thebes by viceroy Panehesy. If Ramesses' XI sovereignty was really recognised in the south, his real power was strongly undermined by pretension of Panehesy to govern independently. There are no grounds to doubt that the mission of Tuthmosis was successful, and the methods adopted to provision the crew at those times were amply described in the LRL no. 47 of approximately the same date.[40] Quite unexpectedly, in the new economic and political situation, the necropolis scribe performed the duties of other officials of the temple and state administration. His new responsibilities made him someone more influential than an "ordinary" scribe of the necropolis. If we compare his duties with those of other high-ranking dignitaries of the era, he can be possibly equated with the scribe of the vizier. As a matter of fact, the role of the scribe of the necropolis during the reign of Ramesses XI can be compared to some extent to that of the scribes of the mat (*sš n tmꜣ*), who used to represent the vizier in the matters of the royal necropolis in the earlier periods.[41] The close links between the vizier and the necropolis scribe, developed during the Ramesside period,[42] did much to increase the status of the necropolis scribe in the administrative system of the Thebaid at the very end of the 20th Dynasty. Later on Tuthmosis was acting presumably along the patterns adopted elsewhere by the royal butlers or other court officials, thus being one of the representatives of the highest authority in the new Theban administrative system.[43]

---

37 Quite possibly Tuthmosis participated in a similar tour in year 14 of the reign, because this part of the document (*verso* of the Turin Taxation Papyrus) was written by his own hand as well, cf. Gardiner, JEA 27, 1941, 35.

38 For the comments as regards their role, see Gardiner, JEA 27, 1941, 20, 25; Černý, Community, 171f.; Ventura, City of the Dead, 108 n. 6.

39 Gardiner RAD, 36, 6; cf. Černý, Community, 226.

40 See below, Chapter 6.

41 Cf. B. Haring, The Scribe of the Mat: From Agrarian Administration to Local Justice, in: DeM in the Third Millennium, 146-150, 152, 156f.; Häggman, Directing DeM, 122 n. 803. As regards the role of the vizier's scribe in the necropolis matters, see J.J. Janssen, in: Gleanings from Deir el-Medîna, 141f. Compare also a vague *sš n št* "scribe of the assessment" of LRLC no. IX ro. 8-9, cf. Janssen LRLC, 44ff.

42 Cf. Häggman, Directing DeM, 127-129.

43 Cf. Valbelle, Ouvriers, 146; Koenig, CRIPEL 10, 1988, 59 (e).

It cannot escape our attention that Tuthmosis' position was strongly reinforced due to his personal relations with the most influential persons in Thebes, as will be clearly visible in the following period. This seems to reflect the profound changes in the administration of Thebaid on the eve of the Renaissance Era, in the period of building of a new bureaucratic system. If Tuthmosis did not bear appropriate titles in connection with his new duties, this is only because the situation in the Thebaid was unstable and the process of the building of the independent pontifical state of Amun was only *in statu nascendi*.[44]

The latest pages of the necropolis journal dating to years 17 and 18 leave no doubts that no work in the Valley of the Kings was conducted at that time whatsoever. These scanty fragments of the necropolis journal (papTurin 1888+2085),[45] were probably written by Tuthmosis as well.[46] His neat and careful handwriting can be recognised among other documents found in the Theban necropolis – in some of the LRL, and the Theban graffiti in particular.[47]

As we know these were the years of the civil war provoked by the viceroy Panehesy, which divided the most powerful representatives of the state administration; just after withdrawal of the Nubian army of Panehesy from the Thebaid, a "Renaissance Era" was inaugurated. Theban graffito no. 1109 can be dated to the period slightly preceding the inauguration of the new era,[48] at the time when the new regime had just started to control the situation in the country. First we hear about prosecution of those implicated in the robberies in the Theban necropolis. There are scanty references to these early years of the Renaissance Era in the dossier connected with the scribe Tuthmosis. Papyrus BM 10052, dating to year 1 of the Renaissance Era, is one of the rare sources mentioning his name explicitly. If this is the case, then we can assume that he was a member of the investigating group participating actively in the prosecutions of the thieves. Thus, in the reports of interroga-

[44] It is quite a different matter that, as it seems, the high-priests of Amun of the 21st Dynasty simply adopted the system developed earlier, in more troubled times at the end of the 20th Dynasty.

[45] Pleyte-Rossi, Papyrus de Turin, pl. 61; Gardiner RAD, 64ff.

[46] See Černý, Community, 360; cf. Gardiner RAD, XX.; Valbelle, Ouvriers, 44. Tuthmosis was mentioned here in ro. 1, 17; 2, 1; cf. Gardiner, RAD, 66, 3 and 5.

[47] As regards Tuthmosis' handwriting, see now Janssen, JEA 73, 1987, 161ff.; Ali, Hieratische Ritzinschriften, 140-141; Kikuchi, GM 160, 1997, 53ff., fig. 2.

[48] Quite possibly it was a period of a relative stabilization of the internal situation, and not of disorder and turmoil, as suggested by those who date the deposition of Amenhotep to those years, cf. e.g. Lull, Los sumos sacerdotes, 58f.

tions of the robbers of the gang of certain Bukhaaf, the scribe Tuthmosis says to one of the culprits: "One tomb is that from which he brought the *tjebu*-vases of silver and [the] fittings (*ip.(w)t*), (but) another one is that from which he brought this inner coffin (*swḥ.t*) – (this is) a second tomb" (papBM 10052, 5, 14-15).[49] Later on in the same document he questioned a slave Sekhahatyamun about his role in the robberies (papBM 10052, 8, 11-12).[50] And again he participated in the interrogation of a wife of one of the robbers, questioning her about the source of the increasing wealth of the robber's family (papBM 10052, 10, 14-15).[51]

The precise role played by the scribe of the necropolis in the robbery trials cannot be evaluated properly. We know, however, that the scribe of the necropolis Nesamenope also participated in the interrogations of the thieves described in the same document (papBM 10052, 1, 19; 5, 17; 5, 21),[52] although not enumerated explicitly among the members of the tribunal headed by the highest authorities of the country. Neither can their connection with the so-called Place of Examination (*t3 s.t smtr*)[53] be proved convincingly. It is noteworthy that Nesamenope appeared in the similar role also in year 2 of the Renaissance Era, as documented in papBM 10403 (ro. 1, 2; vo. 3, 16).[54] If the opening words of papBM 10403 can be taken literally then we can assume that he was one of the leading officials responsible for interrogations of one group of the thieves at least. We can say for certain that Nesamenope was a colleague of the scribe Tuthmosis, as the second "senior" scribe of the necropolis, in supervising all the complicated matters of the necropolis and its staff in those troubled times.[55]

As regards the other mentions of a "scribe Tuthmosis" in the framework of the robbery trials of the beginning of the Renaissance Era, his identity with the scribe of the necropolis must be definitely discarded: certainly this is the case of the information provided by papBM 10403 (ro. 2, 2), and concerning

---

49 Peet, Tomb Robberies, pl. 28=Kitchen, RamInscr VI, 780, 7-8; cf. also Černý-Groll, Late Egyptian Grammar, 67 (Ex. 193); Groll, Non-Verbal Sentence Patterns, 68 (Ex. 216).

50 Peet, Tomb Robberies, pl. 30.

51 Ibid., pl. 31.

52 As regards the role of Nesamenope in the robbery trials, see ibid., 139, 169.

53 We know that officials from the Place of Examination participated also in the interrogations, see papBM10052, 5, 2-3, for the meaning of the term, cf. Boochs, GM 109, 1989, 22 n. 7; McDowell, Jurisdiction, 220 n. 99; id., Village Life, 193, 261 (148); Lesko, Dict. II, 3.

54 Peet, Tomb Robberies, pls. 36-37.

55 Cf. Černý, Community, 213f. (no. 45); Davies, Who's Who at DeM, 137f., 284; Janssen, JEA 77, 1991, 90.

the robberies committed by "the scribe Tuthmosis and the scribe Hori, son of Seni".[56] The identity of the former was specified more precisely in another place of the same document, where he appears among other thieves: "the scribe Tuthmosis, son of Userhat" (papBM 10403ro. 1, 16).[57] It is possible that the houses of both Hori and Tuthmosis were enumerated in the list of houses in papBM 10068 (vo. 6, 9 and 21).[58]

About eight years after the trials, the scribe Tuthmosis, son of Khaemhedje, was in Nubia, far from Thebes and his family. And to this very period dates the bulk of his abundant correspondence, which has been preserved to our times. To fill the gap between the robbery trials of the beginning of the Renaissance Era and the Nubian campaign of Payankh (about year 10 of the era), we can postulate that some of the letters from the family archive of Tuthmosis actually predate his Nubian journey. Quite naturally, the letters written during his stay somewhere to the north of Thebes and in Middle Egypt belong to this group (see below, Chapter 6). The reason of this journey may be compared with that of year 12 of Ramesses XI, when he travelled to the south of Thebes with a mission of collecting taxes. Now the objective of his activity were presumably the rural areas located in Middle Egypt, being presumably under administrative control of the domain of the temple of Amun.[59] PapPrakhov (Ermitage 2969), dated to year 7 (of the Renaissance Era), relates the action of collecting the taxes mainly in the Xth nome of Upper Egypt under the personal supervision of the general Payankh,[60] no doubt authorized by the high priest of Amun to fulfil this task.

The early years of the Renaissance Era are barely documented in the dossier relating to the career of the scribe Tuthmosis. One isolated piece of evidence is provided only by papTurin 2094,[61] with a text on the *verso* dated explicitly to year 2 of the Renaissance Era (vo. 1, 1). The scribe Tuthmosis appears here alongside the foreman Penparei, and his son Butehamun. The

[56] Peet, Tomb Robberies, pl. 36=Kitchen, RamInscr VI, 831, 1-2.

[57] Peet, op.cit, pl. 36=Kitchen, RamInscr VI, 829, 13-14.

[58] Peet, op.cit., pl. 16.

[59] The Wilbour Papyrus from the reign of Ramesses V provides a most detailed information about a land-taxation in this part of the country; as regards the extent of the domain of Amun, see Gasse, Domaine d'Amon I, 175f.

[60] Cf. Berlev, GM 160, 1997, 5ff. As regards papLouvre AF 6345+Griffith fragments, registering tax assessments of agricultural lands in the Xth nome of Upper Egypt, see above Chapter 3. For a map of the area covered by the registers, see Gasse, Domaine d'Amon I, 59; see also Gardiner, JEA 27, 1941, 66ff.; M. Malinine, BiOr 16, 1959, 219f.; K. Baer, JARCE 1, 1962, 32f.

[61] Kitchen, RamInscr VI, 865-868; cf. Helck OPG, 568ff.; Gutgesell, Datierung, 153.

latter, titled simply as "the scribe" (passim), had just started his illustrious career, possibly as an assistant to his father.[62] The appointment of Butehamun to the post occurred in the period of transition, when a new order had taken shape due to the political tensions in the country, though the exact chronology and circumstances of his promotion are wholly unknown to us.

Excursus: The titles of the scribe Tuthmosis

No attention has been given hitherto to the variety of titles borne by Tuthmosis and his descendants, and their meaning in the framework of the administrative system of the epoch. Meanwhile this seems to be a precious source of information concerning not only the personal careers of the scribes but also the history of the royal necropolis in general, and the dating of the particular documents. Quite understandably in most of the contemporary sources Tuthmosis was described simply as the "scribe" or, more officially, the "scribe of the royal necropolis". In the administrative documents of the New Kingdom, the title "king's scribe" was applied to higher officials or even high-ranking dignitaries of the state but sometimes it was given also to the scribes of the royal necropolis, mostly in graffiti and in hieroglyphic inscriptions.[63] Thus Thutmosis is often titled the "king's scribe" in the graffiti, which can be possibly ascribed to him as actually being written by his own hand,[64] having the form of the short formula: "king's scribe Tuthmosis (in the Place of Truth)",[65] besides "the scribe (in the Place of Truth) Tuthmosis".[66] The title "king's scribe" appears also in the graffiti commemorating his father, or else just giving the names of his father or forefathers, as for example graffiti nos.

62 Cf. Davies, Who's Who at DeM, 138.

63 Černý, Community, 17, 44, 225; Allam, ZÄS 133, 2006, 1. Cf. also Černý, Graffiti, 37 (index of titles).

64 For the handwriting, see Ali, Hieratische Ritzinschriften, 140f. Similar handwriting is discernible also in those graffiti, where the name of Tuthmosis is accompanied by the name of his son Butehamun, so the authorship of the latter is surely attested or at least cannot be definitely excluded, cf. e.g. graffiti nos. 1266, 1295a, 1293, 2216, 2217, 2425, 2486, 3089, 3153, 3170, 3368, 3492, 3651, 3951(=1358). As regards the newly found graffito no. 3981a, it is possible that the name of Tuthmosis called Tjaroy was written by his own hand, whereas the rest of the inscription was written by one of his descendants (probably Butehamun), cf. Kikuchi, GM 160, 1997, 54f.

65 Cf. e.g. graffiti nos. 1734, 1954, 2063, 2951, 3073; all of them seem to be written in the same handwriting, cf. Černý, Sadek et al., Graffiti III, pls. 15, 47, 62, 177, 193. Nothing certain can be said about a hieroglyphic inscription of this type: graffito no. 2034 (ibid., pl. 56).

66 Graffiti nos. 145, 295, 405, 1789, 2062, 2064, 2289; cf. Spiegelberg, Graffiti, pls. 19, 33, 46; Černý, Sadek et al., Graffiti III, pls. 26, 62, 95. See also graffiti nos. 2024, 2031, written in a different handwriting, or being just hastily written signatures (?); cf. Černý, Sadek et al., Graffiti III, pl. 55.

1107 and 1109.[67] The exceptional character of the figural graffito no. 1970, with a signature of "king's scribe in the Place of Truth Tuthmosis (justified?)", cannot be explained properly in this context, because its handwriting differs slightly from the examples cited above.[68] Significantly, no person among those mentioned in LRL, including Tuthmosis himself, were given the title of "king's scribe", except general Payankh himself. And this is well in accord with the administrative practice of the New Kingdom.

Certainly there was no necessity to emphasize the other aspects of his activity within and outside the framework of the institution of royal necropolis during Tuthmosis' lifetime, although his career was undoubtedly atypical if we compare it with that of his predecessors in the office. It was only after death of the scribe Tuthmosis that his achievements and extraordinary status were underlined by the new titles attached to his name. There are good reasons to suppose that this was rather a reflection of a personal piety and reverence on the part of his son, who succeeded him on the post of the scribe of the royal necropolis. Thus the set of titles applied by Butehamun to his father's name reflects rather his own ambitions, but also the unprecedented circumstances of the crew's activity on the eve of the new era.

First of all this late prosopographic material relating to Tuthmosis provides us with the title of the "scribe of the *neferu*" (*sš nfr.w*),[69] "the king's scribe in the horizon of eternity (*3ḫ.t nḥḥ*)",[70] and that of "the king's scribe of/in the house of everlastingness (*pr-ḏ.t*)".[71] No doubt, all of them lay stress on Tuthmosis' personal engagement in the process of building of the royal tomb, even if it had never been finished. Similarly, some of the titles of Amennakht son of Ipuy, can be connected also with his function of one of the supervisors

[67] Černý, Graffiti, pls. 8-9; it can be taken for certain that these graffiti were written by his own hand.

[68] Černý, Sadek et al., Graffiti III, pl. 48. It is rather doubtful whether a kneeling figure of graffito no. 1970, holding a fan in his right hand, can be identified with the scribe Tuthmosis, bacause the figure looks rather like that of a prince. Instead, a figure of a boy on the right and a scarab on the left of the kneeling figure can be possibly taken together as a cryptogram of the prenomen of Ramesses X - *Ḫpr-m3ʿ.t-Rʿ* (assuming the figure of a boy as a symbol for *Rʿ* ?).

[69] Graffito no. 1975: Černý, Sadek et al., Graffiti III, pl. 50; IV, 29. For the meaning of the term *nfr.w*, see R.O. Faulkner, JEA 39, 1953, 44f.; A.R. Schulman, Military Rank, Title and Organization in the Egyptian New Kingdom, [MÄS 6], Berlin 1964, 20f.; Haring, Divine Households, 247. As regards the title in a military context ("scribe of the recruits"), see P.-M. Chevereau, Prosopographie des cadres militaires égyptiens du Nouvel Empire, Paris 1994, 216ff.

[70] Graffiti nos. 2038, 3651: Černý, Sadek et al., Graffiti III, pls. 56, 266; see also graffito no. 1285b: Černý , Graffiti, pl. 48; and graffiti nos. 48, 912: Spiegelberg, Graffiti, 7, 75, pls. 8, 101.

[71] Graffito no. 3056: Černý, Sadek et al., Graffiti III, pl. 191; see also graffito no. 1287: Černý, Graffiti, 18, pl. 50; and graffito no. 1359a, written by Ankhefenamun, cf. ibid., 24.

of work on the royal tomb: "the scribe of the *neferu* in/of the horizon of eternity (*3ḫ.ty nt nḥḥ*)", or simply "the king's scribe in the horizon of eternity (*3ḫ.t nḥḥ*)".[72] And these can be compared also with the titles of the scribe Tuthmosis, given to him by his descendants. Moreover, some of them can be found among the titles of Butehamun, and also those of his son Nebhepet, and this might be sought as a true reason of their reappearance with the name of the scribe Tuthmosis. The titles of Butehamun and Nebhepet, relating presumably to their work on the high priest's or the royal (?) tombs, or else in the royal necropolis in general, are the following: "the king's scribe in the horizon of eternity" (Butehamun),[73] besides "the scribe in the horizon of eternity" (Nebhepet),[74] and "overseer of the *neferu* in the horizon of eternity (var.: in the Place of Truth)" (Butehamun and Nebhepet).[75] One more of the Butehamun's titles compounded of the term *pr-ḏ.t* should be noted in this context as well: "overseer of the *neferu* in the house of everlastingness",[76] or else simply "scribe in the Place of Truth (in) the house of everlastingness".[77]

In earlier times, it was the vizier himself who was responsible for the progress of work on the royal necropolis, and this is why the vizier Ta was given the title *imy-r k3.t m 3ḫ.t nḥḥ m pr-ḏ.t* "overseer of work in the horizon of eternity in the house of everlastingness" (graffito no. 528).[78] It is worth noting that similar titles were adopted also by the foreman Anherkhau (II),

[72] Černý, Community, 76 n. 5-6, 349 n. 5 (ushebti figures, Turin Cat. 2534-5).

[73] Coffins Turin CGT 10101(=Cat. 2236), CGT 10102 (=Cat. 2237), and mummy-cover Turin CGT 10103 (=Cat. 2237): G. Maspero, RT 2, 1880, 165; Černý, Community, 77; A. Niwiński, Sarcofagi della XXI dinastia (CGT 10101-10122), [Catalogo del Museo Egizio di Torino, serie seconda, vol. IX], Turin 2004, 42, 151 (1.b), 153 (6.a), 155 (16.a, c), 157 (22.b). Compare also graffito no. 1000: Spiegelberg, Graffiti, 83, pl. 112.

[74] BD papyrus (Turin 1768): Jansen-Winkeln, InschrSp I, 248 (11.122); Niwiński, Funerary Papyri, 365 ("Turin 1"); Černý, Community, 77.

[75] Coffin Turin CGT 10101(=Cat. 2236): Jansen-Winkeln, InschrSp I, 41 (3.79); Niwiński, Sarcofagi della XXI dinastia, 153 (6.a-b); mummy cover of Nebhepet (Louvre E 13047), and his BD papyrus (Turin 1768): Jansen-Winkeln, op.cit., 248 (11.122); Niwiński, 21st Dynasty Coffins, 164f. (no. 333); id., Funerary Papyri, 365 ("Turin 1"); Černý, loc.cit.

[76] Coffins Turin CGT 10101-2(=Cat. 2236, 2237): Jansen-Winkeln, InschrSp I, 41 (3.79); Niwiński, Sarcofagi della XXI dinastia, 151 (1.b), 155 (16.b), 157 (22.b). Compare also a similar title (?) inscribed on the coffin Brussels E 5288, cf. Jansen-Winkeln, loc.cit.

[77] Cf. graffito no. 2055: Černý, Sadek et al., Graffiti III, pl. 59; IV, 34; see also coffin Turin CGT 10101(=Cat. 2236), and mummy-cover CGT 10103(=Cat. 2237): Niwiński, Sarcofagi della XXI dinastia, 42, 153 (6.b).

[78] Spiegelberg, Graffiti, 45, pl. 60; cf. Černý, Community, 78, 81. For other titles of vizier, which connect him with the supervision of work on a royal tomb, cf. ibid., 57f.; Helck, Verwaltung, 23f., 46f.; Häggman, Directing DeM, 116f.

in the early 20th Dynasty.[79] In a later period, the titles *imy-r k3.t n pr-ḏ.t* (var. *m pr-ḏ.t*) and *imy-r k3.t m 3ḫ.t nḥḥ* were also claimed by the scribe of the necropolis Nebhepet,[80] and Butehamun (*imy-r k3.t n/m pr-ḏ.t*).[81] Both terms – *3ḫ.t nḥḥ* and *pr-ḏ.t* – can be connected with a royal tomb,[82] although the latter one originated from the Old Kingdom, when it functioned in a more general sense of the "funerary estate".[83]

As has been rightly observed, it was the illustrious forefather of Tuthmosis, the scribe Amennakht son of Ipuy, who was also titled as *sš-nsw imy-r pr-ḥḏ m ḥw.wt-nṯr.w* "king's scribe and/of overseer of the treasury in the temples (or: chapels) of gods" (graffito no. 473).[84] Furthermore, a simple workman Amennakht, son of the foreman Hay,[85] held the similar title of *sš pr-ḥḏ ḥw.t-nṯr.w m3ʿ-ḫrw* "scribe of the treasury of the temple of gods, justified" (graffito no. 1960a).[86] It is reasonable, however, to connect these particular titles with functions in the administration of the temple in Medinet Habu, and maybe also in other memorial temples on the west of Thebes. Anyway, Amennakht son of Ipuy bears also the title *sš n ḥw.wt nṯr.w* (with variants) in other graffiti as well.[87] In addition, the scribe Amenemope of the early 19th Dynasty was "the king's scribe and superintendent of the treasury in the Place of Truth" besides being the "scribe of the cattle in the Place of Truth".[88]

[79] Černý, Community, 76, 79, 132, 224.

[80] Černý, Community, 77, 80, 224. See also Jansen-Winkeln, InschrSp I, 248 (11.122); Niwiński, 21st Dynasty Coffins, 164 (no. 333); id., Funerary Papyri, 365 ("Turin 1"). Scribe Amenemope of the early 19th Dynasty, the owner of TT 215 (and TT 265, which is a burial chamber, cf. PM I/1², 311f., 346), was termed simply as an "overseer of the gang in the Place of Truth/Place of eternity" (*imy-r is.t m s.t m3ʿ.t/ s.t-nḥḥ*), or else "overseer of work in the Place of Truth" (*imy-r k3.t m s.t-m3ʿ.t*), cf. Černý, Community, 79, 224; Kitchen, RamInscr I, 381ff.; Davies, Who's Who at DeM, 76.

[81] Coffins Turin CGT 10101-2(=Cat. 2236, 2237): Jansen-Winkeln, InschrSp I, 41 (3.79); Niwiński, Sarcofagi della XXI dinastia, 153 (6.a), 156 (20); cf. Černý, Community, 80.

[82] Cf. Černý, Community, 74ff., and 80f.

[83] Cf. R. Hannig, Ägyptisches Wörterbuch, I: Altes Reich und Erste Zwischenzeit, Mainz 2003, 455f., 457; see also M. Römer, ZÄS 134, 2007, 74 (17); id., Or 78, 2009, 4ff.; as regards the graffito of year 4 from the tomb of Haremhab (KV 57): *pr-ḏ.t m p3 ḫr n nsw Ḏsr-ḫpr(.w)-Rʿ Stp.n-Rʿ*, cf. Jansen-Winkeln, InschrSp I, 35f. (no. 61); here possibly only the burial chamber was meant, as suggested already by Reeves, Valley of the Kings, 78; and Peden, Graffiti, 208 n. 469.

[84] Spiegelberg, Graffiti, 41, pl. 55; cf. Bierbrier LNK, 39f., who translated it rather erroneously as "overseer of the treasury or scribe of the treasury".

[85] Cf. Peden, Graffiti, 159 n. 147; Davies, Who's Who at DeM, 20f., Charts 3, and 8 (Amennakht III, son of Hay IV).

[86] Černý, Sadek et al., Graffiti III, pl. 47; IV, 28=Kitchen, RamInscr V, 625, 6.

[87] Cf. Černý, Sadek et al., Graffiti IV, 71, 134 (indexes). Other persons bear similar titles as well, see for example graffito no. 2596.

[88] Kitchen, RamInscr I, 387, 16; 385, 6. The true meaning of both titles remains rather obscure.

Later on it was Butehamun, who was titled as "chief of the cattle in the house of everlastingness".[89] Unfortunately, no such titles can be found in relation to the scribe Tuthmosis, although he was actually involved in the matters relating to the cattle of the estate of the temple in Medinet Habu in year 2 of the Renaissance Era.[90] This possibly means that he did not have any official links with the temple staff, though it is known that in later period some of the members of the gang were in fact in very close relations with the temple personnel in Medinet Habu – some of them held positions of the *wab*-priests within the clergy of the temple.[91]

According to A. Niwiński the graffito no. 1311, recording a visit to the valley of the royal cache at Deir el-Bahari,[92] was written still during the lifetime of the scribe Tuthmosis.[93] His argument based on the placement of the name of Tuthmosis at the top of the text is rather weak in fact. There are a lot of graffiti, where the name of Tuthmosis was written by his son at the very beginning of the text (cf. e.g. graffito no. 3056).[94] Some of these graffiti at least could have been written presumably after the death of Tuthmosis, although no explicit signs of this are included to testify that it was the deceased Tuthmosis who was venerated in this particular way (such as the title *mꜣꜥ-ḫrw* for example). Others were probably written still during Tuthmosis' lifetime, and one can imagine indeed that the period of cooperation of both scribes (i.e. the late years of the Renaissance Era, when Tuthmosis was travelling to Nubia, accompanying general Payankh) may be taken into consideration as well. One way or another, in most cases the appearance of Tuthmosis' name is best explained only as an unquestionable element of Butehamun's filiation.[95]

---

[89] Coffin Turin CGT 10102(=2237): Jansen-Winkeln, InschrSp I, 41 (3.79); Niwiński, Sarcofagi della XXI dinastia, 33, 157 (22.a); cf. Černý, Community, 80.

[90] According to papTurin 2094; cf. Helck OPG, 568; Haring, Divine Households, 254f.

[91] Cf. Peden, Graffiti, 256 n. 810; Häggman, Directing DeM, 372f.

[92] Černý, Graffiti, 20, pl. 59=Jansen-Winkeln, InschrSp I, 38; with a date: year 11, III *shemu* 13 (gr. 1311a: opposite lines 2-3).

[93] Cf. Niwiński, SAK 11, 1984, 149ff. Consequently he dated the graffito to the reign of Psusennes I, thus connecting it with his Tuthmosis "B" and Butehamun "C", according to him different persons than those documented by LRL; for a discussion, see below Chapter 8.

[94] Černý, Sadek et al., Graffiti III, pl. 191; IV, 156; and many others inscribed according to the similar scheme of composition, cf. Davies, SAK 24, 1997, 58 n. 56.

[95] It is still open to question which of the graffiti attest to Butehamun's habit of adding his name underneath an existing graffito of his father, cf. Bierbrier LNK, 130 n. 218. Anyway, it seems that graffito no. 3981a confirms such a custom, cf. Kikuchi, GM 160, 1997, 54f., fig. 2; but not necessarily graffito no. 1311, as suggested by Jansen-Winkeln, GM 139, 1994, 40. As a consequence one can

One could argue perhaps that there is an additional factor in regard to the dating of graffito no. 1311, which would enable us to ascribe the text to the period when Tuthmosis was still alive. He was titled here as the "king's scribe of the necropolis in the Place of Truth", whereas his son and his grandsons (Ankhefenamun, Meniunefer[96]; and written just below (1311b): Nebhepet, Pa[khynetjer], and one of unpreserved name) are simply the "scribes in the Place of Truth".[97] Niwiński was certainly right when he assigned a special significance to the title of the "king's scribe", but nevertheless it is doubtful whether Tuthmosis really deserved it during his lifetime, even if the title was commonly used in this particular social milieu. No doubt the title had clearly a honorific character, as in other cases, when it appears among the Theban graffiti. Here, as a result of its use, a special emphasis was simply laid upon the name of the illustrious forefather, more than on the other living members of the family. Obviously this could be explained merely as a sign of veneration on the part of living members of the family toward the senior scribe, apparently deceased at that time.[98]

It is hardly likely that graffito no. 1311 should be dated to the period of the latest preserved LRL, thus documenting the highly hypothetical 11th year of the Renaissance Era. Let us note that several of Butehamun's sons were enumerated in the graffito,[99] whereas LRL hardly document any of the children of Butehamun, with the possible exception of Ankhefenamun and Meniunefer, the latter evidently still as a child (cf. Chapter 9). More probably graffito no. 1311 can be dated to a slightly later period, namely to the period of the pontificate of Paynudjem I,[100] when Butehamun, accompanied by his

wonder whether some of the signatures left by Butehamun's sons were actually added later to an already existing graffito. The question still needs a further investigation.

[96] These were the eldest sons of Butehamun, provided that Meniunefer was the older one of that name, who predeceased his father, cf. Christophe, BIFAO 56, 1957, 184 (H.1); Černý, Community, 359; Davies, SAK 24, 1997, 56f.; if so graffito 1311a would be dated to the earlier period, whereas 1311b (apparently added later) to the period of activity of younger sons of Butehamun. Such a disctinction would clearly correspond to the chronological scheme proposed by Bouvier-Bouvier, L'activité des gens, 23: their phases III and IV.

[97] Cf. Niwiński, SAK 11, 1984, 150f.

[98] Cf. Jansen-Winkeln, GM 139, 1994, 40; Davies, SAK 24, 1997, 61 and n. 79; Lull, Los sumos sacerdotes, 167.

[99] Presumably the latter unpreserved name may be identified with that of Amenmose. The question is, however, which one of the two sons bearing the name Meniunefer has been listed after Ankhefenamun (see above). As regards other sons of Butehamun, see Davies, SAK 24, 1997, 68 (fig. 1).

[100] As regards the dating of the graffito to the reign of Smendes, see Wenig, ZÄS 94, 1967, 137; Kitchen TIP, 418 (no. 20); Peden, Graffiti, 251 n. 785; Davies, SAK 24, 1997, 65; Lull, Los sumos sacerdotes, 162, 165; Jansen-Winkeln (InschrSp I, 38, 286) related it to Paynudjem I within his new

sons in fulfilling the duties of the scribe of the necropolis, was at the very peak of the career. Other graffiti commemorating the numerous progeny of Butehamun can be related perhaps to this very period.[101] Graffito no. 1285 (a-d), inscribed in "Vallée de la Corde",[102] has a special meaning among these documents, as it gives not only the names of Butehamun's parents – the king's scribe Tuthmosis and the songstress of Amun Bak(et)amun, but also of his daughter – the songstress of Amun Nesymut (gr. 1285d, 2-3), a person unknown elsewhere.[103] At the same time the text can be understood as one more commemoration of Tuthmosis by "his son, who perpetuates his name (*sꜥnḫ rn.f*)", according to the formulation of the text (gr. 1285b, 1).[104] A prayer to Amun (gr. 1285a) located slightly to the right of the main part of the inscription,[105] expresses the author's feelings towards the glorious and beneficial (*ꜣḫ*) god Amun.[106] Consequently the graffito may be securely ascribed to Butehamun, and dated to the period after the death of the scribe Tuthmosis.[107] Quite possibly the nearby graffito no. 1286, written in a similar handwriting,[108] gives the date of execution of the graffito in question: year 10, IV *akhet* 28.[109]

It is worth noting that Ankhefenamun, the grandson of Tuthmosis, went even further in glorifying his grandfather, when he wrote: "The father of his father was the *wab*-priest of Amun in Karnak, who was accompanying the king in every foreign country, king's scribe (in the Place of) Truth, beloved of him (i.e. the king), Tuthmosis, justified" (graffito no. 1018).[110] Obviously,

---

chronological system. An attempt can been made to correlate it with the date of the nearby graffito no. 1310 of year 11 (Černý, Graffiti, 20, pl. 59), recording the progress of some work in the vicinity of TT 320 (cf. Félix-Aubriot-Kurz, Plans de position, pls. 82-82bis) or more probably in the tomb itself, in the period of II *shemu* 6-15; cf. Peden, Graffiti, 216 n. 555, 251f.

[101] For enumeration of graffiti, see Christophe, BIFAO 56, 1957, 184 (H.1-7); Černý, Community, 374f., 362.

[102] Černý, Graffiti, 17, pls. 47-49.

[103] As regards Nesymut, and his second daughter Tadif, see Černý, Community, 358f.; Christophe, BIFAO 56, 1957, 182, 184 (H.7); Bierbrier LNK, 39 (Chart X), 42.

[104] Compare also graffiti nos. 2055, 2216, 2425, 2486, 2633.

[105] For a spatial distribution of the texts (including gr. 1286), see Félix-Aubriot-Kurz, Plans de position, pl. 50 (section 60).

[106] Cf. M. Barwik, Modlitwa wędrowca. Graffiti z obszaru Teb Zachodnich [The prayer of a wanderer. Graffiti from West Thebes], in: Przegląd Orientalistyczny No. 3-4, 2007, 197f.

[107] Cf. Kikuchi, GM 160, 1997, 54f.; Lull, Los sumos sacerdotes, 161.

[108] Cf. Černý, Graffiti, 18, pl. 49.

[109] For attribution of the date to the reign of Smendes, cf. Kitchen TIP, 418 (no.16); Peden, Graffiti, 259 n. 824; see, however, Jansen-Winkeln, InschrSp I, 37, 286 (3.66) – date related to Paynudjem I.

[110] Spiegelberg, Graffiti, 86, pl. 115; Jansen-Winkeln, InschrSp I, 217; cf. Barwik, op.cit., 195; for the

this curious text must be interpreted in the framework of a prayer to the gods of Thebes, as it is a kind of a prayer in favour of Ankhefenamun, still only a *wab*-priest of Amun in Medinet Habu. Of course, there is no doubt about a relative date of the graffito – it was written some time after the death of Tuthmosis, while Butehamun (here called simply "king's scribe in the Place of Truth") was still alive. Ankhefenamun's knowledge about his grandfather's journeys makes an impression, but he obviously distorted the truth, when he used the title "king's scribe" in regard to him. Later on he would be calling himself the "king's scribe" as well (cf. e.g. graffito no. 1021c, and other examples).[111] But this would be related to a profound changes in the administration of the Thebaid and a thorough reorganisation of the necropolis staff and its institutions.

location, see Félix-Aubriot-Kurz, Plans de position, pl. 78 (section 91A); see also a comment by Niwiński, SAK 11, 1984, 150.

[111] Graffito 1021c: Spiegelberg, Graffiti, 87, pl. 115; for other graffiti of Ankhefenamun and his appropriate titles, see e.g. Černý, Community, 199 (nos. 12-13), 362 n. 7, 374f.

6. Chronology of the Late Ramesside Letters

In spite of the problems concerning the chronology of the LRL, their value for the understanding of the history of the period is undisputed. As the author or recipient of the bulk of the preserved letters, the scribe of the necropolis Tuthmosis is the central person of the entire group of letters. The core of the letters are those relating to the Nubian war of general Payankh (see below Chapter 7).Thus we can see Tuthmosis as accompanying general Payankh in his Nubian campaign. After his departure to Nubia it was his son Butehamun who replaced him in the function of the scribe of the royal necropolis.

There are good reasons to suppose that most of the preserved letters belonged indeed to the family archive of Tuthmosis and his son Butehamun. Unfortunately the provenance of the papyri has not beeen ascertained precisely in the available documentation. However, the bulk of the papyri must have been found in the vicinity of the settlement at Deir el-Medina, most probably in the area located in its western necropolis.[1] Scanty information is available only in regard of the provenance of LRL nos. 21, 34-35, and 51.[2] The latter was bought in 1933 so it could have been found during illicit excavations in the same year, when the mission of IFAO excavated in the western cemetery in Deir el-Medina,[3] on the site where the tomb of the necropolis scribe Amennakht should be located.[4]

A well known passage from the LRL no. 9 (from Tuthmosis to Butehamun) must be cited here, as it possibly gives some evidence concerning the hiding

---

1 Cf. e.g. the notes accompanying the copy of papRifaud D: Koenig, CRIPEL 10, 1988, 57, pl. 6; compare also Spiegelberg, Correspondances, 202.

2 Cf. Černý LRL, XVIf.

3 Cf. Bruyère, Rapport (1933-1934), 7f.

4 As regards the location of the tomb, see ibid., 75-77 (no. 1338), 78ff. (no. 1340), fig. 35, pl. II; cf. Černý, Community, 349f.; L.M.J. Zonhoven, JEA 65, 1979, 97; Koenig, BIFAO 81, 1981, 43. It is worth noting that the fragments of the famous plan of the tomb of Ramesses IV (papTurin 1885), were found in the pit tombs nos. 1336, 1337, and 1340; cf. Bruyère, Rapport (1933-1934), 79f. As regards the testament of the scribe Amennakht written on its *verso* (among other texts), see Pleyte-Rossi, Papyrus de Turin, pl. 72; Kitchen, RamInscr VI, 371; Černý, Community, 343f.; J. von Beckerath, in: DeM in the Third Millennium, 1ff.; id., Chronologie, 85.

place of the family archive: "Now you wish to speak, saying: «I am aware of the matter of the documents (*n3 sš.w*) which are deposited (in) the stairwell (?) (*t3 ʿ.t p3-r-ʿ-rd.wy*) ».[5] Now as for the documents upon which the rain had poured in the house (*t3 ʿ.t*) of the scribe Horisheri, my (grandfather), you brought them outside, and we found that they were not obliterated. And I said to you: «I will unbind them again». You brought them down below, and we deposited (them) in the tomb (*t3 mʿḥʿ.t*) of Amennakht, my (great-grand)father. You wish to speak, saying: «I am aware (of this)»".[6] Obviously there is no certainty about relevance of the passage in question for the history of the entire collection of papyri comprising LRL.[7] Quite possibly some group of the letters could have been deposited in a desolated house in the settlement of Deir el-Medina and then transferred to the family tomb located in the western cemetery.[8]

A relatively unexplored field of the studies on the letters is the question of the earliest documents of the family archive of the scribe Tuthmosis. These could possibly shed some new light on the relatively poorly known years of the early career of Tuthmosis, and also the poorly documented period of the early years of the Renaissance Era. The subject will be discussed in the broader context of the matters relating to the functioning of the Theban necropolis in the period preceding the Nubian war of general Payankh.

Early group of letters – before the Renaissance Era

It is still open to question whether LRL no. 1 belongs to this early group of letters, although Wente dated it tentatively to the 6th year of the Renaissance Era or to a later period.[9] It was Bierbrier who noticed that the letter must

5 Cf. Wente, Letters, 191; Lesko, Dict. I, 59, 260; see also Wente LRL, 40 (o).

6 Černý LRL, 18, 12-19, 2; cf. also Černý-Groll, Late Egyptian Grammar, 230 (Ex. 607); 489 (Ex. 1384); Groll, Negative Verbal System, 52 (Ex. 102); Frandsen, Verbal System, 94 (Ex. 12); Winand, Ètudes, 308 n. 29; Sweeney, Correspondence and Dialogue, 154; id., LingAeg 9, 2001, 263 (Ex. 2). For comments on the meaning of the entire passage see Y. Koenig, Notes sur la découverte des papyrus Chester Beatty, BIFAO 81, 1981, 41ff. (esp. p. 42); P.W. Pestman, Who were the Owners, in the 'Community of Workmen', of the Chester Beatty Papyri, in: Gleanings from Deir el-Medîna, 155ff. (esp. p. 157).

7 For example, the data relating to LRL nos. 21, 34-35, decisively points to a different history of this particular group of letters, cf. Erman, ADAW 1, 1913, 14f. As regards their possible origin, see Černý, LRL, XVII; it is worth noting that the letters of this group were bought in 1912, when E. Baraize had cleared the area within enclosure of Ptolemaic temple in Deir el-Medina, cf. ASAE 13, 1914, 19-42; PM I/2², 698ff.; Černý, Ostraca, 126.

8 As for the location of the house of the scribe Horisheri, son of the scribe Amennakht, see Bruyère, Rapport (1934-1935), 315ff. (S.O. II); cf. Černý, Community, 354.

9 Wente LRL, 6-7, 16; id., Letters, 178. As regards its later dating, see especially A. Thijs, Pap.Turin 2018, the journeys of the scribe Dhutmose and the career of the Chief Workman Bekenmut, GM 199,

be much earlier in date, because of the name of the foreman Bak(en)mut mentioned in it as one of the recipients.[10] If this Bak(en)mut held the office of foreman of the right side of the gang after year 17 of Ramesses XI, but before year 2 of the Renaissance Era,[11] when his putative successor the foreman Penparei (I) was documented as holding the office,[12] the letter would predate the Renaissance Era (or can be placed at the very beginning of the Renaissance Era at the latest).[13] However, the dating proposed by E.F. Wente seems to be supported now by the occurence of a mention of the foreman Bakenmut as one of the recipients of LRLC no. III, alongside the scribe Butehamun and the guardian Kar(oy), in a context pointing presumably to the later years of the Renaissance Era, and the Nubian war of general Payankh.[14] It seems this is enough to substantiate Bakenmut's position as the chief of the crew directly after the foreman Penparei (I) son of Nebnefer, in the third decade of the reign of Ramesses XI (thus during the Renaissance Era),[15] even if it disturbs the sequence of foremanship handed over from father to son.[16] In the marriage settlement of the undated papTurin 2021 he appears already as the foreman among the witnesses,[17] alongside the "scribes of the necropolis" Tuthmosis and Efen[khonsu],[18] and also the *wab*-priest and chief worker Ahautynefer (son of Amenkhau), being besides his brother Nebnefer one of the parties in the proceedings before the vizier, as described in the document.[19] Ahautynefer's

2004, 79ff. (based however on his false assumption regarding redating of papTurin 2018 – for arguments against such a supposition, see Chapter 4: Excursus); Davies, Who's Who at DeM, 55; Janssen LRLC, 24 n. 6. Certainly the letter cannot be dated to the period of the Nubian war of Payankh, as suggested by Sweeney, Letters of Reconciliation, 358.

[10] Bierbrier LNK, 35f.

[11] Cf. Černý, Community, 126, 311f.; Bierbrier, CdE 59, 1984, 211; id., LNK, 35f.; Valbelle, Ouvriers, tab. X.

[12] PapTurin 2094, ro. 1; 2; 4: Kitchen, RamInscr VII, 865, 14-15; 866, 1, 3.

[13] See also Häggman, Directing DeM, 352; in another place, however, she dates the letter to the Renaissance Era (ibid., 348).

[14] Janssen LRLC, 24.

[15] See now Davies, Who's Who at DeM, 55, 104, 114, 138f., 280; id., SAK 24, 1997, 62-64; Häggman, Directing DeM, 246 n. 1648, 348f. (the Renaissance Era and the beginning of the 21st Dynasty). Compare, however, my notes in Chapter 4 above.

[16] Cf. Davies, Who's Who at DeM, 55, 138.

[17] Černý-Peet, Marriage Settlement, pl. 15 (4, 11).

[18] Restored wrongly as Efn[amun] by Wente LRL, 9 n. 31; see also Černý, Community, 194 n. 2; compare however Allam HOP, 322; Davies, Who's Who at DeM, 137f. The scanty preserved traces of the name are not certain – compare the photograph published by Allam HOP, pl. 118.

[19] The workman (*k3wty*) Ahautynefer of LRL no. 36 is possibly the same person. See also Chapters 1 and 2 above, as regards his career and chronology of the documents.

position as the "chief of the workmen" is documented in year 12 of Ramesses XI at the earliest,[20] and he was just a simple "workman" in the earlier period.[21]

Even if the exact position of the foreman Bakenmut in the chronological scheme of the period cannot be precisely established (see above), we can take into account another member of the community mentioned in this letter as well. This is the guardian Kadjore, son of the door-keeper Penpamer. Significatly this is the sole evidence relating to this person throughout the corpus of LRL, but a number of sources dating to the period before Renaissance Era mention him as the guardian of the necropolis.[22] The earliest occurrence can be dated perhaps to year 9 of Ramesses IX,[23] and more confidently to years 14 and 17 of the same reign.[24] He remained in the office during the next two decades of the reign of Ramesses XI,[25] and finally he was succeeded by the guardian Kar(oy).[26] A change in the post of guardian had occurred some time after year 17 of Ramesses XI,[27] and it is open to question how long (if ever) Kadjore stayed on the post during early/middle years of the Renaissance Era. Significantly, it was guardian Kar(oy) who was mentioned several times in the LRL, but always in a context pointing clearly to the later years of the Renaissance Era and the Nubian war of general Payankh in particular.[28] The elevated position attained by Kar(oy) in this period can be explained by the mere fact that he participated actively in producing the spears for the army –

[20] PapBM 10068vo. 8, 3: Peet, Tomb Robberies, pl. 16=Kitchen, RamInscr VI, 755, 3.

[21] It is only in the documents dating to the beginning of the Renaissance Era (the acts of trials) that he was deprived of his title, which may be related to his involvement in the robberies.

[22] Cf. Černý, Community, 157-159; Gutgesell, Datierung, 214, 474; Davies, Who's Who at DeM, 200f.

[23] O CG 25742: Černý, Ostraca CG, 89*, pl. 90; cf. Davies, Who's Who at DeM, 200. As regards its dating, cf. Davies, op.cit., 70, 72, 200; Valbelle, Ouvriers, 345; for a slightly later dating of the ostracon, see however Černý, Community, 157 n. 12.

[24] O.Ermitage no. 2973ro., 2-3: J. Černý, ArOr 3, 1931, 396; Turin Necropolis Journal, cf. Botti-Peet, Giornale, pls. 11 (17A, ro. 4, 8), 14 (17B, ro. 1, 2); see also papBM 10053ro. 1, 7 (title unpreserved): Peet, Tomb Robberies, 109 n. 4, pl. 17=Kitchen, RamInscr VI, 506, 12. For his earlier career as a door-keeper, cf. Černý, Community, 168, 170; Gutgesell, Datierung, 456 (oGardiner 249); Davies, Who's Who at DeM, 201.

[25] For the documents, see ibid., 200.

[26] As regards the promotion of Kar(oy), the former doorkeeper (contra Černý, Community, 163, who did not include him into the list of the doorkeepers), to the post of the guardian of the necropolis, see W.A. Ward, in: Pharaoh's Workers, 84 (C.2).

[27] The latest dated reference can be found in the Necropolis Journal of that year: Gardiner RAD, 66, 8; see a comment by Davies, loc.cit (n. 126); Černý, Community, 158f.

[28] Černý LRL, 79 (index: no. 127); see also Janssen LRLC, 23 (3); Demarée, Bankes Papyri, 20.

this is why he appeared among the captains of the crew in LRL no. 28 (name unpreserved), no. 30 and in LRLC no. III as well.[29]

If LRL no. 1 was addressed to the "scribe [of] the [necropolis] Butehamun",[30] the name of the latter does not appear among the persons enumerated at the beginning of the letter in the introductory formula (an "inner address"),[31] where, as it seems, the most important members of the community and close relatives or friends of the scribe Tuthmosis were mentioned by name. Some of them are well known from other sources as well. Besides the foreman Bak(en)mut these are: "the foreman Amen[hotep],[32] the prophet (*ḥm-nṯr*) Amen[hotep],[33] the guardian Kadjore, Pentaumet, Paby, Heramenpenaf, Pakharu, and the workmen of the necropolis in (their) entirety" (ro. 1-3).[34] As regards other persons whom Tuthmosis requested for a prayer for his happy return (vo. 2-3), these are not even members of the gang, but rather their wives,[35] except "the man of the barge (*wsḫ*),[36] and all the men (of the crew)" (vo. 3). Some of these people are known mostly from LRL nos. 4 and 15, but also from other letters. Strangely enough these are not only letters which may be considered as belonging in the "early" group, but also those dated to the period of the Nubian campaign of general Payankh, namely the late years of the Renaissance Era. The following juxtaposition will be helpful perhaps in determining a relations between these letters:[37]

---

[29] His role in manufacturing the weapons is discussed in Chapter 4.

[30] Černý LRL, 2, 14; Wente LRL, 18; id., Letters 179. It may be doubted actually whether the title should be read here as *sš* [*n pꜣ ḫr*], as the reading of the definite article (outside the lacuna?) is doubtful; compare the photographs of the letter in: Janssen LRLC, pl. 65 (vo. 7). In other letters, however, Butehamun was titled as the scribe of the necropolis, cf. e.g. Černý LRL, 76 (no. 39). Compare however LRLC no. III, ro. 1-2, where Butehamun, being one of the recipients, was titled only as "the scribe", which fits better his subordinate position in relation to his father, possibly as the latter's assistant; for the contrary view, see Janssen LRLC, 24 n. 1.

[31] Cf. Černý LRL, XXIII; for the meaning of the term, see Bakir, Epistolography, 35.

[32] Cf. a comment by Černý, Community, 311 n. 4; Davies, Who's Who at DeM, 55, 204 and n. 24.

[33] Probably the same person as the prophet of the deified Amenhotep (I), the author of two letters to the scribe Tuthmosis – LRL nos. 14 and 15: Černý LRL, 27, 3-4; 28, 14-15; cf. Keller, JARCE 21, 1984, 129 n. 118. As regards the authorship of LRL no. 15, see Janssen LRLC, 13 (n. 7), 15; Demarée, Bankes Papyri, 21.

[34] Černý LRL, 1, 1-4.

[35] As regards such a request submitted to the female correspondents, see Sweeney, Women's correspondence from Deir el-Medineh, in: Sesto Congresso Internazionale di Egittologia. Atti II, Turin 1993, 525 and n. 36.

[36] See Janssen, BiOr 25, 1968, 38 (1); followed by Wente, Letters, 179. Anyway, a messenger delivering a letter is probably meant here.

[37] Besides those enumerated below the following workmen appear in LRL no. 12: Kadjadja, Hormes, Neferamun, Panakhtenope son of Panebaku, Wenamun, Awdjar, and Amenhotep; in LRL no. 4:

Pentaumet	– LRL nos. 1,	4,			15	
Paby	– LRL nos. 1,	4,			15	
Heramenpenaf	– LRL nos. 1,	4,		8, 9, 11,	15, 16, 28, 30	
Pakharu	– LRL nos. 1,		5,	12		
Sedjaa	– LRL nos.	4,			15	
Shedsuamun	– LRL no.	4				
Pennestitawy	– LRL nos.			12,	15	
Paherentahatnakht	– LRL no.				15	

One of the earliest letters of the entire corpus seems to be LRL no. 47, which mentions the "commission (*sḥnw*) of Pharaoh" (ro. 4) relating possibly to the royal tomb excavated in the Valley of the Kings.[38] E.F. Wente dated the letter to the 12th year of the reign of Ramesses XI,[39] and such an early dating must be upheld here as well, although a slightly earlier dating cannot be excluded (still before the intervention of Panehesy). The persons mentioned in the letter are those known very well from the sources dated to the early decades of the reign of Ramesses XI, the Turin Taxation Papyrus in particular. A mention of the "doorkeeper (and) guardian Tuthmosis"[40] seems to be most important for the dating of this document, although his position in the line of the guardians of the Tomb, as documented in the sources, remains rather doubtful, though apparently he was the son of the well known guardian Kadjore.[41] Anyway, LRL no. 47 remains the sole evidence of such a combination of the functions of the door-keeper and guardian. In the same letter the two doorkeepers are mentioned side by side, namely Tuthmosis and Khonsumose.[42] It is worth mentioning that a certain Khonsumose and his daughter appear together in LRL nos. 4 and 5,[43] but this time without any title, so there is no certainty about his identity with the door-keeper of LRL no. 47. Both doorkeepers appeared in papTurin 2018: Tuthmosis son of Kadjore in year 8 of Ramesses XI (ro. A1a, 1),[44] and Khonsumose son of Panehesy in entries dated to years

Amenhotep and Amenpnufer; in LRL no. 8: Amenpnufer.

38 Černý LRL, 69, 2 and 15-16; cf. Janssen LRLC, 19; see also Chapter 4 above.

39 Wente LRL, 1-2, 16; upheld in id., Lettters, 171; cf. also Davies, Who's Who at DeM, 201f.

40 Černý LRL, 69, 7; see a comment by Davies, Who's Who at DeM, 202.

41 Cf. Černý, Community, 150; Davies, loc.cit.

42 Černý LRL, 70, 1.

43 Černý LRL, 8, 5; 11, 5.

44 Kitchen, RamInscr VI, 852, 4; cf. Helck OPG, 562. See also an undated entry of ro. D, 8, cf. Kitchen, RamInscr VI, 862, 10 (otherwise Helck OPG, 563). Slightly later, it would seem (entry dated to year 10?), the doorkeeper Tuth[...] appears on the left side of the gang: vo. B2, 12, cf. Kitchen, RamInscr VI, 857, 14;

8 and 10 (ro. A2, 11; ro. A3, 11; ro. A4, 13; ro. C1, 13; ro. C3, 11; vo. B1, 13; vo. Cx+21).[45] Certainly, since we know that Khonsumose started his career as early as year 17 of Ramesses IX, this is not a case of the simple succession, occurring just in year 8 of Ramesses XI, of the doorkeeper Khonsumose to the post after the doorkeeper Tuthmosis.[46] More probably, Tuthmosis acted here as the door-keeper of the temple in Medinet Habu, if he is to be identified with such an official documented in year 12 of Ramesses XI by the Turin Taxation Papyrus, here again in company with the door-keeper Khonsumose.[47]

There are no decisive arguments whatsoever for the early dating of the LRL no. 46 as adopted by E.F. Wente – i.e. approximately the same date as that of LRL no. 47.[48] The question of its authorship cannot be decisively resolved, neither can an addressee be determined. Quite recently an attempt has been made to ascribe it to the scribe Tuthmosis,[49] but this hypothesis has not been accepted.[50] The mention of the person of a certain Henuttawy would be cited as a sole argument in favour of its early dating, provided that she is the same person as the chantress of Amun Henuttawy, being the author of LRL no. 37.[51]

Obviously, LRL no. 37 must be taken as a convenient point of departure in studying these early letters, because it is one of the two preserved letters of the entire dossier which were dated explicitly, although the papyrus is damaged at the place where the year date was written:[52] "It was I who have given 30 *khar* of emmer for [his divine offerings] from [year] 2, [second month] of *akhet*, [day] 27, until the third month of *akhet*, day 2, from the grain which is stored

as regards entry of ro. C2, 14 – its name has not been preserved (cf. ibid., 859, 15); and ro. D, 8 gives the name of the doorkeeper Tuthmosis son of Kadjore (cf. ibid., 862, 10), contrary to the suggestion contained in Helck OPG, 562f. (the doorkeeper Tuth[...]); cf. a comment by Davies, Who's Who at DeM, 201 n. 134.

45 Respectively: Kitchen, RamInscr VI, 852, 14; 853, 8; 854, 8; 858, 16; 860, 11; 857, 12; 862, 8.

46 The earliest evidence is provided by papBM 10053ro. 1, 7: Peet, Tomb Robberies, pl. 17=Kitchen, RamInscr VI, 506, 12; cf. Davies, Who's Who at DeM, 201.

47 Ro. 4, 3; 6: Gardiner RAD, 40, 8; 14; cf. a comment by id., JEA 27, 1941, 25f.; Černý, Community, 168; Helck, Materialien I, (113); Valbelle, Ouvriers, 125.

48 Cf. Wente LRL, 2f., 16.

49 Wente, Letters, 172f.

50 Cf. Sweeney, Idiolects, 312f.; id., GM 158, 1997, 67.

51 It is possible, although not proven, that the letter was written by her own hand, see Sweeney, GM 158, 1997, 74f.; id., Women and Language, 1110f.; id., Correspondence and Dialogue, 180; Janssen, JEA 73, 1987, 167. As regards the chantress Henuttawy in other letters, see also LRL no. 42: Černý LRL, 62, 15; papBM EA 75039: Demarée, Bankes Papyri, 28, pl. 30; and possibly also LRLC no. IV: cf. Janssen LRLC, 27 (2).

52 As regards the lacuna, see a facsimile in Černý LRL, 58a (10c-d); and the photograph in Janssen LRLC, pl. 60; Allam HOP, pl. 101.

under [my] supervision (*w3ḥ ḥr ꜥ.i*)".[53] A purely hypothetical dating of LRL no. 37 to year [1]2 of Ramesses XI must be taken here into consideration,[54] although it is commonly dated to the beginning of the Renaissance Era.[55]

The letter was written by the chantress of Amun Henuttawy, who acted on behalf of the scribe Nesamenope during the latter's absence in Thebes.[56] Her extraordinary position in the administration of the temple in Medinet Habu is corroborated by other documents dated approximately to the same period – in the first instance this is the Turin Taxation Papyrus, but also by other preserved letters (see above). Certainly, her status cannot be viewed simply as due to her own person, but rather as pertaining to her husband, who was himself a member of the staff of the necropolis.[57] On the other hand, we know that the vizier himself wrote to her,[58] which does not seem to be a common practice of the bureaucrats of the time. The quite extraordinary role of the Divine Adoratrices of Amun and their establishment in this period[59] suggests rather an increasing role of the feminine clergy in the domain of Amun, in the spheres of administration and economy of the Theban west bank.[60]

Strangely enough some of the persons participating in the affair described in the letter are also enumerated in the Turin Taxation Papyrus, in the part dated to year 12. This is the case of the fisherman Itnefer,[61] but also the well known scribe of the necropolis Nesamenope, being the recipient of the letter,

[53] Černý LRL, 58, 9-11; cf. Helck, Materialien IV, (616); Allam HOP, 304; Wente, Letters, 174.

[54] For a discussion, see Wente LRL, 4f. (n. 16); Sweeney, JEA 80, 1994, 211f. (n. 40).

[55] Wente LRL, 4, 16; Helck, Verwaltung, 418; Niwiński, Bürgerkrieg, 262; id., BIFAO 95, 1995, 341; cf. also Lull, Trabajos de Egiptología 5/2, 2009, 54.

[56] She was possibly the wife of the scribe Nesamenope, cf. Černý, Community, 214; Helck, Materialien IV, (616); Valbelle, Ouvriers, 240; Sweeney, JEA 80, 1994, 208; Demarée, Bankes Papyri, 28; Häggman, Directing DeM, 208f.; Toivari, JESHO 40.2, 1997, 157, 159f.

[57] Cf. Sweeney, JEA 80, 1994, 208f., 212 n. 49; J.F. Quack, Henuttawis machtlose Unschuld. Zum Verständnis von LRL Nr.37, in: Gallois Chr. et al. (eds.), Mélanges offerts à F. Neveu, [BdE 145], Cairo 2008, 262.

[58] Cf. Černý LRL, 60, 4: "Indeed the vizier has written to me saying ..." (vo. 19).

[59] Cf. Helck, Materialien I, (122)ff.; Naguib, Le clergé féminin, 211ff. Compare also an overall tenor of papValençay I (cf. Gardiner, RdE 6, 1951, 124), besides LRLC no. IX, cf. Janssen LRLC, 43ff.; Haring, Divine Households, 344f. As regards the role of the steward of the estate (*ꜥ3 n pr*) of the Divine Adoratrice Nasamun in the investigations during the reign of Ramesses IX, this can be explained perhaps by the mere fact that the tombs of the chantresses of the estate of the Divine Adoratrice had been robbed at that time (papAbbott, ro. 3, 17-18); for Nesamun and his titles, see Helck, Verwaltung, 520 (36); E. Graefe, Untersuchungen zur Verwaltung und Geschichte der Institution der Gottesgemahlin des Amun vom Beginn des Neuen Reiches bis zur Spätzeit, [ÄA 37], Wiesbaden 1981, I, 105 (n30); II, 106.

[60] See now S.L. Oustine, The Role of the Chantress (*Šmꜥyt*) in Ancient Egypt, [BAR IS 1401], Oxford 2005, 30f. Compare also the letters connected with Henuttawy (see above), Mutenope (LRL no. 36), and in later period those related to Hrere and Nodjmet.

[61] Cf. Černý LRL, 58, 3; Gardiner RAD, 40, 7; see also id., JEA 27, 1941, 26.

who is attested as early as year 12 of Ramesses XI (in the Turin Taxation Papyrus),[62] where conspicuously he appears in company with the songstress of Amun Henuttawy.[63] Nesamenope stayed in office until the beginning of the Renaissance Era, when we hear about him as a member of the investigating tribunal[64] attending the interrogations of the thieves.[65] Some of the persons mentioned in the letter, being possibly the members of the temple staff in Medinet Habu (?) – i.e. the scribe of the offering table Hori, and the god's father Nesamenope – are not identified in other extant sources. Other officials representing the external administration cannot be placed properly in the context of the matters described in the letter. This is the case of an unnamed vizier[66] and possibly also (his?) scribe Saroy. More can be said about the overseer of the treasury and overseer of the granaries Menmarenakht whose activity can be dated securely to the period from Year 17 of Ramesses XI (papTurin 1888+2085) to the early years of the Renaissance Era, when he actively participated in the trials of the thieves.[67] There can be little doubt that he is the same person as the chief taxing master (*ꜥꜣ n št*) addressed by the mayor of Elephantine in papValençay I.[68] The temple officials of the east side of Thebes (?)[69] – the steward of Amun (*pꜣ imy-r pr Imn*) and *wab*-priest Nespamedushepes, and the *wab*-priest of the temple of Mut Pawenesh – are scarcely documented in the Theban sources. As regards the former, he may be the same person as "[...] the *wab*-priest Nespamedushepes" evidenced by papBM 9997 (3, 5),[70] a document with some agricultural accounts of years 14 and 15 of Ramesses XI.

[62] Ro. 2, 10; 3,6: Gardiner RAD, 37, 9; 38, 13. For the position of Nesamenope, cf. Davies, Who's Who at DeM, 284.

[63] She appears alone in ro. 4, 4, and ro. 5, 3: Gardiner RAD, 41, 1 and 13-14.

[64] Hardly likely as "a kind of unofficial counsel for the prosecution", as suggested earlier by Peet, Tomb Robberies, 139.

[65] PapBM 10052, 1, 19; 5, 17, 21.

[66] Nebmaarenakht according to Wente LRL, 4 n. 14 – a supposition based on his proposed dating of the letter; in the case of its earlier dating, an unknown predecessor of the vizier Wennefer should be also taken into consideration; or else Wennefer himself (of whom, as I have discussed above, we know that he visited Thebes on his first official journey in year 17 of Ramesses XI).

[67] Cf. Peet, Tomb Robberies, 123, 136; Wente LRL, 4 n. 14; Helck, Verwaltung, 417f., 384, 505.

[68] Gardiner, RdE 6, 1951, 123. The identity of the chief taxing master of LRL nos. 32 and 46 is still open to question. According to Helck this was the mayor Paweraa, see Verwaltung, 532 (2.8; 2.10); quite possibly Menmarenakht had taken over the title after Paweraa (cf. ibid., 432), and this would provide a precious criterion for the dating of papValençay I.

[69] Less possibly from Per-Ramesse, although both persons enumerated below were writing probably from the North, slightly before LRL no.37 was written.

[70] Kitchen, RamInscr VII, 392, 2. Helck, Materialien I, (30) gave only the reference to LRL no. 37.

It is possible also that the *wab*-priest Pawenesh is the same person as one of the thieves accused at the beginning of the Renaissance Era (years 1 and 2).[71] He was interrogated in year 1, fourth month of *shemu*, day 7:[72] "The *wab*-priest Pawenesh of the temple of Mut was brought. They gave him an oath by the Lord, saying: «If I speak falsehood may I be mutilated and placed on the stake». And they said to him: «What have you to say?» He said: «I did not see anyone. I was living in a small house belonging to the temple of Mut». He was again examined with the stick but he has not confessed" (papBM 10052vo. 11, 17-19).[73] We are informed that he was examined once again in year 2, [x month] of *shemu*, day 15 (papMayer A vo. 8, 1) – this time the name of his father was given in the dossier – but the suspect himself still maintained his own innocence: "Year 2 of the Repeating of Births, [IV month] of *shemu*, day 15.[74] Renewed examination of the thieves. There was brought the *wab*-priest Pawenesh, son of Amenhotep, of the temple of Mut. He was examined again with the stick; an oath was given to him on pain of mutilation, not to speak a falsehood. And they said to him: «When you were standing previously in [front] of the (court) officials, they said to you: Tell the manner of your going (about the thefts), you have never told [it], not knowing that a falling (i.e. theft?) is what your hand (really) did.[75] Painful are the examinations which they will make to you; (so) all you will achieve is a sore hand». He said: «I did not see (anything). It is because of a house of mine that one lied». He was again examined by beating with a stick, with very severe beatings, and he said: «I did not see (anything), but if you bid me lie, I will lie». He was examined again. He was imprisoned in order that he might be examined again" (papMayer A vo. 8, 1-9).[76] In addition, his name recurs in the lists of

[71] Cf. Wente LRL, 4 n. 14.

[72] For the date, see papBM 10052vo. 8,1: Peet, Tomb Robberies, pl. 30=Kitchen, RamInscr VI, 785, 10.

[73] Peet, Tomb Robberies, pl. 32=Kitchen, RamInscr VI, 792, 5-9; cf. Černý-Groll, Late Egyptian Grammar, 370 (Ex. 1048).

[74] For a restoration of the lacuna (IV *shemu*) and emandation of the day number, see Helck, Thronbesteigungsdaten, 129; see, however, reservations expressed by K. Ohlhafer (GM 135, 1993, 63f., 70f.) as regards the latter emendation; in the chronological sequence of the robbery papyri proposed by K. Ohlhafer, the date of papMayer A, vo. 8, 1 falls nine months later than the date of papAbbott-dockets, vo. A, 19 (year 1, II *akhet* 24). As a consequence, the idea of the two phases of the robbery trials in years 1-2 of the Renaissance Era, and the transport of the thieves to the Delta Residence must be taken into consideration; cf. von Beckerath, Chronologie, 90f.

[75] Compare, however, Groll, Non-Verbal Sentence Patterns, 78 (Ex. 251): "not knowing that your hands will be cut"; see also Sweeney, Correspondence and Dialogue, 159 (Ex. 21).

[76] Peet, Mayer Papyri, 14, pl. 8=Kitchen, RamInscr VI, 817,8-818,4; cf. Černý, JEA 27, 1941, 108 (20); Černý-Groll, Late Egyptian Grammar, 61 (Ex. 153), 135f. (Ex. 466), 234 (Ex. 622), 236 (Ex. 628), 332 (Ex. 910); Frandsen, Verbal System, 49 (Ex. 1); Neveu, Grammaire, 269 (Ex. 74).

the thieves (or suspected thieves) of the necropolis (sic!) and the portable chests (*pr-n-sṯ3*), dated respectively to year 1, second month of *akhet*, day 24 (papAbbott-dockets, vo. A 19; the name: vo. B 14),[77] and subsequently to year 2, first month of *akhet*, day 13 (papMayer A vo. 11, 1; the name: vo. 12, 15).[78]

If the proposed identification of both persons can be upheld, then a contradiction appears in regard of the dates given by LRL no. 37 and papMayer A. Thus we are informed that in the "year 2", some time after the third month of *akhet* Pawenesh had written a letter to Henuttawy, while staying in the North (LRL no. 37),[79] whereas according to the data provided by papMayer A he was examined in Thebes in year 1 and subsequently in "Year 2 of the Repeating of Births, [IV month] of *shemu*, day 15". The latter occurrence would have taken place three months before III *akhet* of LRL no. 37, less possibly postdated it (depending of course on the change of date within the Renaissance Era). In both cases, however, the periods of the stay of Pawenesh in the North and in Thebes certainly would be very close in time, if not overlap, if we remember that after an interrogation on "[IV] *shemu*, 15" Pawenesh son of Amenhotep was kept in the prison for further examinations.[80] To avoid this evident contradiction, one must admit that LRL no. 37 predates the Renaissance Era, with the result that its year date should be read rather as [1]2.[81] The consequences of such a hypothesis do not significantly affect our knowledge of the necropolis staff at that period. The absence of the persons enumerated in LRL no. 37 in the list of papBM 10068vo. 2-8, dating to year 12 of Ramesses XI, may be explained by the mere fact that most of them were living outside the administrative complex in Medinet Habu, as clearly demonstrated by the case of Pawenesh. The list of houses was compiled in the aftermath of the disturbances of the civil war, and it would postdate ca. 9 months the presumed date of LRL no. 37.[82] The provisional character of the

[77] Peet, Tomb Robberies, pls. 23, 24=Kitchen, RamInscr VI, 765, 6 (date); 766, 11 (name).

[78] Peet, Mayer Papyri, pls. 11, 12=Kitchen, RamInscr VI, 824, 1 (date); 825, 13 (name).

[79] Černý LRL, 59, 7ff.; cf. Wente LRL, 72; id., Letters, 175. As regards the quotation from the letter written by Pawenesh, see Sweeney, Idiolects, 285 n. 117.

[80] In addition the period needed to send a message, or simply to travel from the Delta residence to Thebes, in those times amounted to ca. 24 days, cf. Helck, JARCE 6, 1967, 139f.; compare Egberts, JEA 77, 1991, 59f.; W.J. Murnane, The Road to Kadesh, [SAOC 42], Chicago 1990 (2nd. ed.), 96f.

[81] Relating of course to the reign of Ramesses XI and not to the Renaissance Era. It is worth mentioning that the chronological scheme proposed by A. Thijs does not remove the contradiction.

[82] The *recto* of Turin Taxation Papyrus with entries dated to year 12, II *akhet* 16 (ro. 1, 1) – IV *peret* 13 (ro. 5, 7), and I *shemu* 9 (ro. 5, 1), completely fills the chronological gap between these two documents; omitted however by Helck OPG, 557, 559.

administration in the Theban area in this period finds its best exemplification in the fact that there was no person responsible for the complex in Medinet Habu (i.e. the *sem*-priest, as one would expect),[83] and the first of the officials enumerated in the list of the houses in its precinct is none other than the scribe of the army Kashuty, followed by other high ranking officials.

Three other letters relating one way or another to the chantress Henuttawy can be connected with approximately the same period – these are LRL no. 42, papBM EA 75039, and possibly also LRLC no. IV,[84] each one of them relating more or less to corn taxation or else dealing with domestic matters.[85]

LRL no. 36, written by the scribe of the necropolis Nesamenope to the chantress of Amun Mutenope, must slightly predate LRL no. 37. We know that the workman (*k3wty*) Ahautynefer mentioned in the former[86] was seriously involved in the robberies committed in the Theban temples so it is highly improbable that he stayed in function still after the legal proceedings documented in papMayer A and papBM 10403, of years 1 and 2 of the Renaissance Era, when he was subjected to interrogation.[87] Significantly, in the legal documents connected with the trials he is always termed as simple worker (*k3wty*), and only in the list of houses of year 12 of Ramesses XI (papBM 10068vo. 8, 3), and in the marriage settlement of papTurin 2021 (ro. 3, 5) he was titled as the "chief of the workmen" (*ḥry k3wty.w*). An analysis of the chronological sequence of the titles held by him inevitably leads to the conclusion that he was probably a simple workman before year 12 of Ramesses XI, and by that year (or slightly earlier) he was promoted to the post of the chief of the workmen. Certainly he cannot be identified with the "gardener (*k3my*) Ahautynefer", enumerated among the members of the *semdet*-staff of the left side of the crew in years 8 and 9 of Ramesses XI,[88] because both of them were the owners of the houses in the complex in Medinet Habu, listed in papBM 10068vo. (5,7; 8,3). In the light of these circumstances, LRL no. 36 can plausibly be dated to the period around year 12 of Ramesses XI (possibly slightly earlier if the Ahautynefer mentioned in the letter is in fact the same

[83] In the case of the domains of the temples of Seti I and Ramesses II these were respectively the prophet (*ḥm-nṯr*) Hapywer and the *sem*-priest Khaemope, cf. papBM 10068 vo. 2, 4 and 15.

[84] For references, see above.

[85] As regards LRLC no. IV, mentioning Nesamenope and the chantress of Amun (name unpreserved): "the letter mostly deals with domestic matters" (Janssen LRLC, 27).

[86] Černý LRL, 56, 9 (vo. 8); as for his identity, see Haring, Divine Households, 450 n. 2.

[87] For this, see also Chapters 1 and 2.

[88] PapTurin 2018vo. A, 1, 13; ro. B, 2, 12 (and probably also vo. B, 2, 18)=Kitchen, RamInscr VI, 855, 1; 856, 10 (and 858, 2).

person as the owner of the house in the complex in Medinet Habu), but after the events connected with the deposition of the High Priest Amenhotep, when Ahautynefer was still in charge of his father's donkeys (cf. papMayer A, vo. 6, 4ff.).

It is a similar case in regard to a certain Aaneru whose participation in manufacturing weapons is mentioned in LRL no. 36.[89] If B. Haring is right[90] that he is identical with an army scribe (of the estate of Amun) of that name, accused of receiving *mery*-wood stolen from the temple and a shrine of cedar, according to the detailed depositions of papBM 10053vo. 4, 20-22,[91] then we have to reach the conclusion that LRL no. 36 must be earlier than the former's "year 9" (or rather year <1>9, as suggested above in Chapter 1). It is noteworthy that one of the houses in the complex in Medinet Habu was owned by "the landworker Paysen belonging to the scribe Aaneri"(papBM 10068vo. 3, 22),[92] and it is open to question whether the latter is the same person as the official referred to in LRL no. 36.

Nothing is known about the recipient of the letter – the chantress of Amun Mutenope. Her close relations with the scribe of the necropolis Nesamenope seems to suggest that in one way or another she was connected with the matters of the west bank of Thebes.[93] Among the persons mentioned in the letter, one official at least belonged to the administrative personnel of the complex in Medinet Habu – this is the deputy of the temple (*ỉdnw n t3 ḥw.t*) Nessobek.[94] As in the case of other officials from Medinet Habu mentioned in LRL no. 37 this person too was not enumerated in the list of houses of papBM 10068vo. 2-8, which seems to suggest a slightly earlier date than year 12 of Ramesses XI. Even less may be said about Ahautyaa, the god's father of Montu, from nearby Armant as it seems.[95]

The circumstances presented in the letter can be placed possibly in the wider context described by the Turin Taxation Papyrus, which documents the methods of collecting the grain for the rations of the workmen of the crew. Obviously the latter document can be rightly connected with the period

89 Černý LRL, 56, 7-8, 10.

90 Haring, Divine Households, 246 n. 8.

91 Peet, Tomb Robberies, pl. 21=Kitchen, RamInscr VI, 763, 3-8.

92 Peet, Tomb Robberies, pl. 14=Kitchen, RamInscr VI, 750, 5; cf. Niwiński, Bürgerkrieg, 246.

93 As regards her possible connection with the community of Deir el-Medina, cf. D. Sweeney, Women's correspondence from Deir el-Medineh, in: Sesto Congresso Internazionale di Egittologia. Atti, II, Turin 1993, 527 n. 4.

94 Černý LRL, 55, 8; cf. Helck, Materialien I, (112); Haring, Divine Households, 453.

95 Černý LRL, 55, 10 and 14; cf. R. van Walsem, in: Gleanings from Deir el-Medîna, 197.

following the deposition of the High Priest Amenhotep and imposition of a military administration on the Thebaid by Panehesy, when special procedures had been followed to stave off the effects of the economic crisis prevailing in the Thebaid. LRL no. 36 demonstrates that some privileged members of the necropolis staff owned the land plots in the vicinity of Thebes, but as in other similar cases it is not easy to distinguish clearly between the purely private character of such agricultural activity and the other official functions of the representatives of the local administration.[96] LRL no. 37 gives a most precious insight into the military administration of the area:[97] the general of the "Place Beloved of Thoth", being a military post or even a fortress located in Thebes,[98] participates in provisioning of the men (of the crew), cooperating with the *sem*-priest of the temple (in Medinet Habu) and the "superior of the house" (*ꜥ3 n pr*), the latter being the overseer of the temple resources.[99]

Letters of the early years of the Renaissance Era (before the Nubian campaign of Payankh)

Hitherto only letters of unspecified dating were included in this group, mostly those predating the letters of the so-called "core group", dated to the times of the Nubian campaign of general Payankh.[100] Apparently all these documents lack any substantial information concerning their precise dating. Nevertheless, some observations can be made, which enable us to fill the gap in the sources pertaining to the early years of the Renaissance Era.

A piece of information provided by LRL no. 12 seems to be especially precious in this regard: "We heard that you have arrived and reached the City (Ne); may Amun receive you with a good reception, and may he do for you all good things. Now we are dwelling here in the temple (i.e., Medinet Habu) and you know the conditions (lit. manner) in which we live both inside and outside.[101] Now the children of the necropolis (*msw-ḫr*) have returned. They

[96] Cf. Katary, in: DeM in the Third Millennium, 177f. A further reference to the subject can be found in LRL no. 5, cf. Eyre, SAK 11, 1984, 203; McDowell, JEA 78, 1992, 196.

[97] Černý LRL, 59, 15-60, 1; cf. Wente LRL, 73; id., Letters, 175.

[98] See above, Chapter 2 (with references).

[99] Cf. Haring, Divine Households, 225ff. As regards the different administrative contexts and meanings of the latter term, see also Gardiner, Wilbour Papyrus Comm., 131; id., AEO I, 34* (no. 1111); II, 267*; id., RdE 6, 1951, 124 n. 2; Helck, MIO 4, 1956, 165, 175; id., Verwaltung, 102, 396; Wente LRL, 74 (z); Graefe, op.cit., II, 81f.; Valbelle, Ouvriers, 139.

[100] Cf. Wente LRL, 5 n. 18, 16f.

[101] Cf. Černý-Groll, Late Egyptian Grammar, 100f. (Exx. 332, 339), 285 (Ex. 774), 292 (Ex. 798); Wente LRL, 44; id., Letters 176; Junge, Neuägyptisch, 124, 216; Janssen, AoF 19, 1992, 14.

have settled in the City (Ne), while I am sitting here alone together with the scribe of the army Pentahutnakhte. Please, let the men of the crew (*n3 rmṯ n p3 ḫr*) who are there, in Ne, be assembled, and send them to me to this side. List of them for you: Pennesuttawy, Neferamun, Hormes, Wenamun, Panakhtenope son of Panebaku, Amenhotep and Kadjadja; total: 7 men. Place them under the supervision of the scribe Butehamun. Let them be brought and hurry up! Do not let them linger at all! – together with Pakharu and Audjar; total: 9 men. (...) Now do not let any youth (*ʿḏd-ʿ3*), whom you will send to stay here with us, indulge in plotting like Hereferniutef or any other like him (...) who might speak with him".[102]

J. Černý expressed the opinion that the fragment in question relates to the youngsters from the community of the necropolis workmen who had escaped conscription during the Nubian war of Payankh.[103] Significantly he placed the events described above at the moment when the crew had left the village in Deir el-Medina and subsequently was transferred to the precinct of the temple of Medinet Habu.[104] No doubt the letter was written to the person who had just returned from a voyage, or else an inspection tour – a suitable job for a deputy of the estate of Amun, as it seems (less possibly a war ?). Actually nothing is known about its recipient, the deputy of the estate of Amun-Ra (*idnw n pr-Imn-Rʿ-nsw-nṯr.w*) Hori.[105] Quite possibly also the "children of the necropolis" (*msw-ḫr*), namely the natives, had just returned to Thebes,[106] not simply fled to the east bank, as suggested by J. Černý's translation.[107] The only possible explanation of their absence outside Thebes would have been their participation in a mission of unknown purpose. The dating of LRL no. 12 to

[102] Černý LRL, 23, 9-24, 7; cf. Černý, Community, 370, 380; Wente LRL, 44f.; id., Letters, 176f.; Černý-Groll, Late Egyptian Grammar, 133 (Ex. 455), 352 (Ex. 998), 406 (Ex. 1129); Groll, Negative Verbal System, 15 (Ex. 27), 35f. (Ex. 75); Frandsen, Verbal System, 8 (Ex. 6), 68 (Ex. 5), 69 (Ex. 10), 204 (Ex. 6), 210 (Ex. 14); Junge, Neuägyptisch, 124, 152; Neveu, Grammaire, 168 (Ex. 18); Häggman, Directing DeM, 321f.; McDowell, Village Life, 239f. (no. 191).

[103] Černý, Community, 380.

[104] Ibid., 370.

[105] Černý LRL, 23, 4; 24, 11. Deputy (*idnw*) Hori son of Pashedmut appears in papPrachov, 8, 12 (Gasse, Domaine d'Amon I, 126, pl. 58), but no conclusion can be reached in regard of his possible indentity with the Hori of LRL no. 12. Another possibility is to identify him with the Hori who is the deputy of the treasury of papTurin 1903vo. 2 (passim), cf. Kitchen, RamInscr VII, 395f.; or else with the homonymous deputy of the Temple in the estate of Amun, attested during the reign of Ramesses IX (papTurin 1881ro. 8, 2), cf. Haring, Divine Households, 453.

[106] See Frandsen, Verbal System, 68 (Ex. 5).

[107] Černý, Community, 370, 380; similarly Wente LRL, 8f.; id., Letters, 176f.; Häggman, Directing DeM, 322.

the early years of the Renaissance Era is generally accepted.[108] It is also true that all of the young men enumerated in the letter are well known from the sources dating to the Renaissance Era.[109] Thus it cannot be excluded that the letter relates to the period when they started their careers as the necropolis workmen – a little bit earlier they were possibly just the "children of the necropolis", as stated here explicitly.[110]

There is some ambiguity in regard to the scribe of the army Pentahutnakhte, a person well known from the sources dating to the earlier period (as a scribe), and to the Renaissance Era (LRL in particular).[111] It is indeed possible that he succeeded the scribe Kashuty in the office of "the scribe of the army of the temple of king Usermaatre-Meriamun, l.p.h., in the estate of Amun".[112] This does not necessarily mean, however, that LRL no. 12 is significantly later in date than the latest of the documents mentioning Kashuty – i.e., the robbery papyri of the beginning of the Renaissance Era, when he was interrogated on account of the supposed robberies committed in the temple of Medinet Habu. It is hardly probable that Kashuty lost his function still before the trials (cf. Chapter 1), his own involvement in the robberies cannot in any case be proved. As regards Pentahutnakhte, there are good reasons to regard him as a contemporary or slightly older than the necropolis scribe Tuthmosis.[113]

---

[108] Cf. Wente LRL, 8f., 16; id., Letters, 176; Valbelle, Ouvriers, 223f., 345 (list X); Haring, Divine Households, 279; Schipper, Wenamun, 329; see however doubts raised by Janssen, BiOr 25, 1968, 38; id., AoF 19, 1992, 14, who dates the letter to the period of the civil war.

[109] Cf. Valbelle, Ouvriers, tab. X (the last column based on LRL no. 12).

[110] It is not clear at all whether the men of the crew and the children (i.e. the natives) of the necropolis (*msw-ḫr*), mentioned in the letter, are in fact two different groups of inhabitants of the west bank, or whether these words refer to one and the same group of young men, who had just returned to Thebes? As regards the meaning of the term *msw-ḫr*, see Ventura, City of the Dead, 35-37; and Chapter 9 below.

[111] Cf. Černý LRL, 76 (nos. 52-53); add papBM EA 75021vo., 3: Demarée, Bankes Papyri, 22f., pls. 23-24. He was also mentioned (as the scribe) in papBM 10403vo. 3, 19, no doubt in relation to the earlier events.

[112] Häggman, Directing DeM, 285, 287; see also Chapter 4 above. The title of Pentahutnakhte in its full form appears in LRL no. 12 (cf. Černý LRL, 23, 5), and in papRifaud D (cf. Koenig, CRIPEL 10, 1988, pls. 4-5, line 1=Kitchen, RamInscr VII, 398, 11-12); the latter of approximately the same date, cf. however Koenig, ibid., 58; Gnirs, Militär und Gesellschaft, 210f. and n. 174. He is noted as the "scribe of the army" also in LRL no. 45 (cf. Černý LRL, 66, 10).

[113] In such a case the scribe Pentahutnakhte (of the temple in Medinet Habu, as it seems), mentioned in the documents of the reigns of Ramesses IX and X, may be the same person, cf. Černý, Community, 209f.; Davies, Who's Who at DeM, 121f. The earliest of the documents mentioning him dates to year 7 of Ramesses IX – papTurin 1881ro. 8, 11: Pleyte-Rossi, Papyrus de Turin, pl. 10; Allam HOP, 313f., pls. 108 (phot.), 110 (Černý's transcription); Peet, in: Studies presented to F.Ll.Griffith, 125f., pl. 10. As regards the dating of the papyrus, cf. e.g. Wente-van Siclen, Chronology, 241f.; Gutgesell, Datierung, 135-7; Bell, Serapis 6, 1980, 12; Janssen, Village Varia, 9-11; Helck OPG 484. Anyway, such a long career may be well enclosed within the lifetime of one generation.

His participation in the provisioning of the crew alongside the chantress Henuttawy and the scribe Nesamenope (LRL no. 37)[114] places him in the social milieu of the Theban necropolis at the beginning of the second decade of the reign of Ramesses XI. This is also the case of the *šrmt*-list of papBM 10068vo. 1, where it has been recorded that 2 *deben* of copper were "handed over (? *w3 n*)[115] to the scribe Pentahutnakhte" (vo. 1, 8).[116] If he succeeded Kashuty as the scribe of the army soon after the latest appearance of the latter (i.e., year 2 of the Renaissance Era), then a dating of LRL no. 12 to year 2 of the Renaissance Era or slightly later seems to be firmly established. This is also the case of papRifaud D, preserved only in the copy made by J. Rifaud,[117] giving the contents of the letter written by the army scribe Pentahutnakhte to the scribe Tuthmosis.

It is difficult to decide whether a vague mention of the Libyans (Meshwesh) in LRL no. 12, as inserted into the words cited above, has any significance in relation to the military operations conducted later by general Payankh or else simply to a raid of the desert dwellers into the Nile valley. Unfortunately the context is too obscure to ascertain the true meaning of the passage in question:[118] "One does not know (about) an arrival of the Meshwesh here. (...) You know that as regards one who comes, it is to this wall (*p3y inb*) that he turns his face because of (*r-ḥ3t*) transfer (?*swḏ/sw3ḏ*). Is it [to] the pilot (*ʿš ḥ3.t*) here that you will give payment?".[119] Certainly this is not the sole mention of the Libyans in the corpus of LRL,[120] and their role in the events of the reign of Ramesses XI still needs further elucidation. The reason of their incursions into the Nile valley is completely unknown. However, two possibilities arise: either they were warlike invaders or else mercenaries incorporated into the army,[121] operating somewhere in Egypt or else in Nubia during the war of general Payankh at a slightly later period. As a matter of

[114] Cf. Černý LRL, 57, 9.

[115] Cf. Lesko, Dict. I, 87.

[116] Peet, Tomb Robberies, 92f., pl. 13=Kitchen, RamInscr VI, 747, 14.

[117] Koenig, CRIPEL 10, 1988, 57ff., pls. 4-7=Kitchen, RamInscr VII, 398f.

[118] Cf. also B. Haring, in: Village Voices, 78; id., Libyans in the Theban region, 20th dynasty, in: Sesto Congresso Internationale di Egittologia. Atti, II, Turin 1993, 162. Quite possibly the second part of the passage in question can be simply taken as a kind of a proverb?

[119] Černý LRL, 24, 6-9; cf. Frandsen, Verbal System, 40 (Ex. 3), 161 (Ex. 2).

[120] See also LRL no. 19: Černý LRL, 35; cf. Sweeney, Correspondence and Dialogue, 202f. (Ex. 24); id., LingAeg 9, 2001, 279 (Ex. 62).

[121] As for the latter possibility, in relation to LRL no. 19, dating to the Renaissance Era, cf. Černý, CAH[3] II.2, 619; Haring, in: Village Voices, 77f.; Sweeney, DE 30, 1994, 208.

fact we can see the chiefs of the Meshwesh (*ꜥ3.w n n3 Mšwš*) in the entourage of the general Payankh (?), forming possibly his guard (thus according to the newly published papBM EA 75019+10302vo. 9-10).[122] Less possibly, the Libyans recorded in the Theban sources from the end of the 20th Dynasty were merely nomads arriving from the desert into the Nile valley in search for sustenance or some opportunities to exchange their commodities or raw materials.[123] It is hardly likely that the Libyans participated in the distribution of luxury goods seized in the royal tombs.[124]

Similarly an undated letter in papLouvre 3169[125] may be possibly connected with the preparations for a military operation, or else some kind of intervention of the Madjoy police against the Meshwesh tribesmen. The letter was sent to Per-hebyt in the Delta, and an unnamed vizier was titled as "the vizer of the land" (*ṯ3ty n p3 t3*), so understandably it does not refer directly to the period of the civil war and its aftermath, although the name of the chief of the Madjoy Ser[montu], would seem to suggest the period of the second decade of the reign of Ramesses XI (see also below).

Here a specific group of letters connected with a journey of Tuthmosis to the north of Thebes, and his subsequent mission in Middle Egypt should be enumerated as well.[126] However, the possible reason of a journey of Tuthmosis to Middle Egypt must be discussed in more detail. The question is why the necropolis scribe was ever sent to Middle Egypt with such an unusual mission? Certainly not only because a large amount of arable land belonging to the temple of Amun was located in the region. The Wilbour Papyrus of the middle of the 20th Dynasty gives the names of some of the temple officials engaged in the administration of the estates dependent on the domain of the temple of Amun in this part of the country. If a member of the necropolis

---

[122] Cf. Demarée, Bankes Papyri, 14ff., pls. 15-16. Part of the document has already been published by Janssen LRLC, 37ff., pls. 23-24 (no. VII).

[123] As suggested recently by Häggman, Directing DeM, 230, 296f., 302-304.

[124] See Jansen-Winkeln, ZÄS 122, 1995, 69; followed by Häggman, Directing DeM, 224. A thesis based solely on the jargon meaning of the word *ꜥḳw* applied to the text of LRL no. 19. However, the case of a certain Nespre, who testified that he acquired some silver from the Meshwesh (papMayer A vo. 8, 14), must be recorded here, cf. Peet, Mayer Papyri, 14, pl. 8=Kitchen, RamInscr VI, 818, 11; for the comment, see Haring, in: Village Voices, 78.

[125] Kitchen, RamInscr VI, 523; cf. McDowell, Village Life, 227 (no. 177); as regards its dating to the reign of Ramesses XI (before the Renaissance Era), cf. Černý, Community, 270; Gutgesell, Datierung, 382 (year 14/15 of Ramesses XI); Haring, in: Village Voices, 77; Jansen-Winkeln, BN 71, 1994, 87.

[126] Wente LRL, 6f., enumerates in this context LRL nos. 1, 5, 14, and 44; according to Wente the letters of this group are dated to year 6 of the Renaissance Era or later; cf. also a comment by Thijs, GM 199, 2004, 86f. Quite possibly this correctly establishes the relative position of LRL no. 1, discussed above.

staff was sent on behalf of the temple administration, it would simply mean that administrative system in the Thebaid had undergone profound changes, although the high priest's responsibility for administering and taxation in this region was not a new factor in the internal policy of Egypt.[127]

Much more complicated is the question of dating LRLC no. II, where Seth "the Ombite" (*Nbwty*/ *Nbty*) was invoked in the preamble (ro. 4).[128] According to J.J. Janssen, the mere mention of Seth "the Ombite" cannot be taken as an argument in favour of connecting it with the LRL no. 47, written by Tuthmosis from Ombos (Vth Upper Egyptian nome),[129] and of an early date of the letter. In his opinion Seth could have been worshipped everywhere as one of the major Egyptian divinities and there is no certainty about a place where the letter was composed. On the other hand, he stresses the mention of "the General" in the letter, and relates it explicitly to Payankh. Consequently J.J. Janssen dates the letter to the period between years 7 and 10 of the Renaissance Era.[130] Apparently we have to accept the above reasoning, at least in regard to the dating of the letter, because "Shed(em)dua and her children, and the daughter of Hemshire" are mentioned in it (vo. 2).[131] So the letter cannot significantly predate other letters of the group dated to the 10th year (LRL nos. 3, and 8), in which the little children of both Shedemdua and Hemshire are referred to continuously (strangely enough no such formula appear in the LRL no. 9, the sole letter explicitly dated to year 10th!).

At the same time J.J. Janssen rightly discarded a dating of the LRLC no. II to the 10th year on the basis of the absence of any Nubian divinities invoked in the preamble. Consequently, I would not diminish the significance of the mention of "the Ombite" among the divinities invoked in the letter, and then its connection with a region north of Thebes appears to be plausible. Presumably LRLC no. II confirms another northern journey of Tuthmosis, after that documented by LRL no. 47, this time accompanying general Payankh, still before the latter's Nubian campaign. Thus the letter should be possibly dated to the middle years of the Renaissance Era (see below), although not necessarily after its year 7 (commonly connected with the

[127] Cf. Černý, CAH³ II.2, 628; O'Connor, in: Trigger et al., A Social History, 227; Gasse, Domaine d'Amon I, 231ff.

[128] Janssen LRLC, 17, pls. 5-6. As regards the god's epithet, see Montet, Géographie II, 82; F. Gomaà, in: LÄ IV (1982), 568.

[129] Cf. Wente LRL, 1.

[130] Cf. Janssen LRLC, 19.

[131] Ibid., pls. 7-8.

investiture of Payankh). Quite obviously pap.Prakhov must be cited here as a precious source concerning Payankh's activity in this part of Egypt in year 7 of the Renaissance Era, and it is open to question whether LRL nos. 23-24 (Wente's "subgroup a"), sent by the second prophet of Amun Hekanefer, son of Payankh were connected with this.[132] Both letters contain a postscript from Penherishefy, the servant (*sḏmy*) of the second prophet of Amun (LRL no. 24), and of the general (LRL no. 23),[133] a person evidenced also by the lintel from Karnak,[134] where he was titled as "the agent" (*ꜥꜣ n*) respectively of the second prophet and of the general. A possible place of stay of the sender of both the letters (somewhere to the north of Thebes, possibly Middle Egypt?) can be deduced only from their contents.[135]

The chronological position of LRL no. 1 in relation to the early letters of the "core group" on the one hand, and to those relating to Tuthmosis' stay in Middle Egypt on the other,[136] would enable us perhaps to reconstruct the sequence of letters of the middle and late years of the Renaissance Era. Contrary to LRL nos. 14, and 44, the texts of LRL nos. 1, and 5 contain clear references to Middle Egypt, having in mind that in both cases Tuthmosis invokes Harsaphes, lord of Heracleopolis, and Thoth, lord of Hermopolis.[137] Unfortunately, a more rigid classification of the onomastic material comprised by the letters is hardly possible.

A rather strange passage from the LRL no. 4 seems to omit any mention of a girl born by Hemshire:[138] "give your attention to the little children, Hemshire[139], and Shedemdua".[140] Even an alternative reading of the passage:

[132] Cf. Wente LRL, 7f.; Sweeney, Idiolects, 279. As regards Hekanefer, see Kees, Priestertum, 167; Kitchen TIP, 42, 253, 481 (tab. 14).

[133] Černý LRL, 38, 9; 39, 14; Penherishefy was possibly a secretary of the second prophet Hekanefer, cf. id., Community, 366.

[134] Gohary, BIFAO 86, 1986, 183ff., pl. 14; Kitchen, RamInscr VII, 387.

[135] Cf. Wente, loc.cit.

[136] Wente's "first group": LRL nos. 1, 5, 14, and 44.

[137] For a possible location of *Namekhay*, recorded in LRL no. 1 (Černý LRL, 2, 3), see Wente LRL, 19 (j).

[138] There is also the case of LRL no. 6, where Hemshire is called by name but not her little daughter; Wente (LRL, 15, 17) dates it with hesitation to year 2 of the Renaissance Era or later. LRL nos. 9, 17 and 31 cannot be counted as a good example, because Hemshire appears only in an address at the beginning of the letter. Other cases where the name of Hemshire appears without her daughter (LRL nos. 10, 24, 43) are of special character. Quite an exceptional example is provided by LRLC no. II, vo. 2, where only "the daughter of Hemshire" was mentioned, but not her mother.

[139] Originally read as *ḥm.w* "servants", but later corrected, cf. Wente LRL, 25 (h); Černý, Community, 367 n. 10.

[140] Černý LRL, 8, 2-3.

"...to the little children of Hemshire and Shedemdua",[141] differs from other places where Tuthmosis usually summons his son and others to pay attention to both women and their children. The little daughter of Hemshire was always mentioned explicitly (although never by the name), but here we have to assume that she was simply incorporated into the group of "the little children" or else that an omission of the daughter of Hemshire in the letter is due to a mere coincidence. The alternative interpretation of the passage would tend towards the conclusion that the daughter of Hemshire had not yet been born when the letter had been written by Tuthmosis. In such a case, the letter should predate slightly LRL no. 5, in which Tuthmosis expressed his concern for the family's welfare in quite unprecedented form: "And you are to look after the little children and take care of them properly just like this daughter of Hemshire, her mother and her nurse (*mnꜥt*). And you shall look after their needs".[142] The appearance of a nurse in this context leaves no doubt that a little daughter of Hemshire was still a newborn baby.

However, it seems highly improbable that LRL no. 4, sent from Elephantine (thus at the very beginning of Tuthmosis' journey to Nubia in year 10),[143] could have been earlier than LRL no. 5 (sent from the Middle Egypt), so it seems that the omission of a mention of the daughter of Hemshire in this particular case has no real value for their relative order. According to the widely accepted view, LRL no. 5 is earlier than LRL.no. 4, and the span of time dividing them would be about 4 years.[144] There are good reasons, however, to reduce the period dividing both letters. This is because of a daughter of certain Khonsumose (see above), mentioned in both of them.[145] In LRL no. 4 Tuthmosis asks his son to take a care (*di ḥr*) of the daughter of Khonsumose, and in LRL no. 5 to look after (*nw r*)[146] her and to cause her to write a letter. As is highly improbable that such a theme could have returned after several years, it seems that LRL nos. 4 and 5 should be placed relatively close in time. In such a case, either the dating of the former should be lowered (but then it would have a consequence for the dating of the Nubian campaign of Payankh),[147] or else the latter must be closer in time to the Nubian campaign

[141] Wente, Letters, 186 (no. 308).
[142] Černý LRL, 10, 9-11.
[143] See, however, some reservations regarding the chronological position of the letter: Wente LRL, 12f.
[144] Cf. Wente LRL, 16.
[145] Černý LRL, 8, 5; 11, 5.
[146] Cf. Janssen LRLC, 18 n. 16.
[147] As a matter of fact in such a case two Nubian journeys of Tuthmosis should be taken into

of year 10, with a consequence that this campaign would have been preceded by another (possibly second?) journey of Tuthmosis to Middle Egypt.

Anyway a more precise dating of both letters cannot be substantiated in the present state of our knowledge. A mention of the chief of the Madjoy Sermontu in LRL no. 5[148] does not provide an essential argument for its dating to a later period, as we know that Sermontu was a simple Madjoy still in the early years of Ramesses XI, as documented by papBM 10068 (vo. 5, 16), where his house in the complex of Medinet Habu is listed. He attained the position of the chief of the Madjoy soon afterwards, since in the accounts of grain supplies, dating to the 15th year of Ramesses XI (papBM 9997, 5A, 2),[149] he appears among other officials – two chiefs of the Madjoy (Amenwahsu and Nesamun) and overseer of the quarter Seramun, whose houses were also listed in papBM 10068 (vo. 3, 20; 5, 11; 7, 7). There are no dated sources referring to Sermontu, which are later than papBM 9997. Papyrus Louvre 3169, apparently mentioning him,[150] is tentatively dated as contemporary with the latter document.[151] Papyrus Louvre 3169 (a letter of unknown provenance)[152] is especially interesting as it gives some details concerning a mission entrusted to Sermontu by the vizier himself (name unpreserved) in connection with some military operations planned against(?) the Meshwesh.[153]

On the other hand, the name of lady Ikhtay mentioned in LRL no. 4[154] cannot be taken as an argument for an earlier dating of the letter, since there is no certainty whatsoever, that it was the former wife of Butehamun who was really meant here.[155] As for the other persons mentioned in the letter, a group of workmen of the crew(?), namely Heramenpenaf, Paby, Pentaumte, and

consideration, compare Wente LRL, 12f.; Thijs, GM 165, 1998, 99f.; id., GM 177, 2000, 66; see also below Chapter 7.

148 Černý LRL, 9, 13.

149 Kitchen, RamInscr VII, 393, 2.

150 Kitchen, RamInscr VI, 523, 3-4: *ḥry Mḏꜣy Sr*[*-Mntw*]; restoration proposed by Černý, Community, 270 n. 5.

151 Cf. Gutgesell, Datierung, 382. The document has been omitted in the sources presented by Helck OPG, 557ff.

152 Its Theban provenance should rather be excluded, cf. Jansen-Winkeln, BN 71, 1994, 87.

153 Cf. Černý, Community, 270; id., CAH³ II.2, 619; B. Haring, in: Village Voices, 77; Häggman, Directing DeM, 303; Morales, GM 181, 2001, 66f.

154 Černý LRL, 8, 11.

155 The letter is addressed to "Butehamun and the chantress of Amun Shed[emdua], cf. Černý LRL, 7, 6-7. The name of Ikhtay is placed among other members of the workmen's community – none of them is Tuthmosis' kinsman. According to Černý, Community, 366f., this was possibly Butehamun's former wife; similarly Baketamun, cited alongside in the same document, was supposed to be the former wife of Tuthmosis.

Sedjaa reappear also in LRL nos. 1 and 15 (cf. a juxtaposition of the names, presented above). This is also the case of the women Irymut and Isis, of whom nothing else can be said, except their possible connection with the crew.

The vessels of green stone (*n3 ḥnw n w3ḏ*) mentioned in LRL nos. 5 and 44[156] seem to suggest that both letters were written approximately at the same period (the former being possibly a direct reply to the latter).[157] The fragmentarily preserved LRL no. 44 does not provide much more detail; even the name of its author remains unknown (possibly Shedemdua?).[158] Interestingly, a newly discovered text on its *verso* contains the name of the army scribe Kashuty of the temple in Medinet Habu,[159] which seems to provide an argument in favour of a relatively "early" dating of the letter – i.e. not later than year 2 of the Renaissance Era, when Kashuty had been succeeded by the scribe Pentahutnakhte in the post of the army scribe in the complex of Medinet Habu. This is well in accord with the mention of "the vizier" (ro. 7), thus probably Nebmarenakht II. It is hardly likely that Herihor or Payankh would be titled in this way in the later years of the Renaissance Era.

In LRL no. 7 Hemshire and her daughter are not even mentioned, although we can find there words of concern about "Shedemdua and her little children (*n3y.s ꜥḏd šri*)".[160] Similarly in LRL no. 1, which can be dated to an early period of the Renaissance Era (see above), there is no reference to Hemshire nor her little daughter, although Shedemdua and her children are referred to. Thus possibly a relative sequence of the four letters commented above would be as follows: LRL nos. 1 – 7 – 5 – 4. If LRL no. 1 still belongs to the early years of the Renaissance Era, then LRL nos. 7 and 5 must be dated to its middle years. It can be taken for granted that LRL no. 4 was written by Tuthmosis from Elephantine, where he was travelling during the Nubian campaign of general Payankh (see Chapter 7). As regards LRL no. 7, it was written by Tuthmosis while he was travelling outside of Thebes, since the following formula can be interpreted only in this way: "(Every day) I pray to every god and every goddess by whom (I) pass".[161] Unfortunately the place

[156] Černý LRL, 9, 8; 65, 6; as regards the meaning of the term, cf. Janssen, Commodity Prices, 217, 303f.; Lesko, Dict. I, 91, 317. It is hardly likely that the vessels were made of emerald; for its use, see B. Aston et al., in: P.T. Nicholson, I. Shaw (eds.), Ancient Egyptian Materials and Technology, Cambridge 2001, 24f.; cf. also Wente, Letters, 204 (n. 2).
[157] Cf. Wente LRL, 6.
[158] Cf. ibid., 6, 16; Sweeney, Idiolects, 317 n. 532.
[159] Cf. Janssen LRLC, 55, pl. 55 (vo. 1).
[160] Černý LRL, 13, 7-8.
[161] Ibid., 13, 3-4.

name given in the letter, i.e. *Yar* (*yꜥr/yꜥrw*), cannot be helpful in determining the place of his stay nor the character of the mission fulfilled by him. *Yar* seems to be merely a wilderness or a "hell-hole", as proposed originally by E.F. Wente.[162] The letter was directed to the guardian Kar(oy), a well known personality from the letters of the Nubian group, but a postscript to the chantress of Amun Tayu[henut][163] was included at the end of the letter. There are no grounds whatsoever to include LRL no. 7 in the "core group" of letters.[164]

E.F. Wente rightly included LRL no. 14, mentioning twice "the general, your lord",[165] in the early group of letters, but his suggestion that it cannot predate the oracular decree of the year 7 of the Renaissance Era[166] must be corrected now in the view of the reassessment of the sources presented above in this book. Here too again its relation to a dossier referring to a voyage of Tuthmosis to Middle Egypt may be only inferred from the following sentence: "And you do not resist from writing me how you are through anyone who will come to the south, so that our hearts will be glad".[167] Provided that it was the author of the letter who stayed in Thebes (he invokes the Theban divinities, including the divine Amenhotep I)[168] Tuthmosis was apparently travelling to the north of Thebes at that moment. As regards the chronological position of the letter, these are the words placed at the very end of the letter, which settle down the question satisfactorily, as it seems: "Another matter to the scribe of the necropolis Tjaroy: Do not worry about the daughter (*tꜣ ꜥḏd*) of Hemshire; she is in good health and there is nothing wrong (*btꜣ*) with her".[169]

One can wonder perhaps why the name of Herihor does not appear among those documented by LRL, all the more if one accepts that the pontificate of Herihor really predated that of Payankh. One possible explanation would be the assumption that Herihor resided at the time in El-Hibeh.[170] On the other hand, one would presume that the royal status of Herihor, usurped by

162 Wente LRL, 19 (j); Lesko, Dict. I, 13, 17. As regards the writings, see Černý LRL, 80 (2).
163 A person unknown elsewhere.
164 Cf. Wente LRL, 7, 17.
165 Hardly likely the title refers to Herihor, as suggested by Thijs, SAK 31, 2003, 300 n. 72; id., GM 199, 2004, 86 (not in LRL no. 1).
166 Wente LRL, 6f.
167 Černý LRL, 28, 7-9; cf. Černý-Groll, Late Egyptian Grammar, 450 (Ex. 1226), 506 (Ex. 1432); Sweeney, Correspondence and Dialogue, 123 (Ex. 29).
168 To whose oracle the author, being himself the prophet of the divine Amenhotep, appealed, cf. Blackman, JEA 12, 1926, 184f.
169 Černý LRL, 28, 9-11; cf. Černý-Groll, Late Egyptian Grammar, 119 (Ex. 414), 286 (Ex. 781); Sweeney, Letters of Reconciliation, 359.
170 Cf. Egberts, JEA 77, 1991, 60 n. 21; for El-Hibeh, see also Chapter 3.

him at the moment of his appearance as a king, effectively prevented middle class officials from direct contacts with the Pharaoh himself. Nevertheless, some of the LRL contain references to an unnamed Pharaoh in rather obscure circumstances. Until now no attempts have been made to explain the meaning of the passages in question, yet these are perhaps most important data relating to the political situation in the Thebaid on the eve of the 21st Dynasty. Significantly enough, only the "early" letters provide such an insight into the personal involvement of the Pharaoh in the matters relating to the local administration at Thebes. Some of the texts would seem to suggest the actual presence of the Pharaoh in Thebes or in the Theban region, a relatively infrequent occurrence in the late Ramesside period, caused mostly by the festival celebrations.[171]

LRL no. 37 is one of the earliest documents which provides detailed information regarding political relations between two parts of Egypt, and the role played in the matters concerning the Theban temples by the Pharaoh himself (that is, it seems, Ramesses XI):[172] "And One (i.e. the king) has given the office of prophet (*ḥm-nṯr*) of Nebet[173] to the god's father Nesamenope, whom Pharaoh, l.p.h., has clothed with an apron (*mss*) as is fitting (*m-šȝw*)".[174] In addition the letter in question informs us in detail about other Pharaoh's interventions regarding the judicial proceedings concerning, it would seem, the legal dispute between a certain Prawenemef and the unnamed father of the recipient of the letter. Quite possibly the subject of the controversy was the cargo of a *ḳr*-ship loaded with "salt and the entire share (*pš* (*mỉ*)-*ḳd.f nb*) of the Northern Region (*ꜥ-mḥ.t*(*y*))".[175] Anyway it is a moot question whether it has anything to do with the provision of the crew of the royal necropolis at Thebes. One way or another, it must have been an important matter if Pharaoh himself became involved in settling the affair. An early dating of the letter to the second decade of the reign of Ramesses XI (less possibly the

[171] In the earlier periods one of the reasons of the southern journeys of the kings, as documented by the extant sources, was their participation in the Opet feast, cf. S. Schott, Altägyptische Festdaten, [AAWLM 10], Wiesbaden 1950, (86)f.

[172] Hardly likely Herihor, as suggested by Niwiński, Bürgerkrieg, 262.

[173] The "Lady" as a reference to any goddess is probably meant here, not necessarily the goddess Nebetuu, as suggested by Černý LRL, 60a (1e-f); similarly Wente LRL, 73; id., Letters, 175; cf. also Häggman, Directing DeM, 209f. n. 1394.

[174] Černý LRL, 60, 1-2; see also Allam HOP, 304; Wente LRL, 73; id., Letters, 175 (no. 290).

[175] Černý LRL, 59, 11; compare Wente LRL, 72, 74 (u); id., Letters, 175; Allam HOP, 304; Sweeney, Correspondence and Dialogue, 179f. For the general comments regarding the affair of the *ḳr*-ship, cf. McDowell, Jurisdiction, 239f.; Sweeney, op.cit., 180; Häggman, Directing DeM, 208f.

beginning of the Renaissance Era) would enable us to date up the actions undertaken by the king and his officials as contemporary in general with those documented in the Turin Taxation Papyrus. Let us remember that the latter document begins with the full royal protocol of Ramesses XI, followed by the titulature of Payankh.

The Pharaoh, whose actions were described so vividly in LRL no. 37, obviously resided in the North (in Per-Ramesse as it seems), the place of prolonged stay of the persons who sent the letters cited by Henuttawy. Nothing is known about Ramesses XI visiting his southern province and Thebes in particular. The possible exception are some rather vague references in one of the "robbery papyri", dated to year 2 of the Renaissance Era, but relating no doubt to much earlier events: "Now when Pharaoh our lord, l.p.h., came to the City, he (lit. One) appointed the *sem*-priest Hori as *sem*-priest of the temple" (papBM 10383, 1,10).[176] In the same document it was stated: "So he went and reported it to Tjawytjawy who was in the City together with Pharaoh. And Tjawytjawy sent saying: «Give the mast (*p3 ḫt-ṯ3w*) to the trader of mine», but the mayor (of the city) refused to give it up without the consent of Pharaoh, his lord. Then Tjawytjawy told the matter of this mast before Pharaoh, and Pharaoh sent a chief fan-bearer, saying: «Give this mast to this merchant of Tjawytjawy», and the mayor said: «I will give it». Behold, it is lying in the possession of this trader of Tjawytjawy behind this fortification-wall of the temple (until) this day"(papBM 10383, 3, 2-7).[177]

We are informed in addition, that there was "the house of Pharaoh" in Thebes at the time of the civil war: "He told the story of this 1200 *deben* of copper belonging to the doors of the house of Pharaoh (*p3 pr n pr-ˁ3*). The *wab*-priest Payseni was brought, who was the guardian (*s3w*) in the house of Pharaoh" (papBM 10383, 2, 4).[178] And similarly in the list of houses of year 12 of Ramesses XI we can find the following information, in the part devoted to the complex in Medinet Habu: "the house of the guardian Pages(?) of the house of Pharaoh (*p3 pr n pr-ˁ3*)" (papBM 10068vo. 8, 4).[179] However, the

---

[176] Peet, Tomb Robberies, pl. 22=Kitchen, RamInscr VI, 834, 11-13; cf. Černý-Groll, Late Egyptian Grammar, 97 (Ex. 317); Frandsen, Verbal System, 66 (Ex. 13). An interpretation proposed by Thijs, SAK 31, 2003, 303 n. 92, that the passage refers to "the coming to Thebes of a 'new' king who until that time had ruled over another part of Egypt", can be viewed only in the light of his proposed alternative chronological system, and seems to be too hazardous.

[177] Peet, Tomb Robberies, pl. 22=Kitchen, RamInscr VI, 835, 11-836, 3; cf. Černý-Groll, Late Egyptian Grammar, 253 (Ex. 686), 429 (Ex. 1171); Frandsen, Verbal System, 45 (Ex. 9).

[178] Peet, Tomb Robberies, pl. 22=Kitchen, RamInscr VI, 835, 5-7.

[179] Peet, Tomb Robberies, pl. 16=Kitchen, RamInscr VI, 755, 4.

role and exact location of "the house of Pharaoh" (*pꜣ pr n pr-ꜥꜣ*), mentioned in the sources as early as the reign of Ramesses IX,[180] cannot be elucidated properly.[181] Even the more detailed description of the place as "the house of Pharaoh inside the temple of Mehit" (*pꜣ pr n pr-ꜥꜣ tꜣ ri.t-ẖnw (n) pr-Mḥyt*),[182] does not make the task easier, because it may be related rather to the estate located in the Thinite region.[183] Evidently it has nothing to do with the *tꜣ wsẖ.t ꜥꜣ.t n tꜣ ḥw.t pr-ꜥꜣ*, cited in the Turin Necropolis Journal of year 17 of Ramesses IX,[184] relating to the great court of the temple in Medinet Habu.

LRL no. 37 convincingly demonstrates that Thebes remained still under Pharaoh's influence for some unspecified period after the deposition of the High Priest Amenhotep. This is quite in accord with the evidence provided by the "robbery papyri" of the beginning of the Renaissance Era, when the king exercised his power over Thebes through the agency of the high-ranking court officials. Such a prominent role of the king in regard to the matters of the Theban region stands in apparent contradiction to the famous statement, contained in LRL no. 21, of general Payankh who slightly later belittled Pharaoh's significance and influence in rather harsh words. It may be surmised whether the letter was written before the appropriation of the full royal trappings by the High Priest Herihor, the new ruler of Thebes and Upper Egypt. Evidently much had changed within the decade dividing the beginning of the Renaissance Era from the period of the Nubian war of general Payankh.

None of the documents dating to the Renaissance Era provides any precise information relating to the king's residence in Thebes. The high priests of Amun as direct successors of the Ramesside pharaohs now played the role of sovereigns of the southern state. It is still open to question whether Herihor or any of his immediate successors ever dwelt in the residential quarter built by Ramesses III

[180] Cf. papBM 10053ro. 4, 1: Peet, Tomb Robberies, pl. 18=Kitchen, RamInscr VI, 510, 1. It was possibly here (or in one of the temples?) that the door-keeper Kar(oy) fulfilled the mission entrusted to him by the necropolis authorities in year 15 of Ramesses IX, as noted in papTurin 2071/224+1960 vo. 1, 11-12: Kitchen, RamInscr VI, 643, 4-5, cf. Häggman, Directing DeM, 110; Helck OPG, 509.

[181] According to Aldred (Tomb Robberies, 93f.) it was "perhaps the palace attached to the temple" (i.e. in Medinet Habu); cf. also Janssen, AoF 19, 1992, 17.

[182] Cf. papBM 10053ro. 7, 14: Peet, Tomb Robberies, 109, 111 n. 20, pl. 19=Kitchen, RamInscr VI, 514, 7f. Compare the Turin Necropolis Journal: Botti-Peet, Giornale, pl. 48 (vo. A 7, 2-4)=Kitchen, RamInscr VI, 597, 15f.

[183] Cf. Müller, in: Libyan Period in Egypt, 259; Fischer-Elfert, JEA 82, 1996, 138f.

[184] Cf. Botti-Peet, Giornale, 38, pl. 43 (vo. B 9, 24)=Kitchen, RamInscr VI, 594, 10f.; similarly in papTurin 2071/224+1960 ro. 2, 12: Kitchen, RamInscr VI, 642, 6 ("gate of the temple of Pharaoh"). In papHarris I, IV, 11f. the temple palace of Ramesses III (to the south of the first court) was termed simply as the "august royal palace (*ꜥḥ*) within it (i.e. the temple)", cf. P. Grandet, Le Papyrus Harris I, II, [BdE 109/2], Cairo 1994, 22 (n. 94).

around his mortuary temple in Medinet Habu, in the eastern High Gate as a royal residence proper, or in the temple palace of Ramesses III transformed perhaps into a "state palace" or a residence.[185] Some traces of adaptation of the latter, dating to the time of Paynudjem I, have been revealed during excavations.[186] Significantly, some possible alterations of the original decoration of the eastern High Gate must be recorded as well. This is clearly visible in the headdresses of some representations of the princesses (originally daughters of Ramesses III),[187] which were transformed into elaborate floral crowns of the type well attested in the late Ramesside period and during the 21st Dynasty.[188] Unfortunately, the exact date of these alterations cannot be established satisfactorily.

Anyway, the administrative centre of Medinet Habu, with the high priest's residence on the spot, would obtain an extraordinary significance, and the role played by the officials of the former administrative headquarters of the necropolis would not be restricted now to their traditional functions connected with the necropolis itself. Some of them presumably were numbered now among the closest entourage of the high priest himself and their function varied distinctly in comparison to the earlier administrative patterns. Certainly, this was the case of the necropolis scribe Tuthmosis, especially during the later stage of his administrative career. One would not understand properly the exceptional role played by him at the side of general Payankh without taking into consideration an abrupt change in the administrative system of the period. No doubt the new regime determined profound changes on every level of the social structure of the local community of Thebes.

---

[185] Cf. R. Stadelmann, Temple Palace and Residential Palace, in: Bietak M. (ed.), Haus und Palast im alten Ägypten, Wien 1996, 228, 230; id., Royal Palaces of the Late New Kingdom in Thebes, in: Bryan B.M., Lorton D. (eds.), Essays in Egyptology in honor of H. Goedicke, San Antonio 1994, 313, 314f.

[186] Cf. U. Hölscher, The Excavation of Medinet Habu III, [OIP 54], Chicago 1941, 54f.; id., Excavation of Medinet Habu V, [OIP 66], Chicago 1954, 3, 36; see also Stadelmann, in: Haus und Palast, 228. For inscriptions of Paynudjem I on the doorjambs and lintel from the temple palace cf. Römer, Gottes- und Priesterherrschaft, 553-555 (nos. 22-23); Jansen-Winkeln, InschrSp I, 20f. (nos. 26-27). For restoration inscriptions of the high priest Paynudjem I in the complex of Medinet Habu, see also Römer, op.cit., 553 (no. 21), 555-558 (nos. 24-26); Jansen-Winkeln, op.cit., 18-20 (nos. 24-25).

[187] Cf. The Epigraphic Survey, Medinet Habu VIII, [OIP 94], Chicago 1970, pls. 630, 639 (?); for other examples of the crowns of this type cf. ibid., pls. 646, 649-655, 657.

[188] As regards this type of the crown in the Ramesside iconography, see Ch.C. van Siclen III, A Ramesside Ostracon of Queen Isis, JNES 33, 1974, 150-153; and a scene from QV 51: Ch. Leblanc, Ta Set Neferou. Une necropole de Thebes-ouest et son necropole, I, Cairo 1989, pl. 112; in addition an undated ostracon from the Valley of the Kings may be cited – oCG 25043ro.: Daressy, Ostraca, pl. 9; see also The Temple of Khonsu 1, pl. 28. For an earlier example however, see a representation in the tomb of Menna (TT 69), cf. Ch. Lilyquist, The Tomb of Threee Foreign Wives of Tuthmosis III, New York 2003, 157 (fig. 93a); and possibly also C.F.A. Schaeffer (ed.), Ugaritica III, Paris 1956, 164ff. (fig. 118), 179ff. (fig. 126).

7. The Nubian campaign of general Payankh

Late Ramesside sources from Nubia are relatively scanty if we compare them with the ample documentation relating to the 19th Dynasty.[1] It is noticeable that during the reign of Ramesses XI, their number markedly decrease in comparison with those of the reign of Ramesses IX. Significantly the geographical distribution of the preserved pharaonic monuments in this period is limited distinctly to the region of Lower Nubia, whereas it reached the southernmost regions of Nubia (as far as Gebel Barkal) still during the reign of Ramesses IX.[2] An unspecified monument (possibly a doorjamb?) from Aswan, dedicated by Ramesses XI to Horus lord of Kubban, seems to be the latest testimony of the Ramesside activity in this part of Egypt.[3] In Nubia the name of Ramesses XI is attested only in Buhen.[4] This is a hieroglyphic graffito left by the viceroy of Kush[5] on a pillar of the Northern temple. Significantly this is not only the sole record of this ruler in Nubia, but also the latest evidence relating to the Egyptian sovereignty over Nubia, although the revenues from Kush (*p3 inw Kš*) used to provide for the institutions of the Theban necropolis will be enumerated still in the early years of the Renaissance Era.[6] Later on, the title of the King's Son of Kush would be held by some members of the high priest's family during the 21st Dynasty,[7] but it must be taken as a purely honorific title without any real significance,

[1] For a convenient enumeration of the sources dating to the late 20th Dynasty, see Peden, Graffiti, 130-133; I. Hein, Die ramessidische Bautätigkeit in Nubien, [GOF IV.22], Wiesbaden 1991, 102ff., 144ff.

[2] Cf. Hein, op.cit., 178 (map 8).

[3] Kitchen, RamInscr VI, 731 (14); S. Farag et al., OrAnt 18, 1979, 282, pl. 19.

[4] R.A. Caminos, The New-Kingdom Temples of Buhen, II, London 1974, 109f., pl. 89 (1-3); Kitchen, RamInscr VI, 842, 10-12 (no. 34); Peden, Graffiti, 133; Hein, op.cit., 47, 104, 146.

[5] His name read is now as Setmose, and not as Panehesy, as once thought, cf. Bohleke, GM 85, 1985, 13ff.; a conjecture accepted by others, cf. e.g. Hein, op.cit., 47, 104, 146. Compare, however, Jansen-Winkeln, ZÄS 119, 1992, 24; Gnirs, Militär und Gesellschaft, 139f. n. 856; both opting for Panehesy.

[6] PapTurin 1903, ro. 1-6: Kitchen, RamInscr VII, 396, 15-397, 2; Helck OPG, 571; cf. Valbelle, Ouvriers, 69.

[7] Cf. Kees, Priestertum, 165f.; Peden, Graffiti, 133 n. 481; Gnirs, Militär und Gesellschaft, 141.

or else merely supporting the claims to revenues from the southern regions (?) of Upper Egypt.[8]

After his defeat in the north, viceroy Panehesy had retreated to the southern province, being his stronghold and recruiting base for his army. Although the name of the real instigator of the counterattack remains unknown, the representatives of the new regime in the Thebaid were strongly determined to regain control of the lost province. It is unknown whether one or maybe more military campaigns were directed against Panehesy. In the later years of the Renaissance Era, general Payankh was in command of the forces operating in Nubia. There are good reasons to believe that the results of the Nubian campaign were apparently negligible, and Nubia soon regained an undisputed independence under the royal dynasty of Kush, reigning from the new capital in Napata.

There are no other sources concerning the Nubian war of general Payankh except the corpus of LRL. As a matter of fact, the core of the letters from the family archive of the scribe Tuthmosis concern the matters connected with the Nubian campaign or campaigns led by general Payankh in Nubia. The letters provide a relatively clear picture of the logistic background of the military campaign but nothing about its real course nor tactics. As demonstrated earlier, there is a significant lack of any decisive information relating to the most important factors concerning the political history of the period. Similarly, the motives of the persons involved in the conflict are also completely unknown to us. Taking into consideration the contents of the letters relating to this period, they can be divided into four distinct groups, which concern in general the following matters:

1. Theban affairs connected with the provision of the army of general Payankh. The scribe Tuthmosis seems to have been one of the persons responsible for this.
2. Tuthmosis travelling to Nubia to meet general Payankh.
3. Tuthmosis in Nubia.
4. Theban affairs supervised by Butehamun in the absence of his father.

[8] See L. Habachi, in: LÄ III (1980), 635. For a contrary view, cf. K. Zibelius-Chen, SAK 16, 1989, 336, 343. Similarly, a revenues or tribute from Syria and Kush in the middle of the 21st Dynasty, as mentioned in the titles of the priest Khonsumose from Karnak, must be taken as purely fictitious. For the document in question, cf. Niwiński, Funerary Papyri, 353 ("Paris 12"). As regards the possible meaning of the title borne by Nesikhonsu, wife of the High Priest Paynudjem II, see Niwiński, DE 14, 1989, 88f.

No doubt all these letters can be dated to the Renaissance Era, and more precisely, to its late years. Nonetheless, the internal chronology of the letters of these four groups is still an open question and depends mostly on the internal relations between them. Only one of the letters of this group can be dated explicitly – this is LRL no. 9. In this the 10th year (undoubtedly of the Renaissance Era) was given as a date of receiving a previous letter written by Butehamun: "This letter of yours reached me through the agency of the retainer (*šmsw*) Djehutyhotep in year 10, first month of *shemu*, day 25".[9]

1) Tuthmosis in Thebes

These are the letters belonging to E.F. Wente's "subgroup b", all of them sent by Payankh to Thebes, and addressed mostly to the scribe Tuthmosis (other recipients are Payshuuben and Nodjmet).[10] This group of letters gives an insight into the scribe Tuthmosis' activities in Thebes, busy with provisioning of the army operating in Nubia (LRL nos. 20, and 22 – the matter of a coppersmith), although very often the character of this activity has not been determined precisely (cf. e.g. LRL nos. 18, and 22 – the matter of Akhmenu). Probably here belongs the case of the bread-rations to the Meshwesh (LRL no. 19). Three letters of Payankh concerning the affair of the two Madjoy (LRL nos. 21, 34, 35)[11] should be attached presumably to this group (for this see also above, Chapter 3). Anyway, the case of a curious political murder, committed on the two unnamed Madjoy policemen,[12] cannot be placed precisely in the context of events of the late Renaissance Era.

Two possibilities arise, regarding the dating of this group of letters concerning the period when Tuthmosis was in Thebes. They either date to before the Nubian journey of Tuthmosis, or possibly date to after his return from Nubia, if he ever returned to Thebes. Nevertheless they concern a period when Payankh was already operating in Nubia, so one should try to make a

---

[9] Černý LRL, 17, 10-11. For the chronological position of the letter, see Wente LRL, 11f.; Kitchen TIP, 21f., 417 (II.5); von Beckerath, Chronologie, 91. Apparently this is the latest attested date of the Renaissance Era; there are no grounds to date LRL no. 41 to a dubious year 12 of the Renaissance Era, contrary to a suggestion proposed by Wente LRL, 17; Helck, in: LÄ I (1975), 885; Kitchen, in: Libyan Period in Egypt, 193 and n. 63; cf. also Vandersleyen, L'Égypte II, 650f.; for this see also below, Chapter 9. As regards a dating of LRL 37, see Chapter 6.

[10] These are LRL nos. 17-22, 34, 35, cf. Wente LRL, 8, 16. The author of LRL no. 17 is the singer of the general, Pentahures, the author of LRL no. 31 of the core group, cf. Sweeney, Idiolects, 279.

[11] All of them written presumably by Kenykhnum, one of general Payankh's secretaries, see Janssen, JEA 73, 1987, 166; cf. Sweeney, Idiolects, 279 n. 40, 303.

[12] Cf. Gardiner, JMEOS 2, 1912-1913, 57ff.; Erman, ADAW 1, 1913, 3ff.; Černý, Community, 381.

distinction between an early and late stage of the war (if not between two different campaigns?). It is impossible to say, however, how much time had elapsed since the beginning of the campaign of Payankh before the preserved documentation begins to supply some of the details about it. Even less information is provided as regards the whereabouts of Payankh himself. Quite possibly LRL no. 20 was sent by Payankh (to Tuthmosis) while travelling to the south, no doubt before he reached his planned destination: "You know about this journey/expedition (*pꜣy mšꜥ*) which I am going to make (*nty tw.i m nꜥy r ir.t.f*)".[13]

One of the letters at least mentions the Theban activity of Tuthmosis as preceding directly his departure to Nubia – this is LRL no. 28, which was written however at the time after he left Thebes.

2) Tuthmosis on the way to Nubia

There are good reasons to suppose that LRL no. 28 was written by the captains of the necropolis soon after Tuthmosis' departure to Nubia. The words cited in the letter seem to describe the circumstances which prompted him to follow his master: "Has not the scribe of the necropolis Tuthmosis reported to you about our searching for a (transport) boat and not having found (it) right away? For he had become depressed[14] when we reached the City (Ne) and when he was told that you had left before we reached our mistress. She said to the scribe of the necropolis Tjaroy: «He said to you: "Follow me!"». (Then) we handed over the clothes to our mistress and she said to the scribe Tjaroy: «Are you not conveying the clothes yourself? It is you who must hand [them] over to your lord!» – so said she, our mistress, to him".[15]

No doubt Tuthmosis followed his master to Nubia to deliver a cargo of clothes according to the demand of the general, expressed through the unnamed female intermediary. Before his departure, however, he wrote a letter to general Payankh, explaining his obvious failure in sending the clothes. Thus we can admit that some time elapsed between the above described events and his final departure to Nubia. In the absence of the scribe Tuthmosis, the necropolis authorities seem to be a little bit lost and disappointed: "As for

[13] Černý LRL, 35, 15; cf. Černý-Groll, Late Egyptian Grammar, 339 (Ex. 927); Winand, Études, 421 (Ex. 1055), 422 (Ex. 1058); Neveu, Grammaire, 78 (Ex. 33).

[14] For an interpretation of the passage, see also Černý, Community, 364 and n. 7; R.J. Williams, JNES 28, 1969, 138; Wente, Letters, 194; Sweeney, Correspondence and Dialogue, 67 n. 153. For a different interpretation, see Satzinger, Neuägyptische Studien, 169.

[15] Černý LRL, 46, 4-12.

this scribe who used to be here in charge of us, he who was appointed (as a scribe)[16], who knows a *ḥy* and who is an influential man, whose father has witnessed that (*iw mtr st p3y.f it*)[17] – (now) he is with you".[18] Obviously this sounds like a complaint of deserted kinsmen, and the reason behind it must be sought of course in the predominant role played by Tuthmosis in supervising the matters of the royal necropolis. At the same time, the tenor of these words seems to suggest that Tuthmosis' departure was a relatively recent occurrence, which seems to be in accord with the observation made above.

Much has been said about the dating of this letter, which is possibly one of the most interesting documents among other LRL. Certainly we must accept the results achieved already by E.F. Wente, who included it in the "core group" of Nubian letters, dating the letter to the 10th year of the Renaissance Era.[19]

Presumably only one of the letters of Tuthmosis was written while he was staying on Elephantine.[20] This is LRL no. 4, in which he briefly described his journey southward: "I have reached my superior. Indeed it was only when they met me in the vicinity of Edfu, that I found out that he had sent a boat to take me. I met him at the town of Elephantine, and he said to me: «Another time you will not have to come»[21] – so he said to me. He gave me bread and beer as previously, and he said to me: «May Montu favor (you)! Now we are moored at Elephantine»; and he says (also): «I shall go up (to Nubia) to attack (*r pḥ*) Panehesy at the place where he is» – so he says".[22] LRL no. 30, which

[16] Or simply: "... who gives", cf. Satzinger, Neuägyptische Studien, 228. This could be a sentence referring to his superior role within the community, or else simply referring to the mental capacity of the man who used to decide and to give advice and instructions, cf. Groll, RdE 26, 1974, 171; Wente, Letters, 195; Sweeney, Correspondence and Dialogue, 56 n. 75. See however, Groll, Non-Verbal Sentence Patterns, 79f. (Ex. 256); Junge, Neuägyptisch, 274.

[17] If we take the dependent pronoun *st* as a variant writing for *sw*, cf. Neveu, Grammaire, 22. Compare also Junge, Neuägyptisch, 272f.; another possibility of translation: "vouched for him" or "testified", cf. Wente LRL, 64 (aj); id., Letters, 195; or else: "whose father had taught him", cf. Sweeney, Correspondence and Dialogue, 56. For the meaning of *mtr* in this context (to inform, to testify), cf. McDowell, Jurisdiction, 21 n. 56; compare also Eyre, SAK 11, 1984, 199 (m).

[18] Černý LRL, 47, 7-9. For the translation of the entire passage, see also Groll, RdE 26, 1974, 171 (VII); Junge, Neuägyptisch, 273f.; Sweeney, Correspondence and Dialogue, 56f.; Häggman, Directing DeM, 224f.; Wente, Letters, 195; as regards the meaning of *ḥy*, see below.

[19] Wente LRL, 10ff., 16.

[20] As regards its chronological position within corpus of LRL, see above, Chapter 6.

[21] Černý LRL, 7, 13; here I follow Wente, Letters, 185; similarly Frandsen, Verbal System, 45 (Ex. 6): "Another time you need not come"; see however Wente, LRL, 24, 25 (d); Černý-Groll, Late Egyptian Grammar, 270 (Ex. 738).

[22] Černý LRL, 7,10-8,1; Černý-Groll, Late Egyptian Grammar, 250 (Ex. 676), 291 (Ex. 791), 378 (Ex. 1061); Groll, Negative Verbal System, 132 (Ex. 283); id., RdE 26, 1974, 169 (I); Sweeney, LingAeg 9, 2001, 263 (Ex. 1). There are no grounds whatsoever to deny that Panehesy is the well

Payankh sent to the authorities of the necropolis, actually confirms the arrival of Tuthmosis: "The scribe of the necropolis Tjaroy and the troop-commander and prophet Shedsuhor have reached me".[23]

Assuan and Elephantine were probably most suitable headquarters for an army operating in Nubia.[24] Probably the fortress on the island of Biggeh was still existing in this period, since we know a name of its commander in the middle of the 20th Dynasty.[25] Payankh could have stay at Elephantine for some time, as well as his wife(?) Hrere. Tuthmosis wrote to his son (LRL no. 2): "I left him (i.e. Payankh?) in Elephantine in the company of (?)[26] Hrere to cause [...]".[27] According to E.F. Wente LRL nos. 38 and 39, sent by Hrere to the troop-commander Peseg, could have been written on Elephantine just about that time,[28] but why should Hrere have acted as a substitute for Payankh in supervising the matters of the Theban necropolis? The only acceptable explanation would be the absence of Payankh who at that time would set out to his military campaign in the south.

It cannot be discerned beyond any doubt at what time Pentahures dispatched a letter to Thebes (LRL no. 31), apparently informing Butehamun that his father had sent him a letter from the south. There are good reasons to believe that Pentahures was then staying on Elephantine, since he invokes "Khnum, Satis, Anukis, and all gods of Elephantine", and an oracle of Khnum is mentioned in it explicitly.[29]

3) Tuthmosis in Nubia

It seems LRL no. 2 can be dated approximately to the same time as LRL nos. 9 and 50, and LRLC no. III; all four of them were written by Tuthmosis while he was travelling from Elephantine to Nubia.[30] In LRL no. 2, recording

known viceroy of Kush, as suggested by Thijs, GM 173, 1999, 187 n. 58. As regards a suggestion that the true reason of the expedition was a negotiation with Panehesy, see Niwiński, BIFAO 95, 1995, 347 and n. 84.

[23] Černý LRL, 50, 5-6.

[24] Cf. Peden, Graffiti, 129.

[25] Cf. Kitchen, RamInscr VI, 100, 15; L. Habachi, JEA 51, 1965, 124f. (no. 4), fig. 2; see also H. Jaritz, CRIPEL 8, 1986, 41f.

[26] Cf. Pleyte-Rossi, Papyrus de Turin, pl. 129; Černý LRL, 3, 7 (ro. 7): *iḳr*; a *hapax legomenon*, cf. Lesko, Dict. I, 49.

[27] Černý LRL, 3, 7-8. According to Wente (LRL, 13) it was Payankh who departed first, though it does not follow from the passage cited.

[28] Wente LRL, 14f., 17.

[29] Cf. Černý LRL, 51, 16; 52, 9-10; cf. Wente LRL, 14.

[30] Cf. Janssen LRLC, 24; see also Sweeney, Correspondence and Dialogue, 22, for the textual interrelations

the departure of Tuthmosis from Elephantine, an invocation to "Amun-Ra, king of the gods residing in Elephantine" can be found; in the latter three these are the gods of Nubia which take a prominent part – "[Horus of Kubban, who dwell in thi]s mountain" (LRL no. 50),[31] "Horus of Kubban and the gods of the land in which I am" (LRLC no. III), and "Horus of Kubban and [Horus of Aniba]" (LRL no. 9). Even if the relative order of these letters cannot be established beyond any doubt it cannot be excluded that the names of the gods invoked are connected with the current place of stay of Tuthmosis. If the restoration of the latter of the above cited passages is right,[32] then we would arrive at the conclusion that Tuthmosis had reached perhaps the region of Aniba (*Miꜥm*) in the very heart of Lower Nubia. Unfortunately there are no relevant sources relating to the geographic setting of the campaign of general Payankh in the south.

It is open to question whether LRL no. 3 really records a meeting of Tuthmosis with his superior in Nubia.[33] We do not know either how long Tuthmosis stayed in Nubia nor how many times he travelled there. If LRL no. 29 can also be dated to the year 10th of the Renaissance Era[34] then one could draw the conclusion that the journey of year 10 was in fact his first visit to Nubia. In this letter, written by Butehamun to the troop-commander Shedsuhor, we read: "Be a pilot for the scribe of the necropolis Tjaroy. You know that (he) is a man who has no experience at all, for he has never before made the journeys on which he is now".[35] A similar request can be found in another letter written by Butehamun (LRL no. 8): "We know that he is a sick man who has never made a jour[ney like this]".[36] As we know that Tuthmosis had several times travelled out of Thebes during his earlier career, the true meaning of these words lay probably in the fact, that he had never joined a military expedition or else simply any journey abroad.[37] In such a case we can

between the letters of this group.

31 As regards the restoration, see Janssen LRLC, 23 n. 4.

32 Only traces of signs are preserved, cf. Černý LRL, 17a (6a-b); compare the photograph in Janssen LRLC, pl. 37 (ro. 3). For this, see also a comment below.

33 As suggested by Wente LRL, 13.

34 See Wente LRL, 13, 17; Wente suggested that the letter reached Tuthmosis (on Elephantine) "shortly before he departed for Nubia".

35 Černý LRL, 48, 16-49, 2. For grammatical comments, see Černý-Groll, Late Egyptian Grammar, 524 (Ex. 1484); Groll, Negative Verbal System, 234 (Ex. 500); id., RdE 26, 1974, 171 (VIII); Winand, LingAeg 5, 1997, 227 (VIIc); id., in: Mélanges offerts à F. Neveu, [BdE 145], Cairo 2008, 299 (Ex. 44). For a literary and stylistic comments see Sweeney, Idiolects, 297 (23); Goldwasser, in: Israel Oriental Studies 15, 1995, 201.

36 Černý LRL, 16, 8-9; see also Wente LRL 34, 37 (v); id., Letters, 188 (310); Neveu, Grammaire, 214 (15).

37 Cf. Janssen LRLC, 20 n. 8: "never so far south" or "never under such dangerous circumstances".

well imagine that in year 10 he travelled to Nubia for the first time during his life. All the dangers of the journey can be discerned in the following passage of the letter no. 29, although the purely literary or even proverbial undertone of the text cannot escape our attention: "A man becomes childlike when he is troubled and he has never seen a fearful face before".[38]

A vivid picture of the circumstances relating to Tuthmosis' stay in Nubia has been created by the prophet of the deified Amenhotep, Amenhotep son Amennakht, in his letter[39] sent to the scribe Tuthmosis (LRL no. 15): "When my letter reaches you, do not go out to see a tumult (of a battle). Indeed you have not been taken (there) as a fighting soldier and you have not been taken as an attendant (*šmsw*) either.[40] It is in order to consult you that you have been summoned (there). Sit down in the boat and keep yourself safe from arrows, spears and sto[nes], and do not abandon us all".[41] Nowhere does Tuthmosis himself describe so expressively the circumstances of the military expedition in Nubia, but it is possible, that the words of Amenhotep were based on a similar passage from one of the unpreserved letters of Tuthmosis, unless we can put it down to the author's imagination and his concern about condition and well-being of the addressee.[42] No doubt the friends of Tuthmosis were well aware of the dangers of this remote country: "And may the gods of the land in which you are save you from every danger (*ḫty*) of this land".[43] Let us cite another passage which sounds similar: "may (they, i.e. the gods) save (you) from arrow(s), from stone(s), and spear(s), and every danger which is there, in that land in which you are" (LRLC no. I).[44]

It cannot be wholly excluded that LRL no. 29 (written shortly before Tuthmosis left Elephantine for Nubia) is significantly earlier than LRL no. 28 (describing the state of confusion of his colleagues in Thebes after his recent departure from Thebes for Nubia), which would raise the possibility that Tuthmosis visited Nubia more than once. Nevertheless there are no decisive arguments to put forward such a hypothesis in the present state of research on

[38] Černý LRL, 49, 4-5; Groll, Negative Verbal System, 234 (Ex. 501); id., RdE 26, 1974, 171 (VIII); Winand, in: Mélanges offerts à F. Neveu, 299 (Ex. 45).

[39] According to Janssen LRLC, 13 n. 7, 15, it may have been written by the hand of Butehamun; cf. also Demarée, Bankes Papyri, 21; Sweeney, Idiolects, 306-308.

[40] For other meanings of the word, cf. Lesko, Dict. II, 124f.

[41] Černý LRL, 29, 10-14; see also Černý, Community, 378f.; Černý-Groll, Late Egyptian Grammar, 390 (Ex. 1088), 448 (Ex. 1218).

[42] Cf. Sweeney, Correspondence and Dialogue, 245.

[43] Černý LRL, 31, 14-15. Similarly ibid., 64, 5-6.

[44] Ro., 6-7; with emendations proposed by Janssen LRLC, 12, 13 n. 7, pl. 1.

the subject (see below).[45] On the other hand, the period of his stay in Nubia was significant enough to enable him to exchange several times correspondence with his Theban kinsmen. Anyway the considerable number of letters of the "Nubian group" can be taken as an indirect indication of this. The second letter, apparently written by Butehamun to Shedsuhor (LRL no. 43)[46] touches on this question more directly, indicating the difficulties in passing the messages to the persons residing in such a distant region: "(I) wrote to you two letters. They were not handed to you – (that is) what they did, just like those which I sent to the scribe Tjaroy – they failed to give them to him (as well)".[47] Similarly in the letter of Tuthmosis to Butehamun (LRL no. 9) we can read: "Now as for the speaking which you did concerning the matter of the letters of yours about which you said: «Have they reached you?» – that is what you said. They have reached me, all of them, except this letter which you gave to the foreigner Seti, the brother of the fisherman Paneferemneb. This is the only one which has not been brought to me".[48]

As we are often informed, the letters were transmitted by messengers. Most probably, they were not always professionals,[49] although sometimes these are Madjoy-policemen or simple attendants or messengers (*šmsw*)[50] who fulfilled such a duty. In other cases, however, the letters were brought by those who were returning home or else travelling to Nubia with other unspecified orders. Some of the letters, as we know, were brought by Hori the Sherden.[51] The practice of transmitting letters in such circumstances was a little bit complicated as it depended on a mere chance of finding a trustworthy messenger. In LRL no. 9 we read: "And dispatch the Madjoy Hadnakhte and send him to me immediately, and do not let him to delay. (I) have already written to you concerning him[52] through Hori the Sherden. And

45 As regards the relative sequence of LRL nos. 28 and 29, see Wente LRL, 13f.

46 The names of recipient and sender are not preserved, but the overall tenor of the letter, comparable to that of LRL no. 29, enables us to identify both of them; cf. Wente LRL, 13; Sweeney, Idiolects, 310.

47 Černý LRL, 64, 14-16. The passage has been commented upon in detail by Sweeney, Correspondence and Dialogue, 131 (with other references).

48 Černý LRL, 17, 13-16. Cf. Groll, Negative Verbal System, 103f. (Ex. 306).

49 Cf. Bakir, Epistolography, 30f.

50 Cf. e.g. Černý LRL, 9, 7; 17, 10-11; 67, 3. For the meaning of the title, see Wente LRL, 28 (a); Černý, JEA 33, 1947, 57; M. Valloggia, Recherche sur les "messagers" (*wpwtyw*) dans les sources egyptiennes profanes, Genève 1976, 215-217; Y. Koenig, in: Hommages à la mémoire de Serge Sauneron, I, [BdE 81], Cairo 1979, 205f.; Demarée, Bankes Papyri, 15.

51 Cf. Demarée, Bankes Papyri, 20.

52 Wente LRL, 38; and id., Letters, 192 (no. 313): "... to you for him"; cf. Winand, in: Mélanges offerts à F. Neveu, 299 (Ex. 41). As a matter of fact this formula can simply denote a postscriptum included in

I have spoken to Heramenpenaf as well, saying: «Let him go to me»".[53] An important passage from LRLC no. I (ro. 14-vo. 2) exemplifies that in a more detailed way: "When the Madjoy Hadnakhte reaches you, you shall dispatch him very quickly. I write to you to inform you through Akhmenu. Write to me (about) your condition <by> Amenopenakhte, who is with <you>".[54] Clearly enough the Madjoy Hadnakhte was on his way to Nubia (or else on the verge of making a journey), when Tuthmosis had already received this letter of Butehamun through Akhmenu. At the same time, Butehamun expected to receive an answer to the present letter through Amenopenakhte, since his journey back to Thebes must have been expected earlier than that of Hadnakhte. No doubt the latter was expected to bring another letter being a reply to the letter he would deliver himself to Tuthmosis in Nubia.[55]

The long distance to be covered by the messengers and certainly also the hardships of such a journey inevitably caused a lot of problems in delivering the letters.[56] Recurring complaints contained in the letters seem to testify that vividly:[57] "(As for) your having written, saying: «The guardian Karoy and the scribe Butehamun caused to have been brought to me [a] letter, while you did not cause (any letter) to be brought to me. What is the point of this disrespect?» – (so) you said. It is a lie! [Ind]eed, I did not show disrespect to you. And if you think that I did not spend a day [...] together with you, and we had (not a supper) together in the evening – say it!"(papBM EA 75020).[58] Thus irregular correspondence was considered a serious matter and it could have put a friendship to the test, but at the same time such complaints about a correspondent's failure to write may be considered as a way of expressing a profound concern and friendly attitude on the part of an author.

The above remarks as well as other observations concerning the communication between Thebes and Nubia have an essential bearing on the relative chronology of the letters forming the core group of the "Nubian letters" of

the letter. Indeed, such a custom is confirmed by a number of the LRL, see for example the special case of the letter of papBankes II: Edwards, JEA 68, 1982, 132f., pl. 13; Demarée, Bankes Papyri, 10f., pl. 7.

53 Černý LRL, 19, 11-14.

54 Janssen LRLC, 12, pls. 1-4.

55 Cf. ibid., 15.

56 Some of the letters had apparently been sent by more than one messenger; compare the contents of LRL no. 31, sent from Elephantine to Thebes, and informing that Tuthmosis sent a letter (from Nubia) to his son (in Thebes) through the agency of Pentahures, the latter being a resident on Elephantine.

57 Cf. Sweeney, Correspondence and Dialogue, 191.

58 Demarée, Bankes Papyri, 19f., pl. 18 (ro. 6-10).

year 10 of the Renaissance Era. Taking into consideration the results achieved mostly by E.F. Wente, and J.J. Janssen the following recapitulation may be proposed here:

1) LRL no. 3 (Tuthmosis to Butehamun) can be securely dated as the earliest of the entire group (partly preserved date restored by Wente as [IV *peret*] 13); LRL no. 8 (Butehamun to Tuthmosis) being a reply to the former.[59]

2) LRL no. 2 (Tuthmosis to Butehamun) was probably written soon after LRL no. 3; it gives a date IV *peret* 21.

3) LRL no. 16 (Butehamun to Tuthmosis) was written after LRL nos. 2, 9 (mentions a date: year 10, I *shemu* 25), and no. 50, because it quotes the material contained in these three letters.[60]

4) LRLC no. III sent by Tuthmosis from Nubia to Thebes my belong to the same group as LRL nos. 2, 9, and 50 (all written by Tuthmosis to Butehamun).[61]

5) LRL nos. 16 and 28 were taken to Nubia by the Madjoy Hadnakhte, who departed from Thebes on I *shemu* 29 (this date is explicitly given in both letters). The letter of papBM EA 75020 was brought to Tuthmosis in Nubia (from an unknown sender) through the agency of Hadnakhte; quite possibly it was brought together with LRL nos. 16 and 28.[62]

6) LRLC no. I was sent by Butehamun to his father in Nubia during II *shemu* of the same year. LRL nos. 29 and 15 were sent to Nubia (respectively to Shedsuhor and Tuthmosis) about the same time, when Tuthmosis was about to depart from Elephantine to Nubia. LRL no. 43 (Butehamun to Shedsuhor) belongs to the same group. LRLC no. I constitutes probably a direct answer to LRL no. 50.[63]

A rather curious and hitherto unnoticed fact deserves special attention in the context of the Nubian travel of Tuthmosis. This is the apparent visit of Hemshire in Nubia,[64] seemingly mentioned in LRL no. 43 (which was sent from Thebes to Nubia):[65] "What is the meaning of this message you sent to me, saying: «It was only after Hemshire was here that you sent a letter»? You

[59] Wente LRL, 9.

[60] Ibid., 10ff.; Sweeney, Correspondence and Dialogue, 22.

[61] Janssen LRLC, 24.

[62] Wente LRL, 10ff.; Demarée, Bankes Papyri, 21; Janssen LRLC, 15.

[63] Wente LRL, 13; Janssen LRLC, 15.

[64] See Černý, Community, 369.

[65] According to Wente (LRL, 13, 17) a letter written by Butehamun to Shedsuhor; compare Sweeney, Idiolects, 310, 317, 318f. (note by J. Winand), as regards the authorship of Butehamun.

would not write me a lie!"[66] Leaving aside all the problems connected with the proper interpretation of the context of this passage let us turn our attention to the quotation from the original letter. I cannot agree with D. Sweeney and P.J. Frandsen that the last part of the passage should be also included in the quotation from the original letter. This sentence seems to be rather an accusation against the unnamed author of the original letter.[67] Surely we can discard the assumption that the place concerned is not Nubia at all. The information provided by LRL 43 leaves no doubt that its recipient was staying in Nubia: "We tell Amun-Ra, king of the gods, to bring you back saved from all danger which is in the upper land in which you are [...]".[68] This should be taken in connection with the notion of bringing somebody back "down (to) Egypt", attested in three other letters (LRL nos. 29 and 50; LRLC no. I). As regards its appearance in LRL no. 50, it is beyond any doubt that it must be taken as a designation of the way from Nubia to Egypt, as this concerns Tuthmosis staying in Nubia.[69] On the other hand the planned journey of general Payankh southward to Nubia was described by the words: "I shall go up" (*ỉw.ỉ (r) ṯsy r- ḥry*).[70] Thus, as for the location of the "upper land" of LRL no. 43, we must agree with the opinion expressed by E.F. Wente that it relates to Nubia.[71]

There is no decisive proof in favour of such a visit of Hemshire in Nubia. Certainly this cannot be supported by another sentence found in LRL no. 10 written by Tuthmosis to the guardian Karoy (and Butehamun), but containing the following words of Kenykhnum to the scribe Butehamun: "If only Hemshire were here concealed!".[72] These words should be taken rather as a complaint of a lonely and despaired man deprived of the very presence of his close relatives. The meaning of the stative *ḥ3p.Ø* at the end of this sentence[73] causes some problems in regard of its meaning. A possible explanation lay in the following sentence if an optative meaning is attributed to it:[74] "... that you might write to me". In such a case, however, we should

[66] Černý LRL, 64, 12-14; cf. a comment by Groll, Non-Verbal Sentence Patterns, 105f. (Ex. 308); id., Negative Verbal System, 147f. (Ex. 334); Frandsen, Verbal System, 48 (Ex. 26), 177 (Ex. 19); Sweeney, Correspondence and Dialogue, 125f., 131 (with an attempt to reconstruct the contents of an original letter).

[67] See Wente, Letters, 200 (no. 322).

[68] Černý LRL, 64, 4-6.

[69] He prays to "[Horus of Kubban] who dwells in [thi]s mountain", cf. Černý LRL, 71, 12.

[70] Černý LRL, 7, 16.

[71] Wente LRL, 77 (d)

[72] Černý LRL, 22, 2.

[73] Cf. Wente LRL, 43 (h); Satzinger, Neuägyptische Studien, 153.

[74] See Wente, LRL, 43 (i); id., Letters, 196 (no. 316).

rather expect that there was a close relationship or even family ties between Hemshire and Kenykhnum, the author of this note.[75] Quite unexpectedly we hear about Hemshire in the letter of the second prophet of Amun Hekanefer to Tuthmosis (LRL no. 24). In a postscript added by Penherishefy, a servant of the prophet and at the same time his secretary: "Hemshire is alive; she is in life [prosperity and health]. Do not worry about her; but you are the one whom she longs to see and whose condition she wishes to hear about [daily]".[76] It seems that the letter was sent from Middle Egypt,[77] where the second prophet was travelling on an unknown mission. What can be said for sure is that the letter was sent from the region located to the north of place where its recipient was staying: "you shall not avoid writing to me about your condition through whoever may come northward (*m-ḫd*)".[78] Thus we should assume that either Hemsheri was then in Middle Egypt or else that the letter was sent from Thebes to Nubia. The latter possibility seems to be highly improbable, because it is Hekanefer and not Tuthmosis who was travelling – Hekanefer prays to the gods whose temples or cult centres he passes by,[79] and Tuthmosis is asked to pray to Amun-Ra, king of the gods, which seems to suggest that he was staying in Thebes. In addition, in LRL no. 23, a document parallel in every respect to LRL no. 24, Hekanefer is asking Tuthmosis to pray for his happy return: "you shall pray to Amun-Ra, king of the gods, Mut, Khonsu, Amun (of) United-with-Eternity, and (all) the gods, lords of Thebes to save me and to bring me back to Ne (Thebes) alive".[80] Nevertheless the reason of Hemshire's stay in Middle Egypt remains completely obscure, just as is the case with her supposed visit to Nubia.

4) Theban affairs supervised by Butehamun

Provisioning of the army of Payankh was the most urgent task entrusted to Butehamun and captains of the necropolis after Tuthmosis' departure to

[75] If this was the case then possibly also LRL no. 43, mentioning Hemshire in even more surprising context, could be connected with Kenykhnum as its possible recipient (?); compare however above, where it is Shedsuhor who is taken into consideration as its recipient.

[76] Černý LRL, 40, 2-3; see also a comment in Černý, Community, 382.

[77] See Wente LRL 7f., 16.

[78] Černý LRL, 39, 11-12.

[79] Ibid., 39, 7: *nty tw.i (ḥr) sš/sny ḥr.w*; similarly: ibid., 39,16-40,1; a common formula found in the letters written by those who were travelling, cf. Bakir, Epistolography, 61f. (with further references to LRL).

[80] Černý LRL, 38, 5-6. A similar wish has been expressed in the postscript by Penherishefy, the same man as that who added a postscript to LRL no. 24, cf. ibid., 38, 14.

Nubia. No doubt Butehamun had assumed responsibility not only for the matters of the necropolis but also the difficult and complicated duty of coordination of the efforts of the local administration to provide Payankh with all the necessary commodities. Sometimes it seems this was evidently beyond his capability, as aptly observed by Tuthmosis who rebuked his son harshly in LRL no. 50: "Another [matter for the scribe Buteh]amun. Look, please: What is (about) the matters which you are saying to me as an answer, [although][81] you [had never] explained them? As for the commission of the coppersmith Hori which you received (i.e. accepted) together with me [...] you [have not] written to me about it, namely its arrangements for seventeen spears of which you said: «I caused [them to be send to the place?] where the general is». And you mentioned (indeed) the matter of the spears, but you have not yet caused the boat [...]. You have not yet named the man[82] to whom you entrusted it, (that is) the matter of the spears, while it is the Sherde[n Hori who brought] them to me, but I do not know the man to whom you gave them and I do not know the boat which [...] a letter, bearing the general's name, about them. What is the meaning of this? I will not be silent to you about it! [...] when I was in [North]ern *Pahedj*[...], and I received them, and I found all the [...] which were in good condition. But the matter of the spears is what I am preoccupied with, for it is not all right. [Do not give me a cause?][83] to write a letter like this again!".[84]

Quite possibly this was one of the earliest letters written by Tuthmosis from Nubia to his son.[85] Fortunately, Butehamun's reply has been preserved (i.e., LRL no. 16), and we can follow his defence in every detail:[86] "As for your saying: «I will not be silent to you at all about the matter of the spears»[87] – so you said. I wrote the letter concerning the arrangements for the spears and I gave it to the guardian Karoy while he was dwelling in Thebes, and I said

[81] Restore possibly: [*iw*]; as for the meaning of *bw.pw.f sḏm* after the circumstantial *iw*, cf. Černý-Groll, Late Egyptian Grammar, 233.

[82] See Groll, Negative Verbal System, 235 (Ex. 503); Černý-Groll, Late Egyptian Grammar, 324 (Ex. 892); Junge, Neuägyptisch, 105.

[83] Cf. Sweeney, Correspondence and Dialogue, 128.

[84] Černý LRL, 72, 8-73, 4. See also Sweeney, Correspondence and Dialogue, 127f., for some interesting comments on this lengthy passage.

[85] The letter does not contain any internal evidence which could be useful in its dating, but its relation to LRL no. 16 (and possibly also no. 10) enable us to include it in the core group of letters, cf. Wente LRL, 10.

[86] Cf. Sweeney, Correspondence and Dialogue, 127f., 133f.

[87] Note that the sentence differs slightly from the original version contained in the letter of Tuthmosis: compare Černý LRL, 32, 5-6 with 73,1 and 74, 2.

to him: «I will not make (*sḫt*)[88] (them) myself while I am living here. (But) I made arrangements for the spears.[89] (So) find out the boat and the man to whom you will give this letter, and sign his name on it» – so I said to him, and he answered me: «It was to Pa(y)shuuben that I entrusted them» – so he said to me. Do I know what he has done with them?".[90] So according to his explanations it was Karoy or Payshuuben[91] who was responsible for the entire confusion regarding the transport of the spears to Nubia. It is possible that also Karoy sent a letter to Tuthmosis containing his excuses in regard of this, and LRL no. 10 could have been a direct reply of Tuthmosis to these apologies or explanations of both persons involved.[92]

An instruction attached at the end of LRL no. 50 seems to be clear evidence that Butehamun was still inexperienced, especially in regard of official relations with his superior, general Payankh: "Now as soon as you learn [that he is writing to you (plural), you shall][93] send (it) to him also. He should write you (plural) a letter first, for it is better that you should not be the first [to write the] letter, until he has written to you. And when you learn that he is writing to you (plural), you shall [send (it) to] him. [In]deed I will not be silent to you about the matter of the spears [about] which you have not written [to me whether you sent][94] them to him. And you have not written a letter in your handwriting (*sš*)[95] to be sent (to) the general, your [superior ...] which (bears) inspectors' (*n3 rwḏw*) names as well".[96] If LRL no. 28 is

[88] Or else "gather (together)", cf. Lesko, Dict. II; 75; Meeks, Année lexicographique II, 347 (78.3782); in consequence *p3 wpw.t*, translated conventionally as "arrangements" or "orders" (cf. Lesko, Dict. I, 97, 99; Sweeney, Correspondence and Dialogue, 133 n. 207), would mean possibly "dispatch","sending" or simply "specification"; for the latter meaning, cf. van Heel-Haring, Writing in the Workmen's Village, 116f. Consequently the matter described in the letter would concern only a transport of the spears to the south.

[89] Wente Letters, 193: "I have drawn up the order for spears"; similarly Černý-Groll, Late Egyptian Grammar, 221 (Ex. 587). Contrary to the opinion expressed by Sweeney (Correspondence and Dialogue, 133 notes 208, 211) I think that Butehamun speaks here about the same arrangements (possibly orders or specification) which he included in the letter drawn by him and handed over to Karoy. It is hardly possible, however, that the latter was responsible for those arrangements.

[90] Černý LRL, 32, 5-12; for translation of the passage, cf. van Heel-Haring, Writing in the Workmen's Village, 114; see also Sweeney, Idiolects, 287 (Ex. 5).

[91] Cf. Sweeney, Correspondence and Dialogue, 133.

[92] See Wente LRL, 10.

[93] According to the restoration made by Černý LRL, 73a (15a-b).

[94] As for the restoration of the text, see Wente, Letters, 190 (no. 312), 204 n. 5.

[95] See Wente, LRL, 84; id., Letters, 190; cf. also Frandsen, Verbal System, 10 (Ex. 6). Compare another use of *sš* as "writing": Černý LRL, 19, 16=Lesko, Dict. II, 78 – LRL 9V11 (definitely not merely "hand-writing", as suggested there).

[96] Černý LRL, 73, 15-74, 4. Compare Groll, Negative Verbal System, 180 (Ex. 400); Černý-Groll, Late Egyptian Grammar, 381 (Ex. 1068), 494 (Ex. 1401); Peust, Indirekte Rede, 107 (Exx. 99-100);

an answer of the necropolis authorities to a letter of general Payankh which has not survived to our times and, which had been sent soon after Tuthmosis' departure to Nubia (see above), then we could assume that it was slightly later than the LRL no. 50. Significantly the lost letter of Payankh mentioned above would probably have been one of the earliest of the series sent to Thebes by the general[97] – if not the first in fact. A final conclusion in regard of this depends mostly on the interpretation of the following words taken from LRL no. 28: "Now we have taken note of the message which our lord sent us saying: «Do not be neglectful of this commission!» – so said our lord, but he did not say: «What is the effect of the message which (I) sent to you previously when I was (going) south»; (and) saying (also): «Cause one to send some of the clothes that have been found. It is after I have departed that you shall send them after me» – so said our lord".[98] It is possible that these words put emphasis on the mere fact that general's letter was not preceded by an earlier instruction concerning the clothes, which should be sent urgently to him. In such a case the second "quotation" which evidently is not taken from general's letter ("he did not say"), cannot introduce the third quotation,[99] being in fact a fragment of the real letter, thus a continuation of the first quotation, evidently taken from the same letter. It seems the passage does not constitute proof of the existence of two letters of Payankh preceding LRL no. 28, and the latter must be an answer to a single letter of Payankh, evidenced only by these scanty citations.

Indeed, when the letter of Payankh had been received by the captains of the necropolis, it caused the whole community to be highly excited and on the alert. According to the instruction included in the LRL no. 50, one might surmise that Butehamun had not been prepared yet to write such an official letter (or never did it). It is conceivable that he was assisted in the task by other more experienced members of the community while writing an answer (i.e., probably LRL no. 28), presumably to avoid any blunder on the part of a still inexperienced junior scribe left in the post by his father. This is possibly

and Wente, Letters, 190 (no. 312), whom I follow here.

97 LRL no. 28 seems to suggest that Butehamun received two different letters from the general within a short span of time – one on I *shemu* 18, and another on I *shemu* 20; cf. Sweeney, Correspondence and Dialogue, 22 n. 146. It is hardly likely that only one letter was concerned here, provided that it was received by Butehamun on I *shemu* 18, and read to the workmen two days later, on I *shemu* 20.

98 Černý LRL, 45, 15-46, 4; cf. Černý-Groll, Late Egyptian Grammar, 449 (Ex. 1222).

99 As suggested by Sweeney, Correspondence and Dialogue, 56 n. 74; 66. Thus in general I follow here the interpretation proposed by Wente, LRL, 60, 62 (q); id., Letters 194.

the true reason of the quite exceptional form of LRL no. 28 in comparison to other letters written by Butehamun:[100] not only because of the full titulature of Payankh which was given in the address placed at the beginning of the letter, but also because its senders, the superiors of the gang, are enumerated here collectively: "the two foremen, the scribe of the necropolis Butehamun and guardian [Kar(oy)]"[101] (in the address of vo. 16 these are simply "the captains of the necropolis"). As for the handwriting of the letter (in which a high percentage of neatly elaborated hieratic forms must be noted in comparison with more cursive ones),[102] and its sophisticated style, it is possible to say that it was written by Butehamun himself.[103] If it really responds to the admonition included in LRL no. 50, then we can assume that Butehamun actually obeyed his father's instruction insofar as the letter was at least drawn up by all the persons responsible for the matters of the necropolis, although written by the hand of the scribe Butehamun, who quite unexpectedly revealed himself in the words placed at the end of the letter: "I am writing to inform my lord...".[104]

One may only surmise that after that Butehamun was more fortunate in fulfilling his duty of the junior scribe of the royal necropolis, entrusted to him in these unprecedented circumstances. Thus we can hear about his involvement in the matters of the necropolis, its workmen and their families, not to mention his concern for the members of his own family and their property.

One of the most enigmatic aspects of the activity of the necropolis scribe in this period are his rather vague connections with the army. As regards Tuthmosis, the senior scribe, his participation in the military expedition cannot be explained in any way unless we take for granted that the institution of the necropolis had undergone profound changes in regard to its organization and administering. Certainly the role of the necropolis crew changed radically after the work on the royal tomb had been abandoned. This issue cannot be reduced, however, to the matters connected only with a supposed recycling of the goods and treasuries hidden in the royal tombs.[105] At the side of Payankh, the scribe of the necropolis played the role of an intermediary (perhaps a

[100] Cf. Sweeney, Idiolects, 295, 297, 298.

[101] Černý LRL, 44, 5-6. As we know, these are exactly the recipients of the LRL no. 30, so it has been suggested that this is the missing letter of the general to the superiors of the crew, cf. Allam, BIFAO 97, 1997, 10 n. 70.

[102] Cf. Janssen LRLC, pls. 39-40; V. Davies, R. Friedman, Egypt, London 2001, 149; N. Strudwick, The British Museum. Masterpieces of Ancient Egypt, London 2006, 239.

[103] Janssen, JEA 73, 1987, 165; Sweeney, Idiolects, 278.

[104] Černý LRL, 48, 2-3.

[105] Cf. Jansen-Winkeln, ZÄS 122, 1995, 72f.

liaison officer?) between his superior and the institutions of the necropolis.[106] If he was an adviser during the Nubian campaign this was not because of his military experience:[107] "Indeed you have not been taken (there) as a fighting soldier and you have not been taken as an attendant (*šmsw*)[108]. It is in order to consult you that you have been summoned".[109] More probably he was responsible for the provisioning of the Payankh's army, if we remember that in the earlier period he operated as an able "taxing officer" or a person accompanying the tax collecting inspection – repeated actions conducted by him in Middle Egypt and in the region to the south of Thebes leave no doubt that he was effective enough to entrust to him such an important task. Evidently logistic operations must have been of vital importance for any military operations in such an inhospitable country as Nubia. Let us return to the letters relating to scribe Tuthmosis' activity both in Thebes and in Nubia which allow us to obtain a vivid picture of the man preoccupied mostly with the arrangement of delivery of army supplies. The letters are however completely silent as regards the food supply for the army in the period of the Nubian war.

Even more complicated is Butehamun's involvement in the matters relating to the military men in the Theban area. Thus in LRL no. 4 Tuthmosis wrote to his son: "And give your attention to the conscript soldiers (*n3 rmṯ mšʿ*).[110] Do not let them flee, nor let them become hungry".[111] A similar instruction, contained in the letter of Tuthmosis (LRL no. 5) written while he was staying in Middle Egypt,[112] seems to suggest that both of them supervised the recruitment of the soldiers in the Theban area. Although the mechanisms of recruitment of soldiers in ancient Egypt are barely known,[113] it cannot be excluded that Tuthmosis, accompanied by his son, actually supervised men being drafted into the army of general Payankh. Anyway Butehamun's participation in it would possibly explain why he was titled

[106] Cf. Häggman, Directing DeM, 219.

[107] Cf. Jansen-Winkeln, ZÄS 122, 1995, 72.

[108] Or simply: "messenger", cf. Wente LRL, 28 (a); cf. above, note 50.

[109] Černý LRL, 29, 11-13. As regards the supposed role of Tuthmosis in peace negotiation with Panehesy, see Niwiński, BIFAO 95, 1995, 347.

[110] Cf. Wb. II, 155 (11); Lesko, Dict. I, 208; A.R. Schulman, Military Rank, Title and Organization in the Egyptian New Kingdom, [MÄS 6], Berlin 1964, 49; R.O. Faulkner, Egyptian Military Organization, JEA 39, 1953, 45. "The men of the army" (*n3 rmṯ p3 mšʿ*) are mentioned in one of the oracle texts, cf. Černý, BIFAO 72, 1972, 52, pl. 16 (no. 42).

[111] Černý LRL, 8, 6-8.

[112] Ibid., 10, 11-12.

[113] Cf. Schulman, op.cit., 76f.

"scribe of the army" (*sš n p3 mšʿ*) in the graffito written at the entrance the tomb of Horemheb (this is the sole evidence however of such a title borne by him).[114] Quite obviously the title did not indicate a military rank, but has a more general meaning, being possibly a result of his close cooperation with the commander-in-chief.[115] On the other hand, it has been suggested that many of the men of the crew were recruited into the army in the period of civil war,[116] and this is why necropolis authorities would have been obliged to take care of them (this would simply mean the necessity of their provision and equipment). Information on these conscript soldiers(?) is in fact scanty, so any conclusions seem to be premature at the moment. It cannot be excluded, however, that some of the members of the community were conscripted when the civil war broke, or else that a special troop of soldiers was detached by Payankh to protect the royal necropolis of Thebes or its vicinity.[117]

When LRL no. 28 was written, the necropolis staff was already commissioned to do a job "for which you have never yet gone".[118] Leaving aside for the moment what is really meant here, two factors should be taken into consideration: (1) the letter should be dated to the 10th year of the Renaissance Era; and (2) the necropolis staff had never taken part in such undertakings as those commissioned by Payankh. We know, however, that there are some incontestable data referring to the restoration of some of the royal burials in the earlier years of the Renaissance Era, under the auspices of the High Priest Herihor (see Chapter 8).

This is enough to have serious reservations therefore about a recent hypothesis put forward by N. Reeves and then developed in more detail by K. Jansen-Winkeln, according to which LRL no. 28 is taken as evidence of a massive plundering of the royal tombs in the Valley of the Kings, instigated by the High Priest Payankh to cover the expenses of his military campaign in Nubia.[119] Nothing at all can be said about the scale and character of the

114 Cf. Jansen-Winkeln, InschrSp I, 35; cf. Peden, Graffiti, 207f. He appears here in company with "the scribe of the general, Kysen". His father Tuthmosis never was titled in this way.

115 Cf. Schulman, op.cit., 64.

116 Černý, Community, 380; idea followed by Valbelle, Ouvriers, 225 n. 8; and Bierbrier, Tomb-Builders, 119, 121.

117 See Jansen-Winkeln, ZÄS 122, 1995, 73.

118 Černý LRL, 47, 4; cf. Junge, Neuägyptisch, 247; Groll, Negative Verbal System, 234 (Ex. 502); Frandsen, Verbal System, 201 (§102: Ex. 7).

119 Reeves, Valley of the Kings, 276-8; id., Ancient Egypt. The Great Discoveries: A Year-by-Year Chronicle, London 2000, 24, 151; Reeves-Wilkinson, The Complete Valley of the Kings, 205; see also E. Hornung, Die Ruhestätte der Pharaonen, Zürich-München 1982, 78; the hypothesis is presented

operations conducted in the Valley of the Kings during the Nubian war of Payankh, as the available documentation dating to the Renaissance Era is in fact very meagre.[120] The role of Payankh in retrieving and despoiling of the royal mummies cannot be evaluated properly in the light of the preserved sources.

No doubt, the supplies of Nubian gold significantly diminished in the period of the revolt instigated by the viceroy of Kush, Panehesy.[121] The Nubian war of general Payankh inevitably led to serious deficiency in gold production from the Nubian gold mining regions. Nonetheless it seems rather doubtful whether any treasures withdrawn from the royal tombs in the Valley of the Kings had any impact on the economic situation of Egypt and the Thebaid in particular.[122] The very character of the Egyptian economic system, based mainly on natural resources of the country and state redistribution of goods, preserved it from any serious disturbances caused by a temporary shortage of precious metals. It is hardly imaginable that such a "deficit" could seriously weaken the Egyptian trade system which can be classified as an intermediate stage between barter and real monetary system.[123] It is possible that some quantity of bronze, and perhaps also linen clothes could have been "recycled", partly to supply an army operating in Nubia. But nowhere can the origin of the metal used for the production of weapon be explicitly determined. The surprisingly small quantities of bronze spears mentioned in the LRL hardly support the assumption that plundering of the tombs for metal objects would had any real commercial significance.[124] On the contrary, it is highly improbable that the royal burials were deliberately robbed by the state officials to obtain such a meagre amount of metal. Precious metals, on the other hand,

in more detail by Jansen-Winkeln, ZÄS 122, 1995, 62ff. The hypothesis now seems to be widely accepted, cf. e.g. Taylor, in: After Tutankhamun, 187-190; V. Davies, R. Friedman, op.cit., 148f.; N. Strudwick, op.cit., 238; Demarée, in: DeM et la Vallée des Rois, 248f.

[120] Cf. Eaton-Krauss, BIOr 49, 1992, 715; and Chapter 8 below.

[121] In the Ramesside period the production of gold from Kush was significantly declining and the gold mining regions of *Wawat* definitely lost their previous significance, cf. J. Vercoutter, Kush 7, 1959, 135-137, 151; B.G. Trigger, Nubia under the Pharaohs, London 1976, 137; Hein, op.cit., 105.

[122] For a critical evaluation of the arguments presented by Jansen-Winkeln, cf. D.A. Warburton, State and Economy in Ancient Egypt. Fiscal Vocabulary in the New Kingdom, [OBO 151], Fribourg-Göttingen, 123f. and n. 333; Graefe, ZÄS 126, 1999, 27ff.; Niwiński, in: Z. Hawass (ed.), Egyptology at the Dawn of the Twenty-first Century, II, Cairo 2002, 417; id., in: BSAK 9, 2003, 300.

[123] Cf. Janssen, Commodity Prices, 545ff.; as regards the significance of the precious metals coming from the robberies in the local trading system, cf. Kemp, Ancient Egypt, 242-244.

[124] A good example is provided by the detailed receipt added at the top of the *recto* of LRL no. 8, cf. Černý LRL, 16, 14-17, 1; Janssen LRLC, pl. 63.

could have been used to buy a raw materials and other commodities abroad, as demonstrated by the story of Wenamun. Unfortunately the range of the foreign trade in this period and its intensity cannot be estimated properly.[125]

Actually we do not know anything about the desecration of the royal burials in the period following the inauguration of the Renaissance Era. It cannot be excluded, however, that some valuables found in the royal tombs during reburial of the royal mummies were in fact appropriated for the sake of the burials of the high priests themselves and maybe the members of their families,[126] including members of the royal family in Tanis at a later period. Anyway, the idea of a massive state looting seems to be an anachronism in pharaonic Egypt, mostly because of the religious significance of the royal burial and its sacred character in particular.[127]

As a matter of fact, there is no firm evidence testifying to such a large-scale action carried out during the pontificate of Payankh. The character of the work made on behalf of Payankh is described in the following fragment of LRL no. 28 (vo. 2-14), which should be presented here in its entirety: "We have taken note of every matter our lord wrote us about – our lord's message, which (he) sent us, saying: «Go and carry out a commission for me, for which you have never yet gone and try to carry it out[128] until (I) reach you!» – so said our lord. How it will be done, namely (the task) which we know about,[129] since we[130] had already been there? «Lay it aside. Do not attend it! »[131] – so said our lord. As for this scribe who used to be here in charge of us, he who

[125] For the subject, see e.g. R. de Spens, in: N. Grimal, B. Menu (eds.), Le commerce en Égypte ancienne, [BdÉ 121], Cairo 1998, 105-126; Sass, Ägypten und Levante 12, 2002, 247ff.

[126] Contra Taylor, in: After Tutankhamun, 189; Warburton, op.cit., 124 n. 334.

[127] Cf. Niwiński, in: Z. Hawass (ed.), op.cit., 417; id., in: BSAK 9, 2003, 300. N. Reeves' idea of the "combined policy of salvage and restoration", applied to the entire period of the Renaissance Era, seems to be more plausible perhaps.

[128] Or better: "work on it eagerly", cf. Groll, Negative Verbal System, 234 (Ex. 502); similarly Junge, Neuägyptisch, 247.

[129] Or: "What can be done, namely (the thing) we know about?". In my translation of this difficult passage I follow Sweeney, Correspondence and Dialogue, 78 (Ex. 57) and n. 222, 105 n. 40; 146f. (Ex. 83).

[130] An emendation is needed, as it seems, as regards the pronoun: 1.pl. c. instead of 2.pl. c., cf. Wente LRL, 63 (ae); id., Letters, 195. The choice between these two possibilities has an essential importance for our understanding of the entire passage, and the question of its attribution to the quotation from Payankh's original letter or not. An alternative is the version given by Wente LRL, 61, with the consequence that the entire passage should be taken as a quotation from the letter of Payankh; compare also Jansen-Winkeln, ZÄS 122, 1995, 67f. See, however, Wente, Letters, 195; and Sweeney, Correspondence and Dialogue, 78 n. 219.

[131] As for *ḫnw*, see an extant comment in Wente LRL, 63f (ag); Spiegelberg, Correspondances, 252 ("prétendre f"); Sweeney, Correspondence and Dialogue, 78 n. 221; see also Gardiner, RdE 6, 1951, 121 (q) – papValençay I vo. 4, 8, 10; Lesko, Dict. I, 381.

was appointed (as a scribe), who knows a *ḥy* and who is an influential man, whose father had testified that [132] – (now) he is with you. Now as soon as he puts the evidence before us also, we will spend between ten and twenty days, while he looks for a *ḥy* daily until he finds (it). Now see, you have written, saying: «Uncover a tomb (*wꜥ s.t*) among the ancient tombs (*nꜣ s.wt ḥꜣ.tyw*) and preserve its seal until (I) return!»[133] – so said our lord. We are carrying out commissions. We will let you find it ready(?)[134] and prepared, namely (the place) which we know about. And send the scribe of the necropolis Tjaroy to cause him to come so that he may look for a *ḥy* for us. Indeed we have to go while we are going astray not (even) knowing the place (*s.t*) where to put our feet".[135]

Undeniably we have to know the true meaning of the word *ḥy* recurring thrice in this letter to ascertain the real value of the passage in question. The wide range of meanings adopted by those who attempted a translation of the passage seems to lead us in one direction: this must be something (less probably a person)[136] pointing out to the location of the tomb in the Valley of the Kings – thus a kind of marker or else a written testimony given by an eye-witness.[137] In the discussion on the subject one important reference has been omitted until now. This is a sentence from papAmbras (1, 1-2), describing the contents of the jars with legal documents relating to the robberies: "Making a list (*šnw*) of the records

[132] Groll (RdE 26, 1974, 171) suggested that this phrase relates to the word *ḥy*; Wente's new translation (Letters, 195) follows this idea. For other possibilities in translation of this phrase, see above, note 17.

[133] This explicit order can be translated with a slightly different meaning, if we take *wꜥ* for a numeral: "Uncover one of the tombs among the ancient tombs", cf. Groll, Negative Verbal System, 237 (Ex. 509); Černý-Groll, Late Egyptian Grammar, 416 (Ex. 1144); cf. however, Sweeney, Correspondence and Dialogue, 51 (Ex. 16), 72 (Ex. 50); Winand, Études, 162 (Ex. 378).

[134] I cannot exclude the meaning "violated(?)" or "disturbed(?)" on the basis of an ambiguous context of papLeopold-Amherst 3, 18; papAmbras 2, 5-6; and papTurin 1880 ro. 3,18a-19; cf. Peet, Tomb Robberies, 51 n. 18, pls. 5 (3, 8), 38 (2, 5-6); Gardiner RAD, 58, 11-12. Compare also Lesko, Dict. I, 89. We could rather expect that the tomb should be just "located" and possibly also clearly "marked" at the time of general's arrival.

[135] Černý LRL, 47, 2-48, 1.

[136] "Inspector(?)" or "supervisor(?)", at least when indefinite article is determined by the sign A1 (Černý LRL, 47, 8 and 16); thus Wente LRL, 61; and Černý, Community, 364; followed by Jansen-Winkeln, ZÄS 122, 1995, 68 n. 54; Junge, Neuägyptisch, 273f.; and Sweeney, Correspondence and Dialogue, 56 n. 76; compare also Caminos, LEM, 272 (papAnastasi V, 26,4). Once the noun is preceded by the indefinite article written without such a sign (Černý LRL, 47, 11) – even here the word is translated in the same manner as in other two instances, cf. Satzinger, Neuägyptische Studien, 85. As a matter of fact, it is highly doubtful whether two different meanings can be ascribed here to the noun *ḥy*.

[137] Cf. Groll, RdE 26, 1974, 171; Wente, Letters, 195; Sweeney, Correspondence and Dialogue, 56 n. 76.

of examinations (*n3 sš n n3 ḥy*)".[138] Here a meaning of the term more plausibly relating to the context of papAmbras has been applied,[139] although its exact meaning cannot be proven after all. Anyway, we can expect that some kind of topographical description was available for those who were engaged in the work on the royal tombs. Indeed, we can imagine that any operations conducted in the necropolis needed a well defined system of topographical markers if not detailed descriptions or even maps.[140] It was suggested that such a role was played by a system of so-called "cairns" located in some parts of the Theban necropolis.[141] And we know that in the Valley of the Kings this function could have been also fulfilled by some of the rock graffiti, as for example graffito no. 557 denoting the location of the tomb of Sethnakht (KV 14).[142] Certainly the scribe of the necropolis must have been well informed about such landmarks or topographical markers in the area of the royal necropolis.[143]

There are some doubts as regards the meaning of the term *ḥ3.tyw* as well. So it is possible to translate the term as "earliest" or simply "first" in regard to time or else as denoting the topographical location of the tomb in question.[144] In his interpretation of the present source, A. Niwiński went even further, suggesting that the term *ḥ3.tyw* denotes possibly the topographical relation of the tomb in question in relation to other tombs, thus locating the tomb at the very entrance to the Valley of the Kings.[145] Notwithstanding the topographical problems connected with the present text it is evident that it gives important information

---

138 Peet's reading *ḥsyw* "the men of old" or simply "blessed ones" (cf. Tomb Robberies, 178, 180, pl. 38), instead of *ḥy*, adopted here, seems to be highly improbable; see above Chapter 1, note 190.

139 For such a meaning cf. F.Ll. Griffith, JEA 12, 1926, 211 (14, 19); Lesko, Dict. I, 300 ("examination"); as a matter of fact Lesko's suggestion regarding the meaning of the term seems to be a result of a misunderstanding of the term as used in papBologna 1086, 13, cf. W. Wolf, ZÄS 65, 1930, 92f. ("Aufsichtsbehörde"); Wb III, 37 (2).

140 The best examples pertaining to such a knowledge are the plan of the tomb of Ramesses IV and the map of a desert region of Wadi Hammamat, both being once in the possession of the scribe of the necropolis Amennakht. No doubt such documents could have been inherited in the family of the necropolis scribes, so it is quite probable, that Tuthmosis owed this information to his father.

141 Cf. H. Carter, JEA 4, 1917, 108; Reeves, Valley of the Kings, 5; compare, however, D. Polz, in: Valley of the Sun Kings, 12f. and n. 28.

142 Spiegelberg, Graffiti, 46, pl. 62=Kitchen, RamInscr V, 624, 4; as regards its location, see Félix-Aubriot-Kurz, Plans de position, pl. 39; cf. Peden, Graffiti, 184f.; Häggman, Directing DeM, 227.

143 Ostracon Cairo JdE 72460 is a good example of a written description of this kind, cf. E. Thomas, in: Studies in Honor of G.R. Hughes, [SAOC 39], Chicago 1976, 209-216; K.C. Lakomy, Cairo Ostracon J. 72460: Eine Untersuchung zur königlichen Bestattungstradition im Tal der Könige zu Beginn der Ramessidenzeit, [GM Beiheft 4], Göttingen 2008; id., GM 216, 2008, 33ff.

144 Cf. Sweeney, Correspondence and Dialogue, 51, 72; Wente LRL, 64 (an).

145 Niwiński, in: BSAK 9, 2003, 300 n. 31; his tentative identification of the tomb as that of Ramesses XI (KV 4), would enable us to shed some new light on the document cited.

concerning some operations conducted by the gang in the Theban necropolis. The question is, however, where actually it had taken place. The term *s.t* used here in relation to the tomb can be connected either with a royal tomb in the Valley of the Kings or a tomb of a queen.[146] J.J. Janssen suggested that a tomb in the necropolis of Deir el-Medina was meant here.[147] The purpose of the proceedings described in LRL no. 28 is unknown either. As far as one can tell, Payankh ordered the finding of a tomb which must be uncovered (not simply opened)[148] but its seals left intact until the return of general Payankh himself. In their reply to his letter, the necropolis authorities promised to carry out this commission, i.e. to find a tomb, which must be ready when general will arrive from the south. The fragment in which the intentions of the necropolis authorities were declared is in fact too obscure. Its interpretation depends on the meaning of two crucial verbs used here (*w3ḥ* and *grg*) and their grammatical form.[149]

It is completely unknown what happened later as a consequence of this exchange of letters. Much has been said about the alleged plunderings instigated on behalf of Payankh but the letter does not relate to it explicitly. Moreover, there are other possible explanations of this enigmatic text. D. Sweeney suggested for example that the tomb could have been inspected as a suitable place to store the royal mummies originating from the royal necropolis in the Valley of the Kings.[150] Such an early date for an evacuation of the royal necropolis certainly cannot be excluded, and we can imagine that the process started soon after first depredations occurring on a mass scale in the Valley of the Kings. In addition, an alternative hypothesis can be presented here. All the proceedings described in the letter can be taken as a memorandum recording a search for a burial place for one of the members of the ruling family in Thebes. It is possible that those

[146] For the meaning of the term, cf. Peet, Tomb Robberies, 35; Černý, Community, 69ff.; id., JEA 15, 1929, 248 (n. 29); Wente, JNES 32, 1973, 225ff.; Thomas, JARCE 16, 1979, 90, 92 (n. 40); Reeves, Valley of the Kings, 231.

[147] Janssen, BiOr 25, 1968, 37 n. 4; cf. Sweeney, Correspondence and Dialogue, 72.

[148] Janssen pointed out to an apparent contradiction between this information and a statement that the workmen of the necropolis have already been in the tomb, cf. Janssen, loc.cit. According to him the tomb could have been entered through the tunnel, without breaking the seal. But what would be a purpose of leaving the seal intact until the return of the general if the tomb had already been entered? Sweeney (Correspondence and Dialogue, 78) observes the contradiction in the orders given by the general to the crew in two successive letters.

[149] Strangely enough both verbs could be also connected with founding and building of the tomb (or perhaps an usurpation of the older one?); cf. Wb.I, 256 (8); V, 186f. As regards a grammatical form and meaning of *grg.tw*, see Winand, Études, 97; Sweeney, Correspondence and Dialogue, 72 n. 188; otherwise Černý-Groll, Late Egyptian Grammar, 198 (Ex. 546).

[150] Cf. Sweeney, Correspondence and Dialogue, 72f.

responsible for it decided to use an old tomb, a fairly common custom in this period. After a careful inspection carried out by the captains of the necropolis, the tomb could have been sealed again, until the return of Payankh. The text does not provide any further details concerning the state of the tomb when it was entered for the first time by the inspectors. Such a scenario has an advantage over other possible interpretations as it provides the explanation of some evident discrepancies enclosed in the text of LRL no. 28.

At present we can add one more letter to the scanty dossier relating to the alleged plundering of the royal tombs in this period. This is one of the letters from the previous Bankes collection (papBM EA 75019+10302),[151] sent by Payankh (only the titles are preserved) to Thebes. This time some precious objects of unknown origin are requested by the general, besides other commodities, and we can only guess about their relation to the activities of the crew in the Valley of the Kings. Even more obscure in regard to this is a passage from LRL no. 19, interpreted by K. Jansen-Winkeln as testimony of the exchange of goods stolen from the royal tombs.[152] More probably the text should be taken literally, then we can simply maintain its connection with provisioning the group of Libyan stragglers or else soldiers of auxiliary troops.[153]

None of the preserved letters informs us about Tuthmosis returning home from the Nubian expedition. Neither do we know whether a request of the captains of the necropolis to general Payankh ever found a response: "And send the scribe of the necropolis Tjaroy to cause him to come ...".[154] It would be tempting of course to classify at least some of the letters of the first group commented above as written after the Nubian journey of Tuthmosis. As stated above, none of the preserved documents can be dated decisively to the period later than the year 10th of the Renaissance Era. It is hardly likely that any of the preserved letters of the archive of Tuthmosis may be related to the period after the Nubian campaign of Payankh.[155] Thus one could presume that he died soon after that date.[156] According to the widely accepted view he would have been aged ca. 65-67

[151] Demarée, Bankes Papyri, 14ff., pls. 13-16.

[152] Jansen-Winkeln, ZÄS 122, 1995, 69.

[153] Cf. Sweeney, Correspondence and Dialogue, 202f. (Ex. 24) and n. 82; id., DE 30, 1994, 208; Haring, in: Village Voices, 77f.; Demarée, Bankes Papyri, 19.

[154] Černý LRL, 47, 15f.

[155] The sole exception seems to be LRL no. 41 (see below, Chapter 9). Significantly enough there are no letters in the archive which could be related to the independent activity of Butehamun, after his father's demise.

[156] As regards a slightly later date, see Peden, Graffiti, 239 n. 718; Thijs, GM 199, 2004, 87.

at the moment of his death,[157] provided that he was a youth ca. 15-20 years old while starting his career in the institution of the royal tomb as a simple workman, early in the reign of Ramesses IX (though only years 16 and 17 are documented). Consequently we may surmise that he was born during the reign of Ramesses VI, at the time when his grandfather Horisheri was the scribe of the royal necropolis.

It is hardly imaginable that the death of Tuthmosis really surprised his kinsmen. Apparently he was chronically ill while accompanying Payankh during the latter's campaign in Nubia, although he often complained about the condition of his health during his earlier travel to Middle Egypt too (see Chapter 6).[158] A major refrain in LRL dating to the period of the Nubian war are words of concern for his health: "Assist him in the boat. Watch (him) vigilantly in the evening as well, while you are around him" (LRL no. 29),[159] and: "Do not neglect the scribe Tjaroy; we know that (he) is a sick man, who has never made a j[ourney like this]" (LRL no. 8).[160] It cannot be excluded that Tuthmosis resorted even to magical spells to heal himself.[161] One of the papyri of the Tuthmosis' archive has been effaced to be reused to write down a magical spell written presumably in a foreign language, probably local to the place where he was, presumably in Nubia.[162] Significantly in the original effaced text we can read what follows: "Indeed, I am alive today, and tomorrow is in god's hands. May he cause that I overcome the illness which flows (*sṯ3*) in (me?)[in pains?]" (papBM EA 75025ro. 7-8).[163] In spite of his illness he was still active, and his position at the side of general Payankh made him one of the most powerful and influential persons among the members of the necropolis staff. His status and his position in the administration of the necropolis were to strongly influence the future of his close relatives, and his eldest son in particular.

None of the documents mentions explicitly the death of Tuthmosis nor its circumstances. The possible exception is an unpublished graffito in the "Vallée des Carrières", in which his son Butehamun prayed to Amun in the following words: "Royal scribe (in) the Place of Truth Butehamun, he said: You are protector of

[157] Cf. Bierbrier LNK, 41; similarly Koenig, BIFAO 81, 1981, 42 n. 2. Different results (ca. 48-51 years) were achieved by Thijs (GM 175, 2000, 101f.) within the chronological scheme of the "short chronology".
[158] For references, see Demarée, Bankes Papyri, 27 (8). Nevertheless, there are no grounds to suspect him of being a hypochondriac, as suggested by Thijs, GM 199, 2004, 87.
[159] Černý LRL, 49, 2-4; for other formulations used by Butehamun in his letters, see Sweeney, Idiolects, 310.
[160] Černý LRL, 16, 7-9; cf. Neveu, Grammaire, 214 (Ex. 15); Wente, Letters, 188; id., LRL, 37 (notes "u" and "v").
[161] Cf. Demarée, in: DeM et la Vallée des Rois, 244.
[162] PapBM EA 75025: Demarée, Bankes Papyri, 27f., pl. 27.
[163] Ibid., 26f., pl. 28.

him, who placed you (lit.: him) in his heart. (Oh) Amun, (Lord) of the thrones of the Two Lands – turn (your) sight (?) to me, (you) who has no face, and save me! I am your servant. Protect (my) body, and let (me) reach the blessed state (*im3ḫ*). Do not as you have done to (my) father, the royal scribe (in) the Place of Truth Tuthmosis" (graffito no. 1573).[164]

It has been generally accepted that Butehamun had in mind the premature death of his father while writing these words.[165] It is possible, however, that the true reason of this complaint was his father's fatal illness, and possibly also death abroad. In such a case we could only speculate about the place of burial of Tuthmosis. It is possible of course that in the case of his death in Nubia his corpse would have been transported to Thebes and laid in the cemetery of Deir el-Medina. A fragment of a canopic vase of blue faience, found in the house "C V" in the settlement at Deir el-Medina, bearing the name of "the king's scribe" Tuthmosis,[166] seems to be an isolated piece of evidence of his burial at that place, although the exact location of his tomb is unknown. It cannot be excluded, however, that Tuthmosis' corpse never reached Thebes and his canopic vessels prepared earlier for his burial were never used for that purpose. The provenience of the piece which was found in the settlement itself cannot help to solve this problem, for the canopic fragment could have been swept down from the upper ground of the western cemetery.

The question arises of the significance of the information provided by the letters from the family archive of Tuthmosis for an overall estimation of the duration of the Nubian campaign of general Payankh. The time needed to traverse the distance of about 320 km between Thebes and Kubban can be calculated at about several days.[167] In such circumstances 5 preserved letters written by Butehamun and 8 letters by Tuthmosis (of the "core group") is not a strikingly

[164] A tentative translation based on an unpublished copy of the hieratic text made by J. Černý, and copied by H. Carter (now in the archives of the Griffith Institute, Oxford – Černý MSS, 6.13. 28); I would like to express my sincere gratitude to Dr. J. Malek for his permission to use this material. The present author was unable to find this important text, while searching for the graffiti in this remote valley of the Theban necropolis. The location of this graffito in Wadi Sikkat el-Agala, given in PM I/2², 594, is obviously wrong, and is based on the rather vague arrangement of the notes written by J. Černý on the basis of descriptions originally made by H. Carter. According to the notebook, this is "the Great Northern Valley"; for this, see also Peden, Graffiti, 236 n. 708. For the translation of the text, see Černý, Community, 374.

[165] See Černý, Community, 373f.; Peden, Graffiti, 192; Häggman, Directing DeM, 332 n. 2213; Thijs, GM 175, 2000, 102; id., GM 199, 2004, 87.

[166] Bruyère, Rapport (1934-1935), 306, fig. 174; Kitchen, RamInscr VI, 875, 12-13.

[167] Compare data cited in Chapter 6, note 80.

large number,[168] having in mind that they were dispatched through any possible person which set out for a journey southwards or in the opposite destination. So it must be admitted that Payankh had campaigned in Nubia for a period not significantly longer than hitherto assumed. As we know that Egyptian military practice was based mainly on yearly (or seasonal) campaigning abroad,[169] it seems to be unlikely that Payankh and his army stayed in Nubia longer than a few months. It was E.F. Wente who already noticed the possibility that Tuthmosis had visited Nubia on two separate occasions.[170] A "second journey (*wḏy.t*) when you are with your superior (*p3y.k ḥry*)", mentioned in the LRL no. 45,[171] would seem to support such an assumption. This is unless the first journey was that which he had embarked upon during his earlier career, travelling to Middle Egypt to collect grain taxes. In such a case, however, we should take as granted, that also during this early expedition he was accompanying his superior, i.e. general Payankh. As a matter of fact papPrakhov informs that Payankh travelled to Middle Egypt in the 7th year. Obviously Payankh's position was elevated enough at that time to enable him to be already the "superior" of the necropolis scribe, or else the formulation of the present text is anachronistic and refers rather to the circumstances connected with the second expedition (i.e. the Nubian campaign of Payankh).

A. Thijs went even further in his recent studies, postulating two successive campaigns led by general Payankh to Nubia.[172] The situation described in two letters (nos. 2 and 4) can be taken into consideration in this context. In LRL no. 4 we can read that while staying on Elephantine, Tuthmosis was informed by the general that he is going to meet Panehesy (and his army). Thus we would reasonably expect that Payankh was on the verge of his journey, just preparing for his march southwards. Meanwhile, it was the scribe Tuthmosis who left Elephantine first, while Payankh and Hrere were still staying on the island (LRL no. 2). Thus the question arises why Tuthmosis was enlisted into the army's vanguard. It is possible of course that he was entrusted the mission of organization of the logistics of transporting and provisioning of the army in an adjacent area south of Aswan.

[168] At least one letter of Butehamun should be added to this number, i.e. LRLC no. I; and presumably one letter of Tuthmosis, i.e. LRLC no. III; nothing certain can be said about a date of papBM EA 75017 (papBankes II).

[169] Very seldom in fact do we hear about a more prolonged period of a military campaign – for example the siege of Sharuhen by Ahmose. The case of the Annals of Tuthmosis III provides ample information in regard of this.

[170] Wente LRL, 13.

[171] Černý LRL, 66, 13-14; id., Community, 377.

[172] Thijs, GM 165, 1998, 99ff.; id., GM 177, 2000, 63ff; id., GM 199, 2004, 79ff.

Would this be the true explanation of those strange words already commented above (LRL no. 29): "he has never before made the journeys on which he is now"? Once again, this can only be mere speculation, as must the question of the possibility of two successive Nubian campaigns of Payankh. Let us also note that Hrere was staying in Thebes, when Tuthmosis had just reached Payankh on Elephantine (cf. LRL no. 30), but unexpectedly she was accompanying Payankh on the island when Tuthmosis left Elephantine for Nubia (LRL no. 2). Two possibilities arise in regard of this. Either Hrere joined Payankh in the relatively short period of time between these two letters, or else these letters relate to two different campaigns.

The circumstances surrounding the beginning of the Nubian war is also a matter of conjecture. Panehesy, although forced out of Egypt, was still a dangerous opponent and neither the high priest of Amun nor Pharaoh would tolerate such a threat for their spheres of influence. The war of the High Priest Amenhotep clearly demonstrated the real power of the viceroy of Kush and his political ambitions. It cannot be excluded that his army, even though weakened during the war in Middle Egypt still preserved its military ability and strength. In such a case it would be hardly imaginable that a war against a rebellious viceroy could be postponed longer than needed to equip an army. It is possible therefore that Pharaoh's army followed him very soon after Panehesy's retreat. As a matter of fact, most of the information provided by the LRL seems to suggest such a scenario. As demonstrated above the LRL no. 28 was written hastily, soon after the departure of the army leaded by Payankh to the south. In this context, however, the supposed date of the letter (year 10 of the Renaissance Era) presents some difficulties in our understanding of the chronology of the Nubian war. Is it possible that the war was instigated 10 or even more years after expulsion of Panehesy from Egypt? Such a delay could be explained of course by a weakness of Panehesy's opponents. There is, however, an alternative explanation for such a delay in undertaking a military action against the viceroy of Kush.

An obscure passage from one of the letters written by Tuthmosis (LRL no. 4) must be taken into consideration here. E.F. Wente has translated it in the following way:[173] "Please tell Amun and the gods of the Temple (of Medinet Habu) to bring me back alive from the enemy also".[174] An alternative translation of the passage is based on the reading of the crucial word as *ḫrwyw* "war":[175]

---

[173] Wente LRL, 25.

[174] Cf. Černý LRL, 8, 12-13.

[175] Cf. Wb.III, 326 (1); Lesko, Dict. I, 372. This meaning is suggested also by Wente LRL, 26 (q); similarly id., Letters, 186 (no. 308).

"...to bring me back alive from this other (or: second?) war".[176] The true meaning of the passage still escapes us, since there are at least two possibilities. Either the next (possibly second?) war after the war conducted in Middle Egypt is meant here or else another (possibly second?) Nubian war. At the present stage of our research, the first possibility seems more plausible, although there can be no certainty about this. In any case, the latter possibility would support the idea of at least two consecutive stages of the military conflict in Nubia. The date of the first hypothetical clash in the south cannot be established at the moment, nevertheless a substantially early date for the beginning of the war in Nubia, and Payankh's pursuit after Panehesy's army, should be taken into consideration.[177]

It is a pity that none of the letters written by Tuthmosis or the officers of Payankh gives any details concerning the course of events and the effect of the operations conducted in Nubia. No doubt this was caused by the very character of the letters being partly a "private" correspondence. Even those letters which are "official" in character are terse and relate only the most urgent matters. On the other hand, we must not forget the realities of ancient Egyptian propaganda, based on the officially sanctioned picture of a victorious pharaoh crushing his enemies. If no such depictions or references were preserved in the sources of the period this is because of the hazardous character of these sources or else the result of a final defeat suffered by Payankh and his army. In the undated graffito no. 714,[178] being the sole mention of Payankh returning home to Thebes,[179] there is no discernible reference to the political situation in the aftermath of the military campaign: "Third month of *shemu*, day 23(?). <Day> of finishing the work in this place (*t3 s.t*) by the crew of the necropolis. The scribe Butehamun crossed over to the City (Ne) to see the arrival of the General in (his) journeying north (*m ḫd*)".

As a matter of fact we know that Payankh's opponent had built a tomb for himself at Aniba.[180] As there are no grounds to suppose that Panehesy was ever buried there[181] the very existence of the tomb does not settle the question of his

[176] See Groll, RdE 26, 1974, 169 (II); similarly Černý, Community, 377 n. 12; Wente, Letters, 186 (no. 308).
[177] Thus contrary to the suggestions made by Thijs, who opted for two campaigns conducted within a relatively short span of time, cf. GM 177, 20000, 69 (with a hypothetical distribution of letters).
[178] Spiegelberg, Graffiti, 57, pl. 76; Kitchen, RamInscr VI, 849 (no. 3); cf. Peden, Graffiti, 191f. n. 372; McDowell, Village Life, 241 (193A).
[179] Cf. Kitchen TIP, 417 (II.5). As regards another interpretation, see Chapter 3 above.
[180] G. Steindorff, Aniba II, Glückstadt-Hamburg-New York 1937, 240f., pl. 29 (c); PM VII, 79; Kitchen, RamInscr VI, 842f.; Hein, op.cit., 29, 104. It was rightly observed that the building of the tomb of the viceroy in Nubia in such a place, and not in Egypt, must be taken as a sign of the waning influence of Egypt in Nubia, cf. ibid., 106.
[181] Except the heart scarab of his wife(?) Tentnub, cf. Kitchen, RamInscr VI, 843, 1. For a contrary

possible last stronghold in the very heart of Nubia. As the centre of Egyptian administration during the New Kingdom,[182] Aniba, located ca. 222 km south of Aswan, provided certainly a convenient operation base for the forces led by Panehesy. Anyway, nothing certain can be said about Panehesy's defeat or else his final withdrawal from the Nubian province.

Among the toponyms enumerated in LRL we can only notice the rather obscure *P3-ḥḏ*[...*mḥt*].*t* [North]ern *Pahedj*[...] (LRL no. 50).[183] No significance can be attached whatsoever to a vague *Yar* –"the place where I am abandoned in this distant land" (LRL no. 9).[184] As demonstrated by E.F. Wente it seems that this is not a genuine geographic locality but rather a proverbial "hell-hole", being a designation of an extremely unpleasant place.[185] On the other hand, quite possibly it is Horus of Kubban, residing in "[thi]s mountain" who was mentioned in LRL no. 50.[186] But he was also invoked in LRL nos. 2, and 9, and LRLC no. III, so it has been observed that Tuthmosis probably travelled southward as far as Kubban (ca. 110 km south of Aswan).[187] In such a case we would admit that Payankh reached the very heart of the territory controlled by Panehesy. It must be remembered, however, that Horus of Kubban (*Ḥr nb B3k*) was worshipped also in the gold-mining regions of Wadi Allaqi,[188] being under control of the fortress of Kubban. It is rather doubtful whether Horus of Miam was mentioned in LRL no. 9,[189] so we cannot be sure whether Tuthmosis went as far as Aniba, where the rebellious viceroy had prepared a tomb for himself. Anyway, Panehesy's tomb had not been ravaged, so it can be assumed that he never lost control over the

view, cf. T. Säve-Söderbergh, in: LÄ I (1975), 276; L. Habachi, in: LÄ III (1980), 635; Zibelius-Chen, SAK 16, 1989, 331f. An ushebti figure (of unknown provenience) with the name of Panehesy (?) cannot be evaluated properly in regard of this, cf. P.E. Newberry, Funerary Statuettes and Model Sarcophagi, [CG], Cairo 1930, 334 (CG 48381); for a highly doubtful interpretation of the item, see Lull, Los sumos sacerdotes, 46.

[182] The headquarters of *idnw n W3w3t* were located there and possibly also the viceroy himself could have been stationed there, cf. Hein, op.cit., 27;

[183] Černý LRL, 73, 2.

[184] Černý LRL, 17, 9-10; see also ibid., 2,3; 4, 3; 13, 9.

[185] Wente LRL, 19 (j); see also above Chapter 6.

[186] Černý LRL, 71, 12.

[187] Cf. Janssen LRLC, 19.

[188] Cf. J. Černý, Graffiti at the Wādi el-Allāki, JEA 33, 1947, 52ff.

[189] Černý LRL, 17, 6 and note a-b; cf. Černý, Community, 377. This text is not included in K. Zibelius, Afrikanische Orts- und Völkernamen in hieroglyphischen und hieratischen Texten, Wiesbaden 1972, 120-122; see however K. Zibelius-Chen, SAK 16, 1989, 331 n. 8.; Demarée, Bankes Papyri, 16. As for the cult centres of Horus of Miam (*Ḥr nb Miʿm*), see Hein, op.cit., 158 (tab. 2).

heartland of his province.[190] As a consequence the military success achieved by Payankh remains highly doubtful in fact.[191]

Despite the local customs of the officials in the Theban area, where they left thousands of graffiti in the desert wadis, there are no such inscriptions in Nubia, which can be related directly to the Nubian campaign of Payankh.[192] Nonetheless we can understand perhaps an apparent unwillingness of Tuthmosis and his colleagues to commemorate the itinerary of Payankh's army. No doubt the hardships of the war in the distant desert country, and the condition of his health prevented him from wandering around in such a hostile and unpleasant environment.[193]

[190] Cf. Kitchen, in: Libyan Period in Egypt, 195 (suggesting a northern border of his province somewhere between Maharraka and Derr).

[191] Cf. Habachi, in: LÄ III (1980), 635; compare also some controversial assertions presented by Thijs, SAK 31, 2003, 299f.

[192] It is well known that dozens of such graffiti can be connected with other Egyptian military campaigns in Nubia.

[193] Cf. Peden, Graffiti, 129 n. 455.

8. Butehamun and his role in the evacuation of the royal necropolis

The early stages of the career of Butehamun[1] are scarcely documented in the sources connected with the functioning of the royal necropolis. The reason for this seems to be quite clear; when he started his activity, first as an assistant to his father, probably as a youth of about 20 years old, the institution of the royal necropolis had ceased to exist in its previous form. The depredations of the period of the civil war and the subsequent policy of restoration undertaken by the high priests of Amun had led to a complete reorganization of the institution of the royal necropolis at Thebes, with the result that some new men appeared within it. Butehamun was certainly one of them. His role at the beginning of the Renaissance Era can be described in fact as that of an assistant of the scribe of the royal necropolis, and he appears as such in the preserved LRL (see Chapter 7). This is why we can see him as accompanying his father, in papTurin 2094 for example, where both are titled simply as the "scribes", and the chief workman Penparei was enumerated in company with them (see Chapter 5).

If Butehamun did not use the title "king's scribe" in the early stages of his own career (in LRL and in some Theban graffiti)[2] this is because he was acting as the necropolis scribe at the side of his father, the latter being the "senior scribe" of the necropolis. Quite understandably he was titled the "king's scribe" in the hieroglyphic texts and in the graffiti dating to the later period. As regards these later texts, especially those written during the pontificate and subsequent "kingship" of Paynudjem I, the title seems to be used according to

[1] The following presentation is based on the assumption that there was only one Butehamun, contrary to the hypothesis presented by A. Niwiński; see below. For a recent discussion on the subject cf. K. Jansen-Winkeln, Der Schreiber Butehamun, GM 139, 1994, 35-40; T. Kikuchi, Das Graffito Nr. 3981a und eine aus den Late Ramesside Letters bekannte Familie der Nekropolenschreiber, GM 160, 1997, 51-58; B.G. Davies, Two many Butehamuns? Additional observations on their identity, SAK 24, 49-68.

[2] Cf. Černý LRL, 76 (index); as regards the graffiti, cf. e.g. nos. 1282, 1301, 1358, 1919 (in all of them with the title "scribe" or "scribe of the necropolis"), which may precede the beginning of the 21st Dynasty; for a comment see Jansen-Winkeln, InschrSp I, 37.

the customs of the epoch, although again a purely honorific character of the title cannot be denied.

One of the earliest documents, besides LRL of the early group (cf. e.g. nos. 1, and 5), which testify to Butehamun's activity, is possibly the graffito written at the entrance to the tomb of Horemheb (KV 57) in the year 4, fourth month of *akhet*, day 22.[3] Here he was titled simply as the "scribe of the army" (*sš n pꜣ mšꜥ*), quite in accord with the state of the Theban administration as it can be reconstructed at the beginning of the Renaissance Era. Another graffito written at the tomb's entrance is dated to the 6th year and gives no name of any member of investigating party except the title of "the vizier and general" followed by the obscure words *ḥry pꜣ* [...].[4] Although an attempt has been made to date both texts from the tomb of Horemheb to the reign of Smendes,[5] both graffiti must be dated to an earlier period, most probably to the Renaissance Era.[6] The title held by Butehamun points rather to such an early date, if one can realize that in the following period (during the reign of Smendes and pontificate of Paynudjem I) he was already the "scribe in the Place of Truth", i.e. the senior scribe of the necropolis. Significantly, inscriptions written on the left jamb of the entrance door mention the "general's scribe[7] Kysen" and names of the scribe Butehamun and king's scribe Tuthmosis side by side. Unfortunately the name of the scribe Kysen is unknown elsewhere, but he can be securely placed in the military entourage of general Payankh in the middle and later years of the Renaissance Era. On the other hand, the titles held by

[3] The graffiti from the tomb of Horemheb are known only from the transcriptions made by A.H. Gardiner (Notebook 70, pp. 68f; Griffith Institute, Oxford), cf. Reeves, Valley of the Kings, 77-79, pl. 6; Niwiński, SAK 11, 1984, fig. 2; Jansen-Winkeln, InschrSp I, 35f. (3.61); Peden, Graffiti, 207-209.

[4] It is hardly likely that any of the titles held by the high-priests of the epoch, being viziers and generals at the same time, started with such words. Thus one can consider whether this is not in fact a partly erased name (Herihor?) – let us note that Gardiner annotated the transcription of this fragment as "unsatisfactory".

[5] Cf. Kitchen, TIP, 417 (I), 418 (III, nos. 7, 8) does not definitely exclude a dating to the Renaissance Era; see also A. Niwiński, SAK 11, 1984, 151 (graffito of the year 4); Peden, Graffiti, 207f.; Jansen-Winkeln (InschrSp I, 35f.) relates both of them to the pontificate of Paynudjem I, not excluding however an earlier date (before the beginning of the 21st Dynasty, cf. ibid., 37, 286). An attempt to correlate them with the period of Herihor's supremacy in the Thebaid seems to be more plausible, for this see Reeves, Valley of the Kings, 234 (nos. 4, 7), 246, 259 (tab. 11).

[6] See Reeves, Valley of the Kings, 234 (nos. 4, 7); see, however, the comment by Eaton-Krauss, BiOr 49, 1992, 715 n. 44. Peden (Graffiti, 207-209) also hesitates between a date in the Renaissance Era or "a very few years later in the early XXIst Dynasty."

[7] "Scribe of the domain (*pr*) of the general" is hardly likely; more probably the sign *pr* should be taken here as a manner of writing the definite article *pꜣ*.

Butehamun and his father fit the situation documented by the LRL very well, where the former always stands in a subordinate position in relation to his father, the senior scribe of the necropolis.

Other sources connected with the operations conducted in the Valley of the Kings during the Renaissance Era are extremely rare. The dating of most of the dockets attributed to this period by N. Reeves (Valley of the Kings, table 10, nos. 4-10)[8] is purely hypothetical.[9] In fact, some of them can be definitely discarded now. This is the case of Reeves' nos. 6 (Year 6, II *akhet* 7), 8 (Year 6, II *akhet* 18), and 10 (Year 6, II).[10] The latter two were written in the tomb of queen Tauseret and Sethnakht (KV 14) in two side rooms (Ka and Kb), exactly at the place where the third building phase of the tomb started, so a connection with the building of the tomb cannot be denied.[11] Thus these graffiti cannot be taken as an argument for Reeves' hypothesis concerning the existence of an intermediary royal cache in KV 14, established during the Renaissance Era.[12] Similarly, there is no reason for dating to such a later period Theban graffito no. 2056a (Reeves' no. 6), written directly above the entrance to the tomb of Seti II (KV 15).[13] It is a mere coincidence that its date is the same as that contained in a docket on the coffin of Seti I (Year 6, II *akhet* 7).[14] The royal butler Setiherwenemef, whose visit is mentioned in the graffito, is well known in connection with the building of the tomb of Ramesses IV, so the dating of the graffito must be much earlier than that supposed by N. Reeves.[15] As a matter of fact, the activity of the royal butler Setiherwenemef is well documented in the sources dating possibly to the reign of Ramesses IV.[16] At the same time, any connection of this graffito with Butehamun, who wrote

[8] See also Reeves, Valley of the Kings, 103, 109ff., pl. 7.

[9] Cf. Eaton-Krauss, loc.cit.

[10] Note that the year date given by N. Reeves (after R.A. Caminos; cf. A. Gardiner, JEA 40, 1954, 43) has been emended by H. Altenmüller, SAK 11, 1984, 44 n. 27; see also below.

[11] Cf. H. Altenmüller, Das Grab der Königin Tauseret (KV 14). Bericht über eine archäologische Unternehmung, GM 84, 1985, 7ff. (esp. pp. 9-10, 14-15); id., Bemerkungen zu den neu gefundenen Daten im Grab der Königin Twosre (KV 14) im Tal der Könige von Theben, in: After Tutankhamun, 141ff. (esp. pp. 149-154).

[12] Cf. Eaton-Krauss, op.cit., 711; Peden, Graffiti, 165f.

[13] Černý, Sadek et al., Graffiti III, pl. 61; IV, 35; Félix-Aubriot-Kurz, Plans de position, pl. 41.

[14] Maspero, Momies royales, 553, pl. 10B; Daressy, Cercueils, 30, pl. 18; Kitchen, RamInscr VI, 838 (30A); cf. Kitchen TIP, 417 (no. 2); Reeves, Valley of the Kings, 234 (no. 5); Helck OPG, 572.

[15] Cf. Eaton-Krauss, op.cit., 715; Häggman, Directing DeM, 175; Kitchen, RamInscr, VI, 146 (A.74); Peden, Graffiti, 198; Helck OPG, 28, 400.

[16] Cf. Janssen, Village Varia, 165ff.; see also Helck, Verwaltung, 274; J. Malek, JEA 74, 1988, 134-136; A.R. Schulman, CdE 61, 1986, 201 (no. 34).

graffito 2056b, is definitely excluded.[17] The latter was simply superimposed on the preceding one, much earlier in time and possibly covered by dirt or patina (and thus invisible) at that time. Anyway, it would be difficult to explain why Butehamun decided to destroy another "contemporary" text left by another member of an inspecting party.

Nevertheless the crew was engaged in some kind of work in the Valley of the Kings, when general Payankh returned home from his Nubian expedition. The undated graffito no. 714, written by Butehamun in the vicinity of the tomb of Tuthmosis III (KV 34) and KV 42, seems to be fairly reliable confirmation of this, if it is rightly dated to the end of the Renaissance Era.[18] One can only guess that the work of the crew was connected with dismantling the royal burials in the Valley.[19]

If the crew was still active after the abandonment of the tomb of Ramesses XI, this can only be because of the necessity to retain it for work on the tombs of the successive high priests of Amun, which must have been built in Thebes. Unfortunately the exact location of none of these tombs can be indicated, except that of Amenhotep (see below). Nothing is known about the original burial place of the lady Nodjmet either.[20] Her two coffins were found in the Royal Cache at Deir el-Bahari, deprived of their original gilding (CG 61024).[21] Their typology, as suggested by Niwiński, points to the period of the pontificate/kingship of Paynudjem I.[22] Other elements of her funerary equipment were found in the cache as well (the canopic chest, and a figure of Osiris hollowed out to contain a funerary papyrus),[23] besides the funerary papyri (see Chapter 3). The mummy itself was covered by a shroud, decorated with a representation of "Osiris Lady of the Two Lands (Mother-of-the-king Nodjmet)|" standing in front of a figure of Osiris.[24] The inscription written on a bandage of her mummy would perhaps provide a decisive argument in regard

[17] Contra Reeves, Valley of the Kings, 112 n. 17.

[18] Cf. Kitchen TIP, 417 (II.5); Jansen-Winkeln, ZÄS 122, 1995, 70: the monthly date of the graffito (III *shemu* 23) postdating ca. 2 month the date of LRL no. 28 (I *shemu* 29); see also Chapter 7 above. As regards the location of the graffito, see Félix-Aubriot-Kurz, Plans de position, pl. 72

[19] See Peden, Graffiti, 192 n. 372.

[20] Cf. however Reeves, Valley of the Kings, 255.

[21] Daressy, Cercueils, 40-50, pls. 25-27.

[22] Cf. Niwiński, 21st Dynasty Coffins, 42, 116f. (no. 72) – "early/middle 21st Dynasty".

[23] Maspero, Momies royales, 592 (9), pl. 21A; cf. A. Dodson, The Canopic Equipment of the Kings of Egypt, [Studies in Egyptology], London – New York 1994, 78, pl. 31b; Jansen-Winkeln, InschrSp I, 33; as regards other objects, cf. PM I/2^2, 662; E. Loring, in: E. Graefe, G. Belova (eds.), The Royal Cache TT 320 – a re-examination, Cairo 2010, 63f.

[24] Maspero, Momies royales, 569; cf. Jansen-Winkeln, InschrSp I, 31.

of the dating of her burial, if it had been documented properly. Unfortunately the text has been only vaguely mentioned by Elliott Smith as "a reference to «the first year of Pinotmou»".[25] A. Niwiński has presented two possible chronological explanations as regards this inscription's vague reference: either it refers (less probably according to him) to the reign of Smendes, or else it should be related to the reign of Psusennes I.[26] If the mummy found inside the coffin was properly identified as hers, then her age at the moment of death can be estimated at ca.30-35,[27] which seems to be too low in comparison with her age as calculated from the historical data,[28] but anyway it would rather favour an early date of her demise.

Nothing certain can be said about the burial place of Payankh either.[29] Presumably there are some grounds to locate it in the region of Heracleopolis Magna (at least an original tomb), due to an inscription there mentioning "the general and overseer of the granaries of Pharaoh", which can be possibly referred to Payankh.[30] Similarly no firm conclusion can be drawn from the commemorative or votive stela of Payankh found in Abydos.[31]

The "place (of the tomb) of the generalissimo" (*ỉwtn pꜣ ỉmy-r mšꜥ wr*), as mentioned in oCairo JdE 72460,[32] is now commonly identified as a reference to the tomb of Ramesses II in the Valley of the Kings (KV 7).[33] The rather curious reference to a "place" or "site" (*ỉwtn*)[34] can be interpreted as an allusion to the entrance of the tomb, which must have been already finished at the

[25] Smith, Royal Mummies, 97; cf. Kitchen TIP, 43, 417 (6); Reeves, Valley of the Kings, 234 (no. 13); Jansen-Winkeln, InschrSp I, 32.

[26] Niwiński, 21st Dynasty Coffins, 43; 117; id., JARCE 16, 1979, 52f.; similarly, Jansen-Winkeln, ZÄS 119, 1992, 26 n. 47; see also Kitchen TIP, 43 n. 182, 417 (III.6) (a preference given to the former possibility); Wente, in: Harris-Wente, Atlas of the Royal Mummies, 270f.

[27] Harris-Wente, Atlas of the Royal Mummies, tab. 6.4 (no. 63).

[28] Cf. Wente, in: ibid., 269ff.

[29] Cf. El-Sayed, BIFAO 78, 1978, 218.

[30] Cf. M.C. Perez-Die, P. Vernus, Excavationes en Ehnasya el-Medina (Heracleópolis Magna), Madrid 1992, 39f. (no. 13), 121 (Fig. 11a); Römer, Götter- und Priesterherrschaft, 45 and n. 139; Jansen-Winkeln, BN 71, 1994, 85; Gnirs, Militär und Gesellschaft, 208 n. 154.

[31] A. Mariette, Abydos. Description des fouilles exécutées sur l'emplacement de cette ville, II, Paris 1880, pl. 57 (b); El-Sayed, BIFAO 78, 1978, 197-99 (Doc.1), pl. 66; R.J. Demarée, The *ꜣḫ ỉḳr n Rꜥ*–Stelae. On Ancestor Worship in Ancient Egypt, [Egyptologische Uitgaven 3], Leiden 1983, 39f. (A11).

[32] E. Thomas, Cairo Ostracon J. 72460, in: Studies in honor of George R. Hughes, [SAOC 39], Chicago 1976, 209-216; see now a thorough discussion in: K.C. Lakomy, Cairo Ostrakon J. 72460: Eine Untersuchung zur königlichen Bestattungstradition im Tal der Könige zu Beginn der Ramessidenzeit, [GM Beiheft Nr.4], Göttingen 2008; id., GM 216, 2008, 33ff.

[33] Cf. Thomas, op.cit., 213; Reeves, Valley of the Kings, 130; Lakomy, Cairo Ostrakon J. 72460, 15-22.

[34] Ro. 1; as for the meaning of the term, cf. Janssen, Commodity Prices, 396; Lesko, Dict. I, 22.

moment when the text on the ostracon was written.[35] This is evident from the fact that the phrase *p3 r-ʿ b3k* ("the work in progress") was used in the same text with regard to the tombs still under construction (ro. 2, and 5; and vo. 1, and 4). It is possible of course that the text could simply refer to the place where the tomb was only planned (?), or else where it was hidden beneath the ground (in such a case possibly an older tomb would be meant here).[36]

Certainly, the dating of oCairo JdE 72460 to the 19th Dynasty (and more precisely to the reign of Ramesses II)[37] cannot be questioned in the light of recent investigation, thus the ostracon cannot be linked to any of the persons of the end of the 20th Dynasty, bearing the title of "generalissimo" (*imy-r mšʿ wr*). More controversial, however, is an assumption presented by N. Reeves, that "the tomb of the generalissimo" (*p3 ḫr n p3 imy-r mšʿ wr*) of papAmbras 2, 8 should be also connected with the tomb of Ramesses II in the Valley of the Kings (KV 7).[38] The coincidence of dates regarding the "renewal of the burial" of the mummy of Ramesses II (Year 6, III *peret* 15),[39] and the date of papAmbras itself (Year 6 of the Renaissance Era) does not satisfactorily explain the chronology of plundering of the tomb of Ramesses II. It should be noted that also what seems to have been the second investigation of the tomb of Horemheb (KV 57) took place in Year 6, II? *akhet* 12.[40] Papyrus Ambras 2, 8-9 mentions a document of "the examination (concerning) the tomb of the generalissimo, which the coppersmith (Pa)uaresi was subjected to".[41] The actual character of activity of this (Pa)uaresi cannot be elucidated in the light of the present text, but it seems that this is the same person as one of the thieves (the coppersmith of the necropolis), mentioned in the depositions of

[35] Cf. Lakomy, op.cit., 24.

[36] Nothing is known about any attempts to conceal entrances of the royal tombs at the beginning of the 19th Dynasty, but the tombs dating to the 18th Dynasty were carefully hidden, so that their locations could only have been remembered or else noted in the documentation of the royal necropolis. In such a case, the tomb of Horemheb could be also taken into consideration, as this Pharaoh even more deserves a designation "generalissimo", the title he really bore during his earlier career (cf. Urk. IV, 2088, 16, 19; 2089, 2; 2091, 9; 2094, 20; 2099, 6, 15; 2100, 17; 2103, 3, 13). Unfortunately, such an assumption does not remove all the topographical problems presented by the Cairo ostracon. In addition, it cannot be excluded that one of the sons of Ramesses II bearing the title of general was really meant here.

[37] Lakomy, op.cit., 7-10, 110.

[38] Reeves, Valley of the Kings, 94; see also Peden, Graffiti, 234 n. 699.

[39] Maspero, Momies royales, 557, fig. 15; Daressy, Cercueils, 32, pl. 22; Kitchen, RamInscr VI, 838 (30B); cf. Kitchen TIP, 417 (no. 3); Reeves, Valley of the Kings, 234 (no. 9); Helck OPG, 572.

[40] Cf. Jansen-Winkeln, InschrSp I, 36; cf. Kitchen TIP, 417 (I), 418 (III.8); Reeves, Valley of the Kings, 234 (no. 7).

[41] Peet, Tomb Robberies, pl. 38 (2, 8-9)=Kitchen, RamInscr VI, 837, 9-10.

the thieves in year 1 of the Renaissance Era (and earlier).[42] Thus the older view that the tomb in question was the tomb of high priest and "general" Payankh[43] cannot be upheld any more, because Payankh was still documented in the later years of the Renaissance Era, in particular after its Year 7 (as exemplified by the Karnak graffito).[44] A possible candidate would be again king Horemheb, whose tomb was presumably disturbed some time before the "Year 4" of the graffito written directly at its entrance.[45] As suggested above, an "early" date of the graffiti from the tomb of Horemheb is satisfactorily supported by the fact that the names of the scribe of the necropolis Tuthmosis and his son were put side by side.

No doubt, the adaptation of the tomb of Ramesses XI (KV 4), or less probably an extension of the tomb for the supposed burial of Pinudjem I took place in the following period.[46] This was the last large building project undertaken in the Valley of the Kings, although the character and purpose of this work cannot be understood properly. It is necessary to discuss in this context an inscription written on the left wall of the first corridor in KV 4.[47] This is undoubtedly the latest of the texts written officially in the Valley of the Kings. The badly preserved text was documented by the Brooklyn Museum Theban Expedition.[48] An older version of the text was inscribed under Ramesses XI as an element of the original decoration of KV 4, and this is just a sketch written in red (and yellow) ink. Then the inscription of the High Priest Paynudjem I was drawn (in red paint) to the right of the older one, and this is an exact copy of the earlier inscription, except the cartouches which were obviously changed.[49] The problem, however, is his prenomen,

[42] PapBM 10052, 14, 15: Peet, Tomb Robberies, pl. 34=Kitchen, RamInscr VI, 798, 14; the coppersmith Pauaresi appears also in Texts B, D, and E in papBM 10054ro. 2, {1}: A. Gasse, JEA 87, 2001, 83, 89 (2); and papBM 10054ro. 3, 2; and vo. 5, 9 (son of Kedakhtef): Peet, op.cit., pls. 6, 9=Kitchen, RamInscr VI, 493, 15; 494, 15. As regards the dating of these pieces of evidence, see Chapter 1.

[43] Černý, Community, 9.

[44] See the discussion in Chapter 3.

[45] It has been suggested that it contains a reference to the burial chamber of the tomb: *pr-ḏ.t m pꜣ ḫr n nsw Ḏsr-ḫpr(.w)-Rꜥ Stp.n-Rꜥ ꜥnḫ wḏꜣ snb*; cf. Reeves, Valley of the Kings, 78; Peden, Graffiti, 208 n. 469.

[46] Reeves, Valley of the Kings, 121ff.; Häggman, Directing, 361.

[47] PM I/2^2, 501 (2); cf. E. Lefébure, Les hypogées royaux de Thèbes, 2 fasc., [Annales du Musée Guimet 16], Paris 1889, 13; Römer, Gottes- und Priesterherrschaft, 57, 563 (no. 36); Jansen-Winkeln, InschrSp I, 21 (no. 28); M. Ciccarello, The Graffito of Pinutem I in the Tomb of Ramesses XI, Brooklyn 1979.

[48] M. Ciccarello, J. Romer, A Preliminary Report of the Recent Work in the Tombs of Ramesses X and XI in the Valley of the Kings, Brooklyn 1979, 8f.

[49] Ciccarello, op.cit., 3, 5f., 8.

written here simply as "High Priest of Amun". Such a form of prenomen of Paynudjem I has no parallels among other examples of his royal titulary,[50] but it is well known that it was used by Herihor and later on by Psusennes I.[51] M. Ciccarello's supposition that the graffito preserves the older priestly title of Paynudjem because it was written in the earliest years of his kingship cannot be substantiated.[52] On the contrary, it seems more plausible to relate it to the royal protocol of Herihor in the form well attested in the epigraphic material from the temple of Khonsu.[53]

The question of the ultimate owner of KV 4 cannot be positively solved on the basis of the remnants of the funerary equipment found in the tomb[54] nor its unfinished decoration. Nevertheless, the contents of the text under discussion may possibly provide some additional information:[55] "Words spoken by Amun-Ra-Harakhte, the great god, who makes festive the Two Lands[56], far striding[57] in the bark of multitude (*ḥḥ*)[58]: (My) beloved son, lord of the Two Lands, lord of strength (High-Priest-of-Amun)| – (I) give to you a kingship, created by him, who is in heaven. Your lifetime on the earth is like (that of the one) from [whom?] you came out,[59] [Osiris?] lord of diadems[60] (Paynudjem, justified)|".[61] For some unknown reason the last two columns of the text were

[50] Cf. J. von Beckerath, Handbuch der ägyptischen Königsnamen, [MÄS 49], Mainz 1999, 183; LR III, 243ff.; compare Römer, Gottes- und Priesterherrschaft, 57: "Andersartige Königstitulatur Painedjems I. mit "HPA" als Pränomen".

[51] J. von Beckerath, op.cit., 177, 179.

[52] Ciccarello, op.cit., 23f.

[53] Cf. Bonhême, Noms royaux, 31f.; id., Livre des rois I, 4ff.; the name was always written with the genitival *n*. As regards similar epithets preceding the prenomen of Herihor, such as those in KV 4, see id., Livre des rois I, 7 (Doc. 21 H.004), 9 (Doc. 21 H.008), 81 (Doc. 21 H.134).

[54] Certainly the fragments of "gilt gesso" found by the Theban Royal Tomb Project cannot be decisively joined with Paynudjem's coffins from the Royal Cache (TT 320), for this see Ciccarello, op.cit., 4.

[55] The following translation differs from that given by Ciccarello, op.cit., 8.

[56] Cicarello is obviously wrong in interpreting the sign *mꜣꜥ.t* as *tꜣ.wy*; so it should be rather emended, cf. Römer, Gottes- und Priesterherrschaft; an emendation accepted also by Jansen-Winkeln, InschrSp I, 21.

[57] Cf. Lesko, Dict. I, 160. The writing of the word *pḏ*/*pd* "to stretch" possibly influenced here by the word *pḏ.t* "bow".

[58] Or else *ḥḥ(.w)*.

[59] Thus the perfect relative form: *pr(.w).n.k m-ḫnt* [...]. The meaning of the horizontal line (?) written after that remains doubtful – certainly not *n*, which was suggested by Ciccarello, op.cit., note 21. It does not look as a suffix pronoun either. Contrary to the versions given by Ciccarello, Römer, and Jansen-Winkeln, its exact position (directly after *m-ḫnt*) was given only in: Reeves-Wilkinson, The Complete Valley of the Kings, 208.

[60] Possibly written over a group *tꜣ.wy*, as suggested by Ciccarello, op.cit., note 22.

[61] Significantly the epithet *mry-Ỉmn*, usually written in this context, was replaced by the mere "justified", cf. J. von Beckerath, Handbuch der ägyptischen Königsnamen, 182f.

superimposed over an older text, which were possibly the remnants of the original layout of the text as planned by those who prepared the inscription of Paynudjem I.[62]

It seems that there is a gap in the last column of the text just above the cartouche of Paynudjem. The partly preserved sign (representing a seated figure with a *w3s* scepter)[63] preceding a royal epithet "lord of diadems" cannot be interpreted as a determinative of the title *nsw*,[64] but rather as a determinative of the "title" *Wsir*, which seems to be a better alternative.[65] None of these words, however, would fill the gap in its entirety. It is possible of course that the supposed gap is quite illusory, but the question cannot be solved decisively without more precise documentation of the text.[66] Nonetheless, it cannot be excluded that the cartouche of Paynudjem I was added to an earlier inscription written possibly on behalf of Herihor, whose prenomen was always written in the form attested by this text. In such a case it can be suggested that undated oCG 25577 found in the Valley of the Kings[67] indeed had a connection with the building or maybe an adaptation of KV 4.[68] The quite exceptional text of the undated oCG 25243,[69] must be also commented in this context in a more detail. It seems to relate to the beginning(?) of the building of the tomb of an unnamed high priest: "Day 14: Piercing of the tomb of the High Priest of [Amun]" (*sd t3 mꜥḥꜥ.t n p3 ḥm-nṯr tpy n* [*Ỉmn*]).[70] The ostracon was found in the Valley of the Kings – in the tomb of Ramesses IX (KV 6) according to G.

---

[62] Cf. Ciccarello, op.cit., 6f. It would be tempting, however, to see in it two different stages of the secondary decoration attempted after the tomb was abandoned during the reign of Ramesses XI, although there is no proof for such a hypothesis. Unfortunately, the peculiarities of the titulary of Paynudjem I, as written here, cannot be satisfactorily explained in this way.

[63] Cf. Ciccarello, op.cit., note 21.

[64] Cf. Wb.II, 325ff. In the texts inscribed on the coffins from the Royal Cache at Deir el-Bahari, Paynudjem's name, written in a cartouche, is always preceded by the title *nsw* (without a determinative), cf. Daressy, Cercueils, 50ff.

[65] As suggested by Ciccarello, op.cit., 8, and note 21. In the texts of the exterior coffin of Paynudjem I the title *Wsir* (without a determinative) often precedes his name (*Wsir nsw P3y-nḏm m3ꜥ-ḫrw*), well in accord with the practice of the royal funerary texts of the New Kingdom.

[66] The sole documentation of the two last columns of the text is provided in: Reeves-Wilkinson, loc.cit.

[67] Černý, Ostraca CG, 51*, pl. 40. As for its dating, cf. ibid., 28; Valbelle, Ouvriers, 346; Häggman, Directing DeM, 356ff. (year 14, most probably of Paynudjem I).

[68] See my comment above (Introduction).

[69] Kitchen, RamInscr VI, 870ff. (A11); VII, 462f. (emendations); Helck OPG, 572f.

[70] For the meaning of the text cf. Černý, Valley of the Kings, 17 n. 8. An alternative rendering would be based on another meaning of the verb *sd*: "to break", "to penetrate", cf. Lesko, Dict. II, 97-99. In such a case, the text in question could be possibly interpreted as referring to the disturbance of the tomb of the high priest.

Daressy.[71] Its provenance, but also the information referring to the Libyans (Meshwesh), who appear frequently in the sources dating to the reign of Ramesses IX, are apparently taken into consideration in dating the ostracon to the reign of this sovereign.[72] In such a case, the tomb which is referred to on the ostracon can be hypothetically identified as the tomb of Ramessesnakht in Dra Abu el-Naga, especially because the term used to describe it (*mꜥḥꜥ.t*) can be applied very well to such a construction but hardly to the royal tomb in the Valley of the Kings.[73] As a matter of fact the text of the ostracon does refer mainly to the works conducted by the crew in the Valley of the Kings (probably on the tomb of the reigning Pharaoh), and the information referring to the tomb of the high priest was just inserted into the sequence of daily dates. Significantly it also means that the workmen of the crew participated in the work on the tomb of the high priest located probably outside the royal necropolis,[74] although the character and duration of their involvement cannot be inferred properly from the text written on the ostracon. A proposed dating of oCG 25243 to the reign of Ramesses XI[75] opens a new perspective for the meaning of this interesting text in the context of a discussion on the location of the tomb of the High Priest Amenhotep, but also in regard to the unknown tomb of his brother Nesamun. So one of them could be a very good candidate for the owner of the tomb related to in the text of the ostracon.[76]

The original burial place of Paynudjem I himself is still an open question too.[77] Although his attempted usurpation of KV 4 seems to be widely accepted,

[71] Daressy, Ostraca, 62. It must be remembered, however, that information provided by Daressy regarding the provenance of the ostraca is not reliable, cf. Keller, in: DeM et la Vallée des Rois, 101 n. 21.

[72] Cf. Valbelle, Ouvriers, 92, 214 n. 6 (number given wrongly); Wimmer, Hieratische Paläographie I, 38f.; similarly Haring, in: Village Voices, 76.

[73] See A. Piccato, A Ramsesnakht Limestone Ostrakon, in: D. Polz et al., MDAIK 55, 1999, 365-70, figs.11-12, pl. 59. For the meaning of the term, cf. e.g. Černý, Community, 14; Bogoslovsky, *Drevne-Egipetskie Mastera*, 257ff.; Valbelle, Ouvriers, 287; G. Lapp, MDAIK 50, 1994, 242.

[74] For a probable location of the tombs of the High Priest Ramessesnakht and his son Amenhotep in the necropolis of Dra Abu el-Naga, see now Polz, SAK 25, 1998, 257ff.; U. Rummel, Grab oder Tempel? Die funeräre Anlage des Hohenpriesters des Amun Amenophis in Dra' Abu el-Naga (Theben-West), in: D. Kessler et al. (eds.), Texte – Theben – Tonfragmente. Festschrift für G. Burkard, [ÄAT 76], Wiesbaden 2009, 348-60.

[75] See Helck OPG, 557, 572f. Such a dating of the ostracon finds a strong support in the name of the Madjoy Anher[tore] (vo. 15), whose office is attested as late as Year 12 of Ramesses XI, cf. Černý, Community, 271 (no. 6). For the dating of the ostracon see also Chapter 4 above.

[76] Cf. also Lull, Los sumos sacerdotes, 47, 61 (Amenhotep; Payankh and Herihor are not excluded either); Römer, Gottes- und Priesterherrschaft, 36 (Herihor or Amenhotep).

[77] See however the hypothesis presented by Reeves, Valley of the Kings, 255 – about the transfer of his mummy from the tomb of Inhapy, which according to him was his original place of burial. On the other hand, the intense activity of the necropolis staff in the area of the Royal Cache in TT 320 during

it cannot be excluded that the idea was finally abandoned.[78] As a consequence, the curious text from KV 4 was tentatively interpreted as commemoration of Paynudjem I's activity in restoration of the royal burials in the Valley of the Kings.[79] As a matter of fact, the diversity of objects left in the tomb must lead to the conclusion that the tomb had functioned as a workshop or atellier for those who prepared the reburials of the royal mummies.[80] A moot question, however, is the earlier history of the tomb and its possible connection with the burial of the High Priest Herihor in particular. Virtually nothing is known about the actual place of burial of Herihor.[81] Thus only a working hypothesis can be postulated here in view of the scanty data commented above: KV 4 would be quite a convenient place for a burial of Herihor, being a direct "successor" of Ramesses XI. No doubt, the idea was finally abandoned, and the tomb was reused as a laboratory or workshop for those who participated in the arduous task of preserving the royal mummies of the past.

---

the pontificate of Paynudjem I, when Butehamun was acting as the scribe of the necropolis (cf. Bouvier-Bouvier, L'activité des gens, 25f., figs. 5, 7.2), may possibly suggest that some important work was conducted there already at such an early date – anyway, two interpretations must be taken into consideration: an early transfer of the royal mummies (or a group of them), or else the preparation of the burial for one of the members of the high priest's family (not excluding the high priest himself?); both explanations, however, are in apparent contradiction with the chronology of the cache proposed by N. Reeves, E. Graefe, and A. Niwiński. A new graffito of Butehamun and his son Ankhefenamun, found recently directly above the shaft of TT 320, would in fact suggest such an early date of its rebuilding or adaptation (for whatever purpose), cf. A. Niwiński et al., in: Polish Archaeology in Mediterranean 12, 2001, 228, 234, fig. 7. As regards the earlier history of the place, and arguments supporting identification of the cache with the tomb of Inhapy, see now Jansen-Winkeln, in: DeM in the Third Millennium, 163ff. (esp. p. 167); compare also S. Rzepka, Graffiti of Nubkheperre Intef in Deir el-Bahari, MDAIK 60, 2004, 149-158.

[78] Cf. e.g. M. Ciccarello, J. Romer, A Preliminary Report of the Recent Work in the Tombs of Ramesses X and XI in the Valley of the Kings, Brooklyn 1979, 10; Reeves, Valley of the Kings, 123; Peden, Graffiti, 245 n. 749.; Häggman, Directing DeM, 219.

[79] Cf. Ciccarello, op.cit., 3, 24.

[80] M. Ciccarello, J. Romer, op.cit., 9; M. Ciccarello, Five Late-Ramesside Lost-Contour Alabaster Ushebties in the Tomb of Ramesses XI, Brooklyn 1979; Reeves, Valley of the Kings, 123. See, however, some doubts concerning this, raised by Eaton-Krauss, BiOr 49, 1992, 712.

[81] For various approaches to the problem of its location, see Černý, Valley of the Kings, 2; Peden, Graffiti, 232-234; id., in: Ch. Lilyquist, The Tomb of Three Foreign Wives of Tuthmosis III, New York 2003, 10; and Niwiński, in: Z. Hawass (ed.), Egyptology at the Dawn of the Twenty-first Century, II, Cairo 2002, 416ff. For the objects tentatively connected with his burial, see H.W. Müller, Goldschmuck und ein Fayencekelch aus dem Grabe des Herihor (?), in: Pantheon. Internationale Zeitschrift für Kunst, no. 3, 1979, 237-247; Egberts, ZÄS 125, 1998, 95 n. 23; Jansen-Winkeln, InschrSp I, 4 (3). According to Reeves (Valley of the Kings, 255) the original place of burial of his wife Nodjmet was possibly in Bab el-Muallaq (WN A) in the "Vallée de l'Aigle", supposed to be the tomb of Inhapy. Recent research carried out in the tomb does not support nor contradict the idea that this was the tomb of Inhapy, or its function as a transitional cachette of the royal mummies, cf. L. Gabolde et al., BIFAO 94, 1994, 175, 228, 230f.

Remnants of the original blocking (plaster fragments with seal impressions) in the tomb of Ramesses XI (KV 4) have been reported by J. Romer,[82] and this observation has an important significance for the history of the tomb in question. First of all, it suggests that the tomb was sealed in antiquity, probably in connection with the burial of one of the persons enumerated above (or else in connection with secondary burials of the Third Intermediate Period).[83] If it was Paynudjem I who instigated the work on "restoration" of the royal burials inside KV 4, it is hardly imaginable that he would decide to adapt the tomb for his own burial, if the tomb had been used earlier[84] as a mere "workshop" for the necropolis workmen.

The final place of the burial of Paynudjem I is unknown. No doubt, however, he was buried in the Theban area, as the remnants of his funerary equipment finally found their way into TT 320. It is important to note that he was buried as a king, and not as the high-priest.[85] It is a matter of conjecture what was the bearing of his "kingly" status on the operations undertaken by the necropolis staff in relation to the reburials of the royal mummies of the New Kingdom. It cannot be excluded that adoption of the royal titles by Paynudjem I resulted in an expression in his reign of the traditional piety shown to the royal ancestors or predecessors. Certainly the same holds true in regard to the pontificate and kingship of Herihor. As a matter of fact, at least two distinct major phases of dismantling and final evacuation of the royal necropolis in the Valley of the Kings can be discerned in the sources contemporary with the pontificates of Herihor and subsequently that of Paynudjem I. In both cases, the very peak of the activity may be related to the period of their kingship. Supposedly all these operations were undertaken with the aim of protecting the mummies of

[82] Cf. J. Romer, Valley of the Kings, London 1981, 260; Reeves, Valley of the Kings, 81 n. 17.

[83] Cf. Reeves, Valley of the Kings, 121, as regards the secondary burial dating to the 22 dyn. As for the secondary burials in the Valley of the Kings in general, cf. Ciccarello, Romer, op.cit., 2; Taylor, Valley of the Kings in the Third Intermediate Period, 200.

[84] It must be noted, however, that there are no means to date operations conducted in the tomb, which resulted in the abandonment of the remnants connected with older royal burials. And it is only Paynudjem's cartouche on the left wall of the entrance corridor which provides the latest possible point of reference. Having in mind the character of the evidence, a later date within the 21st Dynasty cannot be definitely excluded.

[85] Wente, JNES 26, 1967, 168; von Beckerath, RdE 20, 1968, 28. It is worth noting, however, that no royal insignia were placed on his reused coffins, except an uraeus on the exterior coffin, being perhaps a remnant of its original decoration dating to the Tuthmoside period. Anyway, the amulets held in the hands on the covers of both coffins are distinctly non-royal elements of their decoration, cf. Daressy, Cercueils, pls. 28f., 32. For a suggestion that the inner coffin was originally made for Paynudjem I, cf. G. Robins, GM 45, 1981, 65.

the royal ancestors, but other purposes can be discerned as well. Butehamun as the scribe of the royal necropolis certainly participated in all these actions. He was possibly a young man when the works under the auspices of Herihor were conducted in the Valley of the Kings subsequent to the depredations of the period of the civil war. And these resulted in the inspection of the tomb of Horemheb (KV 57) in years 4 and 6 of the Renaissance Era. The existence of another "transitional" cache of the royal mummies in the tomb, as suggested by N. Reeves,[86] cannot be proven convincingly because of the exceedingly poor state of preservation of the objects found inside the tomb.[87] If this was the case, however, one would imagine that it had been organized as one of the earliest hiding places in the very heart of the Valley of the Kings.

If these "early" actions undertaken on behalf of the High Priest Herihor could have been a direct response to the destruction caused by the robbers in the preceding period of the civil war, such a simple explanation does not fit the situation prevailing in the later periods. The complex history of the dismantling of the royal necropolis in the Valley of the Kings is far from being understood properly. First of all the reasons of the consecutive reburials of the royal mummies should be ascertained, since it seems virtually impossible that they were always the result and consequence of a repeating series of robberies. Once the mummies had been desecrated and robbed, the necessity of restoring what had escaped the destruction seems to be inevitable, but also the religious significance of such an attitude towards the remains of the Pharaohs of the past cannot be overlooked. The fate of the objects of the original equipment of the royal tombs is quite a different matter, because precious objects were no doubt appropriated or else reused; this does not necessarily mean that a "state" plundering of the royal tombs, as has been postulated recently, had really occurred. Last but not least, we can imagine that preparations for the burials of Herihor, Payankh, and Paynudjem I heavily influenced the ongoing activities of the necropolis staff, engaged necessarily in searching for an appropriate place of the pontiffs' burials. Although the tombs of the high priests in question have not been located until now, it is possible that they were at least partly equipped with some reused objects originating from the older royal tombs, as a result of the "salvage" actions undertaken by them.

[86] According to Reeves (Valley of the Kings, 77ff., 246, 259) besides the mummy of Horemheb, the mummy of Ay could also have been cached there.
[87] For the summary description, see ibid., 75ff.; Thomas, Royal Necropoleis, 95f.

The final decision to abandon the royal tombs in the Valley of the Kings and to evacuate the burials was certainly the most important factor in the history of the royal necropolis in this period. As a direct consequence of this decision the caches of the royal mummies were organized in the Valley itself and later on in the region of Deir el-Bahari (possibly also in other regions of the Theban necropolis).[88]

It seems that the first attempts aimed at grouping together some of the disturbed mummies was made in selected tombs in the Valley of the Kings. The existence of a royal cache in the tomb of Sethnakht (KV 14) is still a matter of conjecture, as is also the case regarding the supposed cache in the tomb of Horemheb (see above). The existence of a provisional cache in the tomb of Seti I (KV 17) may be dated securely to the later period, namely the pontificate of Paynudjem I, when the mummy of Ramesses II was reburried in (or transferred to) the tomb of Seti I.[89] The earlier hieratic dockets on the coffins of Seti I, and Ramesses II,[90] dated plausibly to the pontificate of Herihor and therefore to the Renaissance Era,[91] refer only to a renewal of the burials of both kings (presumably in their own tombs), according to the formulation preserved in the former text.

N. Reeves' suggestion that subsequently the royal mummies were withdrawn from the cache in the tomb of Sethnakht to another hiding place in the tomb of Amenhotep II in the Valley of the Kings (KV 35), seems to be plausible although not wholly corroborated by the pertinent sources. Anyway, it seems that the latter cache was established in the period of pontificate of Paynudjem I, thus at the height of Butehamun's activity as the necropolis

[88] This is not only the case of a supposed cache in a tomb in "Vallée de l'Aigle" (Wadi en-Nasr), but there were also smaller caches destined for other members of the royalty, as for example that commented in: A. Dodson, J.J. Janssen, JEA 75, 1989, 125-138; supposed to be a cache from the reign of Psusennes I. For an alternative interpretation of the cache, as a collective tomb dating to the 18th Dynasty (the reign of Amenhotep III), see now G. Bouvier, Les Princesses de Gourna, in: D. Kessler et al. (eds.), Texte – Theben – Tonfragmente. Festschrift für G. Burkard, [ÄAT 76], Wiesbaden 2009, 59-69.

[89] On the basis of the linen docket from the mummy of Ramesses II dated to year 15, III *akhet* 6, cf. Maspero, Momies royales, 560, fig. 18; Jansen-Winkeln, InschrSp I, 22f. (3.36); cf. Kitchen TIP, 419 (no. 26); Reeves, Valley of the Kings, 229, 235 (no. 22); Römer, Gottes- und Priesterherrschaft, 560 (29). For the meaning of the text, see a comment by Reeves, Valley of the Kings, 229; Gardiner, JEA 37, 1951, 112 n. 1; Thomas, Royal Necropoleis, 256; cf. also A. Leahy, An unusual spelling of *ḳrśt*, GM 31, 1979, 67-72 (based on later texts).

[90] For references, see above.

[91] Against referring them to the reign of Smendes, cf. von Beckerath, Chronologie der XXI. Dynastie, 51. For a contrary view, see now Jansen-Winkeln, ZÄS 119, 1992, 26; id., in: Ancient Egyptian Chronology, 229; Demidoff, Retour sur une controverse, 100, 102f., 111. A dating of the dockets to year 6 of Ramesses XI (cf. Vandersleyen, L'Égypte II, 651) is obviously out of the question.

scribe. The relatively early date of the cache in the tomb of Amenhotep II may be deduced mainly from the style of the anthropoid coffins in which the royal mummies were placed. In sharp contrast to the material found in the royal cache at Deir el-Bahari, the mummies were deposited not only in the remnants of original royal coffins but also in the reused coffins of non-royalty;[92] the latter of very poor quality and relatively early in date. Most of the coffins can be dated to the Ramesside period, one at least to the 18th Dynasty, but no example datable to the 21st Dynasty has been found in the tomb.[93] In addition the cache in KV 35 is thoroughly different from the character of that in TT 320. This is manifest in the following features:

(1) KV 35 had not been used as a tomb for the high priests and their families;

(2) in KV 35 the cache proper comprised only one or two side chambers of the original tomb – Jb (with the bulk of the mummies), and Jc, the latter with only three uncoffined mummies;

(3) in KV 35 virtually no objects of the funerary equipment of the original burials were transferred into the tomb together with the mummies;[94]

(4) an overall impression of the poverty was strongly emphasized by the apparent disorder in the arrangement of the mummies found in the KV 35 cache.

As regards the date of the creation of the KV 35 cache, the inscriptional evidence may be taken into account, although it is far from being complete. The unpublished hieratic docket written on the shroud of the mummy, described in antiquity as that of Amenhotep III,[95] is dated to year 12 (or 13?), III *peret* 6, and mentions the renewal of the burial (*wḥm ḳrs*) of "king Nebmaatre, l.p.h." by the High Priest Paynudjem I.[96] Though the reading of

92 Cf. Daressy, Cercueils, 242f. (CG nos. 61035-61044).

93 Cf. Wente, JNES 31, 1972, 139; compare also Daressy, loc.cit.

94 Cf. Reeves, Valley of the Kings, 198, 223 (n. 151).

95 In the coffin docket giving the name of "Nebmaatre-Amenhotep, l.p.h.", cf. Daressy, Cercueils, 218, pl. 61; Smith, Royal Mummies, pl. 31; Reeves, Valley of the Kings, 198, 232 (7), 245. As regards arguments against such an identification, see Reeves, op.cit., 226; J.E. Harris, The Mummy of Amenhotep III, in: E. Teeter, A.J. Larson (eds.), Gold of Praise. Studies on Ancient Egypt in Honor of E.F. Wente, [SAOC 58], Chicago 1999, 163ff.; for contrary conclusions based on the analysis of DNA material, see now Z. Hawass et al., Ancestry and Pathology in King Tutankhamun's Family, in: Journal of American Medical Association, Feb. 17, 2010 – vol. 303, no. 7, 638ff.

96 Cf. V. Loret, Le tombeau d'Aménophis II et la cachette royale de Biban-el-Molouk, BIE (3 ser.) 9, 1898, 109; Smith, Royal Mummies, pls. 32, 100-103 (photographs illegible); Thomas, Royal Necropoleis, 250 (no. 13a) – providing a tentative translation made by E.F. Wente; see also Kitchen TIP, 418 (no. 22); Ciccarello, Graffito of Pinutem I, doc.9; Reeves, Valley of the Kings, 226, 235 (no.

the date of the inscription is actually doubtful, its relation to the fragmentarily preserved graffito of an unspecified year 13 written on the rough wall blocking up the entrance to chamber Jb in the tomb of Amenhotep II,[97] cannot be denied. It must be noted, however, that there is no certainty that the wall in question, as found by V. Loret,[98] was a remnant of the original blocking of the chamber in question. It has been suggested indeed that the blocks reused in it might have been transferred from the wall closing the tomb entrance or more probably the sarcophagus chamber itself.[99] As a matter of fact, having in mind the chaotic arrangement of the preserved fragments of the hieratic inscription written on it, the blocks were evidently misplaced due to dismantling of the original wall and its subsequent partial rebuilding – in the same place, or less possibly perhaps, the blocks were transferred from another place in the tomb to be reused here. As a consequence it can be assumed that the inscription dated to year 13 was written after the closing of the tomb (or the side chamber) by the investigating party soon afterwards or possibly at the same time when the mummy of Amenhotep III (or the mummy supposed to be his) had been rewrapped. But this evidently was not the final closing of the cache,[100] which had been entered again at a later unspecified date, although the purpose of this remains completely unknown.[101] The dates in question are commonly interpreted as those of the Tanite king Smendes,[102] and this would provide a convenient point of departure for our study on the activity of the necropolis staff at the period of the pontificate of Paynudjem I (with the dates

18); Jansen-Winkeln, InschrSp I, 22 (no. 3.34).

[97] Cf. Ch.C. van Siclen III, JEA 60, 1974, 129-133, fig. 2; see also Thomas, Royal Necropoleis, 250f. (no. 13b); Reeves, Valley of the Kings, 235 (no. 21).

[98] Cf. Loret, BIE (3 ser.) 9, 1898, 109, pl. 15. V. Loret dismantled five uppermost layers of the blocking wall of the chamber Jb, cf. Thomas, Royal Necropoleis, 250f.; van Siclen, JEA 60, 1974, 129f., fig. 3; compare a modern photograph in: J. Romer, Valley of the Kings, London 1981, fig. opposite p. 117.

[99] See van Siclen, JEA 60, 1974, 133 – with a comment on the original seal impressions made "in a white plaster which was affixed to the sides of several of the blocks", cf. ibid., 130, 131-3.

[100] Cf. van Siclen III, JEA 60, 1974, 131.

[101] It cannot be established when the three mummies deposited in chamber Jc were introduced into the cache. The mummies identified now as that of queen Tiye (despite objections put forward by R. Germer, SAK 11, 1984, 85-90), the unnamed mother of Tutankhamun (so according to the recent research; cf. Z. Hawass et al., op.cit., 640f.), and the mummy of an anonymous boy, were simply laid out on the floor of the chamber without any coffins protecting them, cf. Loret, BIE (3 ser.) 9, 1898, 103f., pl. 11; compare Romer, op.cit., fig. on p. 162. This part of the cache has a conspicuously different character. The same is also true in regard of an anonymous mummy (of Sethnakht?) deposited in the boat found in the antechamber, cf. ibid., 100f., pl. 9.

[102] Cf. e.g. Wente, loc.cit. (he pointed out that there were no mummies dating to the 21st Dynasty or later, in the cache).

referring presumably to the reign of Smendes). It does not settle the question of the date of the establishment of the royal cache in the tomb of Amenhotep II. Available evidence seems to suggest that N. Reeves is right while assuming that the royal mummies had been cached there some time after the inspection of year 13 (of Smendes?).[103]

Ostracon CG 25575[104] is one of the documents which can be connected with the activity of the crew in relation to salvaging and protection of the mortal remains of the pharaohs. It was found in the entrance to the tomb of Siptah (KV 47), at the beginning of the passage dug in the filling of the entrance corridor.[105] The document is dated to year 7, II *akhet* 1, and refers to "ascending (*ṯsy*) of the crew to complete the work at that place" (l. 1-2).[106] Although not explicitly stated what kind of work had been done, the ostracon was possibly left by those who dug out the filling of the corridor (in its upper part) to obtain access to the inner parts of the tomb. N. Reeves plausibly suggested that the operation in question was that of removing the mummy of Siptah from the tomb, and its transfer to the "transitional" cache in the tomb of Sethnakht (KV 14).[107] No doubt the scenario of the events proposed by Reeves fits very well the available evidence, but no exact dates can be attached to this activity. The list of 35 names of the workmen who participated in the work provides exceptionally precious data as regards the number and composition of the crew at this particular period. Most of the workmen enumerated here are also known from other ostraca,[108] and graffiti dating to the late 20th and the early 21st Dynasty.[109] Nonetheless, at present there is no agreement as regards the more precise dating of the piece. Certainly a date for the ostracon as early as year 7 of Ramesses XI[110] cannot withstand criticism, and a dating to the Renaissance Era or else to the reign of Smendes and pontificate of

[103] Cf. Reeves, Valley of the Kings, 197ff., 259 (tab. 11); similarly Eaton-Krauss, BiOr 49, 1992, 714.

[104] Černý, Ostraca CG, 27, 50*, pl. 39.

[105] Cf. Reeves, Valley of the Kings, 107, fig. 34.

[106] Cf. Janssen, Village Varia, 96; Reeves, op.cit., 107.

[107] Reeves, op.cit., 107, 248, 259 (tab. 11). According to Reeves it was transferred later to the cache in the tomb of Amenhotep II (KV 35) "at an as yet undetermined date after Year 13 of Smendes" (ibid., 248). It cannot be excluded, however, that the mummy of Siptah was transferred to the cache in KV 35 directly from his own tomb (KV 47); in such a case oCG 25575 would be dated to a later period than surmised by Reeves, most probably to the period of pontificate of Paynudjem I, which fits better onomastic data contained in it.

[108] These are mostly unpublished ostraca prepared now for publication by R.J. Demarée.

[109] Such a dating of oCG 25575 has been proposed by Černý, Ostraca, 27.

[110] See Janssen, loc.cit.

Paynudjem I currently prevails.[111] Strangely enough, the name of the scribe Butehamun does not appear among the persons enumerated here, although we know that he belonged to this very generation of the necropolis staff engaged in the operations conducted in the Valley of the Kings.

The extensive activity of Butehamun during the pontificate of the High Priest Paynudjem I is explicitly documented by a number of the Theban graffiti, some of them mentioning the name of the high priest himself.[112] The scale of this activity is demonstrated by the fact, that his graffiti were left in every region of the Theban necropolis, including its most distant parts.[113] Their chronological position cannot be understood properly without a more general comment on the chronology of the pontificate and alleged kingship of Paynudjem I.[114] If the datation system of the Renaissance Era can be connected with Ramesses XI, then its existence still after the death of the king would be quite illusory. As a consequence, the latest date of the Renaissance Era can be placed securely within the chronological framework of the reign of Ramesses XI. The latest document dated explicitly according to the Era is LRL no. 9, and other related letters (of the "core group"), dated convincingly to its year 10.[115] Consequently this means that it is inevitable that a new system of dating documents in the Thebaid appeared after the death of Ramesses XI. One can imagine that at that time an attempt was made to introduce a new

[111] Cf. Valbelle, Ouvriers, 346; Peden, Decline of Textual Graffiti, 290 n. 25; Häggman, Directing DeM, 356f.

[112] For enumeration of sources, see Lull, Los sumos sacerdotes, 153ff.

[113] Cf. e.g. Niwiński, SAK 11, 1984, 150 n. 55; Peden, Graffiti, 258ff.

[114] Quite possibly, as has been suggested, his "kingship" may be discussed only in the context of his sovereignty in Upper Egypt (cf. e.g. von Beckerath, RdE 20, 1968, 28f.). A supposed coregency with his son, the Tanite king Psusennes I, or some kind of recognition of his royal status in the North seems to be a mere speculation; cf. P. Montet, La nécropole royale de Tanis II: Les constructions et le tombeau de Psusennès à Tanis, Paris 1951, 182f.; id., BSFE 6, 1951, 29f.; Young, JARCE 2, 1963, 103; Kitchen TIP, 262. For the contrary view, see Kees, Hohenpriester, 27f.; Hornung, Untersuchungen, 102; id., OLZ 61, 1966, 440. Conspicuously Paynudjem I was not included in the lists of the kings of the Tanite dynasty, as compiled by Manetho, cf. W.G. Waddell, Manetho with an English Translation, [The Loeb Classical Library], Cambridge Mass. – London 1964, 154-157; von Beckerath, Chronologie, 62ff.; there are no grounds either to count him among "12 kings of Diospolis" (i.e. the 20th Dyn.), as suggested by Thijs, GM 211, 2006, 83. His royal titulary on two blocks from an unknown edifice in Tanis may be explained perhaps as a part of a filiation of an unknown person connected with the royal court in Tanis (?). Of no significance in regard of this is the goblet with the name of the High Priest Paynudjem I, found in the tomb of Psusennes I in Tanis, cf. Montet, La nécropole royale de Tanis II, pl. 70 (upper); Römer, Gottes- und Priesterherrschaft, 564 (no. 39); Yoyotte, in: Tanis. L'or des pharaons, 65.

[115] Higher dates cannot be decisively attributed to this Era, cf. e.g. Krauss, Sothis- und Monddaten, 164 (in regard to the dates in Butehamun's graffiti). This is also the case of the high dates which are the results of the chronological systems proposed by A. Thijs (see Chapter 1), and Demidoff, GM 177, 2000, 96ff.

system, referring either to the regnal years of the direct successor of Ramesses XI in Tanis (i.e. Smendes), or to the "kingship" of Herihor, if he outlived the last of the Ramessides. If one can accept the idea presented above, that the "kingship" of Herihor might have ended later than admitted hitherto, then we would arrive to the conclusion that his hypothetical "regnal" years formed a basis for the new dating system in Upper Egypt, and those of Smendes respectively in the North. Unfortunately, as stated above, there are no documents datable to the period of "kingship" of Herihor, and this is a weak point of such a hypothesis.[116] After Herihor's demise, it was possibly the regnal years of Smendes which were referred to in the documents written in Thebes. It seems unimaginable, that Payankh (if actually officiating independently after Herihor), and his son Paynudjem I (still only the high priest), ever introduced their own dating systems (see however below).

There are no dates which can be proved beyond any doubt referring to the recognition in Thebes and Upper Egypt of the reign of Psusennes I.[117] A similar situation occurs in the reign of Smendes, though his presence or recognition in Thebes may be evidenced by at least two documents (certainly their number is meagre in relation to the long reign of the king). The most important evidence is provided by the Dababieh stela.[118] Although undated, it is important testimony of activity on behalf of Smendes in Gebelein and in the region to the south of Thebes in particular, after a disastrous Nile flood.[119] An inscription of Smendes in the temple of Montu in Karnak[120] is

[116] A possible explanation would be perhaps the relatively short period of his independent rule in the Thebaid.

[117] See Jansen-Winkeln, InschrSp I, 61; there are doubts about the meaning of a vague reference to "a copy of the register of Pharaoh Psusennes, the great god, (issued) in Year 19", on the stela from Dakhla oasis, dating to the reign of Sheshonq I, cf. A. Gardiner, The Dakhleh Stela, JEA 19, 1933, 22, pl. 6 (line 11); more probably, however, this is a reference to Psusennes II, rather than his earlier namesake; see however Kitchen TIP, 26. Similarly papReinhardt should be dated rather to the reign of Psusennes II or later, cf. S.P. Vleeming, Papyrus Reinhardt. An Egyptian Land List from the Tenth Century B.C., [Hieratische Papyri aus den Staatlichen Museen zu Berlin II], Berlin 1993, 8f.; cf. also Jansen-Winkeln, InschrSp I, 61, 196; M. Römer, GM 200, 2004, 83f.

[118] G. Daressy, Les carrières de Gebelein et le roi Smendès, RT 10, 1888, 133-38; Jansen-Winkeln, InschrSp I, 1-3 (1.3); as regards its location, see also D. and R. Klemm, SAK 7, 1979, 131.

[119] For translation of the text, see BAR IV, 308f.; for a detailed analysis of the text, see now A. Cabrol, Les voies processionelles de Thèbes, [OLA 97], Leuven 2001, 641-646; cf.also Taylor, Horemkenesi, 27 (protection of the Luxor temple?). It is rather doubtful whether the text lends proof to the hypothesis that Smendes visited the southern region in person: *ist ḥm.f sš m sp-snw mi Ḏḥwty* [...] (l. 16); cf. a comment by Cabrol, op.cit., 642f.; the verb *sš/sni* used here is too ambiguous in this context to solve the question properly, cf. Wb IV, 483; Lesko, Dict. II, 79; Junge, Neuägyptisch, 365.

[120] Cf. A. Varille, Karnak[-Nord] I, Cairo 1943, 36, fig. 26, pl. 98 (71); Jansen-Winkeln, InschrSp I, 1 (1.2).

irrefutable testimony in regard of his supposed activity in the Theban area.[121] Such evidence cannot be dismissed in the framework of a discussion of the dating system in the Thebaid in this period. Apparently the sovereignty of the Tanite king was at least temporarily recognised in the Thebaid at this particular moment,[122] probably after the death of Herihor, when the high priest of Amun was Paynudjem I. As a consequence, most of the dated documents from Thebes in the post Renaissance Era may be safely referred to the reign of Smendes.

It must be noted, however, that according to a hypothesis put forward recently by K. Jansen-Winkeln, the year dates referred to in most of the Theban documents of this epoch refer to the high priests of Amun – Herihor, Paynudjem I, and later on Menkheperre.[123] Thus the ample series of graffiti and coffin/mummy dockets referring to the activity of the necropolis staff, and Butehamun in particular, can be attributed either to the regnal years of Tanite king Smendes (according to the traditional view),[124] or else to the pontificate/kingship of Paynudjem I,[125] provided that the latter counted his years from the beginning of the pontificate (thus K. Jansen-Winkeln), and not from the moment of the assumption of the "kingship" by himself. The question of the dating system in the Thebaid during the 21st Dynasty cannot be solved satisfactorily in the present state of our knowledge about the sources relating to this period.

Butehamun's titles making him the man "who opens the doors (in) the necropolis (*r-st3w*)" (coffin Brussels E.5288), and "who opens the doors in the hidden underworld (*dw3t imn*)" (coffin Turin CGT 10102.b),[126] are certainly quite exceptional among those borne by the officials of the Theban necropo-

[121] Significantly there are no references to Smendes in the temple of Khonsu (cf. Thijs, GM 211, 2006, 86), which was the most important Theban monument in this epoch.

[122] Contra Jansen-Winkeln, ZÄS 119, 1992, 34f.; Thijs, GM 211, 2006, 87 n. 41.

[123] Jansen-Winkeln, Relative Chronology of Dyn. 21, in: Ancient Egyptian Chronology, 218ff. (esp. 230ff.); id., ZÄS 119, 1992, 34ff.; cf. also id., InschrSp I, XXXIV and n. 15. See, however, a critical comments against such a hypothesis made recently by Goldberg, GM 174, 2000, 53ff.; Niwiński, JEA 94, 2008, 317ff.; von Beckerath, Chronologie der XXI. Dynastie, 49ff.; id., Chronologie, 67; Kitchen, in: Libyan Period in Egypt, 191f. (§75).

[124] For the sequence of dates, see Kitchen TIP, 417ff.

[125] For the sequence of dates, see Jansen-Winkeln, InschrSp I, 286.

[126] Cf. Jansen-Winkeln, InschrSp I, 41; Niwiński, Sarcofagi della XXI dinastia (CGT 10101-10122), [Catalogo del Museo Egizio di Torino, serie seconda, vol. IX], Turin 2004, 157 (22b); id., SAK 11, 1984, 138. The latter wrongly interpreted both by Niwiński (Sarcofagi, 46) and Guérin (in: Égypte, Afrique & Orient 48, 2007-2008, 24).

lis.[127] The meaning of the titles may be related perhaps to his participation in the evacuation of the royal burials in the Valley of the Kings.[128] Obviously, the famous representation painted on the cover of Butehamun's exterior coffin in Turin (CGT 10101)[129] cannot be taken literally as an irrefutable argument for his participation in the reburial of a group of some members of the Ahmoside family. He was represented here as burning incense, pouring out a libation, and presenting offerings to Amenhotep I, queen Ahhotep (I or II?), queen Ahmose Nefertari, princess Satamun, queen (Ahmose) Meritamun, and king's son (Ahmose) Sapair. Similarly in the inscriptions of the doorjambs from his father's house in Medinet Habu we can read the names of Ahhotep, Ahmose Nefertari and Amenhotep I.[130] Probably no significance should be attached to the fact that the cartouches of Amenhotep I were written on the columns of Butehamun in his house in Medinet Habu,[131] as this may be interpreted simply as an act of devotion to the royal patron of the necropolis. Anyway, it cannot be excluded that it is a mere coincidence that some members of the Ahmoside family were venerated in this way by Butehamun. This would be well in accord with the customs observed in Deir el-Medina – the most explicit example is a scene from the tomb of Anherkhau (TT 359), depicting a row of kings and other members of the royal family, adored by the tomb owner and his wife.[132] Even less significance can be attached to the opening words of the Opening of the Mouth ritual from the mummy-cover of Butehamun (Turin CGT 10103=Cat. 2237), as this can be rather connected with this particular redaction of this version of the ritual[133] which is strongly

[127] And this fact alone provides a solid basis to postulate that the coffin from Brussels was made for Butehamun – a well known personality from the end of the 20th and the beginning of the 21st Dynasty, despite the reservations presented by A. Niwiński (see below). For an unknown reason the coffin was possibly discarded by him, and subsequently reused by an anonymous person; for the comment see Niwiński, SAK 11, 1984, 141; Guérin, op.cit., 20.

[128] Cf. Reeves-Wilkinson, The Complete Valley of the Kings, 205.

[129] Niwiński, Sarcofagi della XXI dinastia, pl. 1; see also Reeves-Wilkinson, loc. cit.

[130] G. Daressy, RT 20, 1898, 75f.; Kitchen, RamInscr VI, 876f.

[131] Cf. PM I/2^2, 773; Černý, BIFAO 27, 1927, 203 (no. 84); Kitchen, RamInscr VII, 401-403.

[132] For this and other examples from the Theban necropolis, see D.B. Redford, Pharaonic King-lists, Annals and Day-books. A Contribution to the Study of Egyptian Sense of History, Toronto 1986, 45ff. According to Redford all these signs of piety can be connected with the cult of the deified Amenhotep I and the royal ancestors in general (cf. e.g. ibid., 38f., 45, 52, 53). One interesting observation should be also made here: the presence of the members of the family of Amenhotep I in this context can be possibly explained by the presence of their cult statues kept in the shrines of Amenhotep I (ibid., 54).

[133] Copied possibly by Butehamun himself, see Guérin, op.cit., 25.

dependent on the Opening of the Mouth ritual of Amenhotep I.[134] It cannot be excluded, however, that the representation of some members of the royal family on Butehamun's coffin has some real meaning in relation to the activities undertaken by him at the very peak of his career.

It is interesting to note that mummies of all the persons represented on the lid of the coffin in Turin were found in the royal cache at Deir el-Bahari (TT 320). There are good reasons to suppose that they were rewrapped approximately at the same time, as suggested by the external linen and coffin dockets (of Reeves' type "A"), written on some of them in the same handwriting and according to a similar scheme.[135] In addition, dated hieratic linen dockets (of Reeves' type "B") were found on the mummies of princess Ahmose Satkamose, prince Siamun and king Ahmose, and these too are written decisively in a similar handwriting.[136] The years 7 and 8 mentioned in them can be referred possibly to the reign of Psusennes I (according to the "traditional" chronological system)[137] or else to the pontificate/kingship of Paynudjem I.[138] If the hypothesis of Butehamun's assistance in these operations is upheld, then a relatively early date within the pontificate/kingship of Paynudjem I emerges as more plausible. In the light of the above reasoning, all the doubts disappear as regards the date of the docket written on the mummy of king Ahmose, being reburied (*rdi.t Wsir*) in year 8, III *peret* 29, by "The majesty of King of Upper and Lower Egypt, lord of the Two Lands (Khakheperre-Setepenamun)| l.p.h., (Paynudjem-Meriamun)| l.p.h.".[139] This would strongly favour the chronological scheme proposed by K. Jansen-Winkeln for the

---

[134] Cf. E. Otto, Das ägyptische Mundöffnungsritual, [ÄA 3], Wiesbaden 1960, vol. II, 8, 34f., 126, 158. The true meaning of the opening words in the version from the mummy-cover of Butehamun still needs further study (see my translation below).

[135] Cf. Reeves, Valley of the Kings, 232 (with references); of the persons represented on Butehamun's coffin, only the mummy of Ahmose Meritamun, and coffins Satamun and Ahmose Sapair, are described in this particular way, cf. Maspero, Momies royales, 538 (facsimile), 539 (facsimile); Daressy, Cercueils, 9f. (transcription).

[136] See Young, JARCE 2, 1963, 102; von Beckerath, RdE 20, 1969, 31 n. 6. E.F. Wente (JNES 26, 1967, 169) expressed his reservations about such an assumption. For a facsimile of the dockets, see Maspero, Momies royales, 534 (fig. 7), 538 (fig. 9), 541 (fig. 12). The handwriting is distinctly different from that of the dockets of type "A", commented above.

[137] Cf. Kitchen TIP, 420 (nos. 39-41); Reeves, Valley of the Kings, 236 (nos. 28-30).

[138] Cf. Jansen-Winkeln, InschrSp I, 21f. (3.31-33), 286.

[139] Maspero, Momies royales, 534, fig. 7; Jansen-Winkeln, InschrSp I, 22 (3.32); Römer, Gottes- und Priesterherrschaft, 560 (30); cf. also Reeves, op.cit., 236 (no. 29) – Paynudjem's prenomen given wrongly; as regards the royal protocol of Paynudjem I, see Bonhême, Noms royaux, 46ff.; von Beckerath, Königsnamen, 182f.

beginning of the 21st Dynasty, and an independent dating system introduced by the High Priest Paynudjem I.[140]

There is another piece of evidence which could confirm such a hypothesis. This is a short hieratic inscription written on the underside of a wooden pectoral,[141] found with the secondary burial of prince Amenemhat in a desolate cliff tomb in the "Vallée du dernier Mentouhotep" (tomb MMA 1021). The text commemorates the workman Paynedjem, son of the foreman Bakenmut, who apparently participated in the work of rewrapping the prince's mummy. There are good reasons to suppose that reburial of prince Amenemhat was conducted approximately at the same time as other members of the Ahmoside family, and queen Ahmose-Meritamun in particular, being possibly the original owner of the tomb in question, and finally transferred to the royal cache in Deir el-Bahari.[142] If the hypothesis formulated by the present author concerning the original ownership of the tomb MMA 1021, and the sequence of events which led to dismantling this burial, is valid, then we would obtain an additional criterion for a dating of the operations connected with reburials of the members of the Ahmoside family in the cache at Deir el-Bahari, or else perhaps in another transitional hiding place(?).

The workman Paynedjem (II), son of the foreman Bakenmut (I), is scarcely known from the sources of the epoch.[143] A possible reason is his low status, so we should not be astonished that Paynedjem's name is not represented among those mentioned in any of the preserved LRL. Nonetheless he was referred to in the Theban graffito no. 1007 and possibly also in 1259.[144] Significantly the graffito no. 1007, giving the name of "servant (in) the Place of Truth Paynedjem, son of the foreman in the Place of Truth Bakenmut",[145] is located on a large boulder in the "Vallée du dernier Mentouhotep",[146] not far from the

[140] A. Thijs' odd and speculative idea about king Paynudjem I as a different personality than the high priest of that name is excessively influenced by his "short chronology" system and apparent over-interpretation of some alterations of the scenes representing Paynudjem in the Khonsu temple; for this see e.g. Thijs, GM 211, 2006, 81ff.; id., ZÄS 134, 2007, 50ff.; for the alterations in question, see The Temple of Khonsu 2, XVIIIf.

[141] W.C. Hayes, The Scepter of Egypt, II, Cambridge 1959, 420, fig. 268; Kitchen, RamInscr VII, 398, 5-8.

[142] For further arguments, see M. Barwik, The owner of cliff tomb MMA 1021 at Thebes, GM 165, 1998, 13-21.

[143] Davies, Who's Who at DeM, 114. Certainly this is a different person from Paynedjem (I), son of the famous scribe of the necropolis Amennakht (V).

[144] For the problem of the dating of the latter graffito, cf. Davies, op.cit., 114.

[145] Spiegelberg, Graffiti, 84, pl. 113; Kitchen, RamInscr VI, 872, 12.

[146] Félix-Aubriot-Kurz, Plans de position, pl. 80bis.

place where the secondary burial of prince Amenemhat took place. Even more interesting in regard of its dating is graffito no. 1085 in "Vallée de l'Aigle", just below Bab el-Muallaq.[147] Here his name was accompanied by that of Ankhef(enamun), no doubt the well known son of Butehamun, because of the partly preserved title of the *wab*-priest of Amun from the temple in Medinet Habu, which strongly supports such an identification.[148]

If the Paynedjem mentioned in papTurin 1888 (2, 9)[149] is the same person as the workman whose name was written on the back of the pectoral, and in the above mentioned graffiti, then we can draw the conclusion that he was active for ca. 30 years, and cooperated both with Tuthmosis and Butehamun, and subsequently with the latter's son Ankhefenamun (probably in the early stage of the latter's career). He would have started his work in the second decade of the reign of Ramesses XI, thus probably following the foremanship of his grandfather Khonsu on the "right side" of the crew.[150] Subsequently he was documented in the ostraca of the late 20th/early 21st Dynasty,[151] when his father was apparently the foreman. As noted above, the position of Bakenmut in the sequence of foremen of that epoch cannot be established precisely.[152] He is known, however, from LRL no. 1 and LRLC no. III;[153] in both cases he was an addressee (besides Butehamun and other members of the community) of the letters written by the scribe Tuthmosis from Middle Egypt and from Nubia respectively. As demonstrated above (Chapter 6), both letters are convincingly dated to the Renaissance Era, respectively to its early and late years. It is hardly likely that Bakenmut's son Paynedjem was still active during the reign of Psusennes I, thus the dating of this phase of the restoration work in the royal necropolis, when the mummies of prince Amenemhat and Ahmose Meritamun were reburied, should be dated presumably to a slightly earlier period than assumed hitherto.

---

147 Ibid., pls. 55, 57.

148 Cf. Černý, Graffiti, 2, pl. 3.

149 Gardiner RAD, 67,6: he appears here in an entry dated to year 17 of Ramesses XI, II *shemu* 10, alongside the deputy Amenhotep, and the workmen (here called simply craftsmen *ḥmww*) Hori, Kanakht, Iyenashenef, and Pamerenamun; cf. also Helck OPG, 566.

150 Cf. Bierbrier LNK, 30 (chart 8); id., CdE 59, 1984, 206; Valbelle, Ouvriers, tab. X; Davies, Who's Who at DeM, 114, chart 7.

151 For example in an unpublished ostracon from the Polish excavations at Deir el-Bahari (inv. no. F.8958ro.,19); and in oCG 25576, 12: Černý, Ostraca CG, 27f., 50*, pl. 37. As regards a date of the latter, see Valbelle, Ouvriers, 346; Häggman, Directing DeM, 358 n. 2424.

152 See above, Chapters 4 and 6.

153 Černý LRL, 1, 1; Janssen LRLC, 22, pl. 9 (ro. 1).

The same holds true in regard to the period of activity of Butehamun, apparently a contemporary of the workman Paynedjem. If he started his career in the crew at the beginning of the Renaissance Era, being a man about 20 years old, it can be reasonably assumed that he could have reached the age of about 55-60 at his death, provided the latest date relating to his activity is year 13 (of Smendes/Paynudjem I),[154] II *shemu* 27. This is the date of the hieratic docket written on a shroud enveloping the mummy of Ramesses III, from the cache in TT 320, on which we can read: "On this day, the high priest of Amun-Ra, king of the gods, Paynudjem (I) son of the high priest of Amun Payankh, commanded the scribe of the temple (*sš ḥw.t-nṯr*) Shedsukhonsu and the scribe in the Place of Truth Butehamun to "osirify" (*r rdi.t Wsir*) king Usermaatre-Meriamun, l.p.h., being firm and enduring forever".[155] It has been suggested that the restoration of the mummy of Ramesses III and other royal mummies had taken place in the complex in Medinet Habu.[156] A unique piece of evidence which can be related to rewrapping the mummies in the Valley of the Kings itself is graffito no. 1282, written in red above the entrance to anonymous KV 49.[157] It records the deposition in the tomb a large amount of linen on two occasions (I *peret* 25, and III *peret* 5), under the supervision of the scribe Butehamun. Though the year was not noted, a large number of the workmen of the necropolis staff enumerated here are well known from other sources dating to the Renaissance Era and the beginning of the 21st Dynasty.[158] It is worth noting that a visit of Butehamun in the tomb of Ramesses III (KV 11), related possibly to the rewrapping (less possibly removal) of Pharaoh's mummy, is recorded in a graffito written in the

[154] For the position of the date in the sequence of dates of this epoch, see Kitchen TIP, 419 (25); Reeves, Valley of the Kings, 235 (20); and Jansen-Winkeln, InschrSp I, 286. Butehamun's prayer of graffito no. 914 must be dated to the next year (14, II *akhet* 15), contrary to Spiegelberg's transcription (Graffiti, 76; compare pl. 102); followed by Wenig, ZÄS 94, 1967, 137; Kitchen TIP, 419 (24); Peden, Graffiti, 251 n. 785; see however Černý, Community, 373; Davies, SAK 24, 1997, 65 and n. 116; Häggman, Directing DeM, 336.

[155] Maspero, Momies royales, 563f., fig. 19, pl. 17; Jansen-Winkeln, InschrSp I, 22 (3.35); Römer, Götter- und Priesterherrschaft, 559 (28); for the photograph, see also Reeves-Wilkinson, The Complete Valley of the Kings, 203.

[156] Cf. U. Hölscher, The Excavation of Medinet Habu V: Post-Ramessid Remains, [OIP 66], Chicago 1954, 5 (with reference to the objects from the royal tombs, found there); Reeves, Valley of the Kings, 230f.

[157] Černý, Graffiti, pl. 45-45A; Jansen-Winkeln, InschrSp I, 36 (3.63); Reeves, MDAIK 40, 1984, pl. 36a (phot.); cf. id., Valley of the Kings, 169, 230f., 235 (19).

[158] Cf. Černý, Community, 15; Demarée, in: DeM et la Vallée des Rois, 248; Häggman, Directing DeM, 361ff. As regards the dating of graffito no. 1282, see Jansen-Winkeln, InschrSp I, 37 (Paynudjem I or earlier); Bouvier-Bouvier, L'activité des gens, 26 n. 25.

burial chamber.[159] This time he was accompanied by two of his younger sons (Meniunefer and Pakhynetjer), and two other persons.

It is difficult to ascertain more precisely Butehamun's age at the moment of his death and the time when it occurred. His mummy has not been preserved (certainly this cannot be the mummy kept in Brussels, as the method of its mummification is not typical for the mummies of the period).[160] In considering this question, a set of coffins belonging to him must be taken into consideration. An exterior and interior coffin as well as a mummy-cover are kept now in the Egyptian Museum in Turin (CGT nos. 10101-10103).[161] A middle coffin belonging probably to the same person (but apparently not to the same find)[162] is in the collection of Musée du Cinquantenaire in Brussels (inv. no. E.5288).[163]

After the long discussion concerning the identity of the owner of the coffins in Turin and Brussels, the hypothesis put forward by A. Niwiński must now be definitely discarded.[164] His attribution of the coffins to a Butehamun "the Younger" ("C"), being in his opinion a different person from Butehamun "the Elder" ("B"), the person well known from the LRL, depends on two factors: the dating of Butehamun's coffins, and the dating of his graffiti. First of all he dates the funerary set from the Turin collection to the middle of 21st Dynasty (the period of the late pontificate of Menkheperre and that of Paynudjem II).[165] As was rightly observed by S. Guérin, all the coffins of Butehamun's funerary set, including the coffin in Brussels, form a homogeneous entity in regard of the iconographic programme of their decoration, and their dating to the very beginning of the 21st Dynasty cannot be discarded.[166] The extant

[159] Cf. Champollion, Notices Descr. I, 414; Spiegelberg, Graffiti, 93 (III-IV); cf. Reeves, Valley of the Kings, 115, 248f.; McDowell, Village Life, 241f. (no. 194); Peden, Graffiti, 245f.

[160] Cf. Niwiński, SAK 11, 1984, 136, 139; Demichelis, BIFAO 100, 2000, 267 n. 7. For a description of the mummy from Brussels, possibly much later in time, see Niwiński, SAK 11, 1984, 139.

[161] See now: A. Niwiński, Sarcofagi della XXI dinastia (CGT 10101-10122), [Catalogo del Museo Egizio di Torino, serie seconda, vol. IX], Turin 2004, 21-47 (with a full bibliography on the subject), pls. 1-7.

[162] According to Niwiński, it was later reused and not included in the funerary equipment of Butehamun, cf. Niwiński, 21st Dynasty Coffins, 112 (no. 47); id., SAK 11, 1984, 141.

[163] B. Van De Walle, L. Limme, H. De Meulenaere, Musées Royaux d'Art et d'Histoire, la collection égyptienne, les étapes marquantes de son développement, Bruxelles 1980, 11-12; Niwiński, 21st Dynasty Coffins, 112 (no. 47).

[164] For a recent discussion on the subject, see Jansen-Winkeln, GM 139, 1994, 35ff.; Davies, SAK 24, 1997, 49ff.; Kikuchi, GM 160, 1997, 51ff.

[165] Cf. Niwiński, Sarcofagi della XXI dinastia, 45f.; see also id., 21st Dynasty Coffins, 172f. (no. 385).

[166] S. Guérin, Les cercueils du scribe royal de la Tombe Boutehamon. L'art de renaître, in: Égypte, Afrique et Orient 48, 2007/08, 17-28 (esp. pp. 25f.); cf. also Jansen-Winkeln, GM 139, 1994, 37; Davies, SAK 24, 1997, 52f.

epigraphic evidence relating to the scribe of the necropolis Butehamun definitely excludes their dating to the middle 21st Dynasty. Typological assertions cannot be taken as a genuine chronology, if not testified by external epigraphic evidence.

As a matter of fact, A. Niwiński depends perhaps too much on the tentative genealogical investigations of W. Spiegelberg, which can be emended now in many points. This is clearly visible for example, when he connects his Butehamun "C" with the family of the chief workman Neferhotep (cf. graffito no. 999).[167] On the other hand, A. Niwiński observes, the set of titles of the owner of the funerary furniture indicates he was an important person in the administration of the west bank of Thebes and its necropolis.[168] The difference between Butehamun's titulature as documented in extant LRL and on his funerary equipment can be explained more convincingly as reflecting the progress of the career of Butehamun. If his early activity, still during the lifetime of his father Tuthmosis, fell in the late years of the Renaissance Era and the pontificate of Payankh, we can be sure that his independent activity fell within the long pontificate and kingship of Paynudjem I. It is to this later period that most of the actions undertaken in the necropolis, in relation to the inspection and preservation of the royal burials, may be referred.

As regards palaeographic arguments proposed by A. Niwiński in his interpretation of the dated hieratic graffiti, these cannot be accepted in any way as supporting the supposed distinction between his Butehamun "B" and "C".[169] His arguments definitely fail in his attempts to undermine J. Černý's readings and corrections of the transcriptions once made by W. Spiegelberg.[170] This concerns in particular the dates given in graffiti nos. 1286 (of year 10, not 30),[171] 1311 (of year 11, not 31), 1021 (of year 11, not 21), 48 and 51 (both of year 11, not 31). As a consequence there are no such high regnal years in

[167] Niwiński, SAK 11, 1984, 144, 153f. (fig. 3); cf. Spiegelberg, Graffiti, 174 (Stammbaum IV); see also Helck, in: LÄ I (1975), 884-885; for a critical comment, see Davies, SAK 24, 1997, 53f., who rightly observes that the graffito no. 999 (Spiegelberg, Graffiti, 83, pl. 112) comprise at least two different graffiti. Similarly any attempt to connect a hypothetical earlier Butehamun with the family of foreman Nekhemmut (I or VI?), on the basis of the hardly legible graffito no. 318a (Spiegelberg, Graffiti, 28, pl. 37), seems to be a mere speculation as well.

[168] Cf. Niwiński, Sarcofagi della XXI dinastia, 46f.; see also Guérin, op.cit., 24.

[169] Niwiński, SAK 11, 1984, 145ff.; id., in: BSAK 9, 2003, 298f. For a similar untenable view, as regards the dates of the graffiti, see Vandersleyen, L'Égypte II, 650f.

[170] Cf. Černý, Community, 372f.; Jansen-Winkeln, GM 139, 1994, 39f.; Davies, SAK 24, 1997, 54f.

[171] Not connected directly with Butehamun, but rightly commented upon by Niwiński in this context (SAK 11, 1984, 145 n. 47).

the graffiti connected with Butehamun. The existence therefore of Niwiński's Butehamun "C", supposed to have been living during the pontificate of Paynudjem II on the basis of such late dates, again appears to be unacceptable.

Similarly an attempt to recognize different handwriting in the graffiti mentioning the name of Butehamun, on the basis of the writing of the hieratic form of sign *w*, is not conclusive proof of the need to make a distinction between two persons of that name. There can be no doubt, that the graffiti commented by A. Niwiński in regard of their palaeography,[172] actually were written by different persons, but these were in fact Butehamun himself (e.g. graffiti nos. 1001 and 1008),[173] and possibly his son Ankhefenamun (e.g. nos. 1000, 1006, 1016, 1018).[174] Other members of the family should be also taken into consideration here as the authors of some of them (cf. e.g. graffito no. 1011). Butehamun's conspicuous style of handwriting is discernible not only in the letters, but also in the graffiti written by his own hand.[175]

According to A. Niwiński, Butehamun's engagement in the reburial of Amenhotep I was explicitly expressed in the opening words of the Opening of the Mouth ritual, as copied on the underside of the lid of his inner coffin and mummy-cover (CGT 10102-10103). The text in question was placed on the underside of the mummy-cover and forms a kind of a title of the entire composition: "Celebration of the Opening of the Mouth (ritual) of Osiris, king Djeser-ka-ra Amenhotep (I), l.p.h., (for)[176] king's scribe in the Place of Truth, Butehamun, in the House of Gold (*ḥw.t nbw*)";[177] the question of the real meaning of this text for our understanding of the role Butehamun played in the reburial of Amenhotep I will not be examined here.[178] Niwiński

[172] Cf. Niwiński, in: BSAK 9, 2003, 299.

[173] Significantly, in both cases only the name of Butehamun was written, thus their authorship cannot be doubted, although graffito no. 1008 does not seem to be complete in its form given by Spiegelbeg, Graffiti, 84, pl. 111.

[174] With the name of Butehamun as an element of filiation. As regards graffito no. 1018, the authorship of which cannot be doubted, see the comment in Chapter 5.

[175] Cf. Ali, Hieratische Ritzinschriften, 142ff.

[176] Or else: "Celebration of the Opening of the Mouth (ritual) (for/ or: for the statue?) of Osiris, king Djeser-ka-ra Amenhotep (I), l.p.h., (and) N, in the House of Gold", which seems to be less probable.

[177] Cf. E. Schiaparelli, Il Libro dei Funerali degli Antichi Egiziani I, Turin 1882, 22; E. Otto, Das ägyptische Mundöffnungsritual, [ÄA 3], Wiesbaden 1960, vol. I, 1 (4); vol. II, 34f. For a photograph of the text, see Niwiński, Sarcofagi della XXI dinastia, pl. 7.2; Egyptian Museum of Turin. Egyptian Civilization. Daily Life, Turin 1988, 35 (fig. 29).

[178] What can be ascertained here is the relationship between Butehamun's version of the Opening of the Mouth ritual and that of Amenhotep I, cf. Otto, op.cit., vol. II, 8, 34f., 126, 158.

explains this[179] by suggesting that the text of the ritual was a kind of "amulet" relating to an older Butehamun ("B") and his achievements which had been appropriated by a younger member of the same family (his Butehamun "C"). This seems highly improbable; quite the contrary, this seems to be an additional argument against Niwiński's hypothesis.

Last but not least, the names of the two wives of Butehamun, provided by the extant sources, cannot be taken as an argument in favour of a differentiation between two Butehamuns.[180] It has been demonstrated convincingly that the handwriting of oLouvre Inv. No. 698, being a letter of Butehamun to his deceased wife Ikhtay,[181] can be ascribed definitely to the Butehamun of the LRL.[182] As a consequence there is no obstacle to accepting the hypothesis that Ikhtay was in fact his first wife, who relatively early predeceased her husband. It may be assumed that she bore Ankhefenamun, the eldest son of Butehamun, whereas the rest of his numerous progeny were presumably the children of his second wife,[183] the lady by the name Shedemdua.

It should be noted here that A. Niwiński's Butehamun "A"[184] is evidently a "ghost" entity as well.[185] This hypothesis was based on false assumptions concerning some of the Theban graffiti, and their dating. First of all none of Spiegelberg's assesments relating to the palaeography of graffiti nos. 938, 971 and 980b can be taken as an argument in favour of their dating to the 19th Dynasty.[186] On the other hand, the apparent presence of royal cartouches in some of Butehamun's graffiti can be explained in another way. The cartouche of Seti (II) cannot be joined with the name of Butehamun in graffiti 2056a-c, since they are in fact three distinct texts written at different periods (see

[179] In: SAK 11, 1984, 141.

[180] Cf. Jansen-Winkeln, GM 139, 1994, 38.

[181] Cf. Černý-Gardiner HO, pl. 80-80A; for a photograph, see Les artistes de Pharaon. Deir el-Médineh et la Vallée des Rois, Paris 2002, 139 (no. 81). For the translations of the text and grammatical comments, see Frandsen, in: Village Voices, 31ff.; Goldwasser, IOS 15, 1995, 191-205; McDowell, Village Life, 106f. (no. 77); Donnat, in: Égypte, Afrique & Orient 25, 2002, 31ff.

[182] Cf. Frandsen, op.cit., 38 (based on an opinion of J.J. Janssen); Sweeney, DE 30, 1994, 205.

[183] Otherwise Bierbrier LNK, 39 (chart X); Davies, SAK 24, 1997, 68 (fig. 1).

[184] Cf. Niwiński, SAK 11, 1984, 144f.

[185] See Jansen-Winkeln, GM 139, 1994, 36; Davies, SAK 24, 1997, 50ff. (with a detailed commentary on the epigraphic sources). Quite recently A. Niwiński has verified his original hypothesis concerning Butehamun "A", cf. BSAK 9, 2003, 296.

[186] In the case of graffito 980b (Spiegelberg, Graffiti, pl. 108) it is self evident because it mentions Ankhefenamun as "*wab*-priest of Amun (of) *Khenemet-neheh*"; for the name of Ramesses III temple in Medinet Habu, see E. Otto, Topographie des thebanischen Gaues, [UGAÄ 16], Berlin – Leipzig 1952, 73; H.H. Nelson, JNES 1, 1942, 127ff.; P. Grandet, Ramsès III. Histoire d'un règne, Paris 1993, 105f. The late orthography of *nḥḥ* also should be noted here, cf. Ali, Hieratische Ritzinschriften, pl. 142.

above), and only graffito 2056b can be connected with Butehamun (and his sons). It is evident that the juxtaposition of the name of Butehamun and the partly preserved royal cartouche of Merenptah in graffito no. 854a is also secondary.[187] Similarly, in the case of graffito no. 1012a, from the "Valée du dernier Mentouhotep", a distinction should be made between graffito 1012a, ll. 1-3, which was written probably by Ankhefenamun, Butehamuns' son, and the rest of the inscription (ll. 4-7), undoubtedly of the reign of Ramesses III.[188] Consequently the first part of the text does not provide any argument in favour of existence of a hypothetical brother of Butehamun "A", Ankhefenamun.[189] There are no solid grounds at all to postulate an existence of a brother of the Butehamun known from LRL.[190]

There is agreement that at least the funerary equipment kept now in Turin could have been found in TT 291 in the western cemetery in Deir el-Medina.[191] Possibly also an amulet with the text of Book of the Dead chapter 100 (papTurin Cat. 1858) can be connected with Butehamun's burial.[192] The inscription left by Butehamun's son in TT 291 (now destroyed) seems to suggest that this was the place of the burial of Butehamun: "Yours is the West, prepared for you. All the blessed ones are hidden in the midst of it. Sinners – (they) will not enter it nor any unjust. Scribe Butehamun has landed in it after (attaining) an old age, his body being sound and complete. Made by the scribe of the royal necropolis Ankhefenamun".[193]

[187] The cartouche can be connected rather with graffito 854b dated explicitly to the reign of Merenptah. The matter still needs further investigation. Anyway, this is a recurring problem with some of the graffiti published by Spiegelberg who often gathered together some graffiti not necessarily written by one and the same hand.

[188] See Kitchen, RamInscr V, 542 (A 175); cf. Peden, Graffiti, 218 n. 576; Häggman, Directing DeM, 337 n. 2263.

[189] As postulated by Niwiński, SAK 11, 1984, 144f. n. 45.

[190] Contrary to Davies, SAK 24, 1997, 58. It seems untenable that a hypothetical son of the scribe Tuthmosis bore the same titles as the well known son of Butehamun. As a matter of fact, an incomplete writing of the name of Butehamun (in line 3) seems to suggest that also the first three lines of the inscription were not written at the same time. Thus the sequence of phrases as they appear on the rock cannot be taken literally, in the manner in which they follow each other.

[191] B. Bruyère, C. Kuentz, Tombes thébaines. La nécropole de Deir el-Médineh – La tombe de Nakht-Min et la tombe d'Ari-nefer, [MIFAO 54/1], Cairo 1926, 56-62; see also Niwiński, SAK 11, 1984, 137f.; id., Sarcofagi della XXI dinastia, 45; Guérin, op.cit., 18.

[192] S. Demichelis, Le phylactère du scribe Boutehamon, BIFAO 100, 2000, 267-273.

[193] Bruyère, Kuentz, op.cit., 56f., pls. 6, 9; S. Sauneron, BIFAO 71, 1972, pl. 52; Černý, Community, 373; Peden, Graffiti, 257; Jansen-Winkeln, InschrSp I, 41; McDowell, Village Life, 73 (44).

9. The aftermath

It is evident that, even though no royal tombs were under construction in Thebes, the activity of the necropolis staff was continued during the 21st Dynasty. In some periods, the available sources even reveal that this activity was exceptionally intensified in the Valley of the Kings and in the adjacent areas where the older royal tombs were located. This raises the question of the direct reason of such intensification of work of the crew. There seems to be an apparent correlation in time between such actions and the burials of the high priests of Amun and members of their families. Quite possibly the burials of the high priests who attained "royal" status – i.e. Herihor, Paynudjem I, and maybe Menkheperre – marked three important turning points in the history of the Theban necropolis in this period.[1] Later on there were the burials of Nesikhonsu, Paynudjem II, and then Djedptahjufankh and Nesinebtasheru, which prompted such increased activity in the necropolis area, as documented by the graffiti and remnants of the burials of the persons in question.

No doubt the preservation and safeguarding of the royal mummies disturbed in the earlier periods was one of the aims of the necropolis staff. This type of action was conducted on a large scale during the pontificate (and subsequently "kingship") of Paynudjem I, although the interpretation of the available sources dating to this period is rather uncertain. All that we have at our disposal are rock graffiti and rare ostraca recording the presence of the necropolis staff in the Valley of the Kings and in other areas of the necropolis. This type of material does not differ significantly from the sources which can be connected with robberies and depredations made in the royal necropolis so there are no grounds to make a distinction between the two groups of sources. Only the dockets written on linen wrappings or coffins can be securely connected with the efforts made to protect the royal mummies. Significantly, such

[1] Neither the tomb nor any remnants of the burial of the High Priest Menkheperre has been successfully localised until now; for this, see Niwiński, in: Z. Hawass (ed.), Egyptology at the Dawn of the Twenty-first Century, II, Cairo 2002, 416ff.

activity in the royal necropolis of Thebes completely ceased in the Libyan period. This is presumably because any ideological and political ties of the Theban high priests with the Ramesside royal family were definitely cut. Understandably enough, the high priests of Amun of the succeeding 22nd Dynasty, related to the royal family residing in the North, were no longer interested in supervising and protection of the old royal necropolis at Thebes. Thus the last entrance to the royal cache in TT 320, occurred some time after the internment there of Djedptahjufankh and Nesinebtasheru in year 11 (and/or 13) of the reign of Sheshonq I.[2] This marks the very end of the long history of the royal necropolis in Thebes together with the practice of the successive reburials of the mummies of the pharaohs of the past.

Strangely enough, it appears that some remnants of the institution of the royal necropolis still existed in the later period of the 21st Dynasty. This is revealed mostly by the graffiti in the Theban area and exceptionally rare ostraca recording inspection tours, or else the progress of work on some mostly unknown building projects. No doubt the institution had changed drastically in comparison with the previous period,[3] but the descendants of Butehamun's family still firmly held the crucial post of the scribes of the necropolis. Scarce evidence attests some foremen of the crew, although their chronological position cannot be ascertained properly.[4] Of the numerous progeny of Butehamun, at least four of his sons were mentioned later in connection with the activity of the necropolis staff. Subsequent to the death of Butehamun, it was Ankhefenamun, presumably his eldest son,[5] who inherited from him the function of the scribe of the royal necropolis. Later on the office of the necropolis scribe was in turn occupied by his younger brothers. The unpublished graffito, found by H. Carter in the remote "Vallée des Carrières", localised recently by the present author, is the earliest dated reference to Ankhefenamun as the necropolis scribe, acting presumably after the death of his father (cf. Pl. 1):[6]

---

[2] Cf. Dewachter, BSFE 74, 1975, 27; Niwiński, JEA 70, 1984, 80; Reeves, Valley of the Kings, 191f., 259 (tab. 11); Jansen-Winkeln, in: DeM in the Third Millennium, 170 (4); E. Graefe, G. Belova, The Royal Cache TT 320 – a re-examination, Cairo 2010, 51, 58, 63, 67, 75.

[3] Cf. Ventura, City of the Dead, 16 n. 99. It is disputable whether the royal workforce was transferred north to Tanis, with only a remnant of the necropolis staff stationed in Thebes "to serve as caretakers of the royal tombs", cf. Davies, SAK 24, 1997, 66.

[4] Cf. Davies, Who's Who at DeM, 280.

[5] See however below.

[6] M. Barwik, Theban Graffito no. 1572 rediscovered and some new texts from the "Valley of the Quarries" (in preparation).

(1) *ḥm-nṯr tpy n Ỉmn M3s3hr*[*ti*] (2) *sš-nsw* (*m*) *s.t-M3ʿ.t ʿnḫ.f*(*-n*)*-Ỉmn* (3) *s3 n sš-nsw Bw-th3-Ỉmn* (4) *rnp.t-sp 16 3bd 2 šmw sw 4*

"(1) High Priest of Amun Masahar[ta]; (2) king's scribe (in) the Place of Truth Ankhefenamun, (3) son of king's scribe Butehamun. (4) Regnal year 16,[7] second month of *shemu*, day 4."

It is noteworthy, that none of the numerous progeny of Butehamun was mentioned in the corpus of LRL. Having in mind the constant concern of both Butehamun and his father about the condition of Shedemdua, Hemshire and her little daughter, it is rather surprising to find that the names of other members of the family were passed over. A possible exception in regard of this is "the scribe Meniunefer" (LRL no. 50; LRLC no. I),[8] apparently one of the eldest sons of Butehamun.[9] If the identification of this Meniunefer with the son of Butehamun is correct, then we must admit that he was merely a child – just an apprentice at the period covered by the LRL, along with his brothers. In one of his letters Tuthmosis instructs his son: "And you shall not allow the children (*n3 ʿḏd šri*) who are in the school (*t3 ʿ.t-*(*n*)*-sb3*) to cease from writing" (LRL no. 5).[10] These words can be related to those boys, who in the future would replace their father as successive scribes of the necropolis.

Significantly only one of the preserved letters (i.e. LRL no. 41) mentions "the scribe of the necropolis Ankhef(enamun)". The title of the scribe of the necropolis suggests that the son of Butehamun was meant here.[11] The letter was written by Bakenkhonsu, "the *wab*-priest of Khonsu and scribe of the king's victuals (*sš n p3 ʿnḫ-nsw*)",[12] a person unattested elsewhere in the avail-

[7] The date is commonly related to the reign of Smendes, cf. von Beckerath, RdE 20, 1969, 31f.; Kitchen TIP, 38, 419 (no. 28); Niwiński, JARCE 16, 1979, 68 (tab. III); id., SAK 11, 1984, 151 n. 57; Davies, SAK 24, 1997, 66; Römer, Gottes- und Priesterherrschaft, 62 (no. 2), 63; Peden, Graffiti, 192 n. 378, 239; Bouvier-Bouvier, L'activité des gens, 23 (III). Alternatively K. Jansen-Winkeln refers the date to the pontificate/kingship of Paynudjem I, cf. id., InschrSp I, 39 (no. 3.75), 286. It has been argued unconvincingly that the regnal year of Psusennes I was referred to, cf. Hagens, JARCE 33, 1996, 153ff. (esp. p. 157).

[8] Černý LRL, 72, 2; Janssen LRLC, 13 n. 10 (with hesitations about his identity), pl. 1, 9. It cannot be excluded that the name of Meniunefer should be also restored in LRL no. 2, in the lacuna preceding the name of scribe Amenhotep, cf. Černý LRL, 3, 9. The reason of this would be exactly the same sequence of names in LRL nos. 2, 50, and LRLC no. I. It has been suggested that Meniunefer and Amenhotep were the eldest of the Butehamun's sons, cf. Davies, SAK 24, 1997, 58, 64.

[9] If he was Meniunefer "the elder", cf. above Chapter 5; the possibility exists, howevere that he was his younger namesake.

[10] Černý LRL, 10, 13-14; cf. also Černý-Groll, Late Egyptian Grammar, 456 (Ex. 1237); Junge, Neuägyptisch, 210; Baines, Eyre, GM 61, 1983, 88.

[11] Thus the scribe of the army Ankhefenamun, son of Ptahemheb, should rather be excluded. The latter was implicated in the robberies, cf. papBM 10052, 11, 9; papMayer A, vo. 8, 16; 12, 14; and papAbbott-dockets, vo. B, 18.

[12] Černý LRL, 62, 4; see also a comment regarding the reading of the second of the titles ascribed to

able sources. This seems to be the latest of the entire group of the LRL,[13] and we can only guess about its connection with the family archive of Butehamun (and/or his descendants?).[14] The document is a palimpsest, but enough has been preserved of the original letter (possibly only a draft letter) to say that it was written by Bakenkhonsu to a chantress (of Amun ?) and/or the *wab*-priest of Khonsu and scribe Dikhonsuiry.[15] An unpublished coffin in the Egyptian Museum in Cairo (from the priestly cache in Bab el-Gusus) belonging to the *wab*-priest of Khonsu and scribe of this name can be possibly connected with the person mentioned in the letter.[16] The coffin has been dated by A. Niwiński to the middle 21st Dynasty (the High Priest Paynudjem II) on the basis of the mummy-braces found on the mummy.[17] Having in mind his priestly titles connecting him possibly with Karnak temples (and his burial place as well) he cannot be connected in a decisive way with a certain Dikhonsuiry, who left some graffiti in the remote region of the south-west valleys, in the Valley of the Kings and in the valley of the Royal Cache (TT 320).[18] It has been rightly observed that no titles at all accompany his name in the graffiti.[19] There are no grounds, however, to doubt the latter's connection with the necropolis staff. As a matter of fact, a certain Dikhonsuiry is mentioned in an unpublished ostracon from Deir el-Bahari (inv.no. F.8958ro., 16), among other workmen of the necropolis of the beginning of the 21st Dynasty.

Significantly, in the original letter Bakenkhonsu was titled as the"*wab*-priest of Khonsu and the general's scribe". This seems to be an earlier variant of the titles held by Bakenkhonsu in the period when a military administration played such an important role in the Thebaid, possibly still during the early activity of Butehamun under the pontificate of Herihor (when Payankh was just a general?). On the other hand, it is open to question what was the true

---

him: ibid., 62a (4a-b); for the meaning of the title, cf. Lesko, Dict. I, 70.

13 Cf. Wente LRL, 15, 17.

14 Cf. Janssen LRLC, 34 n. 4.

15 Cf. Černý LRL, 62a (10a, 12a); Wente LRL, 75f. (not included in: id., Letters, 202).

16 JdE 29733 (unpublished), cf. Niwiński, SAK 11, 1984, 142; id., 21st Dynasty Coffins, 131 (no. 141), pl. 5c; id., BSAK 9, 2003, 297; see also Häggman, Directing DeM, 366. For a mention of a certain Dikhonsuiry on the coffin in Leiden, see Demarée, in: DeM et la Vallée des Rois, 249.

17 Niwiński, 21st Dynasty Coffins, 74, 131 (no. 141). According to Niwiński, the mummy-braces were inscribed with the name of "the High Priest Pinudjem" (ibid., 52 n. 129, 131); see also Daressy, ASAE 8, 1907, 26 (no. 49): "Les bretelles sont au nom de Pinozem". As a consequence, a slightly earlier dating of the burial of Dikhonsuiry cannot be excluded perhaps?

18 Cf. Peden, Graffiti, 243, 252, 262, 264-265.

19 Häggman, Directing DeM, 366f.

meaning of the title of the "scribe of the king's victuals", which it seems he held later, thus referring possibly to the "king" Paynudjem I?[20]

The long period of activity of the members of Butehamun's family, and his progeny in particular, must be explained by the mere fact, that some of them were probably the sons born by the second (younger) wife of Butehamun. As a matter of fact, Shedemdua and "her little children (*ꜥḏd šri*)" were mentioned several times in the preserved correspondence (LRL nos. 1, 3, 7, and 8).[21] According to LRLC no. II these were simply "her children" (*nꜣy.s ꜥḏd*).[22] There is no certainty about the identity of Shedemdua and her relation to Butehamun.[23] Nonetheless her role in LRL may well mean that she was the second wife of Butehamun, even if on the two sandstone lintels from Medinet Habu, it is Ikhtay, who accompanies Butehamun. On the lintel now in Tübingen, Butehamun and Ikhtay are adored as a couple by their daughter Tadif, and son – "the scribe in the Place of Truth Ankhef[enamun] in victorious Thebes". Ikhtay is titled here as "lady of the house, songstress of Amun-Ra, king of the gods", and "his (i.e., Butehamun's) sis[ter] beloved in his heart".[24]

We know of only one of Butehamun's sons as having been born to him by his first wife Ikhtay. It was Ankhefenamun, who has given us the name of his mother in graffito no. 1306.[25] No other member of this family ever gave the mother's name, and this is well in accord with the common custom of the epoch, when the mother's name was only rarely given. In another graffito (no. 1359a)[26] Ankhefenamun gives the name of his father alongside that of his grandfather.[27] The immediate successor of Ankhefenamun in the post of the necropolis scribe was his brother Nebhepet (or Meniunefer the younger).[28] In graffito no. 1138 both Ankhefenamun (who was entitled "the *wab*-priest and

---

[20] Less possibly Herihor, beacuse of the chronology of the career of Ankhefenamun (cf. Černý, Community, 199, 358ff., 374f.).

[21] Černý LRL, 2, 4; 6, 2; 13,8; 14, 15.

[22] Janssen LRLC, 17 (vo. 2), pl. 7; similarly in LRL no. 14, as suggested by Janssen (cf. ibid., 18 n. 15).

[23] Cf. Sweeney, Correspondence and Dialogue, 49 n. 28. Jansen-Winkeln (GM 139, 1994, 38) suggested that she might have been a widowed sister of Butehamun. Compare however, Davies, SAK 24, 1997, 56.

[24] Kitchen, RamInscr VII, 399f.; E. Brunner-Traut, H. Brunner, Die Ägyptische Sammlung der Universität Tübingen, Mainz 1981, 78-80 (No. 1707), pl. 109; for a comment, see Černý, Community, 358.

[25] Černý, Graffiti, 19, pl. 56.

[26] Ibid., 24; H.E. Winlock, The Treasure of Three Egyptian Princesses, New York 1948, 7, pl. 40 (B+C); cf. Peden, Graffiti 262 and n. 846.

[27] The name of his father was given explicitly in graffito no. 2865, besides those innumerable cases, where the father's name appears in the frame of a customary filiation formula.

[28] Meniunefer being only an assistant to his father, and subsequently to his brother Ankhefenamun, cf. Davies, SAK 24, 1997, 66f.; Bouvier-Bouvier, L'activité des gens, 23 (III-IV), 27.

scribe in the Place of Truth") and Nebhepet (title unpreserved) appear side by side, as sons of Butehamun and grandsons of Tuthmosis.[29]

The numerous progeny of Butehamun included no less than seven sons.[30] It has been suggested, however, that Pakhynetjer and Amenmose were not necessarily the younger sons of Butehamun, as is generally accepted, but rather his grandsons, namely the sons of Ankhefenamun.[31] In the graffito no. 1599 from the tomb of prince Montuherkhepeshef in the Valley of the Kings (KV 19),[32] the names of Meniunefer, Amenmose and Pakhynetjer (in this particular order) follow those of Ankhefenamun and Nebhepet, so evidently all of them were commemorated here as the sons of Butehamun. As regards Pakhynetjer, several graffiti specifically present him as the son of Butehamun (cf. e.g. graffiti nos. 1307, 1308, 1309?).

It is possible of course that some of the graffiti can be attributed to the grandsons of Butehamun, but certainly not those which mention Tuthmosis and "his son" Butehamun at the top of the inscription, and then "son of his son" so and so, because the latter formula must be related obviously to Tuthmosis himself. This is the case of graffito no. 3102 for example, which explicitly mentions Ankhefenamun as the grandson of Tuthmosis.[33] On the other hand, graffito no. 2979 can likewise be included in this group,[34] but here the reading of the two parts of the inscription must be reversed: that designed by the editors as "b" must be placed at the beginning, although it was written a little bit to the left of part "a". Only then does the meaning of the text appear to be fairly clear, especially the group "his son", placed after the name of Tuthmosis (and without a continuation according to the older reading). Nevertheless, some of the Theban graffiti enable us to identify some of Butehamun's grandsons, thus the representatives of the third generation of the family active during the 21st Dynasty.[35]

Presumably it was one of the grandsons of Butehamun who wrote a prayer(?) or invocation to Amun on the ostracon found in Deir el-Bahari (oBM EA

[29] Černý, Graffiti, 6, pl. 11.

[30] Cf. Bierbrier LNK, 39; Helck, in: LÄ I (1975), 885; even more according to Davies, SAK 24, 1997, 58ff., 68 (fig. 1) – an opinion based mostly on graffito no. 892.

[31] See Niwiński, SAK 11, 1984, 154 (fig. 3).

[32] Černý, Sadek et al., Graffiti III, pl. 2ter; IV, 2.

[33] Ibid., III, pl. 198; IV, 159.

[34] Ibid., III, pl. 182; IV, 152.

[35] These are graffiti nos. 447, and 1052; cf. Davies, SAK 24, 1997, 59f., 68 (fig. 1); this is hardly likely in the case of graffito no. 1023, which rather documents Nebhepet son of Butehamun and not of Ankhefenamun.

51842):[36] "(O) horizon of eternity, sacred land (or: land of *ḏsr.t*) in truth, the temple of Harakhte; the words (*pꜣ ḏd*) of Amun-Ra, lord of the thrones of the Two Lands, which have been said in it (?). Made by the *wab*-priest of Amun (of) United-[with-Eternity], overseer of young men (*nfrw*) in the Place of Truth, army scribe of the gang of the necropolis *ḥr*[...],[37] son of the king's scribe, overseer of the treasury of the king of Upper and Lower Egypt Ankhef; the father of his father being Buteh[amun], (scribe) of the necropolis". Strangely enough, this unnamed latest scion of the family of the necropolis scribes held titles partly inherited from his illustrious grandfather. Significantly he borne also the title of the "overseer of the young men (*nfrw*) in the Place of Truth" attested elsewhere only in relation to Butehamun and his son Nebhepet.[38] No doubt the impact of the military organization markedly influenced the administrative terminology used in the Theban necropolis at that time.[39] Quite possibly this was one of the results of the civil war which broke during the lifetime of the preceding generations or else the hostilities which disturbed the Thebaid in the time of the High Priest Menkheperre, related in the so-called "Banishment Stela".[40] At the same time it reveals the strongly "military" background of the rule of the high priests of Amun in the Thebaid, which seems to be one of the characteristics of the "Amun theocracy" of the Third Intermediate Period.

It is not easy to decide what kind of works would had been conducted at Deir el-Bahari during the lifetime of the second generation after Butehamun. A significant group of ostraca dating to the beginning of the 21st Dynasty, now studied by R.J. Demarée,[41] can possibly be connected with a hypothetical

36 Demarée, Ramesside Ostraca, 37, pls. 148-149. The parallel text of oBM EA 51843 (ibid., pl. 150) may be possibly attributed to the same person, although the name has not been preserved except the titles and tiny traces of the name at the end (line 5): [... *wʿ*]*b sš* [...]. I am not convinced that the text was written by "a different hand", as suggested by Demarée, ibid., 37.

37 For names beginning with *ḥr*- , cf. Ranke PN I, 251ff. Tiny traces of signs written after the first group would possibly suggest the name Herenamenpenaf, cf. ibid., 252 (5). There is no certainty, however, that the beginning of the name has been preserved here, as it may possibly be read: *ḥr* [*imnt.t Wꜣs.t NN*].

38 Cf. Černý, Community, 45, 77.

39 For *nfrw* as a designation of elite troops, cf. A.R. Schulman, Military Rank, Title and Organization in the Egyptian New Kingdom, [MÄS 6], Berlin 1964, 20f.

40 As regards the latter events, see von Beckerath, RdE 20, 1968, 32ff.; Kitchen TIP, 259ff.; Niwiński, BIFAO 95, 1995, 351ff.

41 Cf. R.J. Demarée, in: DeM et la Vallée des Rois, 245ff.

first stage of work on TT 320[42] (for whatever purpose),[43] or else with some other operations undertaken in the area of the Deir el-Bahari temples. The scale of the activity of the gang in this region of the necropolis can be fully ascertained thanks to the lists of workmen, as preserved on the ostraca. One of the ostraca of the series, found by the Polish Archaeological Mission at Deir el-Bahari in the 1980s (oDeB inv. no. F. 8958),[44] gives a lengthy list of workmen (at least 27 names in the main list) engaged on some building project, which was inspected on "[...] day 13" (ro. 1).

Seven newly found graffiti left by Butehamun and his son Ankhefenamun on the cliff above the Deir el-Bahari temples must be taken as a testimony of the inspection of the area by the necropolis staff at the beginning of the 21st Dynasty.[45] To understand properly this evidence, some new graffiti discovered recently in the temple of Hatshepsut must be also taken into consideration.[46] Of special significance are three testimonies left by an inspecting party on the shaded northern wall of the lower ramp and in the Lower Portico (northern colonnade) of the Hatshepsut temple at Deir el-Bahari. Two of them were scratched on the southern wall of the lower ramp leading to the middle terrace. The third of the texts was written in red paint on the southern wall of the northern wing of the Lower Portico, just a few metres to the west of the preceding two. The latter was once seen by W. Spiegelberg and his transcription of the text is kept in the archives of the Oriental Institute in Chicago.[47] Presumably it was only the high regnal year date comparable to the dated documents of

[42] According to Demarée (personal communication). It is less probable that this is a testimony of a workmen settlement in Deir el-Bahari, as suggested by Demarée, op.cit., 249; A. Peden, in: Ch. Lilyquist, The Tomb of Three Foreign Wives of Tuthmosis III, New York 2003, 11, Häggman, Directing DeM, 16; for its supposed location, cf. also PM I/2², pl. V.

[43] The preparations for the burial (either original or secondary?) of Paynudjem I may be also taken into consideration. For TT 320 as the hypothetical original burial place of Paynudjem I, see O. Berlev, S. Hodjash, Catalogue of the Monuments of Ancient Egypt from the Museums of the Russian Federation, Ukraine, Bielorussia, Caucasus, Middle Asia and the Baltic States, [OBO.SA 17], Fribourg – Göttingen 1998, 5ff.; for the contrary view, see E. Graefe, The Royal Cache and the tomb robberies, in: N. Strudwick, J.H. Taylor (eds.), The Theban Necropolis. Past, Present and Future, London 2003, 79f.

[44] One more ostracon found by the Polish Mission can be dated to the same period – this is oDeB inv. no. F. 8959; although oDeB inv. no. F. 609 is doubtful in dating, it is possibly also of the same period.

[45] Cf. Niwiński, BSAK 9, 2003, 299, figs. 2-9; S. Rzepka, Rock Graffiti above the Temple of Hatshepsut, PAM XI, 2000, 183-190.

[46] Among others these are daily dates and the names of workmen of the necropolis of the 21st Dynasty, scratched on the wall in the lower (northern) portico of the temple. To these may be added an undated graffito, giving the name of Butehamun and some of his sons, found by J. Iwaszczuk in December 2009 to the north of the Upper Portico. The material will be published soon by the present author.

[47] I would like to express my gratitude to Mr. J.A. Larson (Oriental Institute) for his permission to use the data from the notebook of W. Spiegelberg WS 121 (now in the Oriental Institute, Chicago) in the present study.

the last decade of the reign of Tuthmosis III, which led Ch. van Siclen (III) to ascribe the Spiegelberg text to the dossier of the Tuthmoside building ostraca from Deir el-Bahari.[48] As the Spiegelberg file is not annotated properly (just a note: "Der el-Bahri, 1899") Ch. van Siclen (III) formulated a hypothesis that the text is a transcription of an otherwise unknown Tuthmoside ostracon connected with the building of the Tuthmosis III temple at Deir el-Bahari, and a visit of the king himself to the building site.[49] Now, after the rediscovery of the inscription on the wall of the Hatshepsut temple, it is possible to say that this is not the case, and the document in question appears to be in fact a docket left by an inspection party during the 21st Dynasty, possibly in the reign of the Tanite king Psusennes I[50] (cf. Pls. 2-3):

(1) *rnp.t-sp 49 3bd 1 pr.t sw 23 hrw pn* (2) *iy.n ms-ḫr* [...] (3) *r p3 ḏw iw.f* [...] (4) *ḥ3ty-ʿ ʿnḫ-Ḥr-n-3s.t n t3* [*imnt.t*] *W3s.t*

"(1) Regnal year 49, first month of the *peret*-season, day 23: On this day (2) came the "child of the necropolis" [...] (3) to the mountain; he [...] (4) mayor Ankh-Hor-en-Aset of the [west] of Thebes".[51]

Unfortunately, the reason for the visit referred to in the text remains completely unknown. The mention of the "child of the necropolis" would seem to suggest that at least some members of the necropolis staff attended the visiting party, headed possibly by the mayor of the West of Thebes. Nothing is known about Ankh-Hor-en-Aset, apparently the latest among the documented mayors of West Thebes.[52] The very presence of such a high-ranking official (besides the very form of the inscription, written with exceptionally large hieratic signs)[53] indicate the special character of the visit, being possibly an official inspection in the necropolis area. As regards the meaning of the term *ms-ḫr*, it is reasonable to see in it a common designation of the sons of the men of the gang, who did not inherit the position of the workman of the

[48] Ch. van Siclen (III), Trois commentaires sur les ostraca de Deir el-Bahari, RdE 34, 1982-1983, 140-142.

[49] Ibid., 141f.

[50] A high regnal year seems to point out to such a solution, as other candidates – Sheshonq III and Psammetichus I – are hardly probable in this context, having in mind that the former was not recognised in Thebes at such a late date within his reign, cf. Kitchen TIP, 131f. Anyway there is no certainty that he reigned so long, cf. A. Dodson, GM 137, 1993, 53ff. As regards Psammetichus I, the activity in the Assassif area during his reign would certainly favour such a dating, but the additional information provided by two other graffiti from the ramp strongly supports an earlier dating of the inscription in question (see the present author's forthcoming article).

[51] The text will be published soon with a detailed commentary, together with two graffiti from the ramp.

[52] The name is not attested in Ranke PN, except the form Ankh-Hor-sa-Aset, cf. ibid., I, 66 (2). For the mayors of the West of Thebes during the New Kingdom, cf. Helck, Verwaltung, 429-32, 532f.

[53] Height of signs: 3-8, 5 cm.

gang,[54] but were connected in some way with the crew of the necropolis. An inscription on the underside of the mummy-board of lady Tameniut (BM EA 15659),[55] probably of the early 21st Dynasty, refers to the restoration of the coffin of this noble lady, after depredations made by the "children of the necropolis" (*ms.w-ḫr*).[56]

On the other hand, the engagement of the necropolis staff in the construction and successive burials in the tomb of the priests of Amun in Bab el-Gusus,[57] cannot be excluded either. It is perhaps possible to connect this text with the commemoration of the burial of an important person in Bab el-Gusus, dating to the pontificate of Menkheperre.[58] There are good reasons, indeed, to date the text to the pontificate of the High Priest Menkheperre (and not to the regnal years of Tanite king, i.e. Psusennes I),[59] as the dating in relation to his pontificate is explicitly documented in the preserved sources.[60] This is "Year 48 of (*n*) High Priest of Amun-Ra, king of the gods, Menkheperre",[61] very near or even parallel to year 1 (of king Amenemope),[62] documented on a linen from the same mummy.[63] Quite possibly the Year 49

[54] Cf. Černý, Community, 28, 117ff.; Ventura, City of the Dead, 35-37. To these comments on the subject add also J.F. Borghouts, in: Gleanings from Deir el-Medîna, 81 (n. 29); A. Mahmoud, *Msw-ḫr* = the sons of the Tomb, in: Mamdouh Eldamaty, Mai Trad (eds.), Egyptian Museum Collections around the World. Studies for the Centennial of the Egyptian Museum, Cairo, Cairo 2002, 763-76; Häggman, Directing DeM, 66f.

[55] Cf. S. Birch, ZÄS 7, 1869, 26; W. Spiegelberg, RT 17, 1895, 97-99; [I.E.S. Edwards], A Handbook to the Egyptian Mummies and Coffins exhibited in the British Museum, London 1938, 42; Černý, Community, 120; Reeves, Valley of the Kings, 234 (no. 12); Jansen-Winkeln, InschrSp I, 109 (no. 51); for a photograph of the board, see now J.H. Taylor, Death and the Afterlife in Ancient Egypt, London 2001, fig. 128. For the dating of the mummy-board, see Niwiński, 21st Dynasty Coffins, 151 (no. 259).

[56] Cf. Černý, Community, 120.

[57] A general comment on the history of the priestly cache, and its relatively late dating within the 21st Dynasty: Niwiński, 21st Dynasty Coffins, 25-27; id., The Bab El-Gusus Tomb and the Royal Cache in Deir el-Bahari, JEA 70, 1984, 73ff.; id., The Bab el-Gusus Tomb or the Second Cache of Deir el-Bahari, in: Mynářová J., Onderka P. (eds.), Thebes. City of Gods and Pharaohs, Prague 2007, 177-179.

[58] As some additional inscriptional evidence from the Hatshepsut temple seems to suggest (the material will be published soon by the present author).

[59] According to the chronology proposed by K. Jansen-Winkeln; for this, see above, Chapter 8.

[60] According to K.A. Kitchen, these are regnal years of Psusennes I, adopted by Menkheperre, and not the independent "regnal" years of the latter, see Kitchen TIP, 533f. (TIP[3], XVIIf.); id., in: Libyan Period in Egypt, 192; compare also von Beckerath, Chronologie der XXI. Dynastie, 54 and n. 24. The apparent extraordinary meaning of the years 48 and 49 in the dating practice during the pontificate of Menkheperre has been underlined already by Niwiński, JARCE 16, 1979, 56-59; id., BIFAO 95, 1995, 352f.

[61] See G. Daressy, ASAE 8, 1907, 30 (no. 105); with emendations made by Young, JARCE 2, 1963, 103 n. 21; cf. also Römer, Gottes- und Priesterherrschaft, 69, 578 (no. 52); Jansen-Winkeln, InschrSp I, 90 (6.38), 286.

[62] Thus the coregence of both kings may be postulated, cf. e.g., Jansen-Winkeln, ZÄS 119, 1992, 35; id., GM 157, 1997, 70f.

[63] Daressy, ASAE 8, 1907, 30 (no. 105); Jansen-Winkeln, InschrSp I, 106 (7.40).

of Menkheperre is documented also on another fragmentarily preserved linen docket from Bab el-Gusus.[64] Papyrus Brooklyn 16.205[65] can also be dated to the same year, as demonstrated recently by J. von Beckerath (the reign of Psusennes I).[66] And similarly the Year 49 inscribed in a reused tomb in Kom Ombo, being the date of the burial of a certain Wenentawat.[67]

No doubt other locations in the bay of Deir el-Bahari were also visited in those times. This is the case, for example, of the reused tombs in the vicinity of the Hatshepsut temple (i.e., MMA tombs nos. 59, 60, 65).[68] Last but not least the reburial of queen Meritamun in her original tomb located under the northern colonnade of the middle terrace of the Hatshepsut temple (TT 358) in year 19 of Smendes/Paynudjem I, under the pontificate of Masaharta, must be noted as well,[69] although these events were evidently much earlier in date than those referred to in the inscription of Year 49.

Less possibly the burial of the foreman Horemkenesi in the area of the temple of Mentuhotep (II) Nebhepetre[70] can be viewed as an additional factor lying behind such an accumulation of ostraca and other inscriptional evidence in the area of the Deir el-Bahari temples in this period. A newly found ostracon (without an exact provenance but, since it was found among material collected in the past from that site, probably originating from Deir el-Bahari)[71] can be interpreted, however, as a short memorandum of his burial or else its preparation, although its connection with another building chantier in the region, possibly under Horemkenesi's own supervision, cannot be excluded (cf. Pl. 4):

(1) *wꜤb n Ỉmn-RꜤ nsw-nṯr.w* (2) [Ꜥ]*ꜣ* [*n*] *ỉs.t n s.t-MꜣꜤ.t sš Ḥr*-(3) [*m-ḳnỉ*][72]- *ꜣs.t*

[64] G. Daressy, RAr³ 28, 1896, 78; Jansen-Winkeln, InschrSp I, 108 (7.47). Kitchen (TIP, 29, 411f., 421 (no. 47), 531) attributes it to the reign of Psusennes I as parallel to [year x] of Amenemope; similarly von Beckerath, GM 140, 1994, 16; id., Chronologie der XXI. Dynastie, 54.

[65] A.R. Parker, A Saite Oracle Papyrus from Thebes, [BES 4], Providence/R.I 1962, 49-52, pls. 17-19; Jansen-Winkeln, InschrSp I, 101ff. (7.33).

[66] J. von Beckerath, Zur Datierung des Papyrus Brooklyn 16.205, GM 140, 1994, 15-17; cf. Kitchen TIP³, XXVI (Y); date related to the pontificate of Menkheperre by Jansen-Winkeln, GM 157, 1997, 71.

[67] Cf. S. Wenig, FuB 10, 1968, 87, 94; Jansen-Winkeln, InschrSp I, 94 (6.45); id., GM 202, 2004, 71ff.

[68] Cf. PM I/2², 628-630; H.E. Winlock, Excavations at Deir el-Bahri 1911-1931, New York 1942, 93-97.

[69] Cf. H.E. Winlock, The Tomb of Queen Meryet-Amūn at Thebes, New York 1932, 48, 51, 53, pls. 40, 41B; as for the dockets and their dates, see also Reeves, Valley of the Kings, 236 (nos. 24a-c, 25); Jansen-Winkeln, InschrSp I, 28f. (3.52-53).

[70] Cf. J.H. Taylor, Unwrapping a Mummy. The Life, Death and Embalming of Horemkenesi, London 1995.

[71] Inv.no. 781; it was found in one of the magazines located in the "chapels" of the Northern Colonnade on the middle terrace of the Hatshepsut temple at Deir el-Bahari (March 2009).

[72] Only part of the sign *ḳnỉ* (Gardiner, Sign-list D.32) is preserved; as regards its hieratic form, cf. Möller, Paläographie II, 10 (no. 110). Compare the writing of the name in graffiti nos. 1322 and 1343,

"(1) *Wab*-priest of Amun-Ra, king of the gods, (2) chi[ef of] the gang in the Place of Truth Hor-(3)[em-ken]-esi".

Horemkenesi is known to have flourished during the pontificate of Paynudjem I, thus his career may be placed securely at the beginning of the 21st Dynasty.[73] The absence of his name in LRL makes him contemporary with the sons of Butehamun. In graffito no. 1012 he only bears the title of scribe, when Ankhefenamun was the scribe of the necropolis.[74] Consequently Horemkenesi's involvement in the operations conducted in the Valley of the Kings, as documented by graffito no. 2138,[75] must be placed during the lifetime of the sons of Butehamun. At this time, in year 20 (of Smendes/ Paynudjem I), he was already the "chief of the gang", and a group of "the men of the crew" (*n3 wꜥw n is.t*) were accompanying him in "opening (?)[76] of the great valley (*t3 int ꜥ3.t*)", i.e. undoubtedly the Valley of the Kings.[77]

The names of Pakhynetjer and Amenmose can be connected with the very end of the involvement of Butehamun's family in the matters of the necropolis. We can find both of them at the side of Butehamun still in the period when the latter was engaged in the preservation of royal mummies, which simply means that they started their careers still accompanying their father during the pontificate of Paynudjem I. Their independent career fell during the pontificate of Menkheperre.[78] Finally it was the scribe Pakhynetjer who visited the old necropolis at Deir el-Medina, where the tombs of his forefathers were located. In one of the Ramesside chapels of the western cemetery (no. 1331) he left a graffito being at the same time a commemoration of his visits to the tomb and a short prayer directed to Amun:[79] "I was here in the previous year; now (I) have returned (again) this year praying to Amun ...".[80] By that time the institution of the royal necropolis at Thebes was nearing its end.

cf. Černý, Graffiti, pl. 60.

[73] Taylor, op.cit., 16ff.

[74] Spiegelberg, Graffiti, 84f., pl. 114.

[75] Černý, Sadek et al., Graffiti III, pl. 76; IV, 42; for its location, see Félix-Aubriot-Kurz, Plans de position, pl. 42: to the east of the tomb of Seti II (KV 15). As regards translation and comments, see Taylor, op.cit., 18; McDowell, in: Pharaoh's Workers, 163 n. 97; Peden, Graffiti, 243 n. 737; Häggman, Directing DeM, 365.

[76] Or else "inspecting"; compare also graffito no. 1359=3945: Černý, Graffiti, 24; Černý, Sadek et al., Graffiti III, pl. 304; IV, 249; Peden, in: Lilyquist, op.cit., 9f.

[77] Cf. Ventura, City of the Dead, 152; compare, however, Černý, Community, 89.

[78] Cf. Bouvier-Bouvier, L'activité des gens, 24 (V); Černý, Community, 375f.

[79] Bruyère, Rapport (1933-34), 68, fig. 33; cf. Peden, Graffiti, 256f. A sketchy figure of a man in a gesture of adoration with the name of the scribe Pakhynetjer is partly superimposed on it.

[80] What follows is wholly incomprehensible.

Index of the Documents Cited

B. LATE RAMESSIDE LETTERS

Černý LRL

D. GRAFFITI

Plates

1. Graffito no.1572 from the „Vallée des Carrières" (drawn by M. Barwik).
2-3. Inscription from the Hatshepsut temple at Deir el-Bahari, Lower Portico, northern colonnade (photo Z. Doliński; drawing M. Barwik).
4. Ostracon DeB inv.no.781; shale, 9x6 cm (photo A. Kamińska, drawing M. Barwik).

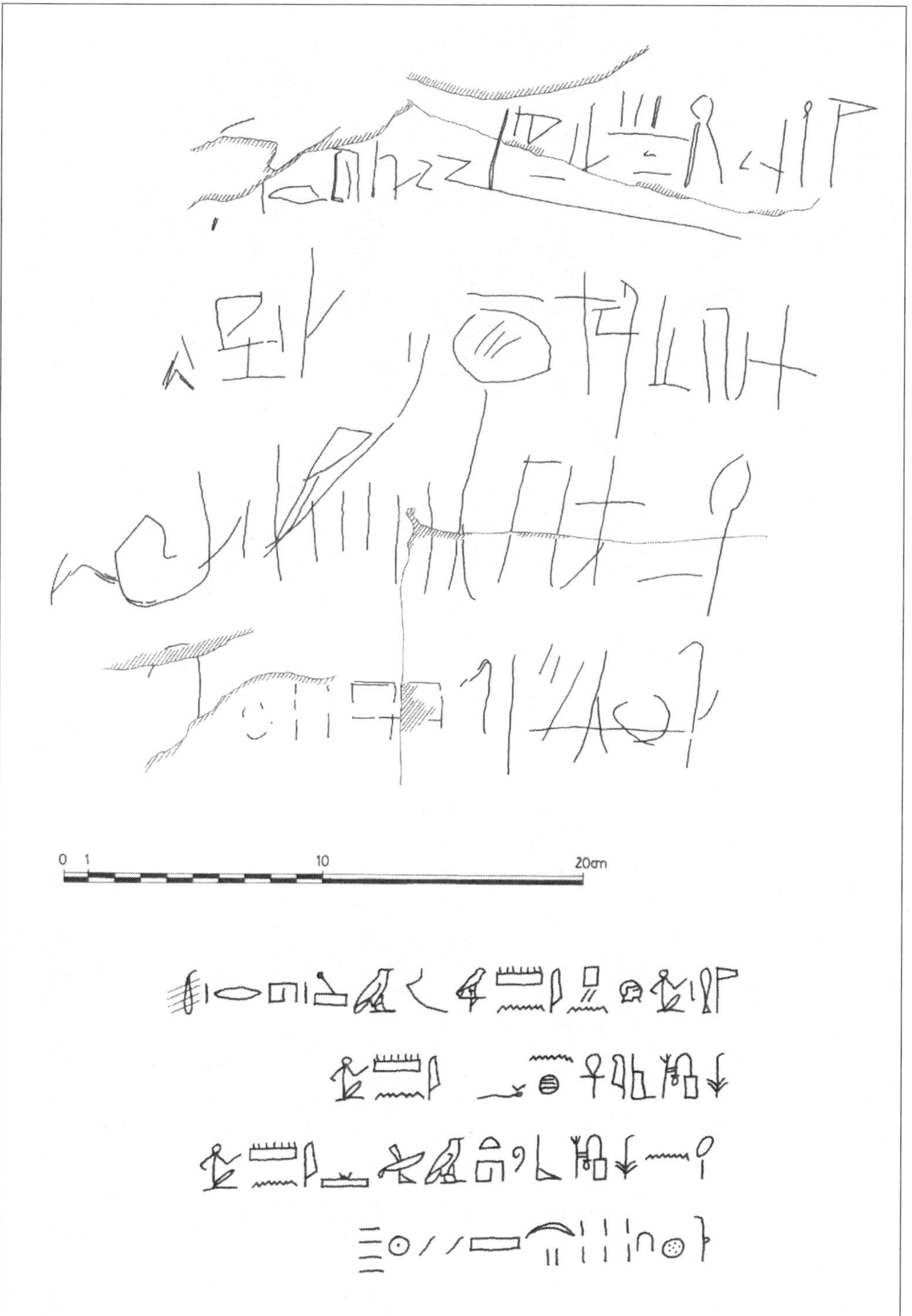
0 1
10
20cm

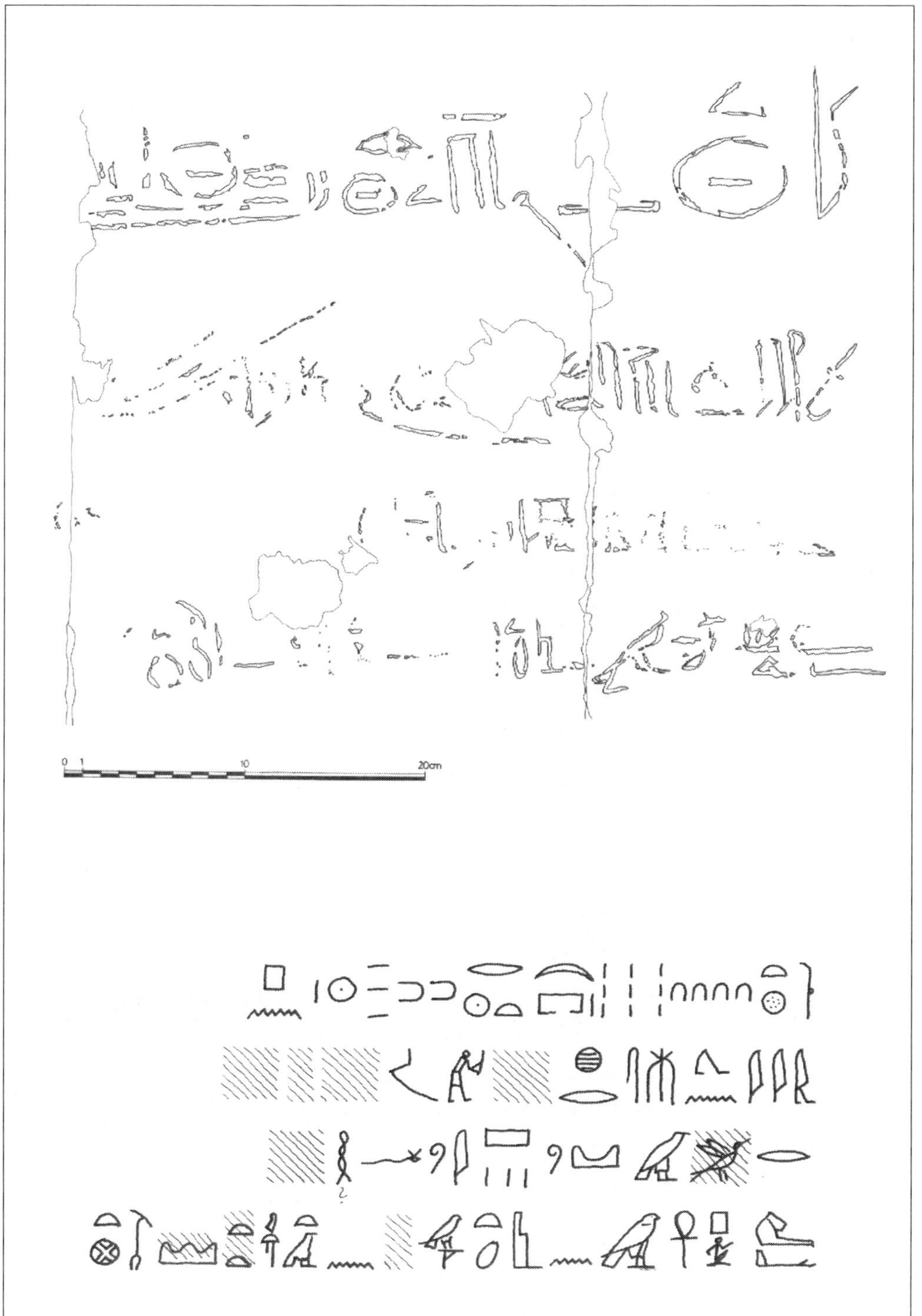
0 1
10
20cm

781

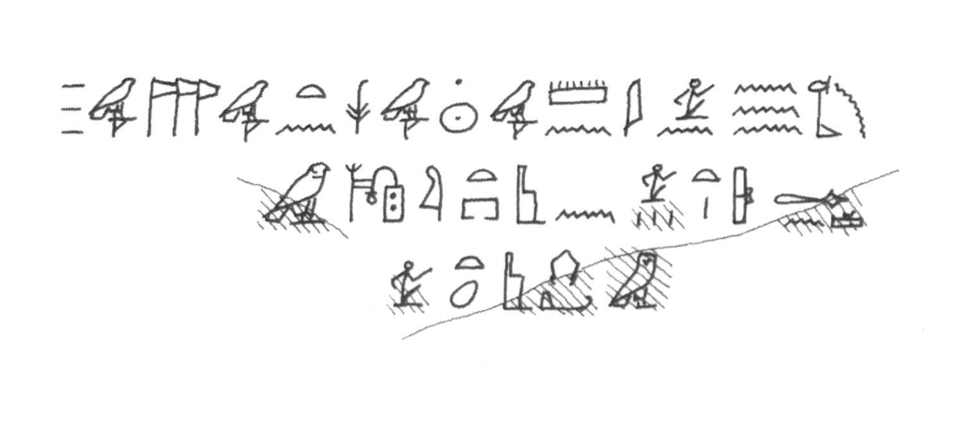